Critical Acclaim for *HCI Models, Theories, and Frameworks*

Not since Card, Moran, and Newell's *Psychology of Human Computer Interaction* was published in 1983 has so much been brought together to advance the science of HCI. This book is a must-read for researchers and Ph.D. students.

I am very impressed with the undertaking of this book and with its results. We have many models and theories in HCI, and this book collects them and encourages people to think about them together. I'm sure good things will come from those who digest this all.

Judith Olson
University of Michigan

Only with slowly evolving frameworks such as these can we understand and guide the advances in technology and their uses that lie ahead. This landmark collection will be of lasting value.

Jonathan Grudin
Microsoft Research

Computing and information technologies are providing profound advances for individuals and society. We have gained new insights from perceiving dynamic visualizations; enhanced our thinking by manipulating flexible representations; increased our knowledge through global search technologies; discovered new modes of communication and collaboration through networked technologies; formed new communities and relationships from near-universal access to the Web; developed new methods of buying and selling; and so on.

The phenomena underlying the relationship between people and technology are complex and varied. Understanding these phenomena is a real challenge, especially given that they span perceptual, cognitive, social, organizational, commercial, and cultural factors.

Practitioners in HCI disciplines (interaction designers, information architects, usability testers, ethnographic field investigators, etc.) offer skills, methods, and practices to design and evaluate these technologies. Researchers in HCI provide innovations and empirical groundings, as well as theoretical perspectives, which are critical for a robust field. But the theoretical work is scattered across many sources, and practitioners are largely unaware of the range of theoretical work that has been done.

This volume is a valuable collection of diverse theoretical perspectives by some of the most articulate advocates in the field of HCI. It is a unique resource for grasping the broad landscape of theoretical thinking that frames HCI. Practitioners should study it to deepen their understanding of the phenomena they are trying to influence, and researchers should study it for inspiration to broaden and strengthen the theoretical foundations of human-computer interaction.

Tom Moran
IBM Almaden Research Center

HCI Models, Theories, and Frameworks
Toward a Multidisciplinary Science

The Morgan Kaufmann Series in Interactive Technologies

Series Editors:

Stuart Card, PARC ■ Jonathan Grudin, Microsoft
Jakob Nielsen, Nielsen Norman Group

HCI Models, Theories, and Frameworks

Toward a Multidisciplinary Science

Edited by

John M. Carroll

MORGAN KAUFMANN PUBLISHERS

An Imprint of Elsevier

AMSTERDAM   BOSTON   LONDON   NEW YORK

OXFORD   PARIS   SAN DIEGO   SAN FRANCISCO

SINGAPORE   SYDNEY   TOKYO

Edited by John M. Carroll
Publishing Director Diane D. Cerra
Senior Developmental Editor Marilyn Alan
Publishing Services Manager Simon Crump
Senior Project Manager Julio Esperas
Editorial Coordinator Mona Buehler
Production Services Matrix Productions Inc.
Cover Design Frances Baca
Cover Image Sisse Brimberg/National Geographic/Getty Images
Text Design Evans & Associates
Copyeditor Sally Scott
Proofreader Sally Scott
Composition & Illustration Technologies 'N Typography
Indexer Edwin Durbin
Printer The Maple-Vail Book Manufacturing Group

Morgan Kaufmann Publishers
An Imprint of Elsevier
340 Pine Street, Sixth Floor
San Francisco, CA 94104–3205
www.mkp.com

Library of Congress Control Number: 2002116251
    ISBN: 1–55860–808–7

This book is printed on acid-free paper.

Contents

5 Notational Systems—The Cognitive Dimensions of Notations Framework 103

by Alan Blackwell, Cambridge University, Cambridge, England
Thomas Green, University of Leeds, Leeds, England

8   Distributed Cognition   193

by Mark Perry, Brunel University, London, England

11   Activity Theory   291

       by Olav W. Bertelsen and Susanne Bødker, University of Aarhus, Denmark

14 Upside-Down ∀s and Algorithms—Computational Formalisms and Theory 381

by Alan Dix, Lancaster University, England

15 Design Rationale as Theory   431

by John M. Carroll and Mary Beth Rosson, Virginia Tech

Acknowledgments

The project of organizing this book was facilitated by support from the National Science Foundation (IIS-0097342), specifically from the Experimental and Integrative Activities (EIA) Division and the Computation and Social Systems (CSS) Program (now the Digital Society and Technologies Program), both part of the Directorate for Computer and Information Science and Engineering. National Science Foundation support allowed some of the authors to gather at Virginia Tech for a weekend workshop to plan this book. I want to personally thank Rick Adrion, director of EIA, and Suzi Iacono, director of CSS, for supporting the concept of a multidisciplinary science of human-computer interaction.

I would also like to thank the Virginia Tech graduate students who took my "Models, Theories, and Frameworks of Human-Computer Interaction" course in the Spring and Fall semesters of 2001. They used the draft chapters of this book as a primary resource and wrote formative evaluation critiques for the authors.

John M. Carroll

1 Introduction: Toward a Multidisciplinary Science of Human-Computer Interaction

John M. Carroll   Virginia Tech

Human-computer interaction (HCI) lies at the intersection between the social and behavioral sciences on the one hand, and computer and information technology on the other. It is concerned with understanding how people make use of devices and systems that incorporate or embed computation, and how such devices and systems can be more useful and more usable. It is the fastest-growing and the most visible part of computer science. Across the world, computer-science graduates are flooding into HCI courses and careers. The exciting, and also sometimes troubling, impacts of computing on societies, economies, cultures, and all sorts of human activities and organizations are impacts of HCI.

HCI professionals analyze and design user interfaces and new user-interface technologies. In the past, they helped to develop and investigate the concepts of the now-pervasive graphical user interface paradigm of windows, menus, icons, and mouse pointing. They created software tools and development environments to facilitate the construction of graphical user interfaces. They pioneered the use of voice and video in user interfaces, hypertext links, interactive tutorials, and context-sensitive help systems. Today, this work continues in the development of input and display devices for mobile computing, information visualizations for digital libraries, and navigation techniques for virtual environments.

HCI professionals also integrate and evaluate applications of technology to support human activities. HCI has developed a large variety of methods for understanding the tasks and work practices of people and their organizations in ways that help frame new possibilities for computer support and that then help assess the obtained utility and usability of devices and systems. Much of the early work in HCI focused on office systems. The ideas that underlie modern word processing and conferencing systems came from this work. Methods work in HCI ranges from the development of checklists, guidelines, and surveys; to various kinds of walkthroughs and interviews; to field studies of workplaces, homes, and other real-world settings; to laboratory experiments; to various kinds of analytic models. Today, this work continues in every sort of application domain—architectural drawing, high school science, Web systems for e-commerce, and so on.

HCI professionals study and improve the work and organizational processes of technology development. One of earliest foci of HCI work was training and supporting professional programmers. HCI work produced notations and tools for design rationale and organizational memory, and concepts and methods for user-centered design and scenario-based design. HCI has become a primary testbed for two broad innovations in design methods, participatory design and ethnographically driven design. Participatory design is the direct involvement of users in design work; ethnographically driven design is the detailed study of work practices to ensure that new technology supports work as it is practiced and not as normatively described in procedures. Today, this work continues in support for end-user programming and component software.

HCI is a young field that is still developing. It has been successful through the past 20 years, and it is important to ask how it can continue to succeed. An important element in the development of HCI to this point, and a key to its future, is its commitment to multidisciplinary science.

1.1   THE GOLDEN AGE

With respect to traditional concerns and subdisciplines of computer science, HCI was originally a joining of software engineering and human-factors engineering. It integrated concerns about tools and methods for software development with concerns about verifying the usability of the software produced. This integration offered solutions to critical problems in both software engineering and human factors.

In the 1970s, software engineering faced a crisis over the so-called waterfall development method, a linear organization of software development activities, each producing interim results—for example, the functional specification document—that are handed off to subsequent stages. The waterfall development method was slow and unreliable; important requirements often emerged only after initial implementation, wasting effort and forcing costly reworking of software. Software human factors also faced a crisis; it was positioned at the end of the waterfall, and thus it became involved only after fundamental design decisions had been taken. It was positioned too far downstream to make more than cosmetic difference in software products. These crises coincided with the dawn of the personal computer, creating a whole new set of challenges for software development, many pertaining to user interfaces and end-user applications. This amplified the sense that computing was in crisis.

Towards the end of the 1970s, cognitive science had coalesced as a multidisciplinary project encompassing linguistics, anthropology, philosophy, psychology, and computer science. One principle of cognitive science was the representational theory of mind, the thesis that human behavior and experience can be explained by explicit mental structures and operations. A second principle was that an effective multidisciplinary science should be capable of supporting and benefitting from application to real problems. Many domains were investigated, including mechanics, radiology, and algebra. HCI became one the first cognitive-science domains.

The initial vision of HCI as an applied science was to bring cognitive-science methods and theories to bear on software development. Most ambitiously, it was hoped that cognitive-science theory could provide substantive guidance at very early stages of the software-development process. This guidance would come from general principles of perception and motor activity, problem solving and language, communication and group behavior, and so on. It would also include developing a domain theory, or theories, of HCI. This first decade of HCI was a golden age of science in the sense that there was wide tacit agreement as to the overarching research paradigm. And a lot got done.

For example, Card, Moran and Newell (1983) developed the Goals, Operators, Methods and Selection rules (GOMS) model for analyzing routine human-computer interactions. This was an advance on prior human-factors modeling, which did not address the cognitive structures underlying manifest behavior. It was a fundamental advance on the cognitive psychology of the time: It explicitly integrated many components of skilled performance to produce predictions about real tasks. There was a relatively broad range of such work. Malone (1981) developed analyses of fun and of the role of intrinsic motivation in learning based on studies of computer-game software. Carroll (1985) developed a psycholinguistic theory of names based on studies of filenames and computer commands. This body of work was a beginning of a science of HCI, but it also contributed to the cognitive-science foundation upon which it drew fundamental concepts. Indeed, much of it was published in cognitive-science journals.

In the mid-1980s, HCI saw itself as an emerging scientific discipline. A vivid indication is Allen Newell's 1985 opening plenary address at the ACM CHI Conference, the major technical conference in HCI (Newell & Card, 1985). In the talk, Newell presented a technical vision of a psychology of HCI. It is striking that the conference organizers had recruited a plenary address describing a program for scientific research. And the effects of the talk were also striking. Newell's talk provoked controversy and new research. It led to alternate proposals, modified proposals, replies, and rejoinders (Carroll & Campbell, 1986; Newell & Card, 1986). It helped to heighten interest in theory and science for at least five years.

1.2   LET 100 FLOWERS BLOSSOM

In the latter 1980s, many new scientific ideas entered the HCI mainstream. One source of new ideas was differentiation within the original cognitive-science community of HCI. Newell's talk is again emblematic; it helped to sharpen latent distinctions. During the early 1980s, a great deal of work had been done on the learning and comprehension problems of novice users. This work lies outside the realm of "routine cognitive skill," outside the realm of GOMS. However, it is within the paradigm of cognitive science. It addressed issues such as abductive reasoning, learning by exploration, external representations, and the development of analogies and mental models. Newell's vision implicitly marginalized this work, motivating the emergence of alternative cognitive-science paradigms.

Another source of new scientific ideas was the growing multidisciplinary constituency of cognitive science itself. Social psychologists, anthropologists, and sociologists entered the cognitive-science discourse, sometimes taking HCI as their empirical touchstone. Suchman's (1987) study of photocopier use described a variety of usability problems with advanced photocopier-user interfaces. She considered the interaction between the person and the machine as a sort of conversation that frequently fails because the participants do not understand one another. She used this study to develop an important critique of planning as it had been viewed in cognitive psychology and artificial intelligence. This was a paradigmatic case of cognitive science, and in particular of HCI as cognitive science. Suchman brought field-study concepts, techniques, and sensibilities from anthropology, ethnomethodology, and sociology, and she applied them to a real problematic situation of human-computer interaction. Her results provided very specific guidance for developing both better user interfaces for photocopiers and better theories of planning.

A third source of new scientific ideas was the increasing internationalization of HCI. This was facilitated by several International Federation for Information Processing (IFIP) conferences held in Europe, and by initiatives within major computer companies. An example is Bødker's (1991) application of activity theory to HCI. Activity theory was originally developed in what is now Russia; its applications to work and information technology were pioneered in Scandinavia. It integrates the analysis of individual behavior and experience with interpersonal cooperation (including division of labor) and culture (including tools and socially developed practices). Its foundation is Marxism, not cognitive architecture. It addresses the achievement of particular goals in the context of broader motivations, human development, and social systems. Activity theory and cognitive science are not incompatible, but they embrace different underlying values and they prioritize conceptual and methodological issues differently. For example, in activity theory, understanding mental representations per se is a secondary issue.

A fourth source of new scientific ideas was technology. The personal computer, and its word-processing and spreadsheet software, were instrumental in the original emergence of HCI. In the latter 1980s and throughout the 1990s, software and systems to support computer-supported cooperative work (CSCW), sometimes called groupware, became increasingly important. Networked computing became more differentiated and sophisticated. In the early 1990s, use of the World Wide Web became widespread, and within a few years it became a universal infrastructure for networked personal computing. Technological support for graphics and visualization, including virtual environments and augmented reality, and for audio and video became far more advanced and accessible. Handheld computers and cellular telephones allowed the use of computing to become increasingly mobile and ubiquitous in everyday life. These technology developments increased the salience of scientific issues in interpersonal communication, coordination, and collaboration; in browsing, search, and information integration; and in many facets of visual perception.

All of these developments contributed to a scientific foundation far more rich, far more diverse than the starting points of the early 1980s. In the mid-1990s, HCI encompassed nearly all of social and behavioral science. Students and scientists from many disciplines bought their research interests and expertise to HCI. The tremendous range of empirical methods and scientific concepts in routine use in HCI has been a source of strength as the field grew to address new problems and issues encompassing new technologies and new applications.

1.3   SCIENTIFIC FRAGMENTATION

HCI has been a successful technological and scientific undertaking. It achieved an effective integration of software engineering and the human factors of computing systems through the concepts and methods of cognitive science. In doing so, it helped to broaden and develop cognitive science itself. No one could have anticipated in 1980 just how HCI would develop. And we cannot know its future course now. However, the progress of the past two decades highlights specific current challenges.

An ironic downside of the inclusive multidisciplinarity of HCI is fragmentation. This is in part due merely to the expansion of the field and its scientific foundations. In the 1980s, it was reasonable to expect HCI professionals, particularly researchers, to have a fairly comprehensive understanding of the concepts and methods in use. Today, it is far more challenging for individuals to attain that breadth of working knowledge. There are too many theories, too many methods, too many application domains, too many systems. Indeed, the problem of fragmentation may be a bit worse than it has to be. Some HCI researchers, faced with the huge intellectual scope of concepts and approaches, deliberately insulate themselves from some portion of the field's activity and knowledge. This tension between depth and breadth in scientific expertise is not unique to HCI, but it clearly undermines the opportunity for multidisciplinary progress.

Fragmentation is also manifest among HCI practitioners. In the early 1980s, in a smaller and narrower HCI community, there was a close coordination of research and practice. The relationship between research and practice in this early period was quite orthodox—the view being that researchers developed concepts, methods, technologies, and prototypes, and practitioners applied and developed them in products. This is actually not a very good model of effective technology development, and it has been supplanted by a more interactive view in which practice plays a more central role in articulating requirements for theory and technology and in evaluating their efficacy in application. However, playing more creative roles in multidisciplinary technology development demands much more of practitioners. It demands that they understand the intellectual foundations of HCI, not merely how to manipulate the tools and methods constructed on those foundations. Although there are many encouraging examples of multidisciplinary HCI practice leading research in highly creative ways, practitioners also often manage the intellectual scope of concepts and approaches by deliberately isolating themselves from some portion of the field's foundations. Ironically, because HCI practice has diversified so rapidly and has incorporated so many new professionals, average expertise among practitioners has never been lower.

The intrinsic difficulties of making sense of a vast and diverse science base are exacerbated by engineering exigencies in contemporary software and systems. During the 1990s, development cycles for new products and services were dramatically compressed. Thus, even among researchers and practitioners with the inclination and skills to pursue a multidisciplinary program of HCI research and application, external factors such as schedule, budget, and compatibility with standard solutions often prevail. This has created an often-overwhelming pressure to streamline methods and techniques so that they can be conveyed to novices in a half-day tutorial, and then put into practice by tutees the very next day. Of course, it is important to manage cost-benefit tradeoffs in methods and techniques, to ensure that the benefits expected merit the effort required. But the pressure to simplify has done violence to some theory-based approaches: Cognitive modeling is frequently conflated with keystroke-level counting, ethnography is conflated with any observational study, and thinking-aloud protocols are conflated with concurrent participant interviews. The pressure to simplify has also led to a higher-than-warranted reliance on checklists and guideline-based usability methods, many of which are grounded in common sense and face validity but not in specific research.

Like most of computing, HCI is a relatively small research community amid a huge community of practitioners seeking to apply HCI knowledge and techniques to practical problems within schedule and budget constraints. This demographic is itself a reflection of the field's success through the past two decades, but it creates pressures to streamline and disseminate concepts and techniques. On the one hand, there is enormous demand for researchers to apply and disseminate concepts and techniques. And on the other hand, there is little enthusiasm or support for researchers to articulate the relationships among concepts and techniques. An example is the current prevalence—both explicit and implicit—of "quick and dirty" ethnography, but without a comprehensive analysis of the consequences of various ethnographic frameworks.

To the extent that the success of HCI through the past two decades was due to its ambitiously multidisciplinary application, fragmentation is a threat to future development. Put more positively, HCI will fully use the leverage of its multidisciplinary science foundation only if it can continually synthesize a coherent methodological framework from that foundation. In the "golden age" of HCI as cognitive science, the underlying rubric for this coherence was the representational theory of mind. This foundation was highly successful in underwriting an engineering practice. But it also helped to raise further questions and to broaden HCI through further disciplinary perspectives. As the multidisciplinary program for HCI science continues to develop, synthesizing a comprehensive and coherent methodological framework will become more challenging but also potentially more powerful.

1.4   TEACHING AND LEARNING

A key to developing a significant science of HCI is teaching and learning. In the early 1980s, many cognitive psychologists joined the HCI project. And throughout the 1980s and early 1990s, these "migrations" continued, from anthropology, communication studies, human-factors engineering, social psychology, sociology, and many areas of computer science. The first generation of HCI professionals necessarily had to adapt and invent what became the subject matter of HCI. But each group of immigrants had only a partial view of the multidisciplinary foundation. Each group faced an immense learning task.

During the past decade, HCI coalesced as a multidisciplinary subarea of computer science. Many handbooks, textbooks, and university courses were developed. A 1988 Association for Computing Machinery (ACM) task force enumerated HCI as one of nine core areas of the computer-science discipline (Denning et al., 1989). And a joint curriculum task force of the ACM and the IEEE (Institute of Electrical and Electronic Engineers) recommended the inclusion of HCI as a common requirement in computer-science programs (Tucker & Turner, 1991). HCI was one of the 10 major sections of the first *Handbook of Computer Science and Engineering* (Tucker, 1997). There have now been two editions of the *Handbook of Human-Computer Interaction* (Helander, 1987; Helander, Landauer, & Prabhu, 1997), and one of *The Human-Computer Interaction Handbook* (Jacko & Sears, 2003). There are four comprehensive undergraduate texts (Dix et al., 1993; Preece et al., 1994; Rosson & Carroll, 2002; Shneiderman, 1998). These handbooks and textbooks all address the science and theory foundations of HCI, but they tend to emphasize individual methods, techniques, and technologies.

During the 1990s, computer-science departments hired HCI faculty and developed new courses. An undergraduate course in HCI became a standard element of the computer-science curriculum. Various advanced and specialized courses were established. For example, it is not uncommon now to see courses in such areas as usability engineering, computer-supported cooperative work, multimedia systems, and user-interface software and tools. These more advanced treatments of HCI generally do not include much discussion of the science or theory underlying practical methods and techniques, or system implementations. And there are very few courses offered anywhere on HCI science and theory as such.

Part of the reason for this is the relative inaccessibility of advanced-level materials on HCI science and theory. Original sources are often difficult for students, lengthy and narrow in scope. They often do not compare and contrast different approaches. Few HCI faculty are able to provide detailed guidance to students in more than a couple of approaches. The upshot is that few if any computer-science graduate students attain more than an undergraduate-survey understanding of approaches to science in HCI. This circumstance is unfortunate, and it will tend to reproduce itself. The next generation of HCI professionals may use and contribute to the multidisciplinary science of HCI no better than has the current generation. Far from ensuring that HCI will benefit from its multidisciplinary scientific foundations, this seems to ensure that it will not.

The objective of this book is to provide a pedagogical survey for the multi-disciplinary science of HCI. The book brings together a range of approaches to science in HCI, presenting them in a common format, at a middle level of detail. The goal is to provide enough detail on each approach, and enough comparative detail across the whole collection, to make primary sources more accessible. A broader goal is provide infrastructure to help raise the level of discourse about models, theories, and frameworks of HCI in academic theses and dissertations, and in technical papers and reports.

Each chapter focuses on a particular approach, briefly describing the motivation for the approach—why it exists, what need or opportunity brought it to prominence in HCI, and for what HCI problems it is typically used. The approach is then compared with its nearest neighbors, in terms of what is common, what is distinct, and how the approaches can (or cannot) work together. Each chapter then provides a brief presentation of an example application to show how the method/approach works and what sort of result or information it produces. The example should be paradigmatic and show the defining strengths of the approach. Subsequent major subsections in each chapter describe the scientific foundations of the approach, some of the most characteristic processes or mechanisms it incorporates, and a case-study application.

Each chapter identifies the scientific field or tradition the approach rests upon, showing how particular principles of a discipline beyond HCI were specialized and developed. This provides a foundation for describing in more operational detail how the approach is employed in HCI work, and illustrating this with one or more examples in which the approach was used in design, evaluation, or other system-development work, emphasizing what sort of result or information it produced. Finally, each chapter briefly comments on the status of the approach described in the field today, suggesting issues that may be important in the next decade.

The chapters are sequenced in the book along a rough dimension of *level of description*. Thus, perception and motor skill are typically thought of as "lower" levels of organization than cognition; cognition, in turn, is a lower level of organization than social interaction. This organization will hopefully make it easier to compare and contrast various perspectives, but it is definitely an idealization. The theories differ in many dimensions. For example, activity theory aspires to provide a comprehensive framework ranging from fairly low-level behaviors within the information-processing range through social and cultural interactions. Chapters on formal approaches and design rationale are not articulated with respect to a level or scope of description, and so they were somewhat arbitrarily placed at the end of the book.

2 | Design as Applied Perception

CHAPTER

Colin Ware   University of New Hampshire

2.1   MOTIVATION

Much of our intelligence can be broadly characterized as the ability to identify patterns, and the visual system is the most sophisticated pattern-finding mechanism that we have. Of our perceptual systems, vision dominates; it is estimated to engage 50% of the cortex, and more than 70% of all our sensory receptors are visual receptors.

This chapter presents a theory of design based on the science of perception. A fundamental assumption underlying this theory is the idea that there is such an entity as "the human visual system." We assume that all humans have essentially the same neural visual architecture, and that processes that operate in this architecture are more or less the same for all humans. Although this is controversial when discussing human cognition, it is not when applied to other aspects of humans: With few exceptions, people have basically the same muscular and skeletal structure (although some, such as athletes and dancers, are much more developed). In cognition, despite the overwhelming evidence for structure, there is a tendency to think of neural machinery as infinitely adaptable, a kind of universal machine. This is not the position taken here. Although it is well known that neural structures are highly adaptive and change in response to different stimuli, it is also the case that the broad neural architecture is preserved in animals that have at least a reasonably normal environment. Thus we can assume a basic set of capabilities in perception that become more-or-less developed in different individuals. This enables us to develop a kind of perceptual and cognitive ergonomics with guidelines for display design based on a model of human sensory processing. Accordingly, a primary goal of display design should be to map data into a visual form that it is matched to our perceptual capabilities. In addition, if we understand how sensory systems can be developed through training, then we may also seek educational strategies for developing perceptual skills.

An extensive body of theory relating to human perception has been developed over the last 100 years. It can be found in the disciplines of neuropsychology, psychophysics, and cognitive science. In addition to theory, there are large numbers of empirical studies that provide such information as limits on the amount of detail that can be seen, limits on stereoscopic depth, the time taken to respond to various kinds of patterns, and so on. The proposition in this chapter is that the same perceptual mechanisms that enable us to perceive the world also enable us to perceive information patterns in computer displays. The approach can be called *information psychophysics*. Where classical psychophysics is concerned with understanding how we see light, color, and simple patterns, information psychophysics is concerned with how we can see simple information patterns (such as paths in graphs or groups of symbols) when these patterns are expressed through light, color, and simple patterns. The resulting theory can be applied both to understanding how existing displays are processed and to developing design guidelines for new displays.

The main part of the argument is presented through an overview of the human visual system, with examples of design rules derived from different levels of processing. The same theoretical points could be illustrated with the senses of touch or hearing; but because vision provides the channel for most computer output at present, however, and for clarity, we focus on vision and neglect the other senses. We conclude with a discussion of the kinds of claims that can be made from this approach and the limitations of these claims. We also briefly consider the kinds of scientific methods that can be applied to developing the science of perception-based design.

2.2   SCIENTIFIC FOUNDATION

A simplified three-stage model of the visual system is useful to provide a framework. This is illustrated in Figure 2.1 and Plate 1 of the color insert. In Stage 1, every part of the visual image is simultaneously analyzed into color, motion, and the elements of form by massively parallel neural processes. In Stage 2, the visual world is segmented into regions and two-dimensional (2D) patterns. Finally, in Stage 3, only a few complex objects can be held in visual working memory. Although information flows from stages 1 to 3, the higher-level processes can modify lower-level processing through feedback loops. For example, it seems likely that objects are held in visual working memory by means of something analogous to pointers back into the lower-level feature space. We can derive design

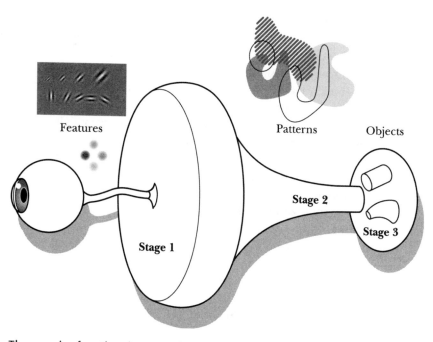

FIGURE

2.1
Three major functional stages of human visual processing include, first, processing incoming information into features, then segmenting it into simple patterns, and finally holding a few more-complex objects in visual working memory. (See Plate 1 of the color insert for a color version of this figure.)

guidelines from each of the three stages, although their robustness tends to diminish as we move from low-level to high-level processes.

2.2.1   Stage 1: Features in Early Vision

By early vision, what is meant is processing that includes the optics of the eye, the characteristics of photoreceptors, and the early stages of neural processing. The science of early vision has been used to provide guidelines for display design for decades. Color vision science contributed in many ways to the design of television and other cathode-ray tubes (CRT) and liquid crystal display (LCD) displays. The most important single fact about color vision is that it is fundamentally three dimensional, because there are three cone-receptor types in the retina. An understanding of this *trichromatic* system is the basis for color science, color measurement systems, and rules for the distinctness of colors. The most widely accepted color measurement standard, the Commission Internationale de l'Eclairage (CIE) XYZ system, is based on the concept of a standard human observer, a set of three empirical functions that represent the human sensitivity to different colors. Because of trichromacy, self-luminous monitors (CRT or LCD) produce mixtures of three colored primary lights. The red, green, and blue phosphors on a CRT are designed to elicit the widest possible range of cone responses, producing the greatest possible range of color sensations.

The television and monitor standards also take into account scientific measurements of the spatial and temporal capabilities of the human visual system. The fact that display refresh is greater than 60 Hz and above is a function of the approximately 50 Hz flicker-fusion threshold of the eye. Studies of luminance perception (roughly, our ability to perceive gray-scale patterns) have resulted in design guidelines for how much detail can be displayed and how much contrast should be provided with text (ideally, at least a 10:1 light-to-dark ratio).

Beyond the receptors, the core theory of color vision is that the receptor signals are processed into separate red-green, yellow-blue, and black-white (luminance) *opponent color channels* in the early stages of neural processing (Hurvich, 1981). Many converging lines of evidence support this, including cross-cultural evidence of color naming, and neurophysiological studies involving recording the signals from single neurons. The concept of opponent colors explains why the colors red, green, yellow, blue, black, and white are special in all societies that have been investigated; this means that if we need color codes to categorize visual information, red, green, yellow, and blue should be used first.

Because the red-green and yellow-blue channels cannot convey detailed patterns leads to a fundamental design rule for information display. Always display detail with luminance contrast. This rule of design comes directly from perceptual theory. It is illustrated in Figure 2.2 and Plate 2 of the color insert.

A knowledge of early-stage processing also tells us how to design symbols to stand out in a cluttered display. The relevant theory here is called *preattentive processing theory* (Triesman and Gormican, 1988). There is a good match between the graphical elements that "pop out" and the characteristics of early-stage neural processors. This early-stage processing is a massively parallel process. Elementary features of the visual image are simultaneously processed into color, elements of motion, texture, and stereoscopic depth. (Approximately 20% of cortical neurons are engaged in this.) Preattentively distinct symbols stand out immediately from their surroundings. This is true for the word "entity" shown on the following page. Color, the elements of shape and form, simple motion, and stereoscopic depth are all preattentive.

Because the luminance channel has a far greater capacity to respond to visual detail, it is essential that whenever detailed information must be conveyed there should be luminance contrast between foreground and background.

Because the luminance channel has a far greater capacity to respond to visual detail, it is essential that whenever detailed information must be conveyed there should be luminance contrast between foreground and background.

FIGURE

2.2

About half way down the image on the left, the text differs from its background only in the yellow-blue color channel. Theory predicts that this will be much harder to perceive than the same information shown with luminance contrast as illustrated on the right. (See Plate 2 of the color insert for a color version of this figure.)

FIGURE

2.3

On the left, the orientation of the ellipse exhibits a "pop out" effect. On the right, the conjunction of orientation and gray value does not pop out.

Often in information display, we wish to highlight some **entity** and make it stand out from other nearby visual entities. Because size and line thickness are preattentive, the word "entity" stands out from other words in this section, even if we are looking somewhere else on the page. There are strict limitations on what can be preattentively perceived, and understanding such limitations is critical in making displays that can be rapidly interpreted. For example, as Figure 2.3 illustrates, a differently oriented ellipse pops out. However, the conjunction of orientation and gray value does not pop out. This means that, in general, if a symbol is to be made clearly distinctive, it must be made different from all the surrounding symbols in terms of some simple basic attribute. Preattentive theory means that the precise rules for making an object stand out from its surroundings are well understood.

2.2.2   Stage 2: Pattern Perception

At a middle level of perception are a set of processes that take the results of low-level processing and discover patterns, such as contours, regions, and motion groups. Understanding this level of perception can provide design guidelines for display layout, and it can help us with interfaces for visual problem solving. Pattern perception is fundamental to visual intelligence; in many cases, to see a pattern is to solve a problem or make a new discovery. Thus, if we can display data in ways that makes patterns easy to perceive, this will facilitate problem solving.

Most modern theories of pattern perception have their roots in the work of the Gestalt psychologists. The Gestalt school of psychology was founded in 1912, and key contributors were Wesheimer, Koffka, and Kohler. They produced a set of laws of pattern perception (Koffka, 1935). These are robust rules describing how we see patterns in visual images; although their theories have not stood the test of time, the laws themselves have continued to provide the basis for theory development. In addition, new explanatory theories based on neural processes have been developed. Independent of the theoretical underpinnings, the gestalt laws themselves can be used to construct design principles for information displays.

The original set of gestalt laws included the following:

+ *Proximity:* Visual entities that are close together are perceptually grouped.
+ *Good continuity:* Smoothly continuous lines are perceived more readily than contours that rapidly change direction. Considerable recent work has provided theoretical underpinnings for the concept of good continuity, together with empirical work that helps define when a continuous contour will be perceived (Field et al. 1992).
+ *Symmetry:* Symmetric objects are more readily perceived.
+ *Similarity:* Similar objects are perceptually grouped.
+ *Common fate:* Objects that move together are perceptually grouped.

To this set, we can add more recent additions:

+ *Common region:* Objects within an enclosed region of space are grouped (Palmer, 1992).
+ *Connectedness:* Objects connected by continuous contours are perceived as related (Palmer and Rock, 1994).

Figure 2.4 illustrates how some of the gestalt laws can be applied in design. In Figure 2.4, the principles of common region, proximity, and connectedness are all applied to labeling objects on a display.

Another application of gestalt laws is in the drawing of node-link diagrams (graphs). Typically the nodes are represented as circles or rectangles, and the links are lines drawn between them. Problem solving with such diagrams can often take the form of finding a path along the links from one node to another. Such paths might, for example, represent an information channel in an organization with a visual analysis revealing information bottlenecks. But this visual analysis will be successful only if the node-link diagram is laid out in such a way that the important paths can be discerned. Hence the subdiscipline of graph layout: the drawing of node-link diagrams for problem solving. Figure 2.5 illustrates how gestalt perceptual principles can be applied to graph layout. On the left, the

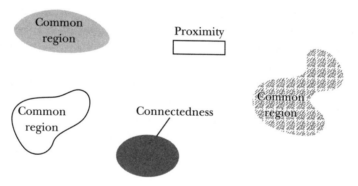

FIGURE

2.4

The Gestalt laws of common region, proximity, and connectedness are applied to attaching labels to visual objects.

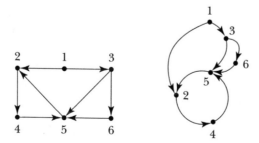

FIGURE

2.5

On the left, the gestalt principle of symmetry is used to emphasize a particular structure. On the right, good continuity emphasizes information flow.

layout emphasizes a spurious symmetry. On the right, the layout uses the principle of continuity to make paths easier to perceive.

One of the most challenging and interesting claims relating to visual displays is that they can somehow support creative thinking and problem solving. The basis for this is the fact that we can only *mentally* imagine quite simple visual images (Kosslyn, 1994). Much more complex information can be analyzed if it is presented *externally* on a visual computer display or a sheet of paper. If the problem to be solved can be represented in this way, then it is possible to try out solutions mentally using the externally presented information. The external image thus becomes a kind of information store for visual problem solving (Zhang and Norman, 1994). For example, with a map in front of us we can mentally construct a route from one city to another, using the external map as a resource. Similarly, with a software diagram we can reason about information flows through the software structures by *perceiving the patterns,* and this can help us improve the design. The diagram in these cases is functioning as both a memory aid, continuously reminding us about the components of the problem, and as a basis for imagining transformations, such as the additions of paths or of changes. This is a form of reasoning that incorporates both internal and external representations. As Zhang (1997) showed with a series of studies on the tic-tac-toe game, details of the visual representation are critical. Certain visual representations will bias toward certain problem solutions. For example, if a key element is placed in a salient position, it will be more readily selected. Thus visual representation per se is not sufficient; it must be a visual representation for which the important patterns are readily perceived.

2.2.3 Stage 3: Objects

Modern models of cognitive processing have at their core functional components called *working memories.* Working memories contain the information stored for problem solving. There are several of these, including visual and verbal working memories (Anderson et al., 1997; Kieras and Meyer, 1997). A key characteristic of all working memories is that they have a strictly limited capacity. In the case of visual working memory, only a few objects can be held in mind at the same time, and these are swapped in or out from either long-term memory or the external environment. However, although only a few objects can be held in mind at the same time, they can be complex.

Kahneman introduced the notion of an object file as a model of how the brain can hold a single complex visual object in mind (Kahneman et al., 1992). This concept can be applied in information visualization in the form of object-based displays. The idea is to encapsulate complex, multi-attribute data objects by mapping attributes to visual characteristics of a visual object (Wickens, 1992). Thus, object shape, color, and surface texture can all be varied to represent attributes of some complex information construct. According to Biederman's theory of structured object perception, we perceive objects as composed of simple, linked, 3D solid-shape primitives that he called "geons" (Biederman, 1987). Color and texture are secondary surface properties of geons. This suggests that we should use the gross 3D shape of visual objects to show the primary attributes of objects, and use texture and color to show the secondary information. It is important to note that there is a considerable difference between high-level object perception and low-level vision. In low-level vision, color is primary for segmenting and in preattentive discrimination. It is only in high-level vision, where objects exist, that color retreats to a secondary role.

Applying this theory, Irani and Ware (2000) used compound objects constructed of 3D shaded geon components to represent information structures. They found that subjects could identify substructures much more rapidly and accurately using this representation, compared to identifying the same information presented using the Unified Modeling Language (UML). Figure 2.6 and Plate 3 of the color insert illustrate.

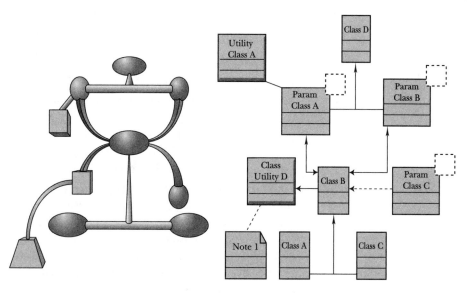

FIGURE

2.6

Because of perceptual mechanisms to analyze the world into structures of three-dimensional primitives, diagrams constructed in this way may be easier to analyze and remember. The diagram on the left is constructed from geon primitives. The one on the right is a UML equivalent. (See Plate 3 of the color insert for a color version of this figure.)

2.2.4   Claims and Limitations

Basing design principles on the science of human perception provides us with design rules grounded in a well-established body of theory and a large variety of empirical results. Because of the presumption of a more-or-less standard human visual system, we can expect cross-cultural validity for the resulting design principles. However, the difficulty lies in distinguishing between aspects of displays that owe their value to culturally determined factors, and aspects that we can somehow trace to innate perceptual mechanisms. For example, the color red in western cultures often stands for a warning. In many Asian cultures red denotes good fortune. This is clearly cultural. However, it is well established that the colors red, green, yellow, and blue are perceptually special in all cultures, and this appears to be due to innate neural structure. Although for these color examples the distinction is clear, often cultural effects and sensory effects are so closely interleaved that it is difficult, if not impossible, to discover which is which.

In addition to the scientific problems, there are pragmatic considerations. Does it really matter if a symbol has some natural perceptual coding, or if it is a cultural product? Heavily over-learned symbol sets, such as the Arabic number system, can be so well established that even if it were possible to design a more perceptually valid number representation system there would be no point. The cost of transforming our number symbols to the ultimately better solution would be impossibly large.

One way of considering the distinction is in terms of time frames. We can think of the neural perceptual machinery as having had a developmental time constant measured in millions of years; some mechanisms have been evolving for hundreds of millions of years, although some minor changes may be as recent as the date of emergence of modern humans about 50,000 years ago. The cultural time constant for symbol systems is much shorter, ranging from hours to a few thousand years. The character set in which this book is written is relatively stable, but some color preferences vary from year to year, and some words may be temporarily redefined for the purpose of a short conversation.

The human perceptual apparatus is extremely flexible and adaptive. This brings into doubt the basic assumption of common perceptual machinery. At the least, it suggests that this assumption may not be particularly useful. Computers tell us that different hardware can run identical software; if socially constructed software dominates the way we use visual information, then the value of understanding the machinery diminishes. As a broad generalization it can reasonably be said that as we move up the processing hierarchy, outlined in this chapter, the importance of the machinery diminishes and the importance of socially constructed symbol systems increases. Thus we are on relatively safe ground when we wish to apply knowledge of perception to the basic issue of how many pixels can be usefully displayed on the 5-centimeter-square screen of a cordless telephone. The problem is much less clear cut when we wish to resolve the issue of whether or not we should design a 3D equivalent to the 2D desktop environment used as the primary computer interface. In the latter case, many tasks must be considered in detail, together with the anticipated habits and skills of the potential users, as well as perceptual issues relating to how well a 3D space can be represented on a 2D screen.

A number of characteristics are common to symbols designed to match human perceptual capabilities, as distinct from design rules that are socially constructed.

Resistance to instructional bias.   Many sensory phenomena—such as contrast effects, after images, and illusions—persist despite our knowledge that they are in fact illusory. In general, this means that there are limits to the flexibility of the visual system. Hence, poorly designed symbols will be inconvenient no matter how familiar they become.

Understanding without training.   If people are given a set of gray color samples of different darkness and asked to order them, they will all come up with the same solution (or a reverse ordering) without further instruction. We can reasonably assume that this is because the gray chips generate a monotonically ordered sequence of neural activity in some sensory mechanism. Given the colors red, green, yellow, and blue, however, people come up with many orderings. Although red, green, yellow, and blue are special in neural color processing, they are not perceptually ordered. Thus, a gray-scale coding of quantity will require less training than a color coding of quantity using the spectrum. Understanding the neural mechanisms tells us which symbols will be more easily acquired.

Cross-cultural validity.   Aspects of data displays that are based on our sensory apparatus will be easily transferred across cultures. Thus, for example, the colors red, green, yellow, and blue will be a useful set of color codes in all cultures. The same colors will stand out for everyone (except people who are color blind). However, the semantics of the colors, such as the connotations of "red," will vary widely; in one society red may represent a warning of danger, in another it may represent good fortune.

Design for perception has only recently become possible, because hitherto we simply did not have the kind of control over color, motion, and texture that is now available. Despite the difficulties, given that design guidelines based on perception will be relatively permanent and are more likely to be valid cross culturally, a relatively greater effort is warranted. Unfortunately, in many cases, we must accept less-than-optimal solutions; the cost of transition from existing symbology is simply too high.

2.3   CASE STUDY

Sometimes a particularly difficult interface problem merits the effort involved in applying vision-research theory and research methodologies. For example, we can consider the problem of providing a usable stereoscopic display for 3D data spaces. Despite the fact that many people regard stereoscopic displays as providing the ultimate 3D experience, such displays are rarely used in practice. Indeed, the many attempts to introduce stereoscopic movies, television, and now computer graphics provide a litany of failure. The following is a brief description of a series of studies described in Ware and colleagues (1998), designed to make a usable stereoscopic display.

> *The problem:* The problem is to provide a usable 3D geographical data visualization system enabling users to interact with 3D stereoscopically displayed data spaces.
>
> *The approach:* There were four components to the search for a solution.
>
> *Component 1:* Study what is known about human stereoscopic depth to attempt to isolate reasons for past failures. Here are some of the major perceptual issues:
>
> ✦ Stereopsis is the ability of the brain to extract distance-from-the-viewer information based on differences in the images in the two eyes.
>
> ✦ Stereopsis is most useful for objects close to the viewer. Beyond about 5 meters, other depth cues are much more important (Cutting, 1997).
>
> ✦ A computer-graphics stereoscopic display fails to simulate reality in a number of important ways. Among them, true depth-of-focus information is not presented because the screen is at a fixed focal distance. Because convergence of the eyes and focusing are coupled visual mechanisms, this interferes with our ability to see stereoscopic depth, causes us to see double images, and is thought to be the cause of eye strain.
>
> *Component 2:* Apply insights gained to develop a method that mitigates perceptual problems. The solution in this case was to develop an algorithm to dynamically adjust the 3D display geometry. This had two important properties. First, it ensured that the near point of the displayed data always lay just behind the screen in terms of stereoscopic depth. This minimized so-called vergence-focus conflict effects. Second, it adjusted the effective eye

separation. This reduced stereoscopic depth for deep scenes and increased it for shallow scenes. The amount of reduction or increase was determined as the result of a careful psychophysical study. This dramatically reduced the likelihood that double images would be seen.

Component 3: Conduct additional perceptual experiments to refine the solution. We carried out studies to find out how disturbing it would be to dynamically adjust stereoscopic-viewing parameters while moving through a virtual workspace. Prior published research suggested certain flexibility in the stereoscopic depth-perception mechanism, and we reasoned that because of this our manipulation would not be seen as disturbing. Our experimental results confirmed this and helped us define parameters for the display algorithm. Except where changes were very rapid, subjects did not notice that the display was being manipulated.

Component 4: Validate final solution in the field and in usability tests. We carried out a study using the algorithm in a realistic setting and found that it was preferred to a stereoscopic display without the algorithm being applied.

The outcome: Our algorithm is being applied in a commercial visualization product called Fledermaus, but the stereoscopic display feature is apparently not widely used except in demonstrations. In general, despite years of work in our laboratory and others around the world, stereoscopic displays remain, for the most part, a "gee whiz" motivational device, not an everyday part of working environments. Part of this can be attributed to the lack of availability of graphics-display hardware.

The introduction of new interface systems is usually far more than simply the invention of a solution to an isolated problem. It is often quite easy to show that a novel input device and display technique can make some task easier to perform, but it is much harder to get novel system components into a working environment. The barriers are many. Manufacturers will not support add-on hardware unless the business case is very compelling. Dell Computer for years clipped off the stereo connectors from the graphics cards in their high-end graphics workstations because they did not wish to provide end-user support for this feature. In addition, system builders avoid adding a new feature, especially if it involves additional hardware, if it adds only a small benefit for one or two tasks.

2.4 CURRENT STATUS OF THEORETICAL APPROACH

The theoretical approach described in this chapter is an applied discipline consisting of the application of the science of human perception to problems of information representation. Because of this, progress closely tracks developments in the underlying science. Color science has more than a century of substantive results, and the application of color science can be traced to nineteenth-century books explaining color theory to artists. The rate of discovery in vision science accelerated from 1960 onward with developments in neuroscience and psychophysics. Work since the early 1990s with functional magnetic resonance imaging have spurred theory development in all areas of neuropsychology. As a result, it is now possible to apply an extensive body of research to the effective use of color, texture, motion, and space perception in coding information. Nevertheless, despite accelerating progress, there are still large areas that are mostly unexplored. In many cases individual phenomena can be modeled, but there is no encompassing theory. For example, we know little about how image information is stored and retrieved.

Although to a great extent the theoretical approach outlined here is based on vision research, it also has some claim to being a separate applied discipline that can be called *information psychophysics*. The goal is not simply to understand how we perceive simple patterns of light and color (as in classical psychophysics) but rather to understand how we perceive elementary information patterns, such as paths in graphs, clusters of related items, or correlated variables. As a separate discipline, information psychophysics is in its infancy, but it is rapidly developing as researchers turn their attention from the development of new computer algorithms to understanding how display algorithms can effectively reveal information.

A body of existing theory that would seem, at first sight, highly relevant to the theoretical approach developed here is based on J. J. Gibson's theory of affordances. Because of its importance, we briefly discuss it here, but we also argue that in fact it has little direct relevance. Affordance theory was constructed by Gibson as a radical alternative to the dominant theories claiming that a world model is cognitively "inferred" from sensory evidence. Gibson proposed that the world is directly perceived based on abundant sensory information (Gibson, 1986). He also claimed that what is perceived is not simply the layout and shape of objects in space, but rather the possibilities for action, which he called *affordances*. Affordance theory has strongly influenced both theory and practice in HCI. The theory suggests a simple design principle: A good design should make the appropriate affordances explicit. However, there is a problem with the concept as he stated it. Gibson insisted that affordances are *physical* properties of the environment *directly* perceived. The problem is that objects on computer screens are not physical objects and we can interact with them only indirectly by using a computer mouse. There are no direct physical affordances in a computer interface. Thus, to be useful, we must develop a cognitive model of affordances—the user interface is perceived as offering opportunities for action. However, this is a radical departure from Gibson's theory because it places the emphasis on perception and cognition, not on Gibson's version of physics—"ecological optics." Also, once we allow that affordances are cognitive, it enables us to propose learned affordances, which means that affordances can be socially constructed. This is about as far from Gibson's intent as it is possible to get. A possible solution is to resort to metaphor. A good user interface is *similar to* a real-world situation providing certain affordances. In addition, the appropriate mode of interaction is *similar to* the real-world interface. Unfortunately, even this is problematic, because the concept of metaphor is not well defined and the notion of similarity requires careful definition if it is not to lead to arbitrariness.

One way that Gibson's theory has been influential in information psychophysics has been through the way he brought researchers' attention to the broad patterns of visual information in the environment (ecological optics). Insofar as perceptual mechanisms are designed to extract these environmental patterns, it may be useful to map data into forms that are common in the environment. However, this view is controversial, and there is little convincing evidence, for example, that 3D information spaces are better than 2D information spaces. In sum, Gibson's theory has little in common with the information psychophysics approach proposed here.

Another way of regarding the theory of information psychophysics is as a component of larger-scale cognitive models such as the Adaptive Control of Thought–Rational (ACT-R) theory of Anderson or the Executive-Process/Interactive Control (EPIC) theory of Kieras (Anderson et al., 1997; Kieras and Meyer, 1997). These models deal with cognitive processing of sensory information as one of the cognitive processes of task performance. As cognitive models become more sophisticated, they will inevitably contain more complete perceptual models that incorporate the pattern-finding capacities of the human visual system. It is to be hoped that information psychophysics can fill the gap, providing an account of pattern finding that feeds into visual working memory and hence to other cognitive subsystems.

2.4.1   Application

In practice, display designers are not likely to use the same methods as vision researchers in evaluating displays. These methods take too much time and provide only limited answers. Instead, a more practical application of vision science to design is through the establishment of design guidelines, initially constructed by researchers. These can be expressed in books, manuals, or, in some cases, standards.

The best developed area is the science of color; the Commission Internationale de l'Eclairage (CIE) has for decades maintained a set of standards relating to how color should be measured, and color-difference formulae that enables us to, for example, make colors that are equally distinct. There is a long history of books for the artist and designer that explain the theory of color perception in more-or-less technical terms and that apply this as a basis for design rules. A recent example is *Computer Generated Color* (Jackson et al., 1994). Other aspects of perception are less well developed, but books such as Wickens's *Engineering Psychology* (1992) and Ware's *Information Visualization: Perception for Design* (1999) are intended to explain the science of perception as it applies to broad issues of display design, ranging from how we deploy visual attention to how we perceive patterns in data.

To conclude, the central argument presented in this chapter is that it is meaningful to consider human sensory systems as computational pattern-finding machines that have certain capabilities embedded in their architecture and neural-processing subsystems. We have shown how visual processing at each stage of the visual system can form the basis of design guidelines. This model works well for early-stage sensory processing, where, for example, scientific color theory has provided the basis for the display devices that are ubiquitous. It works less well at the higher levels of perception, where socially constructed codes are at least as important as innate neural mechanisms.

3 | Motor Behavior Models for Human-Computer Interaction

CHAPTER

I. Scott MacKenzie York University, Toronto, Canada

3.1   MOTIVATION

The movement of body and limbs is inescapable in human-computer interaction (HCI). Whether browsing the Web or intensively entering and editing text in a document, our arms, wrists, and fingers are at work on the keyboard, mouse, and desktop. Our head, neck, and eyes move about, attending to feedback that marks our progress. This chapter is motivated by the need to match the movement limits, capabilities, and potential of humans with input devices and interaction techniques on computing systems. Our focus is on models of human movement relevant to human-computer interaction. Some of the models discussed here emerged from basic research in experimental psychology, whereas others emerged from, and were motivated by, the specific need in HCI to model the interaction between users and physical devices, such as mice and keyboards.

As much as we focus on specific models of human movement and user interaction with devices, this chapter is also about models in general. We will say a lot about the nature of models, what they are, and why they are important tools for the research and development of human-computer interfaces.

3.2   OVERVIEW: MODELS AND MODELING

By its very nature, a model is a simplification of reality. However, a model is useful only if it helps in designing, evaluating, or otherwise providing a basis for understanding the behavior of a complex artifact such as a computer system. It is convenient to think of models as lying in a continuum, with analogy and metaphor at one end and mathematical equations at the other. Most models lie somewhere inbetween. Toward the metaphoric end are *descriptive models;* toward the mathematical end are *predictive models.* These two categories are our particular focus in this chapter, and we shall visit a few examples of each. Two models will be presented in detail and in case studies: Fitts' (1954, 1964) model of the information-processing capability of the human motor system, and Guiard's (1987) model of bimanual control.

Fitts' model is a mathematical expression emerging from the rigors of probability theory. It is a predictive model at the mathematical end of the continuum, to be sure, yet when applied as a model of human movement it has characteristics of a metaphor. Guiard's model emerged from a detailed analysis of how humans use their hands in everyday tasks, such as writing, drawing, playing a sport, or manipulating objects. It is a descriptive model, lacking in mathematical rigor but rich in expressive power.

Neither Guiard's model nor Fitts' model was motivated by issues in human-computer interaction. Yet, today, both are commonly used in the research and development of interactive systems. The reason is simple: They are useful! They are useful because they provide a simplification of the complex interactions between humans and computers. This simplification allows designers to understand and anticipate the impact of a design in a meaningful context. A founding principle of the field of human-computer interaction is that it is multidisciplinary. The field combines work in other disciplines, most notably psychology, cognitive science, and sociology. Fitts' and Guiard's models emerged from basic research in an area within experimental psychology known as *psychomotor behavior* or, simply, *motor control.* Both are widely applicable to many disciplines. The field of human-computer interaction is a beneficiary of this basic research.

Before discussing Fitts' and Guiard's work in detail, we begin with a general discussion on predictive and descriptive models, and we present a few other relevant models within these categories.

3.2.1   Predictive Models

Predictive models, sometimes called *engineering models* or *performance models* (Card, Moran, & Newell, 1983, p. 411; Marchionini & Sibert, 1992), are widely used in many disciplines. In human-computer interaction, predictive models allow metrics of human performance to be determined analytically without undertaking time-consuming and resource-intensive experiments. Predictions so generated are *a priori:* They allow a design scenario to be explored hypothetically, without implementing a real system and gathering the same performance metrics through direct observation on real users. The benefits are obvious.

Hick-Hyman Law

There are many examples of predictive models, some specific to human-computer interaction, others guided by basic theory in perception or motor control. We have already noted that both Fitts' and Guiard's models emerged from basic research in motor control, and we shall have more to say about these shortly. Another example is the Hick-Hyman law for choice reaction time (Hick, 1952; Hyman, 1953). This law takes the form of a prediction equation. Given a set of n stimuli, associated one for one with n responses, the time to react (RT) to the onset of a stimulus and to make the appropriate response is given by

$$RT = a + b \log_2(n) \qquad (3.1)$$

where a and b are empirically determined constants. The Hick-Hyman law has surfaced in a few contexts in interactive systems. Card et al. (1983, p. 74) provide an example of a telephone operator selecting among ten buttons when the light behind a button comes on. Landauer and Nachbar (1985) applied the Hick-Hyman law in measuring and predicting the time to select items in hierarchical menus. Besides confirming the suitability of the law to this category of task, they also found empirical support for their conclusion that breadth should be favored over depth in hierarchical menus. More recently, we have found the Hick-Hyman law useful in predicting text-entry rates on soft keyboards with non-Qwerty layouts (MacKenzie, Zhang, & Soukoreff, 1999; Soukoreff & MacKenzie, 1995). For non-Qwerty layouts, users must visually scan the keyboard to find the desired letter. The act of finding the desired letter among a set of randomly positioned letters is appropriately modeled by the relationship in Equation 3.1.

Keystroke-Level Model

There are numerous predictive models developed specifically for exploring design scenarios for human-computer interfaces. One of the earliest and certainly one of the most comprehensive is the *keystroke-level model* (KLM) by Card et al. (1980; 1983, chap. 8). The KLM was developed as a practical design tool, the goal being to predict the time to accomplish a task on a computer system. The model predicts expert error-free task-completion times, given the following input parameters:

- ✦ a task or series of subtasks

- ✦ method used

- ✦ command language of the system

- ✦ motor-skill parameters of the user

- ✦ response-time parameters of the system

A KLM prediction is the sum of the subtask times and the required overhead. The model includes four motor-control operators (K = key stroking, P = pointing, H = homing, D = drawing), one mental operator (M), and one system-response operator (R):

$$T_{\text{EXECUTE}} = t_{\text{K}} + t_{\text{P}} + t_{\text{H}} + t_{\text{D}} + t_{\text{M}} + t_{\text{R}} \qquad (3.2)$$

Some of the operations are omitted or repeated, depending on the task. For example, if a task requires n keystrokes, t_{K} becomes $n \times t_{\text{K}}$. Each t_{K} operation is assigned a value according to the skill of the user, with values ranging from $t_{\text{K}} = 0.08$ s for highly skilled typists to $t_{\text{K}} = 1.20$ s for a typist working with an unfamiliar keyboard. The pointing operator, t_{P}, is based on Fitts' law. More on this later.

Since its introduction, the KLM has surfaced in many contexts in HCI, such as map digitizing (Haunold & Kuhn, 1994), predicting usage patterns in editors (Toleman & Welsh, 1996), generating power key assignments to reduce typing keystrokes (Nicols & Ritter, 1995), predicting user performance with hierarchical menus (Lane, Napier, Batsell, & Naman, 1993), or predicting text-entry performance for physically challenged users in a word-prediction system (Koester & Levine, 1994).

3.2.2   Descriptive Models

Descriptive models are of a vastly different genre than predictive models. Although they generally do not yield an empirical or quantitative measure of user performance, their utility is by no means second to predictive models. Simply put, descriptive models provide a framework or context for thinking about or describing a problem or situation. Often the framework is little more than a verbal or graphic articulation of categories or identifiable features in an interface. Nevertheless, the simple possession of such a framework arms the designer with a tool for studying and thinking about the user-interaction experience. A simple example is developed in the next section.

Key-Action Model

Computer keyboards today contain a vast array of buttons or keys. Most systems use a variation of the 101-style keyboard, with a row of function keys across the top and a numeric keypad on the right. Have you ever thought about the operation of keys on a keyboard? Here's a descriptive model for this purpose. Let's call it the *key-action model* (KAM). In our KAM, keyboard keys are categorized as either *symbol keys, executive keys,* or *modifier keys.* Symbol keys deliver graphic symbols—typically, letters, numbers, or punctuation symbols—to an application such as a text editor. Executive keys invoke actions in the application or at the system level or meta level. Examples include ENTER, F1, or ESC. Modifier keys do not generate symbols or invoke actions, but, rather, set up a condition necessary to modify the effect of a subsequently pressed key. Examples include SHIFT or ALT. And that's about it for the KAM. It's a simple model, to be sure. It has a name, and it identifies three categories of keys, providing for each a name, a definition, and examples. What do you think of this model? Is it correct? Is it flawed? Do all keyboard keys fit the model? Can you think of additional categories or subcategories to improve the model or to make it more accurate or more comprehensive? Do some keys have features of more than one category? Can you think of a graphical illustration of the model to improve its expressive power? Is the model useful?

The substance of these questions is evidence of the power of descriptive models such as the KAM. The model piques our interest and suggests aspects of keyboard operation that merit consideration, particularly if a new design is contemplated. The most important question is the last. There is no greater measure of the merit of a model than its ability to tease out critical arguments on the potential, the capabilities, and the limitations in a particular interaction domain. We will revisit the KAM later in a case study on the affordances of the desktop interface for two-handed interaction.

Three-State Model of Graphical Input

Another example is Buxton's *3-state model* for graphical input devices (Buxton, 1990). The model is a simple expression of the operation of computer pointing devices in terms of state transitions. It is described simply as a vocabulary to recognize and explore the relationship between pointing devices and the interaction techniques they afford (Buxton, 1990, p. 449). In this sense, it is a paradigm of descriptive modeling. The three states are identified in Figure 3.1, annotated for mouse interaction.

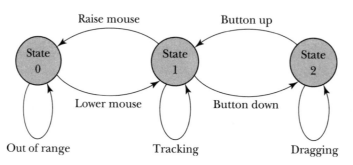

FIGURE

3.1

Buxton's 3-state model of graphical input (after Buxton, 1990).

Left to right in Figure 3.1, the states are *Out of range* (State 0) for clutching or repositioning a mouse on a mouse pad, *Tracking* (State 1) for moving a tracking symbol such as a cursor about a display, and *Dragging* (State 2) for moving an icon on the desktop or for grouping a set of objects or a range of text. The model seems simple and obvious, and we might question its ability to add significant insight to the existing body of pointing-device research. Yet, the model can be extended to capture additional aspects of pointing-device interaction such as multibutton interaction, stylus input, and direct versus indirect input. See Buxton (1990) for further details.

As further evidence of the utility of Buxton's work, we recently used the 3-state model to characterize an interaction technique that didn't even exist at the time the model was introduced. The insight gained led to a redesign of an interaction technique. This work is briefly recounted here. Never shy of innovation, Apple Computer, Inc. (Cupertino, CA) took a bold step in 1994 by commercializing a new pointing device in its PowerBook 500 notebook computer: the TrackPoint touchpad (MacNeill & Blickenstorfer, 1996). And the rest is history. Today, touchpads are the dominant pointing device for notebook computers. (IBM and Toshiba are notable holdouts, preferring isometric joysticks instead.) One of the interaction techniques supported by touchpads is *lift-and-tap*, wherein primitives like clicking, double-clicking, or dragging are implemented without a button. These new interaction primitives are easily represented by Buxton's 3-state model. Figure 3.2 provides a simple comparison of the state transitions for dragging tasks using a mouse and using lift-and-tap on a touchpad.

Diagrams like these are evidence of the descriptive power of models such as Buxton's. Two observations follow: (1) Lift-and-tap necessitates extra state transitions in comparison to a mouse, and (2) the use of state 1–0–1 transitions for lift-

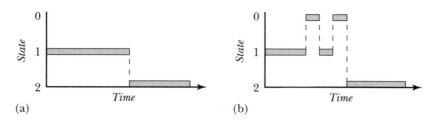

FIGURE

3.2
Dragging tasks: (a) mouse; (b) lift-and-tap touchpad. Dragging begins upon entering State 2 (after MacKenzie & Oniszczak, 1997).

and-tap is confounded with clutching (not shown), which uses the same state transitions.

Among users' frustrations in using touchpads is that these primitives are difficult, awkward, or error prone. For example, if a finger touch following a lift is spatially displaced from the point of lifting, the system often incorrectly enters the Tracking state (State 1) instead of the Dragging state (State 2).

Armed with a deeper understanding of touchpad interaction, we undertook a redesign of the buttonless implementation of state transitions on touchpads. The additional pressure-sensing capability of touchpads was used to implement State 1–2 transitions by "pressing harder." A built-in relay provided both tactile and aural feedback to inform the user of state transitions, much like the feedback in pressing a mouse button. Thus, clicking, double clicking, and dragging were implemented on the touchpad, without a button, yet using the same state transitions as on a mouse. The complete details are presented in the 1997 and 1998 proceedings of the Association for Computing Machinery's (ACM) Special Group for Computer-Human Interaction (SIGCHI) (MacKenzie & Oniszczak, 1997; MacKenzie & Oniszczak, 1998).

Model for Mapping Degrees of Freedom to Dimensions

One final example of a descriptive model will be given. A topic of great interest in HCI is interactive graphics. The vocabulary of such systems includes terms like *dimensions* and *degrees of freedom*. These terms are often used interchangeably; however, the terms are different, and the distinction between them is often poorly articulated. Before proceeding, Figure 3.3 is necessary to establish some terminology.

The figure shows a mousepad and identifies the most common labels for the axes of motion. Left-to-right motion is *translational*, along the X axis; to-and-fro

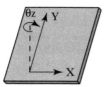

FIGURE

3.3
A mousepad is a two-dimensional surface with three degrees of freedom: X, Y, and θ_Z.

Dimensions		Degree of freedom	Mouse	Two-ball mouse	Other			
					A	B	C	D
3D {	2D {	X	●	●	●	●	●	●
		Y	●	●	●	●	●	●
		Θ_Z	○	●	○	●	○	●
		Z	○	○	●	●	○	○
		Θ_X	○	○	○	●	●	●
		Θ_Y	○	○	○	●	●	●

FIGURE

3.4

Mapping degrees of freedom to dimensions (see text for discussion).

motion is translational along the Y axis. If the mouse is rotated on the pad, motion is *rotational* about the Z axis, labeled θ_Z in the figure. Although most users are quick to declare the mouse a two-dimensional (2D) device (e.g., Zhai & MacKenzie, 1998), this is not quite true. Here's where we see a slight point of confusion between dimensions (D) and degrees of freedom (DOF). A true 2D device has three degrees of freedom (3-DOF), as illustrated in Figure 3.3. If a mouse were a true 2D device, then translational motion along the X and Y axes would be sensed, *as well as rotational motion about the Z axis.* Of course, rotational motion of the mouse is not sensed. This deficiency is illustrated in Figure 3.4. The left two columns show our descriptive model for mapping degrees of freedom to dimensions, using the terminology in Figure 3.3. The third column shows the mappings implemented for a conventional mouse.

The model in Figure 3.4 is a simple tool for illustrating the mappings of degrees of freedom to dimensions for real or hypothetical input devices. The apparent shortcoming of the standard mouse as a 2D input device motivated us to design a new mouse to implement the missing DOF. As shown in the fourth column in Figure 3.4, our two-ball mouse also senses rotational motion about the Z axis. An object acquired in a graphics application with this mouse can be positioned in a single gesture both translationally along the X and Y axis and rotationally about the Z axis, thus negating the need for a "rotate tool." See MacKenzie, Soukoreff, and Pal (1997) for details.

Figure 3.4 also shows the mappings of degrees of freedom to dimensions for other pointing devices. Column A identifies devices that sense only translation along the three axes. An example is the Owl by Pegasus Technologies, Ltd. (Tel Aviv, Israel). Column B identifies true 3D input devices, such as trackers used in virtual reality systems. Such devices sense X-, Y-, and Z-axis translation and rotation. An example is the Isotrak II by Polhemus, Inc. (Colchester, VT). Column C identifies an interesting research prototype known as the Rockin'Mouse. It looks and feels like a mouse, but it has a curved bottom and senses both translation and rotation about the X and Y axes (see Balakrishnan, Baudel, Kurtenbach, & Fitzmaurice, 1997, for details). Column D identifies a hypothetical 5-DOF input device. Because it does not sense Z-axis translation, the device is operated on the mousepad and therefore has that special mouselike appeal.

3.3 SCIENTIFIC FOUNDATIONS AND MODEL DESCRIPTIONS

The two models chosen for detailed study in this chapter are Fitts' law and Guiard's model of bimanual skill. As we shall see, Fitts' law falls within the scope of a predictive model, whereas Guiard's model is an example of a descriptive model.

3.3.1 Fitts' Law

Fitts' Law is one of the most robust and highly adopted models of human movement. The model is, arguably, the most successful of many efforts to model human behavior as an information-processing activity. (For detailed reviews, see MacKenzie, 1991; MacKenzie, 1992; Meyer, Smith, Kornblum, Abrams, & Wright, 1990; Welford, 1968). Fitts was interested in applying information theory to measure the difficulty of movement tasks and the human rate of information processing as tasks are realized. He argued that the amplitude of an aimed movement was analogous to an electronic signal and that the spatial accuracy of the move was analogous to electronic noise. Furthermore, he proposed that the human motor system is like a communications channel, wherein movements are viewed as the transmission of signals. His analogy is based on Shannon's Theorem 17, expressing the effective information capacity C (in bits/s) of a communications channel of bandwidth B (in s^{-1} or Hz) as

$$C = B \log_2(S / N + 1) \tag{3.3}$$

where S is the signal power and N is the noise power (Shannon & Weaver, 1949, pp. 100–103).

Fitts presented his analogy—now his "law"—in two highly celebrated papers, one in 1954 (Fitts, 1954), the second in 1964 (Fitts & Peterson, 1964). The 1954 paper described a serial, or reciprocal, target-acquisition task, wherein subjects alternately tapped on targets of width W separated by amplitude A; see Figure 3.5(a). The 1964 paper described a similar experiment using a discrete task, wherein subjects selected one of two targets in response to a stimulus light; see Figure 3.5(b). It is easy to imagine how the mechanical apparatus Fitts used can be replaced by computer input devices and targets rendered on a cathode-ray tube (CRT) display.

Fitts proposed to quantify a movement task's difficulty—*ID*, the *index of difficulty*—using information theory by the metric "bits." Specifically,

$$ID = \log_2(2A / W) \tag{3.4}$$

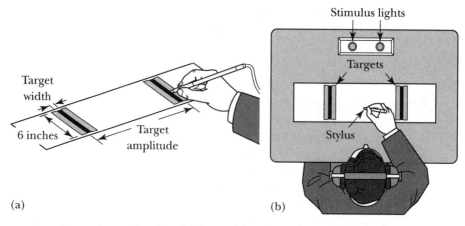

(a)   (b)

Experimental paradigm for Fitts' Law: (a) serial task (after Fitts, 1954); (b) discrete task (after Fitts & Peterson, 1964).

The amplitude (A) and width (W) in Equation 3.4 are analogous to Shannon's signal (S) and noise (N) in Equation 3.3. The following expression for ID was introduced to improve the information-theoretic analogy (MacKenzie, 1989):

$$ID = \log_2(A \,/\, W + 1) \tag{3.5}$$

Because A and W are both measures of distance, the term within the parentheses in Equation 3.5 is without units. The unit *bits* emerges from the somewhat arbitrary choice of base 2 for the logarithm. From Equation 3.5, the movement time (MT) to complete a task is predicted using a simple linear equation:

$$MT = a + b \times ID \tag{3.6}$$

In building a Fitts' Law model, the slope and intercept coefficients in the prediction equation are determined through empirical tests, typically using linear regression. The tests are undertaken in a controlled experiment using a group of subjects and one or more input devices and task conditions.

The design of experiments for Fitts' Law studies is straightforward. Tasks are devised to cover a range of difficulties by varying A and W. For each task condition, multiple trials are conducted, and the time to execute each is recorded and stored electronically for statistical analysis. Accuracy is also recorded, either through the x-y coordinates of selection or through the error rate—the percentage of trials selected with the cursor outside the target. Example data sets for two devices tested in a serial task are given in Figure 3.6. For the purpose of this discussion, the devices are simply referred to as "A" and "B."[1] The figure shows the controlled variables A and W, along with the computed index of difficulty (ID, see Equation 3.5) and, for each condition, the observed error rate (ER) and movement time (MT). Each dependent measure is based on 240 observations (12 participants × 20 trials per condition).

Figure 3.7 shows a common reporting technique for Fitts' Law experiments. The nine MT-ID points for each device in Figure 3.6 are plotted along with the regression lines. The prediction equations for MT as a function of ID are also shown, as are the R^2 statistics for the percentage of variance in the observations explained by the model. It is noteworthy of Fitts' Law in general that R^2 is

---

[1] The data sets in Figure 3.6 are from the fourth block of trials in a Fitts' Law experiment comparing four pointing devices, including a Microsoft Mouse 2.0 (Device "A") and an Interlink RemotePoint (Device "B"). See MacKenzie and Jusoh (2001) for complete details on the devices and the experimental methodology.

A (pixels)	W (pixels)	ID (bits)	Device "A"		Device "B"	
			ER (%)	MT (ms)	ER (%)	MT (ms)
40	10	2.32	2.08	665	1.25	1587
40	20	1.58	3.33	501	2.08	1293
40	40	1.00	1.25	361	0.42	1001
80	10	3.17	2.92	762	2.08	1874
80	20	2.32	1.67	604	2.08	1442
80	40	1.58	1.67	481	0.83	1175
160	10	4.09	3.75	979	2.08	2353
160	20	3.17	5.42	823	1.67	1788
160	40	2.32	4.17	615	0.83	1480
	Mean:	2.40	2.92	644	1.48	1555

FIGURE

3.6

Example data sets for two devices from a Fitts' Law experiment.

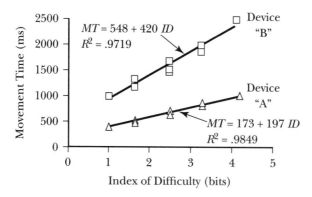

FIGURE

3.7

Scatter plots and regression lines for data sets in Figure 3.6.

usually very high, attesting to the strength of the model as a predictor for rapid aimed movements. For Device "A," for example, the regression equation explains about 98% of the variance in the observed movement times.

Because task difficulty is analogous to information, the rate of task execution is interpreted as the human rate of information processing. For example, if a task rated at, say, ID = 4.09 bits is executed in MT = 979 ms, then the human rate of information processing for that task is 4.09/0.979 = 4.18 bits/s. In fact, this very example is seen in Figure 3.6 for Device "A" for the condition A = 160 and W = 10. Fitts called this measure the *index of performance* (IP), although the term *throughput* (TP) is more common today (Douglas, Kirkpatrick, & MacKenzie, 1999; ISO, 1999).

More likely, the mean throughput is of interest. Reading from the bottom row in Figure 3.6, the mean throughput across all the *A-W* conditions for Device "A" is TP = 2.40/0.644 = 3.73 bits/s. For Device "B," TP = 2.40/1.555 = 1.57 bits/s. Using throughput as a criterion, therefore, we conclude that users' performance with Device "A" was about 3.73/1.57 = 2.4 times better than performance with Device "B."

Unfortunately, the computation of throughput is not as straightforward as just described. In many studies it is reported as the reciprocal of the slope of the regression line (e.g., Card, English, & Burr, 1978; MacKenzie, Sellen, & Buxton, 1991). By this reasoning and from Figure 3.7, we see that throughput for Device "A" is TP = 1/0.197 = 5.08 bits/s. This figure is a nontrivial 36% higher than TP = 3.73 bits/s, computed from the same data except dividing the mean ID by the mean MT. The computation of TP is further complicated by the need to include spatial variability (namely accuracy) to further improve the analogy to Shannon's theorem (Fitts & Peterson, 1964; Welford, 1968). This is accomplished by replacing the target width (W) in Equation 3.5 with the "effective target width" (W_e), computed as follows:

$$W_e = 4.133 \times SD_x \qquad (3.7)$$

where SD_x is the standard deviation in the selection coordinates computed over a block of trials.[2] If only discrete error rates are recorded, as shown in Figure 3.6, then an alternate technique is used to compute W_e (see MacKenzie, 1992, for details). Throughput so computed is extremely useful because in a single measure it captures both speed and accuracy in performance, thus increasing the ability of the measure to reveal overall performance differences between devices or interaction techniques.

If the primary goal in a Fitts' Law experiment is to establish performance differences between devices and/or interaction techniques, then throughput is

---

[2] The coefficient 4.133 emerges from the term $(2 \times \pi \times e)^{1/2}$ in Shannon's original theorem. See MacKenzie (1992) for details.

the best choice as the criterion measure. The recommended calculation is the division of means with the aforementioned adjustment for accuracy:

$$TP = ID_e \,/\, MT \qquad\qquad (3.8)$$

where

$$ID_e = \log_2(A \,/\, W_e + 1) \qquad\qquad (3.9)$$

This is the formula specified in the ISO standard for evaluating computer pointing devices (ISO, 1999). If the primary goal in a Fitts' Law experiment is to generate a movement time-prediction equation, then Equation 3.6 should be used. We will put this equation to work later in a case study.

The first use of Fitts' Law in HCI was the study by Card et al. (1978), in which they empirically established the superiority of the mouse over an isometric joystick. Many other Fitts' Law studies have appeared since (e.g., Accot & Zhai, 1999; Arsenault & Ware, 2000; Douglas et al., 1999; Epps, 1986; MacKenzie, Kauppinen, & Silfverberg, 2001; MacKenzie & Oniszczak, 1998).

This concludes our detailed analysis of Fitts' Law. Later, in Section 3.4, we present a case study showing an application of Fitts' Law in predicting text-entry rates on mobile phones.

3.3.2   Guiard's Model of Bimanual Skill

Humans are not only two handed, they also use their hands differently. This fact has been the subject of considerable study in a specialized area of motor behavior known as *bimanual control* or *laterality* (Kelso, Southard, & Goodman, 1979; Peters, 1985; Porac & Coren, 1981; Wing, 1982). Studying the between-hand division of labor in everyday tasks reveals that most tasks are asymmetric: Our hands have different roles and perform distinctly different tasks. Given this, and the knowledge that people are either right handed or left handed, it follows that an examination of the assignment of tasks to hands is a useful exercise. This is the essence of Guiard's work, as presented in a seminal paper in 1987 (Guiard, 1987). The result of this work is a descriptive model of bimanual skill. Although the model lacks the mathematical rigor of Fitts' Law, it is by no means less valuable as a tool to aid and inform designers of interactive systems.

An important goal for descriptive models is to delineate the critical characteristics in a problem space, and this is precisely what Guiard's model does.

Hand	Role and Action
Nonpreferred	✦ leads the preferred hand ✦ sets the spatial frame of reference for the preferred hand ✦ performs coarse movements
Preferred	✦ follows the nonpreferred hand ✦ works within the established frame of reference set by the nonpreferred hand ✦ performs fine movements

FIGURE
3.8

Guiard's model of bimanual control.

Figure 3.8 identifies the roles and actions of the nonpreferred and preferred hands, as given by Guiard.

The best way to explain the points in Figure 3.8 is through an exemplary illustration and narrative. In Figure 3.9, a right-handed graphic artist is shown sketching the design of a new car. The artist acquires the template with her left hand (*nonpreferred hand leads*). The template is manipulated over the workspace (*coarse movement, sets the frame of reference*). The stylus is acquired in the right hand (*preferred hand follows*) and brought into the vicinity of the template (*works within frame of reference set by the nonpreferred hand*). Sketching takes place (*preferred hand makes precise movements*).

The roles and actions just described provide a provocative and fresh way of describing how humans approach common tasks. This is true both for common tasks and in the narrower context of human-computer interaction. About the same time that Guiard's model appeared, Buxton and Myers (1986) conducted an experiment to investigate two-handed input in computer-aided design (CAD) systems. Their work was undertaken independently of Guiard's work or of other work in experimental psychology on bimanual control or laterality. One of their studies describes a positioning and zooming task where the subtasks were performed by separate hands. The positioning task was performed using a graphics tablet "puck" in the preferred hand, while the zooming task was performed using a slider to control the size of an object. The goal was to manipulate an object so that it coincided in position and size with a similar object. Their second study describes a scrolling-and-selection task. The goal was to select words in a document. The document was sufficiently large that scrolling was necessary to locate the desired words. Their key findings were that subjects—without being instructed—gravitated to a two-handed interaction style, and that task-completion times were smaller when a two-handed strategy was employed.

FIGURE

3.9

Two-handed interaction paradigm. (Sketch courtesy of Shawn Zhang.)

Unfortunately, Buxton and Myers (1986) provided very little insight into the differential roles of the hands in bimanual tasks (cf. Figure 3.8). They concluded only that the subjects' natural tendency toward a two-handed strategy was due to the "efficiency of hand motion" (p. 321). Watershed moments in multidisciplinary fields like HCI often occur when researchers through due diligence locate and adopt relevant research in other fields—research that can inform and guide their own discipline.[3] The union of HCI research in two-handed input and basic research in bimanual control occurred several years later, through the efforts of Paul Kabbash (Kabbash, Buxton, & Sellen, 1994; Kabbash, MacKenzie, & Buxton, 1993). The paper by Kabbash, Buxton, and Sellen (1994) was the first in HCI to cite Guiard's 1987 paper and to be guided by this important model. Subsequent HCI research in two-handed interaction has consistently used Guiard's descriptive model (see Figure 3.8) as a guiding principle in designing new interactive techniques that appropriately engage the hands of users.

---

[3] There are many examples in HCI, for example, Card, English, and Burr's (1978) first use of Fitts' Law (Fitts, 1954), or Norman's (1988) introduction of Gibson's affordances (Gibson, 1979).

3.4 CASE STUDIES

In this section, two case studies are presented. The first is an application of Fitts' Law in predicting text-entry rates on mobile, or cell, phones. The second is an examination of the affordances of the desktop computer interfaces in the context of two-handed input.

3.4.1 Case Study #1: Fitts' Law Predictions of Text-Entry Rates on Mobile Phones

One recent application of Fitts' Law is in predicting text-entry rates on mobile phones. This is particularly relevant today because of the tremendous demand for text messaging on mobile phones. Current volumes are on the order of billions of SMS (short message service) messages per month *(www.gsmworld.com)*.

Text Entry on Mobile Phones

Before presenting our model, the main techniques for entering text on a mobile phone are described. Most mobile phones include a 12-key keypad similar to that in Figure 3.10. The keypad consists of number keys 0–9 and two additional keys (# and *). Characters *a–z* are spread over keys 2–9 in alphabetic order, with the SPACE character assigned to the 0 key. Because there are fewer keys than the 26 needed for the characters *a–z,* three or four characters are grouped on each key, and, so, ambiguity arises. There are two main approaches to text entry on a phone keypad: the *multitap* method and the *one-key with disambiguation* method.

Multitap. The multitap method is currently the most common text input method for mobile phones. With this approach, the user presses each key one or more times to specify the input character. For example, the *2* key is pressed once for the character *a,* twice for *b,* and three times for *c* (see Figure 3.10). As an example, *quick brown fox* is entered as follows:

```
77 88 444 222 55 0 22 777 666 9 66 0 333 666 99
q  u  i   c   k  _ b  r   o   w n  _ f   o   x
```

Clearly, the multitap method bears substantial overhead. In this example, 33 key presses generated 15 characters of text. Calculations using a language corpus

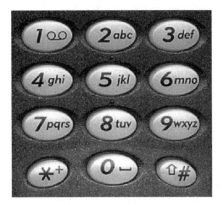

FIGURE   Standard 12-key mobile phone keypad.

3.10

indicate that "on average" the multitap method requires 2.034 keystrokes per character when entering English text (MacKenzie, 2002).[4]

The multitap approach suffers from the additional problem of segmentation. When a character is on the same key as the previous character, further ambiguity arises. For example, both letters in the word *on* are on the *6* key (see Figure 3.10). Successive key presses are segmented (viz., assigned to different characters) using either a timeout or a dedicated timeout kill key. We will say more about these techniques shortly.

One-key with disambiguation.   An alternative way to overcome the ambiguity problem is to add linguistic knowledge to the system. We call this technique *one-key with disambiguation*. An example is *T9* by Tegic Communications, Inc. (Seattle, WA; *www.tegic.com/*). When using *T9*, each key is pressed only once. For example,

```
7 8 4 2 5 0 2 7 6 9 6 0 3 6 9
q u i c k _ b r o w n _ f o x
```

Although each key maps to more than one letter, the system performs beyond-the-scenes disambiguation in determining the intended word. Naturally, linguistic disambiguation is not perfect, since multiple words may have the same key

---

[4] This figure is computed based on entering text consisting of the 26 letters plus the SPACE character. If only letters are considered, the figure is about 2.26 keystrokes per character.

sequence. In these cases, the most common word is the default. A demonstration follows (presses of the 0 key are omitted for clarity):

```
843 78425 27696 369 58677 6837 843 5299 364
the quick brown fox jumps over the jazz dog
tie stick crown     lumps muds tie lazy fog
vie                            vie
```

Candidate words are shown from top to bottom, with the most probable at the top. Of the nine words in the phrase, eight are ambiguous, given the required key sequence. For seven of the eight, however, the most probable word is the intended word. The most probable word is *not* the intended word in just one instance, with *jazz* being more probable in English than *lazy*. In this case, the user must press additional keys to obtain the desired word.

Given the two input methods just described, it is worth speculating on the relative text-entry rates attainable with each. For this, we can develop a prediction model using Fitts' Law in combination with the probabilities of letter pairs, or *digrams,* in the desired language. This is described next.

Predicting Text-Entry Rates Using Fitts' Law

Fitts' Law is not an appropriate model for predicting typing speeds on a Qwerty keyboard, because the task is complex and involves parallel and/or overlapping movements by two hands and ten fingers. If the task is reduced to input via a single finger or stylus, however, then the situation is completely different. With a single stream of motor actions, the task is a standard target-acquisition task conforming to the Fitts paradigm.

Text entry on a mobile phone, for example, consists of aiming for and acquiring (viz., pressing) a series of keys "as quickly and accurately as possible." Users typically perform this task either using their index finger or thumb. The time to press any key, given any previous key, can be readily predicted using Fitts' Law. Models for pressing keys on a mobile phone are reported by Silfverberg, MacKenzie, and Korhonen (2000). For index-finger input,

$$MT = 165 + 52\ ID \qquad (3.10)$$

and for thumb input,

$$MT = 176 + 64\ ID \qquad (3.11)$$

The only ingredients required to build a text-entry prediction model are information on the position and size of keys, the letter assignment to keys, and the relative probabilities of digrams in the target language. These are close at hand. The position and size of keys are easily quantisized for any mobile-phone keypad using a ruler. The standard assignment of letters to keys is shown in Figure 3.10. Tables of digram probabilities are available from a variety of sources (e.g., Mayzner & Tresselt, 1965; Soukoreff & MacKenzie, 1995; Underwood & Schulz, 1960). A final task—laborious but simple—is to put this information together along with the Fitts' Law equations in an electronic form suitable for generating the predictions. A spreadsheet application suffices.

If we limit the model to text entry using 26 letters plus the SPACE character, then there are $27^2 = 727$ target acquisition tasks, one for each letter j given a preceding letter i. The time to enter each i-j sequence is predicted using Fitts' Law, yielding MT_{ij}. The time is weighted by the probability of the digram in the target language, P_{ij}. For English, sequences like t-h or e-SPACE have high probabilities, whereas sequences like g-k or f-v have low probabilities. The sum of the 727 weighted-movement times is the mean movement time per character for the target language for the given interaction technique:

$$MT_L = \Sigma\Sigma \ (P_{ij} \times MT_{ij}) \qquad (3.12)$$

This is converted to a text-entry rate in words per minute (wpm) by multiplying by 60 seconds per minute and dividing by 5 characters per word[5]:

$$WPM = MT_L \times (60 \ / \ 5) \qquad (3.13)$$

Predicted Text-Entry Rates on Mobile Phones

There are a few additional details to accommodate before predictions are available. For the multitap method, keys are pressed one to four times depending on each letter's position on a key. To account for this behavior, we introduce the key-repeat time, MT_{REPEAT}, the time to press a key having just pressed the same key. This is a Fitts' Law task with "zero movement amplitude" (viz., $A = 0$). From Equation 3.5, the index of difficulty is $ID = \log_2(0/W + 1) = 0$ bits. Hence, MT_{REPEAT} is the intercept in the Fitts' Law (see Equations 3.6, 3.10, and 3.11). Thus, to MT_{ij} we add $N \times MT_{REPEAT}$, where N varies from 0 to 3.

---

[5] The average size of a word in English is about 4.5 characters. However, in computing text-entry throughput in "words per minute," it is customary to consider a "word" any sequence of 5 characters, including letters, spaces, punctuation, and so forth.

Method	Predicted Expert Entry Rate (wpm)	
	Index Finger	Thumb
Multitap		
wait for timeout	22.5	20.8
timeout kill	27.2	24.5
One-key with disambiguation	45.7	40.6

FIGURE

3.11

Expert text-entry rate predictions (wpm) for mobile phones (from Silfverberg et al., 2000).

Additionally, the multitap method requires a special technique to segment consecutive characters on the same key, as noted earlier. One technique—*wait-for-timeout*—is to hesitate for a timeout interval (T_{TIMEOUT}) between keypresses for each character. Although durations vary among manufacturers, a reasonable value is $T_{\text{TIMEOUT}} = 1500$ ms. This is the setting on Nokia phones. The other technique—*timeout-kill*—is to press an explicit timeout kill key, thus allowing direct entry of the second character. On Nokia phones, this is implemented using the DOWN-ARROW key. For the timeout-kill strategy, we use $MT_{i\text{-KILL}} + MT_{\text{KILL-}j}$ instead of MT_{ij}, where i and j are on the same key. The user may choose whether to use the wait-for-timeout or timeout-kill segmentation strategy; therefore, a prediction model is built for each strategy. Without further ado, Figure 3.11 gives the predicted expert text-entry rates for mobile phones for the input methods and interaction techniques just described.

Multitap entry rates vary from 20.8 wpm to 27.2 wpm depending on interaction technique (index finger vs. thumb) and the timeout strategy employed. In general, index-finger entry is faster than thumb entry.

A few follow-up comments are warranted. Note the prefix "expert" in Figure 3.11. Indeed, the predictions represent an upper bound. In particular, they do not account for the time to scan the keypad visually to find the next key to press. Zero visual-scan time is reasonable for expert users, but novices must visually attend to the keypad during entry. This will push entry rates down. The predictions also assume error-free input. This simplifies the prediction model, but, in practice, users are fallible and overhead is incurred in correcting mistakes. So, all rates in Figure 3.11 must be viewed in the proper context: They represent only the motor component of error-free expert input.

With predictions above 40 wpm, clearly the one-key-with-disambiguation method is far superior to the multitap method. However, these rates are coincident with rather broad assumptions, and they also must be viewed in the appropriate context. As noted, the rates are for error-free expert input. However, at least two additional assumptions are present for the one-key-with-disambiguation method: (1) all words are in the system's dictionary, and (2) when ambiguity arises, the intended word is the most probable in the list of candidates. Clearly, violations in these assumptions will push rates down, but a detailed discussion of the mechanisms at work is beyond the scope of this chapter. See Silfverberg et al. (2000) for further discussion.

For our next case study, we return to Guiard's model of bimanual control.

3.4.2 Case Study #2: Bimanual Control and Desktop Computer Affordances

Affordances are the action possibilities an artifact offers to a user (Gibson, 1979). A keyboard's keys can be pressed, a mouse can be acquired and moved, mouse buttons can be pressed, and a mouse wheel can be rotated. These are the *what* of desktop computer affordances. Let's consider the *where*.

On a typical desktop keyboard, keys are spread across the device, there is a wide space bar along the bottom, and nonalpha keys are in various locations. Although slight variations exist, the 101-style keyboard is the most common today. An example is given in Figure 3.12, which also identifies the categories of keys as per the key-action model presented earlier.

Of concern here are the "power keys," consisting of *executive keys* (e.g., EN-TER) and *modifier keys* (e.g., SHIFT). On the keyboard's left, we find SHIFT, CTRL, ALT, TAB, CAPS LOCK, and ESC, while on the right we find no less than 18 power keys: SHIFT, CTRL, ALT, ENTER, BACKSPACE, INSERT, DELETE, HOME, END, PAGE UP, PAGE DOWN, ←, ↑, →, ↓, PRNT SCRN, SCROLL LOCK, and PAUSE. Because SHIFT, CTRL, and ALT are mirrored, they do not pose a left- or right-hand bias and are eliminated from further discussion. Only three keys on the left (ESC, TAB, CAPS LOCK) are without a right-side replica; thus, the number of keys are 3 on the left and 15 on the right. These are identified by dots in Figure 3.12. The ratio is 1:5.

Clearly, the keyboard is entrenched with a right-side bias. This was fine in the 1970s; however, the emergence of the graphical user interface (GUI) and point-and-click interfaces in the 1980s changed everything (but not the keyboard, apparently). Most users grasp the mouse in their right hand. A simple observation is that the right hand is busy and, arguably, overloaded. Interactions that involve both power-key activation and pointing are exacerbated for right-handed users: Their options are to "reach over" with the left hand, or to release the mouse and acquire and activate a power key with their right hand.

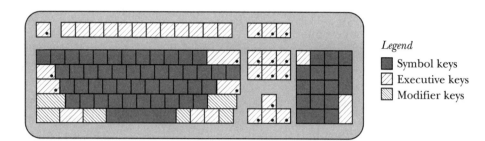

FIGURE
3.12

101-style keyboard and key categories as per the key-action model (see text for a discussion).

FIGURE
3.13

A left-handed user interacting with a desktop system. (Sketch courtesy of Shawn Zhang.)

The scenario differs for left-handed users, however. When they position the mouse on the left side of the keyboard and manipulate it with their left hand, the action possibilities of the desktop interface are dramatically changed (see Figure 3.13). The confounding of power-key activation with pointing operations is greatly reduced.

This brief analysis clearly shows that the affordances of a typical desktop system are substantially different for left-handed users who manipulate the mouse in their left hand. An important question is this: Are left-handed users well-served by the configuration in Figure 3.13? This question is by no means simple to answer. A detailed response would require a checklist-style examination of the myriad tasks typical of desktop use. However, a cursory answer to this question is "yes." Let's examine why.

If we combine the earlier points on affordances and human skill in analyzing common GUI tasks, we see that the bimanual skill model is often violated (viz., preferred hand leads). Of course, there is little gained in suggesting a ground-up redesign of computer keyboards—it's too late! Faced with the unyielding affordances of current keyboards, users (both left handed and right handed) naturally discover and adopt strategies of optimization. In short, users find ways to optimize, often in spite of the interface. The path of discovery seems to favor left-handed users, however. Four examples are cited in Figure 3.14, as performed by left-handed users.

Although multiple techniques are available for the tasks described in Figure 3.14, the example tasks are not only fast for left-handed users, they are *faster* for left-handed users than for right-handed users. (Right-handed readers may wish to reconsider the examples.) The unifying observation is this: *When pointing is juxtaposed with power-key activation (excluding* SHIFT, ALT, *and* CONTROL), *the desktop interface presents a left-hand bias.* This is evident in the Figure 3.14. All the tasks involve a tight coupling of pointing operations with power-key activation. If right-handed users attempt the same tasks, their options are to release the mouse and activate the power key with their right hand, or to reach over the keyboard with their left hand—awkward in either case.

Importantly, the tasks are what we do *all the time.* Note in the third column in Figure 3.14 that trailing movements are also identified as "overlapping." Because the subtasks in the second and third columns are performed by separate hands, there is preparatory trailing movement that overlaps the leading movement. The action point in the trailing movement *immediately* follows the leading movement. And so, left-handed users persistently "cash in" on small-time savings. This leads to a simple conclusion that the desktop interface presents a left-hand bias.

Scrolling

Although Guiard's model of bimanual control alerts us to the differential roles of our hands, the analysis just presented is after the fact. It is unlikely that keyboard manufacturers will launch a redesign of the keyboard—positioning power keys on the left to facilitate right-handed interaction—based on the examples in Figure 3.14. However, Guiard's model does lend credence to one design deficiency worthy of correcting—scrolling. Although scrolling is an extremely common GUI task, affordances are poor for left-handed users *and* right-handed users.

Scrolling is traditionally accomplished by dragging the "elevator" of the scrollbar positioned along the right-hand side of an application's window.

Task	Leading Movement	Trailing/Overlapping Movement
Delete	*Left hand*—manipulate pointer with mouse and select text/object by double clicking or dragging	*Right hand*—press DELETE (probably with little finger)
Select an option in a window (see Figure 3.15)	*Left hand*—manipulate pointer with mouse and click on an option	*Right hand*—press ENTER (Note: OK button is the default; see Figure 3.15)
Click on a link in a browser	*Right hand*—navigate to link via PAGE UP and/or PAGE DOWN keys	*Left hand*—manipulate pointer with mouse and select link by clicking on it
Open a file, open a folder, or launch a program	*Left hand*—manipulate pointer with mouse and single click on an icon	*Right hand*—press ENTER (Note: avoids error-prone double-click operation)

FIGURE

3.14

Examples of common tasks, as performed by a left-handed user manipulating the mouse in the left hand.

FIGURE

3.15

Selecting an option in a window (see Figure 3.14).

Acquiring the elevator is a target-acquisition task taking up to two seconds per trial. More important, this action is in conflict with a basic goal of good user interfaces: unobtrusiveness and transparency. That is, users should not be required to divert their attention from the primary task (reading, editing, etc.) to explicitly manipulate user-interface widgets (Zhai & MacKenzie, 1998).

This we see as an opportunity for design. Scrolling is well suited to delegation to the nonpreferred hand, since its relationship with other tasks conforms to Guiard's model of bimanual control. Evidence of this is presented in Figure 3.16, which contrasts the properties of scrolling with tasks typically performed in concert with scrolling. (The reader is invited to compare the first three bullets in Figure 3.16 with the first three bullets in Figure 3.8, which presents the guiding principles in Guiard's model of bimanual control.)

Desktop affordances for scrolling changed dramatically in 1996 with the introduction of Microsoft's IntelliMouse, which included a scrolling wheel between the mouse buttons. Numerous copy-cat variations have since appeared from other manufacturers. The so-called wheel mouse puts scrolling in the

Task	Characteristics
Scrolling	✦ precedes/overlaps other tasks ✦ sets the frame of reference ✦ minimal precision needed (coarse)
Selecting, editing, reading, drawing, and so on.	✦ follows/overlaps scrolling ✦ works within frame of reference set by scrolling ✦ demands precision (fine)

FIGURE

3.16

Relationship between scrolling and common GUI tasks.

FIGURE

3.17

Scrolling interface example. (Sketch courtesy of Shawn Zhang.)

preferred hand. This is bad news for left-handed users, but it is even worse for right-handed users because of the higher right-side demands presented by the power-key bias noted earlier.

Figure 3.17 presents a scrolling concept for a right-handed user. A touch strip is shown, but a wheel could just as easily be used. There are many implementation issues, such as scrolling sensitivity and support for up/down paging, but space precludes elaboration. Our point is simply that scrolling should be delegated to the nondominant hand. See also Buxton and Myers (1986), Kabbash et al. (1994), and MacKenzie and Guiard (2001).

In this section, we examined common GUI tasks and patterns of bimanual skill. Two important observations emerged: first, current desktop systems are biased for left-handed users; and second, scrolling should be delegated to the nondominant hand. In the absence of a detailed functional taxonomy unifying the actions of the preferred hand and nonpreferred hand with system afford-ances, however, further design recommendations are premature. Broadly stated, such efforts should seek to tightly couple the hands—supporting sequential, co-operative action—with tasks such as power-key activation, pointing, selecting, and scrolling.

3.5   CURRENT STATUS AND FURTHER READING

Both Fitts' Law and Guiard's model of bimanual skill continue as popular re-search tools in human-computer interaction. Fitts' Law remains the preeminent model for pointing-device research. Evidence of this is the recent appearance of Fitts' Law in an ISO standard. The full standard, ISO 9241, is titled *Ergonomic re-quirements for office work with visual display terminals (VDTs)*. Part 9 is titled *Require-ments for non-keyboard input devices* (ISO, 1999). ISO 9241–9 is a comprehensive document that defines evaluation procedures for measuring user performance, comfort, and effort with pointing devices. An experimental protocol defines sub-ject samples, stimuli, experimental design, environmental conditions, furniture adjustments, data collection procedures, and data-analysis recommendations.

Performance is measured on any of six exemplary tasks, three of which are standard point-select tasks conforming to the Fitts' paradigm The depen-dent measure for the evaluations is throughput, computed as noted earlier (see Equation 3.8). The use of ISO 9241–9 should go a long way in bringing con-sistency to empirical evaluations of computer pointing devices. In particular, across-study comparisons are strengthened if studies adopt a consistent method-ology. Reviews of ISO 9241–9 are given by Douglas, Kirkpatrick, and MacKenzie (1999); Douglas and Mithal (1997, chap. 8); and Smith (1996, chap. 3). At least six pointing-device studies have been published wherein the methodology con-forms to ISO 9241–9 (Douglas et al., 1999; MacKenzie & Jusoh, 2001; MacKen-zie, Kauppinen, & Silfverberg, 2001; MacKenzie & Oniszczak, 1998; Oh & Stuerzlinger, 2002; Silfverberg, MacKenzie, & Kauppinen, 2001).

Another active area of Fitts' Law research is in extending its application to a different genre of tasks. Until recently, Fitts' Law was applied only in *time-minimizing tasks* (or *rapid aimed movements*). *Space-minimizing tasks* are distinctly different. In a space-minimizing task, users move a tracking symbol such as a cur-sor while trying to minimize the deviation of the symbol from a predefined path. Accot and Zhai (1997) effectively showed how to model this behavior using a variation of Fitts' Law aptly named the *Steering law*. Examples include navigating hierarchical menus, manipulating an elevator on a scrollbar, or tracing the outline of a shape. Besides the clear need for a prediction model for this genre of tasks, this work is important because it seeks to unify distinctly different motor behaviors within a single theoretical framework. Two related follow-up studies have also appeared (Accot & Zhai, 1999; Accot & Zhai, 2001).

Guiard's work is a continuing source of inspiration for designers of systems for interactive 3D graphics. These systems are generally high-end workstations with graphics accelerators and high-resolution displays. They often support input via graphics tablets and a stylus. The interface is complex, supporting a vast array of functionality. And, so, efforts to improve the interface through two-handed interaction are well invested. Several sources of this work are hereby cited (e.g., Balakrishnan & Hinckley, 2000; Balakrishnan & Kurtenbach, 1999; Fitzmaurice, Balakrishnan, Kurtenbach, & Buxton, 1999; Hinckley, Pausch, Proffitt, & Kassell, 1998; Hinckley, Pausch, Proffitt, Patten, & Kassell, 1997; Kurtenbach, Fitzmaurice, Baudel, & Buxton, 1997; Zhai, Smith, & Selker, 1997a; Zhai, Smith, & Selker, 1997b).

For readings on other predictive models developed with an eye to human-computer interfaces, the reader is directed to several sources. Examples include the Goals, Operators, Methods, and Selection rules (GOMS) model by Card, Moran, and Newell (Card et al., 1983; John, 1995; John & Kieras, 1996; Kieras, Wood, & Meyer, 1997), or the programmable user model (PUM) by Young, Green, and Simon (1989).

For other descriptive models on input devices, including movement characteristics, properties sensed, stimulus-response mappings, and interaction techniques, the reader is directed to several primary sources (Buxton, 1983; Card, Mackinlay, & Robertson, 1990; Card, Mackinlay, & Robertson, 1991; Foley, Wallace, & Chan, 1984; Jacob, Sibert, McFarlane, & Mullen, 1994; Mackinlay, Card, & Robertson, 1990; Ren & Moriya, 2000).

4 | Information Processing and Skilled Behavior

Bonnie E. John   Carnegie Mellon University

4.1   MOTIVATION FOR USING THE HUMAN INFORMATION PROCESSING THEORY IN HUMAN-COMPUTER INTERACTION[1]

Human performance can be enormously enhanced through the use of machines, but the interface connecting human and machine is subtle, and the success of the entire human-machine system turns on the design of this interface. Air-traffic control systems, personal computers with word processors, portable digital appliances—all can make it possible for people to do new things, or, through poor design of the human-machine interface, all can be rendered impractical or even dangerous. This lesson was learned early and often. For example, in recommending a program of research on human engineering for a national air-traffic control system, early researchers noted the following:

> The . . . disregard of physiological and sensory handicaps; of fundamental principles of perception; of basic patterns of motor coordination; of human limitations in the integration of complex responses, etc. has at times led to the production of mechanical monstrosities which tax the capabilities of human operators and hinder the integration of man and machine into a system designed for most effective accomplishment of designated tasks. (Fitts, 1951)

---

[1]   Thanks to Stuart K. Card for his aid in placing human information processing in HCI in historical context.

Many of the early design issues revolved around perceptual and motor activities, and these are emphasized in Fitts' quotation. In psychological terms, these equated to *stimulus-response* and led to the study of stand-alone actions—the time to decode an aircraft display, or the errors made in selecting which aircraft fuel tank to shut off. To design for humans as a component of a larger system, it is useful to be able to describe both sides of the system in uniform terms. Treating the human as an information processor, albeit a simple stimulus-response controller, allowed the application of information theory and manual control theory to problems of display design, visual scanning, workload, aircraft instrument location, flight controls, air-traffic control, and industrial inspection, among others. Fitts' Law, which predicts the time for hand movements to a target, is an example of an information processing theory of this era (see Chapter 3).

But the advent of computer systems emphasized the need for models beyond the stimulus-response-controller models. Models for analyzing human-computer interactions (HCI) needed to deal with sequential, integrated behavior rather than discrete actions. They also needed to deal with content of displays, not just their format. A promising set of developments in psychology and computer science was the information processing models of Allen Newell and Herbert Simon (1961, 1972; Simon, 1969). These models were based on sequences of operations on symbols (as contrasted with the analog signal representations of many of the previous generation of models). The natural form of information processing theories is a computer program, where a set of mechanisms is described locally, and where larger scale behavior is emergent from their interaction. The claim is not that all human behavior can be modeled in this manner, but that, for tasks within their reach,

> it becomes meaningful to try to represent in some detail a particular man at work on a particular task. Such a representation is no metaphor, but a precise symbolic model on the basis of which pertinent specific aspects of a man's problem solving behavior can be calculated. (Newell & Simon, 1972, p. 5)

Figure 4.1 is a generic representation of an information processing system. At the center is some processing executive that acts on a recognize-act cycle. On each cycle, information available through the receptors and from internal memory is matched against a set of patterns, usually represented as a set of if-then rules called *productions*. This match triggers a set of actions (or *operators*) that can change the state of internal memory and/or change the external world through

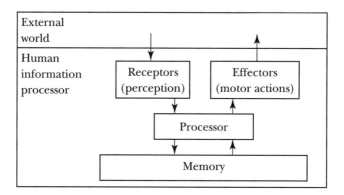

A generic human information processing system.

the effectors. The cycle then repeats. For simplicity of use, some information processing models do not articulate this full structure, but it is implicit in their assumptions.

The need to apply human information processing (HIP) to the design of computer interfaces led to a philosophy composed of task analysis, approximation, and calculation (Card, Moran, & Newell, 1983). These properties separate the models useful in engineering from some of the models used in general psychology. For engineering, it is important to have models that can make predictions from a technical analysis of a task without needing data fitted against an empirical study of users executing the task—zero-parameter models. This is necessary to allow the models to be used early in the design process. "Zero-parameter" models do have parameters, like typing rate or number of search targets, but these parameters can be determined from the task or previous studies in the psychological literature; they are not fit to data measured on the system and the task they are predicting. Note that, to be useful for engineering, the model parameters must be practical to supply at the time the model is to be used. Surprisingly, this requirement excludes some promising models from the psychological literature (Elkind et al, 1990).

Most science and engineering disciplines use approximation, both to make analysis more tractable and to simplify details that are not expected to have major effects on the result. Approximation, though, is a double-edged sword. It can be the key to making a model tractable, abstracting away from irrelevant inputs and approximating the information processing being used. On the other hand, it can also be accused of "looking under the lamp post" because, in making a tractable prediction, relevant variables have been ignored in the name of approximation. In fact, a number of HCI techniques subsequent to the information processing approach have reacted specifically against approximation, giving up the power of quantitative prediction in favor of rich qualitative information unfiltered by what is tractable to the model (e.g., Chapter 13). Indeed, many models in the information processing vein probably did abstract away too much, assuming unrealistically, for instance, that all information available on a cluttered screen was instantaneously and reliably perceived and comprehended by the model (e.g., John & Vera's [1992] initial model of an expert playing a video game made that assumption, but a later model of a novice game-player by Bauer & John [1995] did not). Analysts need to carefully weigh the pros and cons before approximating away from details of the task environment and artifacts. The evaluation of these models is not how much they approximate or whether they are statistically different from the eventual behavior, but whether they predict the behavior to within a particular desired range and whether the mechanisms of the model are insightful for that behavior.

The original examples of HIP models included problem solving tasks and the commission of errors (e.g., crypto-arithmetic, Newell & Simon, 1972), but these were more descriptive than predictive, were difficult to build, and could not easily be used as design tools. Card, Moran, and Newell (1983) introduced the Model Human Processor (MHP), which provided a framework for expressing zero-parameter models, and which could successfully predict short tasks, like matching a symbol to memory, or isolated tasks, like determining the fastest speed that someone would be able to type on several different keyboards. But the MHP was not fully operationalized in a computer program, and thus predicting complex emergent behavior was beyond its scope; newer computational cognitive architectures replaced it in the ensuing decades and will be discussed in subsequent sections.

To produce models of human behavior whose zero-parameter quantitative predictions could be useful in system design, Card, Moran, and Newell concentrated on the common situation of skilled users performing tasks within their area of skill, approximating actual performance by error-free performance (Card et al., 1980a, 1980b; 1983). These models are called GOMS (Goals, Operators, Methods, and Selection rules) models, and they represent an important aspect of HCI design. Many systems are designed with the belief that people will become skilled in their use and will want efficient methods for accomplishing routine tasks; GOMS can predict the impact of design decisions on this important measure of success. Because this is an important aspect of design, because these models have proved successful at predicting performance, and because such modeling has received extensive attention in HCI, this chapter will focus on

GOMS modeling in examples and in the case study. It will return to the more general notion of HIP when discussing the theoretical underpinnings, current status, and future work.

4.2   OVERVIEW OF GOMS

To briefly illustrate a GOMS model, consider the text-editing example in Figure 4.2. The figure shows a sentence that has been marked up for editing; the words "quick brown" must be moved from their current location to earlier in the sentence. We can use this example (which we will refer to throughout as the *fox task*) to make the concepts in GOMS concrete. GOMS is a method for describing a task and the user's knowledge of how to perform the task in terms of *G*oals, *O*perators, *M*ethods, and *S*election rules. Goals are simply the user's goals, as defined in layman's language. What does he or she want to accomplish by using the software? In the next day, the next few minutes, the next few seconds? In the case of our example, the highest-level goal is to edit the text, or, more specifically, to move "quick brown" to before "fox".

Operators are the actions that the software allows the user to take. With the original command-line interfaces, an operator was a command and its parameters, typed on a keyboard. Today, with graphic user interfaces, operators are just as likely to be menu selections, button presses, or direct-manipulation actions. Emerging technologies have operators that are gestures, spoken commands, and eye movements. Operators can actually be defined at many different levels of abstraction, but most GOMS models define them at a concrete level, like button presses and menu selections. The most common operators for analysis are at what is called the "keystroke level" and include moving the cursor, clicking the mouse button, and keying in information. In this example, the keystroke-level operators may involve both the keyboard (e.g., type CTRL-X to cut text) and the mouse (e.g., move mouse to word, double-click mouse button, move to menu, etc.).

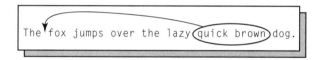

FIGURE   Example of a text-editing task.

4.2

Methods are well-learned sequences of subgoals and operators that can accomplish a goal. For our example, the following method exists in our word processor:

1. Highlight the text to be moved,

2. Type CTRL-X,

3. Move the cursor to the desired location,

4. Click the mouse button,

5. Type CTRL-V.

Notice that this expression of the method is a combination of operators (actions not readily decomposable) and subgoals (easily decomposable to more primitive actions). The operators already at the keystroke level include typing keyboard shortcuts, moving the cursor, and clicking the mouse button. Highlighting the text, however, is a subgoal that can be accomplished through several methods. For instance, the user could choose to mouse-down before "quick" and drag to the end of "brown" to highlight the text. Alternatively, the user could double-click on "quick" and then shift-click on "brown". Other methods for the entire task also exist, such as using the menus to invoke cut and paste through menu items, or deleting the text and retyping it in before "fox", or even deleting the whole sentence and retyping it correctly.

If there is more than one method to accomplish the same goal, then selection rules, the last component of the GOMS model, are required. Selection rules are the personal rules that users follow in deciding what method to use in a particular circumstance. For instance, in the example, if the text to be moved is one or two characters long, then a specific person may delete the text in the wrong location and retype it in the right location. If the text is three or more characters long, that person may cut and paste using keyboard shortcuts. Thus, that person's personal selection rule depends on the length of the word. Another user may have a different selection rule that depends on a different length of word, or on whether she can remember the keyboard shortcuts, or on other features of the task situation. Thus, the fox task in Figure 4.2 has the elements in its GOMS model shown in Table 4.1.

GOMS analysis applies to situations in which users will be expected to perform tasks that they have already mastered. In the psychology literature, this is called having a *cognitive skill,* that is, users are not problem solving and are not hunting around for what they need to do next. They know what to do in this task situation, and all they have to do is act. There are many different types of cognitive skill in human-computer interaction. For instance, there are many single-

Top-level goal	Edit manuscript, or, more specifically, move "quick brown" to before "fox"
Subgoal	Highlight text
Operators	Move-mouse Click mouse button Type characters (keyboard shortcuts)

Methods	For the editing goal:
	    1. Delete-word-and-retype (*retype* method)
	    2. Cut-and-paste-using-keyboard-shortcuts (*shortcuts* method)
	    3. Cut-and-paste-using-menus (*menus* method)
	For the highlighting subgoal:
	    1. Drag-across text (*dragging* method)
	    2. Double-click first; shift-click last (*all-clicking* method)

Selection rules	For the editing goal:
	    If the text to be moved is one or two characters long, use *retype* method
	    Else, if remember shortcuts, use *shortcuts* method
	    Else, use *menus* method
	For the highlighting subgoal:
	    If the text to be moved is not whole words, use *dragging* method
	    Else, use *all-clicking* method

TABLE

4.1.

Possible GOMS elements in the fox task.

user applications where the user tells the system what to do, then the system does it and tells the user what it has done. This is a user-paced, passive system, and GOMS has been shown to work very well for this situation. GOMS has been applied to software such as text editors (Card, Moran, & Newell, 1980a, 1983), spreadsheets (Lerch, Mantei, & Olson, 1989), information browsers (Peck & John, 1992), operating systems (Card, Moran, & Newell, 1983), ergonomic design systems (Gong & Kieras, 1994), CAD systems (Bhavnani & John, 1997), map digitizers (Haunold & Kuhn, 1994), flight-management computers in commercial airplanes (Irving, Polson, & Irving, 1994), oscilloscopes (Lee, Polson, & Bailey, 1989), programmable television sets (Elkerton 1993), and Web pages (John, 1995).

GOMS has also been shown to be valid in single-user, active systems, where the system changes in unexpected ways or other people participate in accomplishing the task. There are GOMS models, for instance, of radar monitoring (Rosenblatt & Vera, 1995) and of video games (John & Vera, 1992), where the system throws new situations at the user at a maniacal pace, and there are GOMS models of telephone operators interacting with customers (Gray, John, & Atwood, 1993). The knowledge gathered by a GOMS analysis is sufficient to predict what a skilled person will do in these seemingly unpredictable situations.

GOMS can be used both quantitatively and qualitatively. Quantitatively, it gives good predictions of absolute performance time and relative learning time. It can therefore be used to help in a purchasing decision (see the case study in Section 4.5), or to see if a proposed design meets quantitative performance requirements, or to compare one system's training time to another.

Qualitatively, GOMS can be used to design training programs, help systems, and the system itself. Because a GOMS model is a careful description of the knowledge needed to perform a given task, it describes the content of task-oriented documentation. You need only tell the new user what the goals are and how to recognize them, what different methods could be used to achieve them, and when to use each method (selection rules). This approach has been shown to be an efficient way to organize help systems (Elkerton, Goldstein, & Palmiter, 1990; Elkerton & Palmiter, 1989; Elkerton & Palmiter, 1991), intelligent tutoring systems (Steinberg & Gitomer, 1993), and training programs (Irving, Polson, & Irving, 1994), as well as user documentation (Gong & Elkerton, 1990). GOMS models can also be used qualitatively to redesign a system. When GOMS uncovers a frequent goal supported by a very inefficient method, then the design can be changed to include a more efficient method. If GOMS shows that some goals are not supported by any method at all, new methods can be added. GOMS may also reveal where similar goals are supported by inconsistent methods, a situation in which users are likely to have problems remembering what to do, and show how to make the methods consistent (Kieras, in Helander et al., 1997).

Since the 1980s, HCI researchers have very carefully tested and retested the predictions of GOMS models, and they have reported these results in refereed conferences and journals. Many studies give rigorous laboratory verification of the predictions made from GOMS models on a number of products. Several studies have used real-world data to verify performance-time predictions of GOMS models. There has also been work with realistic training situations that show the value of GOMS-inspired training programs and help systems (Irving, Polson, & Irving, 1994; Gong & Elkerton, 1990) GOMS is one of the most validated methods in HCI, making it a trustworthy tool for user interaction (UI) practitioners.

4.3   SCIENTIFIC FOUNDATIONS UNDERLYING GOMS

The concepts associated with GOMS are a mixture of several types: task-analysis techniques from the human factors and system design literature, models of human performance on specific tasks, computational models of human cognitive architecture, and loosely defined concepts about human cognition and informa-tion processing. Figure 4.3 displays the relationships among these ideas. The fig-ure is a lattice; at the top is the general idea of task analysis, and at the bottom is a basic conceptual framework for HIP, the *stage model* (where information flows from the outside world through perception to memory, where it can be manipu-lated by cognition, and cognition then commands the motor system to act on the world). Thus the GOMS family consists of ideas for *analyzing and representing tasks in a way that is related to the stage model of human information processing*. This depen-dence on a psychological framework is the distinctive feature of the GOMS ap-proach compared to many other concepts of task analysis in the human factors and system-design literature.

These fundamental assumptions—that both the task structure and the cog-nitive architecture are necessary to describe, and ultimately predict, people's behavior with computer systems—arose from a parable often referred to as "Simon's Ant."

> We watch an ant make his laborious way across a wind- and wave-molded beach. He moves ahead, angles to the right to ease his climb up a steep dunelet, detours around a pebble, stops for a moment to exchange informa-tion with a compatriot. Thus he makes his weaving, halting way back to his home. . . .
>
> He has a general sense of where home lies, but he cannot foresee all the obstacles between. He must adapt his course repeatedly to the difficulties he encounters and often detour uncrossable barriers. His horizons are very close, so that he deals with each obstacle as he comes to it; he probes for ways around or over it, without much thought for future obstacles. It is easy to trap him into deep detours.
>
> Viewed as a geometric figure, the ant's path is irregular, complex, hard to describe. But its complexity is really a complexity of the surface of the beach, not a complexity in the ant. On that same beach another small crea-ture with a home at the same place as the ant might well follow a very similar path. . . .
>
> *An ant, viewed as a behaving system, is quite simple. The apparent complexity of its behavior over time is largely a reflection of the complexity of the environment in which it finds itself.* (Simon, 1969, 63–64, emphasis in original)

Simon asserts that another small creature might follow the same path home, but this applies only to a surface-walking creature; it is easy to imagine that a dig-ging creature might take a subterranean path. The story of Simon's Ant shows that, to predict the ant's path, it is not sufficient to understand the ant alone nor to map the beach alone, but one must understand both in relation to the other. Much psychological research during the next few decades after Simon wrote his parable concentrated on understanding the structure of and constraints on human information processing; that is, it focused on understanding the ant. On the other hand, task analysis, traditionally in the purview of human factors and industrial engineering, concentrated effort on developing techniques to represent the abstract structure inherent in tasks and task environments; that is, on mapping the beach. However, with the advent of widespread computer usage, the emphasis in the HCI branch of HIP research changed to understanding both the human *and* the environment, because, in essence, HCI is about *designing* the beach, not simply describing it. Some research paths embraced rich descriptions of the beach and, importantly, how the ant changes it through use (e.g., Chapter 13). GOMS also embodies Simon's insight, marrying task analysis (maps of the beach) to frameworks of human behavior (the workings of the ant).

Thus, in Figure 4.3, reading down from the top, the top layer consists of task analysis techniques, followed by explicit computational cognitive architectures, and, at the bottom, conceptual frameworks, which are informal statements about how humans can be modeled. As one reads down from the top, or up from the bottom, the ideas get more explicit and detailed; the middle contains approaches whose instantiations are running computer simulation models.

Three things should be noted about the diagram: (1) Because our primary purpose in this chapter is to discuss GOMS models that have been used and useful in HCI, Figure 4.3 emphasizes these techniques and the concepts directly related to them. (2) There are areas in the diagram that are not directly related to GOMS models, and these are indicated with italics. Thus, the diagram is certainly not exhaustive: many more nodes and arrows could be drawn to the literature. What is shown here is only what is central to our discussion of currently documented GOMS models. (3) The diagram shows only generic ideas and approaches, not specific instances of task modeling. Examples of specific instances of using these techniques will appear as needed throughout this chapter.

We will describe the entries in this lattice, starting with the conceptual frameworks, because they form the basis for all GOMS analyses; we will then work through the computational cognitive architectures up to the task-analytic approaches, which are the heart of the GOMS family.

4.3.1   Conceptual Frameworks

The *conceptual frameworks* are so named because they are informally stated assumptions about the structure of human cognition. The conceptual frameworks

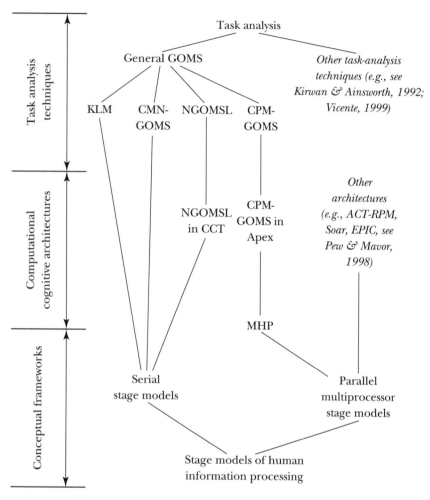

The GOMS family consists of task-analysis techniques that are related to models of human information processing.

shown are all based on a general assertion that human cognition and behavior is usefully analyzed in terms of stages. The conventional notion is that stimuli are first processed perceptually; the resulting information is passed to a central cognitive process that manipulates that information and eventually initiates some motor activity.

The cognitive process that manipulates information is often described as *search through a problem space.* A problem space is defined by a set of possible *states,* which include the information available to cognition internally (from memory) or in the world (through perception). The search involves applying an *operator* to the current state to change it to a new state, and evaluating whether that new state is closer to a desired (goal) state. Operators can be both internal (e.g., mentally adding two numbers) or external (e.g., pulling down a menu to reveal its items). The difficulty of a problem can be assessed by the length and indirectness of the search. In one situation, many plausible operators might be applicable to each state with no knowledge to choose between them. This forces the user to explore, take false paths, and back up to old states. In another situation, there could be few applicable operators at any state (like in a wizard), or the user could have the knowledge of which operator to apply to move closer to the goal. The former situation is called *problem solving* and the latter *skilled behavior,* but in information-processing terms they are both on a continuum of behavior using the same mechanism of search through a problem space.

Figures 4.4 and 4.5 are two problem behavior graphs that show two different paths through a problem space for cutting "quick brown" in the example sentence. Figure 4.4 reflects the behavior of a person who does not know which menu contains the **Cut** command and must search until he or she finds it. This path contains one dead-end state and a back up to a previous state before finding the desired command. This behavior is typical of problem solving. Figure 4.5 reflects the behavior of a person who knows that the **Cut** command resides in the **Edit** menu, and search becomes trivial; this is characteristic of the skilled behavior that GOMS can model.

The stage model of HIP breaks out into two more specific forms. One is that the stages are performed serially, which is sufficient for describing laboratory experiments examining the single-action tasks mentioned in the Motivation section (e.g., decoding an aircraft display or switching off a fuel tank, in isolation from other tasks). The other is that the stages can be performed in parallel to some extent, since different kinds of processing are handled by separate mechanisms, or *processors.* The assumption of parallel operations seems necessary to understand certain types of human behavior, such as transcription typing a long paragraph where the eyes seem to stay several words ahead of the hands, as opposed to typing a single word as it is flashed on a screen.

The Model Human Processor (MHP) that Card, Moran, and Newell (1983) introduced to HCI is a parallel architecture. Perceptual, cognitive, and motor processing are done by separate processing mechanisms, each with their own distinctive types and timing of activities, and with associated principles of operation. Card, Moran, and Newell's important insight was that the empirical human cognition and performance literature could be used to motivate and justify an *engineering model* of human information processing that could be used to predict performance in HCI situations.

State 1:

Text to be cut is highlighted.
Many operators are applicable, e.g., one for pulling down each menu.
No knowledge about which operators to apply, so the first menu is chosen arbitrarily.

State1 transforms to State 1', which now includes the knowledge that **Cut** is not in the **File** menu.

Many operators are still applicable and the second menu is chosen arbitrarily

Apply Operator:
Pull down **File** menu, Search for **Cut.**

Failure:
Back up to State1

Apply Operator:
Pull down **Edit** menu, Search for **Cut.**

State 2:

File menu is visible.
Cut is not in this menu.

State 3:

Edit menu is visible.
Cut is in this menu.
The knowledge to select the **Cut** item is applicable, so the task can continue.

Apply Operator:
Select the **Cut** menu item.

The task continues…

State 4:

Text to be cut has been cut successfully.

FIGURE 4.4   The problem behavior graph showing search through a problem space for cutting "quick brown" when the person does not know which menu contains the **Cut** command.

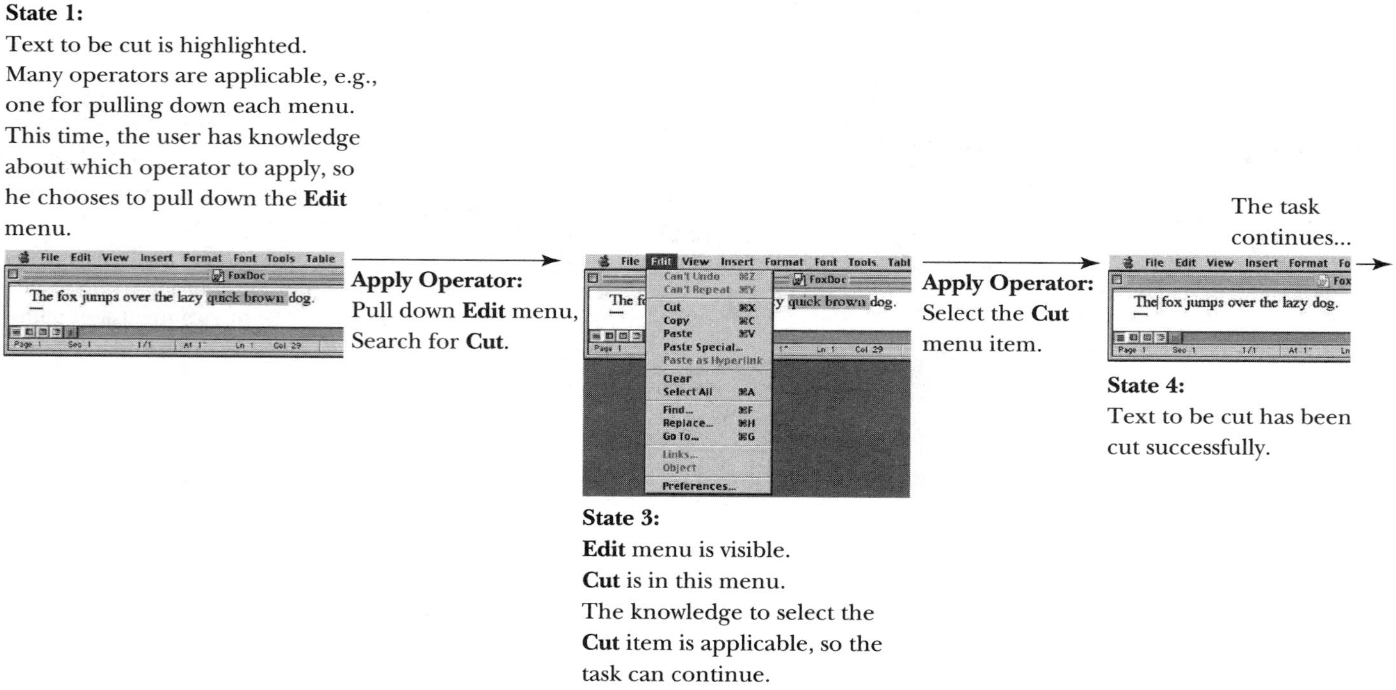

State 1:
Text to be cut is highlighted.
Many operators are applicable, e.g., one for pulling down each menu.
This time, the user has knowledge about which operator to apply, so he chooses to pull down the **Edit** menu.
File Edit View Insert Format Font Tools Table
FoxDoc
The fox jumps over the lazy quick brown dog.
Apply Operator:
Pull down **Edit** menu,
Search for **Cut**.
File Edit View Insert Format Font Tools
Can't Undo ⌘Z
Can't Repeat ⌘Y
Cut ⌘X
Copy ⌘C
Paste ⌘V
Paste Special...
Paste as Hyperlink
Clear
Select All ⌘A
Find... ⌘F
Replace... ⌘H
Go To... ⌘G
Links...
Object
Preferences...
State 3:
Edit menu is visible.
Cut is in this menu.
The knowledge to select the **Cut** item is applicable, so the task can continue.
Apply Operator:
Select the **Cut** menu item.
File Edit View Insert Format
The fox jumps over the lazy dog.
State 4:
Text to be cut has been cut successfully.
The task continues...

FIGURE 4.5 The problem behavior graph showing trivial search through a problem space for cutting “quick brown” when the person does know that the **Edit** menu contains the **Cut** command.

Although the MHP is inherently parallel, only 1 of the 19 examples of reasoning from the MHP presented in Card, Moran, and Newell (1983, Example 7) depends on this fact. The parallel operation of the MHP was made clear in the TYPIST model of transcription typing (John, 1988, 1996), in which the processors could operate in a "pipeline" mode, with information moving through perceptual, cognitive, and motor stages continuously. This model accounted for important properties of skilled typing performance and shows that parallelism can greatly influence the structure and performance of a task.

Although Card, Moran, and Newell provided many examples of how the MHP can be applied to predict performance in some well-understood simple task situations similar to the experimental paradigms in the human performance literature, and they provided simple real-world analogs of these tasks, they did not provide an explicit method for applying the MHP to complex, realistic tasks (the CPM-GOMS methodology to be discussed later provides this explication). In Figure 4.3, the MHP is shown at the border between conceptual architectures and computational cognitive architectures because, while it is more specified than the simple stage concepts, it is not as fully explicit and computationally represented as the ideas in the next level up in the diagram.

4.3.2   Computational Cognitive Architectures

The level called *computational cognitive architectures* in Figure 4.3 lists proposals for how to represent human information processing in terms explicit enough to run as a computer program (such architectures are also called *unified theories of cognition;* Newell, 1990). Representation as a computer simulation is a preferred research tactic in cognitive psychology, based on the assumption that a computational model has "empirical content"—that is, a properly constructed and interpreted model can make predictions of human performance, and these predictions can be empirically confirmed. There are several such architectures under development in cognitive psychology and artificial intelligence, several of which have been applied to topics in HCI, such as ACT-RPM and its predecessors (Anderson, 1976, 1983, 1993; Byrne & Anderson, 2001), Construction-Integration (Kintsch, 1988, 1992), Soar (Newell, 1990), and EPIC (Kieras & Meyer, 1994; Meyer & Kieras, 1994). Each of these architectures makes different assumptions about how cognitive processes such as working memory management, flow of control, learning, and problem solving are handled by the architecture, and testing the empirical content of these assumptions is an active area of psychological research. In principle, all of these architectures could be used to implement a particular GOMS task analysis in a computational model (e.g., John

& Vera, 1992, and Peck & John, 1992, implemented GOMS models in Soar; Gray & Sabnani, 1994, implemented a GOMS model in ACT-R).

However, two computational architectures have a more direct relationship to GOMS and deserve special mention. Cognitive complexity theory (CCT) (Bovair, Kieras, & Polson, 1988, 1990; Kieras & Polson, 1985), a production-rule architecture based on the serial stage model, has been used as the basis for a specific GOMS technique, NGOMSL, which incorporates CCT's assumptions about working memory management, flow of control, and other architectural mechanisms. For brevity, CCT and NGOMSL will not be discussed further, because their mechanisms and contributions are well represented in other HCI literature (e.g. Kieras, in Helander et al., 1997). Apex (Freed, 1998) is an architecture for modeling human behavior in complex dynamic environments such as piloting a Boeing 757 or in air-traffic control; its foundation is the class of AI architectures called *reactive planners* (Firby, 1989). It combines reactive planning with the concept of limited resources (e.g., cognition, right-hand, left-hand, visual perception, etc.) to model human performance. Its concepts and programming environment have been used to build CPM-GOMS models (Section 4.4.3), where the architectural concepts dictate how low-level HCI skills (e.g., typing or using a mouse) can be interleaved to maximize parallelism in skilled performance (John et al., 2002).

4.3.3 Task-Analysis Techniques

At the top of the GOMS family tree in Figure 4.3, the overall node of *task analysis* includes many techniques that generally "map the beach" (e.g., hierarchical task analysis, link analysis, operational sequence diagrams, timeline analysis in Kirwan & Ainsworth, 1992; Vicente's cognitive work analysis, 1999). The node labeled *general GOMS* represents the concept that it is useful to analyze knowledge of how to do a task in terms of goals, operators, methods, and selection rules. Thus, it is a form of task analysis that describes the procedural, "how-to-do-it" knowledge involved in a task. The result of a GOMS-based task analysis will be some form of description of the components of the goals, operators, methods, and selection rules.

There are three critical restrictions on the kinds of tasks that GOMS models can be used for. The first is that the task in question must be usefully analyzed in terms of the "how-to-do-it" or *procedural* knowledge required rather than other aspects of knowledge about the system, like mental simulations of an internalized device model, or analogical reasoning (see Kieras & Polson, 1985, for more discussion). The italicized area to the right under *Task analysis* represents other existing and potential approaches to task analysis that capture other forms of task knowledge. For example, work on electronics troubleshooting (see Gott, 1988) incorporates the person's knowledge of electronic components and the structure and function of the system under investigation, in addition to various kinds of procedural knowledge. Work in analogical reasoning has been applied to understanding consistency in operating systems (Rieman, Lewis, Young, & Polson, 1994).

The second restriction is that the GOMS family can represent only *skilled behavior*, which consists of procedural knowledge that may originally derive from problem-solving activity, or from instruction, but with practice has taken the form of a routinely invocable sequence of activities that accomplishes the goals (see Card et al., 1983, Chap. 11). That is, the search through the problem space to achieve a goal has become trivial. At each state, there are only a few operators already known to move closer to the goal state, and selection between them has also been well learned. Of course, users often engage in problem solving, exploration, and other nonroutine activities while using a computer, and other cognitive modeling approaches and task-analysis techniques can be used to investigate these behaviors (e.g., the Cognitive Walkthrough technique [Wharton, Rieman, Lewis, & Polson, 1994] applies to exploratory behavior by novice users).

We emphasize, however, that most tasks have some element of skilled behavior. Composing a research paper requires the skill of text editing, charting data requires the skill of entering information into spreadsheets, architectural design with a computer-aided design (CAD) system requires routine window manipulation, and so on. Even if the primary task is creative or otherwise not routine, those aspects of the task that are routine are amenable to analysis with GOMS techniques. Applying GOMS to improve the routine aspects of a complex task will reduce the effort necessary to master and perform those routine aspects, getting them "out of the way" of the primary creative task.

The third restriction is that, in all GOMS analysis techniques, the designer or analyst must *start* with a list of top-level tasks or user goals. GOMS analyses and methods do not provide this list; it must come from sources external to GOMS. Typically, this list of goals can be obtained from other task-analysis approaches (e.g., see Diaper, 1989), such as interviews with potential users, observations of users of similar or existing systems, or, in the worst case, simple intuitions on the part of the analyst. Once this list is assembled, GOMS analyses can help guide the design of the system so that the user can accomplish the given tasks in an efficient and learnable way. However, except for possibly stimulating the analyst's intuitions, the subsequent GOMS analysis will not identify any new top-level user goals or tasks that the analyst overlooked, nor will it correct a misformulation of the user goals.

The next level down in the diagram in Figure 4.3 consists of specific proposals for how to carry out a task analysis within a GOMS orientation. It is at this level that the differences appear between different versions of GOMS analyses. Note that the general GOMS concept merely asserts that it is useful to analyze a task in terms of the user's goals, methods, operators, and selection rules. It does not specify any particular technique for doing such an analysis. A particular technique requires (1) more specific definitions of the GOMS components, especially the operators, and (2) guidance and a procedure for constructing the methods in terms of these more specific definitions. These additional details will be presented for three types of GOMS models in the next section.

4.4   DETAILED DESCRIPTION OF GOMS MODELS

GOMS can provide different types of information for the design of an interactive system. John and Kieras (1996a) review its contributions to assessing the coverage and consistency of functionality, and its predictions of operator sequences, execution time, training time, and error-recovery support. The strength of GOMS is in its quantitative predictions of performance time and its qualitative explanations for those predictions. Therefore, this chapter will demonstrate those aspects of GOMS and direct the reader to John and Kieras (1996a) for the others. In addition, there are many different versions of GOMS. Four of them, detailed and related to each other by John and Kieras (1996a, 1996b), appear in Figure 4.3, but others exist with varying degrees of penetration in the HCI community. For instance, QGOMS (Beard, Smith, & Denelsbeck, 1996) is a variant embodied in a graphical tool that substitutes probabilities for selecting a method for the symbolic semantics favored by Card, Moran, and Newell. This section will use three versions of GOMS: the Keystroke-Level Model (KLM), traditional GOMS introduced by Card, Moran, and Newell (CMN-GOMS), and a parallel version, CPM-GOMS, to analyze the expected performance time on the text-editing task shown in Figure 4.2. (For a similar analysis that includes NGOMSL as well as the three detailed here, see John & Kieras, 1996a).

4.4.1   KLM

The Keystroke-Level Model (KLM) is the simplest GOMS technique; it was originally described in Card, Moran, and Newell (1980b) and later in Card, Moran, and Newell (1983, Chap. 8). The KLM makes several simplifying assumptions that make it a restricted version of GOMS. In particular, the analyst must specify the method used to accomplish the particular task of interest, which typically entails choosing specific task instances. Other GOMS techniques discussed later predict the method given the task situation and the knowledge of methods and selection rules, but the KLM does not. Furthermore, the specified method is limited to containing only a small set of preestablished keystroke-level primitive operators. Given the task and the method, the KLM uses duration estimates of these keystroke-level operators to predict the time a skilled user will need to execute the task.

The original KLM included six types of operators: K to press a key or button; P to point with a mouse to a target on a display; H to home hands on the keyboard or other device; D to draw a line segment on a grid; M to mentally prepare to do an action or a closely related series of primitive actions; and R to represent the system-response time during which the user has to wait for the system. Each of these operators has an estimate of execution time, either a single value, a parameterized estimate (e.g., K is dependent on typing speed and whether a key or mouse button click, press, or release is involved), or a simple approximating function (e.g., Fitts' Law estimates for P). The KLM also includes a set of five heuristic rules for placing mental operators to account for mental preparation time.

Subsequent research has refined these six primitive operators, improving the time estimates or differentiating between different types of mental operations (Olson & Olson, 1990), and practitioners often tailor these operators to suit their particular user group and interface requirements (e.g., Haunold & Kuhn, 1994). In addition, the heuristics for placing mental operators have been refined for specific types of subtasks (e.g., for making a fixed series of menu choices, see Lane, Napier, Batsell, & Naman, 1993). In particular, since the original heuristic rules were created primarily for command-based interfaces, they need to be updated for direct manipulation interfaces (John & Kieras, 1996a).

Figure 4.6 provides a sample KLM with computation of execution time for the fox task shown in Figure 4.2, using the operator times supplied in Card, Moran, and Newell (1983, p. 264). Quantitatively, the KLM makes the prediction that this task will take about 15 seconds. Qualitatively, the analyst can use the model to highlight several ideas. The subgoal structure is not explicit in the KLM itself, but an analyst can see it in the model (as annotated) and use it to look for recurring subprocedures that might be combined or shortened. For instance, the analyst has made an annotation to consider a MOVE command instead of CUT and PASTE. A KLM for MOVE would show what time savings this would

Description	Operator	Duration (sec)	
Mentally prepare by Heuristic Rule 0	M	1.35	*mark text to be moved*
Move cursor to "quick"	P	1.10	
(no M by Heuristic Rule 1)			
Double-click mouse button	K	0.40	
Move cursor to "brown"	P	1.10	
(no M by Heuristic Rule 1)			
Shift-click mouse button	K	0.40	*Two commands needed to complete a move. Should we consider a MOVE command instead?*
Mentally prepare by Heuristic Rule 0	M	1.35	
Move cursor to Edit menu	P	1.10	
(no M by Heuristic Rule 1)			
Click mouse button	K	0.20	*cut text*
Move cursor to Cut menu item	P	1.10	
(no M by Heuristic Rule 1)			
Click mouse button	K	0.20	
Mentally prepare by Heuristic Rule 0	M	1.35	
Move cursor to before "fox"	P	1.10	*indicate insertion point*
(no M by Heuristic Rule 1)			
Click mouse button	K	0.20	
Mentally prepare by Heuristic Rule 0	M	1.35	
Move cursor to Edit menu	P	1.10	
(no M by Heuristic Rule 1)			
Click mouse button	K	0.20	*paste text*
Move cursor to Paste menu item	P	1.10	
(no M by Heuristic Rule 1)			
Click mouse button	K	0.20	
TOTAL PREDICTED TIME		14.90	

FIGURE 4.6   A Keystroke-Level Model for moving the text in Figure 4.2 using the CUT-AND-PASTE-USING-MENUS method for the entire task, and the ALL-CLICKING method for highlighting the text to be moved.

provide, which could then be weighed against other considerations like users' prior knowledge or other functionality (e.g. the ability to paste multiple copies).

In terms of underlying architecture, KLM does not need a computational representation because the methods are supplied by the analyst and are expressed as a sequence of operators; all the information processing activity is assumed to be contained in the primitive operators, including internal cognitive actions, which are subsumed by black-box mental operators. Thus the underlying conceptual framework is simply the serial stage model.

The primary advantage of the KLM technique is that it allows a rapid estimate of execution time with an absolute minimum of theoretical and conceptual baggage. In this sense, it is the most practical of the GOMS techniques; it is the easiest to apply in actual interface design practice, and it is by far the simplest to explain and justify to computer-software developers. This simple estimate of execution times can be used to compare design ideas on benchmark tasks, to do parametric evaluation to explore the space defined by important variables (e.g., the length of filenames in a command language), and to do sensitivity analyses on the assumptions made (e.g., user's typing speed) (Card et al., 1980b; Card et al., 1983).

4.4.2   CMN-GOMS

CMN-GOMS is the term used to refer to the form of GOMS model presented in Card, Moran, and Newell (Card et al., 1980a, 1980b; 1983, Chap. 5). CMN-GOMS is slightly more specified than general GOMS; there is a strict goal hierarchy, operators are executed in strict sequential order, and methods are represented in an informal pseudo-code-like notation that can include submethods and conditionals.

In the context of the Card, Moran, and Newell work, it would appear that the CMN-GOMS model is based on the MHP, but in fact Card, Moran, and Newell do not make a tight linkage. In particular, in presenting the CMN-GOMS formulation, they provide no description of how the MHP would represent and execute CMN-GOMS methods. Furthermore, the GOMS concept itself cannot be derived from the MHP as presented by Card, Moran, and Newell, but is only loosely based on two of the MHP principles of operation, the Rationality Principle and the Problem Space Principle, both well developed in the problem-solving theoretical literature (e.g., Newell & Simon, 1972; see Card et al., 1983, Chap. 11). Thus, Figure 4.3 shows that the CMN-GOMS model is based only on the serial stage model, not the MHP.

Card, Moran, and Newell do not describe the CMN-GOMS technique with an explicit "how-to" guide, but present nine models at different levels of detail that illustrate a breadth-first expansion of a goal hierarchy until the desired level of detail is attained. They report results in which such models predicted operator sequences and execution times for text-editing tasks, operating-systems tasks, and the routine aspects of computer-aided VLSI layout tasks. These examples are sufficiently detailed and extensive that independent researchers have been able to develop their own CMN-GOMS analyses (e.g., Lerch, Mantei, & Olson, 1989).

Figure 4.7 is an example of a CMN-GOMS model at the keystroke-level for the fox task shown in Figure 4.2, including details for the MOVE-TEXT goal. Moving is accomplished by first cutting the text and then pasting it. Cutting is accomplished by first highlighting the text, and then issuing the **Cut** command. As specified by a selection rule set, highlighting can be done in two different ways, depending on the nature of the text to be highlighted. Finally, pasting requires moving to the insertion point, and then issuing the **Paste** command.

Quantitatively, CMN-GOMS models predict the operator sequence and execution time. Qualitatively, CMN-GOMS models focus attention on methods to accomplish goals; similar methods are easy to see, unusually short or long methods jump out and can spur design ideas. In this example, the analyst has noticed that issuing commands via the menus will occur often and suggests keyboard shortcuts. In addition, the annotations indicate that this analyst has observed that the VERIFY operator explicitly records points of feedback to the user.

Comparing Figure 4.7 with Figure 4.6, the relationship between the CMN-GOMS technique and the KLM technique is evident. (Note that the expansion of the MOVE-TEXT goal in Figure 4.7 represents the same behavior as the KLM in Figure 4.6.) For instance, there is a one-to-one mapping between the physical operators in the CMN-GOMS model and the Ks and Ps in the KLM. The CMN-GOMS model has other operators at this level: VERIFY-LOCATION and VERIFY-HIGHLIGHT, which have no observable physical counterpart (they could be observed with an eye-tracker, but this instrument has only recently become available and affordable and is not often used in any but the most detailed HCI research). The KLM has no explicit goals or choices between goals, whereas the CMN-GOMS model represents these explicitly. Roughly, the VERIFY operators, goal hierarchies, and selection rules of the CMN-GOMS model are represented as the M operators in the KLM. That is, operators such as VERIFY and goals and selections appear in the CMN-GOMS model in groups that roughly correspond to the placement of Ms in the KLM. This is only approximately the case, as the VERIFY operators sometimes occur in the middle of a group of physical operators, but the approximation is close.

A major difference between the KLM and the CMN-GOMS models is that CMN-GOMS is in program form, so therefore the analysis is general and executable. That is, any instance of the described class of tasks can be performed or simulated by following the steps in the model, which may take different paths depending on the specific task situation. Goals and method selection are predicted by the model given the task situation, and they need not be dictated by the analyst as they must for the KLM.

Given the task specified by the manuscript in Figure 4.2, this model would predict the trace of operators shown with the estimates of operator times in the

```
GOAL: EDIT—MANUSCRIPT
•        GOAL: EDIT-UNIT-TASK...repeat until no more unit tasks
•        •     GOAL: ACQUIRE UNIT-TASK...if task not remembered
•        •     •   GOAL: TURN-PAGE...if at end of manuscript page
•        •     •   GOAL: GET-FROM-MANUSCRIPT
•        •     GOAL: EXECUTE-UNIT-TASK...if a unit task was found
•        •     •   GOAL: MODIFY-TEXT
•        •     •   • [select: GOAL: MOVE-TEXT*...if text is to be moved
•        •     •   •          GOAL: DELETE-PHRASE...if a phrase is to be deleted
•        •     •   •          GOAL: INSERT-WORD]...if a word is to be inserted
•        •     •   • VERIFY-EDIT                                          1.35

* Expansion of MOVE-TEXT goal
GOAL: MOVE-TEXT
•        GOAL: CUT-TEXT
•        •     GOAL: HIGHLIGHT-TEXT
•        •     •   [select**: GOAL: HIGHLIGHT-PHRASE-COMPOSED-OF-WORDS
•        •     •        • MOVE-CURSOR-TO-FIRST-WORD                       1.10
•        •     •        • DOUBLE-CLICK-MOUSE-BUTTON                       0.40
•        •     •        • MOVE-CURSOR-TO-LAST-WORD                        1.10
•        •     •        • SHIFT-CLICK-MOUSE-BUTTON                        0.40
•        •     •        • VERIFY-HIGHLIGHT                                1.35
•        •     •          GOAL: HIGHLIGHT-ARBITRARY-TEXT
•        •     •        • MOVE-CURSOR-TO-BEGINNING-OF-TEXT
•        •     •        • PRESS-MOUSE-BUTTON
•        •     •        • MOVE-CURSOR-TO-END-OF-TEXT
•        •     •        • RELEASE-CLICK-MOUSE-BUTTON
•        •     •        • VERIFY-HIGHLIGHT]
•        •     GOAL: ISSUE-CUT-COMMAND
•        •     •   MOVE-CURSOR-TO-EDIT-MENU                               1.10
•        •     •   CLICK-MOUSE-BUTTON                                     0.20
•        •     •   MOVE-CURSOR-TO-CUT-ITEM                                1.10
•        •     •   VERIFY-HIGHLIGHT                                       1.35
•        •     •   CLICK-MOUSE-BUTTON                                     0.20
•        GOAL: PASTE-TEXT
•        •     GOAL: POSITION-CURSOR-AT-INSERTION-POINT
•        •     •   MOVE-CURSOR-TO-INSERTION-POINT                         1.10
•        •     •   CLICK-MOUSE-BUTTON                                     0.20
•        •     •   VERIFY-POSITION                                        1.35
•        •     GOAL: ISSUE-PASTE-COMMAND
•        •     •   MOVE-CURSOR-TO-EDIT-MENU                               1.10
•        •     •   CLICK-MOUSE-BUTTON                                     0.20
•        •     •   MOVE-CURSOR-TO-PASTE-ITEM                              1.10
•        •     •   VERIFY-HIGHLIGHT                                       1.35
•        •     •   CLICK-MOUSE-BUTTON                                     0.20
```
TOTAL TIME PREDICTED (SEC)   16.25

(handwritten annotation, left:) Is all this feedback in order?

(handwritten annotation, right:) Issuing commands will be used a LOT! Can we shorten this procedure? Consider keyboard shortcuts.

```
**Selection Rule for GOAL: HIGHLIGHT-TEXT:

If the text to be highlighted is a phrase made up of words,
use the HIGHLIGHT-PHRASE-COMPOSED-OF-WORDS method,
else use the HIGHLIGHT-ARBITRARY-TEXT method.
```

FIGURE

4.7

Example of CMN-GOMS text-editing methods showing the task hierarchy and a selection rule.

far-right column. The estimates for the physical operators are identical to the ones in the KLM. The VERIFY-EDIT, VERIFY-HIGHLIGHT, and VERIFY-POSITION operators are assigned 1.35 sec, the same value as the KLM's M operator because this is Card, Moran, and Newell's best estimate of mental time in the absence of other information.[2] Thus, the CMN-GOMS model produces nearly the same estimate for task completion as the KLM. The CMN-GOMS model has one more M-like operator in that it verifies the success of the entire task with a VERIFY-EDIT operator in the EXECUTE-UNIT-TASK goal. Notice that the CMN-GOMS technique assigns time only to operators, not to any "overhead" required to manipulate the goal hierarchy. In their results, Card, Moran, and Newell found that time predictions were as good with the simple assumption that only operators contributed time to the task as they were when goal manipulation also contributed time, but they suggested that at even more detailed levels of analysis such cognitive activity might become more important. Also notice that where the KLM puts Ms at the beginning of subprocedures, the CMN-GOMS model puts the mental time in VERIFY operators at the end of subprocedures. Since mental time is observable only as pauses between actions, it is difficult to distinguish between these two techniques empirically; only appeals to more detailed cognitive architectures can explain the distinction. Pragmatically, however, this difference is irrelevant in most design situations.

4.4.3   CPM-GOMS

CPM-GOMS is a version of GOMS based directly on the MHP, and thus on the parallel multiprocessor stage model of human information processing. It does not make the assumption that operators are performed serially, that is, perceptual, cognitive, and motor operators at the level of MHP processor cycle times can be performed in parallel as the task demands. Research has shown that CPM-GOMS models reflect an even higher level of skill than KLM or CMN-GOMS models (Baskin & John, 1998; John et al., 2002). CPM-GOMS uses a *schedule chart* (or *PERT chart*, familiar to project managers, see Stires & Murphy, 1962) to represent the operators and dependencies between operators. The acronym *CPM* stands for both the *cognitive-perceptual-motor* analysis of activity, and also

---

[2]   Some design situations may require or provide opportunity for using better estimates of specific types of mental operators. Analysts can look at the additional empirical work of Card, Moran, and Newell (1983) in Chapter 5 where they measure many specific mental times, or other HCI empirical work (e.g. John & Newell, 1987, for estimates of time to recall command abbreviations; Olson & Olson, 1990, for mental preparation in spreadsheet use).

critical path method, since the *critical path* in a schedule chart provides a simple prediction of total task time.

To build CPM-GOMS models, the analyst begins with a CMN-GOMS model of a task with operators at a level similar to those in Figure 4.7. These operators are then expressed as goals and implemented with methods of MHP-level operators. Researchers have developed templates of the combinations of MHP-level cognitive, perceptual, and motor operators that implement many different HCI activities like moving a mouse to a target and clicking, reading information from the screen, or typing (e.g., Gray & Boehm-Davis, 2000; John & Gray, 1992, 1994, 1995). Each operator in the templates is associated with a duration estimate, or a set of estimates that also depend on task conditions. For instance, visually perceiving and comprehending a six-character word is assigned a duration of 290 ms (John & Newell, 1989), whereas visually perceiving and comprehending that a symbol is merely present or absent (e.g., the presence of highlighting) is assigned a duration of 100 ms (Card et al., 1983).

CPM-GOMS models were traditionally constructed using project-management software (i.e., MacProject). Templates were preestablished and stored in a library file. The analyst would copy appropriate templates for a task into a blank canvas, then join them together serially to represent the operations necessary to accomplish the task. Finally, the analyst would interleave the templates to take advantage of the parallelism of the underlying conceptual architecture. Recently, a modeling tool built by NASA, Apex (Freed, 1998), has been used to create CPM-GOMS models automatically from CMN-GOMS expressed in a procedure description language (PDL), and by-hand manipulation of operators in project-management software is no longer necessary (John et al., 2002). The schedule chart of the fox task, shown in Figure 4.8, was produced with that tool by encoding the CMN-GOMS model in Figure 4.7 in PDL (Remington et al., 2002).

Quantitative predictions of performance time can be read off the schedule-chart representation of the CPM-GOMS model. Qualitative analysis of what aspects of a design lead to what portions of the performance time are quite easy once the models are built, as are subtask profiling, sensitivity and parametric analyses, and playing "what-if" with suggested design features (e.g., Baskin & John, 1998; Chuah, John, & Pane, 1994; Gray & Boehm-Davis, 2000; Gray, John, & Atwood, 1993; John et al., 2002).

Continuing the fox example of Figure 4.2, Figure 4.8 and Plate 4 of the color insert show the beginning of a CPM-GOMS model. For brevity, the model covers only the portion of the procedure involved with highlighting the text to be moved and pulling down the **Edit** menu; the model continues beyond the figure until it ends at time=4598 msec. Before discussing this model in detail,

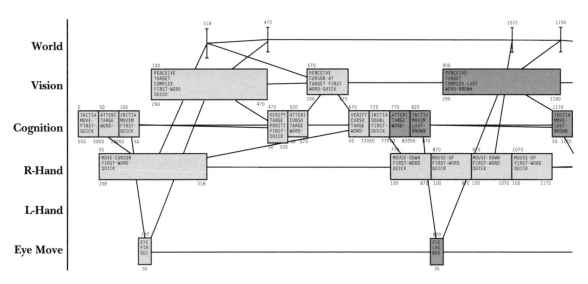

FIGURE

4.8

The beginning of the schedule chart representing the CPM-GOMS model of the fox-task editing example. This part of the chart includes highlighting the phrase to be moved and starting to issue the **Cut** command. Each operator is represented as a box, with its start time in the upper-left corner, its duration in the lower-left corner and its end time in the lower-right corner, in msec. The width of each box is proportional to its duration, so the schedule chart is also a timeline. The green boxes (see the color insert) are the cognitive, perceptual, and motor operators involved in double-clicking on the word "quick". The blue boxes are those involved in shift-clicking on the word "brown". The yellow boxes are those involved in pulling down the **Edit** menu. The purple boxes are the first four operators involved in selecting the **Cut** menu item. The schedule chart continues beyond this figure, until the end of the task at time=4598 msec. (See Plate 4 of the color insert for a color version of this figure.)

however, it is important to note that text editing is not a good application of the CPM-GOMS technique, and we present it here only so that similarities and differences to the other GOMS variations are clear. Text-editing is *usefully approximated* by serial processes, which is why the KLM and CMN-GOMS have been so successful at predicting performance on text editors. The CPM-GOMS technique is overly detailed for such primarily serial tasks and, as will become clear, can underestimate the execution time. For examples of tasks for which a parallel-processing model is essential, and where the power of CPM-GOMS is evident, see the telephone-operator task that appears in the case-study section of this chapter

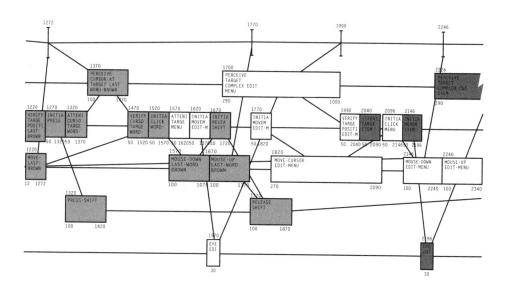

(Gray, John & Atwood, 1993), transcription typing (John, 1988; John, & Newell, 1989), and a highly interactive version of drawing in a CAD system (Baskin & John, 1998).

Although text editing is not the best task to display the advantages of CPM-GOMS, there are several interesting aspects of the model in Figure 4.8 compared to the example models of the text-moving task in the preceding sections. First, there is a direct mapping from the CMN-GOMS model to the CPM-GOMS model, because all CPM-GOMS models start with CMN-GOMS, and the particular model in Figure 4.8 was built with reference to the one in Figure 4.7. For example, the CMN-GOMS operators MOVE-CURSOR-TO-FIRST-WORD and DOUBLE-CLICK-MOUSE-BUTTON in Figure 4.7 become goals in the CPM-GOMS model that are expanded into operators (green boxes) in Figure 4.8; these boxes represent the perceptual, cognitive, and motor operators necessary to move a mouse to a target and double-click on it.

As with the KLM, selection rules are not explicitly represented in the schedule chart because the schedule chart is merely the trace of the predicted behavior. The selection rules are represented in the PDL code, just as they are in CMN-GOMS. The duration times for the various operators, shown in the lower-left corner of the boxes in the schedule chart, are based on the durations estimated by John and Gray (1992, 1994, 1995).

Parallelism is illustrated throughout the model. For instance, in the green set of operators, the eye-movement and perception of information occur in parallel with the cursor being moved to the word QUICK. The information-flow dependency lines between the operators ensure that the eyes must get to the word and perceive it before the new position of the cursor can be verified to be at the right location.

Several goals can be active at one time in CPM-GOMS models, and this is illustrated in Figure 4.8 whenever operators of two colors occur at the same time. For example, the blue operators in service of shift-clicking on BROWN begin before the green operators in service of the double-click on QUICK complete. Later, the yellow operators in service of pulling down the EDIT-MENU intermingle with both the blue operators in service of the shift-click and the purple ones in service of selecting the CUT-MENU-ITEM. This interleaving represents a very high level of skill on the part of the user.

Reading the end time of the final item in the schedule chart (not shown) gives a total execution time through the fox task to be 4.598 sec. Totaling the execution time over the same steps in the other models gives 14.90 sec for the KLM and 16.25 sec for the CMN-GOMS model, making the quantitative prediction of the CPM-GOMS model much shorter than the estimates from the other models. The primary source of the discrepancy between the GOMS variants is the basic assumption in the commonly used form of the CPM-GOMS technique that the user is extremely experienced and executes the task as rapidly as the MHP architecture permits. It should be kept in mind that this particular example task is not really suitable for CPM-GOMS, but it is presented to facilitate comparison with the other techniques, and it shows how CPM-GOMS can represent parallel activities in the same editing task. Some discussion of why the CPM-GOMS technique predicts an execution time that is so much shorter than the others will help clarify the basic assumptions of this form of GOMS analysis.

One aspect of the extreme-expertise assumption is that the example model assumes that the user knows exactly where to look for the to-be-moved-phrase. This means that the model needs only one eye movement to find the beginning and one to find the end of the words to be moved, and that the mouse movements to these points can be initiated prior to the completion of the eye movements. In some real-world tasks, like telephone operators handling calls (see the case study later in this chapter, or Gray, John, & Atwood, 1993), the required information always appears at fixed screen locations, and, with experience, the user will learn where to look. But in a typical text-editing task like our example, the situation changes from one task instance to the next, and so visual search may be required to locate the target phrase. CPM-GOMS has been used to model visual search processes (Chuah, John, & Pane, 1994), but for brevity we did not include this complexity in our example.

A second aspect of the assumed extreme expertise is that the example does not include any substantial cognitive activity associated with selection of methods or complex decisions. Such cognitive activity is represented in the other GOMS variants with M-like operators of about a second in duration. In contrast, in Figure 4.8, the method selection is implicit in the trace produced in the schedule chart, but it does not appear as an operator itself. Likewise, VERIFY-POSITION operators are included in the CPM-GOMS model, but they represent much more elementary recognitions that the cursor is indeed in the location where the model is already looking rather than complex verifications that a text modification has been done correctly as required in the CMN-GOMS model. Thus, Figure 4.8 represents the absolute minimum cognitive activity, which is an unreasonable assumption for a normal text-editing task. However, in an experiment by Card, Moran, and Newell (Card et al., 1983, pp. 279–286), the performance time of an expert user on a novel editing task was well predicted by the KLM; after 1100 trials on the *same task instance,* however, the performance time decreased by 35%, largely because the M operators became much shorter. It is this type of extreme expertise that our example CPM-GOMS model represents. Subsequent research (Baskin & John, 1998; John et al., 2002) has suggested that skilled human performance is well predicted by CPM-GOMS models after about 100 trials of the same task instance, while KLM and CMN-GOMS models predict about the fifth trial quite well. A more elaborate CPM-GOMS model could represent complex decisions as a series of MHP-level operators performing minute cognitive steps serially, as in the earlier work on recalling computer command abbreviations (John, 1988; John and Newell, 1989; John, Rosenbloom, & Newell, 1985). However, the technique for modeling complex decisions in CPM-GOMS models is still a research issue, and so these models currently should be used only for tasks in which method selection is based on obvious cues in the environment and in which decisions can be represented very simply.

A final contributor to the short predicted time is that the mouse movements in CPM-GOMS are calculated using Fitts' Law specifically for the particular target size and distance in this situation, yielding much shorter times than Card, Moran, and Newell's 1.10 sec estimate of average pointing time used in the other models. The 1.10 sec used in the KLM and CNM-GOMS model is the average value suggested by Card, Moran, and Newell for large-screen text editing tasks. But Gong (1993) found that many of the mouse movements involved in using a Macintosh interface, such as making menu selections and activating windows, were faster than 1.10 sec, and that Fitts' Law estimates (see Card et al., 1983,

p. 55) were much more accurate. Thus, Fitts' Law values based on the actual or typical locations of screen objects should probably be used whenever possible in all of the techniques. For CPM-GOMS, moving the cursor to point to an object is a combination of cognitive operators, motor operators, and perceptual operators (see Figure 4.8). The duration of the mouse-movement motor operator itself is calculated using Fitts' Law.

Thus, the CPM-GOMS technique allows one to represent the overlapping and extremely efficient pattern of activity characteristic of expert performance in a task. The main contrasts with the other techniques is that CPM-GOMS models constructed with the current technique do not include the time-consuming M-like operators that the other models do, and that would be expected to disappear with considerable practice if the system interface holds the relevant aspects constant. Furthermore, CPM-GOMS tends to use Fitts' Law for estimates of mouse-movement times (although any GOMS variant could use Fitts' Law, and CPM-GOMS could use 1.100 seconds, as was done by Baskin & John, 1998). Analysts need to consider whether their users are likely to attain the extreme level of skill modeled by CPM-GOMS when deciding which GOMS variant to use. The following case study illustrates a task where this assumption was reasonable and held true.

4.5   CASE STUDY: PROJECT ERNESTINE

Many instances of GOMS modeling have contributed to the design and evaluation of computer systems (see John & Kieras, 1996a, for a description of 11 examples). Perhaps the most economically successful is the case of Project Ernestine (Gray, John, & Atwood, 1993). In 1988, NYNEX, the telephone company then serving New York and New England, considered replacing the workstations used by toll and assistance operators (TAOs, who handled calls such as collect calls and person-to-person calls) with a new workstation. A major factor in making the purchase decision was determining how quickly the expected decrease in average work time per call would offset the capital cost of making the purchase. Because an average decrease of one second in work time per call would save an estimated $3 million per year, the decision was economically significant.

To evaluate the new workstations, NYNEX conducted a large-scale field trial. At the same time, Wayne Gray (at NYNEX) and I (at Carnegie-Mellon University) used CPM-GOMS models to predict the outcome of the field trial. We worked with expert telephone operators to construct models for the current workstation for a set of benchmark tasks. We then modified these models to reflect the differences in design between the two workstations; these included different keyboard and screen layout, keying procedures, and system response time. This modeling effort took about two person-months, but this time included making extensions to the CPM-GOMS modeling technique to handle this type of task and teaching NYNEX personnel how to use CPM-GOMS, compared to the 18-month elapsed time and the scores of people involved in the field trial. The models produced quantitative predictions of expert call-handling time for each benchmark task on both workstations, which, when combined with the frequency of each call type, predicted that the new workstation would be an average of 0.63 seconds slower than the old workstation. Thus the new workstation would not save money, but would cost NYNEX an additional $2 million a year to operate.

This was a counter-intuitive prediction. The new workstation had many technically superior features. The workstation used more advanced technology to communicate with the switch at a much higher speed. The new keyboard placed the most frequently used keys closer together. The new display had a graphic user interface with recognizable icons instead of obscure alphanumeric codes. The procedures were streamlined, sometimes combining previously separate keystrokes into one keystroke, sometimes using defaults to eliminate keystrokes from most call types, with a net decrease of about one keystroke per call. Both the manufacturer and NYNEX believed that the new workstation would be substantially faster than the old one—by one estimate, as much as 4 seconds faster per call. Despite the intuition to the contrary, when the empirical field-trial data were analyzed, they supported the CPM-GOMS predictions. The new workstation was 0.65 seconds slower on average than the old workstation.

In addition to predicting the quantitative outcome of the field trail, the GOMS models explained *why* the new workstation was slower than the old workstation, something which empirical trials typically cannot do. The simple estimate that the new workstation would be faster was based on the greater speed of the new features considered in isolation. But the execution time for the whole task depends on how all of the components of the interaction fit together, and this is captured by the critical path in the CPM-GOMS model. Because of the structure of the whole task, the faster features of the new workstation failed to shorten the critical path.

The pragmatic result of both the empirical results and the CPM-GOMS modeling was that NYNEX decided not to buy the new workstations. The scientific result was that CPM-GOMS modeling was shown to predict real-world performance of skilled users extremely well and it was shown to provide explanations for their behavior that were both reasonable and easy to communicate to users, developers, and managers. The following section will provide some more detail about the task and the models to illustrate the power that CPM-GOMS brought to NYNEX's buy/no-buy decision.[3]

4.5.1   Details of Project Ernestine's CPM-GOMS Modeling Effort

Predicting skilled execution time is a strength of GOMS modeling. Such predictions are successful when the users are experts performing a routine cognitive skill and making few errors. These conditions were satisfied in Project Ernestine, making this task a suitable candidate for GOMS modeling. A TAO handles hundreds of calls each day, and many stay at the job for years (even decades). TAOs recognize each call situation and execute well-practiced methods, rather than engage in problem solving. As for errors, the call-handling system is designed to preclude many types of errors (for example, the workstation will not release a call unless all necessary information is entered), and experienced TAOs make few errors of any type.

Successful GOMS models also depend on the task having clearly identifiable goals, operators, methods, and (if necessary) selection rules. The task of a TAO has these characteristics, as described with reference to the following example.

In 1988, a TAO was the person to whom customers spoke when they dialed "0" (many of the functions handled by TAOs are now automated). A TAO's job was to assist a customer in completing calls and to record the correct billing. Among other duties, TAOs handled person-to-person calls, collect calls, calling-card calls, and calls billed to a third number. (TAOs did not handle directory assistance calls.) For example, consider the situation where a person directly dials a number and has the TAO bill the call to his or her calling card. The dialog is sparse, but typical:

Workstation:	"Beep"
TAO:	"New England Telephone, may I help you?"
Customer:	"Operator, bill this to 412–555–1212–1234."
TAO:	Keys information into the workstation.
TAO:	"Thank you."
TAO:	Releases the workstation to accept the next incoming call by pressing the RELEASE key.

---

[3]   Much of the following section is adapted from Gray, John, and Atwood, 1993, where more detail, including a complete model of a telephone call and details of the empirical study, can be found.

TAOs were trained to answer three questions in the course of a call; these questions correspond to three goals in a GOMS analysis. For each call, a TAO had to determine (1) who should pay for the call, (2) what billing rate to use, and (3) when the connection is complete enough to terminate interaction with the customer. In the above calling-card call, (1) the owner of the calling card pays for the call, (2) the operator-assisted station rate is applied, and (3) the connection is complete when the calling-card number is approved. It was not necessary for the call to actually go through because, if the call did go through, then the correct billing would be applied; if it did not go through, the calling card would not be charged.

To accomplish these goals, TAOs converse with the customer, key information into a workstation, and read information from the workstation screen. In some cases, they also write notes to themselves (primarily to remember callers' names for collect calls). Thus, the GOMS operators for accomplishing the goals include listening, talking, reading, keying, writing, and the cognitive activities necessary to assimilate information and determine action. An additional complexity, beyond the sheer variety of activities, is that TAOs appear to perform many of them simultaneously. The TAO types information into the workstation while listening to the customer and scanning the screen for information relevant to the call. Thus, this task was particularly suited to CPM-GOMS modeling.

Many of these activities had been successfully modeled in GOMS research prior to Project Ernestine. Heuristics for modeling the perception of words on a display screen and for modeling typing had already been developed (John, 1988; John & Newell, 1989; John, Rosenbloom, & Newell, 1985). To handle the variety of activities the TAO must perform on the current workstation, we made extensions to CPM-GOMS to model auditory perception, verbal responses, eye movements to get information from well-known positions on a CRT screen, and system response time. These extensions were made early in the project (John, 1990), and their derivation and general use is discussed in more detail elsewhere (Gray, John, & Atwood, 1993; John & Gray, 1992).

The TAOs accomplished their goals using a dedicated workstation, and the details of the workstation design influenced the CPM-GOMS models. The differences in screen and keyboard layout, keying procedures, and system response times between the current and proposed workstations affected the methods used to process a call, as well as the duration of specific operators within a method (for example, the duration of the horizontal movements to some keys changed between workstations). However, expressing the differences between workstations in the models was straightforward; no extensions to CPM-GOMS were required to express these differences.

Building the CPM-GOMS Models

Figure 4.9 shows the traditional GOMS goal hierarchy and the beginning of the CPM-GOMS model that implements it. We built 36 such CPM-GOMS models, one for each workstation for 18 different benchmark calls selected for frequency of occurrence and importance to NYNEX (e.g., emergency calls are infrequent but important to accomplish in the minimum time necessary). Fifteen of these benchmarks covered more than 80% of the calls handled by TAOs and are included in the quantitative predictions discussed in the next section. The durations of the CPM operators were determined in one of three ways: observed in videos of the benchmark calls, obtained from previous psychological literature, or estimated by the proposed workstation manufacturer.

The durations for all pausing and speaking, by both the TAOs and the customers, were measured from videotapes of the benchmark calls handled by expert TAOs with the current workstation. These included complex auditory perceptual operators, such as the real-time perception and comprehension of the customer's phrase "make this collect," as well as the duration for the TAO's motor operator to say "New England Telephone, may I help you?" Since the same conversations appeared in the benchmark calls for both the current and proposed workstations, these times observed on the current workstation were used in both sets of models. The duration of hand movements for pressing keys on the current workstations were also set from measurements of the videotapes, as were all the system response times for the current workstation (but not the proposed workstation, discussed later).

Normative estimates for unobservable operators were obtained from the psychological literature and can be considered off-the-shelf estimates of how long an average person requires to perform a particular operator. Cognitive operators are assumed to be of equal duration, 50 msec (John & Newell, 1990). The motor operator that makes an eye movement to a known screen location was 30 msec (Russo, 1978).[4] Binary visual perception operators, used when the TAO must detect only the presence or absence of a visual signal, are assumed to be 100 msec

---

[4] Early papers about Project Ernestine used 180 msec for the duration of the eye movement. This was derived from the 1983 Card et al. estimate of 230 msec for an eye movement subdivided into a cognitive operator, 50 msec, to initiate the movement and the movement action itself, 180 msec. We discovered later that the eye movement estimated by Card et al. included some amount of perception and comprehension, which should be separated from the actual eye movement time in CPM-GOMS. Card et al. referred to Russo (1978) for the travel time alone being 30 msec, much shorter than 180 msec. The eye movements never appeared on the critical path of the Ernestine models, and shortening them would therefore not affect the time predictions. All CPM-GOMS models after 1992 use 30 msec for eye-movement time.

GOMS goal hierarchy	Observed Behavior
goal: handle-calls	
. **goal: handle-call**	
. . **goal: initiate-call**	
. . . **goal: receive-information**	
. . . . listen-for-beep	Workstation: Beep
. . . . read-screen(2)	Workstation: Displays source information
. . . **goal: request-information**	
. . . . greet-customer	TAO: "New England Telephone, may I help you?"
. . **goal: enter-who-pays**	
. . . **goal: receive-information**	
. . . . listen-to-customer	Customer: Operator, bill this to 412-555-1212-1234
. . . **goal: enter-information**	
. . . . enter-command	TAO: hit F1 key
. . . . enter-calling-card-number	TAO: hit 14 numeric keys
. . **goal: enter-billing-rate**	
. . . **goal: receive-information**	
. . . . read-screen(1)	Workstation: previously displayed source information
. . . **goal: enter-information**	
. . . . enter-command	TAO: hit F2 key
. . **goal: complete-call**	
. . . **goal: request-information**	
. . . . enter-command	TAO: hit F3 key
. . . **goal: receive-information**	
. . . . read-screen(3)	Workstation: displays credit-card authorization
. . . **goal: release-workstation**	
. . . . thank-customer	TAO: "Thank you"
. . . . enter-command	TAO: hit F4 key

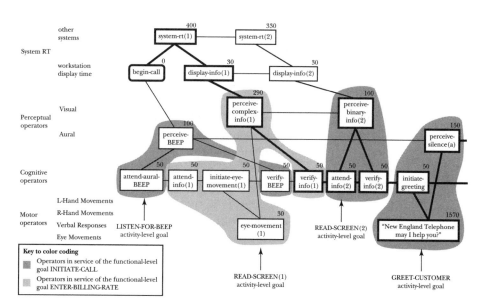

FIGURE 4.9 GOMS hierarchy down to the activity level, and CPM-GOMS implementation of that hierarchy. Shading in the hierarchy corresponds to the background shading of the operators in the CPM-GOMS model. (Adapted from John, 1990, figure 1, pp. 110–111, and Gray, John, & Atwood, 1993, figure 7, p. 254.)

(minimal perceptual operator in the MHP; Card et al., 1983). For example, in Figure 4.9, the perception of info(2) is a binary perception; information processing analysis revealed that the TAO need only detect that a code appears in that spot on the screen, not what the code actually says (because it always says the same thing). In contrast, perceiving info(1) in Figure 4.9 is a complex visual perception because information-processing analysis revealed the TAO must perceive and comprehend the semantics of the code displayed, as well as the presence of the code, to get sufficient information to continue with the call. The complex visual perceptions required of the TAO are all of small words, alphanumeric codes, or numbers, and they are assumed to take 290 msec because they are of similar character to the small-word recognition tasks used to estimate that duration (this is derived from the John & Newell [1989] estimate of 340 msec for the perception and encoding of a short word subdivided into a 290 msec perceptual operator and a 50 msec cognitive operator to verify expectations). Binary auditory perceptual operators, such as detecting the "beep" that signals an incoming call, are also set at 100 msec (minimal perceptual operator of the MHP; Card et al., 1983). The perception of an auditory silence that signals turn taking in conversation is estimated at 300 msec (this is the 400 msec mean interspeaker pause found by Norwine and Murphy [1938] subdivided into a 300 msec perceive-silence operator followed by a 50 msec cognitive operator to verify the silence and a 50 msec cognitive operator to initiate the spoken response). Finally, for the horizontal hand movements required by the proposed workstation, we used Fitts' Law to predict the time to execute that movement. We considered this a "normative" estimate because Fitts' Law is a well-established empirical regularity (see Chapter 3).

To complete the models, the manufacturer of the proposed workstation supplied estimates for the expected response time of the proposed system to various TAO actions. These estimates were used in the CPM-GOMS models of the proposed workstation whenever the workstation had to perform an action like displaying information or looking up a number in a database.

In summary, the models of the current workstation used both normative estimates of durations and measurements taken from videotaped observations of the current workstation. In contrast, the models of the proposed workstation used only preestablished estimates from videotapes of the current workstation, normative estimates from the literature, and estimates of system response time supplied by the manufacturer. The proposed workstation was never observed in operation and might as well have not yet even existed. The models of the proposed workstation could have just as easily been created from a specification of that workstation.

Accuracy of the Models' Time Predictions

The 30 models of the 15 most frequent calls produced quantitative predictions of call-completion time. The most important measure to NYNEX was the difference between the current workstation and the proposed workstation averaged across call categories, but we also examined the absolute and relative predictions for each call category.

When each model was weighted by the frequency of occurrence of its call category, CPM-GOMS predicted that the proposed workstation would be an average of 0.63 seconds slower than the current workstation. For comparison, when the empirical data were weighted by the frequency of call occurrence, the proposed workstation was 0.65 seconds slower than the current one. This overall prediction was the most important one to NYNEX. Pragmatically, with an average decrease of one second per call saving $3 million per year in operating costs, the ability to quantitatively predict performance on the mixture of calls that NYNEX TAOs handled was the most prized prediction. This small difference in work time would cost NYNEX an estimated $2 million per year more than the current workstations' operating costs. The CPM-GOMS models predicted the overall outcome of the field trial with remarkable accuracy. As for predictions of workstation difference for each individual call category, CPM-GOMS predicted the direction of the difference for all but 3 of the 15 call categories.

Looking at the absolute time predictions, the CPM-GOMS models for the current workstation—when weighted by call category frequency—underpredicted the trial data by an average of 4.35%. This underprediction was continued by the models of the proposed workstation, with these models predicting a weighted worktime 4.31% faster than the trial data. These weighted predictions are well within the 20% error limit that previous work (John & Newell, 1989) has argued is the useful range of an engineering model. Because these underpredictions were consistent at about 4%, the relative prediction of the two sets of CPM-GOMS models (0.63 seconds predicted versus 0.65 seconds found in the empirical data) is more accurate than the predictions of absolute call time themselves.

Across call categories unweighted by frequency, the average percent difference between the CPM-GOMS models and the observed calls was 11.30% for the current workstation and 11.87% for the proposed workstation. The correlation between the CPM-GOMS predictions and the trial data was significant with an r^2 of 0.71 for the current workstation and of 0.69 for the proposed workstation. For each workstation and call category, the z scores show that for 14 of the 15 call categories the CPM-GOMS prediction is within one standard deviation of the trial mean for both current and proposed workstations. These data support the conclusion that the CPM-GOMS models predict the trial data in the aggregate with acceptable accuracy.

The individual predictions of worktime per call category were less accurate than the aggregate measures. The percent difference between predicted and observed time per call category for the current workstation ranged from −63% to +49%, with eight call categories more than 20% away from their observed times. Likewise, the percent difference for the proposed workstation ranged from −54% to +49%, with the same eight call categories being more than 20% away from the observed times. These general results—that the overall prediction of work time (both weighted by call frequency and unweighted) is very good while the individual predictions of call category is not as good—are a statistical fact of life. If the individual predictions vary more or less randomly around the actual call times, some being too short and some being too long, aggregate measures will involve some canceling-out of these predictions. Since the aggregate measures are of primary importance to NYNEX, this fluctuation at the level of individual call types is interesting to examine but not too important to the results of the modeling effort. The lesson to be learned for future modeling efforts is to be sure to model a substantial suite of benchmark tasks as opposed to depending on one or two.

Explaining the Differences Between Workstations

Beyond predicting performance time, the CPM-GOMS models provide explanations for their predictions and thereby for the empirical data. Despite its improved technology and ergonomically superior design, performance with the proposed workstation was slower than with the current workstation. A high-order look at the critical paths shows the task to be dominated by conversation and system response time. Seldom is the TAO's interaction with the workstation on the critical path. This pattern is so strong that it was found in our initial model of just one call category (Gray et al., 1989), and so consistent that we declared it confirmed after modeling five call categories (Gray et al., 1990). Thus, the top-order prediction of the CPM-GOMS analyses is that the design of the workstation should have little, if any, effect on the length of calls.

We can look at the details of the models to understand why the proposed workstation is actually slower than the current workstation. The workstations differ in their keyboard layout, screen layout, keying procedures, and system response time, each of which may affect call duration. Here we examine just the keying procedures to illustrate the explicative power of the CPM-GOMS models. The other effects are examined in Gray, John, and Atwood (1993).

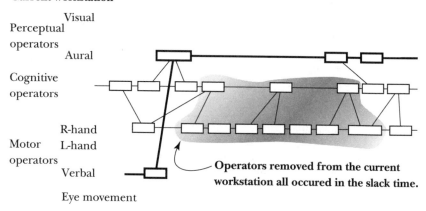

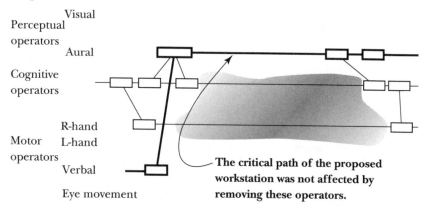

FIGURE

4.10

Section of the CPM-GOMS model from near the beginning of the call. (Adapted from Gray, John, Stuart, Lawrence, & Atwood, 1990, figure 1, p. 32; Gray, John, & Atwood, 1992, figure 1, p. 310; Gray, John, & Atwood, 1993, figure 19, p. 284; Atwood, Gray, & John, 1996, figure 1, p. 108.)

For several calls, the keying procedures for the proposed workstation elimi-nated keystrokes. In some of these calls, this decrease in keystrokes was an advan-tage for the proposed workstation. However, because of the complex interaction of parallel activities in the TAOs' task, merely eliminating keystrokes is not nec-essarily an advantage. For example, Figure 4.10 and Figure 4.11 show the first and last segments of a CPM-GOMS analysis for a calling-card call where new

Current workstation

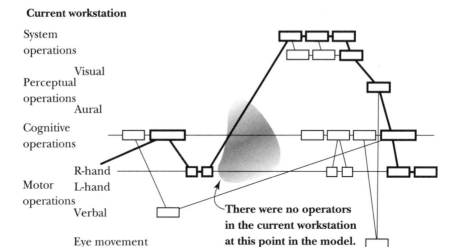

System
operations

        Visual
Perceptual
operations
        Aural

Cognitive
operations

    R-hand

Motor   L-hand
operations
    Verbal

    Eye movement

**There were no operators
in the current workstation
at this point in the model.**

Proposed workstation

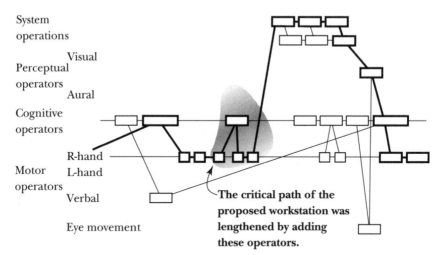

System
operations

        Visual
Perceptual
operators
        Aural

Cognitive
operators

    R-hand

Motor   L-hand
operators
    Verbal

    Eye movement

**The critical path of the
proposed workstation was
lengthened by adding
these operators.**

FIGURE

4.11

Section of the CPM-GOMS model from the end of the call. (Adapted from Gray, John, Stuart, Lawrence, & Atwood, 1990, figure 2, p. 32; Gray, John, & Atwood, 1992, figure 2, p. 310; Gray, John, & Atwood, 1993, figure 10, p. 285; Atwood, Gray, and John, 1996, figure 2, p. 109.)

procedures eliminated two keystrokes from the beginning of the call and added one keystroke to the end of the call, for a net decrease of one keystroke. For each figure, the top chart represents the call using the current workstation, and the bottom shows the CPM-GOMS analysis for the same call using the proposed work station.

Figure 4.10 has two striking features. First, the model for the proposed workstation has 10 fewer boxes than the model for the current workstation, representing two fewer keystrokes. Second, none of the deleted boxes are on the critical path; all are performed in slack time. At this point in the task, the critical path is determined by the TAO greeting and getting information from the customer. The CPM-GOMS model predicts that removing keystrokes from this part of the call will not affect the TAO's work time. Work time is controlled by the conversation, not by the keystrokes and not by the ergonomics of the keyboard.

The middle of the model, not shown (the activities between those shown in Figure 4.10 and Figure 4.11), is identical for both workstations and essentially shows that the critical path is driven by how fast the customer says the 14-digit number to which the call should be billed. TAOs are taught to "key along" with the customer. While a rapidly speaking customer could force the critical path to be determined by the TAO's keying speed, both workstations use the standard numeric keypad, so the critical path (and resulting speed of keying in numbers) would be the same for both workstations in the middle of the call.

If the proposed keying procedures simply eliminated the two keystrokes required by the current workstation in the beginning of the call, then CPM-GOMS would predict equivalent performance. However, for the proposed workstation, the procedure has been changed so that one of the keystrokes eliminated at the beginning of the call now occurs later in the call (four extra boxes in the bottom of Figure 4.11). In this model, this keystroke goes from being performed during slack time at the beginning of the call, to being performed on the critical path at the end of the call. The cognitive and motor time required for this keystroke now add to the total time required to process this call. Thus, the net elimination of one keystroke actually increased call time because of the complex interaction between parallel activities shown in the critical-path analysis. The CPM-GOMS models showed similar clear reasons for each design decision having either no effect on total time, slightly decreasing total time, or, as in this case, increasing the total time of the call.

Value-Added of the CPM-GOMS Models

A simple, seemingly reasonable calculation can be done to predict worktime differences between the current and proposed workstations without cognitive modeling. Such a calculation was made before Project Ernestine, set NYNEX's initial expectations of improved performance with the proposed workstation, and justified the expense of the field trial. Here we work through such a calculation and compare its accuracy to the CPM-GOMS predictions to evaluate the value-added of the human information processing approach in the form of CPM-GOMS.

The benchmark tasks are also used in the non-HIP estimate of workstation differences. First, the proposed workstation changed the keying procedure to eliminate keystrokes for several call categories. From Card, Moran, and Newell, we get an estimate of 280 msec per keystroke for an average, 40 wpm, nonsecretary typist (Card et al., 1983, Figure 9.1, p. 264). For each call category, this time was subtracted for each keystroke that the manufacturer's procedures eliminated. Four keystrokes were eliminated from one benchmark call; two keystrokes from two calls; one keystroke from each of seven calls; zero keystrokes from four calls; and one keystroke was added to one call. Second, the manufacturer estimated that the proposed workstation would be 880 msec faster than the current workstation to display a screenful of information. We subtracted this estimate from every benchmark call because every call displays a screenful of information. From these two facts, we would predict an average advantage for the proposed workstation of 5.2%. When call categories are weighted by their frequency of occurrence, the predicted advantage becomes 18.6% (4.1 sec) for an estimated *savings* in annual operating costs of $12.2 million.

In contrast, the CPM-GOMS models predicted, and the field trial confirmed, that the proposed workstation would actually be about 3% *slower* than the current workstation. Thus, the seemingly reasonable calculation based on the benchmarks and manufacturer's procedures and response-time estimates is wrong in both magnitude and sign. It is important to remember that the non-HIP prediction is more than just a strawman. Large-scale empirical trials such as Project Ernestine are expensive to conduct; this one involved dozens of workstations, scores of people, and many months of planning, training, data collection, and analysis. Expectations based upon such a calculation led NYNEX to commit to the time and expense required to conduct the empirical trial.

Why were the CPM-GOMS predictions so much more accurate than the noncognitive predictions? Two reasons are apparent: (1) Building CPM-GOMS models requires that the analyst understand the details of information flow between the workstation and the TAO, which were overlooked by the non-HIP predictions, and (2) CPM-GOMS models incorporate the complex effects of parallel activities that were important to this task.

For example, the non-HIP predictions assumed that each time a screenful of information was displayed, the proposed workstations' faster system response time would reduce the time of the call. However, the more detailed analysis required to build CPM-GOMS models revealed that the TAO does not have to see the entire screen to initiate the greeting, just the first line, and therefore the TAO is conversing with the customer while the rest of the visual information is being displayed on the screen. Hence, comparisons of how fast the two workstations display an entire screen of information are largely irrelevant. Likewise, the noncognitive model assumes that every keystroke contributes to the length of the call. However, as we discussed above, CPM-GOMS shows that removing a keystroke only speeds the task if that keystroke is on the critical path.

Thus, CPM-GOMS disciplines the analyst to incorporate the right level of detail to evaluate such tasks and correctly calculates the effects of parallel activities to produce accurate quantitative predictions. A non-HIP approach based on benchmarks and design changes alone does not predict as accurately. In addition to producing more accurate quantitative predictions, CPM-GOMS models can provide qualitative explanations for the quantitative results and can also be used as a tool in workstation design (Gray, John, & Atwood, 1993). Clearly, CPM-GOMS adds value over non-HIP predictions.

4.6   CURRENT STATUS

4.6.1   GOMS in Particular

GOMS modeling may be the most active area of the information processing approach in HCI applications. A search for "GOMS" in the HCI Bibliography returns more than one hundred entries, including a 1996 paper in Association for Computing Machinery Transactions on Computer Human Interaction (ACM ToCHI) that profiles 11 cases of GOMS used in industry and government projects (John & Kieras, 1996a). Papers using GOMS appear every year in the ACM Computer-Human Interaction (CHI) conference, and research continues into extending GOMS and making it more accessible. Birds-of-a-Feather meetings at the CHI conference fill the room with scores of interested practitioners and researchers. GOMS appears in many HCI textbooks—Brinck, Gergle, & Wood (2002); Dix, Finlay, Abowd, & Beale (1998); Eberts (1994); Helander, Landauer, & Prabhu (1997); Newman & Lamming (1995); Preece, Rogers, Sharp, Benyon, Holland, & Carey (1994); Raskin (2000); Shneiderman (1998)—and is taught in HCI classes.

Although community interest is high, it is fair to say that few HCI practitioners consider GOMS a ready-to-hand tool to be used routinely in their design practice. One reason may be the lack of readily-available tool support for the techniques. A review of several GOMS tools, GLEAN (Kieras et al., 1995), CAT-HCI (Williams, 1993), and Cognet (Zachary, 1989), highlighted the progress that had been made in this area and the needs still unfulfilled (Baumeister et al., 2000). Other tools are being explored in research labs, such as CRITIQUE (Hudson et al., 1999) and Apex (John et al., 2002), but no widely used commercial-quality tool has emerged at this writing.

4.6.2   Human Information Processing in General

The HIP approach, however, is broader than GOMS. HIP can be used to model more than the routine cognitive skill to which GOMS is restricted. It can be used to model more complex human behaviors like problem solving, learning, and group interaction, which are also crucial for the design of complex systems. Work in these areas of HIP, and in the area of integrating it all within the computational cognitive architectures discussed in Section 4.3.2, lived mainly in the realm of psychology research for several decades (1970s through 1990s), with steady progress in understanding its capabilities and limitations, but with little application to real-world HCI for much of that time.

However, a few highly successful applications of HIP did emerge from research in the late 1980s and early 1990s that dramatically demonstrated the power and potential of the HIP approach for applications. For instance, Project Ernestine demonstrated that the HIP approach could be taken out of the laboratory and used to predict performance on a real-world task with large financial significance.

Intelligent tutoring systems to teach high school mathematics were developed using the ACT-R architecture (Anderson et al., 1995) deployed in real classrooms, and were shown to produce significant improvement in mathematics standardized tests for real students under real conditions. These tutoring systems contain a cognitive model of the problem solving knowledge students are to acquire. The tutors compare student behavior and model behavior step by step, to estimate the student's growing knowledge state, to individualize the problem sequence, and to provide advice as needed. The success of these cognitive tutors demonstrated that HIP could have a significant impact for education. These systems have been commercialized and are currently used by more than 100,000 high school students *(www.carnegielearning.com).*

Finally, the HIP approach embodied in the Soar architecture was used in developing intelligent forces (IFors) for use in simulated theatres of war (STOWs)

(Tambe et al., 1995). These IFors flew simulated airplanes and helicopters in multiday STOWs where only a fraction of the tens of thousands of participants were human. They accepted instructions from commanding officers and planned missions in the same amount of time as human pilots. They communicated with each other to coordinate activities. They flew missions following the plan, but they also reacted to unexpected occurrences as human pilots would. These systems demonstrated that the HIP approach was stable enough and flexible enough to interact for long periods of time, under realistic conditions, and in coordination with each other and with humans. This approach has also been commercialized, and Soar Technology, Inc. produces IFors for several branches of the U.S. Department of Defense *(www.soartech.com)*.

The progress in the research labs and the successes in the field led to an examination of the state of the science of modeling human behavior by a panel of experts convened by the U.S. National Research Council's Committee on Human Factors. The resulting book, *Modeling Human and Organizational Behavior* (Pew & Mavor, 1998), is dominated by the HIP approach (although other approaches are discussed). As well as detailing the state of the science circa 1998, the book maps a route for future research and application. It calls for basic research, application with feedback to research, data collection for validation, and an infrastructure that facilitates scientific progress.

Subsequent to the publication of *Modeling Human and Organizational Behavior,* many new or expanded research and application opportunities have arisen. Several branches of the U.S. armed forces have commissioned HIP modeling efforts both in basic and applied research. Comparisons between different cognitive architectures are being conducted (e.g. Gluck & Pew, 2001). New areas of research are being supported, such as modeling the effects of environmental or emotional stressors on human performance. New arenas of application have opened up, such as modeling the effects of using interactive devices (cell phones, navigation systems, etc.) while driving an automobile (Salvucci & Macuga, 2002) and providing cognitively plausible software agents as video game opponents (Laird, 2001). New communities are also arising around the world, congregating at the International Conference on Cognitive Modeling begun in the late 1990s *(www.hfac.gmu.edu/~iccm/),* as well as having a continued presence in older communities like Human Factors and Ergonomics Society, the Cognitive Science Society ACM SIGCHI, and the Computer Generated Forces and Behavioral Representation conference. In short, 30 years after HIP emerged as a respectable approach in psychology for researching human behavior, it enjoys a vibrant, exciting, and productive role in the creation of human-machine systems.

4.7   FURTHER READING

Readers interested in pursuing the topics covered in this chapter in more depth are referred to the following publications.

4.7.1   Seminal Text in Human Information Processing

Newell, A., & Simon, H. A. (1972). *Human problem solving.* Englewood Cliffs, N.J.: Prentice-Hall.

4.7.2   Human Information Processing in HCI

Card, S. K., Moran, T. P., & Newell, A. (1983). *The psychology of human-computer interaction.* Hillsdale, NJ: Erlbaum.

John, B. E., & Kieras, D. E. (1996a). Using GOMS for user interface design and evaluation: Which technique? *ACM Transactions on Computer-Human Interaction 3*(4), 287–319.

John, B. E., & Kieras, D. E. (1996b). The GOMS family of user interface analysis techniques: Comparison and contrast. *ACM Transactions on Computer-Human Interaction 3*(4), 320–351.

Olson, J. R., & Olson, G. M. (1990). The growth of cognitive modeling in human-computer interaction since GOMS. *Human-Computer Interaction 5*, 221–265.

4.7.3   Human Information Processing Embodied in Computational Cognitive Architectures

Introduces the concept of unified theories of cognition (computational cognitive architectures) and provides the Soar architecture as an example.

Newell, A. (1990). *Unified theories of cognition.* Cambridge, MA: Harvard University Press.

Describes the ACT-R and ACT-RPM (with perceptual and motor modules) architecture.

Anderson, J. R. (1983). *The architecture of cognition.* Cambridge, MA: Harvard University Press.

Anderson, J. R. (1993). *Rules of the mind.* Hillsdale, NJ: Erlbaum.

Anderson, J. R., & Lebiere, C. eds. (1998). *The atomic components of thought*. Mahwah, NJ: Erlbaum.

Describes the EPIC architecture.

Kieras, D., & Meyer, D. E. (1997). An overview of the EPIC architecture for cognition and performance with application to human-computer interaction. *Human-Computer Interaction 12,* 391–438.

Meyer, D. E., & Kieras, D. E. (1997a). A computational theory of executive control processes and human multiple-task performance: Part 1. Basic mechanisms. *Psychological Review 104,* 3–65.

Meyer, D. E., & Kieras, D. E. (1997b). A computational theory of executive control processes and human multiple-task performance: Part 2. Accounts of psychological refractory-period phenomena. *Psychological Review 104,* 749–791.

Reviews the state of the art of human performance modeling. Chapter 3 reviews 11 different computational cognitive architectures.

Pew, R. W., & Mavor, A. S. (1998). *Modeling human and organizational behavior: Application to military simulations. Panel on modeling human behavior and command decision making: Representations for military simulations*. Washington, DC: National Academy Press.

5 Notational Systems—The Cognitive Dimensions of Notations Framework

Alan Blackwell   Cambridge University, Cambridge, England
Thomas Green   University of Leeds, Leeds, England

5.1   MOTIVATION

The field of human-computer interaction (HCI) is gradually achieving sound theoretical descriptions of the activities, context, and cognition of computer-system users. How do these research results get applied by the people who design new user interfaces? Although we have theoretical descriptions of the activities of system users, we have fewer descriptions of the design activities of user-interface designers. There are certainly theory-based design methods prescribing the things that designers ought to do. Almost all of these have been developed from the perspective of descriptions of the user rather than from consideration of the needs of designers—the current vogue for "user-centered design" clearly expresses this emphasis on the user. According to this perspective, if user-interface designers are to apply research into user needs, those designers must be able (and willing) to interpret and apply theoretical results.

Alternatively, there are also many popular approaches to user-interface design that have minimal theoretical grounding. Such design methodologies generally attempt to present designers with a checklist (Nielsen & Molich, 1990) or a procedural list of design activities (Wharton, Rieman, Lewis, & Polson, 1994) that will generate a good design. The reduction of design to a checklist or a predefined procedure is widely proposed in other areas of software development, not just user-interface design. Popular software-engineering texts provide a series of checklists that aim to assure design quality at different stages of a project (Pressman, 1997), while structured and object-oriented design methods prescribe a sequence of design tasks that will generate software from requirements (Booch, Rumbaugh, & Jacobson, 1999).

Although common in software engineering, few other design disciplines proceed according to checklists or predefined sequences of tasks. Software design educators increasingly suggest that such design tools are not sufficient for the design of novel user interfaces either (Winograd et al., 1996). The highly structured (but largely atheoretical) checklist methods have worked reasonably well in the development of user interfaces built from a small set of standard elements, such as Motif widgets, the Macintosh toolbox, or Windows foundation classes. This is because the design choices in arranging menus, buttons, and dialog boxes are relatively few, and the results can sometimes be assessed using checklists such as those presented in style guides for the relevant system (Apple, 1992; Microsoft, 1995). Simple checklists are not so successful when the user interface consists of completely novel graphical elements, composed according to completely novel visual grammars. These notational systems range from complex products such as visual-programming languages, to embedded functionality such as central-heating controls and the ubiquitous computing platforms of the future that move beyond the windows, icon, and menu paradigm.

We do not believe that it will be possible to deal with these new notational systems by creating new checklists. Instead, we emulate other design disciplines by aiming to support the activity of the designers, based on some understanding of the process of design. User-interface design is currently far more of a craft than an engineering discipline. It is subject to elements of affect, fashion, and social acceptance, in addition to technical considerations. For these reasons, we can learn from studies of other design disciplines where the same craft elements apply. For example, a study comparing knitwear designers and helicopter designers (Eckert & Stacey, 2000) observes that a community of designers develops their own vocabulary for design criteria that is created through practice and tradition, rather than being easily accessible outside the community. In the Cognitive Dimensions of Notations framework, we aim to provide the same kind of vocabulary for use by user-interface designers.

5.1.1   Example

Back in the 1980s one of us (TG) was shown a system that he was sure wouldn't work. Yet the received wisdom of 1980s HCI seemed to have no explanation for the problems he foresaw. The system was a speech-to-text dictation system for use with the Pascal programming language. The speech-recognition technology appeared to be entirely adequate for this restricted language. What problem could there be?

What was wrong with the system was an unfortunate combination. First, it was intended for users doing a kind of design activity; second, the language contained many internal dependencies; and third, it severely restricted the user's order of actions. The system worked fine when a document was dictated to it, but real users do not design like that. Design research shows that they continually change things, and they do not start at the beginning but rather in the middle. This system would not allow such behavior.

It is easy to experience the problem. Try dictating a program in Pascal or even Java, in proper order from start to finish. The program *cannot be written down in advance,* because this system was intended for users who were unable to use their hands—suffering from severe arthritis, for example. Correctly dictating even a short program straight from the head is nearly impossible, and the editing commands provided by this system made the problem even harder because they required the program to remain syntactically valid at all times.

This case made it apparent that existing HCI had no way to describe the structure of information, and therefore it had no way to analyze the interactions among (1) the structure of the information, (2) the environment that allowed that structure to be manipulated, and (3) the type of activity the user wanted to perform. In short, the system forced programmers to make decisions before they had the information upon which they needed to base the decisions. We call this *premature commitment**. Moreover, changing those decisions was not easy. We call this second problem *viscosity*†. These are two examples of the cognitive dimensions of the notational system. In the rest of this chapter, we introduce and analyze many others. Brief definitions are given as each term is introduced—more complete descriptions can be found later.

Once dimensions like these have been identified, it is easy to find other cases where they apply. We have seen a prototype conferencing system where, in order to make a contribution to a discussion, a participant had to start by selecting the type of contribution—a query, a rebuttal, or whatever. This is premature commitment again, for how does one know what one is saying before one says it? Maybe the user can look at the draft contribution and decide that on balance it's a query, not a rebuttal, and recategorize it; or maybe the system makes life still harder by making it impossible to recategorize without dumping the text written so far and starting over. (We've all used systems like that.) That's viscosity again.

---

*   constraints on the order of doing things
†   resistance to change

We can easily find similar examples because the description of the problem is short and high level, not a heavily detailed analysis, and because it ignores specifics of representation in favor of the underlying structure of information.

HCI has a gap in that area. It has generated several sophisticated approaches that each address one type of user activity, such as routine cognitive skills or reasoning or menu following. Within their scope, these approaches can offer suggestions for redesign, but they usually focus on representation and they require extensive, detailed modeling. Some other kinds of user activity, notably design activity, have been studied intensively, so we know much about the pattern of activity, but that observational work has not generated much to help design systems that are themselves tools for design. But there is no approach that addresses all types of activity, that can lead to constructive suggestions for improving the system or device, that avoids details, and that allows similar problems to be readily identified in very different situations. The Cognitive Dimensions (CDs) framework fills the gap. It describes necessary (though not sufficient) conditions for usability, deriving usability predictions from the structural properties of a notation, the properties and resources of an environment, and the type of activity.

The motivation for this framework was thus:

+ to offer a comprehensible, broad-brush evaluation (no "death by detail");
+ to use terms that were readily comprehended by nonspecialists;
+ to be applicable not just to interactive devices, which are the usual meat of HCI, but also to paper-based notations and other noninteractive information systems;
+ to be theoretically coherent;
+ and, especially, to distinguish between different types of user needs (such as the difference between dictation tasks and design tasks).

Furthermore, a CDs analysis frequently reveals a variety of interesting design choices. Although its broad-brush nature precludes detailed predictions, the framework can prompt designers to notice effects of their choices that had previously gone unseen. Perhaps most interesting, the framework describes trade-offs between choices, showing how solving one type of user difficulty may create a different type.

5.2   OVERVIEW

The Cognitive Dimensions framework is not an analytic method. Rather, it is a set of discussion tools for use by designers and people evaluating designs.

The aim is to improve the quality of discussion. Experts make sophisticated judgments about systems, but they have difficulty talking about their judgments because they don't have a shared set of terms. Also, experts tend to make narrow judgments that are based on their own needs of the moment and their guesses about what other people may need; other experts don't always point out the omissions. Again, if they had a shared set of terms, and that set was fairly complete, it would prompt a more complete consideration.

In short, experts would be in a good position to make useful early judgments, if (1) they had better terms with which to think about the issues and discuss them, and (2) there was some kind of reminder of issues to be considered. The terms might or might not describe a new idea; most probably, the expert will recognize a concept as something that had been in his or her mind but that had never before been clearly articulated and named.

Discussion tools are good concepts—not too detailed and not too woolly—that capture enough important aspects of something to make it much easier to talk about that thing. They promote discussion and informed evaluation.

To be effective, discussion tools must be *shared*—you and I must have the same vocabulary if we are going to talk. And it is better still if we share some *standard examples*. And it is best of all if we know some of the pros and cons—the *trade-offs* between one solution approach and another.

Discussion tools have many virtues: They elucidate notions that are vaguely known but unformulated; they prompt a higher level of discourse; they create goals and aspirations; they encourage reuse of ideas in new contexts; they give a basis for informed critique; they supply standard examples that become common currency; and they allow the interrelationships of concepts to be appreciated.

Figure 5.1 illustrates a real-life discussion without the benefit of discussion tools; Figure 5.2 shows how it might have been if the participants had possessed shared concepts—shorter, more accurate, and less frustrating. In this version of the discussion, a number of new terms have been introduced, taken from the CDs framework; these are *italicized*.

There is a relatively well-defined series of steps to be taken by designers when applying cognitive-dimensions analysis to a system design.

1. Get to know your system.

2. Decide what the user will be doing with the notation.

3. Choose some representative tasks.

4. For each step in each task, ask whether the user can choose where to start, how a mistake will be corrected, what if there are second thoughts, what

A: ALL files in the book should be identical in everything except body pages. Master pages, paragraph formats, reference pages, should be the same.

B: Framemaker does provide this . . . File -> Use Formats allows you to copy all or some formatting categories to all or some files in the book.

A: Grrrrrrrr. . . . . Oh People Of Little Imagination !!!!!!

Sure I can do this . . . manually, every time I change a reference page, master page, or paragraph format. . . . .

What I was talking about was some mechanism that automatically detected when I had made such a change. (. . . . .) Or better yet, putting all of these pages in a central database for the entire book. . . . . .

C: There is an argument against basing one paragraph style on another, a method several systems use. A change in a parent style may cause unexpected problems among the children. I have had some unpleasant surprises of this sort in Microsoft Word.

| FIGURE 5.1 | An impoverished discussion that would have been better if the discussants had shared appropriate concepts. This is a verbatim transcript from an actual newsgroup discussion, following an irritated message (by A) about how much work he had to do to keep identical formats for all components of a large project (a "book" in the version of Framemaker that had the limitation being discussed). |

A: I'm doing *modification* activities. I find Framemaker is too *viscous.*

B: With respect to what task?

A: With respect to updating components of a book. It needs to have a higher *abstraction level,* such as a style tree.

C: Watch out for the *hidden dependencies* of a style tree. Also, the abstraction level will be difficult to master; getting the styles right may *impose lookahead.* Is the *trade-off* worth it?

| FIGURE 5.2 | An improved discussion (the names of cognitive dimensions are emphasized). |

abstractions are being used, and so on for the other dimensions. This will generate an observed profile.

5. Compare the observed profile with the ideal profile for that type of activity.

The formal apparatus consists of

✦ A list of generic types of notation use activities: in the Framemaker example, the activity is modifying the structure of the notated information.

✦ A list of dimensions: in the Framemaker example, one such dimension is "viscosity," which means resistance to change.

✦ A "profile" for each activity: in the Framemaker example, the activity is modification of structure, which demands low viscosity (among other requirements).

✦ Examples of trade-offs and design maneuvers, to warn of potential problems: in the Framemaker example, the proposed redesign would lower the viscosity but could readily introduce problems such as hidden dependencies and others.

What you get out of this approach is a rough and sketchy evaluation. As we saw back in Figure 5.1, it will correspond to what users talk about. And if you were to consider changing the design, it will alert you to some of the possible trade-off consequences.

An alternative approach to the application of cognitive dimensions is for system users to be given the dimensions as a framework in which to express their experience of using the system. In this case, the nature of the expertise is different. The users of the system may not be expert in the possible design solutions, or in the space of trade-offs, but they do have expertise in the nature of interaction with the system. For this population, cognitive dimensions can provide a vocabulary in which to express the structure of their experience. They can also provide some insight into the possibility of design alternatives, even though the user may never have experienced any system other than the one he or she is familiar with.

It is important to note that the CDs framework is more than a checklist. The list of dimensions (which is included later in this chapter) may loom large in the mind of the reader, because there are quite a lot of them and because some of them have an immediate intuitive appeal. Nevertheless, the list of dimensions is not sufficient on its own to achieve meaningful analysis of a notational system. It is essential to distinguish between different activities and different notations within the system, and to recognize that dimensions are not good or bad in themselves—they simply describe properties of the system with respect to those activities. In our experience, readers coming to the CDs framework for the first time are tempted to regard the dimensions simply as a checklist. However, it is important to understand the rest of the framework in order to start work.

5.3   SCIENTIFIC FOUNDATIONS

There has been a long tradition in computer science of improving system usability by creating new design notations. Early programming languages such as Fortran and Cobol were intended to be reasonably familiar to the users (mathematicians and business people, respectively), while describing system behavior at a relatively high level of abstraction (compared to assembly-language programming). Furthermore, many innovations in software design have been accompanied by diagrammatic notations used to express the design. These extend from the earliest flowcharts to current developments of the unified modeling language (UML) (Booch, Rumbaugh, & Jacobson 1999).

Where graphical editors are used to create, manipulate, and catalog these design diagrams, it is natural to wonder whether the rather mechanical process of generating source code to implement the diagram could not also be automated. The result would be a programming language in which the design diagram was the program—a visual-programming language. This has been an attractive goal for more than 25 years. There is a research journal and a conference series devoted to visual-programming languages—one survey of the field is that by Myers (1986). Some visual-programming languages have become commercially successful—a report of user experiences with the LabVIEW language has been published by Whitley and Blackwell (2001).

Unfortunately, much research into visual-programming languages was not informed by relevant models of human-computer interaction. A survey of the published literature (Blackwell, 1996) revealed that much of it justified the cognitive advantages of visual languages in terms of concepts from popular psychology such as the left-brain–right-brain dichotomy. This was in spite of published research into the usability implications of diagrammatic notations, dating back to the 1970s (Fitter & Green, 1979). Empirical investigations of notation usability have tended to find that, while diagrams are useful in some situations, they are not efficient in others (e.g., Green & Petre, 1992). This is in striking contrast to the occasional claims that visual-programming languages would be a panacea, providing a new generation of universally accessible programming tools.

Green, Petre, and Bellamy (1991) use the word "superlativism" for the belief that there exists some notation that is universally best in its domain, whatever the activity may be. The converse view, which is surely correct (and has been empirically demonstrated in several situations) is *that every notation highlights some kinds of information, at the cost of obscuring other kinds.* Cognitive science and artificial intelligence research has often emphasized the importance of choice of representation in problem solving ("well represented is half solved"). As a result, the effect of notations and external representations on reasoning continues to be a popular research topic. One major stream of this work is in the theory and application of diagrams.

All visual notations have diagrammatic properties—even text has much in common with diagrams. A page like this one contains a great deal of linguistic structure, but it is not purely linguistic. Paragraphs are separated into visual units to indicate thematic structure; page numbers and citations provide overlaid reference schemes; variations in font exploit visual pop-out effects for local emphasis, chapter headings and marginalia offer context and commentary. The textual representation of spoken language has undergone radical improvements in notational usability over the last two millennia, such as the discovery in the fifteenth century that using white space to separate words (BEFORETHAT-THEYWROTEWITHOUTSPACES) enabled scholars to read without speaking aloud (Robinson, 1995). It is not only text that has a surprising degree of diagrammatic content. Even "representational" paintings and photographs include a great deal of diagrammatic structure—compositional elements, conventional symbolization, or meaningful cropped borders (Kress & van Leeuwen, 1996).

Diagrams research generally falls into two classes—detailed explanations of specific properties of notations, and analyses of cognitive tasks employing notations. A good example of the former is Shimojima's formal description of *Free Rides,* in which new information is created simply by following syntactic conventions (Shimojima, 1996). Cheng has described the educational use of Law Encoding Diagrams, in which free rides in the form of geometric relationships express valid conclusions regarding mathematical or physical laws (Cheng, 1998). These analyses give detailed insight into one mechanism for the Cognitive Dimension of *Closeness of Mapping**. One example of a cognitive task employing notations is that of creative ambiguity, described by researchers including Fish & Scrivener (1990), Goldschmidt (1991), and Suwa & Tversky (1997). They describe the process by which designers return to their sketches for new ideas. In order to allow this, the sketches have been left deliberately incomplete or ambiguous. This is an example of one application of the Cognitive Dimension of *Provisionality†*.

The CDs framework does not consider representational issues in themselves: The framework is based solely on structural properties. Questions both of effectiveness (e.g., optimum size of buttons) and of aesthetics are outside its purview. This restriction has two great advantages. The first is that identical (or rather, isomorphic) problems can be spotted even when they occur in very different guises. An early example (from Green, 1989) observed that the file structure of a computer-operating system has much in common with the structure of a pattern sequencer for a drum machine, and therefore that problems and solutions in the one case would probably apply to the other.

---

*   closeness of the representation to the domain
†   degree of commitment to action or marks

The second great advantage of avoiding representational issues is that the CDs framework is thereby applicable to systems long before they reach the stage of being prototyped. Any technique that uses Fitts' Law, such as the Keystroke Level Model, or that considers "whether the user's language is used," such as Heuristic Evaluation, is solely applicable to designs that have at least reached detailed specification.

Despite being applicable to all types of information artifacts, this framework has come to prominence, naturally enough, in an area where conventional HCI techniques have little clear applicability and where a good deal of design activity has been going on—namely, in visual-programming languages and environments. Here, the typical user activity is nonroutine design; the notations (programming language) vary considerably; and the features of the environments also vary considerably: See Burnett, Cao, & Atwood, 2000; Green, 1999; Green & Petre, 1996.

As we stated in the introductory section, we believe that user-interface design and notation design are engineering design crafts, not sciences. Like any other design crafts, they combine elements of science with many other elements: peer-assessed best practice, market pull, fashion, trial and error, aesthetics, individual flair, and whatever else contributes to design. The cognitive dimensions framework only addresses some aspects of this *mélange*. The framework is not the result of importing and specializing any single viewpoint from another science. Rather, it is a synthesis from several sources; because we have much to learn in this area, it constitutes a patchwork or a quilt with holes where suitable pieces could not yet be found.

5.4   DETAILED DESCRIPTION

Every evaluation technique asks one fundamental question. In the CDs framework, that question is: Are the users' intended activities adequately supported by the structure of the information artifact?

And as a supplementary question: If not, what design maneuvre would fix it, and what trade-offs would be entailed?

So the evaluation, in a nutshell, consists in classifying the intended activities, analyzing the cognitive dimensions, and deciding whether the requirements of the activities are met. Note that the term "activity" is used differently in this context than in other chapters of this book. A notational activity in cognitive dimensions is a manner of interacting with a notation. This use of the word is unrelated to Activity Theory or Active User Theory.

incrementation:	adding cards to a cardfile, formulas to a spreadsheet, or statements to a program
transcription:	copying book details to an index card; converting a formula into spreadsheet or code terms
modification:	changing the index terms in a library catalog; changing layout of a spreadsheet; modifying a spreadsheet or program for a different problem
exploratory design:	sketching; design of typography, software, etc; other cases where the final product cannot be envisaged and has to be "discovered"
searching:	hunting for a known target, such as where a function is called
exploratory understanding:	discovering structure or algorithm, or discovering the basis of classification

TABLE 5.1   Six generic types of notation-use activity. Each has different requirements for support.

5.4.1   Activities

No usability analysis can proceed far unless we have some idea of what the artifact will be used for; yet at the same time, there are good reasons to avoid highly detailed task analyses. Such analyses are lengthy to construct, require specialized experience, and in the end do not capture the labile nature of everyday activities. Instead of using a detailed task analysis, the CDs framework just contrasts six generic types of notation-use activity. Note that this list, shown in Table 5.1, was not derived from a single theoretical precursor, but has been extended and refined through contributions from a variety of researchers (e.g. Blackwell, Britton, et al., 2001) since the framework was first proposed. It is assumed that a given artifact will support some of these activities better than others, and the analyst should decide which ones are required. Each activity places different demands on the system. Nothing in what follows is good or bad, except with reference to an activity that we wish to support.

5.4.2   The Components of Notational Systems

Notational systems, as described in this framework, have four components:

an *interaction language* or *notation;*

an *environment for editing* the notation;

a *medium of interaction;*

and possibly, two kinds of *subdevices.*

Interaction Languages and Notations

The notation is what the user sees and edits: letters, musical notes, graphic elements in computer-aided design (CAD).

Editing Environments

Different editors have different assumptions. Some word processors have commands operating on paragraphs, sentences, words, and letters, while others recognize only individual characters. Some editors allow access to history, and others deny it.

Medium of Interaction

Typical media are paper, visual displays, and auditory displays. The important attributes are persistence/transience and constrained-order/free-order. Button presses are transient (unless a history view is available); writing on paper is persistent. Some information structures are successful for their intended purpose only when used with a persistent medium; for example, writing even a short program using speech alone, without access to any persistent medium, is extremely difficult.

Subdevices

Many devices and structures contain subdevices. Two kinds are distinguished.

Helper devices offer a new notational view, such as cross-referencers in programs, outline views in word processors, a history view of button presses. Helper devices are not always so formal, however: If the user typically writes notes on the backs of envelopes or sticks Post-it notes on the side of the screen, these items should be regarded as helper devices, part of the system. The CDs framework is meant to encompass as much of the system as seems reasonable—and if Post-it notes are typically part of the system, they should form part of the analysis.

Redefinition devices allow the main notation to be changed. Macro recorders in contemporary word processors allow a sequence of commands to be replaced by a single command. Macros are a typical abstraction, and systems that allow abstractions to be created or modified always require a subdevice to work as an abstraction manager.

Subdevices, whether helper devices or redefinition devices, often have their own notations or interaction languages that are separate from the main notation of the system, and an independent set of cognitive dimensions. The dimensions of these devices must be analyzed separately. Thus, the macro recorder has different properties from the word processor in which it is embedded.

5.4.3   Notational Dimensions

The main point of the CDs framework is to consider the notations or interaction languages and how well they support the intended activities, given the environment, medium, and possible subdevices. We do this by considering a set of "dimensions." Each dimension describes an aspect of an information structure that is reasonably general. Furthermore, any pair of dimensions can be manipulated independently of each other, although typically a third dimension must be allowed to change (*pairwise independence*).[1]

Here we can discuss only a small number of dimensions, and we can do so very briefly. The full list is currently 14 (although several more have been proposed, as will be discussed later), and each needs far more space than can be given here. A proper presentation for reference purposes should include, besides the brief definition, a thumbnail illustration; an explanation; an account of its cognitive relevance; an estimate of its cost implications; an account of subtypes and examples; and a list of work-arounds and remedies, with their associated trade-offs.

Important: None of these dimensions is evaluative when considered on its own. Evaluation must always take into account the activities to be supported.

Viscosity: resistance to change

A viscous system needs many user actions to accomplish one goal. Changing all headings to uppercase may need one action per heading. (Environments containing suitable abstractions can reduce viscosity.) We distinguish repetition viscosity, many actions of the same type, from knock-on (or "domino") viscosity, where further actions are required to restore consistency.

---

[1] The notion of pairwise independence has caused difficulties to some readers. To illustrate, consider a given mass of an ideal gas, with a temperature, a volume, and a pressure. The volume can be changed independently of the pressure but the temperature must change as well; or the volume can be changed independently of the temperature, but the pressure must change accordingly. Similarly for any other pair of dimensions.

Visibility: ability to view components easily

Systems that bury information in encapsulations reduce visibility. Because examples are important for problem solving, such systems are to be deprecated for exploratory activities; likewise, if consistency of transcription is to be maintained, high visibility may be needed.

Premature Commitment: constraints on the order of doing things

Self-explanatory. Examples: being forced to declare identifiers too soon; choosing a search path down a decision tree; having to select your cutlery before you choose your food.

Hidden Dependencies: important links between entities are not visible

If one entity cites another entity, which in turn cites a third, changing the value of the third entity may have unexpected repercussions. Examples: cells of spreadsheets; style definitions in Word; complex class hierarchies; HTML links. Sometimes actions cause dependencies to get frozen—for example, soft-figure numbering can be frozen when changing platforms. These interactions with changes over time are still problematic in the framework.

Role-Expressiveness: the purpose of an entity is readily inferred

Role-expressive notations make it easy to discover why the author has built the structure in a particular way; in other notations each entity looks much the same, and discovering their relationships is difficult. Assessing role-expressiveness requires a reasonable conjecture about cognitive representations.

Error-Proneness: the notation invites mistakes and the system gives little protection

Enough is known about the cognitive psychology of slips and errors to predict that certain notations will invite them. Preventative mechanisms (e.g., check digits, enforced declaration of identifiers, etc.) can redeem the problem.

Abstraction: types and availability of abstraction mechanisms

Abstractions (redefinitions) change the underlying notation. Macros, data structures, global find-and-replace commands, quick-dial telephone codes, and word-processor styles are all abstractions. Some are persistent, some are transient.

Abstractions, if the user is allowed to modify them, always require an abstraction manager—a redefinition subdevice. It will sometimes have its own notation and environment (e.g., the Word style-sheet manager) but not always (e.g., a class hierarchy can be built in a conventional text editor).

Systems that allow many abstractions are potentially difficult to learn.

Secondary Notation: extra information in means other than formal syntax

Users often need to record things that have not been anticipated by the notation designer. Rather than anticipating every possible user requirement, many systems support secondary notations that can be used however the user likes. One example is comments in a programming language; another is the use of colors or format choices to indicate information additional to the content of text.

Closeness of Mapping: closeness of representation to domain

How closely related is the notation to the result it is describing?

Consistency: similar semantics are expressed in similar syntactic forms

Users often infer the structure of information artifacts from patterns in notation. If similar information is obscured by presenting it in different ways, usability is compromised.

Diffuseness: verbosity of language

Some notations can be annoyingly long-winded, or they can occupy too much valuable "real-estate" within a display area. Big icons and long words reduce the available working area.

Hard Mental Operations: high demand on cognitive resources

A notation can make things complex or difficult to work out in your head, by making inordinate demands on working memory or by requiring deeply nested goal structures.

Provisionality: degree of commitment to actions or marks

Even if there are hard constraints on the order of doing things (premature commitment), it can be useful to make provisional actions such as recording potential design options, sketching, or playing "what-if" games. Not all notational systems allow users to fool around or make sketchy markings.

Progressive Evaluation: work-to-date can be checked at any time

Evaluation is an important part of a design process, and notational systems can facilitate evaluation by allowing users to stop in the middle to check work so far, find out how much progress has been made, or check what stage in the work they are up to. A major advantage of interpreted programming environments such as Basic is that users can try out partially completed versions of the product program, perhaps leaving type information or declarations incomplete.

5.4.4   Profiles

In the CDs framework, evaluation has two steps. The first step is to decide what generic activities a system is desired to support. Each generic activity has its own requirements in terms of cognitive dimensions, so the second step is to scrutinize the system and determine how it lies on each dimension. If the two profiles match, all is well. A tentative tabulation of the support required for each generic activity can be found in Green and Blackwell (1998).

For example, *transcription* is very undemanding. No new information is being created, so premature commitment is not a problem. Nothing is being altered, so viscosity is not a problem. On the other hand, to preserve consistency of treatment from instance to instance, visibility may be required.

Incrementation creates new information, and sometimes there may be problems with premature commitment. The most demanding activity is *exploratory design*. A sizeable literature on the cognitive psychology of design has established that designers continually make changes at many levels, from detailed tweaks to fundamental rebuildings. Viscosity has to be as low as possible, premature commitment needs to be reduced, visibility must be high, and role expressiveness—understanding what the entities do—must be high.

5.4.5   Trade-Offs

A virtue of the CD framework is that it illuminates design maneuvers in which one dimension is traded against another. Although no proper analysis of trade-offs exists, we can point to certain relationships. One way to reduce viscosity

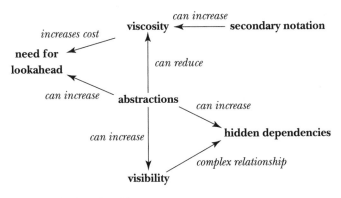

FIGURE   Some typical trade-offs.

5.3

is to introduce abstractions, but that will always require an abstraction manager in which to define the abstractions and some early commitment to choose which abstractions to define. The abstractions themselves may then become viscous, introduce hidden dependencies, and so on. This topic needs much more research, but some of the relationships we have observed are shown in Figure 5.3.

5.4.6   Use by an Analyst

As a usability evaluation technique becomes widespread, its popularity depends more on accessibility and ease of use for the evaluator, rather than on the scientific origins of the technique. The most widely used techniques offer an extensive support apparatus of training and educational resources, analysis tools, and review and tutorial literature. The support infrastructure for CDs has developed from a variety of invited lectures and tutorial sessions at conferences and trade meetings, to a comprehensive written tutorial (Green and Blackwell 1998) now distributed freely from a CDs resources site (URLs are given in the Further Reading Section at the end of this chapter). This written tutorial complements extensive descriptions of each dimension with a strong example, descriptions of the consequences that may arise from problems in that dimension, potential workarounds, likely trade-offs with other dimensions, some design maneuvers and so on. Many aspects of the dimensions are illustrated in simple interactive Web-based devices showing differing designs for the same problem, so that readers can experiment with and experience the usability consequences of the dimensions. These tools allow new users of the framework to develop the required approach to analysis easily.

5.4.7 A Questionnaire Approach

In the context of usability studies, CDs have also been used to structure user-feedback questionnaires. The fact that the dimensions describe generic aspects of usability, rather than features of the system under study, leaves the user free to comment on aspects of the system that the designer may not have anticipated. Users are also encouraged to consider different aspects of their activity beyond their principal use of the system. Furthermore, their responses are grouped in a systematic way that can be related via CDs to the design discourse of the system developers who receive feedback from usability studies.

Kadoda, Stone, and Diaper (1999) first introduced the idea of a cognitive-dimensions questionnaire. Their questionnaire presented only those CDs that they thought were relevant to the system under consideration; to make it easier for the users to pick up the ideas, they paraphrased those CDs in terms of the system under consideration. Their results were promising, but there may be a problem here: Filtering the CDs constrains the respondents to comment on the CDs that the researcher or designer has already identified, and thereby it mixes the HCI expert's evaluation (in choosing the subset) with the users' evaluations. This is particularly dangerous when the questionnaire designer is also the designer of the system, and it will quite possibly completely overlook aspects that are very important to the users.

We therefore set out to develop a questionnaire that presents all the CDs and that lets the users decide which ones are relevant (Blackwell & Green, 2000). We attempted to present the CDs in general terms, rather than presenting descriptions specialized to the system under consideration. On the plus side, this means (1) the users do all the work, (2) the data reflects only their opinions, and (3) the same questionnaire can be used for all systems. On the negative side, it means that the resulting questionnaire is longer, because it has to present all the CDs, not just a subset, and it is possibly harder to understand, because the CDs are presented in general terms. Nevertheless, the result is now being used as an aide to the development of commercial-programming tools (Clarke, 2001). A canonical version of the questionnaire is available from the CDs resource site.

5.4.8   Cognitive Dimensions of Interactive Devices

We wish to avoid the impression that cognitive dimensions apply solely to purely symbolic structures such as classic notations. Although the focus of this chapter has been on notations, many interactive devices can be viewed as information artifacts where the "notation" is the user's actions; such devices are therefore fit for analysis using CDs, offering a useful complement to other evaluative approaches.

For instance, consider a seven-day central-heating controller in which each day can be programmed independently, with, say, three heating periods per day, each defined by a switch-on time and a switch-off time.[2] The user's actions of setting the times form a notation. (An interactive mock-up of such a design is accessible via links from the CDs resource site.) This design suffers from viscosity if most days—all the weekdays, say—are to be set to the same timings; the set-up process takes more effort than it ought to. An alternative design achieves a partial reduction in viscosity by introducing an abstraction, namely a Copy function, which copies the previous day to the next day—Monday's settings to Tuesday, Tuesday's to Wednesday, and so on. (This version is based on a real, commercially available, device, the Horstmann ChannelPlus H17 Central Heating Controller.)

The Copy function is a transient abstraction. Although seemingly simple, experience has shown that just that one abstraction adds greatly to the difficulty of explaining how this device works—the activity of exploratory understanding. The device also has poor visibility: the user cannot readily check the effect of the Copy function.

This analysis is, clearly, not deep. Yet its quick, broad-brush nature is just what we would like to see available when needed. Anyone who is thinking in the terms we have described can immediately, almost trivially, recognize the features of these controllers and thereby come to a better-informed evaluation decision.

---

[2] A virtual version can be seen at *www.ndirect.co.uk/~thomas.green/workStuff/devices/controllers/ HeatingA2.html*

5.5   CASE STUDY: EVALUATING A VISUAL-PROGRAMMING LANGUAGE[3]

Many diagrammatic notations represent information structures as topological graphs—system components are represented by enclosed areas (usually boxes) representing the nodes, while relationships between the components are represented by continuously connected lines extending from one box to another (wires). How usable are such box-and-wire systems? There are many variations. Apparently small notational differences in box-and-wire languages can lead to extreme differences in the programs. Green and Petre (1996) reported a usability analysis of two commercial box-and-wire systems, Prograph and LabVIEW,[4] and how they compared to the old-fashioned Basic language.

In this section we show how one of those languages, LabVIEW, can be evaluated using the CDs framework.

5.5.1   Illustrating the Notation

For comparative purposes, Figure 5.4 and Figure 5.5 show two versions of the same program. This program, which computes the flight path of a rocket, was derived from algorithms used by Curtis et al. (1989) for research into the comprehensibility of flowcharts; Green and Petre (1996) reused them for their research into modern visual-programming languages (VPLs). First, we show the Basic version, then the LabVIEW equivalent.

The LabVIEW notation uses boxes for operations and wires for the data. Conditionals are represented as boxes lying on top of each other, only one of which can be seen at any one time. Loops are represented by a surrounding box with a thick wall.

Viscosity

Green and Petre made a straw-test comparison of viscosity* by modifying each of the programs in the same way, putting in a simple correction for air resistance. Because they wanted to measure the time to edit the program but not the time taken to solve the problem, the modification was worked out in advance; they

---

3   This section draws extensively on Green and Petre (1996).
4   Produced and trademarked by Pictorius Inc. and National Instruments Inc., respectively.
*   resistance to change

```
Mass = 10000
Fuel = 50
Force = 400000
Gravity = 32

WHILE Vdist >= 0
        IF Tim = 11 THEN Angle = .3941
        IF Tim > 100 THEN Force = 0 ELSE Mass = Mass − Fuel

        Vaccel = Force*COS(Angle)/Mass − Gravity
        Vveloc = Vveloc + Vaccel
        Vdist = Vdist + Vveloc

        Haccel = Force*SIN(Angle)/Mass
        Hveloc = Hveloc + Haccel
        Hdist = Hdist + Hveloc

        PRINT Tim, Vdist, Hdist
        Tim = Tim + 1

    WEND
    STOP
```

FIGURE   The rocket program in Basic.

5.4

timed an experienced user modifying the original program (running in the standard environment), working from a print-out of the modification required.

Inserting the material into LabVIEW took a surprisingly long time because all the boxes had to be jiggled about, and many of the wires had to be rebuilt. Prograph was able to absorb the extra code to deal with air resistance with little difficulty—certainly less than evidenced by LabVIEW. This was because the new code was placed in new windows, and relatively little change had to be made to existing layouts. However, this causes poor *visibility and juxtaposability*†. For Basic, the problem is just one of typing a few more lines. Overall time taken was as follows: LabVIEW, 508.3 seconds; Prograph, 193.6 seconds; Basic, 63.3 seconds—an astonishing ratio of 8:1 between extremes. These are differences of a whole order of magnitude, and if the programs were larger we would expect them to increase proportionately (i.e., to increase faster for LabVIEW, slower for Basic). Viscosity is obviously a major issue.

---

†   ability to view components easily

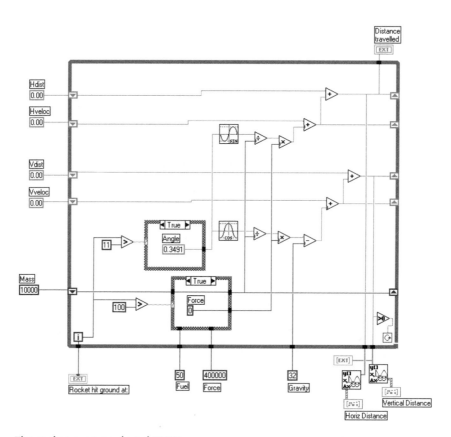

FIGURE 5.5 The rocket program in LabVIEW.

Hidden Dependencies

An important strength of the visual approach is that many of the hidden dependencies* of textual languages are made explicit. Data in a textual language like Basic is transmitted via assignments and use-statements, as shown in Figure 5.6.

The same information in a LabVIEW program is shown in Figure 5.7.

At least one type of hidden dependency is thereby brought into the open. The trade-off in this case, obviously enough, is the use of screen space (*diffuseness†*).

---

* important links between entities are not visible
† verbosity of language

```
x = 1
. . . (possibly many pages of code here . . . )
y = x + 3
```

FIGURE   Hidden dependencies in Basic.

5.6

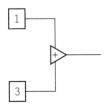

FIGURE   Visible dependencies in LabVIEW.

5.7

Premature Commitment

Green and Petre noted several types of premature commitment* in the construction of these programs: commitment to layout, commitment to connections, and
commitment to choice of construct.

Commitment to layout: Obviously, the visual programmer has to make the first
mark somewhere on the virtual page. As the program takes shape, it may become
clear that the first mark was unfortunately placed, or that subsequent marks were
ill placed with respect to it and each other. Although there is always some way to
adjust the layout, the viscosity may be too high for comfort. That is certainly the
case with complex LabVIEW programs.

Commitment to connections: The two-dimensional layout of VPLs requires subroutines to be associated with their callers by ports with a definite placing. In both
our target languages, one easily finds that the data terminals are not arranged in
the order one wants them for a particular purpose.

---

*   constraints on the order of doing things

Whitley and Blackwell (2001) report the astonishing fact that one of their respondents in a survey on LabVIEW claimed to employ a junior *just to tidy up the layout of the code:*

> One respondent solved the problem by hiring extra help: "Recently, I hired a real nitpicker to clean up my diagrams while they are in progress. That saves me a lot of time and my customers get even neater diagrams than I would have done."

That quotation tells us all we need to know about premature commitment and layout viscosity in box-and-wire diagrams.

Commitment to choice of construct: When a programmer chooses a syntactic construct and then adds code to the construct, it may turn out subsequently that the construct is the wrong one (e.g. a while-loop should be changed to a for-loop). Therefore, programmers may prefer to postpone commitment to a particular construct until the code has been further developed.

   Early versions of LabVIEW suffered the problem that, once a control construct had been selected, it was a tiresome chore to change it. More recent versions of LabVIEW solve the premature commitment problem partly by postponing commitment, as well as by making it easier to change the decision (specifically, it is now possible to draw a loop around existing code, just as a for-statement can be inserted into a textual program).

Abstraction

The abstraction* barrier (the number of new abstractions to be understood by the novice), although probably more than a simple spreadsheet system, is obviously less than, say, C++. Differences in this respect depend more on the choice of primitives than on the requirements of the box-and-wire notational structure itself.

   LabVIEW allows the user to choose to create new subroutines (called "virtual instruments") but does not insist upon it: this language is therefore abstraction tolerant. The abstraction-managing subdevice maintains a hierarchy of "virtual instruments"; its properties will not be analyzed here, but for a full treatment that step would be essential.

---

* types and availability of abstraction mechanisms

```
//–compute the vertical components–//
    Vaccel = Force*COS(Angle)/Mass – Gravity
    Vveloc = Vveloc + Vaccel
    Vdist = Vdist + Vveloc

//–compute the horizontal components–//
    Haccel = Force*SIN(Angle)/Mass
    Hveloc = Hveloc + Haccel
    Hdist = Hdist + Hveloc
```

FIGURE	Secondary notation in the form of comments.
5.8	

Layout abstractions are not in evidence; there are no easy features for group operations when rearranging the components of a program, and much time can therefore be wasted.

Secondary Notation

Designers have apparently not thought hard enough about the need to escape from the formalism. LabVIEW does not have good facilities for commenting, for example. A comment can be attached to a single item, which may seem adequate at first sight, but remember that a text language gives power to comment on a *section* of code, not just a single operation. This secondary notation* is shown in Figure 5.8, as they appear in Basic. Looking back to the LabVIEW program, how would the comments in Figure 5.8 be adapted?

Nor can LabVIEW achieve the same degree of control over spatial layout that Basic achieves over textual layout. The Basic program has been organized to bring related operations into close proximity (which is what makes those comments so effective), but in the visual languages the severity of the constraints on laying out the boxes to avoid clutter and crossings makes it impossible to achieve the same results.

Visibility and Juxtaposability

The visibility† of data flow in the LabVIEW language is excellent.

Where LabVIEW meets trouble, however, is in the juxtaposition of related control branches. The two branches of a conditional cannot both be viewed at

---

* extra information in means other than formal syntax
† ability to view components easily

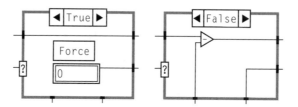

FIGURE

5.9

A LabVIEW conditional from the rocket program, showing both arms. In the LabVIEW environment, only one arm is visible on screen at any one time.

once; although a single mouse click will take you to the next branch, the effect on comprehensibility is very worrying. This is illustrated in Figure 5.9.

5.5.2   Conclusions

The most striking features of these comparisons are, on the one hand, the extraordinarily high viscosity of box-and-wire notations and the very poor facilities for secondary notation, and, on the other hand, the remarkable freedom from hidden dependencies. These give box-and-wire programs a very different feel from textual languages, and they indicate some targets for would-be improvers to aim for.

5.6   CURRENT STATUS

The CDs framework has been adopted by a broad community of researchers, and also by a few practitioners. The bibliography of the CDs resource site currently lists about 60 publications on cognitive dimensions. Future progress on the framework is likely to focus on four issues: making the benefits available to a broader range of software-development professionals, increasing the theoretical rigor in the foundations of the framework, filling in gaps in coverage, and providing new analysis tools based on CDs. We describe some of these continuing research efforts in the following sections.

5.6.1   Dissemination

Most dissemination of the CDs framework continues to be centered on academic venues, via invited talks and tutorials at related conferences. A few specialized symposia have been held, devoted to discussing ongoing research on the CDs framework. There is no centralized organization for these meetings, which have been hosted at institutions with a concentration of CD researchers such as the University of Hertfordshire in England. Several universities are teaching final-year undergraduate courses or masters-level courses including CDs as an analysis-and-design technique. Most of this work is coordinated via the CDs resource site.

5.6.2   Clarification and Formalization

The dimensions are at present defined in informal terms, and in consequence there are areas of overlap and uncertainty. It is imperative to clarify their descriptions and if possible to reduce their number.

Roast and Siddiqi (2000) have developed a system-modeling approach, using system abstractions to lead to closer definitions of the precise meaning of various cognitive dimensions. Detailed consideration of their careful work would take up too much space here, unfortunately, but some flavor of it can be given by looking at the route taken by Roast in examining premature commitment.

Roast's approach provides interpretations based on

+ the goals and subgoals that users may achieve,

+ the user inputs that enable users to satisfy different goals,

+ the objects central to characterizing the goals to be achieved.

Roast describes premature commitment as "the user having to satisfy the secondary goal prior to achieving the primary goal." To develop a formal estimation of premature commitment, he focuses on three facets of the concept: the characterization of how the secondary goal is unavoidable; the relationship between the secondary and primary goals that indicates the inappropriateness of having to commit to the secondary goal first; and the initial conditions. This leads to a new distinction between weak and strong premature commitment, and thence to a detailed formal analysis of the relationship between premature commitment and viscosity. Finally, in a small case study, the formal analysis is applied to an editor used for the specification language Z, and is shown to conform to the difficulties experienced by certain users.

Blackwell is continuing work on a formalized description of user activities, based on an economic model of attention investment (Blackwell & Green, 1999). This model describes the cognitive process of attention to a task in terms of the potential return on investment when that work results in later savings of effort. All programming work can be described as a short-term investment of attention to writing the program, in return for a longer-term saving of effort through automated tasks. The CDs of the notation and environment being used directly affect the factors controlling return on investment in this analysis.

5.6.3   Coverage

Green and Petre (1996), under the heading of "Future progress in cognitive dimensions," observed that the framework was incomplete—but not in the sense that more dimensions were urgently needed. Rather, they emphasized the need for formalization and applicability. Nevertheless, new dimensions do get proposed from time to time. Some of these proposals have been published, but more have been discussed informally. A recent paper outlined future approaches to the process of identifying and defining new cognitive dimensions, illustrating this discussion with descriptions of several candidates (Blackwell, Britton, et al., 2001). Other aspects of the framework, especially the enumeration of design maneuvers and trade-offs, but also fundamentals such as the description of user activities, continue to be refined and expanded.

5.6.4   Analysis Tools

Green (1991), in a work that was further developed by Green and Benyon (1996), offered an extended entity-relationship model of information artifacts in which certain of the cognitive dimensions could fairly easily be identified and in some cases metricated. Viscosity lends itself quite well to this approach. An ERMIA (entity-relationship modeling for information artifacts) model of conventional music notation looks like that shown in Figure 5.10. The figure indicates that the piece of music contains many note symbols, each of which has a height on the staff (the black border indicates a perceptual cue) and a note name. To transpose the key of a piece, every note must be rewritten. The approach even offers a symbolic computation of the cost of change, shown in Figure 5.11.

For this structure, $V = O(n)$, where n is the number of note symbols. (The value of n can run into the thousands.) Note that an alternative representation for music, known as "tonic sol-fa," reduces the viscosity down to a single action!

A very different approach was taken by Yang et al. (1997); they defined simple, *a priori* yardsticks by which to quantify some of the dimensions in the special case of visual-programming languages. They realized that, for practical use, benchmarks with real numbers attached would be more useful for some purposes than mere discussion tools, so they set out to define metrics for some of the

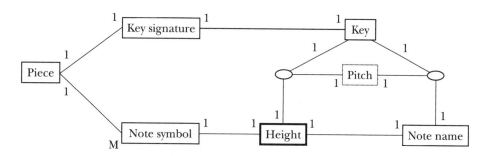

FIGURE

5.10

ERMIA model of music notation.

Transpose Staff Notation
     write Key[1]   *change key signature*
     foreach Note: *change all notes*
          read Note
          compute Note[1]
          write Note[1]

Total actions: #(write actions) = #(Notes)
Working memory storage:
     [1] place-holder , to keep track of notes in the original document

FIGURE

5.11

Symbolic computation of number of actions and amount of working memory storage required to transpose a piece of music written in staff notation, derivable algorithmically for the ERMIA model shown in Figure 5.10.

dimensions. They sensibly restricted their aims to those dimensions that they thought would be of most interest for their purposes of designing and improving visual-programming languages, and their first decision was to concentrate on the static part of a program representation rather than its dynamics—arguing that obtaining a usable static representation was an essential first step.

Eighteen benchmarks are defined in their paper. Examples are:

Visibility or Hiddenness of Dependencies

D1: (sources of dependencies explicitly depicted) / (sources of dependencies in system)

D2: The worst-case number of steps required to navigate to the display of dependency information

Visibility of Program Structure

PS1: Does the representation explicitly show how the parts of the program logically fit together? (Yes/No)

These benchmarks, though admittedly somewhat on the crude side, were applied by the authors to different languages and helped them find overlooked usability problems and encouraged them to redesign the languages. They encourage others to find similar domain-specific benchmarks for their own purposes.

5.6.5   Beyond CDs: Misfit Analysis

Many of the cognitive dimensions may be seen as examples of misfits between the user's view of the domain (related to a mental model) and the device's view. Take viscosity as an instance: The user thinks of a single direct operation, but the device requires an indirect operation or a large number of operations. Other misfits are not so readily expressible as cognitive dimensions, such as inexpressiveness: The user wishes to do something that is part of the conceptual domain but cannot be expressed using the device. As an example, electronic organizers cannot indicate relative importance of engagements, nor links between them, which are important components of diary use (Blandford & Green, 2001). Thus, the concept of a misfit may be more general than the concept of a cognitive dimension.

Ontological sketch modeling (OSM) (Blandford & Green, 1997) is an attempt to develop the idea of misfit analysis. It provides a simple and deliberately sketchy formalism in which to express the user's conceptual models of the device, the domain, and working practices (that is, how the device fits in with the way the user works). Analyzing the degree of fit between these can reveal potential problems of a semantic type that are not revealed by existing HCI approaches.

Misfits cannot be revealed by any approach to HCI that focuses solely on either the user or the device. Traditional task-centered user-modeling for HCI has some very effective results, but it cannot reveal misfits because it does not explicitly consider how the user's conceptual model of the domain and device relates to the model imposed by the device.

In OSM the modeler describes the visible entities, their attributes, and how they are linked within the device; it also describes the entities contained in the user's conceptual model and those embodied within the device that users need to be aware of if they are to use the device effectively. The resulting entities may be private to the device (the user cannot alter them), or they may be private to the user (the device does not represent them), or they may be shared (accessible to both the device and the user). All communication between the two worlds of user and device takes place through the shared entities. If the user-private entities do not fit well onto the shared entities, the device will have usability problems. Similarly, if the device-private entities are difficult to discover or understand, the user is likely to have difficulty learning to work with them. However, the cognitive dimensions were presented entirely informally, and the method of analysis was no more than asking a designer to think carefully about each dimension in turn. With OSM, some of the dimensions can be evaluated algorithmically, once a description of the artifact has been constructed.

5.7   FURTHER READING

Most research and tutorial material related to CDs is available from the CD resource site:

   www.cl.cam.ac.uk/~afb21/CognitiveDimensions/

The site includes an online bibliography of relevant research publications, a variety of introductory papers at different levels, and links to ongoing research. Some key starting points include the CDs tutorial by Green and Blackwell (1998), an extended research presentation by Green and Petre that was published in the *Journal of Visual Languages and Computing* (Green & Petre, 1996), and a description of the use of user questionnaires for CD evaluation (Blackwell & Green, 2000). The bibliography is annotated to direct the reader to other specialist topics.

Related research on usability and cognitive aspects of notational systems continues to be published in venues such as the IEEE conference on Human-Centric Computing, the *Journal of Visual Languages and Computing*, the ACM conference on Computer-Human Interaction (CHI), and conferences devoted to cognitive science, psychology of programming, information design, and diagrammatic reasoning. Most of these topics also have mailing lists, online bibliographies, and resource sites devoted to them:

   www.hcrc.ed.ac.uk/gal/Diagrams/—Diagrams resource site
   www.ppig.org/—Psychology of Programming resource site
   http://hcibib.org/—HCI bibliography

6 Users' Mental Models: The Very Ideas

CHAPTER

Stephen J. Payne Cardiff University, Wales

6.1 MOTIVATION

The user's mental model of the device is one of the most tantalizing ideas in the psychology of human-computer interaction (HCI). Certainly, it is one of the most widely discussed theoretical constructs: It was in the vanguard of early attempts to derive theoretical approaches to HCI that progressed cognitive science at the same time as having a genuine practical impact.

The concept of mental model appealed to theorists of HCI, especially cognitive psychologists, perhaps because it holds out hope that their particular branch of science might really be at the heart of what it means to design technologies that are fit for human purposes and capabilities. It has also appealed to cognitive psychologists engaged in theoretical projects on topics such as reasoning and discourse comprehension. Furthermore, the construct of mental models seems to hold a strong appeal to HCI designers because it captures their intuitions about the ways users come to understand and perhaps misunderstand the devices they use. Thus, much otherwise entirely practically focused writing on user interface design, including commercial style guides, has appealed to the concept (e.g. Mayhew, 1992; Tognazzini, 1992; Apple Human Interface Guidelines, Apple Computer Inc., 1987).

Yet mental models remain a tantalizing—rather than fulfilling—theoretical concept because even a casual inspection of the HCI and cognitive-science literature reveals that the term is used in so many different ways as to be almost void of any force beyond the general idea of users' knowledge about the system they use. Indeed, one might almost say that the appeal of mental models to developers has been due to the fact that these models can be so readily appropriated to any argument concerning the user's need for a working understanding of the device. In this sense, the rapid uptake of the idea of a mental model may have contributed, ironically, to the downturn in interest in theoretical approaches to HCI.

A major motivation of the current chapter is to argue that the construct of a user's mental model is *still* a fruitful area for research in HCI. Much of the literature I will review and attempt to synthesize is somewhat old, by HCI standards, reflecting the state of affairs reviewed in the introduction to this volume—namely, that mainstream cognitive theorizing has, to an extent, lost its position as a central topic in the HCI research community.

Part of the reason for the displacement of cognitive-science approaches is simply a recognition of other vital problems for HCI, which cognitive science has seemed ill equipped to tackle. For example, it is now widely appreciated that the usefulness of a computer system is partly determined by its fit with working practices and organizational structures, including those that moderate collaboration between individuals. It has also been recognized that the relationship between scientific knowledge and engineering is problematic, so that even when a scientific contribution seems highly relevant in principle, making that knowledge effective in a design context can still be a huge challenge.

The expansion of the scientific base of HCI to include more explicitly social and engineering disciplines is surely essential. However, I contend that cognitive science still has a major, even central role to play. It seems to me that "traditional" user-interface issues, such as what makes an interface easy to learn and use, remain vital. And it also seems to me that many of the most radical and influential critiques of cognitive approaches have been over stated, or at least over interpreted. For example, although it is surely true, as Suchman (1987) observed (see Button, Chapter 13 in this volume), that people often cannot or do not plan complete sequences of actions and instead act responsively to local situations, it is also surely true that people sometimes can and do plan sequences of actions and then go on to execute that sequence. (I know that I do.) It seems to me that a cognitive approach offers the best hope of understanding not only the subset of behavior that really is planned, but also the balance between planned and responsive behavior that characterizes any complex activity (see Payne, Howes, & Reader, 2001).

My view, then, is that there is still much to learn about mental models; despite some confusion in the literature, what we already know provides a useful basis for further research as well as some immediately useful concepts and distinctions. A specific motivation of this chapter is to show how the different uses of the term "mental model" can be understood: to uncover relatively weaker and stronger notions that are sensibly labeled "mental models" and that really might hold one of the keys to understanding human-computer interactions, from both a practical and a theoretical (psychological) viewpoint. Much of the theoretically more committed work on mental models has taken place outside the field of HCI, particularly, although not exclusively, in text comprehension and reasoning. Another motivation of the chapter is to bring some of the ideas in this work to the attention of students in HCI, and to argue for its relevance to understanding aspects of HCI.

The confusion over the use of the term "mental model" was well illustrated, and perhaps promulgated, in 1983, when two books with the same title—*Mental Models*—were published. One was an edited collection (Gentner and Stevens, 1983) in which a collection of authors took rather disparate theoretical stances toward a common question: How do people reason about a particular content domain? The domains under consideration were quite various, including, for example, simple electric circuits, electronic calculators, mechanical systems, and sea navigation. The second book (Johnson-Laird, 1983) was a theoretical monograph that presented what was to become a very influential account of text comprehension and deductive inference.

In one case, then, "mental models" picked out a topic for cognitive science, rather than a singular theory: It suggested that it was worthwhile to investigate the theories people construct about specialized, delimited aspects of the environment, and to study how these theories affect their thinking and behavior in that particular domain. In the second, "mental models" stood for a particular kind of mental representation: an analog representation of a state of affairs that might be derived directly from perception, or indirectly from discourse.

In my own opinion, these are both major contributions to cognitive psychology. The *topic* of mental models is an important and still under-researched aspect of the cognitive program, and the *theory* of mental models offers important insights into discourse comprehension and inference. However, the relationship between the two uses of the term (and others) is certainly potentially confusing, as many reviewers have noted (e.g., Moray, 1999). Some of these commentators (including Johnson-Laird, 1989) have tried to argue that the differences are superficial, and that at a deep level the different work on mental models is addressing the same cognitive phenomenon, but I am not convinced. Instead, I think that several independent theoretical commitments have been made under the banner "mental models," with relatively stronger theories supporting a constellation of these claims, and relatively weaker ones only one or two. (In an earlier review [Payne, 1992] I suggested that these commitments were nested in a strict inheritance hierarchy, like a set of Russian dolls, with stronger theories inheriting the commitments of weaker theories. I now think this scheme is too much of an idealization to be sustained. Nevertheless, I have ordered the ideas, with the weaker theoretical commitments earlier in the list.)

Before listing and discussing the key ideas behind the construct, in order to make sense of them it is important to sketch some of the basic explanatory assumptions of cognitive psychology, because all of the theories, however weak or strong, are cognitive theories.

6.2 SCIENTIFIC FOUNDATIONS

Cognitive psychology is often taken to share its main explanatory schema with folk psychology (the psychology of "ordinary folk"). When ordinary folk want to explain human behavior, they will often do so in terms of the agent's knowledge and goals (or beliefs and desires; hence folk psychology is often called "belief/ desire psychology"). So, for example, if you see John crossing the road, you might explain his behavior by noting that he wants to buy some coffee and he knows (or at least believes) that there is a coffee shop on the other side of the road. In such an explanation, the agent is assumed to be rational, that is, to act so as to meet his or her goals according to his or her knowledge. Cognitive psychology, likewise, attributes goals and knowledge to agents in order to explain their behavior. However, it typically goes beyond the mere attribution of rationality. As one of the founders of cognitive science pointed out (Simon, 1955), people often have to act too quickly to allow full consideration of all their relevant knowledge—they do the best they can to achieve their goals according to the knowledge they can bring to mind, and the inferences that knowledge supports, in the time allowed. In this sense, human agents exhibit "bounded rationality": rationality that is bounded by the environmental constraints on their performance, interacting with their limits on access to knowledge and the limits on their ability to process relevant information. According to Simon (1992), "bounded rationality is what cognitive psychology is all about."

Armed with this very abstract characterization of cognitive psychology, I will now list and discuss each of the key theoretical ideas that I take to have been signaled by the term "mental model" in the cognitive literature.

6.2.1 Idea 1. Mental Content vs. Cognitive Architecture: Mental Models as Theories

The first idea of mental models can be introduced as a contrast with more mainstream theorizing in cognitive psychology.

The main approach taken by cognitive psychology to understanding bounded rationality is to seek to understand the general limits of the human information-processing system—the constraints on attention, retrieval, and processing, for example. Thus, cognitive psychology offers general theories of human information-processing architecture: theories of the *structure* of the mind. Considerably less attention, in cognitive psychology, has been given to the *contents* of the mind: what do people believe about an aspect of the world, what is the relation between these beliefs and reality, and how do the beliefs affect their behavior? (The major exception to the rule that cognitive psychology has been obsessed with architecture over content is the work on expertise. The central finding of this work is that experts in a particular domain, such as chess, are differentiated from nonexperts not in terms of their problem-solving skills, or architectural constraints, but in terms of their knowledge of the domain.)

It is an emphasis on mental content over mental structure that is the first (and weakest) theoretical commitment under the name of mental models: People's behavior will often best be explained by appealing to the content of their memories—what they know and believe—independently of any mental mechanisms. This is the claim that is shared by the papers in Gentner and Stevens (1983) and by related papers in the wider literature. For example, the work on naïve physics (e.g., McCloskey, 1983) attempts to explain people's reasoning about the physical world, not in terms of working memory limits or particular representations, but in the terms of the contents of their knowledge—the nature of their theories of mechanics or electricity, for example. (Which is not to say, of course, that there would be no role for any constraints of the cognitive architecture in some account of how naïve theories are constructed, but that question is secondary.)

One reason that most cognitive psychology has focused on structure over content is surely the quest for generality. Cognitive psychology hardly ever tries to explain singular behaviors, such as John's crossing of the road (there are exceptions, of course, such as the detailed analysis of verbal protocols in human problem solving, e.g., Anzai and Simon, 1979). Instead, cognitive psychologists hope to explain a wide variety of behavioral phenomena by theorizing the mental mechanisms that are used across a wide variety of tasks.

Yet the explanation of singular behaviors is often of critical importance in HCI. It is, for example, a staple of usability labs, in which the analysis of critical incidents arising in "walkthroughs" leads to diagnoses about misleading features of an interface design.

Furthermore, there may, of course, be interesting generalizations to be made across the content-domains of which people's mental models are studied that do not rely primarily on mental mechanisms, but instead on epistemic properties of the domains and relations between them. Later in this chapter, I will try to develop such an approach for mental models of interactive artifacts.

One very broad generalization that emerges from a great deal of work on content-models is that people rely on analogies with familiar, readily envisaged domains to build mental models of less-familiar, less-visible domains.

As an illustration of the models-as-theories claim, consider a very simple study of my own (Payne, 1991). I interviewed students about automatic teller machines. Adopting the methods of Collins and Gentner (1987) and others, I asked "what if" style questions to uncover students' theories about the design and functioning of cash machines. For example, students were asked whether machines sometimes took longer to process their interactions, what information was stored on the plastic card, and what would happen if they "typed ahead" without waiting for the next machine prompt.

I discovered a huge variety in students' beliefs about the design of bank machines. For example, some had assumed that the plastic card was written-to as well as read-from during transactions, and that it thus could encode the current balance of their account. Others assumed that the only information on the card was the user's personal identification number, allowing the machine to check the identity of the card user. (Both these beliefs are incorrect!) A conclusion from this simple observation is that users of machines are eager to form explanatory models, and they will readily go beyond available data to infer models that are consistent with their experiences.

Another observation concerning students' "models" of bank machines was that they were fragmentary, perhaps more fragmentary than the term "model" might ordinarily connote: The models were collections of beliefs about parts of the system, processes, or behaviors, rather than unified models of the whole design. Students would happily recruit an analogy to explain one part of the machine's operation that bore no relation to the rest of the system. This fragmentary character of mental models of complex systems is an oft-noted and important aspect (see, e.g., Norman, 1983). One implication of this observation is that users' mental models of single processes or operations might be worthwhile topics for study and for practical intervention (in design or instruction).

Finally, I discovered a simple example of a widely held belief that affected the students' behaviors as users. Almost all respondents believed that it was not possible to type ahead during machine pauses. At the time the study was conducted, this was true for some but not all machines. Consequently, in some cases transactions were presumably being needlessly slowed because of an aspect of users' mental models.

A more recent study in this spirit is an investigation of users' models of the navigation facilities provided by Internet browsers (Cockburn & Jones, 1996).

Web browsers, like Netscape or Internet Explorer, maintain history lists of recently visited pages, providing direct access to these pages without needing to enter the URL or to follow a hyperlink. The "Back" and "Forward" buttons provide an extremely well used mechanism for browsing history lists, but do users have good mental models for how these operations work? Cockburn and Jones (1996) showed that many do not.

The full complexities of history lists and Back buttons depend on the particular browser in question, and they are beyond the scope of this chapter. Nevertheless, a brief and approximate description is enough to show the users' difficulties.

The history list of visited pages is best thought of as a stack. A stack is a simple last-in-first-out data structure to which elements can be added (pushed) or taken out (popped) only from the top (consider a stack of plates). When a new page is visited by following a hyperlink, or by entering a URL, it is pushed onto the top of the stack. This is true even if the page is already in the history list, so that the history list may contain more than one copy of the same page. However, when a page is visited by using the Back button (or, at least typically, by choosing from the history list), the page is not pushed onto the stack. So, what happens when the currently displayed page is not the top of the stack (because it has been visited via the history list) and a new link is followed (or a new URL entered)? The answer is that all the pages in the history list that were above the current page are popped from the stack, and the newly visited page is pushed onto the stack in their place. For this reason, the history list does *not* represent a complete record or time line of visited pages, and not all pages in the current browsing episode can be backed-up to. In Cockburn and Jones' study, few users appreciated this aspect of the device.

6.2.2   Idea 2. Models vs. Methods: Mental Models as Problem Spaces

One important characterization of skill in any domain (including skilled use of a computer system) is a collection of methods for achieving tasks. When novices in some domain attempt a task, they have to solve a problem, which, according to established theory in cognitive psychology (Newell & Simon, 1972), involves searching through a mentally constructed problem space of possible states. With practice, novices might remember the successful sequence of moves, so that if they attempt the task again, they can simply apply this remembered method. This transition from search to routine method-application is the major dynamic in most contemporary theories of skill acquisition (e.g., Anderson, 1987).

When real users interact with real systems, however, a state of perfect skill (a remembered method for every task, if you like) is seldom reached. Thus, problem-solving activity will coexist with routine skill, and the users' behavior will remain, to some extent, dependent on search of a problem space. This classification of human behavior into routine skill or problem solving is commonplace in cognitive science and HCI (see Card, Moran, & Newell, 1983) and parallels the influential approach to plant operators by Rasmussen (1983), who distinguished knowledge-based, skill-based, and rule-based behavior (see Chapter 9). Knowledge-based behavior is essentially problem solving, and it thus relies on knowledge in the form of a problem space to search. Skill-based and rule-based behavior are both types of routine skill, dependent on learned methods. The distinction between skill-based and rule-based behavior, as I understand it, is closely related to the well-known distinction between automatic (rule-based) and controlled (skill-based) behavior.

The distinction between automatic and controlled behavior is not spoken to by the construct of a mental model, yet the construct does suggest a different subdivision of method-based skill. The encoding of methods themselves can be more or less elaborate and flexible, according to the representation afforded by the mental model of the problem space that the methods traverse. The difference between elaborate and simple ("rote") method encodings may not affect the ordinary use of the methods, but it will affect the transfer and reworking of the methods to similar tasks.

In summary, then, mental models of machines can provide a problem space that allows more elaborate encoding of remembered methods, and in which novice or expert problem solvers can search for new methods to achieve tasks.

A classic illustration of mental models providing a problem space is the work of Halasz and Moran (1983) on Reverse Polish Notation (RPN) calculators. RPN is a postfix notation for arithmetic, so that to express 3 + 4 one would write 3 4 + . RPN does away with the need for parentheses to disambiguate composed operations. For example, (1 + 2) * 3 can be expressed 1 2 + 3 * with no ambiguity. RPN calculators need a key to act as a separator between operands—this key is conventionally labelled ENTER—but they do not need an equals key, as the current total can be computed and displayed whenever an operator is entered.

Halasz and Moran taught one group of students how to use an RPN calculator using instructions, like the introduction given above, which merely described the appropriate syntax for arithmetic expressions. A second group of subjects was instructed, using a diagram, about the stack model that underlies RPN calculation. Briefly, when a number is keyed in, it is "pushed" on top of a stack data structure (and the top slot is displayed). The ENTER key copies the contents of the top slot down to the next slot. Any binary arithmetic operation is always performed on the contents of the top two slots, which leads to the result being in the top slot, and the contents of slots 3 and below moving up the stack.

Halasz and Moran discovered that the type of instructions made no difference to participants' ability to solve routine arithmetic tasks; the syntactic "method-based" instructions sufficed to allow participants to transform the tasks into RPN notation. However, for more creative problems, such as calculating (6+4) and (6+3) and (6+2) while keying the number 6 only once, the stack group were substantially better. Verbal protocols showed that these subjects reasoned about such problems by mentally stepping through the transformations to the stack at each keystroke.

This kind of reasoning, stepping through a sequence of states in some mental model of a machine, is often called "mental simulation" in the mental-models literature, and the kind of model that allows simulation is often called a "surrogate" (Carroll & Olson, 1988; Young, 1983). Yet at an abstract level, as I have pointed out, the mental activity in such a simulation is exactly the classical search in a problem space: Operators are applied to problem states so that the next problem state is generated. From one perspective, then, the key thing is that a kind of behavior that is richer and more flexible than mere rote-method following is enabled (this is the perspective that I have stressed). From another perspective (when one considers, for example, "running" a mental model of a mechanical device), the key thing is that reasoning is performed by sequential application of completely domain-specific rules (rather than abstract logical rules) and thus (in keeping with the first mental-model commitment) is knowledge bounded rather than architecture bounded.

A second example of mental models providing a problem-space elaboration of rote methods comes in the work of Kieras and Bovair (1984). Their work was similar to that of Halasz and Moran, in that they compared the learning performance of two groups, one instructed with rote procedures, the other additionally with a diagrammatic model of the device on which the procedures were enacted. Their device was a simple control panel in which each rote procedure specified a sequence of button pushes and knob positions leading to a sequence of light illuminations. The model was a circuit diagram showing the connections among power sources, switches, and display lights.

Kieras and Bovair found that the participants instructed with the model learned the procedures faster, retained the procedures more accurately, executed the procedures faster, and could simplify inefficient procedures that contained redundant switch settings. They argued that this was because the model (circuit diagram) explained the contingencies in the rote-action sequences (e.g., if a switch is set to MA, so that the main accumulator circuit is selected, then the FM, fire main, button must be used).

6.2.3   Idea 3. Models vs. Descriptions: Mental Models as Homomorphisms

The third idea is that mental models are a special kind of representation, sometimes called an *analog* representation—one that shares the structure of the world it represents.

To get an intuitive grasp of this idea, compare a picture with a verbal description. Let's consider how either form might represent a room, say a room with a few chairs in it. A verbal description, for example the one just given, relies on arbitrary word meanings and some minimal syntax, neither of which bear any structural relation to the state of affairs being described. A phrase describing a room with more chairs in it would not necessarily have more words, or more anything (although it might, and there are indeed some devices in English that seem to utilize analog representations, such as "it was a long long long time ago"). A picture, on the other hand, is very constrained in the way it can represent something. A picture of a room with a few chairs in it would have to represent a particular number of chairs, and to represent more chairs there would have to be more tokens (more pictures of chairs) in the picture. In this sense, pictures share the structure of the states of affairs they represent.

The idea that mental models are like pictures, in as much as they share the structure of what they represent, is a definitional property in the work on reasoning and comprehension by Johnson-Laird (1983, 1989) and also in the theory of Holland, Holyoak, Nisbett, & Thagard (1986) and Moray (1999). However, there are different nuances to the claim, which must be considered. And, in addition, there is a vexed question to be asked, namely, what is the explanatory or predictive force of this commitment to analog representational form?

The focus of Johnson-Laird's work has been the construction of temporary models of very simple *static* situations, combining the information from multiple verbal premises in order to draw deductive inferences. The focus of Holland and colleagues' work, and of human-factors work on interaction with machinery (as exemplified by Moray, 1999), is the use of long-term memory representations of complex dynamic systems (a focus shared with most of the chapters in Gentner and Stevens, 1983).

In the case of simple static models, the idea of an analog representation closely parallels our example of the chair-filled room. A mental model, like a picture, is taken to be an isomorphic representation of such situations, with each object and relation in the represented world being represented by a token and relation in the model.

Consider, for example, the following sentences:

The spoon is to the left of the fork
The knife is to the left of the spoon

According to Johnson-Laird (1983), when you read each sentence, you build an analog model of the situation described. So, after reading the first sentence, your model would be something like

spoon fork

The information in the second sentence is combined with this model to construct a single integrated model:

knife spoon fork

Such a model allows deductive inferences to be "read off." For example, one can use the model to confirm that the knife is to the left of the fork, even though this is not explicitly mentioned in the text.

The sense in which dynamic models are often taken to share the structure of the world (in the work of Moray and of Holland et al.) is less exact, in two ways. First, such mental models are proposed to be homomorphisms rather than isomorphisms (i.e., they are many-to-one rather than one-to-one mappings of objects, properties, and relations). Second, they may not share structure at all at the level of static relations, but only at the level of state-changes. Thus, such models have the character of state-transition networks, making the commitment to structure sharing in this case no stronger, it seems to me, than that typically made in the work on models as problem spaces.

Neither of these positions concerning the analog nature of mental models makes very clear the empirical consequences of such a claim. I will tackle this issue in Section 6.3.2, and in so doing I will argue that the stronger idea of analog representations (the Johnson-Laird view, rather than the Moray/Holland et al. view) is, after all, relevant to interactive systems.

6.2.4   Idea 4. Models of Representations: Mental Models Can Be Derived from Language, Perception, or Imagination

The simple spatial description used earlier to illustrate the idea of an analog representation also illustrates a second key idea in Johnson-Laird's work, and in all the work on "situation models" in text comprehension (see Zwaan & Radvansky,

1998, for a review). This is that mental models can be constructed by processing language, but the same models might also, in principle, have been constructed through interaction with and perception of the world. Therefore, a mental model provides a way of mapping language to perception.

According to this theory of text comprehension, readers (or listeners) first form representations of the text itself (surface form and propositional content) and then compute a mental model of the meaning of the text. The model represents the situation described by the language, rather than the language itself (thus, the name "situation model," which is often preferred to "mental model" in the text-comprehension literature).

One potential problem for this idea is that propositions might be consistent with an infinite number of situations (how far apart were the spoon and the fork in the earlier description?). The proposed solution (see, e.g., Johnson-Laird, 1989) is that a single model is used as a representative sample. In this sense, then, models go beyond the information in the textual propositions.

In the work of Kintsch and followers (e.g., Kintsch, 1998), this idea looms large, particularly the idea that situation models are the product of integrating the reader's general knowledge with the information in the propositional textbase.

6.3   DETAILED DESCRIPTION

The aim of this section is, in a sense, to add a personal twist to the ideas previously reviewed above. First, I describe a theoretical framework that extends the idea of models of representations to computational devices, and that thus elaborates the notion that models provide problem spaces. Second, I worry about what is at stake in the idea that models are analog, structure-sharing representations, and I suggest a reworking of the idea with more immediate empirical consequences.

6.3.1   Idea 5. Mental Representations of Representational Artifacts

If a reader's goal is just to understand a text, then the text-representation can be discarded once a model has been constructed. However, there are many tasks of text *use*, in which it is necessary to maintain a representation of the text, alongside a mental model of the meaning of the text. Consider, for example, the tasks of writing and editing, or of searching for particular content in a text. In such tasks, it is necessary to keep in mind the relationship between the surface form of the text—wording, spatial layout, and so on—and its meaning. Text is a representational artifact, and to *use* it in this sense one needs a mental representation of the structure of the text, the "situation" described by the text, and the mapping between the two.

According to the yoked state space (YSS) hypothesis (Payne, Squibb, & Howes, 1990), this requirement is general to all representational artifacts, including computer systems. To use such artifacts requires some representation of the domain of application of the artifact—the concepts the artifact allows you to represent and process. The user's goals are states in this domain, which is therefore called the *goal space*. However, states in the goal space cannot be manipulated directly. Instead, the user interacts with the artifact, and therefore he or she needs knowledge of the artifact and of the operations that allow states of the artifact to be transformed. Call this problem space the *device space*. In order to solve problems in the goal space by searching in the device space, the user must know how the device space represents the goal space. In this sense, the two spaces need to be yoked. The minimal device space for a certain set of tasks must be capable of representing all the states in the corresponding goal space. More elaborate device spaces may incorporate device states that do not directly represent goal states, but that allow more efficient performance of tasks.

To put some flesh on these bare definitional bones, let us first consider, very simply and approximately, the central core of text-editing functions provided by a modern word processor. (For more detailed treatment of the same device, see Payne, Squibb, & Howes, 1990.) The goal space for this device comprises text structures: A document is a sequence of paragraphs (separated by blank lines), each of which is a sequence of sentences, each of which is a sequence of words (each of which is a sequence of alpha characters) separated by punctuation marks and spaces.

Users' tasks are transformations of the goal space, such as insertion or deletion of words, or sentences, or paragraphs. But to accomplish these goals, users need to apply device operators to the device space, and therefore need to have a model of the device space and of how it represents the goal space. A key aspect of this model is that strings of characters represent all the elements of the goal space, including blank lines and the spaces between words, as well as words, sentences, and paragraphs. Thus, once the user knows how to delete a character and a string of characters, that user knows how to delete sentences and paragraphs and how to eliminate the space between text. Early studies of word processors showed that the device-space concept of characters, and its mapping onto the goal-space concepts of space and lines, was nonobvious to novice word-processor users.

These days, of course, word processors typically have internal representations of constructs like word and sentences (as well as a general representation in terms of strings of characters). These representations may allow additional, specialized shortcut methods for some transformations, but they may also cause problems of their own. These issues will not concern us here; instead, we will use the very simple treatment to introduce another important aspect of mental models of devices that the yoked state space hypothesis illuminates: the elaboration of the minimal device space.

The minimal device space for core text-editing functions, then, is one that distinguishes several types of character (space, punctuation mark, letter) and allows any of these characters to be sequenced into a string. Device operators allow the specification of positions within the document (mouse point and click), and insertion and deletion of characters and strings. Characters and strings allow all the goal-space text objects to be represented.

Now consider how users might learn about the **Copy** operation. They may read or be shown that a copy operation can be achieved by a sequence of operators: First mark the string to be copied; then select **Copy** from the **Edit** menu or by using a shortcut; then point to the destination in the document; then select **Paste** from the **Edit** menu. This entire sequence clearly specifies a transformation of the minimal device space—it copies a substring from one place to another in the document-string. However, each step of the sequence does not affect the minimal device space. In particular, selecting **Copy** from the **Edit** menu does absolutely nothing to the minimal-device space. The user might happily live with this, giving the **Copy** action what I have called an "operational account," that is, no independent semantics of its own, merely as a part of the sentential **Copy** operation. However, this operational account of **Copy** makes for an inflexible method. Consider the task of copying a string of text to two separate locations. Payne et al. (1990) observed many novice users who executed the entire sequence of operations twice to accomplish this task.

The more productive alternative is to construct a figurative account of the **Copy** action, by elaborating the minimal-device space so that the action does indeed transform the device state. The idea of a copy buffer, into which the string is copied when **Copy** is selected, provides exactly such a figurative account. Payne et al. (1990) found that, by renaming **Copy** as **Store,** more novice users were inclined to construct such an account and could therefore achieve copy-to-two-places by repeating only the final point-click-**Paste** part of the **Copy** method.

The work of Halasz and Moran (1983) can readily be assimilated into the YSS framework. The no-model condition was provided with enough information to translate algebraic expressions into their Reverse Polish (RP) equivalent; in their understanding of RP expressions, however, the ENTER key was given merely an operational account, it worked simply as a separator of operands, and it did not transform the device state. The stack model, however, provides a figurative account of the ENTER key.

This discussion illustrates a practical lesson for the design of interfaces and instructions. In the case of the copy buffer and the calculator stack, the standard interface does not allow the appropriate device space to be induced readily, so that conceptual instructions must fill the gap. (The obvious alternative, which has been developed to some extent in both cases, is to redesign the user interface so as to make the appropriate device space visible.) These examples suggest a simple heuristic for the provision of conceptual instructions, which may help overcome the considerable controversy over whether or not such instructions (as opposed to simple procedural instructions) are useful (see, e.g., Wright, 1988). According to this heuristic, conceptual instructions will be useful if they support construction of a YSS that the user would otherwise have difficulty inducing (Payne, Howes, & Hill, 1992).

6.3.2   Idea 6. Mental Models as Computationally Equivalent to External Representations

The importance of structure sharing, or analog form of mental representations, is controversial. One well-known argument by Anderson (1978) contends that there is no empirical force to the distinction, because some propositional representation can always mimic the representational properties of an analog model (but see Johnson-Laird, 1983 for a rebuttal). It is beyond the reach of this chapter (or its author!) to resolve this controversy, but I contend that a more abstract claim, at the level of function rather than structure of mental representations, can provide exactly the empirical force that is intended in the idea of mental models as iso- or homomorphisms. The key to this reworking is the distinction between computational and informational equivalence of representations (Simon, 1978).

It is obviously possible to have two or more distinct representations of the same information. Call such representations "informationally equivalent" if all the information in one is inferable from the other, and vice versa. Two informationally equivalent representations may or may not additionally be "computationally equivalent," meaning that the cost structure of accessing the information is equivalent in both cases, or, as Larkin and Simon (1987) put it: "information given explicitly in the one can also be drawn easily and quickly from the information given explicitly in the other, and vice versa." As Larkin and Simon point out, "easily" and "quickly" are not precise terms, and so this definition of computational equivalence is inherently somewhat vague; nevertheless, it points to empirical consequences of a representation (together with the processes that operate upon it) that go beyond mere informational content.

I propose that it is clearer to use *task-relative* versions of the concepts of informational and computational equivalence. Representations are informationally equivalent, *with respect to a set of tasks,* if they allow the same tasks to be performed (i.e., contain the requisite information for those tasks). The representations are, additionally, computationally equivalent with respect to the tasks they allow to be performed, if the relative difficulty of the tasks is the same, whichever representation is being used. (Note that, according to these definitions, two representations might be computationally equivalent with regard to a subset of the tasks they support but not with regard to the total set, so that in Larkin and Simon's sense they would merely be informationally equivalent. The task-relative versions of the constructs thus allow more finely graded comparisons between representations.)

This idea can express what is behaviorally important about the idea of an analog mental representation of a state of affairs: An analog representation is computationally equivalent with respect to some tasks, to external perception and manipulation of the state of affairs it represents. This is the idea behind the classic demonstrations of mental rotation (Shepard & Metzler, 1971). When the task is to compare two objects (e.g., letters) in different rotations, people take longer to confirm that the letters are the same the further apart they are in degrees of rotation. In this sense, their mental processing of the letter-images is computationally equivalent to physical rotation of the external representation of the letters.

The idea can also be seen readily to apply to the mental model of a simple spatial arrangement previously discussed. The ease with which various inferences can be "read off" the mental model is equivalent to the ease with which they could be read off a real physical representation of the same state of affairs (or indeed the diagrammatic representation used to stand in for the model on the page of this book).

The idea seems to run into trouble, however, with states of affairs or situations that cannot themselves be readily inspected. I can just about imagine how a mental model of a nuclear power station might share the structure of the power station, but it is hard to see how drawing inferences from the model could be computationally equivalent to probing and inspecting the real power station. So what are the empirical consequences of the analog constraint in cases like these?

This is, it seems to me, an open question. However, I do believe that the idea of task-relative computational equivalence can be rescued to provide a partial answer. If structure-sharing is taken to be an important property of mental models, then a mental model derived from text shares the structure of the situation, not of the text. However, it is not clear that this distinction extends to mental models derived from "reading" other representational artifacts, such as maps or diagrams.

The case of maps is particularly instructive. A large empirical and theoretical literature has grown up around the concept of a "cognitive map," meaning a mental representation of a physical environment that enables navigation through that environment. To consider just one, well-known, study, Thorndyke and Hayes-Roth (1982) showed that, with prolonged exposure to an environment (the RAND building in California), people could develop knowledge of that environment that was equivalent to the knowledge of people who had studied a map. In particular, both these groups of people could produce direction estimates from one location to another, and estimates of as-the-crow-flies distances between locations that were independent of the complexity of a walking route between the two places. In contrast, people who had not studied a map and who had less experience of the building seemed not to have built a cognitive map, but rather to derive these estimates from their memory for specific routes, so that accuracy was correlated to the complexity of the route. (In passing, I might note that Ruddle, Payne, & Jones [1997] obtained a broadly similar pattern of results from people navigating desktop virtual environments.)

This study suggests that a cognitive map can usefully be defined as a mental representation that is computationally equivalent, with respect to the tasks of direction and distance estimation, to an external map. Yet the ordinary definition of a cognitive map is extremely closely related to the analog-representation definition of a mental model. Just as a mental model is taken to be true to the structure of the described situation, rather than to the text from which it was derived and therefore "source independent," so a cognitive map is taken to be true to the global structure of the experienced environment and not to the particular experiences and therefore "route independent." Perhaps, then, all mental models might be defined as mental representations that are computationally equivalent with external, diagrammatic representations.

This is a stronger claim than I can defend, but it does not seem to me implausible. Perhaps it is the fact that we can readily diagram situations like that described by "the spoon is to the left of the knife" that makes the mental models of such situations so easy to construct and inspect. A similar case for the reliance of internal representations on external representations has been made by Rumelhart, Smolensky, McClelland, and Hinton (1986).

6.4   CASE STUDY

Let us briefly take stock. We have reviewed six separate theoretical "ideas" that underpin the concept of a user's mental model. The ideas range from the relatively weak and more universally accepted to the relatively strong and contentious. The first idea is that it is important to try to systematically investigate what people believe to be true about particular domains (such as interactive devices). The second idea is that mental models can furnish a problem space—a mental structure of possible states of the world that the user can search in order to plan their behavior. The third idea is that mental models might in some sense share the structure of the physical world that they represent. The fourth idea is that models can be derived from perception, or from language or imagination. These four ideas are all extant in the literatures on mental models. The first two ideas are the mainstay of mental models research in HCI, whereas the third and fourth ideas are fundamental to the more theoretically inclined work in cognitive science, particularly the work of Johnson-Laird (1983). The fifth and sixth ideas are an attempt to take a next step, incorporating the four foundational ideas into a more specific theory of the relation between cognition and cognitive artifacts.

The goal of this section is to try to further illustrate how these ideas can shed light on aspects of HCI. First, I will show that the construct of yoked state spaces can motivate an informal analysis of the fit between the representational capacities of a device and the purposes of a user, using the appointment diary or calendar as an example artifact (after Payne, 1993). Second, I will review some experiments I did with Bibby (Bibby & Payne, 1993, 1996) that support the idea of *internalization* (i.e., computationally equivalent mental versions of external representations), with respect to diagrammatic descriptions of device models.

6.4.1   A Yoked State Spaces Analysis of Calendar Design

The original idea behind the yoked state space (YSS) framework was that it might be used to analyze the conceptual complexity of devices. Such an analysis begins with a description of the task domain that the device addresses (the goal space) and then describes the concepts and operators in the device space and how these are used to represent and traverse the goal space. Payne et al. (1990) illustrated such an analysis for core word-processor functions, as briefly reviewed earlier, and Payne (1991) reported a similar exercise considering the MacDraw graphics package.

The YSS conception also suggests a different kind of analysis, at a coarser level. This analysis, called a task-entity analysis, begins with an enumeration of the conceptual entities and relations in the goal space and simply inspects the extent to which the device allows these entities and relations to be expressed. Such an analysis assumes a prior coherent scope for the goal space, as opposed to the first kind of analysis, in which the goal space is defined by the scope of the device. It thus might offer some insight into the functionality of the device in question, as well as its usability.

According to Payne (1993), a coherent and important task domain in need of device support is Prospective Remembering (PR)—remembering what to do in the future, and when. The important concepts in this domain are the to-be-remembered items—let's call them *intentions*—and the temporal context into which the intentions are placed and, eventually (one hopes) enacted.

Intentions have many kinds of relations one to another, which are critically important for the tasks of PR. First, intentions have a nested structure. As I write, my intention of a few weeks ago to email the editor of this book was part of a broader intention to deliver this chapter in good time (not all intentions succeed). Intentions also have a dependency structure; some things have to be done before others. Finally, and obviously, intentions have a relative importance: Some can fail without dire consequences, others cannot.

Considering now the attributes of single intentions, a critical attribute is the particular temporal constraint on the intention. Some intentions have a particular critical time at which they must be enacted, such as a doctor's appointment; others have a tolerant window of opportunity, such as the intention to call a friend sometime next week. Ellis (1988), in drawing this distinction, called the former class of intention a *pulse,* the latter a *step.* A third class of intention, or perhaps a subclass of steps, is intentions that must be enacted before a particular deadline. Yet a fourth class is those that are constrained not by time per se, but by the time of other events—for example, you might intend to have a haircut the next time you're in town.

Turning to the temporal context in which intentions are remembered, we can distinguish several conceptions of time that are relevant to the task of PR. First, we can distinguish the personal from the conventional time line. The conventional time line has a hierarchical structure of years, months, days, and so forth, which is subject to accurate, public measurement and therefore potentially accurate placement of events, both past and future. The personal time line has a more narrative structure, which again may be hierarchical. Events occur in both time lines, of course. Furthermore, individuals must orient themselves (keep track of "now") in both time lines (Freidman, 1990).

Finally, we can note that time has cyclical as well as linear aspects. Both conventional and personal routines are cyclical at different levels: days of the week, seasons, lecture courses, and so on.

Armed with this informal specification of the important psychological properties of the goal space for appointment diaries, we can ask the question, How are these properties represented by the device in question? The answer, with respect to conventional paper diaries, is not at all well.

No between-intention relations can readily be represented, and there is a clear preference for intentions planned for a single day. Uses of diaries adopt ad hoc typographic conventions to try to get round these representational weaknesses—drawing lines that cut across the regions of the calendar, writing in the margins of the page, and so on. Both the conventional and the personal time lines are represented to some extent in a calendar. Both the linear and the cyclical aspects of the conventional time line are represented in the printed layout of the pages, and the linear structure of personal time is represented in the entered appointments. However, the narrative structure and the cyclical structure of personal time are not directly represented but must be extracted by the reader.

Orientation to "now" is only crudely handled in most paper calendars—by a bookmark, for example. Many users leave their calendars open on their desk to support orientation. (Nevertheless, Payne [1993] reported a few critical incidents of users noting appointments in the wrong week.)

This lack of match between the representational capabilities of paper calendars and the conceptually important properties of intentions suggests many design opportunities for electronic artifacts. For example, it should be possible to allow users to enter notes for arbitrary time windows, and to allow the linking and browsing of between-event dependencies. Electronic calendars have continuous access to a clock, and they should take advantage of this to cue the current time, perhaps by making "now," today, this week perceptually distinctive.

6.4.2   Experiments on Internalizaton of Device Instructions

Bibby and Payne (1993, 1996) tested the "internalization hypothesis" in the domain of HCI, using a computer simulation of a device derived from that studied by Kieras and Bovair (1984). The device was a multiroute circuit, in which setting switches into one of several configurations would make a laser fire; various indicator lights showed which components of the circuit were receiving power.

Bibby and Payne asked all participants to repeatedly perform two types of task: a switch task, in which all but one switch were already in position to make a laser fire (the participant had to key the final switch), and a fault task, in which the pattern of indicator lights was such that one of the components must be broken (the participant had to key the name of the broken component).

Participants were instructed about the device with either a table showing the conditions under which each indicator light would be illuminated (Table), or with sequences of switch positions enabling the laser to be fired (Procedures). Both instructions were designed to be sufficient for both switch and fault tasks—they were informationally equivalent with respect to those tasks. However, with the Table, the fault task was easier than the switch task, whereas with the Procedures the switch task was easier than the fault task.

In the first two blocks of practice, participants were allowed to consult the instructions, and this pattern of relative difficulty was confirmed by a crossover interaction in response times. Furthermore, when the instructions were removed from the participants, so that they had to rely on their mental representation of the device, the crossover interaction persevered, demonstrating that the mental representations were computationally equivalent to the external instructions.

In subsequent experiments, Bibby and Payne demonstrated that this pattern persevered even after considerable interaction with the device (it was still evident after 20 examples each of the fault and switch tasks, interspersed with 80 examples of an interactive operating task in which switches had to be set so that the laser would fire despite some broken components, or identified as broken to the extent that it could not fire). Such extended interaction might have been expected to provide an opportunity to overcome the representational constraints of the initial instruction. The crossover interaction eventually disappeared only after very extended practice on the particular fault and switch task (80 examples of each, perhaps because of asymptotic performance having been reached). At this point, Bibby and Payne introduced two similar but new types of task designed so that, once again, the Table favored one task whereas Procedures favored the other. (However, the device instructions were *not* re-presented.) At this point, the crossover reappeared, demonstrating that participants were consulting their declarative knowledge about the device, and that this was still in a form computationally equivalent to the original external representation of the instructions.

What are the implications of Bibby and Payne's work? Practically, they show that the exact form of instructions may exert long-lasting effects on the strategies that are used to perform tasks, so that designers of such instructions must be sensitive not only to their informational content but to their computational properties. In this light, they also suggest that one instructional representation of a device is very unlikely to be an optimal vehicle for supporting all user tasks: It may well be better to provide different representations of the same information, each tailored to particular tasks. In this sense, perhaps instructions should mirror and exploit the natural tendency, noted earlier, for users to form fragmentary mental models, with different fragments for different purposes.

In terms of theory, Bibby and Payne's findings lend support to the suggestion developed previously that mental models of a device that are formed from instructions may be computationally equivalent to the external representations of the device. This idea gives a rather different twist to the standard line that mental models are analog, homomorphic representations. It also supports a somewhat ironic, recursive suggestion concerning future research. The premise of this chapter is that understanding users' mental models can enrich our understanding of the use of cognitive artifacts. But perhaps an excellent way of further developing our understanding of the nature and genesis of mental models is to study the use of simple diagrammatic representations.

7 | Exploring and Finding Information

Peter Pirolli   Palo Alto Research Center

7.1   INTRODUCTION

This chapter will discuss recent theories that address how people forage for information in their environment. The emergence of the global information ecology has created enormous pressures for users who seek useful information. Understanding how people adapt to these pressures has led to the development of information-foraging theory and the notion of users following information scent. Information-foraging theory is grounded in computational theories of human cognition and optimal foraging theories from biology. Applications of the theory to a novel browsing system (called Scatter/Gather) and the World Wide Web illustrate the utility of the approach.

7.2   MOTIVATION: MAN THE INFORMAVORE

The psychologist George Miller (1983) characterized humans as a species of *informavores:* organisms hungry for information about the world and themselves. We are curious creatures who gather and store information for its own sake, and we explore and use this wealth of information in order to better adapt to our everyday problems. We are not unique in this respect. There are other species that seem to be inherently driven by curiosity and a penchant for exploration and learning. We are, however, distinct in the extreme degree to which we have used technology to accelerate our evolution as informavores. This technology-boosted evolution is not without its tensions. Even though the amount of available information grows at an exponential rate,[1] our unassisted perceptual and cognitive capacities have not changed in any fundamental way since long before the invention of writing. Technological advances that increase the volume and flux of available information create pressures that must be met by technological advances that enhance our capacities for exploring, searching, and attending to that information. This chapter presents theoretical developments that aim to explain and predict how people will explore, search, and attend to the information environment, and how the information environment can be better shaped to people.

Much of the focus in this chapter will concern *information-foraging theory* and the concept of *information scent*. Information-foraging theory deals with understanding how user strategies and technologies for information seeking, gathering, and consumption are adapted to the flux of information in the environment. Information scent concerns the user's use of environmental cues in judging information sources and navigating through information spaces. These ideas evolved in reaction to the technological developments associated with the growth of globally distributed, easily accessible information, and the theoretical developments associated with the growing influence of evolutionary theory in the behavioral and social sciences.

7.2.1   Emergence of the Global Information Ecology

Information-foraging theory arose during the 1990s, coinciding with an explosion in the amount of information that became available to the average computer user, and with the development of new technologies for accessing and interacting with information. Hard-disk capacity grew 25% to 30% each year during the 1980s.[2] The number of Internet hosts grew at an exponential rate from 188 in December 1979 to 313,000 in October 1990 to 28,611,177 sites in March 2001.[3] Processing capacity continued to double every 18 months, inexorably following Moore's law.[4] Widespread deployment of improved scanners and fax machines meant that more documents were moving into, and flowing through, the digital world. High-resolution, high-performance, interactive graphics workstations enabled the development of novel information visualization and

---

[1] See *www.sims.berkeley.edu/how-much-info/* for a variety of ways of measuring this growth.

[2] James Porter of Disk/Trend, as cited in Toigo (2000).

[3] See the Hobbes' Internet Timeline © at *www/isoc/guest/zakon/Internet/History/HIT.html*

[4] Named after Gordon Moore, who observed that computer memory chip-capacity doubles every 18 months.

interaction techniques for large volumes of information. Whereas the average personal computer user of the early 1980s had access to perhaps dozens of files in local storage on their isolated machine, the average user in 1995 had access to about 275 million documents on the World Wide Web. It is estimated that the average user in 2001 had access to 525 billion Web documents.

The late 1980s witnessed several strands of human-computer interaction (HCI) research that were devoted to ameliorating problems of exploring and finding electronically stored information. It had become apparent that users could no longer remember the names of all their electronic files, and it was even more difficult for them to guess the names of files stored by others (Furnas, Landauer, Gomez, & Dumais, 1987). One can see proposals in the mid- to late-1980s HCI literature for methods to enhance users' ability to search and explore external memory. Jones (1986) proposed the Memory Extender (ME), which used a model of human associative memory (Anderson, 1983) to automatically retrieve files represented by sets of keywords that were similar to the sets of keywords representing the users' working context. Latent Semantic Analysis (LSA) (Dumais, Furnas, Landauer, Deerwester, & Harshman, 1988) was developed to mimic human ability to detect deeper semantic associations among words, like "dog" and "cat," to similarly enhance information retrieval.[5] This new work on ME and LSA, which was aimed at the "average" user, was contrasted with work in the "traditional" field of information retrieval in computer science, which had a relatively long history of developing automated systems for storing and retrieving text documents (vanRijsbergen, 1979). The 1988 CHI conference in which LSA was introduced also hosted a panel bemoaning the fact that automated information retrieval systems had not progressed to the stage where anyone but dedicated experts could operate them (Borgman, Belkin, Croft, Lesk, & Landauer, 1988). Such systems, however, were the direct ancestors of modern search engines found on the Web.

Hypermedia also became a hot topic during the late 1980s, with Apple's introduction of HyperCard in 1987, the first ACM Conference on Hypertext in 1987, and a paper session at the CHI 1988 conference. The very idea of hypertext can be traced back to Vannevar Bush's *Atlantic Monthly* article "As We May Think," published in 1945 (Bush, 1945).[6] Worried about scholars becoming overwhelmed by the amount of information being published, Bush proposed a mechanized private file system, called the Memex, that would augment the

---

[5] Latent Semantic Analysis proved to be surprisingly successful in addressing psychological facts about human vocabulary learning (Landauer & Dumais, 1997)—an example of application-oriented research making a contribution to fundamental science.

[6] See Buckland (1992) for a discussion of the developments that preceded Bush's publication.

memory of the individual user. It was explicitly intended to mimic human associative memory. Bush's article influenced the development of Douglas Englebart's NLS (oNLine System), which was introduced to the world in a tour-de-force demonstration by Englebart at the 1968 Fall Joint Computer Conference. The demonstration of NLS—a system explicitly designed to "augment human intellect" (Englebart, 1962)—also introduced the world to the power of networking, the mouse, and point-and-click interaction. Hypertext and hypermedia research arose during the late 1980s because personal computing power, networking, and user interfaces had evolved to the point where the visions of Bush and Englebart could finally be realized for the average computer user.

The confluence of increased computing power, storage, and networking and information access and hypermedia research in the late 1980s set the stage for the widespread deployment of hypermedia in the form of the World Wide Web. In 1989, Tim Berners-Lee proposed a solution (Berners-Lee, 1989) to the problems that were being faced by the Conseil Européen pour la Recherche Nucléaire (CERN) community in dealing with distributed collections of documents, which were stored on many types of platforms, in many types of formats. This proposal lead directly to the development of HyperText Markup Language (HTML), HyperText Transfer Protocol (HTTP), and, in 1990, the release of the Web. Berners-Lee's vision was not only to provide users with more effective access to information, but also to initiate an evolving web of information that reflected and enhanced the community and its activities.

The emergence of the Web in the 1990s provided new challenges and opportunities for HCI. The increased wealth of accessible content, and the use of the Web as a place to do business, exacerbated the need to improve the user's experience on the Web. It has been estimated that

+ 65% of virtual shopping trips on the Web end up in failure (Souza, 2000),

+ for every 1 million visitors, 40% do not return because of problems in Web site design, at a cost of $2.8 million (Manning, McCarthy, & Souza, 1998),

+ Web site redesigns that failed to solve such problems were estimated to cost $1.5 million to $2.1 million in 1999 (Manning et al., 1998).

Such figures translate into an enormous loss of potential revenue and profit for a global industry expected to top $1 trillion in 2003. [7] This has created a strong

---

[7] Source: SearchEngineWatch.

demand for theory, technologies, and practices that improve the usability of the Web.

The usability literature that has evolved surrounding the Web-user experience is incredibly rich with design principles and maxims (Nielsen, 2000; Spool, Scanlon, Schroeder, Snyder, & DeAngelo, 1999), the most important of which is to test designs with users. Much of this literature is based on a mix of empirical findings and expert ("guru") opinion. A good deal of it is conflicting.[8] The development of theory in this area can greatly accelerate progress and meet the demands of changes in the way we interact with the Web. Greater theoretical understanding and the ability to predict the effects of alternative designs could bring greater coherence to the usability literature, and it could provide more rapid evolution of better designs. In practical terms, a designer armed with such theory could explore and explain the effects of different design decisions on Web designs before the heavy investment of resources for implementation and testing. This exploration of design space is also more efficient because the choices among different design alternatives are better informed: Rather than randomly generating and testing design alternatives, the designer is in a position to know which avenues are better to explore and which are better to ignore. Unfortunately, cognitive-engineering models that had been developed to deal with the analysis of expert performance on well-defined tasks involving application programs (Pirolli, 1999) had no applicability to understanding foraging through content-rich hypermedia, and consequently new theories were needed.

7.3   SCIENTIFIC FOUNDATIONS

This chapter presents two related strands of theory. These strands roughly correspond to the two aspects of Berners-Lee's vision for the Web: one strand dealing with the individual users' interactions with vast amounts of information, the other strand dealing with the phenomena that emerge from communities of interacting agents and knowledge. The connection among these strands is that they take an *adaptationist approach*. Users are viewed as complex adaptive agents who shape their strategies and actions to be more efficient and functional with respect to their information ecology. System designs (including hypermedia content) are similarly analyzed with regard to how they engage more functional

---

[8] This state of affairs in recognized in the maxim of one "guru" who claims that the only hard-and-fast principle is "it depends."

and efficient user behavior, and how they are adaptive with respect to user needs. By assuming many interacting complex adaptive agents, one may develop models that predict emergent phenomena that arise when many people produce and consume content, and when they interact with one another on the World Wide Web.

7.3.1   Influence of Evolutionary Theory: Adaptationist Approaches

The rise of adaptationist approaches in the study of human behavior during the 1980s deeply affected evolutionary biology as well as the behavioral sciences.[9] The approach gained currency in cognitive science during the 1980s as a reaction to *ad hoc* models of how people performed complex cognitive or perceptual tasks. At that time, models of cognition and perception were generally *mechanistic*, detailing perceptual and cognitive structures and the processes that transformed them.[10] The Model Human Processor (MHP) and Goals, Operators, Methods, and Selection rules (GOMS) (Card, Moran, & Newell, 1983) are cognitive-engineering examples that derive from this approach. The MHP specifies a basic set of information storage and processing machinery, much like a specification of the basic computer architecture for a personal computer. GOMS specifies basic task-performance processes, much like a mechanical program that "runs" on the MHP.

Around the same time that GOMS and MHP were introduced into HCI, there emerged a concern among cognitive scientists that mechanistic information-processing models, by themselves, were not enough to understand the human mind (Anderson, 1990; Marr, 1982). A major worry was that mechanistic models of cognition had been developed in an *ad hoc* way and provided an incomplete explanation of human behavior.[11] It had become common practice to cobble together a program that simulated human performance on some task and then claim that the program was in fact a theory of the task (Marr, 1982, p. 28). Anderson (1990, p. 7) lamented that cognitive modelers "pull out of an infinite grab bag of mechanisms bizarre creations whose only justification is that

---

9   Adaptationism has been a controversial idea in the behavioral and social sciences because it raises questions regarding the fundamental nature of mankind and a host of moral issues. A fascinating account of this "opera" can be found in Segerstrale (2000).

10   Mechanistic models of complex behavior, like problem solving, were an enormous advance in and of themselves.

11   Note that Marr and Anderson are only more recent proponents of the stance.

they predict the phenomena in a class of experiments. . . . We almost never ask the question of *why* these mechanisms compute the way they do" (emphasis added). Miller, in his article about "informavores," commented on the incompleteness of the mechanistic approach by using the following analogy: "Insofar as a limb is a lever, the theory of levers describes its behavior—but a theory of levers does not answer every question that might be asked about the structure and function of the limbs of animals. Insofar as the mind is used to process information, the theory of information processing describes its behavior—but a theory of information processing does not answer every question that might be asked about the structure and function of the minds of human beings" (Miller, 1983, p. 112).

Roughly speaking, the adaptationist approach involves reverse engineering. Human behavior, and the human mind behind that behavior, have adapted to the environment through evolution. This approach leads one to ask *what* environmental problems are being solved and *why* cognitive and perceptual systems are well adapted to solving those problems. For instance, Anderson and Milson (1989) analyzed the particular mathematical functions that characterize forgetting from human memory. Memories tend to decay very rapidly if they are not used frequently or have not been used recently. The specific mathematical form of this decay function was shown to be optimal given the likelihood of information recurring in the environment and the assumption that the cost of searching memory increases with the number of items stored. Later, Anderson and Lebievre (2000) proposed that theoretical memory mechanisms would give rise to those functions. In other words, Anderson and Milson started by asking the question "what problem does memory solve" and assumed that the answer was "to recall events relevant to ones that reoccur in the environment." They then proceeded to analyze the structure of this environmental problem and proposed an optimal mathematical solution (a kind of engineering-design specification). Anderson later proposed a specific mechanistic design (a computer simulation of human memory) that satisfied this design specification.

The mind is a fantastically complex, cobbled-together machine, which has been incrementally designed by evolution to be well tailored to the demands of surviving and reproducing in the environment. The adaptationist approach recognizes that one can better understand a machine by understanding its function.[12] Children can figure out quite a lot about the operation of a VCR by

---

[12] This notion of a scientific observer trying to understand something on the basis of its design is called an *intentional stance* (Dennett, 1988). This is very close to Newell's notion of understanding a system at the *knowledge level* (Newell, 1982, 1993). When the design is assumed to be driven by evolution, it is called an *ecological stance* (Bechtel, 1985).

understanding its purpose with virtually no knowledge of its mechanism. Some cognitive scientists realized that human information processing was an extension of human biology and that "nothing in biology makes sense except in the light of evolution" (Dobzhansky, 1973).

In cultural anthropology, adaptationist approaches arose as a reaction to the lack of systematic theory in that area (Harpending, 1993), which is also common in many areas of HCI:

> Mainstream sociocultural anthropology has arrived at a situation resembling some nightmarish short story Borges might have written, where scientists are condemned by their unexamined assumptions to study the nature of mirrors only by cataloging and investigating everything that mirrors can reflect. It is an endless process that never makes progress . . . and whose enduring product is voluminous descriptions of particular phenomena. (Tooby & Cosmides, 1992, p. 42)

Adaptationist approaches grew in reaction to sociocultural researchers whose aim was no more than recording and taxonomizing observed behavior in an atheoretical manner.

7.3.2   Information-Foraging Theory

One strand of theory that addresses information-seeking behavior by individuals is information-foraging theory. Some essential ideas behind this theory include:

✦ *Exaptation of food-foraging mechanisms and strategies for information foraging.*[13] Natural selection favored organisms—including our human ancestors—that had better mechanisms for extracting energy from the environment and translating that energy into reproductive success. Organisms with better food-foraging strategies (for their particular environment) were favored by natural selection. Our ancestors evolved perceptual and cognitive mechanisms and strategies that were well adapted to the task of exploring the environment and finding and gathering food. Information-foraging theory assumes that modern-day information foragers use perceptual and cognitive mechanisms that carry over from the evolution of food-foraging adaptations.

✦ *Information scent.* In exploring and searching for information, users must use proximal cues—cues they can perceive in their local environment—to judge

---

[13] An *exaptation* is a feature that evolved as an adaptation to one kind of problem but then became an adaptive solution to another problem.

distal information sources and to navigate towards them. Underlined link text on Web pages or bibliographic citations in an online library catalog are examples of proximal cues that users use in this manner.

✦ *The economics of attention and the cost structure of information.* The late Nobel Laureate Herbert A. Simon observed that a wealth of information creates a poverty of attention and an increased need to efficiently allocate that attention. In an information-rich world, the real design problem to be solved is not so much how to collect more information, but, rather, to increase the amount of relevant information encountered by a user as a function of the amount of time that the user invests in interacting with the system. If a user can attend to more information per unit time, then the user's information processing capacity is increased, thereby amplifying cognition. The structure of the physical and virtual worlds determines the time costs, resource costs, and opportunity costs associated with exploring and finding information. People have limited attention and must deploy that attention in a way that is adaptive to the task of finding valuable information. Natural and artificial information systems evolve toward states that maximize the delivery of more valuable information per unit cost (Resnikoff, 1989). People prefer information-seeking strategies that yield more useful information per unit cost, and they tend to arrange their environments (physical or virtual) to optimize this rate of gain. People prefer, and consequently select, technology designs that improve returns on information foraging.

✦ *Relevance of optimal-foraging theory and models.* If information foraging is like food foraging, then models of *optimal foraging* developed in the study of animal behavior (Stephens & Krebs, 1986) and anthropology (Winterhalder & Smith, 1992) should be relevant. A typical optimal foraging model characterizes an agent's interaction with the environment as an optimal solution to the tradeoff of costs of finding, choosing, and handling food against the energetic benefit gained from that food. These models would look familiar to an engineer because they are basically an attempt to understand the design of an agent's behavior by assuming that it is well engineered (adapted) for the problems posed by the environment. Information-foraging models include optimality analyses of different information-seeking strategies and technologies as a way of understanding the design rationale for user strategies and interaction technologies.

It should be emphasized that the development of information-foraging theory has proceeded by establishing a narrow but solid base, and that base is just starting to extend to a broader scope of phenomena. The initial focus has been on understanding how people work on relatively well-defined information-seeking problems, such as "find all documents that discuss GOMS." Within this scope, detailed models have been developed that make many strong or simplifying assumptions. Consequently, the models are surely wrong on some details, and they surely will need to incorporate additional complexities in order to deal with a broader range of phenomena. For instance, later, in the discussion of the detailed example in Section 7.4, models are presented that make the simplifying assumption that users maximize the number of relevant documents of a task. This happened to be true of the tasks that were studied to test the model (i.e., the instructions asked study participants to maximize the number of relevant documents found); in real-world tasks, however, one imagines that the initial set of documents retrieved will be useful, but redundant documents encountered later would have no value. The initial model can be modified to deal with this complexity and others by developing appropriate analyses of the utility of information for the user's task. The scientific bet is that the simple, strong models will provide comprehensible basic insights that can provide a foundation for tackling more complex problems and productively generating further insights. Like all analogies, the one between information foraging and food foraging breaks down at some point. For instance, information can be easily copied and distributed, but food cannot. Search in food foraging is constrained by locomotion in three-dimensional Euclidean space, but the information forager can move through information spaces in much more complex ways. Information-foraging theory draws many ideas from food-foraging theory, but many of those ideas must be modified in the process.

7.3.3   Optimal-Foraging Theory

Optimal-foraging theory (Stephens & Krebs, 1986) seeks to explain adaptations of organism structure and behavior to the environmental problems and constraints of foraging for food. Consider a hypothetical predator, such as a bird of prey. Its fitness will depend on its reproductive success, which in turn will depend on how well it does in finding food that provides energy. The environment surrounding this bird will have a patchy structure, with different types of habitat (such as meadows, woodlots, ponds, etc.) containing different amounts and kinds of prey. For the bird of prey, different types of habitat and prey will yield different amounts of net energy if included in the diet. Furthermore, the different prey types will have different distributions over the environment. For the bird of prey, this means that the different habitats or prey will have different access or navigation costs. Different species of birds of prey might be compared on their ability to extract energy from the environment. Birds are better adapted if they have evolved strategies that better solve the problem of maximizing the amount of energy returned per amount of effort. Conceptually, the optimal forager is one that has the best solution to the problem of maximizing the rate of net energy returned per effort expended, given the constraints of the environment in which it lives.

Now consider an office worker or academic researcher facing the recurrent problems of finding valuable task-relevant information. The environment surrounding these foragers will also be patchy in structure and will contain different types of external media, such as books, manuscripts, or access to online documents with different kinds of interfaces and content designs. The different information sources will have different profitabilities, in terms of the amount of valuable information returned per unit cost in processing the source. Access (or navigation costs) to get the information will vary. The optimal information forager is one that best solves the problem of maximizing the rate of valuable information gained per unit cost, given the constraints of the task environment. In the information sciences, Sandstrom (1994) has suggested that optimal-foraging theory may successfully address the information-foraging behavior of academic researchers in a field.

Optimization models are a powerful tool for studying the design features of organisms and artifacts. Optimization models in general include the following three major components:

+ *Decision assumptions,* which specify the decision problem to be analyzed. Examples of such information-foraging decisions include how much time to spend processing a collection of information or whether or not to pursue a particular type of information content.

+ *Currency assumptions,* which identify how choices are to be evaluated. Information-foraging theory will assume information value as currency. Choice principles include maximization, minimization, and stability of that currency.

+ *Constraint assumptions,* which limit and define the relationships among decision and currency variables. These will include constraints that arise out of the task structure, interface technology, and the abilities and knowledge of a user population. Examples of constraints includes the rate at which a person can navigate through an information-access interface, or the value of results returned by bibliographic-search technology.

In general, all activities can be analyzed according to the value of the resource currency returned and costs incurred, which are of two types: (1) *resource costs* and (2) *opportunity costs* (Hames, 1992). Resource costs are the expenditures of time, calories, money, and so forth that are incurred by the chosen activity. Opportunity costs are the benefits that could be gained by engaging in other activities, but are forfeited by engaging in the chosen activity. The *value* of information (Repo, 1986) and the *relevance* of specific sources (Saracevic, 1975; Schamber, Eisenberg, & Nilan, 1990) are not intrinsic properties of content (e.g., documents, Web pages) but can be assessed only in relation to the embedding task environment.

The use of optimization models should not be taken as a hypothesis that human behavior is actually optimal—as if the individual had perfect information and infinite resource to make decisions. A more successful hypothesis about humans is that they exhibit *bounded rationality* or make choices based on *satisficing* (Simon, 1955). Satisficing can often be characterized as localized optimization (e.g., hill climbing) with resource bounds and imperfect information as included constraints.

7.4   DETAILED DESCRIPTION: SCATTER/GATHER

Scatter/Gather (Cutting, Karger, & Pedersen, 1993; Cutting, Karger, Pedersen, & Tukey, 1992) is an interaction technique for browsing large collections of documents that is based on automatically identifying clusters of related documents. Studies of the Scatter/Gather system (Pirolli, 1997; Pirolli & Card, 1995, 1999; Pirolli, Schank, Hearst, & Diehl, 1996) illustrate the adaptationist approach embodied in information-foraging theory. A detailed analysis of the cost structure of the information environment was performed and models from optimal foraging theory were borrowed to develop predictions about the optimal strategies for users to undertake in interacting with Scatter/Gather. This analysis was then used to develop a detailed mechanistic computer program to simulate individual users. This computer simulation was, in turn, used to evaluate potential design improvements (Pirolli, 1998).

It is not unusual for corporate and e-commerce Web sites to contain tens of thousands of documents. Portals such as Yahoo! are far larger. Web designers for large sites face the difficult task of developing site organizations and links that, on the one hand, get people to the information they seek and, on the other hand, provide some overview of all the content on the site. One technique is to develop a hierarchically organized categorical structure, much like that used in library catalog systems (this is the main approach used in Yahoo!). Users interacting with such structures follow links that seem to lead to progressively more refined topics that match their information goals (Spool et al., 1999). In general, a hierarchically organized search is extremely efficient, and a general model of search costs in such systems is presented in Section 7.5.1.[14] Web site designers face the daunting task of creating category structures that make sense to as many users as possible. One problem, however, is that even the same subject domains may be conceptualized in different ways by different types of people. In addition, the effort required to maintain a hierarchical directory structure by human means has a number of scaling problems. Increased person power is required as more documents are added to a Web site, as the rate of document change increases, or as the user base changes or becomes more diversified. Scatter/Gather (Cutting et al., 1992) addresses these issues by providing a reasonably fast automatic document-clustering technology that organizes the contents of a collection in a hierarchical manner that is continually modified in reaction to user interests.

Figure 7.1 presents a typical view of the Scatter/Gather interface. The document clusters are separate areas on the screen. Internally, the system works by precomputing a *cluster hierarchy,* recombining precomputed components as necessary. This technique allows the interactive reclustering of large document collections in reasonable amounts of time. The clustering in Scatter/Gather depends on a measure of interdocument similarity computed from vectors that reflect the frequency of words in each document (vanRijsbergen, 1979). The Scatter/Gather clustering method summarizes document clusters by *metadocuments* containing profiles of topical words and the most typical titles. These topical words and typical titles are also used to present users a summary of the documents in a cluster. Topical words are those that occur most frequently in a cluster, and typical titles are those with the highest similarity to a centroid of the cluster. Together, the topical words and typical titles form a *cluster digest.* Examples of these cluster digests are presented in each subwindow in Figure 7.1.

7.4.1 Task Analysis

The user may *gather* those clusters of interest by pointing and selecting buttons above each cluster in Figure 7.1. On command, the system will select the subset of documents in these clusters and then automatically *scatter* that subcollection into another set of clusters. With each successive iteration of scattering and gathering clusters, the clusters become smaller, eventually bottoming out at the level of individual documents. At any point, the user may select a set of clusters and request that the system display all the document titles in those clusters. These appear in a scrollable "titles" window. The user may select a title from this window

---

[14] An analysis of the physical card catalog system (Resnikoff, 1989) that used to be found in most libraries suggests that most were near-optimal in their arrangement.

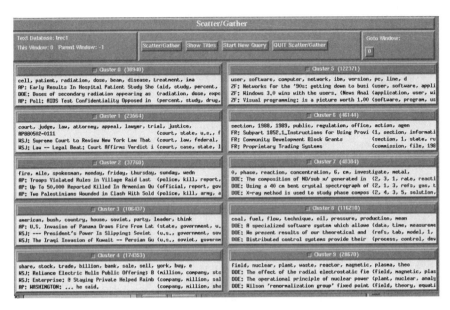

FIGURE

7.1

The Scatter/Gather interface. Each subwindow represents a cluster of related documents.

and request that the contents of the document be displayed for reading. Figure 7.2 presents a flow chart that captures the processing of a cluster window by a user.

Figure 7.3 presents an overview of the user-interaction process. For simplicity, the example in Figure 7.3 assumes five clusters per iteration rather than ten as depicted in Figure 7.1. Assume that a user is interested in papers written about robot planning. At the top level, the system presents the user with five cluster summaries (similar to those in Figure 7.1) that the user judges to be about "Law," "World news," "Artificial intelligence," "Computer science," and "Medicine." From these clusters, the user selects two clusters ("Artificial intelligence" and "Computer science") as being the ones likely to contain relevant papers, and he requests that the system scatter those documents into five new clusters. The user judges these new clusters to be about "Language," "Robots," "Expert systems," "Planning," and "Bayesian nets." The user then selects two clusters ("Robots" and "Planning") and requests that the system display all the titles in those clusters in the scrollable titles window. The user then scans that list of titles and picks out ones to read.

The models and simulations presented in the following sections address data collected in user studies with Scatter/Gather (Pirolli & Card, 1995; Pirolli et al.,

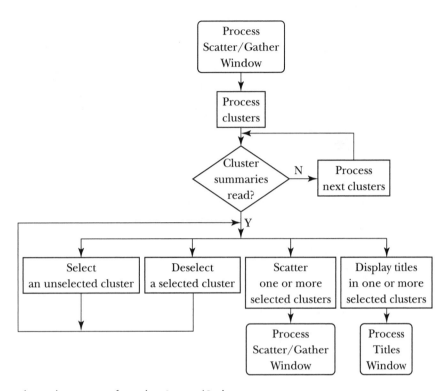

The task structure for using Scatter/Gather.

1996). Those studies used a document collection and a set of user tasks that had been compiled for the Text Retrieval Conference (TREC). These tasks typically asked users to find all of the documents relevant to some topic, such as new medical procedures for cancer. The tasks varied in how many relevant documents could be found.

7.4.2 Simulating Users

Pirolli (1997) developed a computer model to simulate the actions performed by individual Scatter/Gather users. The model was developed by integrating optimal-foraging models with the ACT-R architecture (Anderson & Lebiere, 2000), which is both a theory of psychology and a computer simulation environment. The resulting model was called ACT-IF (for ACT Information Forager).

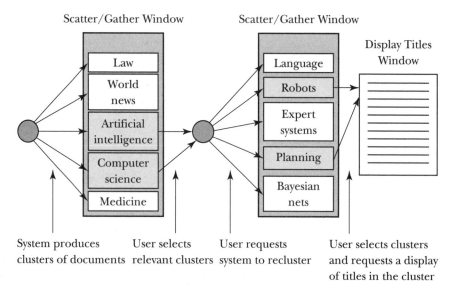

System produces   User selects   User requests   User selects clusters
clusters of documents   relevant clusters   system to recluster and requests a display
                                                                  of titles in the cluster

FIGURE   A schematic view of using Scatter/Gather. The user repeatedly selects (gathers)
         clusters from the Scatter/Gather Window and requests that the system recluster
7.3   (scatter) the selected clusters until the user decides to display and scan titles
         from the selected clusters.

ACT-R consists of a *production memory* and a *declarative memory*. The declarative memory basically models the information being attended to and information that has been recalled from long-term declarative memory. In simulating Scatter/Gather, the declarative information mostly concerns the user's goal and the information that is presented on the Scatter/Gather screen. The production memory contains *production rules*. In the case of Scatter/Gather, the productions represent the elements of task knowledge used by the user—that is, the elements of knowledge that enable users to perform the task specified in Figure 7.2.

For instance, the following production rules represent three elements of task knowledge for working with Scatter/Gather:

    P1:   IF   the goal is to process a Scatter/Gather Window
           &   there is a task query
           &   there is an unselected cluster
          THEN select that cluster

    P2:   IF   the goal is to process a Scatter/Gather Window
           &   there is a task query

>   **&**   some clusters have been selected
> **THEN**   select the Display Titles Window button
>
> **P3:**   **IF**   the goal is to process a Scatter/Gather Window
>   **&**   there is a task query
>   **&**   some clusters have been selected
> **THEN**   select the Scatter/Gather button

Each production rule has the form IF *condition* THEN *action*. The conditions of the rules are patterns that describe the cognitive state of the user. When these patterns match the cognitive state of the user, their actions may be applied to change the cognitive state and perform motor actions. Rule P1 matches when the user perceives an unselected cluster and specifies that the cluster be selected. P2 matches when the user perceives that several clusters have been selected and specifies that the user request that the system display the titles of the documents in the selected clusters. Rule P3 matches when the user perceives that several clusters have been selected and specifies that the user request that the system gather the clusters and rescatter them. In all, Pirolli (1997) represented the Scatter/Gather task using 15 production rules like P1, P2, and P3.

ACT-R operates on a *match-execute cycle*. During the match phase, the condition part of the production-rule patterns are matched against information in working memory—that is, the rules are matched against the current cognitive state of the user. Typically, more than one rule may match the cognitive state of the user. For instance, all three of the production rules listed above may match if there are selected and unselected clusters on a Scatter/Gather Window. In ACT-IF, those production rules that match are ranked by information-foraging evaluations (i.e., evaluations of the gain in valuable information that is expected by selecting a particular rule). These information-foraging evaluations assess the economics of different actions in the Scatter/Gather interface. The production rule with the highest information-foraging evaluation is selected, and then the selected rule action pattern is executed. The information-foraging evaluations are based on perceptions of information costs and value that have come to be called *information scent*.

7.4.3   Information Scent

The text in the Scatter/Gather cluster digests is much like the text used to label links on the Web. These text cues provide information scent. Users estimate the relevance of distal sources of information based on the small snippets of text available to them on their screen displays. An effective model of users' judgments of information scent is a computational model based on *spreading activation* mechanisms used in the study of human memory (Anderson, 1993; Anderson & Pirolli, 1984). Activation may be interpreted metaphorically as a kind of mental energy that drives cognitive processing. Cognitive structures, such as concepts, are called *chunks*. Activation spreads from a set of chunks that are the current focus of attention through *associations* among chunks in memory. Generally, activation-based theories of memory predict that more activated knowledge structures will receive more favorable processing. Spreading activation is the name of the process that computes activation values over a set of chunks. The spread of activation from one cognitive structure to another is determined by weighting values on the associations among chunks. These weights determine the rate of activation flow among chunks (analogous to pipes or wires with specific flow capacities). The associations and weights are built up from experience.

A specific version of spreading activation (Anderson & Lebiere, 2000) uses mechanisms based on the analysis of the requirements of an optimal memory system discussed in Section 7.3.1, on adaptationist approaches (Anderson, 1990; Anderson & Milson, 1989). This is the version of spreading activation used to develop a model of information scent. The basic idea is that a user's information goal activates a set of chunks in a user's memory, and text on the display screen activates another set of chunks. Activation spreads from these chunks to related chunks in a *spreading activation network*. The amount of activation accumulating on the goal chunks and display chunks is an indicator of their mutual relevance.

As will be discussed below, spreading activation networks can be computed *a priori* from online text collections and can be used to represent human semantic memory. Figure 7.4 presents a scenario for a spreading activation analysis. Suppose a user is looking for "information on new medical treatments and procedures for cancer" using Scatter/Gather. The representation of this goal in declarative memory is depicted by the small set of concepts linked to the concept "Information need" in Figure 7.4 (the nodes labeled "new, medical, treatments, procedures, cancer"). These nodes represent the main meaningful concepts making up the users' goal. In Figure 7.4, the user is looking at a browser that has retrieved a set of documents. One of the cluster-digest summaries is the text "cell, patient, dose, beam, cancer." The representation of this part of the browser display is depicted by the network of nodes linked to "Screen text" in Figure 7.4. The figure also shows that there are links between the goal concepts and the text-summary concepts. These are associations between words that come from past experience. The associations reflect the fact that these words co-occur in the

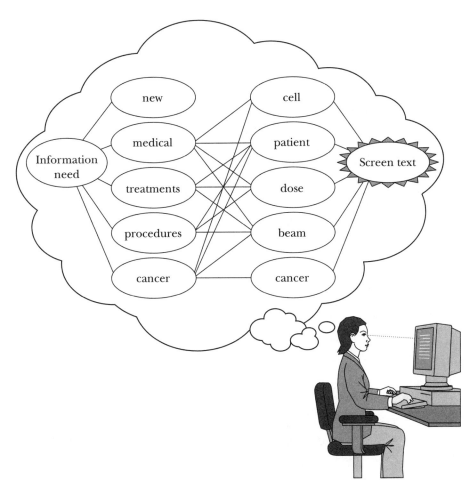

FIGURE   Information scent.

7.4

users' linguistic environment. For instance, the words "medical" and "patient" co-occur quite frequently, and they would have a high weighting of inter-association. Spreading activation would flow from the goal, which is the focus of attention, through the interword associations, to words in the text summary. The stronger the associations (higher weights or strengths that reflect higher rates of co-occurrence) the greater the amount of activation flow. If the goal and browser text are strongly associated, then we expect people to judge them as being highly relevant to one another. At least implicitly, this is what the interface designers of browsers are trying to do when they select small text snippets to communicate the content of large documents to users. They are trying to pick words that people will judge as relevant to their queries. Spreading activation may be used to predict these memory-based judgments of reminding and relevance that are key components of surfing the Web.

Some Web-usability guidelines (User Interface Engineering, 1999) center on the design of effective links that provide "good" information scent that draw users to the information they seek. It would be useful to have automated methods that predict the effectiveness of the information scent of links with respect to user goals. Pirolli and Card (1999) showed how an information-scent model could make accurate predictions of user judgments of information scent (Figure 7.5), and they then also showed how the information scent provided by the Scatter/Gather interface accurately reflected the amount of relevant information in clusters described by the text in cluster digests. Together, these analyses suggest that the text on the cluster digests of the Scatter/Gather browser accurately communicated the location of relevant information. Information-scent models might provide automated methods for evaluating the content design of links on Web pages.

7.4.4   Information-Foraging Evaluations

The information-scent model also provides the basis for understanding how users assess the economics of different actions available in Scatter/Gather. Information-foraging theory assumes that users' choices are directed by cost-benefit analyses: the costs (usually in terms of time) of choosing a particular course of action weighed against the value to be gained by that action. In the case of Scatter/Gather, using the TREC tasks, the value was the number of relevant documents identified by a user. The basic costs of different user and system actions could be determined, in part, by using estimates from the literature (Olson & Olson, 1990), or by measuring system or user times on just the component actions themselves. Figure 7.6 presents a schematic of the action choices that are captured by productions P1, P2, and P3. The square objects represent states of Scatter/Gather interaction (interactions with Scatter/Gather windows are at the top and those with Display Titles windows are at the bottom), and the arrows represent transitions among interaction states that result from the execution of a production rule. For current purposes, let us represent the information-foraging evaluation of productions by the notation *Eval*[*P1: choose cluster*], which should be taken to mean, the evaluation of production P1 that executes

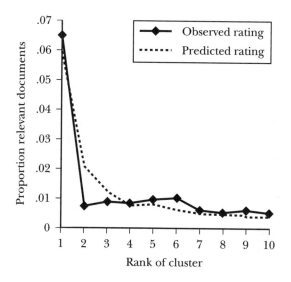

FIGURE

7.5

Ratings of cluster summaries predicted by information scent plotted against the observed ratings produced by users.

the action of choosing a cluster. The following sections describe the evaluations for Productions P1, P2, and P3.[15]

Cluster Selection

The analysis of cluster selection can be developed by analogy to models of optimal-diet selection in optimal-foraging theory (Stephens & Krebs, 1986). The Scatter/Gather display (Figure 7.1) presents users with the number of documents in each cluster, and this can be used by users to estimate the costs of finding relevant documents in each cluster. Assume that the user decided to go through every document title in a cluster and then saved the relevant documents for later reading.[16] There would some cost associated with evaluating every document, and some additional cost of saving the relevant documents. So the profitability for a cluster could be characterized by the following,

---

[15] In Pirolli and Card (1999), a notation was used that was more consistent with the optimal-foraging literature: $\pi = Eval[P1: choose\ cluster]$, $R_{SG} = Eval[P2: rescatter]$, and $R_D = Eval[P3: display\ titles]$.

[16] This could be achieved by displaying the cluster, scanning and scrolling the displayed list, and cut-and-pasting the relevant titles to a file.

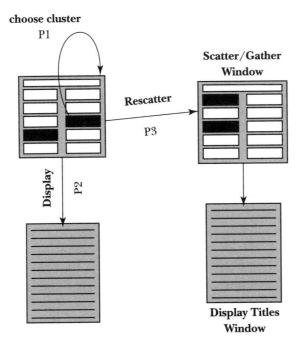

choose cluster
P1

Scatter/Gather
Window

Rescatter

P3

Display   P2

Display Titles
Window

FIGURE

7.6
Basic moves and evaluation parameters for the Scatter/Gather task.

S = proportion of relevant documents in a cluster according to information scent,

N = total number of documents in a cluster (from the Scatter/Gather display),

V = the number of valuable (relevant) documents in a cluster (judged by information scent)

   = $N \times S$

C_1 = the time cost of processing each document,

C_2 = the time cost of processing a relevant document,

$Eval[P1: choose\ cluster]$ = profitability of a cluster in terms of number of valuable documents per unit time,

   = $V/[(N \times C_1) + (V \times C_2)]$

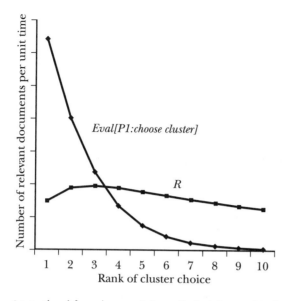

FIGURE

7.7

An optimal foraging model applied to Scatter/Gather. Clusters are ranked by their profitability in this graph. *R* is the rate of gain for the collection of clusters of rank 1 through *i*. Note that these curves vary for every Scatter/Gather Window.

Figure 7.7 shows a typical distribution of profitability values, *Eval[P1: choose clusters]*, over clusters. Suppose the user ranked the clusters by their profitability (which is determined by the proportion of relevant documents they contain), and then selected them in rank order up to some threshold (which is the optimal strategy). Adding more clusters to the "information diet" affects the overall expected rate of gain, R = relevant documents/time, as shown in Figure 7.7. In ACT-IF, R corresponds to the maximum value of the evaluations of P2 or P3,

$$R = \mathrm{MAXIMUM}\,(Eval[P2\text{:}display\ titles],\ Eval[P3\text{: }rescatter]).$$

The evaluations of P2 and P3 are described in more detail below. In other words, ACT-IF will continue to choose clusters (using production P1) until either P2 or P3 has a higher evaluation. At that point, the expected rate of return (R) is maximized. Choosing more clusters will diminish the rate of gain of valuable documents per unit time.

Adding the topmost-ranked clusters tends to improve R because they contain proportionally more relevant documents. Adding the bottommost-ranked clusters tends to decrease R because they contain proportionally more irrelevant documents, which are a time cost for users. The optimal set of clusters to select is the one that produces the highest value of R. When the curves for *Eval*[*P1: choose clusters*] and R are drawn as in Figure 7.7, this optimal point occurs just to the left of the point at which the curves cross. Empirical studies (Pirolli & Card, 1999) indicate that users select clusters in accordance with this model. Users select an optimal-information diet from each Scatter/Gather screen.

Scanning Displayed Titles

Eval[*P2: display titles*] is the rate of gaining relevant documents from selected clusters. At some point, the user selects a set of clusters, displays the titles, and scans them for relevant documents. The document titles are unordered in the scrollable display window. Consequently, the total number of relevant documents encountered as a function of user scan time will be linear. The rate of these encounters will depend on the proportion of relevant documents in the clusters that were selected to be displayed. In general, the proportion of relevant documents in clusters presented to users depends on how many times the user has gathered and rescattered clusters. As the user invests more time in gathering and scattering clusters before displaying titles, the proportion of relevant documents increases in the available clusters, and the rate at which the user will encounter relevant documents when document titles are displayed will also increase. From the proportion of relevant documents in selected clusters, one can determine the rate at which relevant documents will be encountered by a user who chooses to display the titles in those clusters.

Scattering and Gathering Clusters vs. Scanning Displayed Titles

If an ideal user chooses to repeatedly scatter and gather clusters in an optimal fashion, then the total number of documents in the selected clusters will decrease, but the number of relevant documents will decrease at a slower rate. The proportion of relevant documents under consideration will improve as a function of user time. This will improve the rate at which users gather relevant documents once they decide to display clusters. From this analysis, one can determine *Eval*[*P3: rescatter*], which is the rate of gain of relevant documents that would be produced by one more round of gathering and scattering clusters. Figure 7.8 shows a plot of *Eval*[*P2: display titles*] and *Eval*[*P3: rescatter*] over time for an

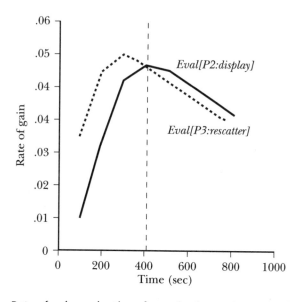

FIGURE

7.8
Rate of gain evaluations for gathering and rescattering clusters *(Eval[P3: rescatter)* vs. displaying documents *(Eval[P2: display])*, as a function of task time.

optimal user interacting with Scatter/Gather. Early in the task, it is optimal to continue scattering and gathering clusters, but there comes a point at which it is optimal to display the titles.

7.4.5   Simulating Users and Evaluating Alternative Scatter/Gather Designs

An engineering model derived from the ACT-IF model of Scatter/Gather users was used to evaluate hypothetical changes to the Scatter/Gather system. That is, rather than perform costly testing of real users, the designs were tested against simulated users. Figure 7.9 shows predictions for two potential design improvements: an increased speed of interaction (by improving the speed of gathering and rescattering clusters) and an improved clustering that puts more relevant documents into fewer clusters. To the question "which improvement is better," the answer is "it depends on the task." If the user has lots of time (soft deadline) then improved clustering is better, but if the user has little time (hard deadline)

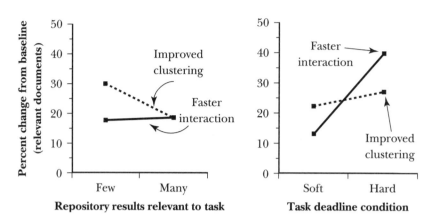

FIGURE

7.9

Predicted tradeoffs of two potential design improvements to Scatter/Gather.

then faster interaction is better. These kinds of "it depends" tradeoffs are rampant in interface design, but user simulations can be more precise about their nature.

7.5   CASE STUDY: THE WORLD WIDE WEB

Users of the Web work in a much richer environment than the Scatter/Gather system, and they often perform far more complicated tasks than simply finding relevant documents. Ongoing research aimed at extending information-foraging theory to understanding Web users and Web designs provides a useful framework that provides much-needed coherence and insight. For instance, the basic notions that users follow information scent and that they optimize the economics of their information seeking helps in understanding behavior at the level of individuals as well as large-scale aggregates of users (such as the behavior of all the visitors to a Web site). These notions also lead to usability guidelines, new user interfaces, and technologies for performing automated analyses of Web site designs.

7.5.1   Information Scent as a Major Determinant of Web User Behavior

Effects at the Level of Individual Users

As was the case with Scatter/Gather, the structure of Web tasks depends in part on the organization of content and the kinds of operations that the user can perform in browsing and searching. Figure 7.6 provided a schematic representation of the Scatter/Gather task structure by identifying common states of interaction and common moves among states. Figure 7.6 is an informal example of a *state-space diagram,* which is a common device used in the cognitive sciences for visualizing problem-solving activity and other forms of complex cognitive activity. A similar state-space representation has been developed for Web interaction. Figure 7.10 and Plate 5 of the color insert present two Web Behavior Graphs (WBGs) depicting the behavior of a user performing two Web tasks: (a) finding a specific movie poster (top of Figure 7.10) or (b) finding a scheduled performance date for a specific comedy troupe (bottom of Figure 7.10).[17] A WBG is a kind of state-space diagram and, more specifically, it is based on *Problem Behavior Graphs,* which can be found in Newell and Simon's (1972) classic investigation of human problem solving. Each box in the WBG represents a state of the user and system. Each arrow depicts a move from one state to a new state. For instance, the sequence S2 → S3 in Figure 7.10 represents that a user visited a particular Web page (S2) and clicked on a link and then visited a second Web page (S3). Double vertical arrows indicate the return to a previous state, augmented by the user's experience of having explored the consequences of some possible moves. Time in the diagram proceeds left to right and top to bottom. Moves within the same Web site are surrounded by the same color in the WBG. This reveals moves within and across Web sites.

Information scent has a significant impact on Web users. The links selected by users tend to be the ones that are scored as having the highest information scent. Poor information scent causes users to flounder because they tend to select links that lead them to useless parts of the Web. This can be seen by inspecting Figure 7.10. The WBG at the top of the figure is much bushier than the WBG at the bottom, involving many more returns to pages previously visited. This

---

[17] The WBGs presented in this chapter are simplified versions of those presented in published reports (Card et al., 2001).

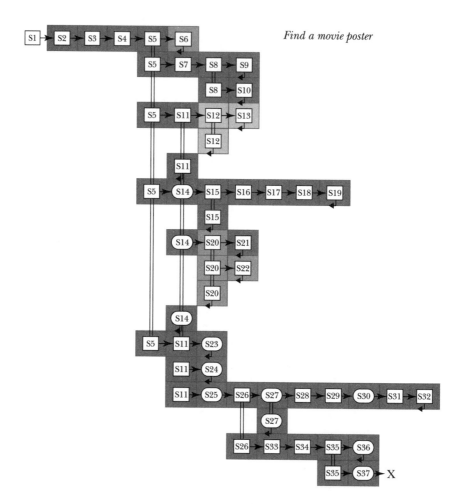

Find a movie poster

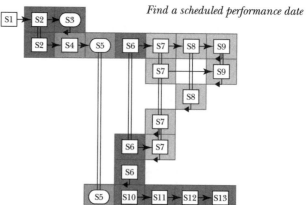

Find a scheduled performance date

FIGURE

7.10

Web Behavior Graphs for a user on two tasks. Each box represents a state of the user-system interaction. Each arrow represents a state change (move). Interaction proceeds left to right, top to bottom. Each move to the right is a move to a new state. Moves down and to the right represent a return to a previous state. Background colors surround interactions with the same Web site. (See Plate 5 of the color insert for a color version of this figure.)

bushiness, or high *branching factor,* in the top WBG is an indication that the user had difficulty finding information scent that led to useful information. Often, users appear to switch from one Web site to another, or they switch from browsing to searching, when the information scent gets low. The propensity to switch to another information patch (e.g., another site or a search engine) when the information scent becomes low is consistent with optimal-foraging theory (McNamara, 1982).

Effects at the Aggregate Level

At the individual level, highly informative and accurate information draws users directly to their goal because they make accurate decisions at every state. The following analysis shows that the accuracy of these scent-based decisions has a profound overall qualitative impact on navigating through information structures like the Web. Concretely, designers can use a number of methods to make link descriptors have more accurate information scent. For instance, including more summary words (up to about 20) seems to improve information scent (User Interface Engineering, 1999). Generally (but not for all tasks), text appears to be superior to images (thumbnails). A combination of text and words called *enhanced thumbnails* (Woodruff, Rosenholtz, Morrison, Faulring, & Pirolli, 2002) combines the search benefits of image thumbnail summaries and text summaries for links (Figure 7.11 and Plate 6 of the color insert).

How important is it to ensure that users get accurate information scent about links and make accurate decisions about navigation? In a study of text, image thumbnails, and enhanced thumbnails as link summaries, Woodruff et al. (2002) calculated the *false-alarm rates* for the different link summaries. These false-alarm rates were the probabilities that a user would incorrectly follow a link—that is, the user thought that the link would lead to relevant information but it did not. These false-alarm rates were in the range of .01 to .15. Although the absolute sizes of these false-alarm rates seem small, such variations can have a dramatic impact. This can be illustrated by considering an idealized case of searching for information by surfing along links in a Web site.[18] Assume that the imaginary Web site is arranged as a tree structure with an average branching factor b. Assume that a user starts at the root page and is seeking a target page that is depth d from the root. If the false-alarm rate, f, is perfect, $f = 0$, then the user will visit d pages. This cost grows linearly with d, the distance of the target from the root. If the false-alarm rate is maximum, $f = 1$, then the user will visit half the

---

[18] The following analysis is based on a method for the analysis of heuristic search costs developed by Huberman and Hogg (1987).

 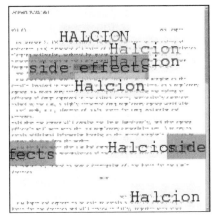

FIGURE

7.11

Enhanced thumbnails. (See Plate 6 of the color insert for a color version of this figure.)

pages in the Web site, on average. This cost grows exponentially with d, since the number of pages grows exponentially with depth.

Figure 7.12 shows the effects of perturbations in false-alarm rates more concretely. The figure displays search-cost functions for a hypothetical Web site with branching factor $b = 10$. The curves represent cost functions for links with false-alarm rates of $f = .100, .125,$ and $.150$. One can see that the search-cost regime changes dramatically as f becomes greater than $.100$. Indeed, for a branching factor of $b = 10$, there is a change from a linear search cost to exponential search cost at the critical value of $f = .100$. Small improvements in the false-alarm rates

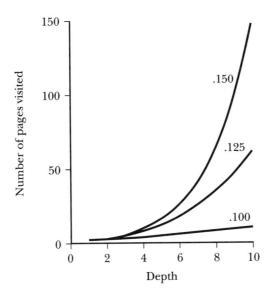

FIGURE

7.12
Changes in the search-cost regimes with changes in information scent. Search cost is in terms of number of Web pages visited in a hypothetical Web site that is 10 levels deep with 10 branches per level. Quantities labeling the curves indicate the probability of a false alarm.

associated with individual links can have dramatic qualitative effects on surfing large hypertext collections. In other words, there is a qualitative shift in the cost structure of navigation costs due to changes in the accuracy of information scent. Web usability experts (User Interface Engineering, 1999) have good reason to recommend that designers focus on designing Web sites with good information scent.

One business model that emerged for Web site producers was to sell advertising and to try to keep users on their sites for as long as possible. Sites that did this effectively were called *sticky*. As discussed earlier, information scent (or the lack of it) appears to determine when users leave a site. A model has been developed (Huberman, Pirolli, Pitkow, & Lukose, 1998) that predicts the distribution of moves (i.e., page visits) that users will make at a Web site. The underlying model is a kind of *random walk model* that has applications ranging from the study of Brownian motion in physics to real options in financial economics. Brownian motion refers to the trajectories made by particles such as pollen suspended in water. To model these trajectories, it is useful to consider each particle as making a random walk in space—each successive step will be a random move in some direction, but the next location must be somewhere near the previous location. Sometimes this model is elaborated to include a notion that there is drift that biases the random moves in some direction. A question (first analyzed by Albert Einstein) is how long it takes a particle to cross an imaginary threshold. The probability distribution of the time it takes particles to cross a threshold (called the *first passage* time) is called an *Inverse Gaussian* distribution. The analogy in the case of the Web is that users correspond to particles moving in a state space of Web pages. Pages are characterized by their information scent (instead of spatial locations), and the user makes moves that drift towards higher scent pages but with some degree of uncertainty (randomness). It is assumed that pages that are linked together tend to be similar in information scent (or at least more similar than pages separated by many links). Users move through this state space until they hit a threshold—for instance, they encounter a page that has high relevance or the information scent gets too low and they switch to another site. If this random walk model characterizes Web users, then we should expect to see an Inverse Gaussian distribution in the time users spend at a Web site (before they decide they have found something or they need to stop and go do something else).

This Inverse Gaussian distribution is shown in Figure 7.13 where it has been fit to usage data from a Web site at Georgia Tech in 1994. The mean and variance of this distribution—that is, the mean number of moves made at a Web site and their variance—is determined by the users' information scent thresholds as well as statistical properties that describe the relationship between the value of the currently visited page and the expected value of a linked page. The statistical properties of the variation of information scent over a Web site determines the particular Inverse Gaussian distribution of moves for a Web site. This is a rather precise way to say that information scent determines the stickiness of a site.

7.5.2   Simulated Users and Usability Evaluation

Chi, Pirolli, Chen, and Pitkow (2001) recently developed techniques aimed at (a) predicting usage patterns at Web sites as well as (b) inferring user goals from existing logs of user behavior. Although these simulations are not as detailed as the ACT-IF model of Scatter/Gather, they can become the basis for engineering tools for Web site designers. The Web usage simulation uses a Web crawler to analyze the content and linkage structure of a Web site. For a given user need (represented by a set of query words), the system computes the link scent for every link on every page. From this, the simulation calculates the probability that a user will go down each link emanating from a page. The simulation proceeds by

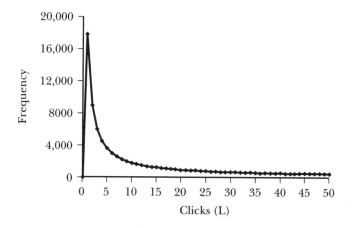

FIGURE

7.13
A fit of the Inverse Gaussian distribution (solid line) to the frequency of users who click L times at the Georgia Tech Web site (data from 1994).

flowing simulated users through the Web site with the flow among pages determined by information scent.

Chi and colleagues also developed a method for inferring the information goal of a user based on the user's traversal path through a Web site. The technique is based on the observation that users communicate a great deal of information about their goals with every link choice they make. At any point in a user's traversal through the Web site, that user has expressed interest in certain links rather than others. The technique developed by Chi and colleagues takes the documents visited by a user and infers a set of keywords that best represent the path taken by the user. Studies by Chi and colleagues indicated that these keywords were effective in communicating the path taken by the user.

A similar system called Comprehension-based Linked Model of Deliberate Search (CoLiDeS) (Blackmon, Polson, Kitajima, & Lewis, 2002) has been developed to evaluate Web sites. CoLiDeS uses a model of information scent based on LSA (Landauer & Dumais, 1997), rather than spreading activation, and achieved success in predicting unfamiliar and confusable links. CoLiDeS is based on an earlier modeling system called Linked Model of Comprehension-based Action Planning and Instruction (LICAI) (Kitajima & Polson, 1997) that addressed how users learn by exploring computer applications by following the labels on interface items such as menus. Such label following is a common strategy in performing actions in computer applications, mobile devices, and control panels. At each choice point in a menu or submenu, the user must assess the information scent of the labels with respect to their goal. Consequently, user models that incorporate predictions about information scent should be applicable not only to the Web, but also to mobile devices and consumer products with menu-driven control panels.

7.6   CURRENT STATUS

This chapter has necessarily focused very narrowly on information-foraging theory as it relates to understanding individual behavior. There is also an emerging field of work that examines the complex emergent phenomena that arise from many agents interacting on the Web. This field of *Internet ecology* uses complex computational models to understand how local actions by individuals are related to complex global phenomena, both social and computational in nature. The relationship between the surfing of individuals and the Inverse Gaussian distribution of number of clicks at a site was one example of this kind of research. This area of research frequently draws upon nonlinear dynamics and statistical physics (recall the application of models of Brownian motion to predict the distribution in Figure 7.13). Some research in this field includes:

+ Internet congestion (Huberman & Lukose, 1997). The Internet is a public good. For the most part, users are not charged for its use. Users may rationally decide to consume bandwidth in a greedy manner while thinking that their behavior will have little effect on the Internet as a whole. This leads to a degradation of Internet performance. A specific model of this "social dilemma" leads to accurate predictions of the statistics of short-lived "spikes" of Internet congestion.

+ The power law distribution of users over sites (Adamic & Huberman, 2000). The number of visits received by Web sites (whether within a particular category, or across all) follows a power law. This is also a characteristic of "winner-take-all" markets. Dynamical models of Web site popularity predict this distribution.

The Internet and the Web provide a fascinating laboratory for detailed quantitative measurements of large-scale ecological phenomena. Now that this laboratory is available, we should expect to see more theories that relate individual behavior to large-scale phenomena.

One novel aspect of information-foraging theory is that it begins to deal with the interaction of the user with information content, rather than just application interfaces. There has been very little research on understanding how people interact with *rich content*—that is, content other than text. Although there has been considerable research in psychology and artificial intelligence on image understanding (for instance, line detection, object recognition), there has been no detailed psychological research on how people browse or navigate through hypermedia that includes images, video, animation, and so forth. There is also a gap in our understanding of how users control their visual browsing of individual displays of content. There has been very little in the way of detailed research on how people visually scan and search for information on Web pages, and such theories could be of great use to designers interested in visual layout.

The studies that have been discussed in this chapter mainly focused on relatively well-defined information-seeking tasks. Most tasks on the Web include information seeking, but are typically broader or more ill defined in nature. They include tasks such as trying to make sense of medical publications about a disease affecting a loved one, choosing a career, finding a good graduate school, and so on. These ill-structured problems dominate our everyday life (Reitman, 1965; Simon, 1973), and they are the ones that require the user to seek and understand as much information as feasible. Information-foraging theory and, more broadly, HCI, will increasingly need to address these complex ill-structured problems and how they might be aided by enhancements in information technology.

AUTHOR NOTES

The writing of this chapter was supported, in part, by Office of Naval Research Contract No. N00014–96–0097. I would like to thank Thomas Green, Julie Bauer Morrison, Mark Perry, and Pamela Schraedley for their reviews. I am also indebted to the students of Virginia Tech's CS 5724 class: Ndiwalana Ali, Stephen Foret, Christian Schaupp, and Akshay Sivananda, who provided thoughtful reviews.

8 Distributed Cognition

Mark Perry   Brunel University, London, England

8.1   MOTIVATION

If you were to think of a typical work situation, it would be hard to imagine some-one working without the most basic forms of interaction with other people. More often than not, we think of busy offices full of people working with one an-other, work floors where teams of employees manufacture and assemble parts, or control rooms where managers coordinate processes. It is therefore perhaps sur-prising that much of the basic research into human-computer interaction (HCI) has not attempted to provide techniques to understand and help design for these situations, preferring to study and provide support for solitary and decon-textualized activities.

One of the reasons for this is that HCI theoreticians and modelers have not had a "way into" the problem—cognitive theory tells us little about social behav-ior, while the social sciences' understandings and explanations of social action are hard to apply directly to design. Yet this is an important area; many team-based safety-critical systems, such as air-traffic control, are being computerized, and this needs to be done with a good understanding of interteam coordination among pilot, copilot, flight engineer, and ground officers. Beyond these areas, the increasing networking capabilities of computers through the Internet has meant that team work can be performed remotely—so that the established social cues that previously moderated team interactions are disrupted. In all of these instances, designers need to have a better understanding of work that goes be-yond the individual, to look at how groups coordinate their behaviors with one another, collaborate, and perform problem-solving tasks.

Similarly, the ways that people adapt and make use of tools in their work to support their cognitive abilities is poorly understood. This is because the theoret-ical approaches and experimental methods that have been applied to the area are not, in general, able to investigate these kinds of behavior. Again, this is a problem for computer-systems designers because so much of human intellectual behavior is mediated through artefacts (i.e., tools) that are artfully appropriated in support of their user's activities. In order to support activities as they occur in the real world, as opposed to laboratory settings, HCI designers need to have a theoretical perspective on this so as to give them a better understanding of the environment in which activities take place.

A number of approaches have been developed or extended to deal with these limitations in HCI and systems design, some of which are discussed in this book. One of these approaches—distributed cognition—grew out of a need to understand how information processing and problem solving could be understood as being performed across units of analysis larger than the individual, to incorporate tool use and the involvement of other people. Rather than developing an entirely new approach to conceptualizing human activity, as many of the other theoretical approaches discussed in the other chapters have, distributed cognition extends the traditional notion of cognition using a similar theoretical framework and ontological basis for describing human activity in these larger units of study. This may well be part of its appeal—HCI researchers trained in cognitive science do not have to abandon their theoretical knowledge and conceptual apparatus to understand distributed cognition.

The most developed framework of distributed cognition uses the same computational basis to understand human behavior as cognitive psychology and applies the same notions of information representations and representational transformations. Where it differs from standard cognitive science is in its theoretical stance that cognition is not just in the head, but in the world (Norman, 1993) and in the methods that it applies in order to examine cognition "in the wild."

8.1.1   Designing Collaborative Technologies

Moving the focus of analysis away from an individual user's desktop, activity in the real world occurs within a context and often in a highly complex social and technological environment. An example of this, which the cognitive approaches have failed to account for, is this notion of the "user": with one person using a computer, this relationship is relatively simple. Within an organizational context, is the user the person who performs the task, or the person to whom the completed task is passed on? In a multiuser environment, such as a video-conferencing or an email system, are they the conglomerate of all of the users, or should the analyst consider the individual perspectives of all of the participants?

A grain of analysis based on the individual cannot easily be adapted to deal with the complexities of what have come to be called computer supported cooperative work (CSCW) systems, and other approaches that can deal with these issues have moved to center stage.

CSCW moves the study of HCI from a focus on the individual toward that of multiple, codependent users, and on the social organization of their work. It involves the analysis and development of tools and technologies to support the interactions of these co-workers. This necessitates a close examination of work and the context that such work is performed within. The role of context in facilitating human activity has become a central feature of research within CSCW, as are the development of appropriate methods for workplace analysis.

Several theoretical approaches, discussed in other chapters in this book, have been developed to analyze activities involving such multitool, multiparticipant behavior. However, these approaches do not attempt to explicate the nature of a fundamental group-based activity—*problem solving*—and focus their attention on the nature of communication and coordination, without bridging the gap between this and what the group are trying to achieve. Despite being outside the "mind" of a single individual, this is still essentially a *cognitive* problem. It is a cognitive problem because the system exhibits "intelligent," purposeful behaviors in problem solving and information processing, but differs in that these are mediated through the expression of features arising through nonneurological mechanisms. If we are to understand that nature of this collaborative cognitive activity, we require an analytical method that makes the mechanisms underlying this problem solving explicit. Understanding the information-processing requirements and processes is vital in pinpointing where the application of collaboration technology could both benefit work and be implemented without disrupting existing practices.

From a theoretical perspective, problem solving involves an intelligent system (of some kind) traversing a "problem space," by moving through various transitory states toward a goal. These problem states are representational in nature, and any analysis must therefore focus on these states and the transformations between them. Collaborative problem solving must involve a unit greater than the individual, who becomes a component of the group's problem-solving resources. To study a smaller unit of work than the group will miss many important features of the work where problem solving is distributed over a network of individuals cooperating with one another to achieve a solution. While the processing of the information available to the group is analogous to an individual's cognitive capabilities, the architecture of this system differs because of the different representational properties of the resources available.

8.1.2   Distributed Cognition in Context

Analysis of systems using distributed cognition permits the inclusion of all of the significant features in the environment that contribute toward the accomplishment of tasks. This is something that the individual disciplines that examine the nature of human action—psychology, sociology and anthropology—fail to do, at least in their conventional manifestations. Moreover, none of these component disciplines are applied sciences, calling into question their immediate value to systems design.

The form of distributed cognition advanced by Hutchins (DCog)[1] has adapted the framework of individual cognition to explain how cognitive resources are organized *within a context,* drawing on actors and other features in the environment to perform problem solving. Hutchins calls this "socially distributed cognition" (1995a). Socially distributed cognition describes group activity in the way that individual cognition has traditionally been described—computation realized through the creation, transformation, and propagation of representational states (Hutchins, 1995a; Simon, 1981). Central to this is the idea of work being distributed over a range of media and over a number of people. It is concerned with representational states and the informational flows around the media carrying these representations. The DCog framework allows researchers to consider all of the factors relevant to the task, bringing together the people, the problem, and the tools used into a single unit of analysis. This makes it a suitable candidate for developing an understanding of how representations act as intermediaries in the dynamically evolving and collaborative[2] processes of work activities. It is therefore an ideal method to use to discover the artifactual, social, and cultural dimensions of work, relating these back to systems development and HCI.

The goal of analysis within DCog is to describe how distributed units are *coordinated* by analyzing the interactions between individuals, the representational media used, and the environment within which the activity takes place. Analyses

---

[1]   This form is differentiated as "DCog" to distinguish it from other disciplines that have appropriated the term, from areas as diverse as ethnomethodology and conversation analysis, social psychology, and activity theory. All of these interpret and use the term *distributed cognition* very differently. What distinguishes DCog from these is its explicitly cognitive stance on symbolic manipulation.

[2]   Strictly speaking, the theoretical development of DCog has grown not from a need to understand collaboration, but from a "correction" to the failures of cognitive science. The term *collaboration,* as it is used in CSCW, is not found in the work of many DCog theorists. However, this is what it describes, even if not using the same vocabulary.

with a distributed cognitive framework have been used to examine the cognitive properties of airline cockpits (Hutchins, 1995b), the navigation systems of naval vessels (Hutchins, 1995a), air-traffic control (Halverson, 1995), shared CAD systems (Rogers & Ellis, 1994), shared-database systems (Nardi & Miller, 1989), collaboration between programmers (Flor & Hutchins, 1992), and even a fishing community (Hazelhurst, 1994). However, there are a number of variations in the use of distributed cognition theory and its application in these areas; it is perhaps most commonly used in an acknowledgment that work is more than simply the activity of a single individual, working alone and without tools. More precise use of the term occurs in describing how mental activity is externalized into the world, as people create external representations to support their own activity or collaborative action. However, the most rigorous application of the term is its application in elucidating the architecture of cognition, where the cognitive activity is not simply mentally represented. The last form is examined in detail in this chapter.

8.2   OVERVIEW

One of these easiest ways to envisage the nature of a DCog analysis is through demonstrating how it can be applied to a real-world problem. The classic application of DCog is in Hutchins's analysis of navigation in the U.S. navy vessel, the *USS Palau* (Hutchins, 1995a). Although the details of the analysis are complex and delve into a level of detail that would be inappropriate to discuss here, Hutchins's analysis can be summarized as the trail of events surrounding the crew taking bearings and the manipulations of this information, resulting in the determination of the ship's location and progress. Essentially, the process of navigation is described in terms of an information-processing activity, although what differentiates it from more standard accounts of human behavior is that this information processing is not characterized in terms of individual cognition but as an emergent process arising from the coordinated actions of the crew.

Hutchins begins his analysis by describing the hierarchical system of naval rank, the relevant crew members, and the roles that these individuals are expected to play in "Sea and Anchor Detail," and, in particular, the "fix taking cycle." He documents the representations in which communications are encoded, and how the combination of all of the interacting parts of the system operate to process information in achieving the navigational system's goal (locating the ship in two-dimensional space). Importantly, at no stage in the process can a single person be said to be navigating the ship. The work of individuals comes together through their assigned responsibilities and in performing roles determined through the prior organization of work.

During the fix taking cycle, information is propagated through a series of artifacts, from the two pelorus operators, who take sightings of landmarks through a telescopic alidade and transmit this information to a "bearing taker." This information on the ship's location in relation to known landmarks (from a navigational chart) is manually entered into a logbook by the bearing taker. This tabulated information is then used by the "plotter" to calibrate a protractorlike tool called a "hoey," which is applied to the navigational chart by matching it up to the known locations of these geographical features. This process allows the vessel's current location and projected course to be calculated by triangulation and compared to the previous projection marked on the map (calculated by the process of "dead reckoning") to see if any navigation discrepancies have arisen. This information is integrated with further readings from other informational sources, and involves the coordination of up to 10 personnel. Through his analysis, Hutchins shows how the coordination of the various activities develops from the naval regulations, standardized training that the team has had, practices that are local to the vessel itself, and the constraints of the technologies used in the system. What we see from this analysis is that navigation arises out of the combined efforts of the collaborating individuals, none of whom can be said to individually determine the course of the process.

The key components of the analysis are two elements—the representations that information is held in and transformed across, and the processes through which these representations are coordinated with one another. Navigational location is often described in textbooks as a complex computation; however, the *computational* element of navigation is no longer a cognitively intensive activity (for an unaided individual), but arises out of a series of seemingly simple activities distributed over several individuals and a variety of media.

8.3   SCIENTIFIC FOUNDATIONS

Simon (1981) has suggested building a "science of the artificial" in which the structures of the physical, social, and organizational environments are studied to examine how they interact with and structure the task in hand. This science would explore the range of internal processes that humans use to organize their activities within their environments. DCog takes on this problem to show how physical, organizational, and social settings can be understood and analyzed within the cognitive realm, but expands on Simon's work to suggest that accounting for the internal, mental processes of an individual is not an appropriate level of analysis to understand such systems. This section explores the background to this development and demonstrates the importance of the approach.

The study of behavior, in particular within HCI, has been dominated by a psychological perspective within the cognitive sciences. The search to uncover the fundamental processes behind behavior has concentrated on human mental capabilities and attempts to formulate an architecture of cognition (c.f. Anderson, 1983; Newell, 1990). In doing so, the other subdisciplines of cognitive science have been sidelined—in particular anthropology, deemphasizing the roles of context and culture—in favor of a stance focused on unsupported mental processes. The development of computer systems to support human performance in the workplace has provided an impetus for reexamining this stance, because in these settings individual cognitive effort is only of value when integrated with that of others.

Traditionally in HCI, a microstructural analysis of behavior was considered to be the appropriate grain of analysis for developing computer interfaces. The experimental cognitive paradigm and the information-processing approach (Newell and Simon, 1972) was initially adapted to examine an individual's behavior as problem solving, in terms of the problem structure of the activity. Task analyses (see, for example, Johnson, 1992) were developed from this, breaking down the structure of activities into their component parts, often to the level of reaction times, such as the Goals, Operators, Methods and Selection rules (GOMS) and keystroke level models (John, Chapter 4, this volume). A range of such techniques, including refinements to GOMS (e.g., Kieras, 1997) and task-action grammars (Payne & Green, 1986), among others, were developed, but these methods are rarely applied to mainstream systems design outside safety- or time-critical systems. A fundamental problem with these forms of analysis was that they fail to take account of the larger task that such molecular activities are embedded within. The task analyses also focus on the knowledge held by users about the system, and they do not account for resources in the environment that are used to organize behavior (although see van der Veer, Lenting, & Bergevoet, 1996).

The gradual acknowledgment that a "microstructural task-based analysis" did not consider the macrostructure of the larger task that such microlevel activities were embedded within has been hugely influential in recent years. Research has moved toward a greater concern with ecological validity (Neisser, 1967) than these early approaches, encompassing more artifact centered, contextual, and organizational studies of activity. The importance of developing "ecological" approaches is particularly appropriate in studying collaborative work because of the nature of teamwork, which operates in an environment rich in organizing resources, such as tools, other people, and a structured approach to problem solving. The problems with these individually oriented experimental approaches in dealing with such real-world situations have led to *the turn to the social* (Anderson, Heath, Luff, & Moran, 1993), and this has been most noticeable in the area of CSCW where sociological and anthropological methods have achieved particular prominence.

While it has many advantages over the conventional experimental approaches, the turn to the social has not been unproblematic. The methods and techniques used by social science have been hard to adapt to the design of technology. This is largely because of their historical development—they were never intended to be used in support of computer-systems design. Nevertheless, the social dimension and the possibilities that such analysis brings to systems design is important in sensitizing designers to the social aspects of technology use (Anderson et al., 1993). In particular, the ethnographic method—an anthropological approach to collecting information on the problem domain—has become a central feature of CSCW, achieving a degree of acceptance in the wider domain of HCI and information systems development (see also Button, Chapter 13, this volume).

8.3.1 External Support for Thought and Systems Perspectives on Cognition

Cognition, as we know it today, is a relatively recent concept, achieving prominence in the 1950s and 1960s. Initially, cognition was assumed to be a purely mental activity, and early proponents such as Neisser (1967) and Newell and Simon (1972) wrote about it as involving single individuals. Neisser (1967, p.4) defined cognition as referring "to all of the processes by which the sensory input is transformed, reduced, stored, recovered, and used." The focus of such studies into cognition, or "cognitive science," was on problem solving and the organization of knowledge about the problem domain.

The dominant paradigm for cognition, information-processing theory (Newell & Simon, 1972), proposes that problem spaces (the representation of the operations required for a given task) are abstract representations—there is no theoretical reason that the theory need be restricted to a single individual. Indeed, Neisser's definition of cognition does not delineate what architecture cognition is actually implemented in. The cognitive perspective on analysis does not, therefore, have to be limited to the unaided individual: Any unit performing these activities could be described as a cognitive entity. In support of cognition, humans develop and use environmental resources—tools—as individuals as well as in support of group behavior. Key to this book, these tools include computer systems. On this basis, individuals can use elements of their environment in cognition; but perhaps most powerfully, this approach allows us to describe how problem-solving behavior by groups of people—mediated through artifacts in their environment—could be described in terms of the cognitive paradigm.

Arguably, one of the most important abilities that humans have is this ability to create and use tools, or artifacts (manmade or modified objects; Cole, 1990). One particular subset of these artifacts are those that aid cognition—known as *cognitive artifacts* (see Norman, 1991). Cognitive artifacts include external representations of "knowledge in the world" (Norman, 1988) as memory aids, such as checklists, books, diaries, and calendars. However, they are also used to augment information processing itself, not just in increasing memory capacity. A fundamental feature of cognitive artifacts is that they do not simply augment, or "amplify," existing human capabilities. Rather, they transform the task into a different one (Cole, 1990; Norman, 1993), allowing resources to be reallocated into a configuration that better suits the cognitive capabilities of the problem solver. This is the basis of cognitive engineering. Such cognitive artifacts include intellectual devices such as numeric systems (Zhang & Norman, 1995), computational devices such as slide rules or calculators, or a combination of both intellectual and physical resources. Indeed, cognitive artifacts do not simply support the cognitive processes of individuals (Norman, 1991). An example of this is language (Cole, 1990), which allows humans to spread their cognitive load over a group of people, and which changes the task from an individual cognitive problem to a distributed problem dispersed over social space. Verbal language is often combined with other representational media, providing an indexical focus (something to refer to and point at) in conversation to coordinate interpretation of representation-bearing artifacts in context.

As a consequence of the overly reductionist stance of traditional cognitive science and HCI research that ignores cognitive artifacts and social interaction, a number of theoreticians have moved toward what Norman (1993) calls the "systems perspective." Such systems-based perspectives attempt to describe all of the features active in a work or activity system: people, artifacts, and, importantly, the means of organizing these into a productive unit. For these researchers, it is the system, rather than the cognitive properties of an individual or the design of an artifact, that determines overall performance at a task. One group of these researchers are those investigating what is loosely called "situated cogni-tion" (see Agre, 1993; Lave, 1988), applying an anthropological approach to the examination of cognitive activity:

> "Cognition" is seamlessly distributed across persons, activity, and setting . . . thought (embodied and enacted) is situated in socially and culturally struc-tured time and space. (Lave, 1988, p. 171)

To Lave, the unit of analysis should not be those of cognition or culture, but that of "activity-in-setting." She goes further and states that the environment can-not be simply considered as a resource for consulting (for example, as an exter-nal memory), but as an active resource in achieving the system goal, allowing cognition to be stretched over mind, body, activity, and setting. Lave gives an ex-ample of this to show how mathematical division is often done in the real world: a study participant was asked how to divide a serving of cottage cheese—three quarters of two thirds of a cup of cheese. However, participants did not do a mental calculation on the fractions (the solution being half a cup). Rather, they filled the cup two thirds full, tipped it out and divided it up into four parts, re-moving one quarter of this. As an abstract cognitive computation, this would have been relatively demanding, but by making use of the environment and the solution pathway represented in the question itself, the task solution appeared to be simple.

Other approaches that make use of a systems perspective are the theories of distributed representations (Zhang & Norman, 1994, 1995) and external repre-sentations (Kirsh, 1995; Larkin & Simon, 1987; Vera & Simon, 1993; Woods & Roth, 1988). These fall more squarely into traditional cognitive science; within this set of approaches, humans use aspects of the environment to decompose tasks into different forms of representations, and where "the representation of the world provided to a problem solver can affect his/her/its problem solving performance" (Woods & Roth, 1988, p. 26). These theories posit two forms of representations—internal (in the mind, as mental symbols), and external (in the world, as physical symbols). These representations are combined into an abstract task space during problem-solving activity. By making use of representations in the world, cognitive agents do not need to maintain complex mental representa-tions. Perceptual information may represent part of the cognitive task, and ex-ternal representations thus become a component part of the cognitive system. The physical constraints on activity that these external representations bring to cognition are important in reducing the rule base required to comprehend the world, simplifying the task at hand, and fundamentally changing the nature of the task from one that is solely mentally represented (Zhang & Norman, 1994).

Both theories of distributed representations and social cognition take Simon's (1981) notion of the human as a mundane processor of information to its logical conclusion through using the environment as a practical resource for problem solving. This is possible because humans are able to make use of their perceptual mechanisms in information processing (Kirsh, 1995; Ware, Chapter 2, this volume). So far, situated-cognition and distributed-representation approaches have been applied effectively only to individual behavior rather than problem solving in social groups, but it is possible to envision how these or similar approaches could be extended to include other actors[3] within a social context.

8.4 DETAILED DESCRIPTION

By performing simple manipulations on external resources, humans can logically process information without performing logic operations in their heads (c.f. Rumelhart, Smolensky, McClelland, & Hinton, 1986). Preece et al. (2002) describe the process of "external cognition" as people creating and using information in the world, rather than simply within their heads to do three key things. These involve externalizing information to *reduce memory load* (such as reminders); to *simplify cognitive* effort by "computational offloading" onto an external media; and in allowing us to *trace changes,* for example over time and space, through annotation (such as crossing items off a list or marking progress on a map), or in the creation of a new representational form to reflect this change. Although this description is a good characterization of how external cognition operates, at least for an individual, DCog attempts to place a stronger theoretical framework around this. We need to investigate the computational character of how cognition is distributed over this extended system before we can make any grander claims as to its theoretical validity.

The key to understanding the application of DCog is in its use in uncovering how systems *coordinate* transformations on representations in *goal-seeking* behavior. Bringing representations into coordination with one other involves a process of mapping a representation from one media onto another. This coordination may be at an individual level, as an individual creates or manipulates representations, with a focus on the coordination of how the representation is propagated

---

[3] The term *actor* rather than *agent* is used here to differentiate between real-world people acting within settings, and theoretical constructs within cognitive models (agents). Moreover, agents need not be human.

between the representational media in pursuit of their goal; or at a group level, with a focus on the coordination of representations that are propagated between individuals through a variety of media.

The aim of DCog is to understand how intelligence is manifested *at the systems level* and not the individual cognitive level (Hutchins, 1995a). Analysts require a means of describing the components within this system to explain the mechanisms that coordinate groups of collaborators. In cognitive science, these properties are described in terms of the representations and computational processes of individual thought. This cognitive framework can be expanded to examine larger units, to include individuals interacting with external representations, and the interactions of multiple individuals in a work setting.

DCog is explicitly aimed toward the redevelopment of systems through their technological media and internal organization (Flor & Hutchins, 1992; Rogers & Ellis, 1994) to better take advantage of human capabilities and to provide support for their limitations. Its goal is to extract information that system designers require in order to make better-informed judgments about the information-processing requirements of systems of collaborating agents. DCog analyses achieve this through deriving the external symbol system (c.f. Newell & Simon, 1972) that captures the elements of processing (representations and processes) that transform system inputs into outputs for particular tasks. The form of this analysis involves detailed studies of the workplace to analyze the role of technology and work practice in system behavior. The method by which this is achieved is through performing a *cognitive ethnography* (Hutchins, 1995a); that is, through fieldwork that places emphasis on the representational and representation-transforming characteristics of the system under observation.

8.4.1   Computation and Cognition

Building a new approach to the study of cognition requires us to look deeply at the foundational elements of what we are looking at—cognition. Through expanding cognition across a unit greater than the individual, to computational accounts of group cognition, the identification of the representational states used by a system allows analysts to examine the information-processing capabilities of the extended cognitive unit.

The importance of the representation in DCog comes from the information-processing metaphor of cognitive science, by which information is transformed computationally in problem solving (Newell & Simon, 1972). The human mind is assumed to be an instance of a Turing Machine that operates through computational mechanisms (Pylyshyn, 1984). Within this computational view, changes to the form of the representations are a part of problem solving: Changing the representation of a problem changes the problem itself, and successive transformations on a representation can transform the initial state into the desired state (Simon, 1981). The computational transformation of a problem state (a representation of the problem) through a "problem space" (composed of the start state, goal state, resources, and constraints) into a goal state occurs through the propagation of that representation across various representational structures (Hutchins, 1995a, 1995b; Simon, 1981). In the human mind, these representational structures would be neural pathways. From the DCog perspective, cognition takes the form of a computation involving "the propagation of representational state across a variety of [representational] media" (Hutchins, 1995a, p. xvi), and not just within the mental domain. There is no distinction between the representational media—internal or external—that form the system's "boundary." Instead, the boundary to the distributed system is constrained by the set of resources appropriated into the problem's resolution.

In DCog, a larger granularity of analysis is used than in the study of individual cognition: The computation may be realized through any number of representations, people, computerized artifacts, or nontechnological artifacts. The word *representation* is used here to describe the way in which a system stores knowledge about a domain. Representations may be encoded internally in the individual (i.e., mentally), or in the environment (in an artifact). They may encode knowledge about things, or about the organization of things. The same knowledge can be encoded in different ways that are functionally and logically equivalent (i.e., problem isomorphs), yet can be manipulated by individuals or systems in different ways. Many processes can change these representational states, so that incoming information is processed into an output by the larger cognitive system. This can be seen more clearly in the diagrams shown in Figures 8.1(a) and 8.1(b), from Halverson (1995). These diagrams illustrate how a framework to examine the mental process of cognition can be expanded to a larger unit, the group, using the same categories—input, output, process, and representations.

Within a distributed cognitive system, actors and artifacts are considered to be equally important in problem solving, and together, these make up the *functional system*[4] of activity. Historically, this concept appears to be derived the "activity system" of activity theory (see Bertelsen and Bodker, Chapter 11, this volume), which has a similar meaning. The functional system has different

---

[4] The terms *functional system* (Hutchins, 1995a), *functional unit* (Rogers & Ellis, 1994), and *complex cognitive system* (Flor & Hutchins, 1992) have all been used to describe the system under examination, and are interchangeable.

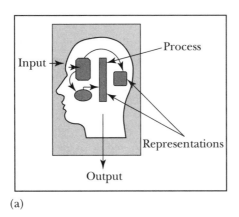

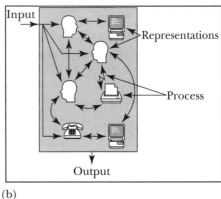

FIGURE

8.1
(a) Mental cognition, (b) Distributed cognition.

properties to the individuals participating in the activity or system; it, and not the individuals, performs the task, and the functional system should therefore be treated (at least functionally) as an intelligent entity. The use of the functional system as an entity within DCog is different to the use of the activity system by activity theorists, who view cognition as an individual activity situated within this wider setting. Within DCog, the entities operating within the functional system are not viewed from the perspective of the individual, but as a collective. In the analysis, both people and artifacts are considered as representational components of the system, using the same theoretical language to describe their properties.

Another way that we can discuss cognitive systems is through abstraction away from their implementation in a physical substrate. Abstraction away from the mechanisms of cognition is commonly used in cognitive science, which allows system descriptions in terms of the functional attributes of a cognitive processor without regard to the details of its implementation—the doctrine of *functionalism*. By disregarding the specifics of implementation, and looking to the higher-level terms of what the system *does* rather than *is* (i.e., a functional description), the most basic constituents of a cognitive system could be said to consist of a sensory system, a system memory, a processor, and a means of acting on that processed information if necessary. The same is true within DCog. These components are shown diagrammatically in Figure 8.2 (from Perry, 1997) and discussed in the light of DCog:

✦ The *sensory mechanism* takes its inputs from outside the cognitive system and passes it to the information-processing unit in the form of representation.

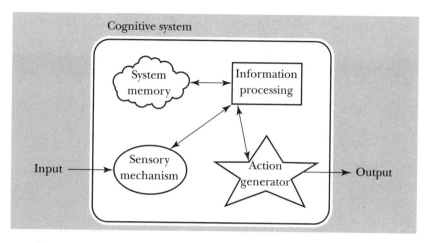

FIGURE

8.2

Functional description of a cognitive system.

+ The *action generator* allows the production of outputs from the cognitive system. It may also provide feedback to the information processor about the performance of the actions executed.

+ *Memory* involves a representational state that is stored to organize subsequent activities; it receives representations from the information processor and, when required, passes them back to it. This storage function may be systematic or serendipitous, arising through features in the world that are interpreted to inform the system of its past, current, and possible future states.

+ The *information processor* receives representations from the sensory system and acts upon them, to transform them, combine them, or even destroy them. These representations may be stored in the system memory, acted upon to create outputs, or used to prime the sensory system to attend to particular inputs.

None of this should be regarded as controversial, as it simply describes the mechanism of information processing.[5] Indeed, it is not radically different from John's model human processor (see Chapter 4, this volume). This is not to say that the implementation of the cognitive system is unimportant; as we shall see,

---

[5] As an aside, it is interesting to consider Simon's background to the development of cognition, in understanding organizations as adaptive cognitive system (March & Simon, 1958). In a sense, DCog returns to this theme, showing relationships between individual and group behavior.

the nature of the representations themselves are important in determining the resources and constraints on the system's behavior.

The implementation of a distributed cognitive system in a real-world example can be highly complex: the four units of the functional cognitive system may not map neatly onto individuals—single or different actors might perform the four functions of the system. The functional description provided within this framework allows the analysis of problem solving with any size of cognitive unit, because individuals are no longer the central focus of enquiry, although they may make up components of the system.

When the cognitive system is socially distributed over a number of interdependent actors, cooperation among these individuals is required so that they can bring their problem-solving resources into conjunction with one another. The coordination of these resources is crucial to their cooperative action. This activity is analogous to human cognition in deciding what to do in a given situation; for example, in catching a ball, the perceptual system must locate the visual position of the ball, the cognitive system must both understand that the ball must be caught and communicate this to the motor system, which must move the body into a position that enables the ball to be caught. This takes place with feedback occurring at every stage. Failure of the coordination mechanisms will usually result in failure to catch the ball. The same case exists in coordinated multi-participant activity. Each independent actor brings resources to the problem and must engage in communicating ideas to the other participants, using feedback to modify their behavior in the light of the other actors' actions. Failure to coordinate these mechanisms will result in the failure to produce a good problem resolution, or a solution at all.

Although the theoretical basis of DCog has drawn from the classical interpretations of cognitive science that abstracts problem solving into logical and programmatic manipulations on representations, the development of DCog has also drawn inspiration from the PDP—parallel distributed processing (Rumelhart, McClelland, & The PDP Research Group, 1986), or connectionist approach to individual, neuronally based cognition. PDP is closely linked to the way we understand how neurons operate—not as silicon-based computers with programs, but as a series of highly interconnected pathways that learn and organize interaction between themselves based on "weightings" and "thresholds." In PDP systems, the whole pattern of agent activation is the meaningful unit of analysis in cognitive behavior, and the cognitive system is seen as multiply connected and controlled, much the same as in human society.

Despite their lack of explicit rules of intelligence or logic and their apparent simplicity, PDP systems appear to exhibit intelligence and logic (Norman, 1986). This clearly has parallels to groups of individuals collaborating on tasks, albeit being wildly different in form. However, instead of electrical or electrochemical interfaces between the processing units, DCog operates through socially mediated protocols between the units of the information-processing system. There are few "rules" of social action, although there are norms of behavior that we are expected to follow, as well as legal and organizational requirements.

A classic feature of PDP systems is what is known as graceful degradation—the ability of the system to continue functioning (with a gradual loss of performance) as the units of processing are removed (Rumelhart, McClelland, & The PDP Research Group, 1986). This is also seen in distributed cognitive systems, because of the redundancy of the representations in use. In most distributed cognitive systems, there is duplication in the systems, so that systems do not fail critically when a single processing component fails, because other media (artifacts or agents) can compensate. The existence of multiple representations within a system also means that cross checks between the representations can be made (known as *assistive redundancy;* Hutchins, 1995b) to ensure that the computation has been performed correctly.

While systems of individuals are not as easily specified or homogenous as PDP systems, the PDP approach does show that self-organizing systems of information processors can work together to produce apparently intelligent and cognitively functioning systems. As with the PDP systems, investigation of the (social) protocols that maintain and coordinate the individual processors is important in specifying the structure of the cognitive processor.

8.4.2   The Social Organization of Group Problem Solving

One of the problems faced by groups in performing collaborative work is organizing the task into component parts that can be performed by individuals. This must be managed so that the parts can be integrated back together again after the component parts of the task have been processed. Attendant to this process is an issue of coordination to ensure that the individually assigned parts are performed both correctly and in a form that can be reintegrated with the whole. In shared problem solving, the collaborating agents must organize an effective distribution of labor to bring together their individual expertise to resolve their shared problem, and they must do this by communicating with each other. There may be many ways to organize groups of agents to distribute the computational load among them, some of which may be better than others (in terms of their speed, processing resources required, and proneness to error). This division of labor determines the computational architecture of the problem-solving unit, because it establishes the resources and processes that can be brought to bear on the problem representations. However, as problems and situations evolve during performance of the task, this will necessarily involve an ongoing division of labor that develops and changes to adapt to the situation.

Although the structure of the environment is important in determining action, actors do not passively use existing structures. As humans, we do not simply make use of the environment as a resource, but we adaptively organize the environment (or "cognitive ecology") within which we exercise information processing—so that social, cultural, and historical elements are crucial components of these systems. Within DCog, this proactive *structuring* is central in coordinating the actions of collaborating individuals. Such adaptive structuring involves organizing and reorganizing the physical and cognitive artifacts in the environment, and modifying the social context in which the behaviors on these artifacts occur. These organizing structures can be retained as representations (either internal memories, or externally as written rules or checklists), or as constraints on behavior (embodied in the physical artifacts and work environment). The structure of these constraints in the workplace therefore plays a role in determining the architecture for the information-processing activities of the functional unit and helps determine the division of labor between people and over artifacts.

8.4.3   Communication and Coordination of Distributed Knowledge

Distributing work across a group of agents must involve the organization of that group to coordinate activity through some form of communication. Indeed, within DCog, communication is not differentiated from the computations involved in information-processing work. Knowledge is propagated around the functional unit through a number of communicative pathways (Rogers & Ellis, 1994): verbal, nonverbal, intermodal transformations (e.g., verbal to text), and by constructing new mental representations in combination with external representations (e.g., operations on tools). All of these can be observed directly. The organization of knowledge is important in determining its use, because it constitutes the system's expertise and because it is possible that no single person will be aware of this organization. This knowledge is distributed across the heads of actors *and* in the organization of tools and the work environment (Hutchins, 1995a).

For a cognitive artifact to be used in problem solving by the distributed cognitive system, the representation encoding the information must have a universally understood meaning between the sender and recipient. Universal comprehension of the medium may derive from common experience or training, or through its use in the setting. This meaning (or mapping) may be self-evident, mirroring features of the environment, such as a picture (an analogue representation); or they may be more abstract and complex, such as text, which require transformational rules for interpretation. Different forms of representational media have particular properties that constrain the uses to which their representations can be put and how they can be accessed.

This is clearly shown in Hutchins's (1995a) example of the computational activities and representational transformations in the "fix cycle" of a navigational system, where the navigational system captures knowledge in the world as representations and successively rerepresents them until they can be applied to a chart to represent a physical location (the system's goal). The representations are propagated through a complex set of media, and the goal of spatial orientation (navigation) is achieved through bringing the representational states of these media into coordination with one another. The forms of representational media used, the organization of the media, and the interactions of the actors are therefore critical to the task operations performed by the functional system.

It may be useful here to contrast DCog's views on the nature of coordination with ethnomethodology (see Button, Chapter 13, this volume). Ethnomethodologically informed ethnography is focused on the ordering of activity—its "coordination"—but not in the *work* itself (i.e., the activity *around* the task necessary to organize the collaborative resources for the task, and not activity *on* the task). To use Button's own distinction, his analysis is of the order-of-production but not of the production. To a large extent, and, in particular, for certain types of work, this coordination may be the most difficult part of the work, but in many other cases it is only a component part of it. This perspective is extended to the studies of artifacts in work—ethnomethodological analysis centers on members' use of body position, language, and other artifacts in the presentation of self—and orientation toward the perspectives of others. This neglect of the primary role of artifacts in the computational part of the task (i.e., not just as devices for mediating the coordination of members' perspectives) is a serious problem with the simplistic application of such ethnomethodological studies. This is not to say that this perspective is useless, but it cannot show a full picture of the work—missing out on a very necessary part of work that is relevant to systems design. Fortunately, in HCI and CSCW, a more pragmatic approach is generally applied, and the ethnographic data is used to describe the task. DCog, however, does not separate these two elements of work, and coordination around the task and the task itself are considered together in the analysis.

Having identified what socially distributed cognitive labor involves, we are now in a position to discuss methods with which to investigate distributive cognitive systems.

8.4.4   "Doing" DCog

Traditional approaches to data collection in cognitive science examine how information is represented within the cognitive system, and how these representations are transformed, combined, and propagated through the system. The added benefit of examining cognition within systems extending beyond the brain is that many of the representations are physically manifested in artifacts and do not require the indirect methods of examination that experimental psychology has to use. In essence, the analyst can physically "enter" the cognitive system (Hutchins, 1995a). Some representations will be held mentally, but in the case of DCog the level of granularity in the analysis is only concerned with the inputs and outputs to actors and not their internal representations.

Access to the visible representations involved in an activity allows analysts to determine the *resources* used in the performance of problem solving. We do not need to know the internal mental processes, as the analysis is not concerned with the coordination of mental representations, but with how actors make their actions and intentions available to others (similarly to ethnomethodology) in the form of representations and organizing behaviors to aid interpretation and processing of those representations. Artefacts are the physical embodiments of representations and the media through which representations are operated on. Understanding the role of representations and the processes involved in transforming them gives an insight into the nature of the resources used to perform collaborative work and design.

As a framework for describing and explaining group cognition, DCog is not a method—its practitioners are therefore able to be eclectic in the approaches they can apply. However, while the analyst is therefore free to select the method of data collection that is most appropriate to the functional system under examination, one method, ethnography (Hutchins calls this "cognitive ethnography"), is the most commonly applied form of data collection. Ethnography is a form of naturalistic research that allows us to "describe what happens in the setting, how the people involved see their own actions and those of others, and the contexts in which the action takes place" (Hammersley & Atkinson, 1995, p. 6). The ethnographic method was developed independently of the distributed cognitive framework (see Button, Chapter 13 in this volume, for a review) and has had to be adapted to fulfill its requirements as a tool for data collection. This is developed in the context of cognitive science and its requirements for the collection of data that is explanatorily adequate. This (cognitive) ethnography is not radically different to sociological or anthropological ethnography, but its focus on information processing within the functional system has more in common with the cognitive sciences. Its is, nevertheless, viewed as an interpretive approach that is very different from the positivistic tradition of its parent discipline.

The unit of analysis for DCog is the functional system, which may be formed of a collection of individuals and artifacts and their relations to each other. Analysis therefore begins by determining an appropriate system goal around which a functional system operates. The analyst will then have to specify the units involved in information processing within the functional system; once these have been identified, he or she will have to examine how representation transforming activities are coordinated to achieve the system's goal. This will result in a description of the pathways that information flows through, and the external structures that are created and used prior to the solution of that goal. Flor and Hutchins (1992) describe this as the equivalent of examining the systems' mental state. The work involved in data collection—the cognitive ethnography—is observational: DCog researchers look for information-representation transitions (Flor & Hutchins, 1992) that result in the coordination of activity and computations. Rogers and Ellis (1994) specify the four areas involved in these knowledge transitions to be examined:

+ the way that the work environment structures work practice,
+ changes within the representational media,
+ the interactions of the individuals with each other,
+ the interactions of the individuals with system artifacts.

Analysis of systems using DCog can also be applied at a number of different levels of granularity. Indeed, it may be hard to develop an analysis from a single level of granularity. It would be hard to describe the process of navigation simply from the level of the representational transformations on taking bearings during the fix cycle without examining how those transformations fit into the wider organizational picture of navigational work in general—after all, what are the navigators trying to achieve? It may therefore be useful to describe human-activity systems as being composed of several layers of embedded functional systems that are related to one another. Analysis may be carried out at one or more of these levels.

In practical terms, the DCog analyst will need to describe: (1) the background to the activity—the goals of, and the resources available to, the functional system. They will then need to (2) identify the inputs and outputs to the functional system, (3) the representations and processes that are available, and (4) the transformational activities that take place in the problem solving when achieving the functional system's goal. This rather abstract characterization of doing a cognitive ethnography is clarified in the examples drawn from real data and analysis in the case study that follows.

8.5 CASE STUDY: ENGINEERING DESIGN AND CONSTRUCTION

The field study that illustrates the application of the DCog approach is derived from fieldwork carried out in the United Kingdom on a road-building project. To build what was known as the "permanent works," or permanent road structures, the construction team had to design and build "temporary works." Temporary works are nonpermanent structures that included scaffolding, concrete moulds, and supply roads. These temporary works were developed out of the designs of the permanent works, but they had to take into account current site conditions (such as slope, weather, soil conditions, and existing structures) and the available resources (money, time, materials, equipment, and labor) that were not accounted for in the designs of the permanent works.

In this case, the *goal* of the functional system was to construct a road, following the permanent works designs and contractual details, with commercial constraints (cost) without causing a danger to trains running on a nearby railway line or a potential for environmental damage.

The top-level functional system involved elements from within a construction company (ConsCo), made up of a *construction team,* comprising a team leader, 7 engineers of varying experience and with different responsibilities, and about 45 team laborers and site supervisors. The team operated on-site, away from the main site office, and they were supported by a *design coordinator.* The design coordinator worked closely with a *design engineer* (off-site) to develop the team's requirements into a temporary-works design solution. Several other individuals and groups external to ConsCo were also involved in the design process, including a *resident engineer,* who checked that the road was built to contractual standards, a *railway operator,* and an *environmental agency,* each with their own responsibilities. Note here how the *work activity* determines the boundaries of the analysis and not the commercial boundaries of the organization.

The transformational activity performed by the functional system at the construction site involved taking inputs into the system, transforming them into representations that could be applied in the temporary works' design process, and rerepresenting them until they matched the desired goal as an output to result in a constructible set of temporary works structures.

The analysis and empirical work could have been performed in a number of ways—even for this small part of the construction process—as several subsystems could have been considered as independent functional systems. However, in determining the high-level system goal as the temporary-works design process, this set the outer boundaries of the functional system. This did not mean that the analysis would focus only on a single level of granularity; on the contrary, several levels are described in the following examples.

8.5.1 Organizational Coordination and Control in Representation Transformation

The process of coordination in ConsCo was highly operationalized into a formal organizational set of procedures, equivalent to Hutchins's (1995a) description of the naval regulations governing Sea and Anchor Detail (or the Watch Standing Procedures). Similar processes are used throughout the construction industry in many different areas, but for the sake of this chapter the focus here is on the use and control of drawings and their associated documentation.

While the temporary-works drawings were created from the design brief by the temporary-works designer, the construction team had to coordinate with him to ensure that the design matched their expectations and the constraints of the site. The temporary-works designer also had to coordinate planning with the resident engineer to see whether the design was contractually valid, and with the other interest groups to ensure that it met their specific requirements. A final inspection then had to be made to check that the design was internally consistent and structurally sound. At each of these stages, it was important that the various parties' comments were recorded and that any resulting changes did not interfere with those of the other stakeholders. Changes and negotiation around these temporary-works designs were managed through a versioning control system to ensure that these superseded other drawings or that unfinished drawings were not used in the construction process.

When working alone, document-version control can be difficult; even in writing a short document such as this chapter, I have gone through about 10 major revisions with duplicate files stored on at least three computers. The construction team had a much harder task because of the large number of people involved, in addition to having duplicate copies of the drawings for use on-site—

staff often being on-site and unavailable—and having a huge number of often similar-looking drawings in circulation. As a consequence, a system of document control has been developed within ConsCo, drawing from engineering practice and experience (developed over millennia) to prevent accidental errors in document use. In the language of DCog, this is a *system of coordination.*

At each stage in the design process, the design representation (i.e., the drawing) would be modified to demonstrate that a change to its status had taken place. The preliminary drawings and sketches derived from the "design brief" were initialed by the temporary-works designer and stamped with the word "preliminary." When these drawings met the construction team's approval, they were stamped with the words "for discussion." These "for discussion" drawings were then presented to the resident engineer and the other groups involved. Each would sign the drawing when their approval was achieved. Following approval by all stakeholder groups, the drawing would be stamped with the words "for inspection." After a final check of the designs by an independent engineer, the drawings would be signed and stamped with "for construction," whereupon they could be used in the construction process by the team. Just stamping the drawings was not seen as sufficient to demonstrate a document's status. Red ink was used on these stamps so that unauthorized copying would not result in "uncontrolled" drawings, because duplication would result in black copies. This meant that a drawing's user could determine which drawings represented the current design, and which were duplicate copies that had possibly been superseded.

Notably, in this coordinated set of representational transformations, the approval and stamping process did not involve the design representation being changed into another medium. Rather, it involved a change to the structure of the medium. Each of these changes determined what the representation could be used for, and what design process should next be applied to it. While the design representation underwent a great deal of change, the medium carrying it was only slightly modified. The consequences of these small iterative changes to its medium were far reaching and significantly changed its meaning.

What we can clearly see from the design process within ConsCo was that a great deal of effort was put into the process to ensure that changes to the representational status of the drawings were made *clearly visible.* The necessity of this was largely because the external media used in the design process were often changed only through these simple and often trivial modifications to their structure. Use of such a system means that the work of drawing control changes from a computationally complex task of communicating with all of the other stakeholders to ensure that they are aware of the state of the design, to a simpler one of proving a single physical representation and ensuring that this is up to date.

8.5.2   Representational Transformations in Information Processing

DCog claims that in order to process information from several sources and different formats, representations have to be *coordinated* with one another. For Hutchins (1995a), this involved rerepresenting information from the ship's compass and visual position onto the navigational chart so that they could be combined into a representation of spatial location. In construction, this coordination occurred through a wide range of representational media and coordination processes.

A description from the field study about how representational transformations were performed at the level of an individual is described here. The example demonstrates how information represented in one rich medium is extracted and synthesized into a simpler representation with a structure that is appropriate for a particular task: comparing the design to the physical conditions on site. In practice, this transformed the engineer's activity from a complex computational task of mentally comparing and interpreting abstract data from tables and drawings into a simple visual comparison of marks on a physical artifact.

A graduate engineer had been observed spending some time poring over a drawing, taking measurements of the planned gradient of section of the road, and writing these into a table of measurements. He then manually transferred these measurements onto a sketch he had made of the area. However, this new representation was scaled differently to the original drawing. While the original drawing had been a plan *overview* of the road (i.e., viewed from above), the sketch showed a section *through* the structure (viewed from the side). In addition to the different aspects of the drawing and sketch, the engineer had changed the axes on the sketch so that they exaggerated the gradient, making deviations and discrepancies in the more easily visible data: the horizontal axis was on a scale of 1:250, while the vertical scale was 1:10. The engineer then populated the sketch with information taken from a table of his own recordings on the actual site conditions (see Figure 8.3).

When he had completed the sketch, the graduate engineer left it on the senior engineer's desk, with a note attached to it explaining that he had found a discrepancy between the expected and actual gradients. The note further commented that he was going to be away from his desk for the rest of the day, but that he would be working at a particular location if further information was required.

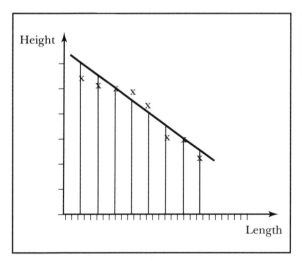

FIGURE   Sketch of a road gradient.

8.3

In the example, information was transformed from the design drawings onto different representations (tables of measurements) and then onto a graphical representation (the "section view" sketch) that more clearly demonstrated the relationships between the two datasets. Information was propagated through a series of representations, from the tabulated site data and the original drawing, through their representation onto a new medium (the sketch) that was more appropriate for comparing gradient differentials. However, this solution was useless in itself unless it could be communicated to someone who could resolve this and who could check whether this differential was important. To bring the representation into coordination with the design representations held by the senior engineer (both mental and physical), the junior engineer attached a text explanation to the sketch. What we have done here is to describe the situation in terms of its informational and information-transforming activities, albeit for a relatively simple case, making the role of the media used in information representation and in the coordination of those representations explicit. A simple diagram of these state changes in the system is shown in diagrammatic form in Figure 8.4.

While it oversimplifies the information processing carried out, the diagram shows key representational transformations and coordinations used in the computation as the engineer resolves the problem and communicates this information onwards.

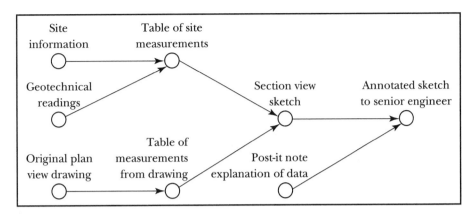

FIGURE

8.4
Diagram of representational state changes in the creation and use of a sketch.

8.5.3   Coordination of Representational Transformations

Although the previous example shows the computational transformation that occur through propagation of a representation through a set of media, this process was largely mediated and coordinated through the actions of a single individual. This is a very limited view of design work on-site, which often involved close collaboration between individuals.

The nature of multiparticipant and multiorganizational coordination processes used in the example of ConsCo could be partially gleaned from the project documentation, in the contract for the project with the client organization (a governmental agency), as well as from the Contract Quality Plan and the Planning and Temporary Works Handbook (a set of internal, but industry-led standards). However, the practical descriptions of representational mappings in this documentation were too abstract for direct application without interpretation in context. In the majority of cases, these documents described only *when* changes to representations had to occur and *what* the computations to the media should result in, but not *how*. In practice, such collaborative work was largely socially mediated, scaffolded by the available artifacts, organizational and cultural constraints, and the participants' professional standards and training.

An example from the fieldwork at ConsCo demonstrates an instance of such a multiparticipant representational coordination. Here, the construction team's senior engineer discussed a design problem with the temporary-works design coordinator, as they attempted to develop a design brief for the temporary-works design engineer. As they discussed the problem, they elaborated on previously generated sketches by jotting on them. They also referred to features of the drawings in speech by pointing at them:

> (from fieldnotes)
>
> Senior engineer (SE): If you look here, there's a barrel run there (points at sketch generated in the meeting of a section view through a design structure)
>
> Temporary-works design coordinator (TWC): Yes, I see.
>
> SE: So if we dig here . . . (he holds one hand to the sketch and runs a finger on the other hand along a permanent-works drawing [in plan view] beside the sketch, indicating a line of reference)
>
> TWC: No you can't do that because of drainage problems . . . (pauses) . . . No, no, I see now.
>
> SE: So if we cap these piles here . . . (indicates several points on the sketch)
>
> TWC: Yeah. OK. Lets do that.

The discussion demonstrates how a common understanding of the problem was negotiated by cross-referencing two different forms of external representation. In DCog terms, this is clearly a process of coordination—the bringing together and aligning of representations in collaborative information processing. The senior engineer mediated this coordination of representations by using his hands to demonstrate the relationship between the drawing and the sketch. This allowed him to indicate where the digging represented on the sketch (seen from the side) would have to be performed on the site, represented on the drawing (from an aerial view). By physically using his body to mediate the coordination of these two representations, the senior engineer created a new, shared viewpoint of the information on the representation that could then be used by the temporary-works coordinator in developing a design brief for the temporary-works design engineer. Notice how this social and physical set of actions can be considered in terms of their informational and information-transforming properties. Key features are summarized in Figure 8.5.

The diagram shows some of the key representational transformations and coordinations that help the senior engineer and design coordinators resolve their problem; however, it differs from Figure 8.4 in the way that the actors socially coordinate the computation. Note that although the analysis refers to mental states (i.e., mental representations), no claim is made about the nature of

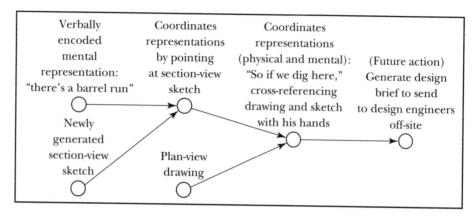

FIGURE

8.5

Diagram of representational state changes in the discussion of a design problem.

these internal and invisible states, focusing on the media and manipulations to the artifacts involved.

8.5.4   Summary

The data, although brief, show the various coordination mechanisms through which information is propagated around and processed with a functional system. Progressive rerepresentations of information through a range of media result in computational work, with little cognitive effort on the part of individuals—other than in the coordination of representations and in the generation of new, more appropriate representational forms. Of course, this is not to trivialize this form of work, but these are more generalizable skills and can be taught, and work systems can be designed to simplify this process. The mental work of actors within the functional system can be seen not so much as one of task-based information processing, but rather of the representational coordination of task-based artifacts. This coordination of representations is key to understanding how problem solving takes place in multiparticipant activities: The coordination of representational media and the knowledge of how and when to use and modify these representations means that the heavy computational work of the problem is distributed into the environment. HCI designers need to be made aware of this so as not to disrupt such practices by introducing different representational forms of information to users.

8.6   CURRENT STATUS

It is important to remember that DCog is a developing framework for understanding human activity. It is not a clearly established discipline with a well-defined set of acknowledged characteristics and boundaries that are accepted by its practitioners. In some instances, we see sloppy language being used: "you can clearly see distributed cognition happening here . . .". The area is also hotly debated within cognitive science, outside of its application in HCI and CSCW. Even within the best-known form of DCog—described here and originating directly from Hutchins's work—there is some dispute. For example, it is questioned whether DCog is an emergent property of work systems involving actors, artifacts, and other organizing resources in their environments, or if it is simply a useful analytical device for describing activity within settings.

The analysis of activity from a computational perspective that brings out the mechanisms by which representational transformations are coordinated cannot be applied to the design of computer and CSCW systems in a straightforward manner. Perhaps this is true of most of the approaches in this volume—creative interpretation of the analysis is a necessary part of the design process. The value of DCog as an approach in HCI and systems design is that it describes human work systems in informational and computational terms; understanding the role and function of the representational media in use clearly has implications for the design of technology in the mediation of that activity, because the system designers will have a stronger model of the work. Further to this, DCog frames human problem-solving activity in terms of representations and processes, terms that are well understood by systems designers, because this is also the way in which they think about computers. An issue here is that, although DCog may be appropriate for analyzing situations that involve problem solving, not all activities are best described as doing so, and the approach is inappropriate in these instances.

The descriptions from the "cognitive ethnography" and its interpretation provide designers with a description of the informational characteristics of work. Clearly, this is of interest to systems designers as they are most usually interested in developing and introducing *information* technology, because it allows them to understand the representational properties of the informational media in use and their functions. This form of description highlights both the information bottlenecks and the communication breakdowns that may make existing systems less effective, but it can also be useful in helping designers understand where not to attempt to introduce technologies that will in themselves introduce new bottlenecks and breakdowns.

In light of the novelty of the approach, which emerged only in the mid-1990s, there are few published DCog papers in the HCI literature, and many of these are theory based. While there are few studies of its application outside of university PhD theses, the published DCog material is heavily cited and informs systems thinking in HCI and CSCW, even if it has not been applied directly. This is certain to change over the next decade as more material is published and as the subject is taught as a mainstream approach in cognitive science and HCI courses at universities.

AUTHOR NOTES

This work was developed at Brunel University in London and at the Center for the Study of Language and Information, Stanford University in California. The writing of this chapter was supported, in part, by Brunel University, which granted me study leave in 2002.

FURTHER READING

Hutchins, E. (1995). *Cognition in the wild*. Bradford: MIT Press. Essential reading on DCog. A deep and insightful review of the area. Powerful ethnography of navigation in large ships, although now slightly dated in the light of Global Positioning System (GPS) technology.

Norman, D. A. (1993). *Things that make us smart*. Reading, MA: Addison-Wesley. Written in a easily readable and digestible style; the book has a short chapter on distributed cognition, and covers distributed representations and related phenomena.

Rogers, Y., & Ellis, J. (1994). Distributed cognition: an alternative framework for analyzing and explaining collaborative working. *Journal of Information Technology, 9*, 119–128. A short review of DCog, with a good introduction to theory and application.

Various authors. (1996). Book review. *Mind, Culture and Activity, 3*(1), 46–68. A discussion and critique of Hutchins's book and a response from the author.

9 Cognitive Work Analysis

CHAPTER

Penelope M. Sanderson   University of Queensland, Australia

The experience with the early process computer installations . . . clearly indicated the pressing need for analysis of operators' cognitive tasks and guidelines for interface design. Because of the slow transition in psychological research away from behaviorism and the preoccupation of the early research in artificial intelligence with games and theorem proving, we found it impossible to wait for guidelines from such sources. It appeared to be necessary to start our own selective research program to find models useful for engineering design. From analysis of many hours of verbal protocols recorded during real work situations in workshops and control rooms and of hundreds of incident reports (in particular, from nuclear power plants), we developed a conceptual frame of reference that served us well in formulating our problems in concepts that could be related to control system design. (Rasmussen, 1986, p. ix)

9.1   MOTIVATION

Cognitive engineering is commonly viewed as the analysis, modeling, design, and evaluation of complex sociotechnical systems. The field acquired its current identity after the Three-Mile Island nuclear power plant accident in Pennsylvania in 1979. The term *cognitive engineering* was first used by Norman (1980, 1981) and *cognitive systems engineering* by Hollnagel and Woods (1983).

Cognitive work analysis (CWA) is one of several analytic approaches to cognitive engineering. CWA emerged from the work of Jens Rasmussen and his group at Risø National Laboratory in Denmark; from the 1960s through the 1990s, they were charged with helping the Danish government introduce safe nuclear power to Denmark (see Vicente, 1999, for a history). The Risø group were required to advise how to design human-machine systems, such as nuclear power plant control rooms, so that they would be safer and more reliable. After several years of investigation, the Risø group found ways to ensure high technical reliability for such systems. However, accidents and incidents still occurred, usually when human operators were required to handle situations and abnormalities that system designers had not anticipated. In such situations, operators effectively had to "finish the design" of the system—that is, through their activities and the information available to them, the operators had to compensate for the information or resources that were missing in order to preserve the purpose of the system.

Finding ways to support operators performing such adaptive compensation became very important. However, Rasmussen and his colleagues found contemporary academic research unhelpful. So they developed their own way of analyzing human cognitive work (Rasmussen, 1986), which later came to be called *cognitive work analysis* (Rasmussen, Pejtersen, & Goodstein, 1994; Vicente, 1999). The scientific foundations of CWA are various—a "conceptual marketplace," as Rasmussen has described it—because they have been appropriated to fulfill a practical need.

CWA has grown to be an effective approach for describing the forces that shape human cognitive work in complex real-time systems. In such systems, human operators need to understand and control complex physical processes—a nuclear-fission process, a chemical reaction, a forest fire, a complex network-management task—that usually has a quite separate existence from the information and communications technology that couple the operator with the process. A poorly designed interface can separate a human operator from the sense of engaging directly with the process of interest. In particular, CWA is an approach to cognitive engineering that helps analysts find ways to support the human operator in unexpected situations where the operator will have to behave adaptively.

9.1.1   Connection of CWA with Other Areas

Figure 9.1 is a simplified map of the relation among CWA, cognitive engineering, and ecological interface design (EID). Cognitive engineering draws upon many areas of research, not shown here, such as cognitive science, systems engineering, control engineering, organizational theory, work analysis, and so on. The cognitive engineer's focus is not human interaction with the mediating information and communications technology, but instead human interaction with the complex physical system that lies *on the other side* of the technology.

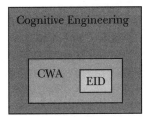

The relationship among cognitive engineering, CWA, and EID.

CWA draws strongly upon work psychology, ecological psychology, and systems thinking. EID is a set of principles to guide interface design that emerges from the part of CWA that is particularly strongly influenced by ecological psychology.

9.1.2 Designing for Unanticipated Events in First-of-a-Kind Systems

The distinction between supporting operators in anticipated versus unanticipated situations is crucial for CWA. It is different from the more common distinction between supporting operators in normal versus abnormal conditions. Many abnormal conditions can be anticipated by designers, and many interfaces can be developed that will help human operators handle anticipated abnormalities and faults. The goal of the Risø group, however, was to help designers build interfaces that let human operators safely handle *unanticipated* abnormalities and faults, possibly by putting together procedures that had never been seen before and judging the effects in the context of the first principles of operation of the system.

A further motivation for CWA has been the rapid pace of technological change. Although the technical needs of industry and organizations usually evolve gradually, from time to time industries and organizations will evolve very rapidly, posing challenges about how the human operator should best be supported. Therefore, a basis for performing *revolutionary* rather than just evolutionary design is needed. The need for conceptual tools that support a leap in design away from current systems is brought home when cognitive engineers must provide advice about human-system integration in first-of-a-kind systems, as we will see in Section 9.5.2.

In the face of these needs, the Risø group developed a way of analyzing human work that Rasmussen and colleagues describe as follows:

> It is clear . . . that analysis and design of modern, dynamic work systems cannot be based on analysis and design of work systems in terms of stable task procedures. Instead, analysis of work systems must be in terms of the behavior shaping goals and constraints that defines [sic] the boundaries of a space within which actors are free to improvise guided by their local and subjective performance criteria. (Rasmussen, Pejtersen, & Goodstein, 1994, pp. 24–25)

Rasmussen (1997) later noted that theory development in many of the disciplines contributing to cognitive engineering had gone through three phases: a normative phase (how things should be done); a descriptive phase (how things actually are done); and a "predictive" phase (what requirements should be satisfied for the system to behave in a new, desired way). Theorizing about work or task analysis seems to have done the same thing. Briefly, normative work analysis methods lean toward prescribing the best way or ways of performing tasks, but they result in activity trajectories that will be limited by the situations that can be imagined. Descriptive work analysis methods focus on a faithful description of work methods in practice, but they tend to provide information about human work that is inextricable from the current means for carrying it out and tend to identify design needs that are limited by the situations that can be currently observed. Neither really helps us to understand how to support human operator adaptability in the face of unanticipated variability, especially for systems that do not yet exist (Vicente, 1999).

The conclusion of the Risø group was that, rather than analyzing behavior, they should analyze the constraints that shape behavior (Rasmussen, 1986; Rasmussen et al., 1994). The constraints ranged from properties of the work domain itself through to cognitive strategies possible in the current situation, as will be discussed in Section 9.3. This is the "predictive" approach mentioned earlier, which, for clarity, has since been renamed the *formative* approach (Sanderson, 1998; Vicente, 1999). A formative model is a "model that describes requirements that must be satisfied so that a system could behave in a new, desired way" (Vicente, 1999, p. 7).

A formative work analysis method will aim to represent first principles of the system and requirements for successful functioning, out of which successful activity will emerge. Rather than specifying exactly what the activity should be, a formative work analysis model specifies the principles that will constrain the kind of activity that will make sense. For example, a task analysis method that focuses on constraints to be satisfied by activity, rather than instructing exactly what activity should be performed, is formative. The result is not restrictive, but instead defines a "bounded but infinite" (Vicente, 1999) set of action possibilities for the human. In this way, CWA is a formative approach to work analysis.

9.2   OVERVIEW OF CWA

To introduce the ideas behind CWA, we provide an example of its use that is both simple and complete. We use Vicente's (1991, 1996, 1999) analysis of a small thermohydraulic system, DURESS (DUal REServoir System). A mimic diagram (physical layout) of DURESS is shown in Figure 9.2. The purpose of the studies with DURESS has been to understand and test principles that would lead to interfaces that support human operators well when they are faced with unanticipated variability.

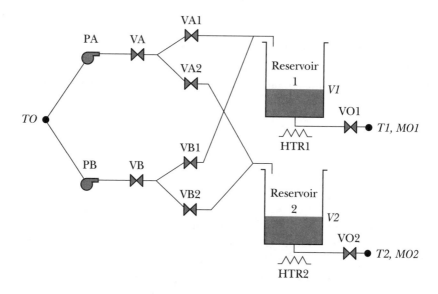

FIGURE	Vicente's (1991) DURESS system shown as a mimic diagram; the diagram also
9.2	shows the basic elements of the "P" (physical) interface for empirical evaluations.

Phase of Analysis	Kinds of Information	Modeling Formalisms	Image of Typical Modeling Formalism
Work domain analysis (WDA)	Purpose and structure of work domain	Abstraction-decomposition diagrams and abstraction hierarchies	
Control task analysis (CTA)	What needs to be done in the work domain	Maps of control task coordination, decision ladder templates	
Stategies analysis (SA)	Ways that control tasks can be carried out	Information flow maps	
Social-organizational analysis (SOA)	Who carries out work and how it is shared	Annotations on all the above	Annotations on other models
Worker competencies analysis (WCA)	Kinds of mental processing supported	Skills, rules, and knowledge models	

FIGURE 9.3   An overview of CWA showing phases of analysis, purpose of each phase, typical modeling formalism used, and graphical image of modeling formalisms.

9.2.1   Phases of CWA

In this section, we will outline how various phases of analysis within CWA were used to identify the information needs of the human operator and how some of the previously cited information was used to develop and evaluate a new display for DURESS. The phases of analysis as described by Vicente (1999) are presented in Figure 9.3 and will be discussed more fully in Section 9.4. (There are minor differences between Rasmussen et al. [1994] and Vicente [1999] in how some phases are classified; here we adopt Vicente's simpler convention.)

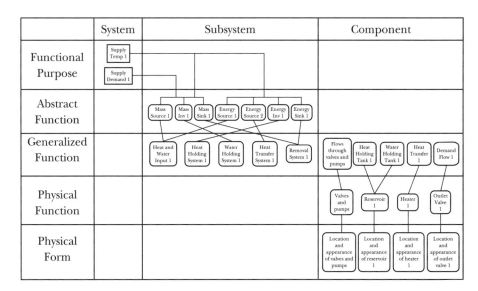

	System	Subsystem		Component	
Functional Purpose	Supply Temp 1 / Supply Demand 1				
Abstract Function		Mass Source 1, Mass Inv 1, Mass Sink 1, Energy Source 1, Energy Source 2, Energy Inv 1, Energy Sink 1			
Generalized Function		Heat and Water Input 1, Heat Holding System 1, Water Holding System 1, Heat Transfer System 1, Removal System 1		Flows through valves and pumps, Heat Holding Tank 1, Water Holding Tank 1, Heat Transfer 1, Demand Flow 1	
Physical Function				Valves and pumps, Reservoir 1, Heater 1, Outlet Valve 1	
Physical Form				Location and appearance of valves and pumps, Location and appearance of reservoir 1, Location and appearance of heater 1, Location and appearance of outlet valve 1	

FIGURE 9.4   An abstraction hierarchy representation of DURESS showing means-ends links (from Vicente, 1999).

Work Domain Analysis

The CWA analyst first analyzes the system or "work domain" itself—in this case, the DURESS system. Exactly how the work domain has been put together will constrain the kinds of goals and tasks that are possible, so it makes sense to analyze the work domain before thinking about the human operator's goals and tasks. Figure 9.4 shows the kind of analysis that results for DURESS. It combines information about physical process, productive functions, and mass and energy balances that need to be preserved, and it shows how they all link together. This step helps the designer specify sensor locations and the higher-order information to be derived, and it identifies the "system image" to be shown to the human operator in a display.

Control Task Analysis

The second phase of analysis involves identifying the control tasks that need to be performed, independently of the strategies to be used or who will perform them. Control tasks emerge from work situations or work problems, and they transform inputs (current state, targets, etc.) into outputs (decisions, control actions, etc.) subject to physical and performance requirements of DURESS. For example, DURESS must start up safely and efficiently. Knowing the control tasks helps designers specify information that will help the human operator recognize when control tasks are needed, and that will help the human operator monitor the impact of control tasks on system functioning.

Strategies Analysis

The third phase of analysis involves identifying strategies that could be used to carry out the control tasks, regardless of who does them. For example, DURESS could be started up so that just the A water stream is used to feed the two reservoirs, or both the A and B streams could be used. The first strategy is easier, but it leaves the system exposed if there is a component failure along the A water stream. This phase helps the designer specify human-computer dialogs to support and guide activity.

Social-Organizational Analysis

The fourth phase of analysis involves identifying how responsibility for control tasks and strategies might be divided between different human operators or between humans and computers so as to best meet the purposes of DURESS. For example, the operator could control one feedwater stream, and automation could adjust the second feedwater stream to reach a global production goal from DURESS while maximizing flexibility of operation. This phase helps define role allocations and also the best organizational structure for responding to contingencies.

Worker Competencies Analysis

The fifth phase of analysis involves identifying the kinds of cognitive and perceptual activities the human operator might have to engage in when carrying out different control tasks. This phase helps the analyst see if there are regularities in the work domain, the control tasks, or the strategies that might be more directly conveyed to the human operator so that workload is lower and understanding is higher.

Vicente (1991) used some of these forms of analysis to develop and test a new interface for DURESS (see Figure 9.5) that contrasts with the so-called physical or P interface shown in Figure 9.2. The new "physical + functional" or PF interface reveals information from some of the uppermost levels of the work domain analysis in Figure 9.3 and displays them in a way that shows relations

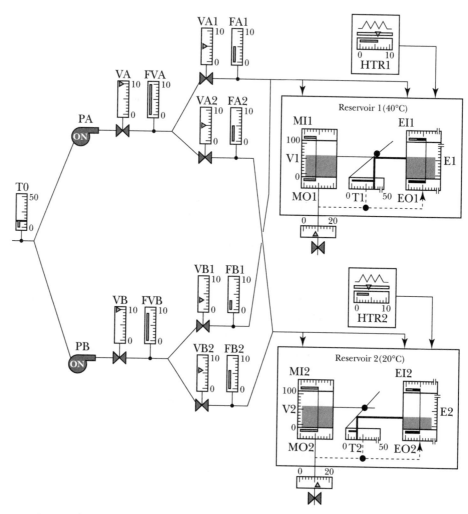

FIGURE
9.5
The "PF" (physical + functional) interface for DURESS, (adapted from Vicente, 1999).

between them. A series of studies have shown that operators not only understand the effects of their actions better with the PF interface than with the P interface, but they can also perform complex configurations more efficiently, manage and diagnose unexpected and unfamiliar faults much more easily, and usually demonstrate a better fundamental knowledge of how DURESS works (Vicente, 1996, 1999). Effective operators also show greater variety in their control activity than less effective operators, but tighter capture of operating targets and production goals (Yu, Lau, Vicente, & Carter, 2002; Hajdukiewicz & Vicente, in press).

In summary, the experiments with DURESS were the first strong empirical proof of what, for many years, the Risø group had known analytically, observed in the field, or seen informally in simulator studies. An analysis of work that identifies behavior-shaping constraints, from the work domain itself through to the cognitive competencies of workers, leads to the design of interfaces that better support human operators when they face unanticipated variability.

9.3   SCIENTIFIC FOUNDATIONS

We now consider the scientific foundations of CWA. CWA developed slowly as a response to a practical need, which was to design information and control environments to support human-operator adaptation when unanticipated variability occurs, so that human-machine systems would be more reliable. CWA is therefore not an application of preexisting theory to a new need. Rasmussen's comments (1986) given at the start of this chapter indicate that the Risø group developed its own approach because of lack of appropriate guidance from the existing scientific literature.

Instead of a scientific foundation, CWA has something closer to a scientific justification that practitioners have developed in parallel with the approach itself. As Rasmussen (1986) notes:

> the conceptual framework that we developed turned out to be very useful for relating our system design problems to discussions in the scientific literature in general. (Rasmussen, 1986, p. x)

CWA developed alongside an awareness of intellectual developments in cognitive and ecological psychology, sociology, anthropology, systems science, safety science, decision science, communications theory, control theory, and so on, rather than as a direct result of any of them (Rasmussen, 1986; Rasmussen et al., 1994; Vicente, 1999). However, the scientific justification of CWA is, in some areas, sufficiently robust that it supports unique, empirically testable predictions about human adaptation in work contexts (Flach, Hancock, Caird, & Vicente, 1995; Hancock, Flach, Caird, & Vicente, 1995; Hajdukiewicz & Vicente, in press).

In the following sections we examine the scientific justification of CWA from the perspectives of systems thinking and ecological psychology, and we will also touch on the role of cognitive science in CWA.

9.3.1   A Systems Perspective

CWA is an approach to understanding human work that rests strongly on a systems perspective—the idea that "the whole is more than the sum of the parts." Systems theorists believe that the properties of a whole system cannot be inferred by studying properties of its parts, but instead they must be inferred by studying relations between the parts (von Bertalanffy, 1968). If we study the parts of a system and, from our understanding of the properties of the parts, hope to understand the properties of the whole, we are taking a "reductionist" or analytic view. On the other hand, if we identify the properties of the parts of a system and then identify the arrangements and relations between those parts with a view to understanding properties of the whole system, we are taking an "antireductionist" or systems view. By doing the latter, the systems theorist hopes to discover properties that emerge from certain arrangements of elements. Those properties may be relevant across a wide variety of systems, regardless of whether those systems are biological, ecological, social, engineered, and so on.

As is consistent with an antireductionist systems perspective, CWA takes the whole human-environment system as the unit of analysis. Early researchers in the area of human manual control of vehicles and industrial systems learned that modeling the human, then modeling the environment, and then putting the two together in hopes of understanding human-system interaction, does not work (Moray, 1986; Rouse, 1980; Sheridan & Ferrell, 1974; Taylor, 1957). Instead, modeling the environment (for example, modeling what an engineered system is meant to do and how it is constructed) constrains what models of its human controller will be sensible and what kind of modeling languages might be useful.

The concept of control raises a second aspect of the systems perspective that is relevant for CWA—the distinction between open and closed systems. An open system is one that is subject to disturbances or input from the environment, whereas a closed system is not. An open system therefore will usually require intervention (control) from time to time if it is to continue functioning according to some criterion. The area of systems theory that deals with how open systems function and how they are regulated in the face of disturbances is known as *cybernetics* (Ashby, 1956). These days, human control of complex systems is aided by automatic controllers and intelligent aiding systems that undertake much of the responsibility for following targets and compensating for anticipated disturbances (Sheridan, 1987). The role of the human operator is typically simply to monitor how well the automatic controllers are working and to make further adjustments if needed. However, when a disturbance occurs that is beyond what the automatic controller understands—so-called unanticipated variability—the human operator will need to take compensating action that is effective. A key goal of CWA is the modeling, analysis, design, and evaluation of information systems that support the kind of adaptation that will restore control.

The systems perspective is also evident in the fact that CWA concepts come from a wide variety of disciplines—indeed, Rasmussen and colleagues (1994) described the conceptual foundations of CWA as "a cross-disciplinary market place" and pointed to the need to develop a conceptual framework for integrating very different ideas:

> The cross-disciplinary problem is to identify or develop compatible paradigms in the involved disciplines and to become familiar with their different terminologies. Of course, this creates very difficult, but also very stimulating problems—first in the efforts to establish a common framework and terminology . . . and second, in maintaining concepts and terms that can serve the communication within the communities of the individual academic disciplines. (Rasmussen et al., 1994, p. xv)

Providing abstract unifying frameworks of the kind seen in CWA is very much a preoccupation of systems thinking. For the group at Risø, a key unifying concept within the CWA framework was the concept of behavior-shaping constraints being passed from one domain of discourse within the framework to another, as we will see in Section 9.5.

9.3.2   An Ecological Orientation

The ecological orientation is particularly strong in CWA. Rasmussen and colleagues (1994) talk of building "ecological information systems" that human operators can operate with something closer to the ease with which they navigate the natural world. Rasmussen and Vicente (1989) and Vicente and Rasmussen (1990, 1992) also propose "ecological interface design" (EID), which is an approach to building interfaces using specific principles of CWA.

Ideas from ecological science—and from Gibsonian ecological psychology in particular—enter the Risø group's work from the early 1980s onwards (see Rasmussen, 1986). As Carroll and Rosson (Chapter 15, this volume) note, "ecological science rests on the principle that systems in the natural and social world have evolved to exploit environmental regularities." Ecological *psychology* proposes that much human perception and action can be understood as an evolved response to higher-order environmental regularities that allow a direct perception of the significance of information (Gibson, 1979). Ecological psychology could therefore be characterized as the study of the way organisms perceive and respond to regularities in information.

A key concept behind ecological psychology is that environments and information should be described in terms that reveal their functional significance for an actor rather than being described in objective actor-free terms. A classic example is Warren's (1982) work on stair climbing, in which he finds that there is a constant ratio between stair riser height and an individual's leg length that minimizes energy expenditure and maximizes the subjective experience of comfort when climbing. Neither the riser height nor the leg length alone accounted for effectiveness and comfort. Instead, it is the relationship between the two for each individual actor that accounted for effectiveness and comfort.

A further concept is the idea of affordances. The affordances of an object are the possibilities for action with that object, from the point of view of a particular actor (Gibson, 1979; McGrenere & Ho, 2000). Those possibilities may or may not be discerned by the actor—that is a separate question. One goal of EID is to make affordances visible.

A final concept is the idea of direct perception, which proposes that certain information meaningful to an actor is automatically picked up from the visual array. A classic example is Lee's (1976) discovery that vehicle-braking behavior is controlled by direct visual information in the flow of optic information about time-to-collision, rather than by inferences constructed from lower-level information such as distance-to-go, speed, and acceleration. While the concept of direct perception has been heavily challenged from other areas, the concept underlies much of EID, a derivative of CWA.

The ecological influence on CWA emerged most strongly after a series of interactions in the late 1980s between the Risø group and a group of scientists based around the University of Illinois who combined interests in cognitive engineering with interests in ecological psychology. Flach (1995) provides a personal historical account of these interactions. The ecological approach to human factors that emerged is the application of ecological psychology to *engineered systems* rather than to natural habitats (Flach et al., 1995; Hancock et al., 1995). Engineered systems are tools for achieving purposes and involve information transactions with humans. However, they have higher-order regularities that humans have not yet evolved to pick up directly, often making the perception of significance difficult. Moreover, regularities in engineered systems change as quickly as technologies and industries change, so we cannot expect humans to evolve fast enough to pick up new regularities in each generation of engineered systems.

One response to this problem has been to build increasingly sophisticated diagnostic tools and decision aids to relieve the human of the intense cognitive load usually required to understand the state of a system and to choose what to do. However, this often means that, if something goes wrong, the human has a struggle to get back into the picture (Bainbridge, 1983). An alternative approach—the response preferred by those taking an ecological approach—is to determine how engineered systems might be designed to take advantage of human perceptual-motor efficiencies that have *already* evolved to show how the system is (or is not) functioning according to its first principles to achieve goals. Such a system would make it easier for the human operator to directly perceive the system state and to select actions to restore safe functioning in a way that respects the first principles. An example of this approach will be given in Section 9.5.

There is a strong link between the systems perspective discussed in Section 9.3.1 and ecological psychology in the scientific justification they provide for CWA. Both emphasize the need to take the human-environment system as the unit of analysis, and both emphasize the logically primary role of the environment in any analysis of goal-oriented behavior. Ecological psychology, however, provides us with a particular orientation on how the environment should be analyzed. It emphasizes an *observer-dependent* analysis of the environment rather than an observer-independent analysis. It challenges us to find higher-order regularities in the environment that might map to functional properties of a task and to actions of a skilled operator (Flach, 1995; Kirlik, 1995).

9.3.3   The Role of Cognition

Given that CWA stands for *cognitive* work analysis, cognitive science plays a smaller role than might be expected, even though that role is essential. Vicente (1999) even explains the name CWA as a historical accident, stating that CWA might have been better called *sociotechnical* work analysis. It is important to realize that CWA is not a theory of cognition or even a cognitive model of work, but instead a way of analyzing constraints that shape work-related cognition. As we move through the phases of CWA, we are moving from environmental determinants to cognitive determinants of activity.

For CWA, it is important, first, to understand what environmental constraints should be identified and conveyed to human operators, before turning to an analysis of human cognitive constraints—cognitive strengths and limitations (Flach, 1995; Vicente, 1999). For example, human factors and human-computer interaction (HCI) researchers sometimes claim that interfaces should be designed to be compatible with the mental models of human operators. However, where there is an external physical system being controlled, it is more important to determine what the *correct* model of the system and possibilities for action are that should be conveyed to the human operator (Rasmussen, 1986). Vicente (1999) provides a full development of this argument with examples of the dangers of basing design on the mental models of even the most experienced human operators.

Once the correct model to convey has been identified, then cognitive science can help determine *how* that correct model might be conveyed to human operators, what cognitive competencies human operators might bring to the situation, and how human performance might be supported. Many areas of cognitive science become relevant at this point, and CWA provides a meta-framework for organizing their contributions. When we describe CWA in detail in Section 9.4, and particularly the CWA phase known as Worker Competencies Analysis, the role of cognitive science in CWA will be clearer.

9.3.4   Summary

Overall, CWA is a multidisciplinary approach to cognitive engineering with a systems orientation that has strong ties to psychology, sociology, decision theory, control theory and to the technology related to the domains in which CWA is applied. Although the concepts and models related to those fields present scientific hypotheses about human-work interaction, CWA does not do so in the same sense. Instead, CWA presents a framework for the design of work places and work systems. Therefore, the formulation of the CWA concepts as an approach to design is not falsifiable in the way a scientific hypothesis would be, but the results from its use for design are falsifiable (Rasmussen, personal communication, January 12, 2003).

9.4   DETAILED DESCRIPTION

In this section, we describe CWA in more detail. First, we discuss the analytic phases of CWA. Then we describe each phase and give an example of the kind of analytic products that come out of each phase. Finally, we show how the phases of CWA are relevant at all points in the system life cycle.

9.4.1   Overviews of CWA

Using the terms introduced earlier, CWA is an approach to analyzing human cognitive work that will lead to systems that better support human-operator adaptation when operators are confronted with unanticipated variability. A key

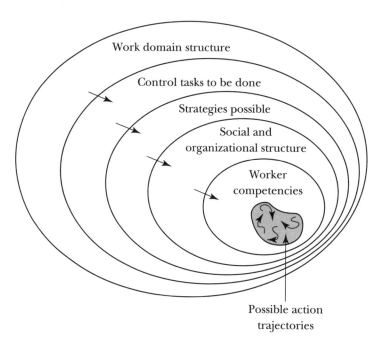

Possible action
trajectories

FIGURE   A space of action possibilities is represented as a malleable form, shaped by five
                classes of constraint.
9.6

idea behind CWA is that human work activity is shaped by a nested set of constraints ranging from determinants in the work domain itself through to cognitive competencies in the human operator. Repeating Rasmussen and colleagues'
(1994) description:

> analysis of work systems must be in terms of the behavior shaping goals and
> constraints that defines [sic] the boundaries of a space within which actors
> are free to improvise guided by their local and subjective performance crite-
> ria. (Rasmussen et al., 1994, p. 25)

The five classes of constraint relate to the five phases of CWA that were outlined in Figure 9.2. Researchers have found various ways to illustrate how these
classes of constraint are nested. Figure 9.6 combines several of these views. In
the center of the figure is a "dynamic space of functional action possibilities"
(Vicente, 1999, p. 339) from which workers choose a set of actions that will help
them achieve their goals. However, the action possibilities for the workers are
not limitless. Instead, they are constrained by the way the work domain works,

the control tasks that are possible within the work domain, the strategies that can be used to perform those control tasks, the social-organizational structures available to carry out those strategies, and the cognitive competencies of the actors who carry out the strategies. Each class of constraint removes options for what an appropriate and possible course of action might be. In this way, the set of actions that both make sense and are possible are progressively narrowed down to a set of actions from which the worker chooses.

9.4.2   Description of CWA Classes of Constraint

In the discussion that follows, we use Vicente's (1999) five CWA phases as the key classes of behavior-shaping constraint. We briefly describe each phase and introduce the analytic formalisms typically employed with brief examples.

Work Domain Analysis (WDA)

The work domain is the set of physical and purposive constraints within which activity takes place, but the work domain does not describe activity. By "purposive," we refer to the reasons that a technical system exists and must be controlled. Analyzing the work domain might involve analyzing a natural or engineered physical system, or a socially constructed system of work. For example, a WDA of the work domain of a navy frigate involves analyzing the physical and purposive structure of the frigate and also the constraints imposed by the natural environment in which the frigate finds itself (Burns, Bryant, & Chalmers, 2001).

WDA usually involves an analysis along two orthogonal dimensions—abstraction and decomposition—to make an abstraction-decomposition space (see Figure 9.7). Rasmussen (1979a, 1985) has always identified five levels of abstraction: functional purpose, abstract function, generalized function, physical function, and physical form. These are shown in Figure 9.7 with a description at left. In each level of the abstraction hierarchy, the same system is fully described, but the descriptive languages relate to the physical elements of the work domain at the bottom two levels and to the intention or purpose of the work domain at the top three levels. Connections between an element at one level to an element at the next level above indicates *why* the first element exists, whereas connections to an element at the next level below indicates *how* the element has been instantiated or engineered. In this way, the physical functioning of a system is connected with its purposive functioning.

Figures 9.2 shows Vicente's (1991) DURESS system with its abstraction hierarchy (AH) representation showing connections between levels as graphical

Description of Level	Level	System	Subsystem	Unit	Component
The intended effect of the system on its environment.	Functional purpose (FP)	FP of whole system	FP of subsystems	FP of units	FP of components
Priorities, values, balances, and relations to be conserved for the system to have its intended effect and to fulfill the functional purpose.	Abstract function (AF)	AF of whole system, taken together	AF within subsystems	AF of units	AF of components
Functional properties and flows that emerge when physical functions are configured to serve the functional purpose of the work domain.	Generalized function (GF)	GF of whole system, taken together	GF of subsystems	GF of units	GF of components
Basic functional properties of objects at the physical-form level.	Physical function (PFu)	PFu of whole system, taken together	PFu of subsystems	PFu of units	PFu of components
Physical form—objects, structures, and configurations.	Physical form (PFo)	PFo of whole system, taken together	PFo of subsystems	PFo of units	PFo of components

FIGURE
9.7

The abstraction-decomposition space most frequently used for WDA, with a definition of each level. Areas in the abstraction-decomposition space usually developed during WDA are shaded.

links. The links connect means and ends in terms of the structure of the work domain, not in terms of activity that is performed on it. This is an important distinction that will become clearer after examining Control Task Analysis.

Decomposition involves breaking down the work domain from wholes into its constituent parts. It can be performed independently at each level of abstraction because each level describes the whole system (see Bisantz & Vicente, 1994, for an example). Decomposition clarifies part-whole relations in the work domain, which are distinct from the structural means-ends relations that connect levels of abstraction.

It is easy to confuse WDA with task analysis, especially as many forms of task analysis are a hierarchical decomposition of how observable behavior emerges from goals. Vicente (1999, 2000) notes that task analysis is an analysis of *trajectories* of behavior (trajectories seen or trajectories possible), whereas work domain analysis is an analysis of *fields of constraints* that will mold trajectories of behavior. For example, navigational directions give you specific routes for getting from place to place. However, a map displays the field of constraints (roads, terrain, etc.) that allows you to construct your own route or even to make a detour around an unexpected obstacle. The directions are a task-based description, whereas the map is a representation of the constraints that will mold behavior. WDA therefore does not include representations of events, tasks, strategies, actions, or actors.

In summary, WDA starts to narrow down the "dynamic space of functional action possibilities" by defining the physical functionality and purposive structure of a work domain. However, it does not specify events, tasks, strategies, actions, or actors.

Control Task Analysis

Control Task Analysis (CTA) defines what needs to be done for a work domain to be effectively controlled. As Vicente notes, "a control task analysis should identify what needs to be done, independently of how or by whom, using a constraint-based approach" (Vicente, 1999, p 183). Control tasks might be completed by automation or intelligent agents just as readily as by humans.

Control tasks need an overall coordinative framework. Rasmussen and colleagues (1994) distinguish a kind of control task analysis that identifies work coordination needs versus a kind that identifies decision needs:

> The pattern of interaction between people and their work environment, as well as their mutual cooperation, is more or less continuous and dynamic. In order to analyze this interaction, it is necessary to decompose the pattern into meaningful elements that are manageable for separate analysis. . . . Activities must be decomposed and analyzed in terms of a set of problems to solve or a set of task situations to cope with. (Rasmussen et al., 1994, p. 58)

The work domain is now instantiated as a set of situations or functions, on which more detailed analyses can be performed. An analysis of activity using work functions is therefore "a focus on the degrees of freedom left for meaningful activities by the constraints posed in time and functional space by a particular task situation" (Rasmussen et al., 1994, p. 29). Figure 9.8 shows an initial analysis of an air defense work domain in terms of work situations (phases of mission) and general classes of work functions (prototypical problems that need to be solved) (Sanderson & Naikar, 2000). It provides a framework for showing constraints on how work functions are coordinated over time.

Once a general framework has been developed for showing how control tasks are coordinated with each other, CTA provides us with tools for identifying constraints on how control tasks might be executed. For this, Rasmussen's (1983) decision-ladder formalism is often used. The decision ladder is not a model of human decision making but instead is a template of possible information-processing steps that allow a controller, human or automatic, to take information about the current state of the system and execute appropriate actions in response. Given the needs of different control tasks, and because of the nature of expertise, some information-processing steps are sometimes omitted. Figure 9.9 shows associative leaps between nonadjacent states of knowledge

	On ground Not in aircraft	On ground In aircraft	On way to station	On station	Returning to base	On ground In aircraft	On ground Not in aircraft
Mission planning and reporting		Mission planning				Mission reporting	
System set-up, configuration, and shutdown		System set-up / System configuration				System shutdown	
Surveillance activity				Surveillance			
Control activity			Control				

FIGURE

9.8

Framework for performing Control Task Analysis using work functions. Example shows an air defense work domain (from Sanderson & Naikar, 2000).

and shunts from information-processing activities to a state of knowledge that bypasses a lot of intervening information processing.

When invoked, an information-processing step in the decision ladder receives inputs (events, goals, system states) that it transforms into outputs (control adjustments), subject to constraints based in the human controller's knowledge of possible and proper functioning of the work domain. The CTA therefore defines an envelope within which actors can operate to fulfill the functional purpose of the system, but it still leaves open the exact strategies and adjustments used. Superimposed on the decision ladder in Figure 9.9 is a control task involving a routine adjustment, where observation leads immediately to a corrective task, bypassing much intervening information processing (based on Rasmussen, 1980).

In summary, CTA continues to narrow down the "dynamic space of functional action possibilities" by defining constraints that must be satisfied when work functions are coordinated over time and when effective control is exercised over the work domain. CTA indicates what needs to be done, but not how it should be done or by whom. Control Task Analysis is therefore different from cognitive task analysis (Schraagen et al., 2000), which usually includes assumptions about who is doing the task and how.

Strategies Analysis

Strategies Analysis (SA) is the phase of CWA at which *how* control tasks can be done is analyzed. The focus is not on the details of actual observed strategies, but

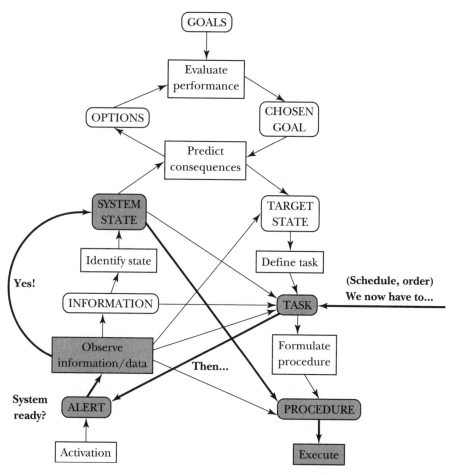

FIGURE

9.9

Decision-ladder template for identifying information-processing steps when conducting Control Task Analysis (from Rasmussen, 1980).

instead is on general classes of strategies and their intrinsic demands, regardless of who or what is carrying them out (Naikar & Pearce, 2001). As noted by Rasmussen (1981):

> System design must be based upon higher level models of the structures of effective mental processes which the operators can use and their characteristics with respect to human limitations and preferences so that operators can adapt individually and develop effective strategies. Rather than descriptions of the course and content of actual mental processes, we need descriptions

of the structure of possible and effective mental processes. (Rasmussen, 1981, p. 242; quoted in Vicente, 1999, p. 215)

Usually a control task can be carried out in many different ways, each with costs and benefits. Verbal protocols of electronics technicians diagnosing faults in laboratory equipment showed that the technicians used a variety of problem-solving strategies, often jumping between different strategies (Rasmussen, 1981; Rasmussen & Jensen, 1973, 1974). Some strategies involved simply trying to localize the fault by moving through the circuitry doing "good/bad" tests of components. Other strategies used the information from tests to indicate system state, rather than fault location, either by matching the data pattern to patterns associated with particular faults, by guiding a search strategy in a rule-based manner, or by supporting logical inferences about possible fault location. Each time a strategy was carried out, it was different in its details but still retained general properties (such as its tactics and its demands on cognitive resources) that made it a member of that class of strategies.

SA often results in flowchart templates that show strategies in prototypical form. As was the case for the decision ladder, the details of particular instances can then be superimposed on the template. Figure 9.10 compares three strategies for starting up the DURESS microworld: The first opens just one feedwater stream, the second opens both feedwater streams for one side, and the third opens both feedwater streams for both sides (Vicente, 1999). The second and third involve greater computational complexity than the first, but they lead to greater production with a configuration that is more robust if a valve fails. The general classes of strategies may differ across work domains and control tasks, even though there can be higher-order similarities between them (Naikar & Pearce, 2001). Instead, the strategies available to the human operator will reflect the control task in question and the work domain in which the control task is being performed.

In summary, SA continues to narrow down the "dynamic space of functional action possibilities" by defining constraints associated with different classes of strategies that might be used to perform control tasks. SA identifies how control tasks might be carried out, but not by whom.

Social-Organizational Analysis

Social-Organizational Analysis (SOA) looks at how the responsibilities for executing strategies are divided among humans, or between humans and automation, and how the different agents involved might communicate with each other. Since the goal of CWA is to support human-operator adaptation in the face of

a) Single:

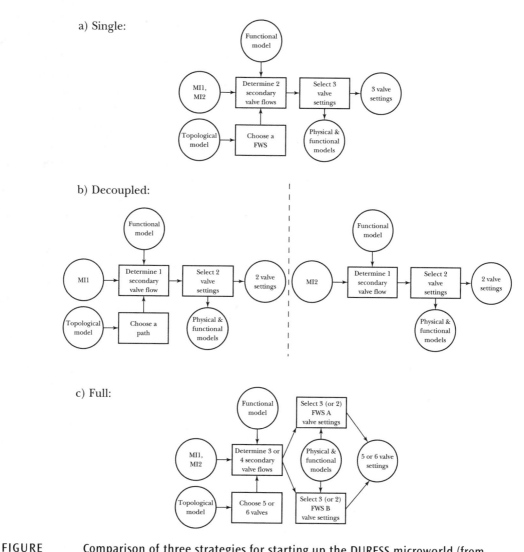

b) Decoupled:

c) Full:

FIGURE

9.10

Comparison of three strategies for starting up the DURESS microworld (from Vicente, 1999).

unanticipated variability, Rasmussen and colleagues (1994) and Vicente (1999) emphasize the need to support social coordination that is *self-organizing*. They distinguish two dimensions contributing to SOA:

✦ The division and coordination of work (the *content*),

✦ The social organization of the workplace (the *form*).

The division and coordination of work refers to how work is divided and co-ordinated between actors. Factors influencing this will be load sharing, the need to couple or decouple functions, safety considerations, and so on. Exactly how work is divided and coordinated will determine the *content*—or information—that must be available for individual actors and that must pass between actors. To show this, SOA typically takes analytic products of CWA (for example, the abstraction-decomposition space, the decision ladder, an information flow diagram, and so on) and overlays them with information indicating which actor or group of actors is responsible for which parts. For example, when responsibility for control tasks is divided across actors, responsibility for the functioning of different parts of the work domain will fall to different actors. Figure 9.11 shows an example from the nuclear power plant domain (Gualtieri, Roth, & Eggleston, 2000).

The social organization of the workplace refers to the organizational architecture of the workplace, whether imposed by management or emerging from social interactions and conventions. The result is the *form*—or behavioral protocol—of communications. As Rasmussen and others (1994) note, examples include autocratic organizations, authority hierarchies, heterarchical structures, or anarchy. If conditions change and it seems that a new organizational structure would be more effective, the actors should be able to move toward the new structure. Again, the form of social organization can be overlain on analytic products of CWA. We will see an example in Section 9.5 that led to a decision about team structure.

In summary, SOA continues to narrow down the "dynamic space of functional action possibilities" by defining constraints imposed by how work is coordinated among actors (through division of work) and how social interaction is controlled (through reporting structures). SOA identifies how "actors"—human or computer—will share responsibility for executing a control task with a specific strategy. However, it does not identify the cognitive demands of a strategy, and therefore the cognitive competencies the human operator should have in order to carry out a control strategy.

Worker Competencies Analysis

Worker Competencies Analysis (WCA) provides a way of classifying different kinds of cognitive control needed if the human operator is to carry out control strategies successfully. WCA helps the analyst determine how those demands might be met or aided, given what is known of human cognition. Rasmussen's (1983) Skills-Rules-Knowledge (SRK) taxonomy is a key tool in WCA. It distinguishes three ways that the human operator's thinking and actions may be

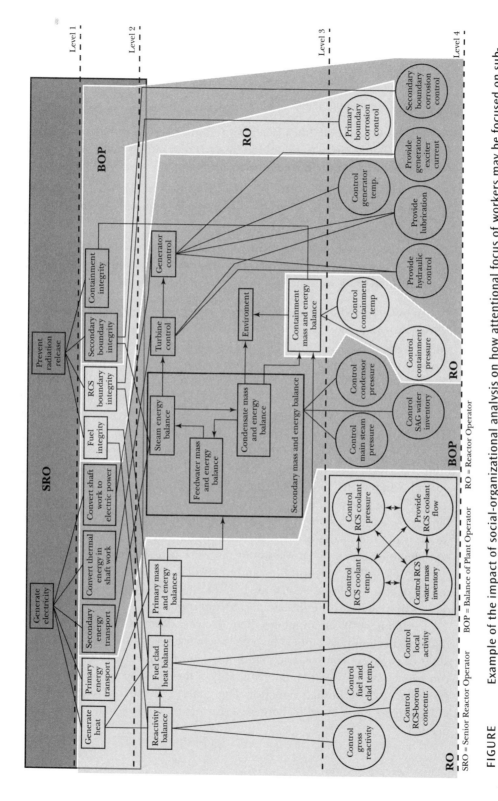

FIGURE   Example of the impact of social-organizational analysis on how attentional focus of workers may be focused on sub-
9.11   sets of the work domain, depending on role (from Gualtieri, Roth, & Eggleston, 2000).

guided by the constraints in the work situation. Three different kinds of cognitive control are distinguished:

+ Skill-based behavior (SBB) is behavior tightly coupled with space-time signals from the environment, or guided by signs that rapidly evoke a sensorimotor response without further cognitive processing.

+ Rule-based behavior (RBB) is behavior guided by signs from the environment that trigger an association between a required system state and a course of action.

+ Knowledge-based behavior (KBB) is behavior guided by states of the system that are symbols whose significance must first be determined. KBB usually requires reasoning with the first principles of the domain.

An experienced operator will move fluently between different levels of cognitive control in response to the familiarity of the work situation, how the work situation manifests itself, and the tools available for responding to the situation. Figure 9.12 shows how cognitive control is channeled into a category based on how the work situation is interpreted (left side) and how ready-at-hand a response is (right side). SBB is the least resource demanding, and human operators will prefer to work in that region when it is feasible and safe. This is an insight that we will return to when discussing EID in Section 9.5.

As Sanderson and Harwood (1988) have emphasized, SRK is not a model of human performance or a model of human skill acquisition similar to those proposed by Anderson (1982) or Fitts and Posner (1967). Instead, it is a taxonomy for classifying how cognition is controlled by the way information is presented in the environment. Despite this, WCA is the most "cognitive" of the CWA phases. If we carry out the phases of CWA successively, then by the time we reach WCA, a considerable amount is known about the work ecology, how the system works, what people will do to it and how, and who will do it. Analyzing the cognitive demands of action helps us determine how an interface should be designed and indicates how operators might be selected and trained.

In summary, WCA completes the narrowing down of the "dynamic space of functional action possibilities" by providing a framework for classifying different kinds of cognitive control. Each kind of cognitive control reflects how the work constraints are represented, the familiarity of the situation, and the training and experience of the human operator. The general category of cognitive control will point to more specific human-performance models that can be used as needed.

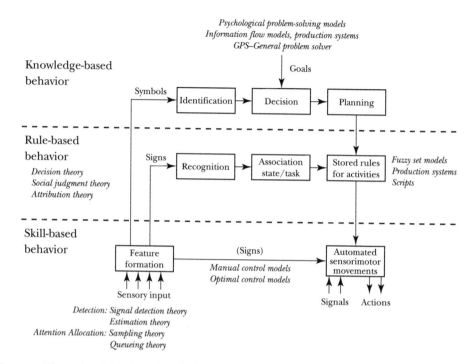

Psychological problem-solving models
Information flow models, production systems
GPS–General problem solver

Knowledge-based behavior

Goals

Symbols → Identification → Decision → Planning

Rule-based behavior

Decision theory
Social judgment theory
Attribution theory

Signs → Recognition → Association state/task → Stored rules for activities

Fuzzy set models
Production systems
Scripts

Skill-based behavior

Feature formation

(Signs)

Manual control models
Optimal control models

Automated sensorimotor movements

Sensory input

Signals   Actions

Detection: Signal detection theory
Estimation theory
Attention Allocation: Sampling theory
Queueing theory

FIGURE
9.12

Diagram of skill-based, rule-based, and knowledge-based behavior, showing how the availability of responses channels processing either to a response (right side) or to a qualitatively different kind of processing (left side).

9.4.3   CWA and the System Life Cycle

Because of CWA's focus on providing work environments that allow human operators to adapt to unanticipated variability, there is often a large focus on interface design. However, CWA can guide decision making about human-system integration at all points in the system life cycle (SLC) (Sanderson, Naikar, Lintern, & Goss, 1999). Stages of the SLC include requirements definition, modeling and simulation, tender evaluation, operator training, system upgrade, and system decommissioning. Each of the five phases of CWA can in principle be applied to each stage in the SLC. This approach has been useful in several defense establishments around the world, including Australia's Defence Science and Technology Organisation (DSTO). CWA has been used by DSTO personnel to provide advice to defense customers (Naikar & Pearce, 2001; Naikar, Pearce, Drumm, & Sanderson, 2002; Naikar & Sanderson, 1999; 2001) that ranges across evaluating tenders, determining the best crew composition for a new platform, defining training and training-simulator needs, and assessing risks in upgrading existing defense platforms (see Section 9.5). Recently, Hori, Vicente, Shimizu, and Takami (2001) have taken the idea represented in the SLC and have shown how CWA satisfies ISO standards for building in usability during the system life cycle.

Not all applications of CWA—whether for requirements definition, interface design, training, or system upgrade—use all phases of CWA to the same degree, or even at all. The questions at hand dictate where the analytic effort should be focused. However, analytic products developed at one stage in the SLC for a particular system can be reused at later stages, resulting in economy of effort and greater ease of communication with and between professionals involved at each level.

9.5 CASE STUDIES

Because no case study covers all the phases of CWA equally well, or a representative selection of points along the system life cycle, a variety of case studies will be presented here. They fall into two general categories: display design and evaluations of human-system integration.

9.5.1 Display Design

One of the most useful byproducts of CWA is EID (Vicente & Rasmussen, 1990, 1992; Vicente, 2002). The goal of EID is to find a way of displaying information to the human operator about the work domain that lets the operator function at the least resource-demanding level of cognitive control that is practical, while still being able to reason from first principles if needed. EID is based on two ideas from CWA:

+ Analyzing the work ecology as a structural means-ends hierarchy. This involves using the abstraction hierarchy, which is the key analytic template for WDA.

+ Supporting human cognitive work at the most appropriate level of cognitive control. This involves using the SRK distinction, which is a key analytic template for WCA.

Three design principles emerge from the SRK distinction, described by Vicente (2002, p. 4) as follows:

✦ Skill-based behavior (SBB)—workers should be able to act directly on the interface.

✦ Rule-based behavior (RBB)—there should be a consistent one-to-one mapping between the work domain constraints and the perceptual information in the interface.

✦ Knowledge-based behavior (KBB)—the interface should represent the work domain in the form of an abstraction hierarchy to serve as an externalized mental model for problem solving.

EID uses the WDA and WCA phases of CWA and combines them with ecological concepts—specifically, the idea that answers to questions should be directly picked up from the interface whenever possible, rather than being laboriously inferred.

Many interfaces have been developed and evaluated by the Risø group and colleagues using concepts later formalized in the EID framework (Goodstein, 1968). The first interface explicitly built using EID principles and subjected to controlled experimental investigations was the PF interface of Vicente's (1991) DURESS system (see Section 9.2). Here, however, we turn to a more complex example by Ham and Yoon (2001a, 2001b) based on the secondary side of a nuclear power plant (NPP; see Figure 9.13).

Following EID, Ham and Yoon performed a WDA of the system using an abstraction hierarchy representation in order to determine what should be displayed. Figure 9.14 shows an AH representation of the NPP secondary side. Structural means-ends links are shown.

Ham and Yoon (2001a) sought to answer a criticism that some experimental comparisons of EID displays with conventional displays have been confounded because an EID interface not only uses configural graphics but also contains more information than a conventional interface does (Maddox, 1996). This is a difficult criticism to answer, because part of the rationale behind EID is that functional information—too often omitted from interfaces—is needed alongside physical information. However, Ham and Yoon sought to answer this criticism by several means:

1. As much as possible, retain the same representational format across conditions being compared rather than changing information and format at the same time.

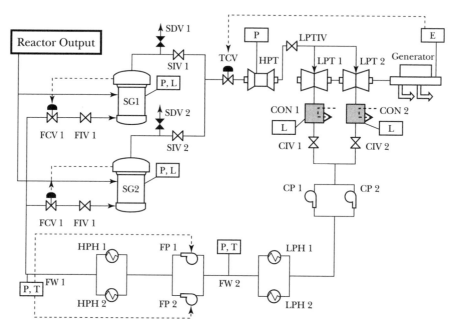

FIGURE

9.13

Physical form representation of Ham and Yoon's (2001a, 2001b) nuclear power plant secondary-side simulation.

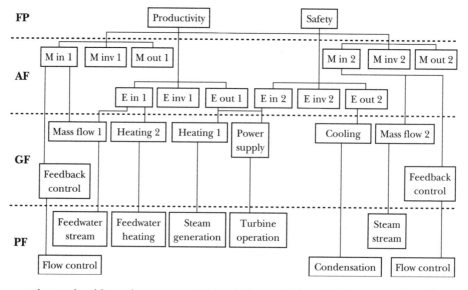

FIGURE

9.14

Abstraction hierarchy representation of Ham and Yoon's (2001a, 2001b) nuclear power plant secondary-side simulation, showing structural means-ends links.

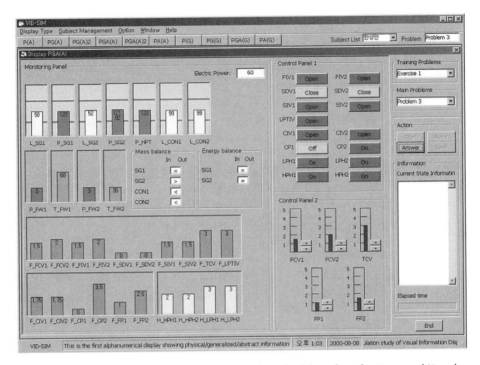

FIGURE

9.15

PGA (physical, generalized, and abstract function) interface for Ham and Yoon's (2001a, 2001b) nuclear power plant secondary-side simulation. (See Plate 7 of the color insert for a color version of this figure.)

2. Perform comparisons that control for the amount of information as much as is consistent with EID.

3. Perform comparisons that test aspects of EID that do not depend on manipulating the amount of information displayed.

In a series of studies, Ham and Yoon (2001a, 2001b) compared interfaces containing different combinations of information from physical function (PF), generalized function (GF), and abstract function (AF) levels of the abstraction hierarchy. Ham and Yoon (2001a) compared the effectiveness of a PF-only interface (P) with a PF-plus-GF interface (PG) and a PF-plus-AF interface (PA). Figure 9.15 and Plate 7 of the color insert show Ham and Yoon's (2001b) PGA interface. The P interface was similar except that both the GF (lower-left bars) and AF (mass and energy balances at center) information was left off. The PG interface omitted the AF information, and the PA interface omitted the GF information.

Subjects used one of the three displays to monitor and diagnose faults while controlling the plant. Results for diagnosis time, amount of information-gathering actions, number of warning alarms, and number of exceed alarms showed that the P interface led to the worst performance, PG the best, and PA in between. The PG interface was best probably because it preserved the natural connection between the adjacent levels of abstraction PF and GF. In contrast, the PF and AF levels in the PA interface were too remote from each other, and the intervening GF information had to be deduced.

Ham and Yoon's (2001b) Experiment 1 compared the PG interface with two interfaces containing information from all the levels of abstraction but displayed slightly differently (PGA and PGA', see Figure 9.15). There was only a weak indication that the PGA interfaces led to better fault diagnosis performance. Ham and Yoon conjectured that the faults being used were not truly creating unanticipated variability that would require human operators to work with the fundamental constraints and principles of operation of the system at the AF level if they were to handle the system effectively.

In Experiment 2, then, Ham and Yoon (2001b) compared fault diagnosis performance with the less complex faults of Experiment 1 versus much more complex faults that created highly cognitively loading situations in which AF information was needed to monitor plant stability. A further PGA interface highlighted means-ends relations between levels of abstraction (PGA-R). Results comparing performance with PG and the PGA and PGA-R interfaces showed that having the AF level of information helped operators with routine faults to a certain extent. However, when there were nonroutine cognitively demanding faults, the PGA interfaces supported better performance than PG. The operator could keep the plant stable with the PGA interface even while handling complex faults. The benefits of showing GF and AF information was strongest of all when the relations between the levels of abstraction were highlighted in the PGA-R interface with means-ends grouping, allowing high-level functional information to be extracted using RBB rather than KBB.

Subsequent studies by the same research group show that a similar pattern of results holds when graphical P, PG, and PGA interfaces are compared (Han, Kim, Ham, & Yoon, 2001). Moreover, unpublished comparisons between graphic and nongraphic versions of displays indicate that the graphical displays are superior, possibly because they clarify means-ends relations even further (Ham, personal communication, January 16, 2002).

In summary, Ham and Yoon's research shows that EID can lead to interfaces that support better human performance under truly unanticipated and complex conditions. The best levels of performance are seen only when all the information from the AH is included in the interface, and interface enhancements expose the structural means-ends relations in the work domain.

9.5.2   Systems Engineering and Human-System Integration

The second case study moves us away from interface design to system evaluation and design of teams for the Commonwealth of Australia's forthcoming AWACS-style air defense platform—Airborne Early Warning and Control (AEW&C). This work shows how Australia's DSTO organization used CWA for revolutionary rather than evolutionary design. It moves our focus from the CWA phases most relevant for EID (WDA and WCA) to CTA and SOA. It also moves our focus from empirical studies to field studies. Finally, it shows how analytic products of CWA developed for one part of the SLC can sometimes be used with relatively little adjustments at other parts of the SLC.

The first need was to evaluate three different designs for AEW&C that had been submitted by three tenderers for the contract. Naikar and Sanderson (2001) used WDA to help in the tender evaluation and selection process. Usually, tenders are evaluated against technical specifications only, and there is no systematic way of relating what is being technically delivered to whether the higher-level purposes of a system are being supported—for example, whether the concept of operations for the platform is being supported. Because WDA provides a way to relate physical structure to the purposes of a system, it was felt that WDA might provide a useful additional tool in the tender-evaluation process.

A WDA was developed for the AEW&C work domain that provided a framework for the Commonwealth's tender-evaluation teams to relate evaluation of technical capabilities at the physical form and function levels to purposive functions at generalized function and abstract function levels of the WDA (see Naikar & Sanderson, 2001, for further details). As Figure 9.16 and Plate 8 of the color insert show, the evaluation subgroups focused on specific technical areas. For each tendered design, the evaluation subgroups judged how the quality of technical solutions affected how well the generalized functions would be supported under that design. Then the head of the overall evaluation team (1) summarized the findings of the subgroups in terms of how well the generalized functions were supported overall, (2) evaluated how well the generalized functions supported the abstract functions, and (3) evaluated how well the abstract functions supported the functional purpose. Finally, the three designs were compared to see how well all levels of the AH were supported, and the designs were ranked.

Although the final decision to award the contract depended upon other processes than the WDA process alone, when the AEW&C Project Office briefed the deputy secretary of the Department of Defence on the evaluation process, WDA was singled out for mention because of its usefulness. WDA had provided a systematic basis for evaluation that integrated the work of different experts.

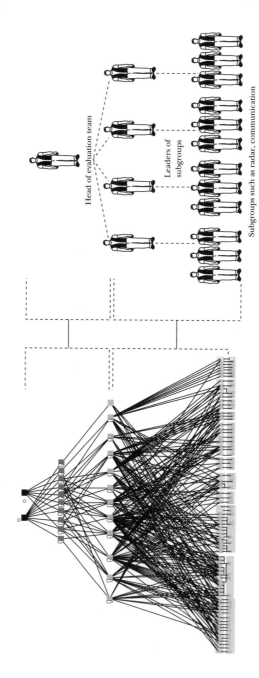

FIGURE   Work Domain Analysis for AEW&C at left (overview) and organizational structure of AEW&C

9.16   tender-evaluation working groups (TEWGs) and sub-TEWGs at right (from Naikar & Sanderson,

            2001). (See Plate 8 of the color insert for a color version of this figure.)

Moreover, it had allowed evaluators to systematically shift their focus from low-level technical factors to high-level functional properties of AEW&C that were independent of particular missions or scenarios.

The next issue on which the Commonwealth needed advice was the best team structure for AEW&C: specifically, how many crewmembers there should be and whether they should be trained in dedicated roles or should be multi-skilled. As before, the advice had to be given on the basis of the limited information available. CWA promised to be useful because of its formative properties, allowing the analyst to focus on behavior-shaping constraints rather than relying upon actual trajectories of behavior (Naikar & Pearce, 2002; Naikar, Pearce, Drumm, & Sanderson, 2002).

To attack this issue, Naikar and colleagues used WDA, a variant of CTA that analyzed more general work functions rather than control tasks, and SOA (Naikar & Pearce, 2001; Naikar, Pearce, Drumm, & Sanderson, 2002). The original WDA from the tender-evaluation work was updated to better reflect structural means-ends relations and was simplified. Naikar and colleagues then extended the work function analysis shown in Figure 9.8, using a variant of a cognitive walkthrough technique with subject-matter experts (SMEs) that involved three steps: (1) working with SMEs to design a general AEW&C operational scenario that would strongly challenge a crew and dividing the scenario into significant epochs, (2) performing a non–real time walkthrough assuming a certain crew structure and keeping records of simulated crew activity and communications, and (3) representing the results of how the scenario unfolded using the work functions.

A general framework for the analysis is shown in Figure 9.17. The work functions or work problems to solve were identified with input from the SMEs and are shown as circles within bands that extend over partially overlapping phases of mission. Figure 9.18 and Plate 9 of the color insert show the results of applying this general representation to the results of the crew cognitive walkthrough process. The crew cognitive walkthrough starts with one specific crew structure assumed. However, once the interplay between work functions and the probable communication demands had been identified, the same scenario could be hand simulated with a different crew structure to examine the effects. In this way, SOA is superimposed on the work-function analysis. Figure 9.18 shows simulated activity for a six-person crew of multiskilled specialists whose roles are given at left (in the figure, four further roles are not staffed). The arrows show the communications required as the mission commander supervises a change of responsibilities for the specialists. By comparing how a scenario plays out under different assumed crew structures, it was possible to draw conclusions about the cognitive workload, communications load, and reliability of information flow among crewmembers in the different cases.

| ON GROUND NOT IN AIRCRAFT | ON GROUND IN AIRCRAFT | EN ROUTE TO STATION | ON STATION | EN ROUTE TO BASE | ON GROUND IN AIRCRAFT | ON GROUND NOT IN AIRCRAFT |

* Recognized Air Sea Picture
† Situational Awareness

FIGURE
9.17

Activity analysis for AEW&C: Identification of work functions and their placement in a frame-of-work situation (from Naikar, Pearce, Drumm, & Sanderson,
2002).

Using this approach, Naikar was able to infer that a seven-person crew with
flexibility not only in skills but also in social-organizational form would be best
equipped to take advantage of multiskilling without undue load on the mission
commander in monitoring role changes. The result is shown in Figure 9.19 (see
also Naikar & Pearce, 2001; Naikar, Pearce, Drumm, & Sanderson, 2002). This
new team design had not previously been considered by the AEW&C project office. Because the new team design was considered better than other solutions
they had considered, the project office adopted it for AEW&C.

* Recognized Air Sea Picture
† Situational Awareness
** Electronic Sensing Measures

FIGURE

9.18

Allocation of work functions to actors in AEW&C showing communications patterns at a selected epoch of the scenario (from Naikar, Pearce, Drumm, & Sanderson, 2002). (See Plate 9 of the color insert for a color version of this figure.)

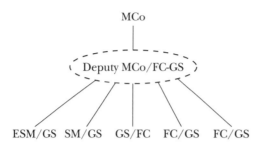

FIGURE

9.19
Proposed team structure for AEW&C based on an analysis of work functions (from Naikar, Pearce, Drumm, & Sanderson, 2002). *MCo* = Mission Commander, *FC* = fighter controller, *GS* = general surveillance, *ESM* = electronic sensing measures, *SM* = sensor management. Slashes indicate multiple roles.

In summary, the AEW&C case study shows that CWA can be used to make recommendations about human-system integration even when very little is known about AEW&C's structure and functioning. For the crew structure case study in particular, the work function analysis and the SOA phase of CWA were used to narrow down the "dynamic space of functional action possibilities" to a point where deductions about crew performance could be drawn, without even knowing the details of their tasks, and inferences could be drawn about a better crew structure that was recognized by SMEs for its validity.

9.6   CURRENT STATUS

Although its constituents have been around since the 1970s, CWA has seen tremendous development over the last decade. Two seminal monographs have been published (Rasmussen et al., 1994; Vicente, 1999), and there has been widespread interest in EID from the research-and-development community.

EID is where the greatest current application of CWA is seen. Although the benefits of EID are still to be proven in large-scale industrial installations—an area where uptake of any new design philosophy is bound to be conservative—evaluations in large-scale industrial simulator environments are emerging (Jamieson, 2002). Experimental studies and simulator evaluations continue to support the benefits of the approach (Vicente, 2002). In the near future, researchers will probably tackle the thorny issue of how EID-based requirements can be turned into physical designs, a process that is still more craft than science (Liu, Nakata, & Furuta, 2002; Reising & Sanderson, 2002c). We will also see more work on the spatial and temporal integration of large information spaces

(Burns, 2000a, 2000b) and possibly work on extending the precepts of EID to auditory and haptic displays (Sanderson, Anderson, & Watson, 2000).

However, an area of extensive growth for CWA in the next decade may involve system life cycle (SLC) issues unrelated to interface design. CWA has a role to play in all stages of the SLC. Recent work on the use of CWA for tender evaluation (Naikar & Sanderson, 2001), software requirements analysis (Leveson, 2000), engineering instrumentation requirements analysis (Reising & Sanderson, 1998, 2000a, 2000b, 2002a, 2002b), training needs analysis and simulator design (Naikar & Lintern, 1999; Naikar & Sanderson, 1999), and crew design (Naikar et al., 2002) point to such potential.

It has often been felt that CWA applies best to physical or engineered work domains rather than social or intentional domains, where the work domain consists of social practices and conventions such as command and control (Lind, 1999; Wong, Sallis, & O'Hare, 1998). Certainly, proper functioning and behavior-shaping constraints are much easier to identify in physical domains than in intentional ones. However, recent CWA work in a variety of intentional domains—and specifically some military domains—suggests that CWA applies to these domains as well. Examples are network management (Kuo & Burns, 2000), defense systems (Bisantz, Roth, Brickman, Gosbee, Hettinger, & McKinney, in press; Burns et al., 2001), and ambulance dispatch (Chow & Vicente, 2002).

Whatever the domain and whatever the purpose, CWA involves detailed modeling, which can be very time consuming. There have been attempts to provide software support for some of the modeling frameworks used for CWA. A prototype software system has been developed for performing WDA, termed the Work Domain Analysis Workbench, or WDAW (Sanderson, Eggleston, Skilton, & Cameron, 1999; Skilton, Sanderson, & Cameron, 1998). The WDAW's graphical user interface provides an abstraction-decomposition space in which nodes and links of different types can be created and manipulated to form a WDA. User-defined highlighting allows analysts to trace certain classes of means-ends and part-whole relations. There are hyperlinks to external documents and applications, such as design documents, simulations, videotaped SME interviews, and so on, so an analysis can become the hub of a distributed system of information about the work domain in question. In another effort, Potter, Roth, Woods, and Elm (2000) have incorporated some of the phases of CWA in a large-scale tool designed to infuse cognitive engineering methods into the software development process. Other efforts are ongoing. Overall, well-designed software support for CWA would help make the approach more accessible and should also help the conceptual development of the approach.

Research-and-development communities composed of people with different scientific backgrounds often find CWA a useful framework for integrating their concerns because of its "systems" qualities. For human-factors psychologists,

CWA can provide a framework for scaling up an analysis from a concern solely with individual cognition to a concern with teams in a rich real-world context. For engineers, CWA can provide a simple way to introduce key factors relating to human cognition and decision making that will influence the effectiveness of human-system interaction. For systems developers and software engineers, however, there is a structural similarity between CWA and existing software engineering techniques, and notions of abstraction on both sides are easy to confuse. As Leveson (2000) has noted, though, CWA can provide a framework for capturing the design intention behind a proposed system that can guide the technical evolution of the system throughout its lifetime.

At present, CWA is practiced by a relatively small but growing school of cognitive engineers. Its future depends on whether it continues to provide conceptual tools to handle new problems in the design of human-system integration environments; whether it does so sufficiently better than other techniques so that the effort of learning it is justified; whether CWA analytic products prove to be useful across the whole system life cycle; and whether methods for applying the CWA approach can be sufficiently well defined so that a wide variety of practitioners can learn and reliably perform them. However, the future of CWA also depends on how easily practitioners adapt its basic underlying principles and synthesize constraint-based methods for the purpose at hand. Ultimately, CWA's success will depend on whether it continues to provide practitioners with unique areas of usefulness.

FURTHER READING

Key references include Vicente (1999, 2002), Rasmussen, Pejtersen, & Goodstein (1994), and Reising (1999). Vicente (1999) provides the first textbook dedicated to CWA. It is the most accessible introduction to Rasmussen's ideas, which can otherwise be difficult to grasp. Rasmussen and colleagues (1994) is the most comprehensive expression of the Risø approach to cognitive engineering. Reising (1999) provides a medium-sized review of Rasmussen and colleagues (1994). Reising provides an invaluable introduction to the book's themes, plus a suggested order for reading the chapters of the book that differs from their printed order. Naikar and Lintern (2002) provide a similarly sized review of Vicente (1999) that gives a further overview and critique of CWA.

10

CHAPTER

Common Ground in Electronically Mediated Communication: Clark's Theory of Language Use

Andrew Monk   University of York, England

Human-computer interaction (HCI) has come to encompass technologies that mediate human-human communication such as text-based chat or desktop video conferencing. The designers of equipment to electronically mediate communication need answers to questions that depend on a knowledge of how we use language. What communication tasks will benefit from a shared whiteboard? When are text messages better than speech? Thus, the theory that informs the design of these artifacts is a theory of human-human interaction.

Previous theories of language use divide into the cognitive and the social. Most psycholinguistic accounts of language production and comprehension are very cognitive. They are solely concerned with the information processing going on in an individual's head. Ethnomethodological and other sociological accounts of language use are, in contrast, social. They concentrate on the structure that is observable in the behavior of groups. Herbert Clark has developed a theory of language use that bridges these two camps and that can make practically relevant predictions for the design of facilities to electronically mediate communication.

The key concept in Clark's theory is that of common ground. Language is viewed as a collaborative activity that uses existing common ground to develop further common ground and hence to communicate efficiently. The theory (1) defines different kinds of common ground, (2) formalizes the notion of collaborative activity as a "joint action," and (3) describes the processes by which common ground is developed through joint action.

The first section in this chapter explains why a purely cognitive model of communication is not enough, and it defines what is meant by the phrase "collaborative activity." Section 10.2 introduces the idea of common ground and how it is used in language through an example of two people communicating over a video link. Section 10.3 indicates where the interested reader can find out about the antecedents to Clark's theory. Section 10.4 sets out the fundamental concepts in Clark's theory. Section 10.5 uses three published case studies of mediated communication to illustrate the value of the theory.

10.1   MOTIVATION

Previous chapters have been concerned with understanding how humans interact with computers, as would seem quite proper in a book on theory in human-computer interaction. However, the discipline of HCI has come to include the study of electronic devices for the purpose of communication, such as video-conferencing systems, text-based chat, and email. Some of the questions designers need to answer about these systems are concerned with human-computer interaction, such as how to use the limited display on a mobile phone, but others are concerned with the way we use language, such as what communication tasks will benefit from a shared whiteboard. As we stated earlier, the theory that answers these questions is a theory of human-human communication.

A common view of human-human communication conceptualizes language as a sender producing some utterance that is then comprehended by a receiver. While this has value, it is not the whole story.

10.1.1   Production Plus Comprehension Equals Communication

The upper part of Figure 10.1 depicts a much simplified model of how two computers communicate with one another. Computer A sends the sequence of characters forming an email message by looking up a digital code for each letter. Each digital code is then translated into a pattern of voltage changes on a wire. Computer B reverses this process. It registers the pattern of voltage changes, converts this into a digital code, and looks up the letter. When enough letters have been accumulated, it can display the email. This conception of information transmission was used by Shannon & Weaver (1949) to formulate a mathematical theory of communication that has been used by communication engineers for many years.

The lower part of Figure 10.1 takes the information-transmission model as an analogy for human-human communication. Some representation of the meaning of a word in Person A's head is looked up to find its phonemic

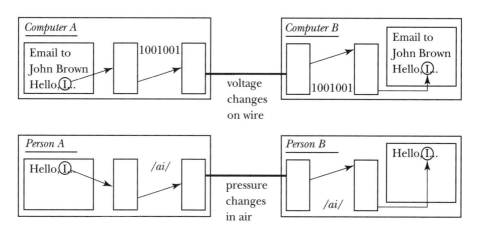

FIGURE

10.1

The information-transfer model of communication, shown in the top panel as applied to communicating computers, and shown in the bottom panel as the encoding-decoding model of human-human communication.

representation, and that is then converted to sound-pressure changes in the air by Person A's vocal apparatus. Person B's ear registers these pressure changes, and auditory processing in Person B's brain converts them to a phonemic representation and then to a representation of the meaning of the word.

This information-processing model allows one to decompose the process of communication into two parts, speech production and speech comprehension. Speech production is the process of converting meaning to sound-pressure changes, and speech comprehension is the process of converting speech-pressure changes back into meaning. Figure 10.1 is a simplified version of current understanding. The linguists, psycholinguists, and speech scientists who study what goes on within each of these two processes have developed sophisticated models hypothesizing many different representations that may be generated along the way (see, for example, Altmann, 1997).

The models developed have resulted in many practical advances. Research on speech comprehension has led to improvements in digital hearing aids and speech-recognition software. The research on speech production has led to speech-synthesis software and speech-therapy programs for stroke victims. This approach to languages use has, however, proved less useful in providing guidelines for the design and configuration of electronic communication systems. For example, if one is designing a video-conferencing configuration, should one use the camera to convey as much information as possible about detailed facial expression and lip movements of the person currently talking, or would it be more valuable to provide a wide angle view of what everyone at the other end is doing? When does text have advantages over speech?

The problem is that models of speech production and speech comprehension are cognitive models. They are models of what goes on in an individual's head. It turns out that to answer the questions posed earlier we need a social model, that is, a model of how a pair or a group of individuals use language as an ensemble. It is not intuitively obvious why this should be so. Common sense says that, if we have one model of how a speaker produces speech and another of how a listener comprehends it, then it should be possible to simply put them together to form a model of language use. The next section explains why we need something more.

10.1.2 Language Use as a Collaborative Activity

Roger: Did you have oil in it?
Al: Yeah, I—I mean I changed the oil, put new oil filters, r—completely redid the oil system, had to put new gaskets on the oil pan to stop—stop the leak, and then I put—and then—
Roger: That was a gas leak
Al: It was an oil leak, buddy
Roger: It's a gas leak
Al: It's an oil ⌐leak!
Roger: └on the number-one jug
Al: It's an oil leak!
Roger: Outta where, the pan?
Al: Yeah
Roger: Oh, you put a new gasket on, it stopped leaking
Al: Uh huh[1]

Consider this conversation. Al has been mending Roger's car. Roger comes to the conversation thinking that the problem involved a gasoline or petrol leak. Al has just fixed an oil leak. What follows is a process of realignment. This language process is described as "repair." It starts when Roger senses "trouble" in the conversation because Al is talking about fixing the oil system. He signals this to Al with the utterance "that was a gas leak." They then collaborate until conversational repair is achieved. Eventually, Roger signals that he now sees there was an oil leak by saying "outta where, the pan?", the pan being the oil sump. Al then signals that he understands that Roger now understands this with his utterance "Yeah."

---

[1] A snippet of real conversation (Jefferson, 1987, p. 90).

This is very different to the picture of communication presented in Figure 10.1. First of all, notice how ill formed and imprecise the utterances are, with repetitions and restarts (e.g., "r—completely redid"). There is also overlapping speech. The tabulation in the dialogue shows that "leak!" and "on the number-one jug" were overlapping in time. Al and Roger get away with this imprecision because communication is a collaborative activity, not just a matter of using a well-defined code to replicate the contents of one person's head in another's.

Al and Roger come to the conversation with different assumptions and priorities. They go away with different assumptions and priorities, but they have developed sufficient common ground to serve each of their separate purposes. The conversation is a collaborative process in which they each endeavor to communicate sufficiently for their own purposes. At the same time, they monitor the conversation for evidence that the other person is or is not communicating sufficiently well for their purposes. Thus, each has an obligation to signal to the other when they sense communication is failing. Each has an obligation to monitor the conversation for such signals and to take appropriate actions to repair the situation until the other signals that all is now well. This mutual pact is the basis of every conversation.

We can now see what the information-transfer model depicted in Figure 10.1 is lacking. Communicating computers have a common code. This is possible because the code is well defined and can be programmed into both computers by engineers. In contrast, everyday spoken language is ambiguous and only works because the parties actively collaborate to make it do so. Experience may have programmed you and me with the same rules for converting sounds into phonemes and for combining phonemes into words. However, when it comes to communicating intent or history, I cannot just look up a recipe that will copy what is in my head into yours. Nor would I want to. Spoken-language use is efficient precisely because only the information relevant to each individual's separate needs is communicated.

This discussion is the starting point for the collaborative model of conversation assumed by Herbert Clark. The remainder of this chapter will describe his theory in more detail and will illustrate how it can be used to explain various observations about electronically mediated human-human communication.

10.2 OVERVIEW

This section introduces the notion of common ground and how it is used in language. Section 10.4 contains a more detailed treatment of the other fundamental concepts in Clark's theory.

Clark's theory is based around the concept of common ground—that is, the things we know about what is known by the person we are talking to. If this seems rather recursive, that is because it is. Clark's definition[2] of common ground implies that:

a proposition *p* is only common ground if: all the people conversing know *p*; and they all know that they all know *p*.

This definition of common ground allows one to move between a view of language as an activity carried out by an ensemble of people (the social viewpoint) and a view of language as an activity carried out by individuals (the cognitive approach). The social viewpoint is developed by providing a detailed description of the activity by which the ensemble of conversants use and increase common ground. The cognitive viewpoint is developed by describing how an individual comes to know what is known by the others.

The nature of common ground is best explained by an example. This example will also illustrate how Clark's theory can help us understand the way that technology may affect the process of communication. Consider two people using a desktop video-conferencing package to discuss an architectural plan. They are wearing headphones with a boom microphone and can hear what each other says without difficulty. They can view changes in the other person's facial expression via a head-and-shoulders view in a small video window. The remainder of the screen is taken up with a shared view of the architectural plan. Let us say that they have never met before. Even so, they can make some assumptions about common ground. First, there will be some common task defined by the work context. Let us say that Anne is an architect and Ben is someone who has hired Anne to design a house for him. The common task, negotiated in their previous correspondence, is to agree what small changes need to be made to make the plan final. They also know they have the common ground that comes from living in the same town.

They can assume certain conventions with respect to the communication process. They will speak English. They will both try to use language that the

---

2 Clark's formal definition of common ground is as follows:
　　p is common ground for members of C if and only if:
　　i. the members of C have information that *p* and that *i*.
　This implies:
　　everyone in C knows *p*,
　　everyone in C knows everyone in C knows *p*,
　　everyone in C knows everyone in C knows everyone in C knows *p*,
　　and so on.

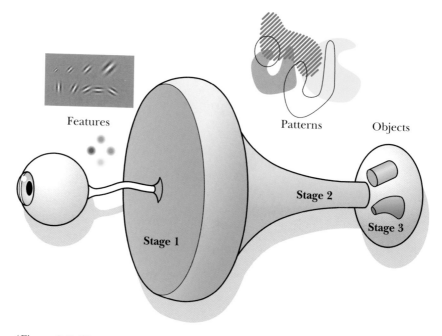

Features   Patterns   Objects

Stage 2

Stage 1

Stage 3

PLATE

1

(Figure 2.1) Three major functional stages of human visual processing include, first, processing incoming information into features, then segmenting it into simple patterns, and finally holding a few more-complex objects in visual working memory.

Because the luminance channel has a far greater capacity to respond to visual detail, it is essential that whenever detailed information must be conveyed there should be luminance contrast between foreground and background.

Because the luminance channel has a far greater capacity to respond to visual detail, it is essential that whenever detailed information must be conveyed there should be luminance contrast between foreground and background.

PLATE

2

(Figure 2.2) About half way down the image on the left, the text differs from its background only in the yellow-blue color channel. Theory predicts that this will be much harder to perceive than the same information shown with luminance contrast as illustrated on the right.

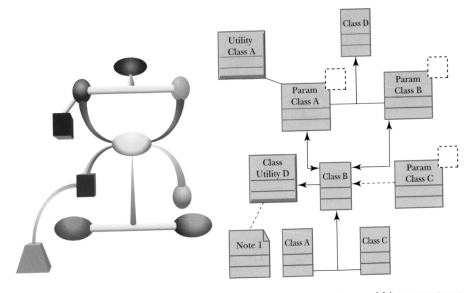

PLATE

3

(Figure 2.6) Because of perceptual mechanisms to analyze the world into structures of three-dimensional primitives, diagrams constructed in this way may be easier to analyze and remember. The diagram on the left is constructed from Geon primitives. The one on the right is a UML equivalent.

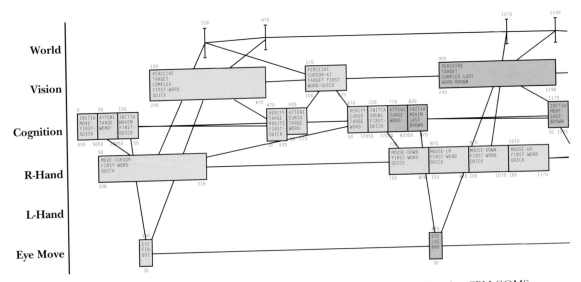

(Figure 4.8) The beginning of the schedule chart representing the CPM-GOMS model of the fox-task editing example. This part of the chart includes highlighting the phrase to be moved and starting to issue the **Cut** command. Each operator is represented as a box, with its start time in the upper-left corner, its duration in the lower-left corner and its end time in the lower-right corner, in msec. The width of each box is proportional to its duration, so the schedule chart is also a timeline. The green

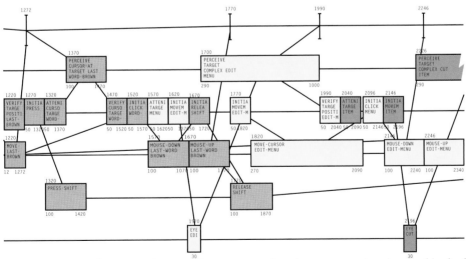

PLATE

4b

boxes are the cognitive, perceptual, and motor operators involved in double-clicking on the word "quick". The blue boxes are those involved in shift-clicking on the word "brown". The yellow boxes are those involved in pulling down the **Edit** menu. The purple boxes are the first four operators involved in selecting the **Cut** menu item. The schedule chart continues beyond this figure, until the end of the task at time=4598 msec.

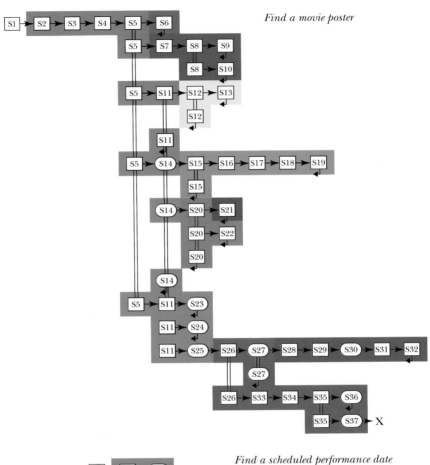

Find a movie poster

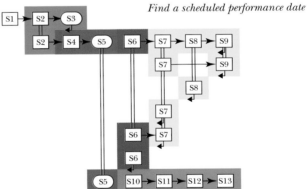

Find a scheduled performance date

PLATE

5

(Figure 7.10) Web Behavior Graphs for a user on two tasks. Each box represents a state of the user-system interaction. Each arrow represents a state change (move). Interaction proceeds left to right, top to bottom. Each move to the right is a move to a new state. Moves down and to the right represent a return to a previous state. Background colors surround interactions with the same Web site.

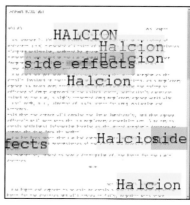

PLATE

6

(Figure 7.11) Enhanced thumbnails.

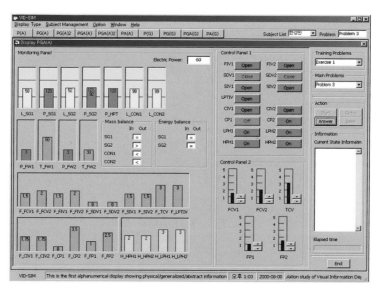

PLATE

7

(Figure 9.15) PGA (physical, generalized, and abstract function) interface for Ham and Yoon's (2001a, 2001b) nuclear power plant secondary-side simulation.

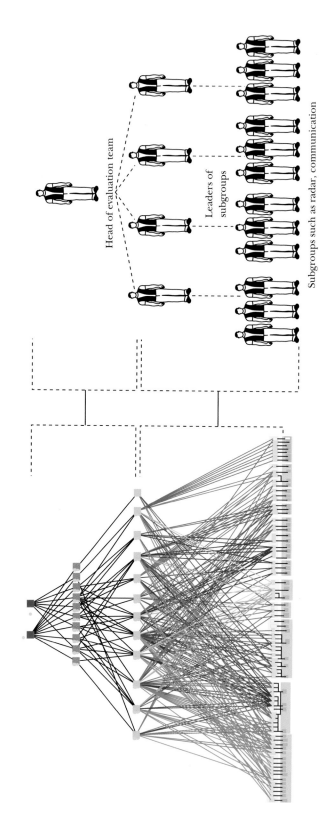

Head of evaluation team

Leaders of subgroups

Subgroups such as radar, communication

PLATE

8

(Figure 9.16) Work Domain Analysis for AEW&C at left (overview) and organizational structure of AEW&C tender-evaluation working groups (TEWGs) and sub-TEWGs at right (from Naikar & Sanderson, 2001).

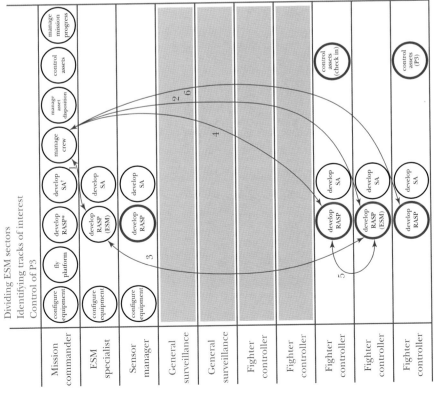

(Figure 9.18) Allocation of work functions to actors in AEW&C showing communications patterns at a selected epoch of the scenario (from Naikar, Pearce, Drumm, & Sanderson, 2002).

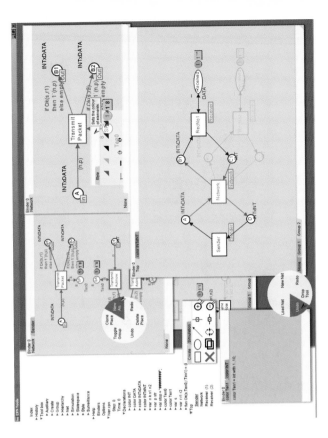

(Figure 11.1) The redesigned CPN2000 binders, palette and marking menu.

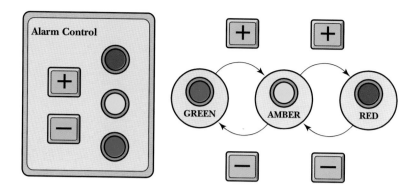

(a) control panel   (b) state transition network

PLATE 11   (Figure 14.2) Top secret control panel.

PLATE 12   (Figure 15.2) The MOOsburg community network system. In the upper left is an exhibit room with three visitors present; the upper right displays a list of tools that can be evoked in this place; the lower left holds a chat tool; and the lower right shows an interactive map that can be panned and zoomed to locate and enter places in MOOsburg.

other will understand and to monitor the conversation for potential misunderstandings. When they feel that they do not understand something sufficiently for their current purposes, they will signal this to the other person.

From the video images, they can make assumptions about their respective ages and genders that may have a bearing on how they express themselves. Also, Anne will assume that Ben will not have the same detailed knowledge of architectural terms that she has. As the conversation develops, she modifies this opinion. Ben uses the term "architrave" correctly, so she tries more technical (and hence more concise) terms in her utterances. These do not cause trouble in the conversation, so she continues to use them. Later, however, Ben does not understand the term "lintel." Anne picks this up from his facial expression and explains it to him. During this explanation, Ben demonstrates his understanding, and they now both assume that this is common ground.

Ben describes how he would like the door of one bedroom moved, the one that faces south. The architectural drawing is larger than the screen, and so this bedroom can be seen only by scrolling from the initial view. In their discussion of a previous detail, Ben has scrolled to this view but Anne has not. He has no way of knowing this. Everyday experience leads him to assume the general principle that what he can see she can see also. This false assumption of common ground causes problems when he uses the phrase "up there on the left." After some time they realize they are talking at cross purposes and go about repairing their common ground.

At the end of the meeting, they check their common ground regarding the original work objective and agree that the drawing can be sent to the builder. As this has legal implications, Anne suggests that she send Ben a paper copy of the modified plan, and Ben agrees to formally accept the plan in a letter. This change of communication medium permits rereading so that each party can ensure that they really have achieved common ground.

The scenario sketched here illustrates the way common ground is used and how technology can affect the process of developing it. The following list summarizes some of the common ground exemplified there under three categories: conversational conventions, communal common ground, and personal common ground.

Conversational conventions

We will each try to be concise as possible but take account of the background of the other person.

We will each make it clear to the other person when we cannot understand something sufficiently for our (individual) current purpose.

Communal common ground

We will speak in English.

We are both professional people.

We both live in the same town.

Personal common ground achieved before the conversation

Our joint purpose is to sign off on the plan.

Personal common ground developed during the conversation

The door on the bedroom that faces south has to be moved.

When we use the term "lintel," we mean the horizontal supporting beam above a door or window.

We can both (now) see the bedroom that faces south on the plan.

The plan can go to the builder.

Conversational Conventions are the assumptions that Clark states we must make in order to converse at all. The two examples given here are not meant to be exhaustive or well defined; Clark takes a whole book to do this! Knowing what communities a person belongs to allows us to make certain assumptions about existing common ground. Communal Common Ground is common ground that can be assumed from our experience of these different communities. Personal Common Ground is the common ground personal to the particular conversants under consideration—that is, the common ground assumed from our experience with the other individual.

By describing language use in this way, we can begin to understand how the technology impinges on the conversation in the way that it does. If Anne had not been able to detect Ben's puzzlement because there was no video image of his face, then Ben would have had to signal it in what he said. In some circumstances Ben might have been loath to do this, and a serious conversational breakdown could have occurred. Ben's false assumption of common ground could have been avoided if scrolling on his machine automatically resulted in scrolling on Anne's (so-called linked scrolling). We can also see why some media are better than others in certain circumstances.

This section has explained what common ground is, as an introduction to Clark's theory. Clark's theory explains the process by which common ground is used and developed in conversation. This, the main part of the theory, is out-lined in Section 10.4.

10.3   SCIENTIFIC FOUNDATIONS

Questions concerning the interpretation of language are not new, and they have been explored by philosophers of language for centuries. In the late 1600s, John Locke, for instance, attempted to conceptualize at an abstract level how simple and complex words are used and interpreted. But it is only relatively recently that social scientists have conducted empirical studies of language use. Techno-logical developments such as audio and video recorders meant that talk as op-posed to text could be documented and analyzed at a level of detail not before possible.

In the late 1970s sociologists such as Garfinkel, Sacks, and Goffman turned their attention to the everyday and the taken-for-granted. As techniques such as discourse analysis developed, it became possible to identify ethnomethods, the taken-for-granted means of accomplishing interaction. In-depth qualitative anal-yses uncovered previously overlooked phenomena such as turn taking—the pro-cess by which we signal that we are about to respond or we wish our interlocutor to respond.

The view of language use as simple information transfer corresponds to many people's common-sense view of what is going on, and so it has taken many years for this alternative notion of language use as a collaborative activity to gain popularity. As indicated above, the prime movers in this shift have been social scientists. Ethnomethodologists such as Goffman (1976) and Sacks, Schegloff, & Jefferson (1974) have been very influential, as have philosophers such as Grice (1957). As social scientists, these authors take an approach that is at odds with the cognitive approach that is more commonly adopted by psychologists. For ex-ample, sociological accounts generally avoid attributing intentions to individu-als, whereas intention is the basis of more cognitive accounts (Monk, 1998). What Clark has achieved is a marrying of these two approaches through his con-cept of a "joint action" (see Section 10.4.1).

Readers with an interest in the building blocks of his approach can consult the following sources. McCarthy & Monk (1994) is a longer tutorial paper along the lines of Section 10.1. Clark's book (1996) is a coherent statement of his whole theory that cites many references to the social science on which it is based. Readers can also consult the original papers cited in these two sources.

10.4   DETAILED DESCRIPTION

Section 10.2 defined different kinds of common ground and informally de-scribed some of the mechanisms by which common ground is developed through an example. This section develops these ideas through some more for-mally defined concepts. The first part of this section sets out Clark's fundamental assumptions. First he argues that face-to-face communication, rather than writ-ten language, should be the basis of a theory of language. He then points out, and defines for his own purposes, some known properties of face-to-face commu-nication; specifically, that it involves more than just words, is a joint action, mini-mizes effort, and develops common ground. The second part of this section outlines some concepts that build on these fundamentals. These are the process of grounding, levels of collaborative activity, layers, and tracks.

10.4.1   Fundamentals

Face-to-Face Conversation Is "Basic"

Much work in linguistics starts from an analysis of well-formed written text. Clark argues that real spoken conversations are a better starting point, even if they are messier. Children appear to learn how to do face-to-face communication sponta-neously. Learning to read and write requires formal instruction. Indeed, a large part of the population of the world has only spoken language. If face-to-face speech is the basis of all our language behavior, then our understanding of other ways of communication should build on our understanding of face-to face com-munication, not the other way around.

Face-to-Face Conversation Involves More Than Just Words

One of the major contributions of ethnomethodologists such as the Conversa-tional Analysts (see, for example, Sacks et al., 1974) has been to describe in de-tail how we use hands, face, eyes, and body in combination with the world we are in to facilitate the conversation. As well as the various cues used to man-age turn taking, these "instruments" can be used to signal meaning to someone else. Table 10.1 is adapted from Clark (1996) and lists examples of how we do this. Normally we think of language just as a process of describing things using words—see the table cell in italics—but we sometimes describe things with our hands. We might describe the shape of something by making our hands into that shape. Pointing is another important signal in language use. Pointing saves a lot

Instrument	Describing-As	Indicating	Demonstrating
Voice	*words, sentences*	"I", "here"	tone of voice
Hands, arms	emblems	pointing	iconic gestures
Face	facial emblems	pointing	smiles
Eyes	winking	eye gaze	widened eyes
Body	junctions	pointing	iconic gestures

TABLE 10.1 Methods of signaling. The voice is not the only instrument for communication in a face-to-face conversation. Adapted from Clark (1996, p. 188).

of words and can be done by voice (e.g., "that there"), with a finger, or even with the eyes and face. Clark's final category of signal is demonstrating. We can demonstrate a gesture or tone of voice by imitating it. Clark suggests that a smile is best thought of as a signal that demonstrates one's happiness to someone else.

Face-to-Face Conversation Is a Joint Action

As explained above, it does not make sense to think of language use except as a joint action involving two or more people. As such, it presents the same problems as any other joint action such as playing a duet or shaking hands. In particular, there is a need for "coordinating devices" such as conventions or jointly salient perceptual events that are part of common ground. Clark uses this observation to explain many of the more detailed characteristics of language use described in his book. The key characteristics of a joint action are that both people involved intend to do their part and they believe that the joint action includes their part and the other's. He uses a recursive definition of joint action.[3]

Ensemble A-and-B is doing joint action *k* if and only if:

0. The action *k* includes 1. and 2.
1. A intends to be doing A's part of *k* and believes 0.
2. B intends to be doing B's part of *k* and believes 0.

This definition, which applies to all joint actions including language, implies:

A believes *k* includes A's part plus B's part.
A intends to do A's part.

---

[3] I am aware that some readers of this chapter may not find these quasimathematical formalisms as useful as I do. If you are such a reader, you should be able to follow the argument from the text surrounding them.

B believes A intends to do A's part.

A believes B believes A intends to do A's part.

And so on.

Face-to-Face Conversation Uses Common Ground to Minimize the Effort Required to Communicate

As should be apparent by now, the key concept in Clark's theory is common ground.

> Everything we do is rooted in information we have about our surroundings, activities, perceptions, emotions, plans, interests. Everything we do jointly with others is also rooted in this information, but only in that part we think they share with us. (Clark, 1996, p. 92)

As was pointed out in Section 10.2, we make our assumptions about common ground on various bases. Some relate to the groups we belong to. Very soon after meeting you, I will be able to make assumptions about the extent and detail of our common ground coming from our languages, nationalities, genders, ages, and occupations. Other bases for making assumptions about common ground depend on our history together.

By making assumptions of common ground, face-to-face conversation becomes extremely efficient. Even a grunt can communicate meaning in a context that is well understood by both conversants. This extreme efficiency is possible only because the joint action of language includes an intention to communicate efficiently. I must be able to assume that you are intending that I should understand what you are saying. Furthermore, I must be able to assume that you are intending to do this in the most efficient way possible; otherwise, ambiguities will arise. This notion of efficiency was reformulated by Clark and Brennan (1991) as a matter of minimizing communication costs and then used to predict the effects of different ways of mediating communication (see Section 10.5.1).

Face-to-Face Conversation Develops Common Ground

The effect of conversation is to test, reformulate, and add to our common ground, so the most important source of common ground is our history of joint actions together.

One example of this personal common ground is the private lexicons of words that lovers develop together. Another more mundane example is the use of whiteboards or flip charts in meetings to form easily accessed references to previously established common ground. Thus, someone can point at a somewhat cryptic heading on a whiteboard and, in a single gesture, refer to the common ground that may have taken several minutes to establish in the first place. So economical and effective is this form of common ground that people talking in the corridor have been known to construct imaginary "air whiteboards" that they can point to later in the conversation.

10.4.2 Grounding, Levels, Layers, and Tracks

The previous section presented the concepts on which Clark's theory is based. Before going on to describe how these concepts relate to studies of electronically mediated communication, four further constructs need to be explained. They are the process of grounding, levels of joint action, layers, and tracks.

Figure 10.2 depicts the micro-structure of the process that Clark describes as "grounding," that is, the process of developing common ground.

(a) Anne presents an utterance u for Ben to consider. Anne takes account of the common ground that already exists between them in order to present u in a form she believes Ben will understand. Ben attempts to infer the import of u, interpreting it as u'.

(b) Ben provides some evidence e that, from his point of view, all is well with the conversation. This might be simply to continue with the next turn in a sensible way. Alternatively, Ben might rephrase the utterance and play it back to Anne. Anne interprets e as e'. On the basis of e' and the common ground they have already developed, Anne then has to make a judgment about whether or not Ben has understood u "sufficient for current purposes."

(c) Finally, Anne signals to Ben that she understands that he has an understanding sufficient for current purposes. Again, this is most commonly done by simply continuing with some relevant next utterance. If necessary, words like "yeah" or "uh-uh" can also serve this purpose. If she is not satisfied that e' meets the grounding criteria, she can query e or re-present u.

This notion of a closely coupled grounding process is used in Section 10.5.2 to explain the problems observed with a computer-supported cooperative work (CSCW) system.

The process of grounding just described elaborates the sequence in which common ground is observed in the structure of face-to-face conversation. The notion of levels of shared action further elaborates the process by describing all the joint actions that have to be in place for this process to work.

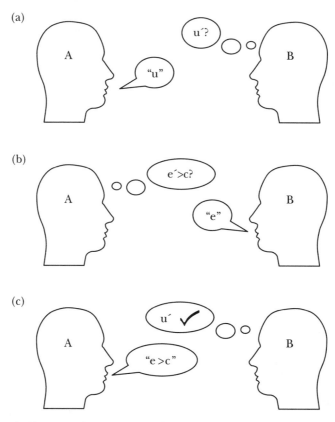

FIGURE

10.2

Clark's grounding process. *u* = utterance, *u'* = understanding of utterance,
e = evidence of understanding sufficient for current purposes, *e'* = understanding of evidence of understanding sufficient for current purposes,
c = grounding criterion.

Table 10.2 lists the four levels of shared action that Clark suggests are necessary for effective conversation. They can be thought of as an "action ladder" to
be read from the bottom. The first requisite is that A and B have joint action 1.
Refer back to the definition of a joint action in Section 10.4.1. Joint action 1 has
two parts—one for A (behaving for B) and one for B (attending to A). The
definition of a joint action implies that they are both intending to take these
parts and believe that the other is doing likewise. Joint action 2 is for A to present
signals to B and B to identify them. Joint action 2 depends on joint action 1 happening simultaneously. If B is not attending, then he cannot identify the signal.
Clark describes this as the principle of upward completion. Joint action 3, which

Level	Speaker A's part	Addressee B's part
4	A is proposing a joint project w to B	B is considering A's proposal of w
3	A is signaling that p for B	B is recognizing that p from A
2	A is presenting signal s to B	B is identifying signal s from A
1	A is executing behavior t for B	B is attending to behavior t from A

TABLE

10.2

The action ladder. The levels of simultaneous joint action needed to converse.

depends on and happens simultaneously with joint actions 1 and 2, is where A signals some proposition and B recognizes that A means that proposition. Finally, joint action 4 is where A proposes a joint project and B considers it.

The example Clark uses to illustrate this is an occasion when he bought something in a drug store. Clark walks up to the counter where the assistant is busy checking stock. The assistant says "I'll be there." At level 1, Clark and the assistant have engaged in a joint action where the assistant says something and knows that Clark will listen. At level 2, they are similarly engaged in a joint action where the assistant utters the words "I'll," "be," and "there," knowing that Clark will identify them. At level 3, the assistant knows that Clark is engaged in recognizing this signal as a proposition. Of course, what the assistant was really doing was the level-4 joint action of proposing a joint project. Clark's part in this joint proposal is to wait, the assistant's part is to finish what he or she is doing. The notion of levels of joint action is used in Section 10.5.3 to predict the effects of media on conversations where there is a "peripheral party."

The concept of tracks is a way of distinguishing between "the official business" of a conversation and talk about the communicative acts by which that business is conducted. When Al says "uh huh" in the conversation described in Section 10.1.2, he is not making a contribution to track 1, the business of discussing the repair of the car. He is instead contributing to track 2, talk about the communicative acts that achieve track 1. When Al says "uh huh," he is commenting on Roger's signal that the conversational repair had been successful.

The concept of layers is used to cope with the problem of pretence in fiction, irony, teasing, and so on. When I say "There were an Englishman, a Scotsman, and an Irishman standing in a field," you know I am telling a joke. Layer 1 is to pretend layer 2, layer 2 is me proposing the proposition that there were an Englishman. . . . Clark's concepts of tracks and layers have not, to my knowledge, been used to discuss mediated technology. They are included here for completeness.

10.5   CASE STUDIES—APPLYING THE THEORY TO THE DESIGN OF TECHNOLOGY FOR COMMUNICATION

This chapter takes as case studies three published papers that have applied Clark's theory to the design of technology to mediate communication. The theory was developed to explain unmediated face-to-face conversation. As explained in Section 10.4, Clark sees this as the logical starting point for a theory of any kind of language use; indeed, his book's title is *Using Language*. However, it is unreasonable to assume that the theory should be able to explain or predict the effects of mediating technology without further elaboration, and each of these case studies has to extend the theory accordingly. Part of the interest in developing these examples is to examine how much has to be added to make the theory useful in design.

10.5.1   The Costs of Grounding (Clark & Brennan)

A basic principle in Clark's theory, explained in Section 10.4.1, is that conversants seek to minimize the effort required to communicate; this is, in a sense, the purpose of developing common ground. Different communication media present different costs to different parts of the grounding process. For example, typing a text message will take more effort than speaking on the phone. However, reading complex instructions from the computer screen may be easier than having them read to you over the phone. Clark and Brennan (1991) elaborate the theory by analyzing these costs as they apply to different communication media. The extended theory can then be used to explain some of the problems people have with media in particular contexts.

Clark and Brennan (1991) characterize the differences between different communication media in terms of which "constraints on grounding" they do and don't provide. In everyday life, "constraints" may be thought to be bad; in this context, they are good as they reduce ambiguity. Take the first constraint copresence. Say we are in the same room and I can see you are looking at a vase of flowers. I can use this common ground to construct an efficient utterance— "dead eh?" to which I might get the expected reply "OK, I'll get rid of them." Had we been conversing on the phone, I would have had to construct quite a long utterance to engage you in the same shared project—"I don't suppose you could possibly chuck out the flowers in the vase on the hall table, please?" The phrase "dead eh?" is too ambiguous without the constraints provided by copresence. You might prefer to think of constraints on grounding as "resources for grounding." Here we will stay with Clark and Brennan's terminology.

Clark and Brennan's (1991) complete list of constraints on grounding is given in the list below. Equipment for mediated communication that provided all these constraints would be very good. All these constraints can be viewed as an analysis of the findings from many studies of mediated communication in terms of Clark's theory. The first six of the constraints are advantages of face-to-face conversation that might be absent in mediated communication. These come from Clark's theory in the sense that mechanisms identified by Clark will not be possible if these constraints are absent. For example, many of the methods of signaling enumerated in Table 10.1 will not be available without the constraints of copresence and visibility. The tightly coupled process of grounding, described in Section 10.4.1, will be difficult without audibility, contemporality, simultaneity, and sequentiality. The last two constraints in the list below are advantages of written communication identified in studies comparing written and spoken electronic communication.

Copresence: A and B share the same physical environment

> If I am in the same room as you, I can see and hear what you are doing, and I know what you can see and hear and what you are looking at.

Visibility: A and B are visible to one another

> If we are video conferencing, I can see you but will not have all the information I would have about you if we were copresent.

Audibility: A and B communicate by speaking

> If we are on the phone, I can hear you but will not have all the information I would have about you if we were copresent.

Contemporality: B receives at roughly the same time as A produces

> On the phone, you understand what I say at the same time or very soon after I speak. If we are communicating by voicemail, this is not the case.

Simultaneity: A and B can send and receive simultaneously

> Face to face, I can nod or grunt to show I understand while you are speaking. Other devices may not allow this.

Sequentiality: A's and B's turns cannot get out of sequence

Misunderstandings often arise when emails are read in a different order to that in which they were sent. This is unlikely to be a problem on the phone.

Reviewability: B can review A's messages

Written material can be reread and revisited. Speech fades quickly.

Revisability: A can revise message for B

Emails can be read and revised before they are sent. Voice communications have to be repaired in subsequent turns or with extra words in the same turn if trouble is anticipated.[4]

In order to predict the problems users may have with a new communication medium, one simply asks which of these constraints are present or absent. The consequence of some medium lacking one or more of the constraints is to increase the costs of some part of the grounding process. For example, if the conversation between the architect Anne and the homeowner Ben developed in Section 10.2 had taken place without the video window, Ben would have had to use words to indicate that he did not understand the word "lintel." This would have been more costly in terms of effort and possible loss of face than looking puzzled. Had they been communicating by writing in a chat window, the cost in effort of signaling, detecting, and repairing this trouble in the conversation is potentially even larger.

People evaluate costs in ways that depend on the purpose of the conversation. Two lawyers communicating about a case may choose the medium of typed letters because it affords the constraints of revisability and reviewability. Here the cost of an inappropriate joint project being construed by either party is considerable, and so the cost of losing all the other constraints is justified. Also, they already have extensive common ground as they are both lawyers who have dealt with this kind of case before. They may choose to meet their clients face to face. This is because they need all the constraints they can muster to create some common ground. They know that their view of the case, as a technical problem that must be formulated within a particular legal framework, is quite different to the client's view of the case as a personal problem.

Clark and Brennan's approach has the potential to make detailed predictions about the costs and benefits for using different media for different

---

[4] Clark and Brennan's (1991) constraints for grounding.

purposes. However, it has yet to be fleshed out in sufficient detail to allow some-one not immersed in the theory to make predictions using mechanical rules or heuristics.

10.5.2   Why Cognoter Did Not Work (Tatar, Foster, & Bobrow)

Cognoter was a software tool for use in electronic meeting rooms developed in the 1980s at Xerox PARC (Palo Alto Research Center) as part of the Colab project. The Colab electronic meeting room contained networked computers arranged so that a small group of people could have a meeting together. In a conventional meeting room, people use a whiteboard to coordinate the work. Cognoter was to emulate and enhance the function of a whiteboard through the networked computers and a large-screen central display. The obvious advantages of such a system is that material can be prepared in advance, displayed to the others, changed by the group, and saved for future use. These are all things that are much less easy to do in a conventional meeting room. In addition, Cognoter was designed to facilitate brainstorming by allowing participants to work in parallel. Participants created "items" in an edit window. Items were then displayed to the others on an item organization window as a short catch phrase or title. Anyone could move an item in the item organization window or open it to read and edit the content.

The experiences of users of Cognoter were mixed, and so Tatar, Foster, & Bobrow (1991) recruited two groups from outside the Colab research team to study it in detail. Each group consisted of three long-term collaborators who were asked to brainstorm about some subject of their own choosing that would be useful in their work. It was observed that neither group was able to use the item organization window in the way intended. Also, there were numerous conversational breakdowns where Cognoter got in the way of the work they were trying to do. Tatar et al. (1991) concluded that the designers of Cognoter had used an inappropriate model of communication, corresponding to the information-transfer model depicted in Figure 10.1. The idea of a Cognoter item as a parcel of information that is constructed and then transmitted to the others may be good for individual brainstorming, but it simply does not fit in with what happens in the rest of the meeting when discussing what to do with the ideas generated. If one views language use as a closely coupled process of collaborative activity, as depicted in Figure 10.2, a very different picture emerges. From this perspective, Cognoter items have two functions: as elements in the conversation (signals), and as elements that may be conversed about (common ground). Cognoter did not support either function very well.

When someone is writing on a whiteboard, other participants in the meeting know that they are doing so and can coordinate their actions accordingly. Creating an item with the item editor was a private activity, making this difficult. Also with a conventional whiteboard, the other participants can see the emerging text as it is written. This allows them to propose modifications and otherwise negotiate and signal common ground as described in Clark's process of grounding. With Cognoter, the author of an item had no idea whether the others had read or even seen it. He or she could make no assumptions about its status in terms of the level of joint action it was involved in. In terms of Table 10.2, they could not make any assumptions about levels 1 and 2 in the action ladder. In terms of Clark and Brennan's (1991) analysis presented in Section 10.5.1, Cognotor did not provide the normal grounding constraints expected from copresence, even though all the participants in the meeting were in the same room.

There was a further problem when people tried to refer to items on the item organization window, because the others were likely to be looking at a different version of the display. This was due partly to network delays (an absence of Clark and Brennan's contemporality constraint) but mainly because each display could be scrolled independently. A participant might have scrolled the item organization window so the item another person was referring to was not visible. To add to the confusion, the central screen could be displaying a third view onto the item organization window. As was indicated in Section 10.4.1, pointing is a very effective conversational resource (see Table 10.1). Pointing may be done with a finger, by voice, or with your eyes, and it is known in this literature as *deixis*. Deixis broke down when the person making the reference was looking at a different version of the display to the version the others were looking at. This is another breakdown in the normal grounding constraints provided by copresence. Because of our experience of face-to-face conversation, we expect that what we can see everyone else can see too, and so it is quite difficult to repair these breakdowns.

Tatar et al. (1991) suggested some modifications to Cognoter. The features they suggested are now commonly accepted as advantageous with this kind of system and have been implemented in commercial systems such as Timbuktu and Netmeeting. They are: (1) fast communication and update of displays; (2) shared editing, where everyone can see the message being composed, letter by letter, backspaces and all; and (3) consistent positioning of windows and linked scrolling so that if I scroll so do you. Point (2) comes under the more general design guideline of maximizing "awareness," making everyone aware of what everyone else is doing. Point (3) is an example of the design guideline What I See Is What You See (WISIWYS). These now widely accepted design principles are given a sound theoretical underpinning by Clark's theory and may even have been, to some extent, inspired by his ideas.

10.5.3 Predicting the Peripherality of Peripheral Participants (Monk)

Watts & Monk (1999) studied doctors (general practitioners, GPs) in their treatment rooms communicating over a videophone with medical specialists in a hospital. Figure 10.3 presents a schematic of this arrangement. The GP was usually in the presence of a patient. There might also be other legitimate overhearers. For example, in one observed consultation the patient was a young girl accompanied by her mother. The consultant was talking to the girl over the video link and asked if she "ate well," to which she replied in the affirmative. The mother disagreed with this and was eventually able to break into the conversation and make this clear.

Watts & Monk (1998) characterize the legitimate overhearers, who are not currently actively involved in the work of the conversation, as *peripheral participants*. The people currently actively involved in the work are described as *primary participants*. So, in the above case the primary participants were the consultant in the hospital and the girl in the treatment room. The mother and the GP were, at that time, peripheral participants. When the mother heard the child indicate that she was a good eater, the mother felt the need to change her participatory status.

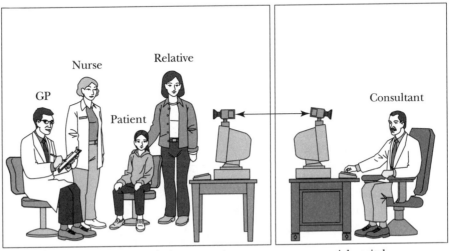

The treatment room (primary care)　　　　A hospital

FIGURE　　Schematic of the video-conferencing context studied by Watts and Monk (1999).

10.3

Another example of a legitimate overhearer might be a nurse. Two of the visited sites had a nurse who organized the video link and who would generally be present during the consultation. The same nurse might well be involved in treating the patient after the consultation. Having heard the discussion of treatment among GP, patient, and consultant, as a peripheral party, this nurse was in a better position to explain the treatment to the patient. In Clark's terms, the nurse had additional personal common ground due to overhearing.

At all the sites visited, the camera was positioned to give a limited view of the person sitting directly in front of the video link, hence peripheral participants in the treatment room were unlikely to be visible to the consultant in the hospital. On the basis of Clark's theory, Watts and Monk (1999) formed the hypothesis that, if the specialist in the hospital could not see a peripheral participant, this might make them more peripheral. It might be harder for them to change their participatory status and join the conversation. Also, the primary participants might make fewer allowances for them, in their use of language, for example.

The challenge for Clark's theory, then, is to predict how a particular audio-video configuration could affect how peripheral a peripheral participant will be. Monk (1999) extended Clark's levels of joint action (Table 10.2) to do this. The starting point is a Participant Percept Matrix (PPM) (Watts & Monk, 1998). This shows who can see and hear what. Table 10.3 is a PPM for the situation just described. The GP, patient, and nurse are copresent, so they can all see and hear one another. However, because audio is via telephone handsets and the image is of limited scope, not all the percepts are available to all the participants.

| | | *Participants* | | |
Percepts	**Specialist**	**GP**	**Patient**	**Nurse**
Specialist's face	—	yes	yes	yes
GP's face	yes	—	yes	yes
Patient's face	no	yes	—	yes
Nurse's face	no	yes	yes	—
Specialist's voice	—	yes	no	no
GP's voice	yes	—	yes	yes
Patient's voice	no	yes	—	yes
Nurse's voice	no	yes	yes	—

TABLE 10.3   Participant Percept Matrix for one instance of telemedical consultation. The specialist and GP are communicating with telephone handsets, and the camera provides the specialist with a limited scope image that shows only the head and shoulders of the GP.

Level	Speaker A's part	Side participant C's part
4	No joint action	No joint action
3	A is signaling that p for B and C	C is recognizing that p from A
2	A is presenting signal s to B and C	C is identifying signal s from A
1	A is executing behavior t for B and C	C is attending to behavior t from A

TABLE 10.4 Levels of joint action with a close peripheral participant (a side participant).

Level	Evidence leading speaker A to consider side participant C	Evidence leading side participant C to consider speaker A
4	No joint action	No joint action
3	C has responded appropriately to previous signals (H); A can hear verbal back channels from C (H); A can see visual back channels from C (S)	A's signal is directed at B and C (H); A's signal refers to common ground specific to C (H)
2	Only by downward evidence	Only by downward evidence
1	A can see C is attending (S)	C can see A's behavior is directed at B and C (S)

TABLE 10.5 Evidence that the other person is taking part in the joint action, speaker, and addressee. (H) = must be able to hear other; (S) = must be able to see other.

Table 10.4 extends Clark's theory as represented in Table 10.2 for a two-person conversation to the case of a three-person conversation where C is a close peripheral participant, that is, someone who is really a part of the conversation but is not the addressee. See Monk (1999) for a full explanation of the term "side participant."

Table 10.5 then lists the evidence that might lead A and C to assume that the other is taking part in each level of joint action. There is no joint action at level 4 because C is only a side participant. However, C may feel able to assume they are part of lower-level joint actions. Some of this evidence comes from being able to hear the other person ("H" in Table 10.5), some from being able to see them ("S" in Table 10.5). When using this table, one should also recognize Clark's principle of downward evidence in the action ladder. A level-3 joint action is possible only if the corresponding level-1 and -2 joint actions are too. This means that evidence that the other person is joining you in a level-3 joint action is also evidence that he or she is joining you in the corresponding level-1 and -2 joint actions.

Table 10.5 can be used to determine what evidence is available to a primary participant, say the specialist, that would lead that participant to consider a peripheral participant, say the nurse, to be a side participant, and vice versa. Combining this with an analysis of the evidence available to the other primary participant, the GP, allows an assessment of the overall peripherality of the nurse, that is, how easy it will be for the nurse to join in the conversation.

This account shows how Clark's model can be elaborated to make predictions about the effects of small changes to the way a video link is configured. Monk and Watts (2000) presented a laboratory experiment where such predictions were made and tested with encouraging results. However, much more data is needed before we can say with confidence that the model has real predictive power.

10.6   CURRENT STATUS

The three case studies presented here demonstrate that elaborated versions of Clark's theory are capable of making useful predictions in the area of electronically mediated communication. As with any theory, the question then becomes "how realistic is it to apply the theory in a real design context?" In an ideal world, a theory should be encapsulated as a set of guidelines or rules that could be used by a designer with very little background in human factors of human communication. Failing this, the theory should be formalized as principles that could be used by a human-factors consultant who has had the time to get to understand the theory and the background material needed. At the earliest stages, which is where we are now with Clark's theory, the theory is only really usable by researchers with a specialist's knowledge of the area.

The reason for this can be seen in the case studies. In two of the three, the theory has to be added to before it can make predictions. Clark and Brennan (1991) had to add the concept of a grounding constraint to complete their analysis. Monk (1999) had to generalize Clark's levels of joint action to three participant conversations and specify the evidence that leads participants to consider they are being joined in a joint action. Only Tatar, Foster, and Bobrow (1991) were able to use the framework with little modification. As more researchers use the theory to reason about electronically mediated communication, the bounds of the theory and the additional assumptions needed will become more apparent. It is to be hoped that it will then be possible to set out principles that could be used by our hypothetical consultant. The next phase of development will be to gain sufficient practical experience of using the theory in real design contexts to make the next shift to a set of well-specified guidelines for use in particular contexts—guidelines for configuring multiparty video conferencing, guidelines for desktop video, guidelines for asynchronous communication, and so on. We are a long way from this ideal state at the moment. I very much hope that this chapter will serve as a stimulus to taking some steps in this direction.

10.7   FURTHER READING

Readers interested in the background material (scientific foundations) that Clark's theory draws on should read the tutorial review paper by McCarthy and Monk (1994).

Clark's book (1996) is an accessible and coherent statement of his whole theory. It has useful orienting summaries at the beginning and end of each chapter. Also, the first and last chapters provide accessible summaries of the whole book. He also goes to some lengths to explain the scientific foundations of his work. Before this book was published, it was hard to find a coherent statement of Clark's framework that could be described as a theory; the concepts were distributed in a number of papers. For this reason, the work had not had a large impact. Readers interested in this theory are strongly recommended to find the book and get it straight from the horse's mouth.

Other readers may wish to find out more about the research literature on electronically mediated communication. Finn, Sellen, & Wilbur (1997) is a comprehensive set of papers (25 chapters, 570 pages) on video-mediated communication. The CHI, CSCW, and ECSCW conferences are also good sources of papers (see, for example, Kraut, Miller, & Siegel, 1996; McCarthy, Miles, & Monk, 1991; Neuwirth, Chandhok, Charney, Wojahn, & Kim, 1994; Tang, 1991; Veinott, Olson, Olson, & Fu, 1999; and Vertegaal, 1999).

Of the case studies, Clark & Brennan (1991) is very accessible. Tatar, Foster, & Bobrow (1991) is rather lengthy, whereas Monk and Watts' work on peripheral participation is distributed among several papers. Watts & Monk (1997) is a good two-page starting point.

ACKNOWLEDGMENTS

The author was supported by the UK EPRSC (Grant GR/M86446) and the PACCIT programme (Grant L328253006) during the period of this work. I would also like to acknowledge the help of members of York Usability Research, students, and other authors in this volume for their comments on previous drafts of this chapter.

11 | Activity Theory

Olav W. Bertelsen
Susanne Bødker   University of Aarhus, Denmark

11.1   MOTIVATION

Since the mid 1980s, activity theory has been explored as a basic perspective on human-computer interaction (HCI). In order to understand why this form of HCI came into being, let us consider the Scandinavian research on computer technology use and design of the early 1980s. The 1970s had been a period in which, in general, conventional theory had been challenged in the universities, at the same time as many new areas, such as computer science, evolved. In the Scandinavian context, this led to research projects that critically reconsidered the introduction of computer technology in the workplace. The projects developed an action research approach, emphasizing the active cooperation between researchers and "those being researched," suggesting that researchers need to enter an active commitment with the workers of an organization to help improve their situation (Ehn & Kyng, 1987). In the early 1980s, concerns evolved for the maintenance and development of skills of the involved workers and for technological alternatives (e.g., Utopia; Bødker et al., 1987). These projects were situated in a context where insights from social psychology and industrial sociology were necessary—some of the inspiration came from activity theory through German work psychology and Scandinavian critical psychology.

11.1.1   Through the Interface—Artifacts Used in Context

The rise of the personal computer challenged the focus, in traditional-systems developments, on mainframe systems for automation of existing work routines. It furthermore brought forth a need to focus on how to work on materials and objects through the computer. In the search of theoretical and methodical

perspectives suited to deal with issues of flexibility and more advanced mediation among human beings, material, and outcomes through the interface, it
seemed promising to turn to the still-rather-young HCI research tradition that
had emerged primarily in the United States (for further discussion, see Bannon
& Bødker, 1991).

This tradition, however, already faced problems, as outlined by Norman
(1980):

> The problem seemed to be in the lack of consideration of other aspects of
> human behavior, of interaction with other people and with the environ-
> ment, of the influence of the history of the person, or even the culture, and
> of the lack of consideration of the special problems and issues confront-
> ing an animate organism that must survive as both an individual and as a
> species. (p. 2)

Specifically, the cognitive science–based theories lacked means of addressing
a number of issues that came out of the empirical projects (see Bannon &
Bødker, 1991):

+ Many of the early advanced user interfaces assumed that the users were the
  designers themselves, and they accordingly built on an assumption of a generic user, without concern for qualifications, work environment, division of
  work, and so on.

+ In particular, the role of the artifact as it stands between the user and her materials, objects, and outcomes was ill understood.

+ In validating findings and designs, there was a heavy focus on novice users,
  whereas everyday use by experienced users and concerns for the development of expertise were hardly addressed.

+ Detailed task analysis was seen as the starting point for most user-interface
  design, whereas much of the Scandinavian research had pointed out how
  limited explicit task descriptions were for capturing actual actions and conditions for those in use (Ehn & Kyng, 1984). The idealized models created
  through task analysis failed to capture the complexity and contingency of
  real-life action.

+ Classical systems focused on automation of routines, and this perspective on
  qualifications was carried over to HCI. As an alternative, the tool perspective
  was formulated (Ehn & Kyng, 1984) to emphasize the anchoring of computer applications in classical tool use—the craftsman surrounded by his
  tools and materials with a historically created practice as his basis. However,

this perspective was in dire need of a theoretical foundation that would make it applicable in the design and evaluation of computer applications; available HCI theory had no answer to this.

✦ From the point of view of complex work settings, it was striking how most HCI focused on one user/one computer in contrast to the ever-ongoing co-operation and coordination of real work situations (this problem later led to the development of computer-supported cooperative work, or CSCW).

✦ Users were seen mainly as objects of study. This was in striking contrast to the early Scandinavian experiences with active user participation, where users obviously were an active source of inspiration in design.

11.1.2   In Search of a New Theoretical Foundation

Because of these shortcomings, it was necessary to move outside cognitive science–based HCI to find or develop the necessary theoretical platform. European psychology had taken different paths than had American, with much inspiration from dialectical materialism (Hydén, 1981; Engeström, 1987). Philosophers such as Heidegger and Wittgenstein came to play an important role, primarily through discussions of the limitations of artificial intelligence (AI) (Dreyfus & Dreyfus, 1986; Winograd & Flores, 1986). Suchman (1987), who had a similar focus, introduced ethnomethodology into the discussions; and Ehn (1988) based his treatise of design of computer artifacts on Marx, Heidegger, and Wittgenstein.

The development of the activity-theoretical angle was carried out primarily by Bødker (1991, 1996) and by Kuutti (Bannon & Kuutti, 1993; Kuutti, 1991, 1996)—both with strong inspiration from Scandinavian activity-theory groups in psychology. Bannon (1990, 19991) and Grudin (1990a, 1990b) made significant contributions to the furthering of the approach by making it available to the HCI audience. The work of Kaptelinin (1996) has been important for connecting to the earlier development of activity theory in Russia. Nardi produced the most applicable collection of activity theoretical HCI literature up to that time (Nardi, 1996).

11.1.3   What Does It Offer?

As a consequence of this historical development, activity-theoretical HCI has come to focus on the following:

✦ analysis and design for a particular work practice with concern for qualifications, work environment, division of work, and so on;

✦ analysis and design with focus on actual use and the complexity of multiuser activity. In particular, the notion of the artifact as mediator of human activity is essential;

✦ focus on the development of expertise and of use in general;

✦ active user participation in design, and focus on use as part of design.

Activity-theoretical HCI offers a set of conceptual tools, rather than a collection of tools and techniques ready for practical application. This chapter will demonstrate these concepts, along with some selected techniques that we have successfully applied ourselves.

11.1.4   How Is It like Other Theories?

Through numerous practical examples, Don Norman (1988, 1991) has pointed out how malfunction is more easily demonstrated than well-function, and how artifacts often stand in the way of human use rather than mediating it. Norman bases his work in part on Gibson's ecological psychology. This theory has been the starting point of several attempts (e.g., Carroll et al., 1991; Hutchins et al., 1996; Rasmussen, 1986; Rasmussen et al., 1994) to move away from the separation between human cognition on the one hand and human action on the other. Activity theory shares with these approaches an interest in actual material conditions of human acting. However, these approaches often lack a concern for motivation of actions, a level of analyses that activity theory adds through the notion of activity. Activity theory shares the idea that a hierarchical analysis of human action is valuable with means/ends analysis, task analysis, and alike. It insists, however, on flexible hierarchies, as we shall see later, rather than on static decomposition of wholes into parts. It further insists that activity takes place on all levels at the same time, and not in sequence (such as Norman's 7-stage model [1988]).

11.1.5   What Sets It Apart?

Because activity theory understands human conduct as anchored in collective/shared practice, it addresses more than just individual skills, knowledge, and judgment, and it is not restricted to the "generic" human being. In other words, we can talk about the appropriateness of a certain tool for a certain practice, and we can study how the introduction of a particular artifact changes practice and how practice may change the use of the artifact. As practice develops over time, concern for the historical context of an artifact in use is essential to activity-theoretical HCI. Learning, accordingly, is not a matter of how the individual adapts, or gets adapted to the artifact; it is also a matter of how the collective practice develops, in small steps or larger leaps. To design an artifact means not only to design the "thing" or device, which can be used by human beings as artifacts in a specific kind of activity. As the use of artifacts is part of social activity, we design new conditions for collective activity, such as a new division of labor and new ways of coordination, control, and communication. In actual use, artifacts most often mediate several work activities, and the contradictions and conflicts arising from this multitude of use activities are essential for activity-theoretical artifact analysis and design.

11.2   OVERVIEW

In this chapter we will use a project that we have been involved with as an example to convey both the basic concepts of activity theory and their potentials in HCI analysis and design. The application developed was a graphical editor and simulator environment for Colored Petri Nets (CPNs). This editor is a (re-)design of a tool, Design/CPN, that is used by more than 600 organizations around the world, both in academia and industry. Design/CPN is a complex application that supports the construction and evaluation of complex CPNs. Typically these CPNs are used for verification of software protocols, such as in alarm systems; in such production applications, nets can contain thousands of places, transitions, and arcs, which are structured into hundreds of modules. Users are not individuals but (parts of) project groups cooperating around the nets, the protocols they model, and the design of the software and hardware on which these would run. Design/CPN has a traditional interface based on direct manipulation, menus, and dialog boxes.

The formal definition of CP nets goes like this: A Petri net is a bipartite graph with two kinds of nodes: *places* (depicted as circles or ellipses), and *transitions* (depicted as rectangles). Edges of the graph are called *arcs* and can only connect places to transitions and transitions to places. Places hold tokens, which represent the current state of the system. Simulating the net involves moving tokens from place to place by firing transitions according to predefined rules. CPNs (Jensen, 1992–1997) are an extension of Petri Nets for modeling complex systems. CPNs can be hierarchical. Hierarchical nets make it possible to structure a complex net into smaller units that can be developed and tested separately.

The redesign of Design/CPN, called CPN2000 (Beaudouin-Lafon & Lassen, 2000), aimed to design an interface for the next 10 years, based on actual experiences with the existing tool. The project applied a participatory design process, involving users from the early stages of brainstorming all the way through the design process (see Mackay et al. [2000] for details).

In order to study the practice and conditions of use, the process took as its starting point a number of studies-of-use situations involving videotaping novice as well as expert users. In parallel with this, to seek inspiration from advanced technology, a number of brainstorming sessions took place, including exploration of advanced interface ideas, such as tool glasses (Bier et al., 1993). To provide hands-on exploration, prototypes were built and explored in workshops with users. A first version of CPN2000 was used by a small group of CPN designers for production work. This use was studied in order to inform the next round of the iterative design process.

Design/CPN is used both as a professional tool and as an educational tool, defining from the outset two different types of use activities to be understood as the basis of design. The educational activity is typically one where one to two students work in front of a computer, in a room with other students attending the same class (where the tools and nets have been introduced). In contrast, the professional users work in an environment where they share some nets with others and where the purpose of building the nets is mainly a tool for the design process as such—for example, when building an alarm system. The designers take over nets from one another; they take notes from reviews and meetings and adjust Webs accordingly; they redesign protocols based on earlier products; and they only rarely design new nets from scratch. When Design/CPN works well for a particular designer, it does not get in the way of his attention on these other foci, which is why we talk about the computer application as *mediator.*

Design/CPN is a mediating artifact that allows the user to produce CPNs. However, such CPNs are in turn mediating how users verify alarm protocols; creating a CPN rarely has a purpose in itself. We can go on like this, illustrating how a particular artifact most often mediates a multitude of activities, and how what is sometimes the object of the activity is in other instances itself a mediator. To fully understand the use of an artifact such as Design/CPN, we must find out which activities the artifact is used in and how these are connected. This is why we talk about *webs of activities.*

Accordingly, the webs of activities that Design/CPN is part of in the two situations (educational and professional) are rather different, the purposes of use differ, the qualifications and experiences of the users differ, and the focus of attention is different for the two groups: When students explore a new tool, their focus is primarily on the interface and its very narrow surroundings (how to create an arch, how to move a label, etc.); whereas the professional user may have her focus mainly on solving a tricky protocol problem or on remembering what her co-workers said in a meeting, at the same time that she works through a CPN to handle these issues. The professional user has developed a repertoire of operations that allows her to work through the artifact, whereas the student user still lacks this repertoire and needs to be conscious of how to handle the artifact. As an example, our user studies showed how an experienced user continuously reformatted a net on his screen while he was busy explaining some feature or other displayed on the screen to us.

The development of a repertoire of operations for handling Design/CPN is not the only difference between the student and the professional user, but it is a very important one for analysis and design of HCI. As a matter of fact, it happens to anyone even with the most mundane artifacts that they use everyday—somehow their attention is drawn toward the artifact, and they have to be conscious about the use of the device. For example, a small difference in layout of a key pad prevents the user from typing her PIN code, and she has to think and remember to reproduce it. Such halts are examples of what we call *focus shifts*, and they are essential for our analyses of HCI. An analysis of the foci of users in real work/use situations was important for the analysis of Design/CPN and design of CPN2000. This analysis technique will be presented in detail in Section 11.5.

There is no trivial move from the analysis of an existing artifact to the design of a new one. However, our analyses gave us reason to believe that we should get away from overlapping windows, and from traditional pull-down menus, and provide more direct tools for formatting nets. Furthermore, Beaudouin-Lafon (2000) developed a theoretical model regarding instrumental interaction on which the interaction design was based. This model reflects fundamental concepts of activity theory, as we shall illustrate later.

Accordingly, CPN2000 applies tool glasses, traditional tool palettes, contextual marking menus, and two-handed input. The idea was to move beyond WIMP (windows, icons, menus, and pointing devices) interfaces—specifically, that any entity in the interface should be accessible as a first-class object. Commands should apply to as many different types as possible. The CPN2000 interface requires a mouse and keyboard plus a trackball for the nondominant hand. A large window, the workspace, contains an index to the left, a set of floating palettes that can be turned into tool glasses, and a set of binders containing pages.

Floating palettes (Beaudouin-Lafon & Lassen 2000) are similar to those found in traditional interfaces: clicking a tool activates it. The tool is then held in the dominant hand and applied by clicking or dragging.

Tool glasses (Bier et al., 1993) are positioned with the nondominant hand and operated by a click-through of the dominant hand, typically the right hand.

Marking menus (Kurtenbach & Buxton, 1994) are available throughout the interface by clicking with the right mouse button. All the commands accessible through these contextual-marking menus are also available through palettes/tool glasses. The marking menus have at most eight entries per menu and at most one level of submenus.

An important characteristic of the interface is that it supports multiple working styles. Floating palettes are efficient when a single tool needs to be applied to multiple objects; a marking menu is more efficient when multiple commands are applied to the object in succession; tool glasses support a mix of these and are particularly efficient for editing the graphical attributes (color, thickness) of a set of related objects.

In the following, we use examples from CPN2000 and its design process to further illustrate *why* we apply activity theory to HCI, *what* we do, and *how* it is done (Figure 11.1 and Plate 10 of the color insert).

11.3   SCIENTIFIC FOUNDATIONS

Historically, activity theory originated as a dialectical materialist psychology developed by Vygotsky and his students in the Soviet Union in the beginning of the twentieth century. As a psychological theory, it was aimed at understanding the mental capacities of a single human being. Activity theory rejects the isolated human being as an adequate unit of analysis, insisting on cultural and technical mediation of human activity. The unit of analysis accordingly includes technical artifacts and the cultural organization that the human being is both determined by and actively creating.

Vygotsky and colleagues (1978) analyzed human activity as having three fundamental characteristics; first, it is directed toward a material or ideal object; second, it is mediated by artifacts; and third, it is socially constituted within a culture. Historically, activity theory is an answer to the problem of studying isolated individuals in the laboratory setting. Instead of dealing with the isolated relation between the subject (S) and an object (O), from which the subject is perfectly separated, Vygotsky introduced a mediating X, which is culturally constituted. This mediating X is also referred to as *instruments,* which can be either

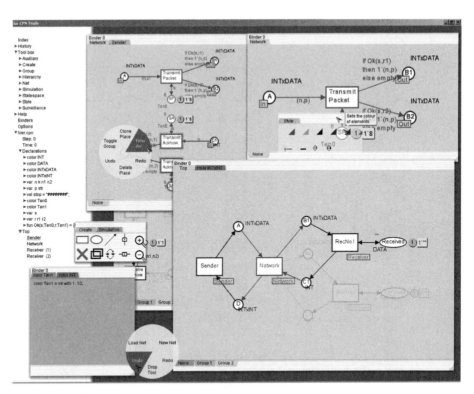

FIGURE

11.1
The redesigned CPN2000 binders, palette, and marking menu. (See Plate 10 in the color insert for a color version of this figure.)

technical instruments (tools) or psychological instruments (signs). Psychological instruments like language and concepts are internalized during childhood development, following which it is not possible to experiment with or even to talk about a basic, universal, unmediated, cognitive apparatus; activity theory as such does not exist. Vygotsky distinguishes between meaning and sense in language. Meaning is stable and is what the sign points at or denotes, whereas sense is the fluctuating contents of the sign determined by the use of the sign in practice.

A. N. Leontiev (1978, 1981) was a student and co-worker of Vygotsky who, in the division of labor in Vygotsky's group, was assigned the task of describing the development of natural history, from one-celled organisms to human beings. Leontiev's work resulted in a slightly different basic model in the analysis of cognition. In describing this development, the hunt becomes an important laboratory for thought. In natural history, the first important step in the development

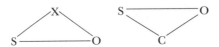

FIGURE

11.2
Triangles of activity. On the left is human activity mediated by artifacts (Vygotsky); on the right socially mediated activity (Leontiev).

from cell to human is when animals start to work together in fulfilling their needs. Thus for Leontiev the basic triangle is not S-X-O, but the pre-human S-C-O where C is community (Figure 11.2). At the level of animals it is possible to identify embryonic forms of mediation of S-O relations in form of *ad hoc* tools, mediation of the S-C relation as emerging rules and rituals, and mediation of the C-O as emerging division of labor, such as in the hunt.

At a point in the phylogenic history, these embryonic mediations gradually become permanent parts of the systemic structure of human activity. According to Leontiev (1978), human activity can be analyzed into a three-level hierarchy of activity, action, and operation, each of which reflects the objective world. Activity is directed to satisfy a need through a material or ideal object. The subject's reflection of (including expectation to) this object is the motive of the activity. Human activity is carried out through actions, realizing objective results. These actions are governed by the conscious goals of the subject. Goals reflect the objective results of action. Actions are realized through series of operations, each "triggered" by the conditions and structure of the action. They are performed without conscious thinking but are oriented in the world by a nonconscious orienting basis, as described in Table 11.1. (See Bærentsen [1989] and Bærentsen & Trettvik [2002].) Goals that are different from the motive, but still realizing it, are possible only in human activity; in animals, goal and motive are always the same. According to Bærentsen & Trettvik (2002), operations may be cultural-historically developed or naturally evolved and ecologically determined. Accordingly, operations may realize internalized cultural-historical patterns of conduct or inborn species-specific patterns of behavior, and they may result from appropriated use of tools, educated manners toward other human beings, or movements in the physical world according to concrete physical conditions.

The three levels of activity are not fixed (Figure 11.3); an action can become an operation through automation/internalization, and an operation can become an action through conceptualization in breakdown situations (Bødker, 1991). A separately motivated activity in one context can be an operation in another. The focus of activity theory on how human acts transfer between the different levels of activity is an important feature that distinguishes this framework

Levels of activity	Mental representation	Realizes	Level of description	Analytical question
Activity	Motive (need)—not necessarily conscious, but may become conscious	Personality	The social and personal meaning of activity; its relation to motives and needs	Why?
Action	Goal—conscious	Activities (systems of actions organized to achieve goals)	Possible goals, critical goals, particularly relevant subgoals	What?
Operation	Condition of actions (structure of activity)—normally not conscious; only limited possibilities of consciousness	Actions (chains of operations organized by goals and concrete conditions)	The concrete way of executing an action in accordance with the specific conditions surrounding the goal	How?

TABLE 11.1   Activity as a hierarchically organized system, showing the relationship among the three levels.

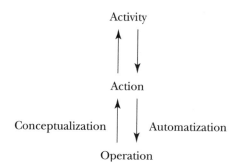

FIGURE 11.3   The dynamic relationship among levels of human activity.

from the mainstream of cognitive theories, for example, Card and colleagues' (1983) engineering psychology, where acts are classified as belonging to static categories such as time bands. In short, development is a basic feature in the framework of activity theory.

Leontiev's notion of human activity can be depicted as embedded triangles (Figure 11.4)—the Subject-Object-Community triangle of prehuman activity expanded with societally constituted forms of mediation: instruments, rules, and division of labor (Engeström, 1987). The specific form of the triangular figure is

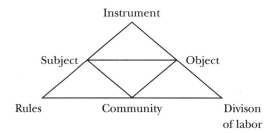

FIGURE
11.4   Leontiev's theory of human activity as depicted by Engeström (1987).

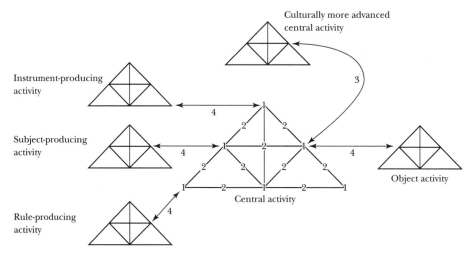

FIGURE
11.5   The relation between activity systems in terms of classes of contradictions.
(1 = primary, 2 = secondary, 3 = tertiary, 4 = quaternary)

not very important. The important thing is that activity is an intertwined system;
if one corner changes, the system becomes unstable and must develop to obtain
renewed stability.

   Activity systems are fundamentally marked by contradictions. In dialectical
thinking (Hegel, Marx, etc.), dynamics are understood as the eternal resolving
of inner antagonist contradictions. Engeström (1987) classifies contradictions
within and between activity systems as the driving forces in human learning and
development (Figure 11.5). The *primary contradiction* is the contradiction of com-
modity between use and exchange value. This double nature is a basic feature of

the capitalist economy, penetrating each corner of the activity system as an eternal source of instability and development. Though an example from CPN2000 may be a bit farfetched, there is, in this project as in any design project, the tension between the best possible solution and what may be designed with the time and resources available. *Secondary contradictions* are between the corners of the activity system—between the students' understanding of CP nets and assumptions about distributed systems underlying Design/CPN, between documentation standards of the alarm company and flexibility of documenting with CPN2000, between early graphics editors and the need for support for production of CP nets, and so on. *Quaternary contradictions* are contradictions between the activity looked at and the neighboring activities. Examples include contradictions between the institution educating the alarm engineers to become natural scientists and the need for skills in cooperation and decision making in the alarm company, and contradictions between the producers of Design/CPN wanting a conceptually clean tool and engineers needing support for discussion and documentation. *Tertiary contradictions* are contradictions between the considered activity and the activity (existing or nonexisting) it potentially could become. Such tertiary contradictions can be generated deliberately by finding examples and developing visions in the process of developing a community of practice to a new stage. The use of bimanual input in advanced 3D animation environments can be seen as generating a tertiary contradiction in the CPN2000 project.

Activity is constantly developing as a result of contradictions and instability, and as a result of the development of new needs. Activity theory understands human beings as dialectically re-creating their own environment. Subjects are not merely choosing from possibilities in the environment, but they are also actively creating the environment through activity.

The historical development of activity implies a development of artifacts and environments. Modes of acting within an activity system are historically crystallized into artifacts; in this sense, the historical development of activity can be read from the development of artifacts mediating the practice, to some degree (Bærentsen, 1989; Bannon and Bødker, 1991).

> Artifacts can be characterized as crystallized knowledge, which means that operations that are developed in the use of one generation of technology are later incorporated into the artifact itself in the next. (Bannon & Bødker, 1991, p. 243)

Activity is crystallized into artifacts in two ways. First, they are externalizations of operations with earlier artifacts; second, they are representations of modes of acting in the given activity. Artifacts mediating human activity are not just more-or-less suitable attachments to human practice; they also constitute activity.

Vygotsky's theory has a strong focus on developmental psychology and pedagogy. In understanding learning and development, the concept of the zone of proximal development is central. Originally it was aimed at changing the focus of developmental psychology (which is, in practice, a foundation for teaching strategies) from already acquired skills to potential skills "waiting" to mature in the individual. Learning is seen as a voyage through the zone of proximal development. Inherent in the concept is an emphasis in activity theory treating potentiality and development as basic aspects of human activity and stating that learning and development are socially mediated. People are understood not in terms of what they are but in terms of what they are becoming.

The concept of *the zone of proximal development* has been widely applied outside the areas of pedagogy and developmental psychology. It is central in Engeström's (1987) framework of expansive learning, as well as in approaches to the design and use of computer artifacts. In such contexts, the zone of proximal development has come to mean the possible future practices, or developmental potentials, spanned out in confronting existing practice with other ways of doing similar things. In other words, development takes place in the meeting of what is in one way or another different from what the learners already are capable of doing.

11.4   DETAILED DESCRIPTION

We outline here a series of key principles of activity theory, formulated with emphasis on HCI.

Activity theory takes motivated activity as its basic, irreducible unit of analysis. This unity implies that human conduct cannot be understood as the mere aggregation of behavioral atoms, and that consciousness is rooted in practical engagement in the world. Computer artifacts are looked at in use and not in isolation. Looking at computer artifacts in use sometimes means focusing on the narrow-use activity and the handling of the computer artifact, typically in HCI studies. In other cases, the context is much wider, such as focusing on the web of activities of use and design. One of the forces of activity theory is, however, that it allows for studies of all these levels of activity to be combined, applying one and the same set of concepts.

In the CPN2000 case, we studied the activity of alarm-protocol design, where Design/CPN mediated cooperation between designers and the actual validation of a protocol, to mention a couple of the distinct activities identified. In both cases, the CPN tool mediates a designer's work on a CPN. In one instance, the designer's purpose is to capture all the changes to the protocol agreed upon in a meeting; in the other, it is to see if the designed protocol works.

Human activity is mediated by socially produced artifacts, such as tools, language, and representations. This means that, in their immediate relation with their surroundings, human beings extend themselves with artifacts that are both augmentations of and external to the person.

The particular Colored Petri Nets are fundamental artifacts to the group of designers. The Design/CPN supports construction and validation of nets, but the formalism is also independent of the tool and used for such activities as scribbling notes from a meeting.

Activity can be understood as a systemic structure. Activity is object oriented: It is a (possibly collective) subject's active engagement directed toward an object. This engagement is socially mediated by the community in which the activity is embedded or constituted. Changing parts of the systemic structure disturbs the balance or the entire structure.

As illustrated here, designers used Design/CPN in order to build alarm systems. Only some people who were part of this activity used Design/CPN or CPN. Others worked on hardware or management, for example. In this particular case, we do not know if changing the hardware platform or management strategy (e.g., division of work in the project) would have influenced the use of Design/CPN, though we suspect it would.

Activity is realized through conscious actions directed to relevant goals. Actions are realized through unconscious operations triggered by the structure of the activity and conditions in the environment.

In our studies, we have seen how users construct CPNs using the Design/CPN tools to create places, transitions, annotations, and so on. The same act can change among the three levels in the course of learning and due to changed condition.

The expert user keeps reformatting the net through operations, whereas the students we studied had their point of focus on the formatting, when they carried this out.

When the guidance for an act is transformed from conscious interaction with external objects into an unconscious internal plan of action, internalization takes place. Externalization takes place when activity with one generation of an artifact is crystallized into the next generation of the same artifact.

CPN2000 is ultimately a crystallization based on the operations, actions, and activities of using Design/CPN.

Before the existence of CPN tools, the formalism was used by drawing nets by hand or by using general-purpose drawing programs. In such manual construction of nets, the person constructing the net spends time checking the syntax of the net as she draws it. Also, different styles in laying out the nets were developed. In Design/CPN as well as in CPN2000, this checking of syntax as well as elements of layout is crystallized into the tool. However, in the redesign from Design/CPN to CPN2000, the introduction of two-handed input is an example of development by design that cannot be understood in terms of crystallization. This is because it transcends the existing ways of working with CPN in an abrupt manner.

11.4.1   Mediation

Computers mediate our daily activities, whether these are in relation to things or other human beings. Activity theory has been concerned with this kind of mediation by a variety of mundane tools (see Kaptelinin, 1996) and by information technology (Bannon & Bødker, 1991; Bannon & Kuutti, 1993; Bertelsen, 1996; Bødker, 1991, 1999). Activity theory gives a useful handle for understanding the mediators, and how they are shaped, in a dialectical relationship with the changing practice of use.

Because activity theory takes purposeful acts as the basic unit of analysis, we have to study what happens when users focus on their job (or other purposeful act) while applying the computer artifact. With the hierarchical structure of activity, this means that the situation tends to be routine when the object of the user's (conscious) action is the same as the object of work, whereas the user directs unconscious operations to the mediating artifact. The computer artifact becomes a transparent tool.

In studying the CPN tools, we may identify the activity of the protocol designers as shown in Table 11.2.

In the further analysis of mediation, the next step is to look at the actual objects of focus in this work and the various possible locations of the objects (things or persons), as they are present inside or outside the computer or both. These "real" objects of our activity—our objects of interest (Shneiderman, 1983) or domain objects (Beaudouin-Lafon, Berteaud, & Chatty, 1990)—constitute the anchoring of the further analysis. Each location of the object has its own characteristics, with regard to how directly it can be accessed by the user. The syntax shown in Figure 11.6 is used to map the interaction of a particular artifact.

If we look at the CPN example, we see that the actual objects are alarm protocols (Figure 11.7). The CPNs are examples of objects that exist both outside

Why?	Making good alarm systems (and ultimately building and selling alarm systems)
What?	Building and verifying alarm system protocols by constructing CP nets using Design/CPN (various subgoals of this process)
How?	Adding new places and transitions, moving arcs, changing arc curvature, changing markings, pulling down menus, etc.

TABLE

11.2

Applying the analytical questions from Table 11.1 to CPN use.

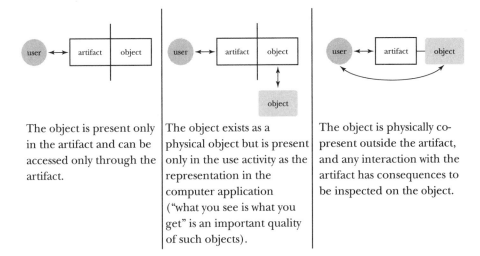

The object is present only in the artifact and can be accessed only through the artifact.	The object exists as a physical object but is present only in the use activity as the representation in the computer application ("what you see is what you get" is an important quality of such objects).	The object is physically co-present outside the artifact, and any interaction with the artifact has consequences to be inspected on the object.

FIGURE

11.6

Objects as they are encountered in or through the artifact—a graphical syntax.

and inside the computer. Printouts are used for discussions and annotations in meetings with the remaining project group, and the changes are later entered into Design/CPN by a protocol designer. Accordingly, these printouts mediate the cooperation in the design group in ways that Design/CPN does not. At the same time, the CPN "in the computer" has numerous capabilities for simulation, and so forth, that the printout does not. In this manner, most computer applications are most appropriately seen as clusters of artifacts rather than singular ones. Beaudouin-Lafon (2000) mentions some of these artifacts, namely what he calls meta-instruments. Meta-instruments are, in his understanding, instruments to create instruments. In activity theoretical terms, meta-instruments belong with the cluster of artifacts that mediate the total interaction, and may be

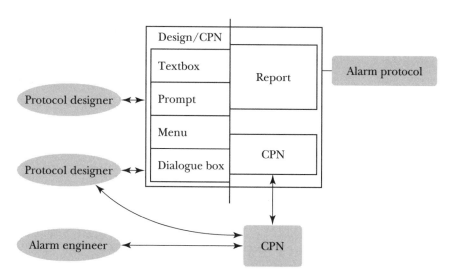

FIGURE

11.7

The ultimate object of Design/CPN is the alarm protocol. While using Design/CPN, other objects are in focus, such as the net (CPN) that exists in the computer as well as a printout, and the simulation report in the computer. Meanwhile, the users focus on many objects (textbox, prompt, etc.) that belong to the handling, as meta-instruments, or because they attract the attention of the users. Some users—the alarm engineers—use only the printed-out net, while others—the protocol designers—interact with the alarm protocol through Design/CPN and perhaps through a printout.

differentiated analytically and designwise when necessary. The instruments created or modified through meta-instruments are, at the same time, examples of objects that are objects exactly while modifying them (but preferably not otherwise), and objects that exist only in the artifact.

We further (Bødker, 1991) analyzed the levels of mediation in computer-mediated work as follows:

✦ The physical aspects support operations toward the computer application as a physical object. Pushing keys and mouse buttons, as well as movements of pointing devices, are the physical aspects; Mackenzie's (Chapter 3, this volume) discussion of mouse degrees-of-freedom and dimensions are concerns that belong mainly with the physical aspects.

✦ The handling aspects support operations toward the computer application. The handling aspects are the conditions that allow the user to focus on the "real" objects and subjects of the activity. A typical example of a concern at this level is the scroll bar and how scrolling affects the window on which it has effect.

◆ The subject/object–directed aspects constitute the conditions for operations directed toward objects or subjects that we deal with "in" the artifact or through the artifact (see Figure 11.6).

In Design/CPN, the *handling aspects* are about creating places and transitions, adding new places and transitions, moving arcs, changing arc curvature, changing markings, pulling down menus, and so on. The *physical aspects* are related to the use of the mouse to move and place things, and the use of parameters to chance curvature. As a matter of fact, changing the physical aspects of the tools was a major concern in CPN2000 and an important reason to choose bimanual interaction. The choice of a different set of physical aspects gave new possibilities for the handling of the CPNs, such as through the two-handed click-through of tool glasses. The *subject/object directed aspects* are about how pieces of nets may be reused in other configurations, for example, and how a hierarchical structuring of complex nets may be carried out.

Computer artifacts not only mediate in a toollike transparent way. A great deal of learning takes place before and during normal use, as will be illustrated in the example in Section 11.5.1 where we analyze the use of Design/CPN by novice users.

It is possible to use the questions of why, what, and how to capture important stereotypes of computer artifacts. We use the terms *system, tool,* and *media* to capture these stereotypes, as shown in Table 11.3.

A system mediates between the individual contributors of actions and operations and their object. At the same time, the system is the instrument of the acting subject, who is not directly contributing to the production of the outcome. A tool mediates the relationship between the subject and the material object being worked on. And a medium mediates the relationship between the acting subject and the practice surrounding the subject and the activity.

Almost no real-life computer application can be understood in terms of only one of these stereotypes. Accordingly, the stereotypes can be used analytically by tracing and characterizing the use of the artifact in the historical development of use, or in the web of different activities that takes place around the computer artifact. It is particularly interesting to understand the contradictions among the different use activities.

Design/CPN is used by individual users to construct and analyze CPNs. It is intended as a tool mediating this work, although, as we shall see, there are situations where the users do not find themselves in control.

	system	*tool*	*medium*
why?	planning/control	material production	communication
what?	data entry +extraction	shaping material	creating and interpreting signs
how?	"low risk" data entry	transparency: good access to material	transparency: undisturbed interpretation

TABLE   Characteristics of the system, tool, and media perspectives.

11.3

11.4.2   Internalization—Externalization

Activity theory does not assume a fixed separation between mental representations and external representations, as in cognitivist approaches to human cognition. In contrast, the unity of consciousness and activity is taken as a basic feature of human cognition. Cognition cannot be separated from the outward acts in which the individual engages. The principle of internalization and externalization deals with the development of mediation. When learning addition of natural numbers, the child first uses external representations like fingers, pebbles, or an abacus, but gradually these artifacts are internalized and the child is able to perform addition without external props. Externalization, on the other hand, may take place in a situation of a need for repair, such as when the numbers are too large to add by mental arithmetic, in which case an abacus or a piece of paper may be used for external representation. Likewise, externalization is needed when two or more persons work together; speaking aloud or using the abacus are means supporting this type of externalization as well. When internalized acts take place, they enable simulation and rehearsing as well as monitoring of the invisible.

CPN tools are examples of rather massive externalization. Not only are CP nets externalized means for making sense of distributed systems, but making automated simulations is a further externalization of the process of checking the behavior of the system under various conditions.

Considering the three types of use situations—editing a net, modifying a net to do something else, and constructing a net from scratch—the user studies strongly indicated that the three situations required increasing competency. Students had no problems editing nets, whereas modification was harder for them, and creating a net from scratch was very difficult because it also involved wrestling with the tool, the formalism, and the idea of modeling a system. In dealing with such complex situations, it is important to have internalized handling of the tool, the CPN formalism, as well as concepts of the domain to be modeled. However, users rarely work from a blank page; more often they modify and change layout of existing nets in a sort of bricolage. Thus, earlier nets are used as externalized experience with making nets.

11.4.3   Computer Artifacts in a Web of Activities

In much activity-theoretical research, the unit of analysis is, in one way or another, a particular work or educational activity, with its community of practice, actors, rules, division of work, and tools. In particular instances, this analysis is expanded to several interlinked activities—be these interlinked historically, in what Engeström (1987) calls activity systems, or in what we call *webs of activity*. When moving the focus from activities to computer artifacts as mediators of activities, we are faced with certain theoretical possibilities. First of all, what allows us to generalize our investigations beyond sheer individual use of technology is practice. By anchoring an analysis in practice, the historically developed ways and means by which groups of people undertake a particular activity, we are able to balance the analysis between the general and the particular. Furthermore, as is often the case with interface design, we need to explore an artifact that is not yet there; the existing practice is a valuable starting point for that, as illustrated by the CPN2000 example (Bødker & Grønbæk, 1996).

Studies of computer artifacts in use need to focus on the narrow-use activity and the handling of the computer artifact, as well as on the wider context of use and design. One of the forces of activity theory is that it allows studies of all these levels of activity to be combined. It allows us to change scale and to study connections on multiple levels of activities where computer artifacts are used and designed, without establishing a permanent hierarchy in the analysis (Bardram, 1998; Raithel, 1992, 1996).

Bødker (1999) summarizes how a computer application may have positions in a variety of activities in the web of design/use activities. As discussed by Engeström (1987), as well as by Mathiassen (1981), it is the tensions or contradictions between these positions that are the source of change. In Engeström's model of work development, he sees contradictions in the activity system as the major driving force of such change: He bases his analysis on contradictions within the activity and between this activity and surrounding activities, because they constitute the basis for learning and change; he looks at contradictions in how tools, objects, and subjects are seen. An interesting contradiction that we shall return to is whether the CPN tool always works on a valid CPN or whether it is all right to work on sketches that are incomplete.

Engeström suggests studying contradictions between, for example, the tools currently used and the object created, or the norms that are part of practice and the division of work. Looking at things from the point of view of the artifact, which is shaped and used in several different activities, makes it very difficult to identify and delimit the activity system that is of interest for the analysis. This would potentially include all use activities, all teaching and artifact production activities, as well as ideals for the change of all of the use activities. Despite this, *awareness toward contradictions is an important component in our analysis.*

The CPN2000 case identified two distinctly different use activities—that of alarm-protocol design, and that of learning about distributed systems. As indicated by the example analyses that we present here, the difference between these two transcends all levels of use, including the handling of the CPN tool. Furthermore, the analysis indicates that Design/CPN has many users who do not understand CPN well enough to design a CPN from scratch, whereas they are able to make changes and adjustments to nets created by others.

As indicated by the example, activity theory allows for a focus of attention to technical solutions that crosses boundaries between activities, or that supports several coexisting activities simultaneously (Engeström & Escalante, 1996). Heterogeneity as a conceptual frame of analysis has come out of actor-network theory. In the context of human-computer interaction, heterogeneity has been emphasized not least in the work by Star (1996). However, it is also profoundly embedded in many studies of webs of activities. One early example is Engeström and Engeström's (1989) joint work with doctor-patient construction of a patient diagnosis, where they point to the profoundly different understandings and models that the two persons carry of the particular disease. Another example is Bødker and Grønbæk's (1996) analysis of cooperative prototyping. The focus on heterogeneity points to the profoundly different conditions that various groups (and individuals) have for participating in activities of design and use of information technology.

11.4.4   Development

The most distinct feature of activity theory, when compared to other materialist accounts in computer science, is the emphasis on development. Because human activity is historically constituted and constantly developing, human use of technology cannot be meaningfully understood in terms of stable entities. Rather than labeling levels of consciousness, activity theory offers concepts like automation, conceptualization, internalization, and externalization as handles for understanding the dynamics between levels of the hierarchical structure of activity and of computer use (Bannon & Kuutti, 1993).

Activity-theoretical analyses have served as a basis for studying how people operationalize their use of artifacts of various sorts. Bærentsen's (1989) analysis of the development of hand weapons goes beyond that in presenting an analysis of the historical development of hand weapons interlinked with the development of their use as well as their context in terms of conditions of use. Existing practice is historically shaped, and activity-theoretical analyses help create links between the past, the present, and the future, which are important for the design of interaction artifacts. Bertelsen (1996) has analyzed how practice is crystallized and transformed in the case of a checklist used in planning a music festival. Bødker (1993) used the tool, systems, and media metaphor to characterize different stages in the development of a particular computer artifact. This makes it possible to focus on how the purpose of the use of the artifact changes along with changes in actual objects and in ways of handling the artifact (why, what, and how).

Engeström's seminal work (1987) points to activity theory as a basis for development of work as such, and it points to a number of instruments for this that make sure that we look to the past as well as to the future throughout the design process. As regards the specific design of computer artifacts, these instruments have been crystallized and developed in the following:

+ User interface styles

+ Theory-informed checklists

+ Extreme (plus/minus) scenarios (Bødker, Christiansen, & Thüring, 1995; Bødker, Graves Petersen, & Nielsen, 2000).

Bardram & Bertelsen (1995) used the concept of the zone of proximal development in the context of developing transparent interaction. At first sight, this appears to contradict the concept, as there does not seem to be any social mediation going on in the one man–one computer situation. However, computer artifacts are not only tools mediating users' relations to their object of work; they are, at the same time, media mediating the relation between designers or culture and users. Computer artifacts are social mediation in the same sense as books, and accordingly the designer leaves traces that help her to be present as a more capable peer, guiding the user through the zone of proximal development.

Design—Use

As illustrated by Gasser (1986) and Bødker (1999), the use of rather rigid computer applications develops beyond pure adaptation by the users; as such, the computer application (even when built) is a source of changing practice. From this perspective, design never seems to stop (Floyd, 1987).

The interlinking between design and use, however, goes further than that. The design activity is constrained by the computer in various ways, through the actual, available materials as such, and through the past experiences of designers and users (Bødker et al., 1987). The introduction of two-handed interaction in CPN2000 depended on the availability of trackballs for PCs, and it gave rise to many concerns regarding how one could support two-handed interaction as well as alternative and more traditional one mouse–one hand interaction. The choice of two input devices opened up a new design space because it made it possible for designers to focus on new possibilities, such as tool glasses. The iterative design process set up for CPN2000 aimed to make active use of experiences from use in the continued design. Hence, experimental use of prototypes by experienced CPN designers was introduced to inform the iterative design process.

Designers and users are, in general, parties in a number of interlinked and partly overlapping activities that we need to understand in order to make better designs, and ultimately to create better computer artifacts. In these multipractical design situations, the experiences, resources, tools, and so forth, of designers meet and sometimes clash with those of the users and others involved. The CPN2000 project involved a number of designers and implementers of different backgrounds—some with primary experience in and concern for the programming tools, some with a background in Petri Nets, and some with an interest in advanced interface design. The PN people were also designers and users of the old tool, whereas most of the rest of the group had no or little experience with Design/CPN. This introduced many conflicting interests into the process. These differences, however, in the end added to the creative design that resulted. But it was indeed necessary to create a process where these conflicts were elaborated and turned around to something positive through such springboards as scenarios from use and through video prototypes (Mackay, 2002). In Bertelsen and Bødker (2002), we have discussed such differences in terms of general discontinuities in design and pointed out that it is vitally important for innovation and dynamics of design to mediate and explicate the discontinuities rather than to eliminate them. In the CPN2000 project, the divergent perspectives enabled the group as a whole to go beyond established conceptions of what tool support for CP nets could be.

Summary—A checklist for situating computer applications in use

To situate the computer application in use, one should

- ✦ situate work and computer application historically,

- ✦ situate the computer application in a web of activities where it is used,

- ✦ characterize the use according to the stereotypes of systems, tools and media,

- ✦ consider the support needed for the various activities going on around the computer application, and the historical circumstances of the computer application,

- ✦ identify the objects worked on, in, or through the computer application,

- ✦ consider the web of activities and the contradictions in and between activities.

FIGURE	Situating the computer application in use.
11.8	

11.4.5 Activity Theory in Practical Design and Evaluation

Bødker (1996) summarizes how to make an analysis situating a computer application in use, followed by a focus shift analysis of an actual use activity. This summary is outlined in Figure 11.8. Though these analyses are outlined as having a certain order among them, the analyses have really been taking place in interaction and iteration.

A similar kind of checklist can be found in Korpela et al. (2000), as shown in Figure 11.9.

Yet another similar example, but one based in abstract considerations, is the activity checklist (Kaptelinin, Nardi, & Macaulay, 1999), which is based on the formulation of the five basic principles of activity theory: object-orientedness, hierarchical structure of activity, internalization and externalization, mediation, and development. Mediation is "folded in" with each of the other four principles, resulting in the four categories of concerns: means/ends, environment, learning/cognition/articulation, and development. For each category, a series of questions are asked with the purpose of understanding the use-context that the artifact is intended to support. The main problem with respect to that list is

The checklist included the following questions to identify the main constituents of the central activity:

+ 1a. **Outcome:** What services or products do we produce?

+ 2a. **Object and process:** What raw materials or prerequisites do we start from? How do we produce the services or products from the inputs we have?

+ 3a. **Instruments:** What kinds of physical tools and knowledge, skills, and so forth, do we need for this work?

+ 4a. **Subjects:** Who are we—what different kinds of people are needed to produce these services or products?

+ 5a. **Social relations and means:** When we work to produce the services or products, what kinds of rules, division of labor, communication, and so forth, apply between us?

The following questions were included to identify the network of activities:

+ 1b. **Outcome:** Who needs our services or products? Why do they need them—to produce some services or products for some others?

+ 2b. **Object:** From whom do we get our "raw materials"? How do they produce what we need?

+ 3b. **Instruments:** From whom do we get the tools and knowledge we need? How do they produce them?

+ 4b. **Subjects:** Where do we come from—who educates and raises the kinds of people needed here? How does that happen?

+ 5b. **Social relations and means:** Who sets the rules for us? How are the rules generated?

FIGURE Situating the computer application, part 2.

11.9

that it leaves out concerns for contradictions, thus disabling the theoretical framework's analytical power.

11.5 CASE STUDY

According to Engeström (1987), activity theory does not offer ready-made techniques and procedures for research; rather its conceptual tools must be

Summary—A checklist for HCI analysis through focus shifts

For each specific focus, ask:

- ✦ what is the purpose of the activity/actions for the user?
- ✦ which object is focused on by the user? where is this object located (in, through, or outside the computer application)
- ✦ what is the instrument? where is it located (in, through, or outside the computer application)

When more users are cooperating, ask:

- ✦ are the purposes, objects, and instruments in accordance or conflicting (between the individuals, as well between the group and individuals)?

For each focus shift, ask:

- ✦ from what focus/object to what?
- ✦ breakdown or deliberate shift?
- ✦ what causes the shift? in particular, is it the physical, handling, or subject/ object-directed aspects of the computer application that are involved.

FIGURE

11.10

HCI analysis through focus shifts.

concretized according to the specific nature of the object under scrutiny. However, we do see several crystallized techniques emerge, such as the checklists shown in Figures 11.8 and 11.9 and the focus-shift analysis that follows. The second example in this section is concerned with the design implications of activity theory–based concepts.

11.5.1 Focus and Focus Shifts

The objects of work identify the points of focus from which the analysis starts. The focus shifts that indicate the dynamics of the situation are, however, the main points of concern in the analysis. These are summarized in Figure 11.10.

In making this analysis, we apply a mapping technique that creates an overview of the answers to these questions. This will be illustrated through the later example from our analysis of Design/CPN, and we start by summarizing the situation and artifact:

Mary and Sue are students of computer science, using the Design/CPN tool for the first time after seeing it demonstrated in a lecture. They are generally well acquainted with the Unix environment, opening and closing windows, menus, and so on. They take a class in distributed systems, in which CPN is used for analysis and verification.

They have particular assignments to do in order to explore the tool. The teacher who has designed the assignments is well acquainted with the tool.

The objects that they focus on are primarily the CPNs, though these are parts of something wider—learning about distributed systems, doing exercises, or, as in industrial settings, modeling network protocols so as to analyze them.

They sit next to each other, each doing the assignments on a computer. The camera is on Mary and the computer screen she works on. The camera-person also acts as interviewer, but has no knowledge of the tool and cannot give advice.

The timer on the camera shows 14.50 when this example starts. The actual events last for about 30 seconds.

By carefully reviewing the tape, we see that it contains nine focus points and eight focus shifts. The focus points are identified through looking at the actions on the screen and identifying what is talked about.

Three objects of focus are concerned with the actual activity and accordingly supported by the subject/object directed aspect of Design/CPN: the exercise, the Petri Net, and a report that is generated as part of the exercise. The user shifts among focuses of solving the problem outlined in the exercise, creating the net, and creating a report as part of the exercise. Of these objects, only the exercise is outside Design/CPN because it lives on a sheet of paper. The remaining objects are inside the Design/CPN. In the remaining four categories of focus points, the Design/CPN tool imposes itself on the user, and accordingly they are, more or less sufficiently, supported by the handling aspects of Design/CPN. The four focus points are: a textbox, a menu, a dialogue box, and a prompt. In actual fact, we are dealing with more than one menu, more than one prompt, and so on.

The exercise sheet is the only object accessible through tools other than the computer application; that is, it can be written on with a pen.

In the analysis, we use a form where the objects of focus are outlined in one dimension, and a time/progression of the interaction is outlined in the other. In this dimension, we also place the transcript of the conversation taking place and the screen images used to identify foci. An asterisk * is used to indicate the point of focus, and the trace left by the series of asterisks is accordingly a trace of focus shifts—as shown in Figure 11.11.

The immediate observations that we make from this analysis are that novices in this type of training situation have much of their focus on the tool. This is not

Transcript	Picture	Subject/object directed aspects			Handling aspects			
		exercise	Petri net	report	text box	menu	dialogue box	prompt
(14.50.00)	S14		*					
M: It says that I have to make a textbox, that's what I'm trying to do so that I can see the report S: I did (. . .), that's what he said in the lecture				*				
	S15		*					
M: why doesn't it show up?					*			
	S16				*			
	S17						*	
S: it is gigantic M: well, if I can close it, I should be able to . . .					*			
	S18							*
(14.50.37)	S19			*				

FIGURE
11.11

Tracing focus shifts.

surprising. What is more surprising is that they have severe difficulties orienting and remembering where functions are located in the many long menus. As shown in Figure 11.12, things pop up as very large windows on top of others, adding to the problem of orientation. Error boxes and other elements pop up on top of nets, disturbing the focus on the net. Some elements of the nets, such as arcs, are, however, small and difficult to grasp, move, and annotate.

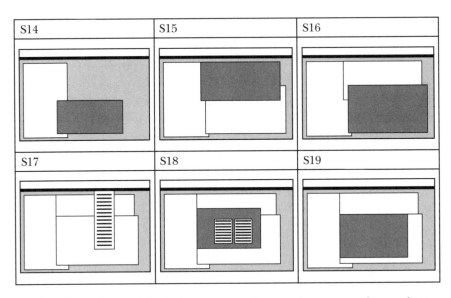

FIGURE

11.12

Sketches illustrating which window or menu the user focuses on. The numbers refer to the transcript in Figure 11.11. The shaded window indicates which window or menu is in focus of use.

11.5.2   The Concept of Artifacts in Use as a Tool in the Redesign of the CPN Tool

Many ways of bringing activity theory to design have not yet crystallized into formalized techniques or methodical prescriptions. Thus, the influence of activity theory often seems indirect, taking effect only through the way designers understand the situation at hand. An example of this "application" of activity theory in the CPN2000 project is the influence of the concept of artifacts in use in the initial discussions in the CPN2000 HCI group.

A concern early in the design process was to determine what the basic data structure for the tool should be. This was important because the basic data structure would be determining the overall architecture of the tool. The textbook definition of a CP net states that it is a "bipartite graph with places and transitions. . . ." Thus, the obvious and consistent solution would be to have representations of nets according to the formal definition as the basic data structure in the tool. This was the approach taken in the old tool as well. The formal, presentation-independent net was the basis for the editor as well as the validator and simulator.

In a historical perspective, the tools used in working with CP nets have developed from pen and paper through general-purpose graphics editors (only supporting presentation of the nets) to tools like DesignCPN directly based on the formal semantics and syntax of the nets, enabling automatic verification and so forth. Whereas this development is an obvious advantage for construction of nets, it is also striking that the need for additional data structures in the tool related to the presentation of nets became a source of inconsistency.

This dilemma between basic data structures based on formal definitions and practical use of the tool was not new. In syntax-directed source-code editors, it is a well-known problem that editing tools cannot determine to which parts of the syntactical structure comments belong, thus marginalizing the use of comments and jeopardizing the maintainability of the code. Similarly, in an earlier study an object-oriented source code debugger (Bertelsen & Bødker, 1998), we observed a discrepancy between the strictly object-oriented principles that the tool was built on and the programming practice that the tool was intended to support. The general emphasis in activity theory on understanding artifacts in use, rather than in isolation, in this case becomes operational in the analysis, through the concept of the debugger-in-use (not as container for principles).

The concept of Petri-nets-in-use was formative in setting up the user studies. The focus was not only on how the existing tool was used and what limitations it had. Focus was as much on understanding the kind of work the tools and the CP nets were going to support. In addition, the concept of Petri-nets-in-use was a possible handle for transforming studies of use into considerations for the system architecture.

Focusing on CP nets in use implies that not only is the CPN tool seen as a means for working with the nets *per se,* but that the nets are seen as means for doing something else purposefully. In this respect, a CP net is not only a well-defined formal description of some phenomena, but it is also a means for communicating design ideas, for documentation, and so on. Thus, the layout of nets became a first-order aspect in the concept of Petri nets in use. In the CPN2000 tools, this is reflected, for example, in the use of tool glasses for reapplying the styling of one part of a net to other parts of the net.

The concern for artifacts in use moves the focus of HCI from being mainly at the interface to the whole work arrangement, as well as inward to concerns for system functionality and system architecture.

11.5.3   The User Interface

As mentioned earlier, Beaudouin-Lafon (2000) has developed an interaction model for CPN2000 and for computer applications in general. In line with the framework of activity theory, his idea is to understand user-interface elements such as scroll bars and windows as mediators/artifacts, and hence to view the entire user interface as a cluster of artifacts where interaction with domain objects, as well as with the artifacts themselves through meta-instruments, take place.

He develops ways of describing the relationships among the physical, the handling, and the subject/object–directed aspects of the interface through the following:

✦ The degree of indirectness—the temporal and spatial distance between the object on the screen and the instrument that operates on it.

✦ The degree of integration—the relationship between the degrees-of-freedom of the physical pointing device and the logical device (e.g., scroll bar) on which it operates.

✦ And the degree of compatibility—the relationship between the movement of the physical device and the domain object; for example, the relationship between the direction of the mouse and the direction of the object when dragging an object.

This model is used to characterize and compare standard interface components, and to discuss the notion of direct manipulation in general. It strongly supports the idea, in activity-theoretical HCI, that mediation is essential rather than directness as such, and it points to a number of ways in which user interfaces may be designed to mediate better.

11.6   CURRENT STATUS

In her collection of papers regarding the application of activity theory to human-computer interaction, Nardi (1996) suggests that activity theory is a powerful descriptive tool rather than a predictive theory. It offers a set of perspectives on human activity and a set of concepts describing this. In this chapter, we have explained the descriptive concepts of activity theory, but we have also presented a number of concrete techniques used to focus on computer-mediated activity, more commonly known as HCI.

A recent issue of *Scandinavian Journal of Information Systems* (volume 12, 2000) presents a series of studies of activity-theoretical HCI as well as of the wider activity of use, such as the changing character of work influenced by information technology, distribution of activities, and the emergence of interorganizational communities. Not least does the volume deal with design of these technologies so as to accommodate for use in the narrow as well as in the wide. As with the rest of HCI, activity-theoretical HCI must be concerned with wider activities because of the changing application of computer technology in society in general and in work in particular. As an example of this, the use and design of one piece of software running on one hardware platform rarely takes place in isolation. People switch between many computer applications, running on many pieces of hardware, including handhelds and electronic whiteboards. As a consequence, Nielsen and Søndergaard (2000) explore webs-of-technologies to be considered in use and in design. These webs-of-technologies, together with the webs-of-activities, make us focus on contradictory demands and needs, and make us see these contradictions as important driving forces of change.

HCI is increasingly becoming an interdisciplinary science. Engeström and Miettinen (1999) map out the relationships of activity theory to most recent theoretical trends in the social sciences, including pragmatism, symbolic interactionism, actor-network theory, Wittgensteinian approaches, situated learning, and semiotics. It is largely these same theories that have found their way into HCI. Nardi (1996) as well as Plowman and colleagues (1995) combine activity theory and ethnomethodology. Star (1996) has worked to combine symbolic interactionism and activity theory in CSCW and in information systems design, and Engeström and Escalante (1996) have combined activity theory and actor-network theory in their study of design and use of a public-information system. Activity theory has become a theoretical tool for ethnographical studies (e.g., Nardi, 1996; Spasser, 2000), for participatory design (Beguin & Rabardel, 2000; Bødker & Grønbæk, 1996; Bødker & Petersen, 2000; Timpka & Sjöberg, 1994), as well as for psychological approaches (Bærentsen, 2000; Greif, 1991).

Activity theory has served well to inform analyses of computer artifacts in use, in particular in work. A wide array of methods and tools support this perspective, from historical analyses and ethnographical studies to schemes for focus-shift analyses. Similarly, activity theory is getting a foothold for understanding design activities, structurally and processually (Bødker 1999; Koistinen & Kangajosa 1997; Korpela, 1994). The change-oriented perspective on computer applications in use implies direct demands on how we do design, so as to accommodate further change. And it needs to address further the technical constitution of the artifact. Bertelsen (1997, 1998) has started to address issues of why object-oriented technology seems appropriate for an activity theoretically inspired design process. It seems to be one of the really big challenges for an activity theory–informed design—how far can one actually be able to go? How close to technology? How design oriented?

The Finnish developmental work-research tradition (Engeström et al., 1996) offers, for the time being, the most complete methodological approach to activity-theoretical work analyses and design, emphasizing the continuous development of work. In the developmental-work tradition, computer artifacts may be one instrument of such development, as described by Helle (2000). However, Helle's paper is in a sense an exception within a tradition where very few examples, thus far, have addressed the issues of IT in use and design. This forces practitioners such as Korpela and colleagues (2000) to seek their own approaches based on the theoretical frame of developmental work research.

Two interesting issues in activity theory–based HCI approaches to study in the future are the crystallization of activity theory–based design instruments, like the activity checklist and the focus shift analysis, and the development of technical concepts based on activity theory. For the latter concern, we have seen that the concept of artifacts in use is leading to considerations of basic system architecture and data formats.

11.7   FURTHER READING

Bannon, L., & Bødker, S. (1991). Beyond the interface: Encountering artifacts in use. In J. M. Carroll (Ed.). *Designing interaction* (pp. 227–253). Cambridge, UK: Cambridge University Press.

Bannon, L. J., & Kuutti, K. (1993). Searching for unity among diversity: Exploring the "Interface" concept. In S. Ashlund et al. (Eds.), *INTERCHI '93: Conference on Human Factors in Computing Systems. INTERACT '93 and CHI '93 Bridges Between Worlds* (pp. 263–268). New York: ACM Press.

Bardram, J. E., & Bertelsen, O. W. (1995). Supporting the development of transparent interaction. In B. Blumenthal, J. Gornostaev, & C. Unger (Eds.), *Human-computer interaction. 5th International Conference, EWHCI '95 Moscow, Russia, July 1995. Selected Papers* (pp. 79–90). Berlin: Springer Verlag.

Bødker, S. (1991). *Through the interface—A human activity approach to user interface design.* Hillsdale, NJ: Erlbaum.

Engeström, Y., & Middleton, D. (Eds.) (1996). *Cognition and communication at work.* Cambridge, UK: Cambridge University Press.

Nardi, B. (Ed.) (1996). *Context and consciousness. Activity theory and human computer interaction,* Cambridge, MA: MIT Press.

12 | Applying Social Psychological Theory to the Problems of Group Work

Robert E. Kraut   Carnegie Mellon University

12.1   MOTIVATION

In the work arena, groups are a major mechanism for organizations to tackle problems that are too large or complex for individuals to solve alone. For example, modern software packages, like Microsoft's Excel, consist of millions of lines of computer code, whereas a good programmer typically writes a few thousand lines of code a year (Somerville, 2000; see Boehm et al., 1995, for more precise estimates of productivity in software engineering). To construct these massive applications, companies bring together individuals with skills in such disparate topics as interviewing, requirements analysis, software architecture, algorithms, databases, programming, graphic design, user interfaces, evaluation, and the application domain. Very few people are polymaths, with skills in all of these areas. Thus, both the scale and the scope involved in building large software applications demand group effort of some sort.

The subfield of human-computer interaction (HCI) known as computer-supported cooperative work (CSCW) attempts to build tools that will help groups of people to more effectively accomplish their work, as well as their learning and play. It also examines how groups incorporate these tools into their routines and the impact that various technologies have on group processes and outcomes. Computer-supported cooperative work, as a subfield, grew out of dissatisfaction with the individualistic emphasis in early research in HCI, with its overwhelming concern with single individuals using computers to perform routine tasks. This individualistic emphasis contrasts with the everyday observation that much paid work is done by interdependent individuals who collaborate (or compete) on ill-structured tasks.

We try to create technology to support groups for two primary reasons—to support distributed groups and to make traditional, collocated groups more effective. First, we want to get the benefit of groups in settings and for tasks where they had not previously been practical. Distributed work has existed since at least the days of the Hudson Bay Company in colonial America (O'Leary, Orlikowski, & Yates, 2002). However, the large numbers of interdependent teams whose members are located in different locations is a modern phenomenon, brought about by consolidation, acquisition, and globalization in corporations and enabled by improvements in telecommunications and computing technology. For example, engineering teams building modern aircraft have designers in multiple locations around the world (Argyres, 1999). Teams building large telecommunications software systems have members in North America, Europe, and Asia. Large consulting firms are likely to draw upon experts drawn from multiple offices scattered around the globe to get advice. These are not isolated examples. A recent study of a large telecommunications corporation showed that about 50% of the project teams in this company were composed of members who were located in different cities (Cummings, 2001). Distributed groups are typically not as effective as ones whose members are collocated (Cramton, 2001), so one goal of CSCW research has been to develop technology that would allow distributed teams to work as if they were collocated.

A second goal of CSCW systems is to help both collocated and distributed teams perform better than they would otherwise. As already mentioned, the reasons for creating groups to do work is so that they can accomplish tasks that are beyond the scope of individuals. Across many tasks, groups do perform better than the individuals who belong to them. Yet combining individuals into groups often leads to poorer performance than one would expect if the combination were "frictionless." For example, people work less hard in teams than they do when working individually (Karau & Williams, 1993). They fail to take advantage of the unique knowledge and skills they bring to the group, and they reach decisions without exploring many of the relevant alternatives (Larson et al., 1996). They have difficulty coordinating their contributions (Diehl & Stroebe, 1987). Finally, the very diversity for which they were formed often leads to dissatisfaction and conflict (Williams & O'Reilly, 1998). Steiner (1972) coined the term *processes loss* to describe the decline in performance from some theoretical maxim that groups typically show. But CSCW systems can be designed to ameliorate some of these process losses.

The contention of the current chapter is that both of these goals of CSCW require deep knowledge of the factors that make groups effective or that undermine them. This knowledge, for example, can help us understand what makes distributed teams perform more poorly than collocated ones and what is needed to support them (Cramton, 2001; Kraut, Fussell, Brennan, & Siegel, 2002; Olson & Olson, 2000). It will also suggest remedial actions to take to overcome known inefficiencies in groups. The next section provides an introduction to the field of computer-supported cooperative work. The remainder of the chapter will provide an introduction to the relevant social psychological literature. We will also show how social psychology theory can help explain and solve a well-understood problem—the failure of brainstorming groups to deliver more or better ideas than what is known as a "nominal group," that is, a noninteracting collection of individuals.

12.2   AN OVERVIEW OF CSCW RESEARCH

Figure 12.1 is a conceptual map of the CSCW area, showing the variety of research issues it addresses, differing in approach, focus, and scope. The prototypical CSCW research project (the center of the figure) examines small groups interacting with computer or telecommunications applications. CSCW researchers differ in their approach. Some researchers build systems to support small group work; they typically come from the engineering-oriented disciplines of computer science and electrical engineering, which put great value on the engineering and building of systems and applications (e.g., Boyle, Edwards, & Greenberg, 2000). Others come from the social science disciplines of psychology, sociology, anthropology, and communication studies. These disciplines typically value the ability to describe a social phenomenon empirically and to identify the causal mechanisms that influence it. Their CSCW research often describes how applications were used and the consequences of their use (Orlikowski, 2000).

There is variation around the modal research in terms of the focus and group size they are concerned with. The modal research is concerned with small groups interacting with an application. Further away from this core, on the engineering side, research topics range from software architectures, which are necessary to support CSCW applications (e.g., Dewan, 2000), to enabling software and telecommunications infrastructures. On the social science side are applied, empirical studies of groups performing tasks (e.g., (Olson, Olson, Carter, &

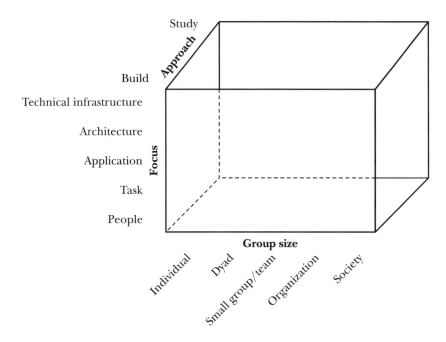

FIGURE   Variations in CSCW research.

12.1

Storrosten, 1992; Hughes, King, Rodden, & Andersen, 1994; Suchman, 1987) and more basic empirical research on the behavior of groups (Clark, 1992; McGrath, 1993). These empirical studies often provide fundamental knowledge and can serve to set requirements for the CWCW applications to support group work. CSCW research also varies in the size of the social collective it considers. The typical size or scope of the social collective treated in most CSCW research is small groups or teams of between three and a dozen people. However, the scope can range from dyads (Clark & Brennan, 1990; Monk, Chapter 10 this volume) to organizations (Button, Chapter 13 this volume), to communities (Preece, 2000) and beyond.

12.3   SCIENTIFIC FOUNDATIONS

Since the turn of the twentieth century (Ross, 1908) and especially since World War II, the field of social psychology has developed a rich theoretical base for understanding and predicting group behavior. The goal of this chapter is to provide a brief introduction to the nature of groups and to give the reader a taste of social psychological theories about group behavior and how they can contribute to the design of collaborative systems. I use the term *social psychological theories* advisedly. There is no unified theory in modern American social psychology with pretensions of explaining all of social behavior. Rather, the intellectual style has been to build and test a large number of medium-level theories, each attempting to account for an interesting social phenomenon in a limited domain. However, unlike theories in cognitive psychology, this theoretical base has been inadequately mined in the HCI and CSCW literatures.

This chapter will only scratch the surface of the literature on groups in social psychological and organizational behavior research. Our overview will start with McGrath's classic review of the small group laboratory literature up to the mid-1980s. Even though the empirical review is dated, McGrath provides an excellent framework for thinking about research on groups. More recent texts and handbooks in social psychology provide citations to the current literature (Aronson, 1999; Baron & Kerr, 2003; Gilbert, Fiske, & Lindzey, 1998; Hogg & Tinsdale, 2001).

12.3.1 Input-Process-Output Models of Group Functioning

There is substantial agreement among social psychologists about the classes of factors that influence group outcomes. Among the most useful frameworks for thinking about groups and their effectiveness are the input-process-output models summarized by Steiner (1972), Hackman (1987), and McGrath (1984). Figure 12.2 illustrates the basic features of an input-process-output model. These models hold that the success of a group (its outcomes) depends upon inputs or resources that the group has to work with (e.g., the skill of its members and the task they have been assigned) and the interaction among team members (e.g., smooth communication, competition). We begin this discussion by considering the outcomes or success criteria for a group, because understanding them highlights relevant inputs and interaction.

Outcomes

Production outcomes.   Input-process-output models emphasize that the outputs of a work group are multidimensional. Often when lay people think of work groups they judge their success exclusively in terms of production—task outcomes that are acceptable to those who receive or review them, produced as efficiently and effectively as possible. For example, one might judge a software-engineering

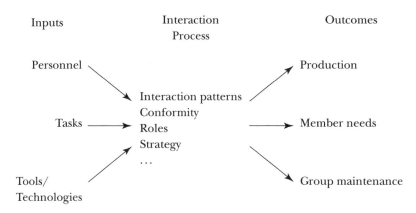

Inputs

Interaction
Process

Outcomes

Personnel

Interaction patterns
Conformity
Roles
Strategy
. . .

Production

Tasks

Member needs

Tools/
Technologies

Group maintenance

**FIGURE
12.2**   Elements of an input-process-output model of groups.

team based on the quality and quantity of the software it produces, a factory team based on the number of cars it assembles, a team of scientists based on the importance of the theories they develop or empirical observations they collect, or a design team based on the new product ideas they have. By the production criteria, groups are successful if they meet their production goals, and useful technologies help them do so more efficiently or in new configurations. By these criteria, the success of groups is analogous to the success of individual work—more efficient or effective production.

The experimental literature shows that groups on average perform better than the average of their members or than a member selected at random. For example, they produce more and better ideas than a single individual when brainstorming, and they solve problems more accurately than the typical person in the group (Gigone & Hastie, 1997; Hill, 1982). Groups do better than individuals through two basic mechanisms—aggregation and synergy. First and most simply, the different individuals who make up a group bring unique resources to it. They bring energy and differences in knowledge, skills, and attitudes that are often essential for accomplishing some task. As we indicated in the case of software engineering, the large size of software projects and the range of knowledge and skills they require mean that no single individual could construct a large software project individually.

Second, and more difficult to explain, is synergy. Synergy is the increase in effectiveness that comes about through joint action or cooperation. It is the result of groups building upon the resources that its members contribute and going beyond them. It is, for example, the creative solution that occurs when members with different points of view or different backgrounds try to solve a problem and achieve a solution that goes beyond what any of the members knew before they got together. To make this concrete, consider IDEO, one of the most successful new product-design firms in the United States. When trying to develop a new design for some product, such as a shopper-friendly, child-safe grocery cart that resists theft, it routinely mixes biologists, engineers, historians, and designers together on its design teams (Kelly & Littman, 2001). To generate this synergy, it creates a physical environment and work process to bring together ideas from different disciplines in new and creative ways (Hargadon & Sutton, 1997). For example, it maintains archives of toys and gadgets, has an organizational structure that downplays status differences among managers and employees, evaluates employees based on helpfulness to others as well as creativity, and emphasizes brainstorming meetings as a way to share ideas.

Group maintenance and member support.   Besides production, groups also need to have the capability to work together in the future (group maintenance) and to support the needs of individuals within the group (member support) to be successful (Hackman, 1987). Consider a scientific team putting together a research proposal to a granting agency. Their proposal convinces the reviewers and the granting agency, and they receive a grant for $800,000. By a production criterion the group was successful, because it produced a high-quality proposal acceptable to the reviewers. However, the team also needs to maintain itself as a group to be successful. If the process of writing the proposal was so filled with conflict that the team was unwilling to work together once they received their funding, that group would not be successful by the group-maintenance criterion. Similarly they would need to recruit graduate students, convince department heads to grant them space, and perform a host of other activities to maintain themselves as a group.

In addition to production and group maintenance, successful teams also support their members. For example, we would consider the scientific team more successful if working together made members more satisfied with their work, helped them meet personal career goals, or enabled them to learn from each other.

Relationships among outcomes.   These outcomes of groups do not change in lockstep. In many real-world groups, for example, productivity and job satisfaction, a component of member support, are only weakly correlated (Judge, Thoresen, Bono, & Patton, 2001; Oliver, Harman, Hoover, Hayes, & Pandhi, 1999). Interventions designed to improve one of these outcomes may have a debilitating effect on another. For example, in a classic experiment, Leavitt (1951) demonstrated that increasing structure in group communication by having all messages flow through a single coordinator can improve the efficiency when the group performs simple distributed problem-solving tasks. However, the same intervention also harms members' satisfaction with the group. Similarly, Connolly and Valacich (1990) have shown that having a skeptic in a brainstorming group causes the group to generate more ideas of higher quality. Again, however, this intervention decreases members' satisfaction with the group.

Inputs

According to input-process-output models, both inputs to the group and the processes that group members use when working together influence whether groups will be effective in achieving their production goals, meeting members' needs, and maintaining themselves over time. By influencing the group process, inputs have both direct and indirect effects on group effectiveness. Inputs include such resources as personnel, task, and technology.

Personnel.   Obviously, groups composed of more highly qualified people—having appropriate knowledge, skills, and motivation—will on average be more effective than groups with less highly qualified members. Work groups that are functionally diverse have a larger stock of ideas to draw upon, and they have differences in assumptions that allow them to generate more creative solutions. As we have seen in the case of IDEO, new product-development teams with members who have expertise in a wide variety of disciplines have the potential to be highly creative, bringing together old ideas in new ways (Hargadon & Sutton, 1997).

However, diversity can be a mixed blessing. McGrath's (1984) and William and O'Reilly's (1998) reviews demonstrate that functional diversity, demographic diversity, and variation of length of time with an organization can lead to crippling frustration and conflict within a group. It is difficult for individuals from divergent backgrounds to share a common enough language to communicate efficiently (Isaacs & Clark, 1987). In addition, they are likely to have different values and beliefs about what is important (Pelled, Eisenhardt, & Xin, 1999). Language and other differences among visual designers, engineers, and marketing personnel on a new product team, for example, may cause them to talk past each other rather than being a source of synergy. They may all desire elegance of design, but for the designer this means a visually appealing one, for the engineer it is a solution that efficiently solves a problem, and for the marketer it is one that appeals to consumers' tastes.

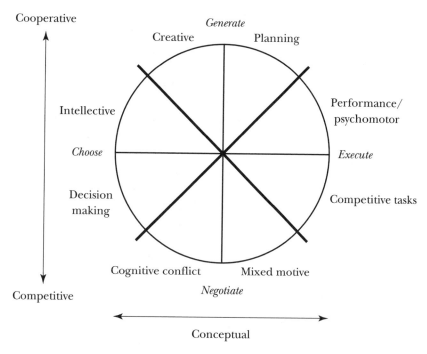

FIGURE

12.3

Taxonomy of group task (adapted from McGrath [1984]).

Task. As mentioned previously, on average groups do better than their individual members on many tasks. But the extent to which they exceed the capabilities of individuals and the processes by which they achieve this success depend upon the characteristics of that task. McGrath (1984) has developed an influential taxonomy of the tasks that comprise group work (see Figure 12.3). The taxonomy was originally developed to describe the artificial tasks that characterize laboratory experiments on group behavior. In the real world, any group is likely to engage in most of these tasks to varying degrees. Despite this limitation, the taxonomy is useful for highlighting how even small changes in task definition are likely to influence group effectiveness.

The upper-left-hand quadrant of McGrath's circumplex consists of cooperative cognitive tasks. Among these, McGrath distinguishes among *generative tasks,* such as brainstorming, where groups develop new ideas; *intellective tasks,* in which groups answer math or other problems with correct answers; and more open-ended *problem-solving tasks.* A typical brainstorming task asks groups of individuals to identify new uses for a fork or to solve a problem on a college cam-pus of an imbalance between the demand for parking spaces and their supply. In these brainstorming tasks, groups produce more good ideas than does any single individual (Gigone & Hastie, 1997; Hill, 1982). The primary mechanism seems to be mere aggregation, in which multiple people, even if they are not interact-ing, are likely to generate more unique good ideas than any single one of them. However, synergy can also play a role, because in interacting groups one person's ideas may spark variations from others (Paulus, Larey, & Dzindolet, 2000).

In one subset of intellective tasks, including anagrams and Eureka problems, the solution can be easily verified once generated. For example, consider the brainteasers in Figure 12.4. On these tasks, groups tend to be as good as the best person in them on any trial (Gigone & Hastie, 1997; Hill, 1982). These tasks fol-low a "truth wins" rule. Once any person in the group solves the problem and communicates the answer to the group, the group accepts it. Again, aggregation is the key, because a collection of individuals is more likely to contain at least one individual who can figure out the correct answer than is any one of them se-lected at random. Finally, ambiguous problem-solving tasks are those with multi-ple acceptable solutions or where the correct answer cannot be easily verified. These include world-knowledge problems (e.g., the morbidity rate for black males) or difficult math problems. In these tasks, groups tend to be as good as the second best person in them in any trial and seem to follow a "trust-supported" heuristic. Interaction in the group allows the group to pool informa-tion and to fix errors though a process of both aggregation and synergy. For ex-ample, when a group is trying to estimate a morbidity rate, one person may be knowledgable about health risk and death, while others may contribute knowl-edge of accidents and violence.

BB AA RR	go it it it it	we**lie**ight
I'M you	my own heart a person	long do
knee light light	XQQME	search and

FIGURE

12.4

Examples of Eureka puzzles.

Answers, left to right and top to bottom: Parallel bars, Go for it, Lie in weight, I'm bigger than you, A person after my own heart, Long over due, Neon lights, Excuse me, Search high and low.

Technologies. The focus in much of the research in CSCW is on building technology that helps both conventional and distributed groups to be more effective. The social-science tradition considers technology broadly to include both the ways in which groups and tasks are structured and the artifacts they use. Thus, for example, the assembly line in an automobile plant uses the technology of division of labor, which breaks down a large task into a sequence of subtasks performed by specialized workers, and the technology of conveyor belts, which moves components from one station to another. To give another example in the CSCW domain, researchers have developed technologies to reduce interruptions among team members. They include scheduling conventions, which distinguish between quiet times, when communication is discouraged, and interaction times, when communication within the group is permitted (Perlow, 1999). They also include sophisticated filtering algorithms, which permit electronic communication only when a recipient isn't busy (Horvitz, Jacobs, & Hovel, 1999).

Just as groups should be more effective if they have more qualified personnel, it is obvious that they would also be more effective if they had appropriate technology to support their activities. Technology can be as simple as the office arrangements and the physical proximity that permits members of a group to communicate frequently and interactively. Most organizations collocate individuals who need to work together precisely to take advantage of physical proximity. When group members cannot be collocated because of the nature of the task, the availability of relevant staff, competition, or other factors, teams must use telecommunication—literally, communications at a distance. These telecommunication technologies include telephones, video-teleconferencing systems, electronic mail, instant messaging, shared computer-file systems, databases, and screen-sharing software. These technologies are not as effective as physical proximity for communication. Groups are less likely to form among people who are geographically separated. If distributed groups are formed, they have more difficulty in setting direction, in coordinating their work, and in forming successful working relationships than do teams whose members are collocated (Cramton, 2001; Kraut et al., 2002; Olson & Olson, 2000).

Technology for groups goes beyond simple communication facilities. For example, the distributed teams of engineers who design modern aircraft use sophisticated software tools that combine communications, databases, computer-aided design, and simulation (Argyes, 1999). The engineers can use three-dimensional digital software to see parts as solid images and then simulate the assembly of those parts on the screen, easily correcting misalignments and other fit or interference problems among parts that need to interoperate and that were designed by other engineers.

Inputs such as people, tasks, and technology have a dual impact on group effectiveness. They can influence outcomes directly, and they can influence outcomes by changing the ways that group members interact with each other. For example, groups are generally better able to complete a well-defined task, because it is easier for them to figure out and evaluate solutions against clear criteria. This is an example of a direct effect of task on performance. In contrast, having a well-defined task may make it easier for groups to establish a clear division of labor, in which each member knows his or her responsibilities and how subtasks will be integrated. In this sense, the task is influencing group effectiveness by changing group interaction and reducing coordination costs.

Interaction Processes

The way that group members interact with each other can directly influence group outcomes and can mediate the impact of inputs on the group. Factors such as the following can all influence groups' outcomes in terms of production, maintenance, and member support: communication, conflict, conformity, socialization, leadership, status, and in-group-out-group differentiation. For example, group members are strongly influenced by the beliefs, attitudes, and behaviors of those around them (Asch, 1955; Sherif & Sherif, 1969). Some consequences of the conformity pressures in groups are that, over time, diversity in a group tends to decline (Latane & Bourgeois, 2001), that group members perceive more homogeneity in the group than actually exists (Latane & L'Herrou, 1996), that members feel comfortable with the homogeneity of the group, which helps group maintenance (Williams & O'Reilly, 1998), and that groups sometimes fail to sufficiently explore options (Janis, 1972).

Given the range of interaction processes in groups, the influences on them, and their consequences, this chapter cannot adequately review the relevant literature. We focus here on communication, perhaps the most important component of group interaction. One can characterize group communication in terms of its volume, its structure, its content, and its interactive features. A large literature in social psychology and organizational science shows that for tasks involving interdependence and uncertainty, team members must have a substantial amount of interpersonal communication to be successful (Thompson, 1967; Van de Ven, Delbecq, & Koenig, 1976). For example, without swift communication including feedback, pairs have difficulty constructing simple objects (Chapanis et al., 1972; Krauss, Garlock, Bricker, & McMahon, 1977). Pairs who can communicate are less likely to devolve into self-destructive behavior in prison dilemma settings (Macy, 1991). Pelz and Andrews (1966), in their classic study of scientists in organizations, show the importance of within-team communication for success, and these findings have been replicated often. In a more recent study, Cummings (2001) showed that teams in a multinational corporation were evaluated more highly when the members communicated more with each other. Conversely, Kiesler, Wholey, and Carley (1994) showed that novice software-engineering teams failed when they didn't communicate enough.

However, even communication is not an unalloyed good. Communication takes time away from individual production (Perlow, 1999). Organizational contingency theorists hold that no one way of behaving in a group or organization is appropriate for all groups, and that the technology needed to support a group varies greatly with the tasks that typically confront the group. They emphasize uncertainty as a key feature of tasks that determines whether a particular technology will be appropriate (Galbraith, 1977; Lawrence & Lorsch, 1970).

Consistent with organizational contingency theory, a basic finding from both laboratory experiments and field studies in organizations is that the right combination of volume, structure, content, and interactivity in group communication depends upon the task. For example, in classic experiments Leavitt (1951) demonstrated that in a simple distributed problem-solving task, having all messages flow through a communication coordinator increased efficiency. In this task, groups of five were required to identify a unique card among a set that had previously been distributed to them. Here, having a wheel communication structure, shown in Figure 12.5(a), in which all messages were given to person C, who in turn passed them on to their destination, was more efficient than the fully connected graph shown in Figure 12.5(b), where each group member could directly connect with every other one. However, in a more complex task, in which the group needed to solve a more difficult problem, the fully connected graph was superior to the wheel (Shaw, 1964).

Field studies of teams in organizational settings show similar results. Tushman's research on research and development labs (Argote, 1982; Katz & Tushman, 1979) compared teams performing tasks differing in uncertainty: for example, teams doing relatively certain service work (e.g., maintaining laboratory equipment) and teams doing a more uncertain and complex basic research. When service teams were organized hierarchically, with a supervisor central to both communication and coordination, they were more successful than when they were organized in a self-managed way, with less supervision and more peer-to-peer communication. In contrast, basic research teams were more successful when they engaged in more peer-to-peer communication and had a diminished role for the supervisor. (See Argote [1982] for similar results among hospital emergency-room crews dealing with either routine or more unusual cases.)

These results have implications for communication tools and technologies to support group work. In groups performing relatively certain tasks in stable

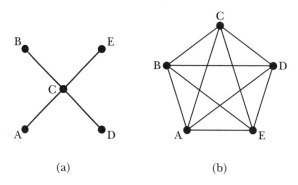

(a)   (b)

FIGURE   (a) Wheel structure, (b) fully connected structure.

12.5

environments, the current generation of CSCW, which does not easily support highly interactive communication among multiple individuals, may suffice. At one extreme are highly routinized tasks conducted in a stable environment, such as those done by the staff in a fast food restaurant. In this environment, communication among workers assembling an order of burger, fries, and a shake can be highly ritualized. The counter clerk can enter the order on the keypad of the cash register, which then updates a queue on a video screen behind the counter. By glancing at the list on screen, the fryer and griller know how much food to cook, and the assembler can grab fries and the burger from the staging area and pour a shake, without any direct communication with other team members. More extensive, direct communication among them is unnecessary and is likely to interfere with their ability to keep up with demand during peak meal times. In contrast, technologies that restrict communication would be less acceptable in environments where the task is more uncertain. For example, communication among research scientists collaborating on a project or members of a hospital emergency room must be more direct and interactive (Argote, 1982; Katz & Tushman, 1979; Tushman, 1979). Teams might need to be collocated to work effectively, and distributed teams might need to meet frequently. Uncertainty can increase because of interdependence among team members, tight time constraints, or greater variability, among other factors (e.g., Kraut & Streeter, 1995).

12.3.2   Process Losses

Even though groups typically perform better than an average member, for many tasks groups do worse than the theoretical maximum one would expect, given the resources that members bring to the group. Steiner (1976) terms this the general problem of *process loss,* in which the mere fact of being in a group degrades performance from what the members could be capable of producing. Consider the problem-solving tasks described previously: The basic finding was that groups perform as well as their second best member, and that an individual's answer on one of these tasks is accepted only if a second member supports it (McGrath, 1984). This means that in many groups, at least one group member had a better answer than the answers that the group as a whole agreed upon.

Analogous phenomena occur in real-world groups as well. One might expect, for example, that teams with greater diversity should outperform more homogeneous teams, because the diverse teams can bring a richer, nonredundant set of resources to bear on problems. Yet, despite these expectations, reviews of the research literature show that functional and demographic diversity in work groups have mixed effects (Williams & O'Reilly, 1998). They only occasionally lead to production benefits, and they frequently lead to dissatisfaction with the group and turnover in membership.

Process losses come about through two distinct processes: miscoordination problems and reductions in motivation.

Coordination problems: Groups are inherently different from individuals performing the same task because of the need to coordinate. Whenever the work of individuals is interdependent, they must coordinate to achieve success (Van de Ven, Delbecq, & Koenig, 1976). This process of coordination takes effort, which could otherwise be directed toward production. Indeed, Malone and Crowston (1994), among others, define coordination as the extra activities that people must do when working in concert to accomplish some goal, over and above what they would need to do to accomplish the goal individually. Coordination consists of broad alignment of goals, as when a management team sets a direction with implications for marketing and engineering. It also consists of detailed alignment of behavior, as when a coxswain shouts "stroke" to coordinate the behavior of a rowing crew. When coordination is high, a unit of individual work will translate into more team output. Conversely, when coordination is low, the same quality and quantity of individual work will result in less group output.

A wide variety of distinct mechanisms leads to process losses because of coordination problems. Table 12.1 provides a sampling of these mechanisms. Several of these mechanisms partly account for the failure of functional diversity in groups to result in the expected gains in creativity and production. For example, people with different functional backgrounds often have different vocabularies, standard operating procedures, values, and goals. Differences in these factors make it more difficult for them to coordinate. Experimental research shows that group productivity is hurt when people have incompatible personal goals

Coordination problem	Definition
Coordination effort	Time and effort invested in coordination deducts times and effort from production and group maintenance.
Misaligned goals	Value differences or political differences among group members prevent them from pursuing common goals.
Misaligned communication	Individuals have difficulty communicating with each other because of differences in assumption, vocabulary, location, and other impediments to achieving common ground.
Conformity pressures	Individuals are less likely to express personal beliefs and ideas because of social influences, such as imitation or evaluation apprehension.
Synchronization problems	Output offered by one individual in a group does not meet the input needed by another, because it is of the wrong form or arrives at the wrong time.
Production blocking	Scarce resources, such as time in a meeting or production tools, can't be simultaneously used, and some group members remain idle while others work.

TABLE   Examples of coordination problems.

12.1

(Mintz, 1951). On April 14, 1994, two U.S. Air Force F-15 jets shot down two U.S. Army helicopters in Iraq's no-fly zone. Differences among army and air force pilots in vocabulary, standard operating procedures, and values were partly responsible for this accident (Snook, 2000). For example, the army's value of flexibility and the air force's value of precision in planning led to different standard-operating procedures, in which the army helicopters received their flight routes just moments before a flight, whereas the air force had detailed flight plans in place 24 hours before their flights. Thus the jets didn't expect to see friendly aircraft in the area and fired on the helicopters. These problems were compounded by a number of others.

Motivational problems. In addition to the coordination problems in having to align, schedule, and integrate individual efforts, working in a group also influences the motivations of the group members. Sometimes being in a group enhances individual motivation, and other times it undercuts it. Groups, for example, establish norms about how hard members should work. "Rate-boosters" and "slackers" are terms for people who expend more or less effort, respectively, in relationship to an implicit group norm. Group members tend to pressure those who deviate from the group norm to conform. Whether the group norm is to work hard or to slack off often depends on history, on explicit goals that are set for the group (Locke, Latham, & Erez, 1988), and on whether group members directly participated in the goal-setting or whether it was imposed upon them (Coch & French, 1948). For example, members generally conform more closely to production goals if they have a hand in setting them.

Sometimes merely being in the presence of another is sufficient to change motivation. Social facilitation is one of the oldest phenomena identified in social psychology. Triplett's 1898 experiments on pacing and competition examined the consequences of the mere presence of others on an individual's behavior (Triplett, 1898). Zajonc (1965) reviewed evidence to show that merely being in the presence of another seems to increase individual arousal across many species, including humans. A basic principle of behavioral theory is that increased arousal makes the most dominant response (i.e., the one most poised for being emitted) in a situation even more dominant. Findings that animals eat more in the presence of others and that people laugh more when watching a comedy in the presence of others are consistent with this proposition (Zajonc, 1965). The implication is that the presence of other people will facilitate performance when a task is well learned, but will degrade performance with new tasks. For example, all else being equal, compared to working alone, people working in a group should have more difficulty learning a complex new task, but should perform better executing well-learned tasks.

12.3.3   Social Loafing

Social loafing is another phenomenon in which group membership degrades individual motivation. The basic empirical phenomenon is that individuals typically work less hard when they are part of a group than when they are working on their own. The issue here isn't the mere presence of others. Rather, social loafing occurs when people think that the outcomes of their efforts are being pooled with the efforts of other group members. The phenomenon was first identified by Ringelmann (cited in Kravitz & Martin, 1986). A group of volunteers pulled on a rope connected to a strain gage; as the number of volunteers increased, the force they exerted declined from the amount one would expect by adding up the volunteers' efforts when they worked individually. By comparing blindfolded volunteers who believed that they were pulling alone to those who thought that they were jointly pulling on the rope, Ingham, Levinger, Graves, and Peckham (1974) demonstrated that the effect was the result of decreased effort and not failures of coordination. By the time of Karau and Williams' review (1993), researchers had demonstrated the phenomenon in more than 80 experiments in both laboratory and field settings, using a wide variety of tasks, including physical ones (e.g., rope

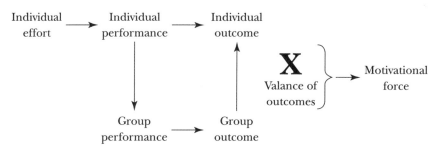

FIGURE

12.6
A collective effort of social loafing (from Karau & Williams, 1993).

pulling, swimming) and cognitive ones (e.g., brainstorming, evaluating poems, keeping vigilance).

Although social loafing is a robust phenomenon, the extent to which being in a group leads to social loafing varies with the nature of the task and the nature of the group. In particular, an individual will engage in less social loafing if the individual is working in an attractive group; if the task is personally satisfying or engaging; if the individual thinks other members will perform poorly; if the individual thinks his or her own contribution is unique; if the individual's own output is visible to other group members; or if the individual is a woman, was raised in an Asian culture, or is a child.

Karau and Williams (1993) developed an integrated theory of social loafing, which accounts well for prior research. This is illustrated in Figure 12.6. The basic assumption is that people will work harder (greater motivational force) if they think their effort will lead to some performance that will help them to achieve some valued outcome. This relationship is easy to see when individuals are performing alone. One might expect a runner to race harder if he thinks his effort will increase his chances of winning and if he values winning. Performing in a relay race complicates the picture, because there is a less direct link between his effort and the chances of his team's winning, and because his evaluation of winning is likely to be influenced by his liking for the group. This model predicts that, when working in a group, individuals would work harder when they think that their contributions are unique or that other members will perform poorly, because in these cases their effort is more necessary for group success. In addition, individuals should work harder if they like the group, because this increases the value of the outcome for them. In Section 12.5, we explore the implications of this theory for design.

12.4   DETAILED DESCRIPTION: EXPLAINING PRODUCTIVITY LOSS IN BRAINSTORMING TEAMS

The performance of brainstorming teams is an excellent example of the benefits that groups bring and the way that process losses undercut their effectiveness. We have seen that on brainstorming tasks, groups produce more good ideas than any single member is likely to produce. However, a group of interacting individuals is likely to produce fewer good ideas than a "nominal" group, that is, a group of comparable individuals who work independently and pool their contributions. In this section, we consider how social psychological theories that account for process losses might apply to this phenomenon. We can use our understanding of the reasons for the process loss in this case to evaluate the likely success of the design of commercial brainstorming tools. In Section 12.5, we try to show how, using Karau and Williams' theory of collective effort, we might redesign other social-technical systems, like list servers or online discussion groups, where content is often undercontributed.

There are three plausible explanations for why interacting groups produce fewer ideas than collections of similar individuals working independently—social pressure, social loafing, and production blocking. Social pressure and social loafing are examples of motivational problems, whereas production blocking is a coordination problem. There is evidence that all three processes frequently occur in groups of many kinds, including brainstorming groups. However, production blocking seems to be the major cause of production loss in interacting brainstorming groups. In this section we consider the evidence that leads to these conclusions and suggest how this attribution of causation has consequences for the design of group systems for brainstorming.

Social pressure.   Although there are many forms of social pressure, in the case of brainstorming one might expect that individual contributions may be inhibited because of evaluation apprehension—an individual's fear that others might think badly of him or her for coming up with silly or impractical suggestions. Osborne's (1963) directions for successful brainstorming, which emphasize the nonjudgmental contributions in the early stages of brainstorming, try to guard against this inhibitor.

Social pressure in general and evaluation apprehension in particular reduce participants' willingness to contribute ideas in a brainstorming session. This is especially true for people who offer minority points of view or controversial ideas (McLeod, Baron, Marti, & Yoon, 1997). Diehl and Stroebe (1987) directly manipulated evaluation apprehension among individuals who were brainstorming by telling some of them that their contributions would be judged by peers or expert judges (high evaluation apprehension) or not (low evaluation apprehension). Individuals who expected judgment produced fewer ideas than those who did not, especially when the discussion topics were controversial.

To reduce evaluation apprehension, some researchers have recommended anonymity in electronic brainstorming systems (Nunamaker, Dennis, Valacich, Vogel, & George, 1991), and most commercial brainstorming systems enforce anonymity. As Dennis and Williams note in their recent review, however, evidence about the benefits of anonymity are equivocal at best (Dennis & Williams, 2002). Connolly, Jessup, and Valacich (1990) examined the effects of anonymity and evaluative tone on the performance of 24 computer-supported four-person groups. Participants in the nonanonymous groups were introduced to each other and their ideas were identified with their names, while those in the anonymous groups were not introduced and their contributions had no names attached. These researchers also manipulated the evaluative tone of the experiment by having confederates offer critical or supportive comments in response to others' contributions. They found a strong effect of evaluative tone, with groups containing a critical confederate generating more ideas, but only weak effects of anonymity. Research by Cooper, Gallupe, Pollard, and Cadsby (1998) showed anonymity raised the productivity in electronic brainstorming groups by 10 to 20%. However, similar research by Dennis and Valacich (1993), Jessup, Connolly and Galegher (1990), Prentice-Dunn and Rogers (1982) and Jessup, Connolly and Tansik (1990) found little evidence that anonymous groups produced more or better ideas than ones where members were identified.

Does evaluation apprehension account for the productivity loss in brainstorming groups? To test this, one would need to show that the difference in brainstorming productivity between interacting groups and nominal groups is reduced when one controls for evaluation apprehension. Diehl and Stroebe (1987, experiment 4) conducted this test by comparing brainstorming groups who believed their contributions would be judged by peers or experts (high-evaluation apprehension) with those who thought their contributions would not be judged (low-evaluation apprehension). They found that the high-evaluation apprehension groups produced fewer ideas than the low-evaluation apprehension ones, but only when they believed that the judgments reflected upon the individual contributor rather than the group a whole. However, regardless of the evaluation-apprehension condition, nominal groups produced almost twice as many ideas as interacting groups. This pattern of results suggests that, whereas evaluation apprehension inhibits the generation of ideas, it does not account for differences between nominal and real groups.

Social loafing. Social loafing might account for production loss in interacting brainstorming groups compared to nominal groups, because participants working in a real, interacting group might be less motivated to contribute. To test for the effects of social loafing, researchers typically compare individual-assessment groups of coacting individuals (i.e., groups in which individuals work in the presence of others, but believe that their outputs will not be pooled) with collective-assessment groups (i.e., groups in which individuals work in each others' presence and believe that their outputs will be combined). Social loafing does reduce brainstorming effort, as it does many other outcomes. Research comparing individual- and collective-assessment groups shows that social loafing reduces contribution in brainstorming tasks. For example, Diehl and Stroebe (1987, experiment 1) conducted a brainstorming experiment with two independent variables—type of session (individual versus real interacting four-person group) and type of assessment (individual versus collective). In the individual-assessment condition participants were led to believe that their individual contributions would be tallied, while in the collective-assessment condition they were led to believe that the contributions would be pooled among all people in an experimental condition before being tallied. Collective assessment reduced contributions. Subjects in the collective-assessment condition reduced their contributions by 24%, showing the effects of social loafing. However, the effects of type of assessment were much weaker than the effects of being in a four-person group or of working individually. Subjects in the group sessions reduced their contribution by 63% compared to those in the individual sessions (i.e., what others have called nominal groups). Moreover, the productivity loss from being in an interacting group was approximately the same whether subjects thought their contributions would be evaluated individually or collectively. These results suggest that while social loafing can decrease productivity for brainstorming tasks, it cannot account for differences between nominal and interacting groups.

Production blocking. Conventional, face-to-face brainstorming groups experience some degree of production blocking, because multiple members of the group cannot talk simultaneously without drowning each other out or interrupting each other. Therefore, to determine whether production blocking accounts for productivity losses in brainstorming groups, researchers have added production blocking to conditions under which blocking would not typically occur. For example, Diehl and Stroebe (1987, experiment 5) compared five experimental conditions. To replicate traditional research, they compared interacting groups and nominal groups (isolated individuals brainstorming independently). In addition, they included three other conditions, in which subjects believed they were in groups whose members were distributed in different rooms. Red lights, which glowed when other members of their distributed groups were talking, regulated when they could contribute, to different degrees. In one condition (blocking, communication), they heard the other people by headphones and were told to refrain from contributing when the red light was on. In the blocking, no-communication condition, they were told to refrain from contributing when the red light was on, and they could not hear the other parties. In the no-blocking, no-communication condition, the red lights glowed when others were talking, but subjects were told that they could contribute "whenever they wanted and that they need not pay any attention to the lights." Results were consistent with the production-blocking explanation, showing that both blocking manipulations reduced brainstorming contribution to 50% of the level of the interacting groups, while seeing the light without the blocking instruction had no effects on brainstorming. The details of this experiment are shown in Figure 12.7.

Gallupe, Cooper, Grisé, and Bastianutti (1994, experiment 3) used a similar approach. They compared two electronic brainstorming systems, in which people typed their contribution. In the electronic, no-blocking condition, participants could type in parallel and enter ideas simultaneously. In the blocking condition, subjects could enter material only when a previous contributor had verbally indicated that he or she had finished entering an idea. They compared these two electronic conditions with a conventional interacting, face-to-face brainstorming group whose members spoke their contributions (face-to-face), and a face-to-face group whose members had to wait until others were finished speaking before making a contribution (face-to-face, first in). Subjects in the electronic, no-blocking condition produced about a third more nonredundant ideas than subjects in either of the other conditions, which did not differ from each other.

Together, the results of this research show that evaluation apprehension, social loafing, and production blocking can all reduce production in brainstorming groups. However, production blocking seems to be the primary factor that explains why nominal groups (individuals whose contributions are pooled) typically produce more ideas than interacting groups. Electronic groups whose members interact in parallel can perform as well as or better than nominal groups (Dennis & Williams, in press). Introducing blocking into the electronic group eliminates the advantages of working independently.

12.4.1   Application to System Design

Knowing whether social pressure, social loafing, or production blocking is the primary cause of production loss in group brainstorming has implications for

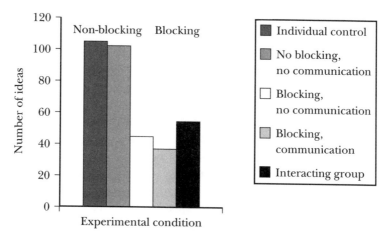

FIGURE

12.7
Brainstorming contributions (from Diehl & Stroebe, 1987, experiment 5).

designing effective brainstorming tools. If social pressure and evaluation apprehension are the major culprits, one design solution is to enforce anonymity in contributions. Disguising the identity of contributors should reduce their fears that others will think poorly of them for outlandish contributions and thereby reduce inhibition. As Nunamaker and his colleagues note (Nunamaker et al., 1991), "anonymity can affect EMS [electronic meeting support] use by reducing or eliminating evaluation apprehensions and conformance pressures, as well as social cues. The reduction of evaluation apprehension and conformance pressure may encourage a more open, honest and free-wheeling discussion of key issues" (p. 55). Based on this logic, most commercial-meeting support systems, including those with electronic brainstorming features, enforce anonymity (e.g., *www.groupsystems.com*).

In contrast, if social loafing is a major cause, then enforcing anonymity would be counterproductive. Both theory and Karau and Williams's (1993) empirical literature review suggest that making an individual's contributions visible decreases social loafing and encourages people to contribute. One type of positive social pressure in a group is to set a production standard. Knowing that others can observe and evaluate one's output discourages group members from slacking off, at the same time that it discourages them from contributing outlandish or controversial ideas. Perhaps these conflicting outcomes are the reasons why anonymity does not seem to have consistent effects on the quality and quantity of performance in brainstorming sessions.

Finally, if production blocking is the major source of the problem, then manipulating anonymity is irrelevant. Production blocking occurs when simultaneous contributions overtax some scarce resource, such as time or working memory. Production blocking occurs because in face-to-face settings two people can't talk at the same time or because the act of listening to others' contributions prevents an individual from simultaneously generating new ideas. If production blocking is the major cause, then the solution is to devise procedures or technologies that allow simultaneous input. Virtually every research-oriented and commercial group-decision support system has a module for electronic brainstorming and has procedures for simultaneous input. For example, the brainstorming module from *www.groupsystems.com* circulates lists of suggestions among the participants. Each participant initiates a list by making a contribution. When participants submit a contribution, they are randomly given one of the circulating lists, to which they can append another new idea or a comment on a previous one. In this arrangement, multiple participants can contribute simultaneously. They also have an opportunity to see the contributions of others for the potential stimulation this might provide.

Although we have used the phenomenon of production losses in brainstorming as a vehicle to understand the application of various social psychological theories, these theories are not limited to this domain. In the next section we discuss how a theory of social loafing might be used to increase contribution rates in various online communication forums.

12.5   CASE STUDY: APPLYING SOCIAL PSYCHOLOGY THEORY TO THE PROBLEM OF UNDERCONTRIBUTION TO ONLINE GROUPS

12.5.1   Social Loafing and Online Groups

One of the benefits of the Internet is its support of online groups and communities (Preece, 2000). The Internet supports computer-mediated communication among groups of individuals who may or may not have offline relationships as well. People can communicate in near real time, using synchronous communication services like the multi-user domain (MUD) Dungeons and Dragons games, chats, and instant messaging. Alternatively, they can communicate without having to be simultaneously available, using asynchronous communication services like electronic mail distribution lists, list servers, and electronic bulletin boards.

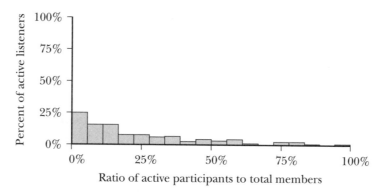

FIGURE

12.8

The distribution of the activity level of members in 39 email-based distribution lists (from Butler, 1999).

For example, *www.lsoft.com/catalist.html* and *www.tile.net/lists/* provide listings of literally thousands of electronic-mail based discussion lists, a large proportion of which are open to the public. These online groups can be recreational, as are many Dungeons and Dragons–based MUDs or movie fan–based distribution lists. They can provide technical, product, or hobby information, such as distribution lists for computers and programming languages. Many, such as the numerous health-oriented chats and distributions lists, provide both social support and information for their participants. A common characteristic of online groups is their highly uneven distribution of contributions. In almost all, a small fraction of the members contribute most of the content, with the remainder acting as "lurkers" or subscribers who only read. Figure 12.8 shows the distribution of active participants in a sample of 39 active email-based distribution lists on a wide variety of topics (Butler, 1999). More than 50% of the individuals subscribing to these lists posted no messages at all, and in fewer than 10% of the lists do even 50% of the subscribers contribute anything. The vast majority of messages were contributed by a small number of posters.

Imagine that your goal, as a sponsor of an online group for cancer support, such as OncoChat *(www.oncochat.org/)*, or the breast-cancer distribution list at *bcsupport.org*, was to increase participation rates, so that more of the subscribers contributed. In some sense, the problem of low contribution rates is a social dilemma, analogous to paying taxes or donating to public television. If no one contributed to these online groups, then the social benefit that members get from them would disappear.

As an exercise, one could take Karau and William's (1993) theory of social loafing and use it as the basis for creating design guidelines to increase participation rates in this group. To my knowledge, no one has yet formally conducted such an exercise or built an online group based on these guidelines. Existing online groups are consistent with these guidelines to varying degrees. The proposal sketched in this chapter is admittedly speculative and should be treated as a set of testable hypotheses rather than established fact. Table 12.2 lists the variables that reduce social loafing, according to Karau and William's meta-analysis. The second column indicates how this variable is linked to Karau and Williams's collective effort model. Remember that this theory says people will be motivated to work on a task to the extent that they perceive that their successful performance on the task will lead to an outcome that they find attractive. Finally, the third column provides design suggestions based on this variable. As an oversimplification we will treat thematically oriented, synchronous systems like MUDs, synchronous, unstructured systems like chats, and asynchronous bulletin boards and list servers as instances of online groups. We recognize, however, that there are important differences in the ways they operate and probably important differences in the ways that the variables associated with social loafing will influence members' behavior.

These suggestions in Table 12.2 are intended to illustrate the generative power of social-psychological theory. For the purposes of this illustration, we are assuming that Karau and Williams's theory is a complete and accurate theory of social loafing. Whether the suggestions derived from this theory will in fact improve participation rates in online groups and the health of the groups more generally depends upon four factors. First, are the suggestions an accurate derivation from the theory? Second, are they implemented well? Third, are there other factors besides social loafing, such as differential commitment to the group, that lead to the unequal participation rates, and will interventions that counter social loafing have a beneficial or at least a neutral effect on these other processes? Finally, do the efforts to increase participation rates affect other valued outcomes from the online group, such as communication volume, the satisfaction that members get from the group, or their longevity with the group?

The discussion that follows fleshes out a few of the design suggestions in Table 12.2, to illustrate the potential utility of the theory. Consider suggestions related to increasing the attractiveness of the group. The empirical literature shows that social loafing is reduced when members are more attracted to a group. We can term this the *attractiveness principle*. One can increase the attractiveness of a group either by influencing members' connections to particular others in the group or by influencing their identification with the group as a whole. A long-standing topic in social psychology has been understanding the factors that lead to liking among individuals. For example, people typically like others who are similar to themselves; who are good-looking, intelligent, or have

Variable	Link to theory	Design implication (Examples)
Identifiability	Direct deterrent to loafing; individuals are accountable because behavior is directly connected to them	Do not allow anonymity or aliases in the group.
Attractiveness of task	Increases the valence of individual outcomes	Provide opportunities for interactivity, because interactive communication is more attractive and less effortful than asynchronous communication. Sharply define the topic of the group, since this will recruit members interested in the topic. Do not constrain content of online communication, since free communication is more attractive (at least to sender).
Attractiveness of the group	Increases the valence of group outcomes	Sharply define the topic of the group, since this will recruit members who are similar to each other and will help define group boundaries. Recruit members who have prior relationships outside of the group (e.g., organizational or geographic connection), because multiplex relationships are stronger than single-stranded ones. Develop management policy, norms, or tools to reduce inappropriate behavior.
Group size	Larger groups lower the probability that one's individual effort will lead to valued group outcomes	Place size limits or entry thresholds on new membership. Split active groups into subgroups, to maintain small group size. Cull nonparticipants to reduce size of group.
Uniqueness of own contribution	Intensifies the probability that one's individual effort will lead to group outcomes	Mix members with different approaches to same topics (e.g., MDs, caregivers, past patients, and currently ill patients in support groups), helping members to see their unique role.
Expectation that others will perform poorly	Intensifies the probability that one's individual effort will lead to valued group outcomes	Mix novice and experts within a single group, making expertise more essential.

TABLE
12.2

Design ideas for online groups based on Karau and William's collective effort model (1993).

other positive social attributes; who have provided them favors; and with whom they have a history of interaction. (See Berscheid & Reis [1998] for a fuller discussion of the basis of interpersonal attraction.) Translating these principles into criteria for the design of online groups requires creativity.

Because people like those who are similar to themselves, members of topically oriented groups should have their joint interest in the organizing topic as a basis for similarity. Thus, they should be more likely to form friendships with others who subscribe to specific online groups with sharply defined topics, such as the usenet groups that concentrate on a particular soap opera (e.g., *alt.tv.days-of-our-lives*) rather than more general groups that encourage discussion of all soap operas (e.g., *rec.arts.tv.soaps*). Similarity is desirable in its own right and provides a basis for conversation on a wide variety of topics, through which additional bases for friendship might emerge. Because relationships that support a variety of exchanges (termed *multiplex relationships*) tend to be deeper and longer lasting than those based on a single type of exchange, list owners who run online groups should encourage wide-ranging and hence off-topic discussion in their groups. This is the logic behind recommendations to define group membership sharply around a topic, but to not moderate group conversation or discourage off-topic conversation once people are members.

A second way to encourage members to increase their commitment to a group is to emphasize properties of the group itself, instead of the people who constitute it. For example, people feel more committed to groups that have clear boundaries, which differentiate group members from outsiders (Tajfel, Billig, Bundy, & Flament, 1971). This is another argument for constituting online groups with well-defined topics. In addition, people become more committed to groups for which they sacrificed to achieve membership (Aronson & Mills, 1959). Together, these two principles suggest the design of online groups where members must be vetted by a group owner or membership committee. Vetting would contrast with the practice in many discussion groups, where joining is as simple as sending "SUBSCRIBE" in an email message. People like to affiliate more with high-status groups that have achieved success (Cialdini et al., 1976). Archives from a group and lists of frequently asked questions (FAQs) that emphasize the group's accomplishments may help in this regard.

The social-loafing research shows that people expend more effort on groups where they believe their own contributions are likely to be unique and other group members are less competent or skilled than they. Working through the implications of what we might call the *uniqueness principle* is substantially more difficult than working through the implication of the attraction principle. The practice in technical groups and health-support groups of mixing experts with novices is consistent with the uniqueness principle. Constant and his colleagues (1996) showed that experts in a technical distribution list responded to "does anyone know" questions simply because they knew they had expertise that would be valuable to other subscribers. Most health-support groups, like the usenet group *alt.support.depression,* encourage participation by a variety of participants with complementary resources. They consist of those who actively have a disease, those who have previously had it, those who are providing support for someone with the disease, and medical professionals. Each type of member can provide unique contributions, ranging from questions about symptoms, diagnosis, and treatment, to information about these topics, reports on subjective experiences, and expressions of concern and support. Some people become members of these groups to receive information and support, while others become and remain members to provide it.

To some extent, however, the uniqueness principle is at odds with the attractiveness principle. Online groups filled with novices are likely to turn off the experts, because they are so dissimilar, because their presence tends to detract from the stature of the group as a whole, and because the majority of exchanges in the group are likely to go from expert to novice. To keep these countervailing tendencies in balance, online groups often develop FAQ archives to relieve the burden on experts from handling the most mundane questions. (See *www.faqs.org/faqs/* for an index of FAQs for many usenet groups.) Some researchers have attempted to create software that integrates database lookup of information with advice from actual group members (e.g., Ackerman, 1998), so that when experts are asked advice they can be assured that their contributions are unique and haven't previously been asked and answered.

12.6   CURRENT STATUS

The thesis of this chapter has been that social psychology provides a rich body of research and theory about principles of human behavior, which should be applicable to the design of HCI applications, especially applications to support multiple individuals who are communicating or performing some task. Simply put, as members of a discipline social psychologists know an enormous amount about how people form attachments to each other, how they make judgments of each other, how groups form and develop, and how groups organize to work together productively. Like the research reviewed here on social loafing, most tend to be mid-level theories, providing insight into a single aspect of human behavior in groups, rather than into groups in general. As in the case of the research literature on social loafing, these theories of group behavior and behavior in groups have implications for the design of computer systems to support groups.

However, researchers and developers in the field of HCI have rarely taken advantage of this trove of empirical phenomena and theory. There are several reasons why this body of research has been underexploited. First are the standard problems of disciplinary inbreeding. In CSCW, as in many fields, researchers tend to know about and therefore refer primarily to research reports published in the restricted set of journals that they consider core to their discipline. As Finholt and Teasley note (1998), researchers in HCI and CSCW primarily refer to articles published in proceedings for the Human Factors in Computing Systems (CHI) and the CSCW conferences and rarely refer to the reference literatures in cognitive psychology, sociology, anthropology, or social psychology.

The other, major reason is the mismatch of goals and values of HCI and CSCW research with those of social psychology. HCI and CSCW are primarily engineering disciplines, where the dominant goal is problem-solving. In solving a practical problem, it is likely that engineers will have to bring together many strands of knowledge. For example, in solving the problem of underparticipation in online communities, those with an engineering ethic might bring together ideas from social loafing in psychology with ideas about public goods in economics (Fulk, Flanagin, Kalman, Monge, & Ryan, 1996). Public-goods economics examines problems of collective action (Olson, 1971), such as people's unwillingness to contribute to public television and other public programs, or their overreadiness to pollute the environment. In these cases, behavior that is rational at the individual level has pernicious social consequences when many people make the same decision.

In contrast, social psychology views itself as a behavioral science, whose goal is to uniquely determine the causes for social phenomena. Although researchers who identify with the behavioral and social sciences are active in HCI and CSCW, they are active as applied scientists, importing ideas and methods from their home disciplines to solve design problems. In contrast to an engineering-oriented researcher, a discipline-oriented social psychologist's goal would be to distinguish the independent influence of the social psychological and the economic factors in causing undercontribution to groups. A standard research strategy in social psychology is to use experiments to manipulate one potential causal variable at a time while holding all other variables constant. For example, theories of social loafing attempt to explain why individuals are less productive in groups than when working individually. To distinguish the effects of believing oneself part of a group from the effects of the mere presence of others, for example, social-loafing experiments constrast individuals working alone or in the presence of others under conditions of either individual or collective assessment. This strategy allows the researcher to identify one factor, such as the pooling of output, as a true cause, even though in the world outside of the laboratory other causes may also be present.

This research strategy of holding other variables constant while examining the impact of a variable of interest makes it difficult to compare the strength of effects of different causal factors. This problem is compounded in laboratory experiments, because the strength of a variable depends on the way an experimenter operationalized it, rather than on how the variable is distributed in the world outside the laboratory.

In solving real design problems, contextual details are frequently important. For example, in solving the problem of undercontribution to online communities, the solution may depend on whether the community is intended for adults or children, whether it has commercial or nonprofit content, or whether it uses an asynchronous technology, like email, or a synchronous one, like chat. In contrast, the norm in much social psychological research is to abstract these contextual details away. The goal is to have a theory that is as general as possible. Thus a theory of social loafing, for example, is more successful to the extent that it holds for both physical and mental tasks, that it applies to college students and adults, or that it applies to history-less laboratory groups and to real-world groups with real histories, like swimming teams. Refinement of theory often requires specifying conditions under which phenomena of interest occur. Thus the finding that social loafing is less likely to occur when people are attracted to the group helps to define the theory. For a social psychologist examining social loafing, the source of the attraction should be irrelevant. To someone designing a real online community, however, whether a group is attractive because members are rich, intelligent, or good-looking, because they share a common interest, or because they are familiar with each other are crucial details.

A result of these fundamental differences between the values of problem-oriented designers and theory-oriented social psychologists is that the knowledge produced by the psychologists doesn't fit with the designers' needs. It is often not detailed enough. As we have seen, social loafing, for example, is less likely to occur when members are attracted to a group. However, the research on social loafing does not provide guidance on how to make a group attractive, or on the implications of different methods. We have also seen that social loafing is less likely to occur when members consider themselves unique. However, a participant's perceived uniqueness is likely to make the group less attractive to him or her. The social-psychological research doesn't indicate which of these phenomena is more powerful. This lack of concreteness leaves the designer to improvise when attempting to apply social-psychological knowledge to solve design problems. It is perhaps for this reason that, when CSCW researchers turn to the social-science literature outside their own field, they are more likely to consult ethnographic research than experimental social psychology. Ethnographic research is filled with a wealth of concrete detail, often at the expense of generalizability. From an ethnographic study such as Orlikowski's research on the use of Lotus notes in a software company (2000), one might learn how one company induced help-desk personnel to contribute to a shared database. Judging the generalizability of the conclusions is an exercise for the reader.

Writing this chapter was supported by a grant from the National Science Foundation NSF 9812123.

13 | Studies of Work in Human-Computer Interaction

Graham Button   Xerox Research Centre Europe, Grenoble, France

13.1   MOTIVATION

In 1990, Jonathan Grudin argued that human-computer interaction (HCI) had passed through a number a stages in its development and was, at that time, moving from the fourth stage, which he characterized as "a dialogue with the user," to a fifth stage, which would be focused on the work setting. During the decade or so that has passed since he made this argument, HCI has indeed increasingly emphasized research into systems that support the interactions and collaborations among people in their workplace. This has been particularly evident in the field of computer-supported collaborative work (CSCW) and has involved turning to the disciplines that have been traditionally associated with research into the work setting, most notably sociology. Consequently, since the latter part of the 1980s, HCI researchers have increasingly looked to sociology for their understanding of work and the workplace (cf. Sommerville et al, 1992). In addition, sociologists have themselves, increasingly, become directly involved in HCI and CSCW research (cf. Luff et al., 2000).

Sociology is, however, a far-from-unified field, and it is possible to see that a variety of sociological theories and methods have been courted and used as resources in HCI (Shapiro, 1994). Dourish and Button (1998) have argued, however, that one particular type of sociology, ethnomethodology, has come to predominate the emergent HCI concerns with the workplace. It utilizes an ethnographic/fieldwork approach rather than drawing off a particular social theory; it is empirical inasmuch as it is concerned with the *analysis* of work and the workplace; and it owes much to the methodology of ethnomethodology and conversation analysis. This chapter is concerned with studies of work that can be characterized in this way.

A number of precipitating developments have led to its adoption. The publication of *Plans and Situated Action* by Lucy Suchman in 1987 was a particularly defining moment for a significant minority in HCI, especially those concerned with the then-fledgling interest in CSCW. Suchman's attack upon the cognitive-science understanding of human behavior resonated with those within HCI who were attempting to move away from the predominant focus on the *individual user* and were attempting to place the computer within a *social context* of use. A cognitivist approach may have enabled HCI to address the individual's use of the computer, and to facilitate interface design, but it is a limited resource for the consideration of social relationships despite recent, but unconvincing, forays into "distributed cognition" theory.

Suchman's critique of cognitivism went much deeper than pointing out its limited scope, however. She mounted an attack on iconic figures in cognitive science, such as Herbert Simons, not just for their failure to take into account the social world, but also for their failure to understand that human action is situated in the social and cultural world, which has important implications for the way in which human action can be appropriately explained. In particular, she undermined the idea that human action can be explained in terms of *mental predicates* such as "plans," an important concept in the development of artificial intelligence. Suchman's rebuttal of an "interior" explanatory framework made reference to the fact that all action takes place within a swarm of sociocultural contingencies that cannot be covered in full, and in advance, by a plan—an argument that owes much to ethnomethodology.

A second precipitating development in the adoption of studies of work in HCI was the development of CSCW itself. CSCW was emphasizing the design of interactive systems. In part, this recognized the fact that many undertakings and people's working environments involve collaboration and the concertion of action, something that the cognitive approach within HCI was not well equipped to handle. Suchman's work resonated with this community, and she supplied it with a theoretical underpinning for its position. However, she offered this community more than just an anticognitivist argument, because she also demonstrated that work could be *studied* as part of the process of designing systems for the workplace. These studies were not, however, the traditional experimental situations characteristic of much HCI research at the time, but rather they involved studying work in the actual workplace in which systems were being used. At this stage of her career, Suchman drew heavily from the fields of conversation analysis and ethnomethodology within sociology. Suchman was thus furnishing those within HCI who were dissatisfied with its individualistic and cognitivist approach with a powerful critique of its predominant theory and the beginnings of a new empirical method of study based upon ethnomethodology. CSCW was a ripe area for populating with studies of work; without the CSCW movement, Suchman's ideas may not have been as readily embraced within HCI as they were.

A third precipitating moment in the development of studies of work was the Scandinavian Participatory Design movement (cf. Greenbaum & Kyng, 1991). Members of this movement had, for a number of years, argued that the requirements for technology should be developed directly from within and around the work situation of the technology's users. An important part of doing this was to directly involve the workers in the design process. The Participatory Design movement had developed methods and perspectives on interactive-systems design from this position and emphasized the following issues: the flexibility of work activities, the idea that work is an accomplished rather than a mechanical matter, and the idea that workers' voices should be heard with respect to workplace management and development. Again, Suchman's emphasis upon *work practice,* derived from ethnomethodology, resonated with their practical attempts to develop interactive systems for the workplace.

The study of work as a method in HCI has proliferated in the past ten or so years. Not all studies were conducted under the influence of Suchman's work, nor under the auspices of ethnomethodology, though most would claim to be ethnographic. This chapter will not examine the varied ways in which work has been studied in HCI but rather will concentrate on the attempts to develop a method for HCI that involves studying work for the purposes of rigorous interactive-systems design based on ethnomethodology and conversation analysis. It does so because this is by far the most systematic and developed orientation to the studies of work undertaken within HCI, and certainly the most prolific.

13.2   OVERVIEW: A PARADIGMATIC CASE

There are a number of ways in which ethnomethodologically grounded studies of work have been applied in HCI. One way, which we will use as an introductory example, has been to analyze the impact that a system has on the work that is done in the setting into which it is introduced. This has often led to a *critique* of a system for its dysfunctional consequences on the organization of the work and the setting. Studies of work have thus been used to analyze the organizational principles, or methods, behind a domain of work; to analyze the impacts of a system on these methods; and to critique its design when it conflicts with these methods. These methods and critiques then become available for the design of subsequent technologies.

One family of technologies in the workplace that has attracted a great deal of interest in HCI deals with the coordination of work (see Suchman [1994] and the subsequent replies and commentaries in Volume 2, numbers 3 and 4, 1994, of the journal *Computer-Supported Cooperative Work*). Often, it has been found that these coordination technologies clash with the methods through which a domain of work is itself coordinated. The designer, rather than studying this "natural" coordination, has often produced an idealized model of coordination that, when it is applied to the work setting, overconstrains the work, with the result that it is now more difficult for people to accomplish their work assignments than it was without the new technology. Coordination technologies that have been developed to better support coordinated work have thus been criticized for having the opposite consequences: making it more difficult for people to coordinate their work. A study by Bowers, Button, and Sharrock (1995) is a case in point.

Bowers and colleagues studied the introduction of a production-management system into the print rooms of a number of production printers in the United Kingdom. They studied the methods through which production was organized before introducing the system, and then, once the system had been introduced, analyzed how it played into these methods. An intended outcome of the "natural" coordination methods used by print operators, administrative staff, and management was the smooth flow of work across the print-room floor, in such a way that machines and operators were fully occupied and that the print jobs were produced on time. However, following the introduction of the new production system, this smooth flow of work was severely disrupted; during the first month many sites were significantly behind on their workload and had failed to meet many of the contracted deadlines they had with their customers. In order to work around the problems that the system had caused, the management in many of the sites disabled the system, although it had cost them many tens of thousands of pounds to install.

The problems encountered could not be passed off as "teething problems." Rather, the problems were caused by designers who had inappropriately modeled the workflow that the system enforced. On the face of it, it might seem that the relationships among the various stages that make up printing are simple and straightforward. A job is first processed by the administrative staff who, among other things, give it a job number; it then goes to the origination department who set it and do the art work. From there, it moves either to plate making, if it is a wet-ink job, or directly to printing, if it is to be electronically printed. If the job had gone to plate making first, it then goes to printing; all printed jobs are then passed on to the finishing department, where they are cut and bound. The last stage is dispatch.

All of the sites studied by Bowers and colleagues had a number of processes that controlled the relationships among the various stages and that were routinely used in this type of business. The production-management system was designed to control the workflow of the job through the various stages in accordance with these processes. However, Bowers and colleagues had found that, prior to the system's introduction, in order for the processes that controlled production to be used in actual situations, it was necessary for everyone involved to exercise their judgment as to how the processes could be fitted to a particular occasion. In this respect, a number of practices, which were not covered by the formal processes themselves, had developed across sites in order to achieve the results the processes had been designed to achieve, but that due to contingencies would not eventuate "on this occasion." These *ad hoc* practices were familiar methods that had developed in print shops in order to make the formal processes work "on the ground." The use of these methods was an important factor in achieving the result that was the intended outcome of the formal process—the smooth flow of work across the printshop floor in such a way that operators' time and machine capacity were maximized.

In this respect, Bowers and colleagues described a number of methods that machine operators, administrative staff, and management used to fit the processes to particular circumstances. For example, sometimes operators would "jump the gun" and start a printing job when that job had not yet been assigned a job number—although, according to the formal processes, operators were not supposed to commence work on a job until it had been given a job number by the administrative staff. When, for example, a job did not have to go to the origination department but could go straight to printing, the result could be delay and the interruption of a smooth flow of work. This would happen when an operator had completed one job but did not have a new job to start work on because the administrative staff had not yet completed the task of allocating a job number to it. In order to overcome this delay, operators would look to see what jobs lay on the administrators' desks and which ones were awaiting processing. Much of the work at these types of printshops involved repeat runs, so it was an easy matter for the operators to find jobs about which they already knew the details, set them up, and start to run them. They were thereby jumping the gun because they were starting work on the job before the administrative staff had completed their work. However, the operators exercised their judgment in the circumstances and were able to achieve the result the processes were designed to achieve: the smooth flow of jobs across the printshop floor in such a way that operators and machines were working to full capacity.

The system that the company introduced to support production management and work coordination had a formal model of the workflow, and it enforced the relationships among the tasks that made up the work of the print room. Thus, the system enforced the formal work processes. For example, under the new system's regime, it was not possible for an operator to start work on a job unless it had a job number. The operator had to log onto the system by entering his or her identifying operator's code number and the job number, and the system would not recognize the operation unless both were entered. Operators could work on the job without entering it into the system, but the records produced by the system would then have no entry for the operator during that time, and he or she would consequently be deemed to have been idle during that time. Previously, the operators would have just entered the job into their paper logbook once the job number had caught up with them, and they would put the record straight. The system overly constrained the operators, which led to the production problems the sites were experiencing as a result of using the new system. All of the staff involved were prevented from exercising their judgment in the situations that confronted them, which resulted in the problems that Bowers and colleagues witnessed. As a result, the system was at best only partially used.

Not only does this study of work analyze the methods through which a domain of work is organized by those who are party to it, from the inside; it also makes clear that modeling a workflow using formal process as a resource only partially grasps the work that a system is meant to automate or support. This example may be an extreme one, but the general point can be taken: Studying work reveals a domain of work practices and methods that are crucial for the efficient running of an organization. This can be characterized as the "hidden" work of organizations. This hidden work may not be remarked on by orthodox design methods, with detrimental results for the work to be supported. Bowers and colleagues treated work as a methodical matter, and they tried to uncover the methods through which people order their work, on the ground, to reveal this hidden work. By surfacing it, they were able to not only critique a bad design and a bad design methodology that overformalized the work, but they were also able to make the hidden work available for the purposes of design.

13.3   SCIENTIFIC FOUNDATIONS

Studies of work in HCI draw from a number of interrelated analytic and methodological developments in sociology and anthropology. These are, primarily, ethnography, situated action, and ethnomethodology.

13.3.1   Ethnography

There are a number of ways in which the phenomena of work have been understood within the human and behavioral sciences such as sociology, economics, and psychology. The most predominant of these has been to *theorize* work, and to thereby account for activities and interactions in the workplace according to a particular theory of human behavior or a particular social theory. Introductions to organizational behavior and organizational theory range across a vast territory from scientific taylorism, to the human relations school, to labor process theory. Although each theory stoutly contests its difference, and despite the fact that each is radically opposed to the other, they all have a common stance on what it is to actually account for work. They cast work in terms of a *general* theory of human behavior and societal relationships. A second and often allied approach is supposedly more empirical in nature. This is to give a positivistic rendition of work by analyzing it in terms of the personal attributes of the workforce such as gender, age, class, race, religion, education, and the like. Within this statistical approach to work, certain types of occupations are consequently found to be predominantly staffed by people possessing similar social or psychological features.

These theoretical and statistical approaches to work provide, however, only an abstract account of work, neither actually tackling the question of what people are doing when they engage in their job of work in their own terms, nor discussing how they are actually doing their work. The theorizing and positivistic tradition in the human sciences may furnish descriptions of the characteristics of people in a particular domain of work, or what, in undertaking a job of work, people may be doing at a societal level, but it is difficult to understand what someone's day's work looks like or how it actually appears to them. Thus, labor process theory, to pick a predominant theory of work (cf. Braverman, 1974), may describe work as the reproduction of capital or labor but does not provide more than a casual and glancing reference to the "content" of the work.

Contrasted against the more structural orientations to work displayed in theorizing and statistical approaches, there has been, within the area of the sociology of work, an *interactionist* approach that has attempted to develop an understanding of work from the inside. This has often involved observing work within the actual workplace; some sociologists even undertake the work themselves. This approach to work was initiated by the sociologist Everett Hughes (Hughes, 1971) and led to a wave of observationally based studies; although they had their heyday in the last century, these studies still continue today. Symbolic interactionists employed a methodology that had been previously developed within anthropology, that of *ethnography*.

An anthropologist, Malinowski, first developed ethnography in a foundational series of studies of the Trobrianb islanders (Malinowski, 1967). During this study, he lived among the islanders; learned to speak their language; recorded first-hand recollections of their culture, rituals, and magical incantations; listened to their stories and folklore; participated in their customs; and learned, at their knees, about their myths and history. In this way, Malinowski became immersed in the life of the tribe he was studying and developed a description of Trobrianb islanders' society from the *inside*. Ethnography, as this method was termed, became the established method for anthropology.

Everett Hughes, drawing off his anthropological training, applied ethnography to his own society, implying that it is possible to gain an insight into the ways of life of *one's own* society from the inside, just as it is for other societies. However, Hughes was concerned with investigating domains of society rather than society itself, and he concentrated on work, occupations, and the professions—trying to build an understanding of their distinct characteristics by studying them in the ethnographic mode and deploying the fieldwork techniques of anthropology. Since the time of Hughes's initial studies, a considerable body of literature has developed on work-related themes such as "the value of work," "changing perceptions of work," "the management of social relations," and "the formal and informal structures of work."

Studies of work within HCI and CSCW have tended to employ an ethnographic approach. What this has meant in practice is that researchers have adopted the fieldwork techniques of anthropology and early interactionist studies. They have not utilized the social theories of functionalism and interactionism that underpinned, respectively, Malinowski's and Hughes's work. As Anderson (1996) points out, ethnography in HCI has really stood as a proxy for "fieldwork," grounded, we could add, in ethnomethodology (Randall et al., 1995).

13.3.2   Situated Action

The distinguishing feature of many of the fieldwork techniques associated with ethnographic fieldwork in HCI is that work is observed as it happens and as it unfolds. Thus, the participant observer who may be "shadowing" a particular individual is witness to many of the circumstances that a person is involved in during the course of a workday. The analyst who uses videotaped material can capture the fine detail of work that might elude him or her the first time around, but that might be the very stuff of the work to those who undertake it. This distinctive cast of ethnography plays very well into another of the foundations of studies of work in HCI that originated in Lucy Suchman's *Plans and Situated Action.*

Suchman (1987) argued against the predominant cognitive model of human behavior abroad in psychology and cognitive science. The principle Cartesian underpinning of this model is that human action is accounted for in terms of inner mental processes. Thus, cognitive science uses otherwise mundane terms such as "plans" as if they were causal perquisites of action. In this respect, the mind is a processing unit, just like a computer, and all human action or interaction is accounted for in terms of interior mental predicates. Human action can thus be accounted for in terms of "purposes," "intentions," "goals," "motives," and, in the example that Suchman was attacking in the field of artificial intelligence, "plans." In order to understand how people act, it has been posited by Schank and Ableson (1977), one has to understand how they followed a script or a plan. Thus, their actions can be broken down into particular elements that are then accounted for in terms of parts of the plan, and, consequently, "in-order-to" types of explanations are given for their actions.

Contrary to this idea, Suchman argued that all human action takes place within a swarm of contingencies that are demonstrably oriented to by people in the conduct of their actions. It is in light of these contingencies that people construct and engage in their social actions and in their interactions with one another. A simple but telling example is illustrated in Schegloff's (1986) analysis of the opening turns of conversation, where what one speaker might say as part of the opening depends on what a prior speaker has said, or what they believe a following speaker could say. By their very characterization as contingencies, it is not possible to project in detail just how any one conversation may unfold before the participants engage in their course of social interaction. For example, we may well plan to tell someone about our wonderful vacation, but we decide not to do so when they tell us about their recent bereavement.

In this respect, the formulation of a plan before engaging in action will not be able to take into account the contingences that develop in the course of engaging in a course of action and that decisively shape it. In this respect, a plan cannot determine the course of someone's action. A plan can be a guide for some actions, but it will have to be applied in a context of contingencies, which cannot be formulated in advance of the action (Lynch, 2001). Consequently, the cognitive-science treatment of plans as causal antecedents is problematic. Furthermore, there are, indeed, many occasions in which actions are undertaken with no plan at all.

In Suchman's argument, social action is, then, always situated within some complex of social arrangements. Studies of work within HCI have oriented to this feature of social action in their attempts to study work as it unfolds within the actual circumstances in which it occurs. Often this has involved reference to its organizational context (Button & Sharrock, 1997), but, as work done by Christian Heath (cf. Heath & Luff, 1991) and by Chuck and Candy Goodwin (cf. Goodwin & Goodwin, 1993) has shown, this can also involve fine details of what a collaborator in the workplace is doing. These details can be subsequently built into the work of others who, by doing so, demonstrate their importance for the organization of work. In this regard, Goodwin and Goodwin's (1993) study of the control room in a U.S. regional airport showed how baggage-crew dispatchers would monitor the "sing-song voice" of a controller in order to find, in the buzzing noise of the control room, the information they required to do their work. Hearing the voice, they would attend to its content and thus ensure that baggage crews were ready and waiting when the plane docked at its landing stage.

The idea that human action is oriented to the context of its production, and the idea that what constitutes context is situationally determined, problematize concepts such as plans or tasks. They also offer the opportunity to adopt an *analytic* mentality. That is, social action can be analyzed within the situations in which it occurs in order to find, in the materials themselves, how a course of action has been put together. It is just this type of analytic mentality that is characteristic of studies of work undertaken within HCI. Thus, not only do studies of work within HCI use materials that have been ethnographically generated, but they also treat those materials as a matter for analysis.

13.3.3   Ethnomethodology

Ethnography and fieldwork techniques have been used by a variety of sociological perspectives. Ethnographic-based studies of work within HCI, which draw from a number of the different sociological perspectives, have also been pursued. However, by far the greatest proportion of ethnographically based studies of work that have been undertaken for the purposes of system design are founded on one particular methodological orientation in sociology, that of ethnomethodology and conversation analysis. Ethnomethodology was also one of the sources on which Suchman's work on situated action was based.

Sociologist Harold Garfinkel originated ethnomethodology in the 1960s (Garfinkel, 1967). It has proven to be a small but persistent area within sociology. It would not be properly accurate to call ethnomethodology a perspective or theory within sociology because it proposes an alternative theory. A primary concern of ethnomethodology as originally articulated by Garfinkel is with *social order*. Social order has been a traditional topic within the human sciences, overtly announced by Thomas Hobbes, but worked on by many varied perspectives and theories. The way in which social order is examined by ethnomethodology emphasizes how it breaks with a sociological orthodoxy.

Garfinkel radicalized the question of social order in two ways. First, order had, prior to Garfinkel, always been addressed as a societal matter, and questions were oriented to the structural properties of, and the conditions for, social order. Garfinkel, however, argued that social order was a much more essential matter than sociologists had previously considered, and he argued that people, in the conduct of their activities, display their orientation to the ordered properties of actions and interaction, and use those orderly properties when carrying out their social conduct. There are two consequences to this. First, order is to be found, as Harvey Sacks (1993a) remarked, "at all points," and consequently order is not just a societal matter—it is a matter that pervades all aspects of social life. However, being all-pervasive, order is not just a matter for professional human scientists, it is a matter for ordinary members of society; it is a *members' phenomena,* as Garfinkel put it. That is, people themselves attend to the ordered properties of conduct, and they use those ordered properties in the achievement of their conduct.

This leads to the second distinguishing characteristic of social order for Garfinkel, which is that order is a member's *accomplishment;* it takes actual work to bring off. The traditional way in which order has been considered in the human sciences is to posit mechanisms whereby social structure provides for the actions of individuals. The mechanisms that have been offered have been varied and relate to the social theories that abound within the human sciences. Thus, Talcott Parsons, from the structural-functionalist perspective, emphasized how order is the product of consensus brought about through reciprocally shared normative values and rules (Parsons, 1937), whereas Marxist sociology has argued that order is the product of constraint—people being subject to the power of a coercive state exercised over them by its various institutions.

Counterpoised against this way of construing social action, as the product of some posited external structure, Garfinkel brought attention to the ways in which it is organized in its very doing. Participants to its production then constantly work at order in social life. This emphasis on the way in which people achieve the order of their activities dovetails well with the other underpinnings of studies of work in HCI. It requires an analytic mentality to render this order, and it requires materials for analysis, as provided through ethnographic fieldwork. Ethnomethodology has explored the *in situ* production of social order through two broad domains of interest: conversation analysis and ethnomethodological studies of work, both of which have been used within HCI as part of a study of work methodology.

Conversation Analysis

Sociologist Harvey Sacks originated conversation analysis (CA) (Sacks, 1993a, 1993b). Although there is a vast literature in CA, the seminal work, written by Sacks and his colleagues Emanuel Schegloff and Gail Jefferson, is "The Simplest Systematics for the Organisation of Turn-Taking for Conversation" (Sacks et al., 1974). In this piece, Sacks and colleagues provide a description of the way in which turn taking in conversation is organized by participants on a moment-by-moment basis, and how that organization is worked on, as an interactional matter, in the unfolding course of a turn at talk. Turn taking is thus an interactional phenomenon, relating to multiple participants, and organized as a collaborative matter. Sacks and colleagues provide for the turn taking in conversation in terms of two components and what they describe as a set of rules that participants orient to in the production of their talk. Although the production of social order is a thoroughly normative affair, the use of the vocabulary of rules should not lead readers to suppose that Sacks and colleagues were merely positing a set of abstract rules that, if followed, would result in people taking turns during a conversation. Rather, their description of the rules involved in speaker transfer in conversation embodies the very work that people engage in, as a situated matter, to orient to some norm of conduct. Their description also displays an understanding of how norms of conduct have to be worked for the details of a particular context. Lastly, it displays just how detailed an understanding of context there can be, for participants can show that they are orienting to tiny episodes of, for example, speaker overlap, and pause, which are consequential for how they build their activities.

Conversation analysis has developed as the study of turn taking in conversation, and in that respect it may seem to have little to do with the idea of studying work as part of a methodology for systems design and evaluation in HCI. However, as we will see Section 13.4.1, this is far from the case, for CA has underpinned some of the ways in which the study of work has been approached, and CA has also been invoked in the development of natural-language interfaces.

Ethnomethodological Studies of Work

The second major preoccupation of ethnomethodology is its interest in work. However, ethnomethodological studies of work stand in contrast to other ways in which work has been studied in sociology. In line with ethnomethodology's unease with the traditional trends in sociology to theorize or to statistically apprehend its phenomena, ethnomethodological studies of work have distanced themselves from the predominant themes in the sociology of work such as labor process, demography, gender, and the like that epitomize the current way in which work is treated in sociology. In addition, ethnomethodological studies of work have also distanced themselves from the interactional studies conducted in the tradition of Everett Hughes.

Garfinkel (1986) credits his interest in work to Harvey Sacks's remarks on the "interactional whatness of work," by which Sacks means just how the work is constituted in the interactions of those party to it (reported in Lynch, 1993). Garfinkel gives an example of the types of problems he has with other ethnographically based studies of work, such as interactionism, by taking a well-known study of jazz musicians by Howard Becker (1963). Garfinkel compliments Becker on some of his detail. Thus, through reading Becker's work, we know much about the culture of jazz musicians: what they like to play versus what they are forced to play by clients, how they talk about the rest of us, the clothes they wear, how they spend their days and nights, and the rest. However, Garfinkel points out that, although we now know about these matters, we still do not know how they make their jazz together, how they make their music through their collaborations and interactions, and how they work together, in real time, in actual occasions, to create their music. What is missing from Becker's interactionist account is the constitutive features of making music, the interactional *what* of the music making.

Ethnomethodological studies of work have taken up this issue, and they have attempted to examine domains of work in order to understand what are the particular constitutive features of courses of work and how, in their interactions with one another, people are recognizably engaged in doing their work. Many of the foundational studies in ethnomethodological studies of work have been concerned with the work of scientists, developed particularly by Garfinkel and his students (cf. Garfinkel et al., 1989, and Lynch, 1993). However, as the study of work has developed as a method within the field of system design, this has had a reciprocal effect upon ethnomethodology itself; a range of ethnomethodological studies of diverse work domains has now accumulated as a result of ethnomethodology's deployment within HCI.

13.4   DETAILED DESCRIPTION

Studies of work in HCI have been used for a number of design purposes. Studies of the way in which people have to work with, and often work around, a system have been used to *critique* the design methodologies that stand behind a range of systems designs. It is a critique of how to approach design based on an essential understanding of some of the organizing principles of how people interact and work with one another. A second purpose has been to use studies of work to *evaluate* particular designs in use and to provide for the reiterative design of the system. However, one of the first domains of interest in HCI that was elaborated on in studies of work is that of *requirements analysis*. This is the way in which studies of work can provide technology requirements of a different order of concern to those rendered through other requirements methodologies. Lastly, studies of work have been used to offer *foundational reconceptualizations* in HCI.

13.4.1 Critique

One way in which studies of work have been used within HCI is to critique existing design methodology. This has been seen with respect to the study by Bowers and colleagues (1995) that was seen earlier in this chapter. The stark conclusion of that study was that workflow systems that are based on abstract and formal understandings of work might encounter difficulties when they are deployed in real work settings because of the situated, *ad hoc* character of the organization of work. In this respect, it is not so much the *design* of the particular system that is questioned, but the approach behind the design. This methodology is one that construes work as a set of formal stipulative processes, when, as revealed through detailed study, work is a much more flexible phenomena involving *ad hoc* practices and contingent operations in its accomplishment. Work is not so much organized as "rule following," but in the contingencies and improvisations of applying rules.

A strong example of this orientation to design, which is in part based on conversation analysis and on Suchman's understanding of the notion of "situated action" is Suchman's (1994) critique of Winograd and Flores's *the coordinator*. Winograd and Flores (1986) had developed this workflow system based on "speech act theory" as elaborated by Searle (1983). Speech act theory is concerned with felicity conditions—for example, the conditions that have to be present in order for someone to correctly "make a promise." These conditions inevitably lead to an emphasis on a speaker's intentions, for to correctly make a promise one must, for example, intend to keep it. If, when you promise to meet someone at 10:30 outside the bookstore, you do not intend to be there, then, in Searle's account, you are not correctly doing "making a promise." Speech act theory thus posits that it is possible to provide for human action in terms of sets of rules and conditions for their correct enactment.

The coordinator is intended to regulate the relationships between people in organizations based on this conception of human action. Thus, people's activities are regulated by conditions and rules for doing their work and for enabling that work to be related to or moved onto others. Thus, for example, it is only possible to pass work further down the line once all of the conditions associated with a particular task that one is undertaking have been met.

The thrust of Suchman's criticism is not so much directed to the system itself, but to the methodology behind it: the adoption by Winograd and Flores of speech act theory as a heuristic in their design. Drawing partly on conversation analysis, Suchman challenges the constrained and cognitive picture of language portrayed in speech action theory, emphasizing that conversation analysis has demonstrated that meaning and intention are interactionally contingent. As we have seen, conversation analysis underscores the situated and unfolding character of conversational exchanges. Speech act theory, however, with its emphasis on necessary and sufficient conditions, cannot encompass the contingent character of people's interactions with one another. Consequently, Suchman argues, *the coordinator* cannot support this feature of ordinary action and interaction. Suchman goes further and argues that this feature of action and interaction is actually violated because the system imposes a stipulative organization on people's actions.

Suchman's argument is generalizable. Based on an understanding of the situated and contingent character of work, action, and interaction, she is questioning the appropriateness of designing technologies, such as coordination technologies, around formal and stipulative theories and methodologies. Part of the problem she develops is the moral and political efficacy of so doing: Should systems constrain their users? Another part is the practicality of so doing: Can people work effectively? Both are serious matters for HCI.

13.4.2   Evaluation

Studies of work in HCI are also being used to evaluate particular technology designs. By conducting studies of the actual use of a system in the workplace, it is possible to gather detailed data on the application of the technology that can be used in its evaluation and the subsequent reiteration of the design. An example of the evaluative use of this method is Heath and Luff's (1993) study of a media-space in a research laboratory.

The researchers studied by Heath and Luff had found that the physical arrangements of their new systems laboratory were not conducive to the collaborative nature of their work. Rather than being in close proximity to one another, which they considered to be essential for promoting collaboration, the researchers found that they were scattered throughout a three-story building. Their problems were compounded by the layout of the floors. Ideally, they would have preferred to work in an open environment that promoted the possibility of inter-actions among lab members, which they believed was essential for their work. However, in practice they were faced with small areas carved up into individual rooms, with small and unworkable common areas.

In response to the limitations of the building, they designed and imple-mented a media space that supported cooperative work between the physically distributed researchers. This infrastructure allowed the researchers, and also the administrative staff, to initiate and establish audio and visual communication with one another while in their respective offices, and to have access to the pub-lic areas within the building. One of the ways in which technology was being par-ticularly used was to develop long-term "office shares" between researchers who were collaborating on a project. Thus, typically, two individuals would preserve a connection over a number of weeks or even months, and through the technol-ogy would establish a strong sense of copresence.

Although the media space system was used and did allow the researchers to overcome some of their problems, users felt that its deficiencies prevented it from being all they hoped for. These problems involved difficulties in establish-ing interaction with remote parties through the system and then sustaining that interaction once initiated. Heath and Luff made video recordings of the way in which technology was being used in the course of the researchers' work, and through analyzing these episodes found that the technology resulted in what they called "asymmetries" in interpersonal relations that were not present in or-dinary face-to-face encounters. In particular, although the technology provided the participants with mutual visual access to each other, it also undermined their ability to engage in other forms of conduct, such as gestures and off-camera events, which were important for their work. This evaluation was fed into the re-design of the system, and the designers introduced new audio cues that signified important activities that could not be seen, and that supported activities such as glancing.

13.4.3   Requirements

An early example of how studies of work were used to generate systems require-ments is still instructive. Bentley and colleagues (1992) describe how a study of the work of British air-traffic controllers was used to design a prototype flight strip. The flight strip is a manual system in which strips of paper represent partic-ular aircraft in a controller's field of operation. The flight strip carries relevant details about that aircraft, and it is placed in a rack of flight strips being used by a controller. Bentley and colleagues make the point that the study does not so much lead to detailed systems requirements as they are conventionally thought of, but, rather, it provides what they call *pointers* to appropriate design decisions.

They give a number of examples. An obvious advantage of developing a computer system to replace the manual system is that many of the manual processes can be automated. In this regard, Bentley and colleagues make the point that it would be an easy matter to automate the ordering of flight strips, and that a systems designer might believe this to be an obvious decision to take. However, one of the observations made by the study is that the actual manipulation of the flight strip into its correct position by a controller worked to focus attention on this and the other flight strips. This need to pay specific attention to the strip actually worked as a safety device because it allowed the controller to identify possible trouble early on. Automated positioning was then deemed by Bentley and colleagues to be inappropriate.

Again, flight strips are manually placed into different colored holders that distinguish the heading of a flight. A design decision to automatically assign the correct colored border to the electronic flight strip based on the aircraft's heading could also have been made. However, manually assigning colors is a method that forces controllers to check their data and, thus, is again an important safety device. Bentley and colleagues also make the point that studies of work may not only ground design requirements and decisions in the real world of work, but they can also be used to stand in for actual users in the early stages of systems design.

13.4.4   Foundational Reconceptualizations

In many of the examples that we have used so far, there is something of a disjuncture between the study of work and the actual design. That is, a study of work is undertaken and then some sort of design activity, or some design activity followed by a study of work. This disjuncture is reinforced when it is also noticed that a division of labor exists between those who do the study and those who do the design. The two elements in the division of labor—the designers and the social scientists—may be brought together in a design space, but knowledge of the work setting gained through its study *has generally been transferred* from the social scientist(s) to the designer(s).

In contrast, Dourish and Button (1998) have attempted to develop a more foundational relationship between one of the underpinnings of studies of work—ethnomethodology—and design in their proposition: *technomethodology*. Fundamentally, their concern is not with the findings of particular ethnomethological studies of working settings, but with the actual analytical framework within which those studies are conducted. Similarly, they are not so much immediately concerned with the design of any particular system but with the design of systems per se.

They give an example of this foundational approach by drawing together a relationship between the notion of "abstraction" in system design and the notion of "accountable action" in ethnomethodology. Both elements are conceptually central to the respective disciplines of design and ethnomethodology. Abstraction is viewed as a fundamental tool in systems design. For example, user-interface behavior such as file copying or file printing are abstractions of the behavior of the programs they control, as are sets of abstractions that programmers manipulate to control the computer. The description "accountable action" in ethnomethodology draws attention to the fact that social actions are not just done, they are done so that they can be recognized as such. Actions are *accountable,* that is, it is possible to give an account of them.

Dourish and Button explore the extent to which this foundational respecification of action in ethnomethodology can be used to reflect on the idea of abstraction in design. They give an example of file copying. Many systems represent this in terms of a percentage bar that tells a user how much copying has been done as a percentage of the total copying to be done. They envisage a scenario in which the copying is being done on a remote volume and in which the copying fails when it is 40% done. There are many reasons why this may have occurred, but there are no resources for determining the actual reason in any particular case. Yet, why the failure has occurred can be important for what a user does next.

Using the idea that human action is accountable (done so that it can be recognized), Dourish and Button suggest that abstractions can be developed in such a way that they act as a way of viewing the mechanisms at work when, in this example, copying is taking place. That is to say, copying is made to appear in such a way that what is being done is recognizable. Thus the system is able to provide an account of what it is doing as it is doing it, which enables users to better determine any remedial action that may be required.

13.5   CASE STUDY

Bentley, Button, and Pycock (1999) describe InterSite, a distributed production-management system for multiple production print factories that was designed following extensive studies of the work practices found in these organizations and reported in Bowers, Button, and Sharrock (1995) and in Button and

Sharrock (1997). The study by Button and Sharrock revealed that the work of managing production involves methods for making the order of the work visible. These methods primarily involved the use of paper documents. For example, a simple forward loading board consisting of a sheet of paper with print machines listed on a vertical axis and days of the week along the horizontal axis was used in many sites to assign jobs to machines within a timeframe. Another paper device was a job ticket that contained the details of the job such as its job number, its due date, the instructions for what work had to be done on it, and the like. Yet another paper form was the job flag. This included information such as the job number, its due date, and a part number and was inserted into stacks of printed material on the printshop floor.

These simple devices were used by the various managers who, between them, were responsible for organizing and moving a job through its production phases in such a way that two conditions for the organization of the print site were met: (1) keep the site at full production with all machines and operatives fully working throughout the working day, and (2) meet the deadlines agreed on with a customer. They used the devices in order to make visible the orderly properties of the production process so that they could attend to any problems that might occur. For example, the printshop floor at any one time contains pallets of printed material, positioned in the aisles or behind machines. These pallets have inserted into them the job flags and also have the job tickets resting on top of them. Through these devices, the production manager is able to view a stacked pallet not as just a pallet of printed material, but as, for example, a "late job." By viewing the details of the job on the job ticket, it is possible to make determinations such as "this job is going to be late if it is not moved into the next production process now." It thus furnishes relevant personnel with information they need to take remedial action and hurry up its progress.

Another example is that, by consulting the forward loading board when a job request is received, the administrative staff can quickly ascertain if they have spare capacity and can take on the job in the time requested. In addition, the forward loading board can be quickly consulted should it become necessary to reorder production if, for instance, a machine goes down. By looking to the forward loading board, the scheduler and the production manager can make decisions to reorganize the printing schedule for various machines in order to work around the ailing one.

It is also a simple matter to know where in the production process a job is because the job ticket, which accompanies the job throughout its production phases, makes that explicit.

The devices that are used by factory production printshop managers have the following characteristics. First, they are on public display: they are either on desks, which are in public places within the print shop, or they are placed on jobs, which are in full public view. Second, they can be consulted by anyone to check on the status of jobs for whatever reason. Third, they can be consulted at a glance: The information they contain is simple and is visually rendered either, as in the case of forward loading boards, pictorially, or, as in the case of the job ticket, through standard and patterned formatting. Fourth, they can be used collaboratively between people: They are sites at which people involved in the management of production can collaborate, and devices through which they collaborate. Fifth, the devices are all paper based.

In sum, it is the public, shared, and visible character of the devices that constitute their effectiveness in the work of managing the order of production in print factories, and their paper medium is convenient and portable.

This investigation into the work of managing production printing was done within the context of changes that were taking place in communication infrastructures, which meant that it had become an easy matter to move print files between geographically remote sites. The fact that most, though not all, print jobs come into the print factory as electronic files provided the systematic possibility of print factories working together in new ways, either coming together as coalitions to share work across the coalition, or for load balancing within a company with many sites. Thus, for example, a new form of distributed print production could take place in which sites could easily collaborate with one another. For instance, should one site receive an order that it cannot complete by the due date, it can now collaborate with another site to have the job printed by merely sending them the file over a computer network. There was, then, the opportunity to use the new technology for printing and to use the new communication infrastructures to maximize printing capacities of confederations or collections of print factories.

However, a problem that the study revealed was that, while it was possible to easily move files from one site to another, it was not possible to systematically select which site to collaborate with. This was the case because, in contrast to the situation with regard to single sites where the production capacity was visible, the production capacity of remote sites was not visible. The study examined a company that had more than fourteen production sites, which it intended to network. However, for any job that one site needed to have printed elsewhere, the following question existed: Which of the other thirteen sites had spare capacity? To find out, factory managers would have to phone the another sites to ascertain if they had production holes, with all the hit-and-miss consequences attendant to that process. Furthermore, sites would be unable to ascertain the production status of jobs they were responsible for and that were being produced by remote sites, again simply because the whereabouts of the job in the production cycle was not immediately visible to them.

Bentley and colleagues describe InterSite, which is designed as a solution to this problem. Importantly, InterSite is based on both the methods that mangers use to order the production process and the types of tools they use. Thus, artifacts such as the forward loading board and the job ticket form the basis of Bentley and colleagues' approach to supporting production management in the case of distributed production—by making the order of production visible within the new distributed environment. Their solution uses the World Wide Web to support the sharing of these artifacts with other print shops and thereby allows visualization of the status of production across the network. The idea behind the InterSite approach is to use the network to share representations of production status in a form that is familiar to printshop personnel, to allow them to use the same methods for managing production in a distributed environment as they use in their own printshops. InterSite thus facilitates the sharing and presentation of *documents* to support existing human decision making, negotiation, and coordination practices. This contrasts with commercial production-management systems, which see the problem as one of sharing *data* between distributed database systems to allow the automatic coordination of production management across different sites.

Bentley and colleagues' approach to supporting distributed document production is to interleave the system with existing production processes, to broaden the options for printshop managers. As well as having the options of taking a job for inhouse production or rejecting the job, they add the option of accepting a print job for production at a different location. Determination of whether to distribute a job is of course dependent on being able to locate a shop capable of producing the job to the required quality and within the required timeframe. To support this, InterSite provides facilities for registered print shops—collectively, the "coalition"—to electronically "publish" their production schedules (the forward loading boards) to an InterSite server at a central location. From the InterSite home page, it is then possible for managers of printshops who participate in the coalition to access the published schedules as required, and to try to identify potential partners with spare capacity on appropriate machines.

InterSite thus allows the sharing of forward loading boards in a distributed environment and consequently allows personnel to analyze production states of other factories in much the same way as they are able to analyze their own production state using their forward loading boards. This overcomes one of the major barriers to distributed production, allowing the production state of the whole network to be visible to participants within the coalition. Another major barrier is that of not knowing, once work on a job has begun, where in the production process the job is. Information on job status is required to identify potential problems such as overloading of particular production processes, or to answer customer queries. By maintaining an awareness of the production status, shop managers can project the likely situation on the factory floor in the future and take action to mitigate problems before they occur.

Button and Sharrock (1997) had described how printshop managers spend a large part of their time walking round the factory floor identifying where each job is in the production cycle in order to maintain awareness of the production status. This practice relies on the properties of the job ticket, and the fact that it never leaves the job as it moves around the factory floor. The job ticket's location indicates the stage of the job's process, what has been done, what is still to be done, who is working on it, and more. To address this, InterSite provides facilities for remote job tracking. As with the forward loading board display, the job-tracking facilities build on existing working practices in the printshop and, in particular, the properties of the artifacts—in this case the job ticket—that are employed to manage production.

InterSite provides an interface for receiving tracking information from external clients, allowing automatic routing of the electronic job folders. These clients must provide two identifiers—one corresponding to a job folder and the other to an in-tray where the job is now located. The identifiers for these objects are automatically and uniquely generated when they are first created. This then allows the connection of a variety of sensors that detect the presence of a work bag and can read the associated job identifier and send this information, along with a location identifier, to InterSite where the electronic job will automatically be routed to the appropriate location and the status display updated. As an example, Bentley and colleagues describe how they connected a barcode reader using this interface; the barcode can be programmed to send a specific location identifier and can read the job identifier encoded as a barcode on the job ticket. Again, a feature of single-site production is pressed into service electronically in such a way that production mangers are able to use the obvious visibility of the production status that their work relies on in its accomplishment.

InterSite is a complex system with numerous features, and it is not possible to fully describe it here. However, it has a lightweight impact upon the methods used to do the work of managing print production, and it demonstrates the possibility for radical design that attention to the methods through which work is organized can have. The radical nature of this design is particularly brought out when compared to other production-management systems that exist. These emphasize the transfer of data and the outcomes of processing that data; by comparison, InterSite leaves the decision making in the hands of mangers but allows them to operate in new infrastructural environments.

13.6   CURRENT STATUS

During the past ten years or more, considerable progress has been made in recognizing the importance of the social world for considerations in systems design. In many quarters of HCI, especially CSCW, there has indeed been a move away from the individual user to the work setting as predicted by Grudin (1990). There has been a considerable body of studies assembled, and studies of work are being extensively used as a resource for systems design in industrial and academic environments. Studying work as a method in HCI design is, however, still something of a novelty for those areas of HCI that are not concerned with the collaborative and interactive character of human behavior, and it is more abundant in CSCW than in mainstream HCI.

One characteristic of the use of studies of work in HCI has, however, tended to be constant throughout this decade—the division of labor between the social scientists and the designers. Thus, those whose fulltime preoccupation is with the organization of work mainly undertake the studies of work, while those from within the design sciences do the design that uses these studies. Some may protest this description because it is possible to find that actual designers of a system may go into the field, and they may even claim to be studying work in an ethnographic tradition. However, from the point of view of the type of work examined in this chapter, these studies are often inadequate. They are either a superficial overview of the setting, lacking any analytic sensibilities, or they are used as *post hoc* rationalizations for design decisions they have already been made, or both.

Two possible developments may be considered for the future. First, it may be possible to train people in HCI to undertake serious and rigorous studies of work so that they can, themselves, engage in studies of work as part of their methodological arsenal. Including this chapter in this book on HCI method is an instantiation of this possibility. Also, the fact that university computer-science departments have now started to hire people whose main preoccupation is with studying work may result in centers of excellence in which social-science research and design blend into each other through recurrent practice.

The second possible development is a continuation of the current trend in which there is collaboration between different disciplines within a working division of labor articulated within a design space. In this future, it is the collaboration between specialisms on a design team that is the hallmark. Studies of work, which are done for the purposes of design, can be articulated within the parameters of design problems and issues. This is a trend that can be evidenced in a number of academic and industrial organizations. A research question that permeates this trend, however, is one of mutually aligning the different disciplines involved so as to affect an appropriate consummation of the relationship.

Whatever the particular future of studies of work will be in HCI, two issues are clear. First, the alignment of studies of work and design will be refined in practice and good example, not in methodological or theoretical fiat. Second, HCI has had the door onto the workplace opened for it. It has been shown that the ways of work and the workplace require and make relevant interactive systems, and that these ways are themselves available as resources for the design of those systems. Closing that door is not an intellectual nor a practical option.

13.7   FURTHER READING

Button, G. (ed.). (1993). *Technology in working order: Studies of work, interaction and technology.* London: Routledge.

Luff, P., Hindmarsh, J., and Heath C. (eds.). (2000). *Workplace studies: Recovering work practice and informing system design.* Cambridge, UK: Cambridge University Press.

Suchman, L. (ed.). (1995). Representations of work. Special edition of *Communications of the ACM, 38* (9).

Thomas, P. J. (ed.). (1995). *The social and interactional dimension of human-computer interfaces.* Cambridge: Cambridge University Press.

14 Upside-Down ∀s and Algorithms—Computational Formalisms and Theory

Alan Dix Lancaster University, England

14.1 MOTIVATION

The time delay as Internet signals cross the Atlantic is about 70 milliseconds, about the same time it takes for a nerve impulse to run from your finger to your brain. Parallels between computation and cognition run as far back as computers themselves. Although at first it feels as if the cold, abstruse, more formal aspects of computation are divorced from the rich ecology of the human-computer interface, the two are intimately bound. Mathematics has also been part of this picture. Indeed, the theory of computation predates digital computers themselves, as mathematicians pondered the limits of human reasoning and computation.

There are a number of aspects of this interplay between computation, mathematics, and the human-computer interface.

First, understanding your raw material is essential in all design. Part of the material of human-computer interaction (HCI) is the computer itself. Theoretical and formal aspects of computing can help us understand the practical and theoretical limits of computer systems, and we can thus design around these limits.

Second, diagrams, drawings, and models are an integral part of the design process. Formal notations can help us sketch the details of interaction, not just the surface appearance, of an interactive system, and we can thus analyze and understand its properties before it is built. This is the area that is typically called "formal methods" within HCI, and we'll look at an example of this in Section 14.2.

Third, various techniques from mathematics—simple counting to sophisticated equations—may be used to reason about specific problems in HCI. In this book, we see chapters including Fitts' Law, a logarithmic regression; information-foraging theory, which involves differential equations; not to mention the heavy reliance on statistical modeling and analysis of virtually all quantitative empirical work.

Finally, the design artifact of HCI involves people and computers working together within a sociotechnical whole. Among the many political, social, and emotional aspects of this interaction, there is also an overall computational facet. The theory of computation has, from the beginning, spanned more than mere mechanical computation, and conversely an understanding of digital computation can help us understand some of the complexity within rich organizational ecologies.

14.1.1   What Is Formal?

As with all words, "formal" is used to mean different things by different people and in different disciplines. In day-to-day life, formal may mean wearing a dinner jacket and bow tie or using proper language. That is, formal is about the outward form of things—a formal greeting may belie many emotions beneath the surface.

Taken strongly, formalism in mathematics and computing is about being able to represent things in such a way that the representation can be analyzed and manipulated without regard to the meaning. This is because the representation is chosen to encapsulate faithfully the significant features of the meaning.

Let's see what this means in simple mathematics. One night you count the cockroaches on the wall—213. The next night you count again—279. Now because 279 is bigger than 213, you can assert that there were more cockroaches on the second night than the first. How do you know? Did you line up the cockroaches in queues? No! You know because you compared the numbers. The numbers 213 and 279 represented faithfully the significant feature of the cockroaches. Of course, the cockroaches on the first night might have been bigger, a different color, more friendly, so the numbers don't capture everything.

Even looking at something as simple as cockroaches, we can see both the power and limitation of formalism. It allows us to discuss certain features succinctly and with precision, but without the things they represent being present. However, by its nature it excludes features that are not represented.

When we write, when we speak, when we draw, symbols stand for things that are not present. In interfaces, a drawing of a potential screen design allows us to discuss that design even though it is not there. However, the drawing does not allow us to discuss the dynamics (perhaps a storyboard might allow this for a single scenario) or the effects of actions on underlying data, on the world, or on other users. Certain formal descriptions of a system allow this. Think again of the cockroaches. If we were comparing cockroaches in two different rooms, it would, in theory, be possible to collect them in jam jars and then line up the cockroaches to see which room had more. However, if we had collected the first night's cockroaches in a jam jar, we would not have had 279 cockroaches the second night to collect as some would be stuck in the jar. The formalism of counting not only makes the comparison easier, it makes it possible.

Formal descriptions often include place holders for unspecified things, for example, a furniture designer may draw a homunculus with limbs in the right

proportions. The homunculus stands for *anyone* of the relevant height, arm length and so on. Notice how powerful this is—not only can we talk about a specific person who isn't present, but we can talk about anyone at all with particular properties. This is used to particular effect in mathematics where we can say things like: "for any number n, $n+1$ is greater than n." Here the place holder "n" stands for any number whatsoever. This power to talk about an infinite amount of things (every number!) in a finite expression is one of the things that makes mathematics so powerful.

Because the real thing does not need to be present, it may be something abstract, including something like a sequence of interactions. A storyboard would allow us to talk about one example of a fixed sequence of interactions, whereas in a formal system we can usually talk about things we would like to be true of any interaction sequence. And, more abstract again, we can talk about any system of a particular kind and all the possible interactions a user could have with that system For example, Mancini and I worked on issues surrounding **Undo** and were able to show that any system with particular kinds of **Undo** would need to be implemented in effectively the same way (Dix & Mancini, 1997; Dix, Mancini, & Levialdi, 1997).

Finally formalisms force you to think. It would be easy to look at the wall one night and think "there are more cockroaches than yesterday." Perhaps the wall just looks more densely covered. However, when we start to count the cockroaches, we need to be a lot more clear. What counts as a cockroach—should I include that mess where I hit a cockroach with my shoe? The cockroaches keep running in and out of cracks—do I mean every cockroach including those hidden in the cracks (perhaps I could put spots of paint on them), or do I just mean every cockroach that is out at a particular time, say 11 P.M.?

when you count cockroaches you have to decide what counts as a cockroach

Sometimes forcing things into conceptual boxes is unproductive (think how many hours have been wasted arguing whether a platypus is a bird or a mammal), but often the very act of being precise makes us think more clearly about problems. While using formal methods to model various aspects of interaction, I have often found that it is the process of creating the model that is more important than anything I do with it.

14.1.2   The Myth of Informality

There is a fashionable tendency to decry the formal, mathematical, or precise in favor of softer, more informal techniques. This is always a popular stance, perhaps because of the rise of post-modernism, perhaps because people feel powerless, like cogs in the unbending bureaucracies of modern society. Seminal books such as Suchman's *Plans and Situated Actions* (1987) and Winograd and Flores' *Understanding Computers and Cognition* (1986) have been successful in part because they appear to present atheoretic, highly contextual, and aformal approaches. (In fact, both have strong theoretical stances of their own and were written in the context of an overformal design environment at the time.)

As already noted, there are many other disciplines and many aspects of HCI where this is the right approach, and attempts to formalize such areas are misguided. However, maintaining the opposite view, the myth of informality, and eschewing formalism completely is both illusory and ultimately dangerous.

The design process may well be informal, but the designed product is anything but. A computer is the most formal artifact possible; *all* it does is interpret meaningless symbols according to formal rules.

Maintaining the myth of informality means that the effects of the intrinsic formality of a computer system have not been considered during design. Would you buy a ship from an engineer who lived in the Sahara?

There are arguments for and against formalizing certain phenomena, but not computer systems. Any design process that produces computer systems as part of its final product (albeit within a rich sociotechnical whole) is dealing with formality.

The choice is simple: Do we deal with the formality in knowledge or in ignorance?

14.1.3   Chapter Structure

The next section will examine some simple examples in order to demonstrate the utility of this approach. We will then look at some of the history of the use of formalism in mathematics and computing from Aristotle to Alan Turing. This will then lead to a more detailed review of the different ways in which formal methods and computational theory have been used in HCI. In order to validate this, a more substantial case study will show how adoption of a simple formal notation for dialogue design led to a 10-fold improvement in productivity and more robust systems. The final section of the chapter will establish the current state of the field and will look forward to the future potential of these techniques, especially in emerging application areas such as ubiquitous computing.

14.2   OVERVIEW OF ISSUES AND FIRST STEPS IN FORMALISM

In order to show some of the aspects of formal methods in interaction design, we'll look at the way simple diagrammatic formalisms can help us examine two simple devices, a wristwatch and an alarm panel. From these, we will see some important general lessons about the advantages of using more formal techniques.

14.2.1   Two Examples

Some years ago, my daughter had a digital wristwatch. The watch had two buttons and came with a set of closely written instructions covering a slip of paper about 2 inches wide (5cm) and 15 inches long (40cm). Figure 14.1 shows one diagram on the paper (much larger than life size!). The two buttons were labeled A and B; this diagram was intended to show the main functions of button A.

From this diagram, we can see that button A switches the watch between four main modes:

Time display: normal mode showing current time and day

Stop watch: timing to seconds and hundredths of a second

Time setting: to set/update the time

Alarm setting: to set the built-in alarm

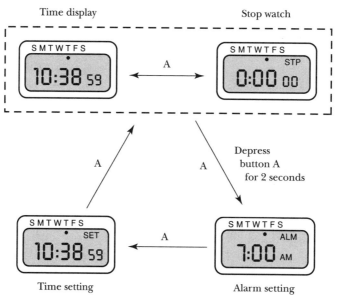

FIGURE   Digital watch instructions.

14.1

This diagram, produced as part of the user documentation, can be seen as a state transition network (STN), a type of formal specification of part of the functions of the watch. STNs have been used extensively in interface specification. They are often written as small circles or boxes representing the potential states of the systems, with arrows between the states showing the possible transitions. The arrows are labeled with the user action that initiated them. Describing states is always difficult, and the digital watch instructions do this by simply drawing what the watch will look like in the state.

Consider an even simpler interface—perhaps the security control panel at a top secret establishment, shown in Figure 14.2 (a) and Plate 13 of the color insert. It has two buttons labeled "+" and "−"—these control the current alarm state, which can be at three levels, or three lights, green, amber, or red.

Imagine we have been given a state transition network for this panel; see Figure 14.2 (b). Just looking at the STN—without knowing what it is about—we can ask some questions: What does the "+" button do when the state is red; what does the "−" button do when the state is green? This is a formal analysis—we don't need to know what the STN means, but we can see just from the pattern that something is missing. In many applications, such as a remote control for a television, we would probably want the "+" button to cycle back round from red

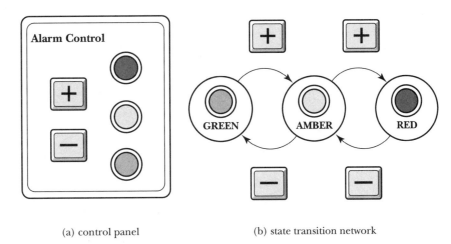

(a) control panel   (b) state transition network

FIGURE   Top secret control panel. (See Plate 13 of the color insert for a color version of
              this figure.)
14.2

to green, but in this application—an operator under stress perhaps—we would probably not want to risk accidentally changing from red alert to green. The formal analysis tells us *that* something extra is needed; the contextual understanding tells us *what* it is.

Looking again at the digital watch, there is a similar story. At first it looks as though it is complete. Only one button is being considered, and the diagram shows what it does in every state. Or does it? What happens from the Time setting state—does it go to Time display, Stop watch, or perhaps whatever state it was in before going into Alarm setting? In fact, after a quick bit of experimentation, it turned out that it always goes to the Time display state.

Also, look at the transition labeled "Depress button A for 2 seconds." This suggests two things:

✦ Time is important.

✦ We need to think about depressing and releasing the button as separate events.

This immediately prompts a series of questions:

✦ Does time matter in either of the "setting" states?

✦ Do the transitions labeled simply "A" mean "when A is depressed" or "when A is released"?

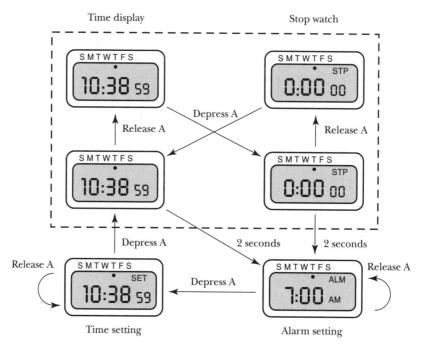

FIGURE 14.3   Digital watch states in detail.

Further experiments showed that the transitions between "Time display" and "Stop watch" happened when the button was pressed. However, clearly the system "remembered" that the button was still down in order to change to "Alarm setting" state after two seconds. Figure 14.3 shows the full picture with the "Time display" and "Stop watch" states each split in two to represent this "remembering."

14.2.2   Lessons

These examples demonstrate several key features of formal descriptions.

formal analysis. It is possible to ask questions about the system from the formal description alone. For example, in the alarm system, we noticed that "+" was missing from the red state. We didn't need to know anything about what the diagram meant (nuclear meltdown, or simply color chooser); we just used the *form* of the diagram alone.

early analysis. In the case of the watch, we actually had the artifact; because we could look at the diagram, however, we could have performed the same analysis before a prototype was available. Even with rapid prototyping, this can save precious resources.

lack of bias. If we had been testing the alarm system without the formal analysis, we might not have thought to try out "unusual" actions like pressing "+" when the alarm was already in "red" state. Testing is often biased toward "normal" behavior—what the designers expect the users to do. Formal analysis helps to break this bias.

alternative perspective. In a single diagram, the formal description looks at the system with every different potential user input. Drawings of the watch early in design would show what it was like (but in greater detail) at individual moments of time. A fully working prototype would give a better feeling for what interaction with the watch was really like, but it still does not let you see different possibilities except by repeatedly experimenting. Different representations therefore allow us to see different things about a design. Furthermore, different kinds of formal representation can allow yet more views on the artifact during design.

forcing design decisions. The watch example is taken from the user documentation and so would not be expected to show all possible fine behaviors (it would simply be confusing). However, one wonders whether the detailed behavior in Figure 14.3 was the result of the designer thinking about what was wanted or arbitrary decisions made while coding the internals of the watch. Using formal representations, the designer is forced to make these user-interface decisions explicitly and to communicate those decisions to the implementor.

On the other hand, the example in Figure 14.3 shows only the behavior of one of the two buttons of a pretty simple device. Formal descriptions, by making you be precise, can become complex through sheer level of detail. However, this extra detail is not being created for the sake of the formal description but is simply exposing the extra decisions that will be there in the final artifact. If they aren't there in the design documents, they will be in the code!

14.3 SCIENTIFIC FOUNDATIONS

In this section we'll look at the history of formalism and how this feeds into current uses of formal notations, formal methods, and general computational theory. Much of this story is about the gradual discovery of the fundamental limits of human knowledge in general and computation in particular.

14.3.1   A Brief History of Formalism

The roots of formalism go back a long way, certainly to Euclid's axiomatization of geometry and to Aristotle and the formalization of logical inference (Rouse Ball, 1908). It is Euclid who had the most significant impact on mathematical education. It is amazing to think that Euclid's *Elements* was still being used as a high school text book 2200 years after it was written! However, it is Aristotle who is the more "modern" thinker. Despite coming through the Platonic school of perfect forms, he was able to look to the world as it is—the beginnings of empiricism. But he also based this on two pillars of self-consistent and sufficient basic truths in theology and logic (or mathematics).

Of course, many things happened over the next 2000 years: Arabic mathematics with the introduction of zero and the modern digits, and the development of calculus (differentiation and integration), which enabled the formulation of modern physics, engineering, economics, and much more. However, this is not the story of mathematics, but formalism, so we'll skip forward to the nineteenth century.

Galois is one of my heroes.[1] He set "group theory" on a formal footing. Group theory is, in one sense, a very abstract branch of mathematics; yet, like numbers, it is an abstraction of common phenomena, such as the number of ways you can put a computer back into its box (upside down, rotated 180 degrees, etc.). Group theory can tell us that the slider puzzle shown here cannot be solved, and it also underlies modern quantum mechanics, but above all Galois set it in a formal framework that is the pattern for much of modern mathematics. That is why he is an important step in the story of formalism, but not why he is my hero. Galois' theory did all this and also was the key to solving a whole range of open problems about the roots of polynomials and what can be constructed with ruler and compasses, many of which were unsolved since the height of Greek geometry 2000 years previously. I particularly like the fact that his theoretical framework largely proves what you can't do, foreshadowing some of the great results of the twentieth century. And he did all this before, at the age of 20, he was killed in a duel. Beat that!

The nineteenth century saw Cantor's formulation of set theory, which is at the heart of virtually all mathematics and is also the foundation of many "formal"

---

[1] Evariste Galois, born in Paris in 1811.

methods in computing.[2] For example, it is set theory that gives us the vocabulary to talk about the set of possible keys the user could press:

```
Input = { 'a', 'b', . . . , 'z', '0', '1', . . . }
```

From this and functions between sets, we can talk about the set of states of a system, and the function that maps the current state to the new state depending on the current input:

```
update: State × Input → State
```

Although there were problems and setbacks, the nineteenth century in mathematics, as in so many fields, was one of rising optimism. At the turn of the century, mathematicians' success was so great that they began to ask fundamental questions of the discipline itself: Could all mathematics be performed strictly formally, without insight or understanding, simply by playing out the rules? Various major steps were taken, and problems in the theory of infinite sets were solved (problems uncovered by Bertrand Russell's paradox of the set of sets that don't contain themselves). Whitehead and Russell began a monumental work of proving basic mathematics with total rigor from logical foundations. It took a major volume to even get as far as statements such as $1+2=2+1$, but progress was being made, and the pair worked their way through several more tortuous volumes.

Not only was mathematics itself progressing, but throughout the nineteenth century mathematics was being used as the language of creation: formulating and integrating the basics of physics, especially in Maxwell's equations, which brought magnetism, static electricity, and electrical current within a single coherent mathematical theory. It seemed as though there would be no end to this progress; the complete and final formulation of all things was within human grasp.

Remember Aristotle's twin pillars: theology and logic. Towards the end of the nineteenth century, Nietzsche, reflecting this spirit of humanistic optimism and self-sufficiency, declared the "death of God," and in the process discarded one of Aristotle's pillars.

By the 1920s, however, the foundations of this optimism had been systematically undermined. The discovery of quantum mechanics and relativity showed that the complete, comprehensive treatment of physics was not around the

---

[2]   Georg Cantor (1845–1918), German mathematician and professor at Halle.

corner and that the world did not behave in ways that made sense at all. World War I hardened an already growing postcentennial cynicism and laid to rest, with the corpses in Flanders, the belief in the moral ascent of man.

But Aristotle's second pillar stood firm and, in the cloistered halls of Cambridge University, Whitehead and Russell labored on. Then, in an obscure conference hall, a young mathematician, Gödel, stood up and announced the death of mathematics. The last pillar had fallen.

14.3.2 The Limits of Knowledge

I said that Galois, in proving the impossibility of many problems, also prefigured the twentieth century. The nineteenth century appeared to be an unstoppable chain of achievement, leading to the belief that everything was possible. In contrast, the successes of the twentieth century have been in understanding what is not possible.

Gödel began this process in mathematics. He proved that any formal system was either incomplete (it couldn't prove some things even though they are true) or inconsistent (proves things that are false), and, moreover, we can't tell which of these is true of any particular system except by applying a different system . . . and then we don't know about that one (Kilmister, 1967).

Gödel showed that our knowledge in mathematics is patchy and full of holes, like Swiss cheese. Not accidental holes, because we haven't got round to finding something out yet, but fundamental holes because they can never be filled.

Given his fundamental reshaping of the intellectual landscape, Gödel should surely rank alongside Einstein. The physics of quantum mechanics and relativity can only be understood through their mathematics, but Gödel cast in doubt the very meaning of the mathematics itself. Gödel found his evangelist in Hofstadter, whose cult book *Gödel, Escher, Bach: An Eternal Golden Braid* popularized many complex issues of incompleteness, self-similarity, and self-reference (Hofstadter, 1979).

14.3.3 The Theory of Computing

The roots of the theory of computation also began during the 1930s, much of it before the first electronic computers. Church and Turing worked on understanding what was possible to compute, whether by clerks in a bank or by a machine, but each dealt with very different models of computation. Church's

Some computer programs finish their job quickly, and others may take a long time but eventually "halt" and give their result. However some programs simply never finish at all; they never halt. Imagine that you have bought a clever program (let's call it `will_halt`) from magisoft.co.uk that tells you whether other programs will eventually halt or not. You then write the following:

```
my_program:
    if will_halt(my_program)
            loop forever
    otherwise stop
```

Does your program halt? If it does, and `will_halt` works this out, then your program will loop for ever; if it doesn't halt and `will_halt` works this out, then it will stop. That is, if it halts it doesn't and if it doesn't it does. Something is wrong! You sensibly return `will_halt` to magisoft as it clearly can't possibly work.

BOX   The Halting Problem

14.1

lambda calculus is a sparse algebraic description of functions using only lines of λs, variables (x,y, . . .), and brackets combined with a small number of "reduction rules." In contrast, the Turing machine consists of a small device running over an infinitely long tape. The magic is that, in a milestone result, it was found that these two models, although different in methods of operation, were exactly equivalent in what they could do. Other models of computation were also found to be equivalent. This is taken as justification (not proof) of the Church–Turing thesis (actually coined by Kleene) and variants, which is a broader hypothesis stating that all computation is fundamentally the same (see the Stanford Encyclopedia of Philosophy).

However, this early theory did more than model computation; it also found its own limits. In a variety of results, most famously the halting problem (see Box 14.1), the theorists of computation found that there were certain useful things that it was impossible to compute.

So, from the very beginning, computation theory has considered its limitations.

14.3.4   Complexity

As important as whether something finishes is how long it takes. If something is going to take 100 years to happen, I don't think I'll wait around. A branch of computing called *complexity theory* deals with these questions "how long," "how much memory," "how many network messages," and, in parallel computers, "how many processors."

Let's think of an electronic newsletter. Each day I email it to my subscribers. If there are 10 subscribers, there are 70 messages per week; if there are 100 subscribers, there are 700 messages per week; for 1000 subscribers, 7000 messages. The number of messages rises linearly with the number of subscribers. If there are n subscribers, this is usually written $O(n)$ (the "O" stands for "order of").

Now let's imagine a mailing list. Each morning, everyone reads all the messages on the list and sends one of their own to *everyone* on the list (including themselves). If there are 10 people, then there will be 700 messages a week—10 people each day sending 10 messages. If there are 100 people, there will be 70,000 messages (7 days × 100 senders × 100 recipients); 1000 people leads to 7 million messages per week. This time, the number of messages rises with the square of the number of people. This is written $O(n^2)$.

Some problems are even worse. Imagine you are a manager trying to work out who should do which job. You decide to try every possible combination and each day assign people accordingly. Say there are two people, Ann and Bob, and two jobs, artist and builder. On day 1 you try Ann as artist and Bob as builder; on day 2 you try Ann as builder and Bob as artist. Two days and you've tried the lot. Now imagine there are three people—Ann, Bob, and Chris—and three jobs— artist, builder, and clerk. This time it is a little more complicated, so you write out the schedule as seen in Table 14.1.

Notice this time that we need six days for three people. When Dave joins the firm, you branch out into medicine and take 24 days to try four people in four jobs. You grow further and find that five people in five jobs takes 120 days, and six people in six jobs takes 720 days. This number is growing as the factorial of the number $O(n!)$. (See Box 14.2.)

At this point you enlist Pete (whom you know is a good programmer!) to write a program that, based on data in the personnel database, simply simulates assigning people to roles and works out the best combination. Pete is good. The program takes only a microsecond to simulate each assignment, so you test the software by running it against your existing six people; in 720 microseconds, less than a millisecond, it gives the answer and agrees with the real experiment. Now that you have solved your personnel-management problems, you happily grow

	Ann	Bob	Chris
day 1	artist	builder	clerk
day 2	artist	clerk	builder
day 3	builder	artist	clerk
day 4	builder	clerk	artist
day 5	clerk	artist	builder
day 6	clerk	builder	artist

TABLE

14.1

Schedule of all possible combinations of jobs for three people.

The factorial of a number is the product of all the numbers less than or equal to it. For example, $6! = 6 \times 5 \times 4 \times 3 \times 2 \times 1$. It grows very rapidly, even faster than an exponential.

n	n!
1	1
2	2
3	6
4	24
5	120
6	720
7	5040
8	40320
9	362880
10	3628800
11	39916800
12	479001600
13	6227020800
14	87178291200
15	1307674368000

BOX

14.2

Factorial

further. When you have 10 employees and 10 jobs, the system checks and finds the best combination: in less than four seconds (3.6288 seconds to be exact) it gives the answer. As you grow to 11 and 12 employees, it seems to be a little sluggish responding, but you put this down to having the monthly accounts running at the same time. However, when you hire your thirteenth employee things start to go wrong. You wait and wait, then ring Pete and get his answering machine; just as he rings back, an hour and three quarters later, the computer comes back to life and gives the answer. "Ah well, it's just one of those funny things computers do," you agree. On the fourteenth employee, you set it going in the morning and then go out to client meetings for the rest of the day. When you get in the next morning, the computer screen looks frozen, perhaps it has crashed; you go to get a cup of coffee and it is waiting there with the answer when you get back . . . curious. But with the fifteenth employee, things are clearly not right—the program seems to run and run but never stop. Pete is on holiday for two weeks, and so you have to wait for his return. When he does, you call him, and he says "ah, I'll have to think about it." The next day he calls and says, "Look at the screen now"—and the answer is there. "That's amazing," you say. "How did you do it?" Then he admits that 15 employees simply took 15 days to complete, but that the sixteenth would require 242 days; if you want to grow to 20 employees, you will need to wait seventy-seven thousand years for the answer. Twenty-four employees would take 20 billion years, longer than the age of the universe. Ah, well, they do say small is beautiful.

It is so easy to assume that computers are fast and can do anything, but if the underlying problem or algorithm doesn't scale no amount of speed will be enough. Problems like the last one that involve trying lots of combinations are known as nonpolynomial as there is no polynomial (power of n) that bounds them. Even quadratic, $O(n^2)$, algorithms grow in difficulty pretty rapidly (as in the mailing list), and to be really scalable one tries to find things that aren't too much worse than linear. For example, simple sorting algorithms are $O(n^2)$, but there are faster algorithms that are $O(n \log_2 n)$. This means that sorting 2 items takes about 2×1 steps, 4 items takes 4×2 steps, 8 items 8×3, 256 items 256×8, and so on. This is longer than linear, but massively faster than a slow quadratic sort (32 times faster for 256 items, and 100 times faster for 1024 items).

14.3.5   Good Enough

Notice that the halting problem is about a program that can *always* tell us whether other programs halt; the personnel allocation program tries *every* combination in order to find the *best* solution. This is traditional algorithmics—deterministic methods that, excepting for simulations, dominated the first 25 years of programming and still form the main part of virtually all current systems and computing syllabi.

However, since the mid-1970s, a second strand has emerged that is focused on *usually* getting an answer, or trying *enough* things to get a *reasonably good* answer. Methods in this strand include simulated annealing, neural networks, and genetic algorithms, but there are also numerous more specialized algorithms that employ elements of approximation or randomness to solve problems that would otherwise be impossible or intractable. Many of these techniques are based on analogies with physical or biological systems: simulated annealing—the cooling of metals; neural networks—brains; genetic algorithms—natural selection; and recent work has been inspired by the behavior of colonies such as ants or bees.

14.3.6   Agents and Interaction

The early theory of computing was also very much concerned with all or nothing computation—you give the computer a problem and then wait for the result. In HCI, we are more interested in interaction where we constantly give little bits of input to a device and get little bits of response. To be fair, computational models that involve interacting agents have been around since the early days of computing. For example, cellular automata (CA), made popular by Conway's Game of Life (Berlekamp, Conway, & Guy, 1982; Gardner, 1970)—see Box 14.3—were originally proposed by von Neumann, one of the pioneers of computing (1956, 1966). However, for a long time such interactions were mainly concerned with what happened *within* a computing system (typically as a computational model or parallel or distributed computing). This has gradually changed, and it is now common to consider models of multiple agents interacting with one another, the environment, and human users.

This view of computation as involving interacting entities has both practical and theoretical implications. My own studies of human processes emphasize the importance of initiative—who makes things happen and when (Dix, 1998; Dix, Ramduny-Ellis, & Wilkinson, 2002). This is certainly a key element in many areas of practical computing, too, but until recently not a major part of the vocabulary of fundamental computation theory. Wegner has suggested (1997) that the fundamentally different nature of interaction may mean that interacting computers are fundamentally more powerful than all-or-nothing computation.

Imagine a large board of squares such as a chess or Go board. Each square either contains a token (is alive) or doesn't (is dead). Now, for each square, you look at its eight neighbors and apply the following simple rules:

> overcrowding: If more than three are alive, the square becomes (or stays) dead.

> loneliness: If less than two are alive, the square becomes (or stays) dead.

> birth: If exactly three are alive and the square is dead, it becomes alive.

> Otherwise, the square stays as it was.

The rules are regarded as operating at the same moment over the whole board (that is, not in sequence).

If you regard each square as a small computational device, Life is a form of cellular automata (CA). CA differ in how many states each device has (just two here, alive or dead), how many neighbors are considered, the geometry of the "board" (2D, 3D, different shaped grids), and the complexity of the rules.

BOX   Conway's Game of Life

14.3

Working at a time when there were no physical computers, Turing was radical in ensuring that the models of computation he used were physically realizable. However, as real computers became available, this view was somehow lost, and computation theory became more and more abstract. And to some extent we now see signs of a more grounded theory as computational devices are scattered among our everyday lives. I call this more physical view *embodied computation* and find that it radically changes the way I personally look at computation (Dix, 2002a).

14.3.7   Notations and Specification

Although a large part of mathematics is about manipulating formulae, it is re-markably laid back about notations. There are some fairly standard symbols (e.g., basic arithmetic, upside down ∀ for "forall" and back to front ∃ for "ex-ists"), but these are regarded as a convention rather than a standard. In individu-al parts of mathematics and in individual papers and books, variants are used for the same thing and special notation introduced on an *ad hoc* basis.

Computing has always been more conservative about notation. Perhaps this is because of its connections with the more "formal" parts of mathematics, per-haps because of links with electrical engineering where standardization is more important (if a mathematician gets confused, she wastes paper; if an electrician is confused, he dies). Possibly, also, it is because computer science has had to cre-ate notations (programming languages) to communicate with computers and has let the same mindset leak into notations to communicate with one another!

No matter the reasons, notation is very important. However, this doesn't mean that there is no *ad hoc* development of notations. Indeed, in some areas of computing—both in programming languages and in formal areas—it seems as if every paper has a new notation. The difference is that the notation itself is seen as significant: the end, not just the tool. The few notations that have become widely used have earned their originators cult status and have found their adher-ents in often hostile factions. Notation is the religion of computer science!

In mathematics, notations are most widely used to talk about general proper-ties of classes of mathematical structure. In contrast, computing notations are most often developed to analyze or specify the behavior of particular systems. Specification, the production of a precise description of an existing or intended system, has become almost synonymous with "formal methods."

14.3.8   Kinds of Notation

The formal notations that have been influential in computing fall into two main camps. The first is *finite process*—notations capturing the sequences and processes of computation in terms of a finite number of stages, phases, states, or steps. This includes many diagrammatic representations such as state-transition networks and flowcharts, and also textual notations such as formal grammars and produc-tion rules.

The second is *infinite state*—more obviously mathematical notations using ei-ther set and function notation, or a more "algebraic" representation. The most common of these is "Z," which was originally developed by the programming research group at Oxford (Spivey, 1988).

One of the enduring problems in computing has been representing and reasoning about *concurrent activity*. One thing at a time is difficult enough, but several things happening at once spell analytic breakdown! However, this is particularly important for HCI, as even a simple interface involves the human and computer working together. Collaboration and networking add to this,

In fact, one of the oldest diagrammatic notations in computing is Petri Nets, which was designed to represent concurrent and parallel activity (Petri, 1962; see also Petri Nets World). This has a small but continuing and dedicated community. Probably more influential (possibly because they look more like programming languages) have been the more algebraic notations for concurrency, CCS (Calculus of Communicating Systems) and CSP (Communicating Sequential Processes) (Hoare, 1985; Milner, 1980). These cover very similar ground to one another and, perhaps because of this, have been the source of some of the deepest internecine strife in computing. CCS has been the basis for an ISO standard notation LOTOS (Language of Temporal Ordering Specifications) (1989). Both Petri Nets and LOTOS have been used extensively in HCI.

14.4 DETAILED DESCRIPTION

In this section, we'll look at how different aspects of mathematical, formal, and algorithmic methods can be used in HCI.

14.4.1 Two Plus Two—Using Simple Calculation

Straightforward mathematical calculations are everywhere in HCI. These range in complexity. At the simplest are simple arithmetic, for example, in the Goals, Operators, Methods, and Selection rules (GOMS) keystroke-level model (Card, Moran, & Newell, 1980, 1983). The models behind information-foraging theory (see Chapter 7, this volume) are more complex, using differential equations. In areas such as visualization, information retrieval, and graphics, mathematics is again central.

Even small, "back of the envelope" calculations can be surprisingly effective in helping one to understand a problem. I recall some years ago thinking through the statement (which I'm sure you've seen as well) that graphical displays have high "bandwidth." This obviously has to be interpreted in terms of

Compare the keyboard with the screen for rate of entry measured in bits per second.

Keyboard:
Take typing times from KLM times quoted in Dix and colleagues (1998).

```
nos targets — 64 keys
good typist — 9 keys per sec.
rate = 9 * log²(64) = 54 bps
```

Screen:
Screen width W with items size S on it. The average distance to target is half the width. To make calculations easier, assume a square screen and that the screen is completely filled with targets.

Fitts' Law—$0.1 \log_2 (D/S + 0.5)$
$D = W/2$
nos items—$(W/S)^2$

$$\text{rate} = \frac{\log_2 ((W/S)^2)}{0.1 \log_2 (W/2S + 0.5)}$$

$$\approx \frac{2 \log_2 (W/S)}{0.1 \log_2 (W/S)}$$

$$= 20 \text{ bps}$$

So, screen clicking is nearly three times slower than typing!

BOX   Back of the Envelope

14.4

visual perception, not just raw pixels per second, but I'll accept it for output. But what about input—do screen buttons and icons increase that? In fact, a quick Fitts' Law calculation shows that no matter what the number and size of the screen buttons, a reasonable typing speed is always faster (see Box 14.4). The difference is that, whereas the lexicon of the keyboard is fixed and has to be interpreted by the user in any context, graphical user interfaces (GUIs) can be contextual, showing appropriate actions. (If you know any information theory, this is a form of adaptive compression.) Notice that a small mathematical argument can lead to a design perspective.

Let's work through a similar example. Often the $7+/-2$ rule (Miller, 1956), which is about working memory, is mistakenly overapplied. One example is for menu systems; you may well have seen suggestions that the number of menu items per screen (e.g., on a Web page) shouldn't exceed $7+/-2$. On a touch screen, large targets are easier to hit, again suggesting that small numbers of larger targets are a good idea. However, the fewer menu items on a single screen, the more menu levels that are required to find particular content. Let's assume there are N items in total, and you choose to have M menu items per screen. The depth of the menu hierarchy, d, is given by:

$$d = \log N / \log M$$

If we look at a single display, the total time taken will be the time taken to physically display the screen and the time taken for the user to select the item, all times the number of levels:

$$T_{total} = (T_{display} + T_{select}) \times d$$

Using Fitts' Law for T_{select} and the formula for d, we get:

$$T_{total} = (T_{display} + A + B \log M) \times \log N / \log M$$
$$= ((T_{display} + A)/ \log M + B) \times \log N$$

Notice that the effect of the increased number of screens exactly balances the gains of larger targets, and the only factor that varies with the number of menu items is the per-screen costs ($T_{display} + A$). This suggests that the more items per screen the better. Look at virtually any portal site, and you'll see that practical experience has come to the same conclusion!

In fact, there are extra factors to consider; for very small targets, Fitts' Law starts to break down, which puts lower limits on target size. Also, errors are significant, as they cause wasted screen displays, so smaller numbers of well-explained items may be better. For larger numbers of items, a further factor sets in—the time taken for the user to locate an item on the display. There is evidence that, for linear menus, the actual select time is closer to linear than logarithmic. Redoing the calculations shows that this visual search becomes the limiting factor for larger screens, leading to a maximum menu size depending on refresh time (which is still much larger than $7+/-2$ for most cases!) However, good design of screen organization and subheadings can push this visual search back toward the logarithmic case (see Larson & Czerwinski, 1998). For WAP (wireless application protocol) with small scrolling displays, the figures are again different.

Notice that being precise forces us to make assumptions explicit, and also, by focusing us on the critical factors, helps us look for potential design solutions.

14.4.2   Detailed Specification

One of the main uses of formal methods in HCI, as in other areas of computing, has been to specify the behavior of specific systems. There are three reasons for doing this:

+ to analyze the system to assess potential usability measures or problems;

+ to describe the system in sufficient detail so that the system that is implemented is what the designer intends;

+ as a side effect of the previous item, the process of specification forces the designer to think about the system clearly and to consider issues that would otherwise be missed.

Some of the earliest work in this area used formal grammars, in particular Reisner's work on BNF (Backus-Naur Form) (1981). The strand of work arising from this is described in detail in Chapter 6.

Closely related to this is the widespread use of diagrammatic representations of dialogue structure, including the uses of STNs (as in Section 14.2). Diagrammatic formalisms are often seen as being less formal, with implications (depending on your viewpoint) of being (1) less rigorous or (2) more accessible. It is certainly the case that, for many people, diagrams are more immediately appealing, but they can be just as rigorous as more obviously "mathematical"-looking notations (see Box 14.5). The main "informality" of many graphical notations is in the labels for boxes and arcs, which are typically important for understanding the real meaning of the diagram, but not interpreted within the formalism. As we'll see in the case study in Section 14.5, this is actually a very powerful feature.

As noted earlier, human-computer dialogue typically involves multiple, potentially concurrent strands of activity. Even something as simple as a dialogue box may have many button groups, each easy to discuss individually, but all can be used in an arbitrary order by the user. The HCI group at Toulouse, France, pioneered the use of an object-based variant of Petri Nets called ICO (Interactive Cooperative Objects) for specifying user-interface properties (Palanque & Bastide, 1995). Recall that the Petri Net formalism was designed precisely to be able to manage concurrent activity. Petri Nets have a long-standing analytic theory, which can be used to analyze the resulting representations of systems, used both in Toulouse and by others who have adopted Petri Nets. The Toulouse

> The idea that graphical equals informal would have been very strange to the Greek geometers and many (not all) mathematicians for whom diagrams are critical for understanding. When Newton wrote his treatise on gravity and motion, *Principia Mathematica,* he deliberately used geometric explanation rather than more textual notations, because he thought the mathematical explanation would make things too easy. Only really clever people would be able to understand the diagrams!

BOX   Newton's *Principia Mathematica*

14.5

group have worked for some years using their formalism in the design of air-traffic-control interfaces and have recently created design and analysis tools for the approach (Navarre et al., 2001).

Another successful approach to concurrency has been the use of LOTOS at the CNUCE Institute in Pisa, Italy. It is interesting to note, however, that this work has found greater external interest since the emphasis shifted from full use of the LOTOS notation to a diagrammatic representation of task hierarchies, called ConcurTaskTrees (CTT), where groups of subtasks are linked using concurrency operators from LOTOS (making more precise the plans in standard HTAs [Hierarchical Task Analysis] [Shepherd, 1995]). The original intention of this was as a bridge toward full use of LOTOS, but it has gradually stolen the limelight. Again, a critical feature has been the introduction of a support tool CTTE (ConcurTaskTrees Editor) (Paternó, 2000; Paternó, Mori, & Galimbert; 2001; Paternó & Santoro, 2001).

These are all notations and formalisms where the principal focus is on the flow of dialogue. Others have used state-oriented notations such as Z to specify systems. One of the earliest examples of this is Sufrin's (1982) specification of a "display editor" (in contrast to command line) back in 1982. Algebraic notations have also been used (Torres et al., 1996). I find that these full specifications really force one to think hard about the system that is being designed.

A simple example I use with students and in tutorials is a four-function calculator. What is in the state? Clearly there is a number that is currently displayed, but many students get stuck there. The parts that have no immediate display are harder to think about as a designer. However, this hidden state is also more confusing for the user when it behaves unexpectedly, so it is more important that the designer gets it right.

```
user types: 1 + 2  7 = − 3
start after 1 + 2
```

action	display	pend_op	total
	2	+	1
digit(7)	27	+	1
equals	28	none	28
op(−)	28	−	28
digit(3)	**283 !!!**	−	28

BOX

14.6

Calculator Scenario

Some of the extra detail becomes apparent when you think about particular user actions—when the = key is pressed, the calculator must know what operation to do (+,−,*,÷) and what the previous value was, so the state must record a "pending" operation and a running total.

The other method I find useful is to play through a scenario annotated with the values of various state variables. Doing this to the calculator (see Box 14.6) shows that an additional flag is needed to distinguish the case when you just typed "2" from when you just typed "1+1." In both cases the display says "2," but in the former case typing an additional "3" would give you "23," whereas in the latter case it would be "3."

Of course, formal notations are not very useful unless they give some benefit. In the hands of an expert analyst, the process of producing a detailed specification will reveal new insights into the usability of the system. However, formal specification also allows the opportunity for more automated analysis. Automatic proof tools have been used, but they are still difficult to use. Because of this, there has been a growing interest in model checking tools that enable (still quite simple) properties to be checked automatically (Abowd, Wang, & Monk, 1995; Paternó & Santoro, 2001). One advantage of these is that, if a property fails, then the normal output of the checking tool is a trace of user actions that would cause the violation—a crude scenario that can be fed back to those not expert in formal techniques.

Dialogue specifications were used extensively in the early user-interface management systems (UIMS) (Pfaff & ten Hagen, 1985). For a period, these were less extensively used, partly because the ready availability of event or object-based GUI builders lead to a more "try it and see" model of UI construction. However, there has been a growing research agenda in computer-aided design and construction of user interfaces (for example, the CADUI conference series).

A significant area within this has been "model-based" user-interface-development environments including UIDE (Foley & Sukaviriya, 1995), MASTERMIND (Szekely et al., 1996), and TADEUS (Elwert & Schlungbaum, 1995). These have some sort of model of the user's task, the underlying application semantics, and the device capabilities. The designer creates the models using a notation or design environment, and then the system automatically generates the actual user interface. This is particularly powerful when targeting multiple devices—for example, PDA (Personal Digital Assistant), WAP, Web, as well as standard desktop interfaces.

14.4.3   Modeling for Generic Issues

The area of formal methods with which I am most associated personally, and which perhaps is the beginning of formal methods in HCI as an identifiable area, is the strand of modeling started in York, England, in the mid-1980s, typified by the PIE model (Dix & Runciman, 1985).

The PIE model takes a general view of an interactive application as a transformer of the history of user actions (for historical reasons labeled P) into a current display and possibly also some kind of additional result (printout, saved document). This model and variants of it were used to specify and analyze a range of general user interface issues, mainly to do with the users' ability to predict future behavior based on the available display and their ability to reach desired goals in the system (Dix, 1991).

$$P \xrightarrow{\;I\;} E \begin{array}{c} \nearrow R \\ \text{result} \\[4pt] \searrow \text{display} \\ D \end{array}$$

This use of formal methods is particularly powerful, because one is able to make inferences about properties of a whole class of systems. The cost of working with very precise models is defrayed over many systems, which are instances of the general class.

Other examples of this kind of activity include work on understanding case-based systems as used in help desks (Dearden & Harrison, 1995), and the modeling of authoring environments for educational media (Kotze, 1997). Abstract formal modeling has even been used to formalize some of the cognitive dimensions properties found in Chapter 5 (Roast & Siddiqi, 1996).

A topic that has been studied intermittently from the very first PIE paper (Dix & Runciman, 1985) onwards has been **Undo.** This is partly because it is a generic issue and so a good one to deal with using such models, and partly because the nature of **Undo** makes it a good candidate for formalization. Some systems try to make **Undo** reverse the effect of any previous command, including itself. Quite early on, we were able to show that (with the exception of two-state systems like light switches!) this was impossible and that **Undo** has to be regarded as a different kind of meta-action. There has been a substantial amount of work since then, including group **Undo** (see Section 14.4.4). However, the most complete treatment of **Undo** has been in Mancini's thesis (1997), which captures the multilevel nature of **Undo.** The same model, "the cube," based on a form of the PIE model, was also used to model "back" and "history" mechanisms in hypertext and the Web, showing how formalism can expose and capitalize on similarities between disparate phenomena (Dix & Mancini, 1997; Dix, Mancini, & Levialdi, 1997).

14.4.4   Computer-Supported Cooperative Work and Groupware

Formal modeling and specification work has not been limited to single user interaction. As well as specifications of particular systems, there are a number of areas that have had more extensive analysis. One example is workflow packages, which are based on various kinds of models of collaborative processes. Here the formal representation is largely in order to build a system, which is reminiscent of the use of formal dialogue notations in early UIMS.

An area that has required deeper formal treatment is distributed editing and group **Undo** (see Box 14.7). The problems with the latter are mainly due to "race" conditions when two people edit parts of the document virtually simultaneously, and messages between their computers pass one another on the network (Dix, 1995a; Ellis & Gibbs, 1989). Group **Undo** problems are perhaps more fundamental as there are similar implementation issues, and it is also unclear what is the right thing to happen anyway! (See Abbowd & Dix, 1992.)

Although there have been a number of papers dealing with specifications of particular computer-supported cooperative work (CSCW) issues (e.g., Palanque & Bastide, 1996), there are few notations aimed specifically at this area. CTT is an exception, as it has been extended to explicitly deal with several people cooperating on a task (Paternó, 2000). My own LADA (A Logic for the Analysis of Distributed Action) notation is another example (Dix, 1995b). As well as using formal methods to talk about the groupware systems themselves, there has been some work in using formalisms to understand the human side of collaboration. Winograd and Flores' (1986) use of speech-act theory embodied in the Coordinator tool is one example. Belief logics and related formalisms (Devlin, 1994;

BOX   Group **Undo**

14.7

Ellis & Wainer, 1994) have also been used to formalize the shared and disparate beliefs and knowledge of collaborating people. This could be seen as a formal parallel of the sort of shared understanding described in Chapter 10. Another example of this type of work has been the use of artificial life and game theory to understand collaboration (Marsh, 1994).

14.4.5   Time and Continuous Interaction

In applied mathematics, for example simple mechanics, one typically deals with continuous phenomena such as the location and velocity of a ball:

$$\frac{dv}{dt} = -g \qquad \frac{dx}{dt} = v$$

In contrast, computing tends to deal with discrete values at clocked time points. Instead of rates of change, we look at state changes at particular events or on clock ticks. Certain types of system include discrete computer controllers interacting with continuous real-world phenomena, for example, a fly-by-wire aircraft or an industrial controller. A branch of formal specification has grown up to deal with such phenomena, called *hybrid systems* (Grossman et al., 1993), but it is very much a minority area compared with the discrete formal-methods community. The hybrid systems area also draws a sharp distinction between discrete computer components and continuous physical ones.

Even in desktop interfaces, there are phenomena that are continuous, such as the movement of the mouse, and others that we perceive as continuous, such as the location of an icon we are dragging. For many years, I have argued that these status phenomena are important and should be dealt with on a par with event phenomena (Dix 1991a, 1991b, 1996, 1998). More recently, virtual reality, ubiquitous computing, and similar areas have further emphasized the importance of these phenomena, and various strands of modeling work have ensued—including a European Union project, TACIT, focused on continuous phenomena, which used notations from the hybrid systems area (Doherty, Massink, & Faconti, 2001) and other work based on systems theory (Wûthrich, 1999).

A related area that has always been a hot topic personally is time. Delays and timing have long been seen as important in HCI (Schneiderman, 1984). However, there was a period from roughly the mid-1980s to mid-1990s when it was assumed that personal computers were getting faster and faster and so problems due to time would go away. This led to implicit design assumptions I called the "myth of the infinitely fast machine" (Dix, 1987). It was an area I have returned to several times in formal and semiformal material (Dix, Ramduny, & Wilkinson, 1998) until, largely due to delays on the Web, it became widely clear that computers just wouldn't get "fast enough." Recent formal work in the area has included attempts to deal with multiple granularity in time (Kutar, Britton, & Nehaniv, 2001).

14.4.6   Paradigms and Inspiration

There has been a rich interplay between cognitive and computational models since the earliest days of computing. Cognitive models have influenced artificial intelligence (AI) research and neural networks, and AI models and computer-like architectures have been used to model human cognition. There is an even longer Pygmalion tradition of constructing humanoids in clockwork, steam, and flesh enlivened with electricity—looking to the latest technology in the hope of capturing the essence of the animus that makes us human. The human as computer model is perhaps simply the latest in this line, but it has been informative and successful despite that.

Computational analogies can similarly be useful as a way of understanding various interface phenomena.

If we assume users have perfect knowledge of the system and its behavior, they should be able to work out an optimal route through the system to their goal. This can be seen as an AI-planning model of human interaction and is the implicit model behind a variety of optimal-path interaction metrics (Thimbleby, Cairns, & Jones, 2001).

However, much of interaction is more contingent. We sort of know what we want, and when we see it we may recognize it or at least see that one state of the system is closer than another. Our interaction with the system is more of a goal-seeking behavior, seeking a partly understood goal within a partly understood system. For such systems, search and optimization algorithms may be better models than planning.

Search and optimization is a huge area within computing, and it is complex partly because many of the problems are intractable (in the sense of exponential time)—you cannot consider every possible solution. One class of methods is called *hill climbing*. You take a partial solution and look at all closely neighboring solutions. If all of them are less good, then your current solution is (locally) the best. If any are better, you take the best of the solutions you considered as your new current solution. This is like walking in the hills and always taking the steepest upward path. Eventually you come to a hill top. The problem with steepest-ascent hill climbing is that you are only guaranteed to get to some hill top, not the biggest. If you start in Cambridge, in England, you are likely to end up at the top of the Gog-Magog hills (approximately 100 meters, or 300 feet); if you start at Kathmandu, the peak you end up at will be much higher! Locations such as the Gog-Magog hills, which are higher than anything close, but not highest of all, are called *local maxima*.

One solution to this, which has been very powerful in AI game-playing algorithms, is to find a *heuristic* (Finlay & Dix, 1996). This tells you not how good a partial solution is, but how good further solutions in a particular direction are likely to be. For example, in chess you can score a board position based on the values of the pieces. With a suitable heuristic, one can perform hill climbing (or variants), but based on the heuristic rather than on the actual value. In real hill climbing, instead of looking at the heights just one step away, one scans the horizon to see which direction looks more mountainous.

In a user interface, this reminds us how important it is for users to be able to predict what will happen if they perform actions. Direct manipulation and graphical interfaces are particularly bad at this because vision is a here-and-now sense (see my discussion of visual versus "nasal" interfaces [Dix, 1996]). Surprisingly few visualization systems give you this sort of "over the horizon" view to enable a heuristic search. Two exceptions are HiBrowse (Ellis, Finlay, & Pollitt, 1994), which allows you to selectively drill down hierarchical attributes in a database, telling you how many items would be selected if you choose particular values; and Influence Explorer (Tweedie et al., 1995), a dynamic slider-based visualization that has histograms of selected items and also (differently colored) items that just miss one or two selection criteria. At a broader level, information scent (Chapter 7) is a form of heuristic.

Another good solution to avoid local maxima in the computer domain is adding randomness, either just starting at random locations and doing a simple hill climb, or being a bit random in one's exploration, not *always* taking the best path (e.g., simulated annealing). Thimbleby and colleagues (2001) model interfaces as finite graphs and use various graph theoretic properties to analyze potential usability. Their methods include constructing Markov models, which measure how likely users are to make particular state transitions (or perform particular actions depending on the current state). In various interfaces, they find that random strategies perform better than typical user behavior, because users have mistaken models and hence planning strategies fail! This is also one of the reasons why children perform better with computer systems and household appliances than adults—they are less afraid to experiment randomly. (See my randomness Web pages for more about algorithms that exploit stochastic properties [Dix, 2002b]).

Search is just one example where we can draw analogies between algorithms and interfaces to give us inspiration for design (and for algorithms). However, search is special, not just because goal-directed exploration is a general interface issue, but also because the process of design itself is a form of goal-directed search.

Consider the normal pattern of prototyping-oriented design:

1. think of an initial design

2. evaluate it

3. consider alternatives to fix bugs or improve the design

4. select the best

5. evaluate that

6. . . . iterate . . .

In fact, this is precisely hill-climbing behavior and has exactly the same problems of local maxima—designs that cannot be incrementally improved but are not necessarily that good.

A really good designer will have some idea of the final solution, based on experience and insight; so the initial start point is more likely to be a "Kathmandu" prototype than a "Cambridge" one.

Given that not all designers are so inspired, traditional graphical design practice usually includes several diverse start-points before commencing more incremental improvements—a form of hill climbing with random start-points.

However, it is analytic and theoretical approaches that can give us the ability to have heuristics, assessing more accurately the potential directions. This is particularly important in novel areas where we have little experience to guide our intuition.

So, if you are a brilliant designer in a well-trodden area—do what you like. Otherwise, a prototyping-based UI development process is essential as we don't understand users or interfaces well enough to produce the right system the first time, but prototyping is fundamentally flawed unless it is guided by an analytic and theoretical framework.

14.4.7   Socio-Organizational Church-Turing Hypothesis

I'll conclude this section by discussing another area where computation can act as a paradigm or inspiration.

An organization has many aspects: social, political, financial. However, among these diverse roles, many organizations perform an information-processing role: transforming orders into delivery instructions and invoices, student exams into degree certificates. Recall that the Church–Turing thesis postulates that all computation is fundamentally equivalent. This only covers what is possible to achieve, not how it happens, which of course is very different!

However, practical experience shows that all practical computational devices tend to exhibit similar structures and phenomena. This is why models of physical computation have proved so effective in cognitive modeling and vice versa. If we apply this to an organization, we get the *socio-organizational Church–Turing hypothesis,* a term coined by Wilkinson, Ramduny-Ellis, and myself at a workshop in York some years ago (Dix, Wilkinson, & Ramduny, 1998; Dix, 2002c). If we look at the information-processing aspects of an organization, we would expect to see similar structures and phenomena to those in mechanical computation devices.

For example, computers have different kinds of memory—long-term memory (hard disks) and short-term memory (RAM and processor registers). In an organization, the former is typically explicit in terms of filing cabinets of paper or computer systems, and the latter is often held in people's heads or scribbled in notes on jotters.

A special part of the memory of a computer system is the program counter, which says what part of a program the computer is currently executing. The organizational analogy is the state of various formal and informal processes. If we look for these *placeholders* for the state of organizational processes, we typically find them either in people's memory or to-do lists, or in the physical

	computational parallels		
	computer	cognitive model	organization
process	program	procedural memory	processes
data	data	long-term memory	files
placeholder	program counter	short-term memory/activation	location of artifacts
initiative	interrupts, event-driven	stimuli	triggers

TABLE

14.2

Structural parallels of the socio-organizational Church-Turing hypothesis.

placement of papers and other artifacts. That is, the office ecology is part of the organization's working memory; cleaners who tidy up are brainwashing the organization!

Table 14.2 summarizes the structural parallels among computers, cognitive models, and organizations.

14.5   CASE STUDY—DIALOGUE SPECIFICATION FOR TRANSACTION PROCESSING

As my case study, I'm going to use not a recent example, but one from more than 15 years ago—in fact, from before I became a computing academic, and before I'd even heard the term HCI! At the time, I was working for Cumbria County Council, in England, working on transaction-processing programs in COBOL, the sort of thing used for stock control or point-of-sale terminals in large organizations.

Why such an old example, rather than a more sexy and up-to-date one? Well, first, because this sort of system is still very common. In addition, the issues in these large centralized transaction-processing systems are similar to those of Web-based interfaces, especially e-commerce systems. Third, it is a resounding success story, which is not too common in this area, and a 1000% performance improvement is worth shouting about. Finally, and most significantly, because it was a success it gives us a chance to analyze why it was so successful and what this tells us about using formalism today.

The other thing I ought to note is that, although this was a successful application of formal methods in interface design, I didn't understand *why* at the time. It is only comparatively recently that I've come to understand the rich interplay of factors that made it work and so perhaps I'm now able to produce guidelines to help reproduce that success.

14.5.1   Background—Transaction Processing

Transaction-processing systems such as IBM CICS have been the workhorses of large scale information systems, stock management, and order processing since the late 1970s. They are designed to be able to accept many thousands of active users.

Architecturally, these systems are based around a central server (or cluster) connected to corporate databases and running the transaction-processing engine (see Figure 14.4). In the system I worked with, this was an ICL mainframe; in Web-based applications, however, it will simply be a Web server or enterprise server. The user interacts with a form-based front end. In the systems I dealt with in the mid-1980s, the front end was semi-intelligent terminals capable of tabbing between fields. Subsequently, in many areas these were replaced by personal computers running "thin client" software and now are often Web-based forms. The centralization of data and transaction processing ensures integrity of the corporate data, but the fact that users interact primarily with local terminals/PCs/browsers means that the central server does not have to manage the full load of the users' interactions.

When the user interacts, the succession of events is as follows:

1. user fills in form on terminal;

2. terminal may perform some initial validation (e.g., numbers vs. letters, range checks, date format, or, on thin PC client or Javascript on Web forms, more complex validation);

3. user checks and then submits form (presses special key or screen button);

4. terminal/PC/browser sends form data as a message to the transaction-processing engine (e.g., CICS or Web server) on the central server;

5. transaction-processing engine selects appropriate application module for message (based on last screen/Web page or information in message);

6. application module interprets message (form data), does further checks, performs any database updates, gets any required data from the database, and generates a new screen/Web page as result;

7. transaction processing engine passes this back to the terminal;

8. terminal presents the screen/Web page to the user.

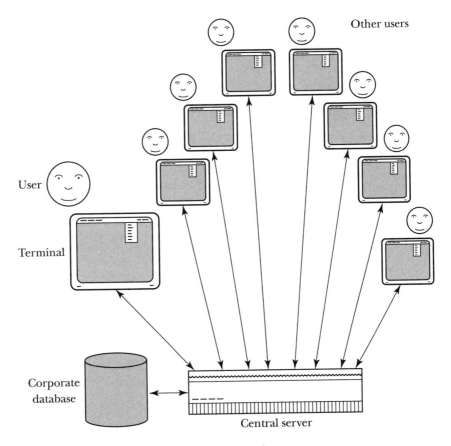

FIGURE

14.4

Physical architecture of a transaction-processing system.

All these stages except the sixth one are managed by the transaction-processing infrastructure. This sounds as if the job in designing this part should be straightforward, as if most of the complexity of dealing with detailed user interactions has been dealt with. But it is not quite as simple as all that.

14.5.2   The Problem . . .

In a graphical user interface (GUI) or any single user interface, the succession of events in the program is straightforward:

1. user event 1 arrives (e.g., mouse press)

2. deal with event and update display

3. user event 2 arrives (e.g., mouse release)

4. deal with event and update display

5. user event 3 arrives (e.g., key click)

6. deal with event and update display

As we know, this can cause enough problems!

In a transaction-processing system, with one user, the application module may receive messages (with form data) in a similar fashion. However, the whole point of such systems is that they have many users. The module may therefore receive messages from different users interleaved:

1. message 1 for user A received

2. deal with message and generate new screen/Web page for user A

3. message 1 for user B received

4. deal with message and generate new screen/Web page for user B

5. message 2 for user B received

6. deal with message and generate new screen/Web page for user B

7. message 2 for user A received

8. deal with message and generate new screen/Web page for user A

The transaction-processing engine deals with passing the new screens back to the right user, but the application module has to do the right things with the form data in the messages. In the case of simple transactions, this may not be a problem; for example, if the application simply allows the user to enter an ISBN (International Standard Book Number) for a book and then returns data about that book, the system can simply deal with each message in isolation. However, a more complex dialogue will require some form of state to be preserved between transactions. For example, a request to delete a book may involve an initial screen where the user fills in the ISBN, followed by a confirmation screen showing the details of the book to be deleted. Only then, if confirmed, will the system actually do the deletion and generate a "book has been deleted" screen. Even a search request that delivers several pages of results needs to keep track of which result page is required and the original search criteria.

Getting back to my workplace in Cumbria in the mid-1980s, the transaction systems in place at that stage dealt only with the simple stateless record-display transactions or multipage search transactions . . . and even the latter had problems. When several users tried to search the same database using the system, they were likely to get their results mixed up with one another! I was charged with producing the first update system. Whereas occasionally getting someone else's search results was just annoying, deleting the wrong record would be disastrous.

14.5.3 All About State

So what was wrong with the existing systems, and how could I avoid similar but more serious problems? In essence, it is all about state.

In most computer programs, you don't need to worry too much about state. You put data in a variable at one stage; if you require the data at a later point it is still there in the variable. However, in the case of transaction-processing modules, the module may be reinitialized between each transaction (as is the case with certain types of Web CGI [Common Gateway Interface] script), so values put in a variable during one transaction won't be there at all for the next transaction. Even worse, if the same module is dealing with several users and not reinitialized, then values left behind from a transaction for one user may still be "lying around" when the next user's transaction is processed. This is precisely what was happening in the search-result listings. Some of the state of the transaction (part of the search criteria) was being left in a variable. When the system was tested (with one user!), there was no problem, but when several users used the system their search criteria got mixed up. Although it was possible to explicitly save and restore data associated with a particular terminal/user, the programmers had failed to understand what needed to be stored. Instead, the existing programs coped by putting state information into fields on the form that were then sent back to the next stage of the transaction. With Web-based interfaces, similar problems occur with session state.

However, there is also a second, more subtle part of the state: the current location in the human-computer dialogue.

In traditional computer algorithmics, the location in the program is implicit. It is only when one starts to deal with event-driven systems, such as GUIs, network applications, and transaction processing, that one has to explicitly deal with this. And of course traditional computer-science training does little to help. Not only are the principal algorithms and teaching languages sequential, but also the historical development of the subject means that sequential structures such as loops, recursion, and so on are regarded as critical and are in lists of essential competency, whereas event-driven issues are typically missing. Even worse, event-based languages such as Visual Basic and other GUI development languages have been regarded as "dirty" and not worthy of serious attention. Possibly this is changing now that Java is becoming a major teaching language, but still the event-driven features are low on the computer-science agenda!

So, computer programmers in the mid-1980s—as well as those of today—were ill prepared both conceptually and in terms of practical skills to deal explicitly with state, especially flow of control.

This was evident in the buggy transaction modules I was dealing with. The flow of the program code of each module looked rather like a twiggy tree, with numerous branches and tests that were effectively trying to work out where in the flow of the user interaction the transaction was situated.

```
if confirm_field is empty // can't be confirm screen
                  // or user didn't fill in the Y/N box
 then if record_id is empty // must be initial entry
      then prepare 'which record to delete' screen
      else if valid record_id
           then read record and prepare confirm screen
           else prepare error screen
 else if confirm_field = "Y'
      then if record_id is empty // help malformed
           then prepare error screen
           else if valid record_id
                else do deletion
                then prepare error screen
      else if confirm_field = "N'
           then prepare 'return to main menu' screen
           else prepare 'must answer Y/N' screen
```

No wonder there were bugs!

Of course, if one looks at many GUIs or Web applications, the code looks just the same—Try using the **Back** key or bookmarking an intermediate page in most multistage Web forms, and you'll probably find just how fragile the code is.

14.5.4   The Solution

A flow chart of the program looked hideous and was very uninformative because the structure of the program was not related to the structure of the user interaction. Instead of focusing on the code, I focused on the user interaction and

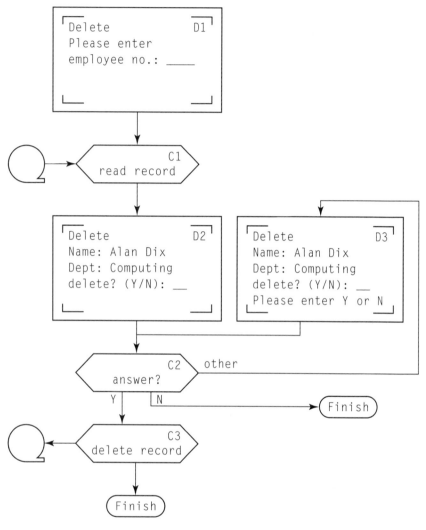

FIGURE

14.5

Flow chart of user interaction.

produced flowcharts of the human-computer dialogue. Figure 14.5 shows a typical flowchart. Each rectangle represents a possible screen, and a miniature of the screen is drawn. The hexagonal boxes represent system actions, and the "tape" symbols represent database transactions. Note that this is not a flowchart of the program, but of the human-computer dialogue, rather like the STNs in

Section 14.2. Note also that the purpose is to clarify the nature of the dialogue, so the system side is only labeled in quite general terms (e.g., "read record"). These labels are sufficient to clearly say what should happen and do not say how the code to do this works in detail. This is because the difficult thing is getting the overall flow right.

Notice also that each major system block and each screen is labeled: D1, D2, D3 for the screens; C1, C2, C3 for the system code blocks. These are used to link the flowchart to boilerplate code. For each screen there is a corresponding block of code, which generates the screen and, very important, stores the label of the next system block against the terminal/user. For example, screen D3 will save the label C2. The first thing the module does when asked to deal with a message is to retrieve the label associated with the user. If this is blank, it is the start of the dialogue (it will generate screen D1 in this case); otherwise the module simply executes the code associated with the relevant system block.

This all seems very mundane, but the important thing is that it worked. Systems that were taking months to develop could be completed in days, and the turnaround time for upgrades and maintenance was hours. That is, systems were being produced at least 10 times faster than previously and, furthermore, with fewer bugs!

14.5.5   Why It Worked . . .

So why is it that such a simple formal method worked so well, and can we use this to assess or improve other formalisms or develop new ones?

Let's look at some of the features that made this method function well:

useful—*addresses a real problem!*

The notation focused on the overall user-interface dialogue structure that was causing difficulties in the existing systems. So often formalisms are proposed because they have some nice intrinsic properties, or are good for something else, but they do not solve a real need.

appropriate—*no more detailed than needed*

For example, there was no problem in producing the detailed code to access databases and so forth, so the formalism deals with this at a crude level of "read record," "delete record," and so on. Many formalisms force you to fill in lots of detail, which makes it hard to see the things you really need them for as well as increasing the cost of using them.

communication—*mini-pictures and clear flow are easy to talk through with client*

Formal methods are often claimed to be a means to improve communication within a design team, because of their precision. However, when precision is achieved at the cost of comprehensibility, there is no real communication.

complementary—*different paradigm than implementation*

It is quite common to use specification methods that reflect closely the final structure of the system, such as object-oriented specification for object-oriented systems. Here, however, the specification represents the structure of the dialogue, which is completely different from the structure of the code. This is deliberate: The notation allows one to see the system from a different perspective, in this case one more suitable for producing and assessing the interface design. The relationship between the structure of the notation and the structure of the code is managed via simple rules, which is what formalisms are good at!

fast pay back—*quicker to produce application (at least ten times faster)*

I have been involved in projects where substantial systems have been fully specified and then implemented, and I have seen the improvements in terms of quality and *long-term* time savings. However, I still rarely use these methods in practice even though I know they will save time. Why? Because I, like most people, like instant payback. Spending lots of time up front for savings later is very laudable, but when it comes to doing things I like to see results. Not only that, but clients are often happier to see a buggy partial something than to be told that, yes, in a few months it will all come together. The dialogue flowcharts didn't just produce long-term savings, but they also reduced the lead time to see the first running system.

responsive—*rapid turnaround of changes*

The feeling of control and comprehension made it easier to safely make changes. In some formal methods, the transformation process between specification and code is so complex that change is very costly (see Dix & Harrison [1989] for a discussion of this). The assumption underlying this, as in much of software engineering, is that well-specified systems will not need to be changed often. Of course, with user interfaces, however well specified, it is only when they are used that we really come to fully understand the requirements.

reliability—*clear boilerplate code is less prone to errors*

Although the transformation process from diagram to code was not automated, applying and modifying boilerplate code templates was a fairly automatic hand process. This heavy reuse of standard code fragments greatly increases the reliability of code.

quality—*easy to establish test cycle*

The clear labeling of diagrams and code made it easy to be able to track whether all paths had been tested. However, note that these are not just paths through the program (which effectively restarted at each transaction), but each path through the human-computer dialogue.

maintenance—*easy to relate bug/enhancement reports to specification and code*

The screens presented to the user included the labels, making it easy to track bug reports or requests for changes both in the code and the specification.

In short, the formalism was used to fulfill a purpose; it was, above all, neither precious nor purist!!

14.6   CURRENT STATUS

To see where formal methods are going in HCI, we'll start by looking back at the progress of formal methods first in computing in general and then in HCI. We'll then move on to examine the trends and potential ways to go forward in the area.

14.6.1   Retrospective—Formal Methods in Computing

There was a period, in the late 1980s and the early 1990s, when every major research project in computing *had* to have a formal methods component in order to be respectable. There were known problems in industrial take-up, but this was widely explained as due to lack of suitably trained personnel. As a new breed of formally adept graduates entered the market, it was believed, formal methods would find its true place as central to computer systems design.

Even by the end of this period, the excuses were wearing thin; certainly by the mid-1990s the popular spirit had moved against formalism: "doesn't scale," "too difficult," "requires too much training." . . . Although there is still a strong formal methods community, the emphasis is more on particular domains where safety, cost, or complexity make the effort of formal methods worthwhile. Within these areas, there have been a continual stream of industrial success stories, and some consulting firms make formal methods expertise one of their market differentiators (see Clarke and Wing's 1996 survey article).

The critique is all sensible, and "problems" in the formal methods community were largely due to overhype in the early days. In other fields, for example structural engineering, one would not expect to apply the same level of analysis to a garden gate as to the Thames flood barrier in London. Even within a single structure, the analysis of a ship's hull would be different from an internal cabin door, and a porthole beneath the waterline may be different from one above deck level.

However, there is another side to this. In so many disciplines that have been fashionable and then fallen into disrepute, one hears, usually from within the discipline itself, that "it has never been used in practice" and has failed somehow to meet (overblown) expectations. However, again and again one finds that this is because the discipline constantly redefines itself to exclude those parts that have become successful and "spun off." For example, artificial intelligence experienced the same hype and decline, but spin-off areas such as natural language processing, computer vision, and aspects of expert systems are all widely used (and used in HCI!).

Looking with less exclusive eyes, we can see a huge growth in the use of structured methods and diagrammatic specifications, especially in the use of the Unified Modeling Language (UML). Many of the notations used to have their roots in what once would have been called "formal," but now is perhaps simply normal. Note too that it is precisely because systems are large and complex that more formal notations are used. It is easy for programmers to get the details right, but they need support in understanding interactions and architecture. Of course, if formal methods are defined to exclude all this, then, true, adoption is low!

14.6.2   Retrospective—Formal Methods in HCI

Within HCI, formal methods have always had a rougher ride as the rigid and cold notations stand in contrast to the richness of human interaction. The area gained somewhat due to the early general formal-methods hype, and certainly that was one of the enablers for the early York work. However, rather than growing dramatically and then suffering reverses (as was the case within computing), the formal-methods subcommunity within HCI has gradually grown and is now able to support not only an annual conference largely of its own (DSVIS), but also a number of other conferences where it is a major facet (CADUI, EHCI, TAMODIA).

Although individuals have very different agendas and are wedded to their own methods, the relatively small formal methods (FM) in HCI community has tended to knit together in the face of the "opposition" from the wider HCI community and so has managed to avoid some of the internal schisms that have bedeviled FM in computing. This has meant that the collections, journal special issues, and conferences in the area have included a wide range of formalisms including logics, set theoretic specifications, diagrammatic notations, and even cognitive task models.

Formal methods has always been criticized for dealing only with toy problems, and to a large extent this would also be a valid criticism of a large proportion of the FM-in-HCI literature. A significant number of papers describe new specification techniques, developments of old ones, or applications of existing methods, and then apply them to simple case studies. This is perhaps reasonable given the need to start simple in order to address problems and issues one at a time. And there are signs of maturity, as some of the longer-established groups and methods (e.g., Toulouse and Pisa) have created support tools and are applying their techniques to problems in large commercial organizations.

We are perhaps still looking for headline success stories to sell formal methods into the mainstream HCI community in the way that the NYNEX study did for GOMS (Gray, John, & Atwood, 1992) (see also Chapter 4, Section 4.5), but it seems as if this is now on the horizon.

The culture clash between postmodern HCI and formalism has always been stronger in the United States than elsewhere, and formal papers in computer-human interaction are rare. However, there has been quite a strong line of papers in CSCW conferences and HCI journals using formal arguments and analyses to deal with issues of distribution and concurrency—for example, in describing the use of "operation transforms" and **Undo**/**Redo** frameworks for managing race conditions and conflicts in group editors.[3] The various "spatial" models in CSCW are also reliant to varying degrees on formal definitions (Benford et al., 1994; Dix et al., 2000; Rodden, 1996; Sandor, Bogdan, & Bowers,

---

[3] For a short bibliography on operation transforms and group **Undo,** see *www.hcibook.com/alan/topics/undo.*

1997). These are both cases where the underlying area is complex and where simpler arguments and explanations fail.

The last of these is an example of creating generic models/specifications to address a broad issue rather than a specific system. I have always found these the most exciting papers, giving the biggest bang for buck, because the understanding gained can be applied to many different systems. However, these publications are relatively rare. Producing such work requires a comfort in using the formalisms and an ability to look at an area in broad terms. It may be that these skills are usually found in different personality types, hence making it difficult for an individual to succeed. However, it may equally well be due to education— it is only in the more "techie" courses that more formal methods are taught (and not always there). The FM-in-HCI community is therefore full of those who (and I caricature) either started off in very technical areas and are gradually learning to understand people or started off in more people-oriented areas and are gradually learning that hand waving is not enough. This of course takes quite a time to mature, but, when it does, it means that the FM-in-HCI community contains the most well-rounded people in IT!

14.6.3   Prospective

So where does this take us?

The areas that have greatest take-up are where the formalisms are simplest (as in my case study) and where there is tool support. Particularly powerful are cases where the formalism can be used to generate interfaces, either early prototypes or as part of the final running system (cf. appropriateness and fast feedback in Section 14.5). This is set to continue; for example CNUCE's CTTE is being used in a growing number of sites.

However, it is also clear that there are application areas that are intrinsically complex, such as the work on distributed group editing and group **Undo.** This area is hitting new complexity limits as the various researchers widen the types of operations they deal with; it seems that some simplifying framework is needed.

Looking more widely, the trend of having many papers about different methods is likely to continue. Each research group has its own focus, and there is a good feeling about working on "your" notation. Rather than fighting human nature, it would be good to see the development of an integrating framework to make the relationships between different notations and methods more clear. Perhaps more important, such a framework is essential to allow interoperation between the growing numbers of formally based interface design and analysis toolkits.

Note that this is still a wish, because there is no real sign of such an integrating framework at present; the closest may well still be the original York modeling work! Perhaps the closest is the work on the syndetic modeling framework (Barnard et al., 2000), which proposes that systems are regarded as lower-level interactors each described by appropriate microtheories and then bound together into higher-level interactors by macrotheories. However, this is more a framework for formulating a broad theory, not the theory itself.

In fact, prompted by the writing of the early drafts of this chapter, I started the process of seeking a unifying framework between HCI formalisms using traces of activity as a common point between widely different notations (Dix, 2002d).

The existing safety-critical application areas, such as flight control, are likely to remain central, with perhaps other high cost-of-failure applications such as e-commerce joining them.

The Web, WAP, and other aspects of global networking are creating new problem areas that are difficult to understand:

- every system is becoming a distributed system, with portions on a user's machine, running as applets, at multiple interacting servers (consider .Net)

- multiple users, machines, and applications engender emergent properties

- state, which we have seen is difficult, is broken up over servers, URL parameters, and multiple frames and windows in a user's browser

- parts of the system are unreliable or insecure

- there are generic components (browsers, Web servers) as well as specific applications

- the **Back** button and bookmarks mean that applications keep "restarting" in the middle!

These all suggest that formal models and reasoning may be not optional but essential! Note that the most recent general collection in this area, Palanque and Paternó's 1997 book, used the Web browser as a common example—and things have got much more complex since then. We are still awaiting the equivalent of a Model-View-Controller (MVC) or Seeheim model of interfaces in this type of environment, and similar issues to those in group editing and **Undo** may be necessary.

The other area that is fast growing in importance is the very small multiple-context-dependent ubiquitous devices that are dynamically linking and reconfiguring themselves . . . to do something useful, one hopes! There has been relatively little work on formal issues in this area, although some colleagues and I have addressed aspects of context and location modeling (Dix, Rodden, Davies, Trevor, Friday, & Palfreyman, 2000). Clearly this is another challenge for which, again, more formal analysis will be essential.

Both global networking and ubiquity lead to emergent properties, which may mean that areas such as artificial life or the still-growing area of critical and complex systems (in the Santa Fe Institute sense) will be needed to understand or model (perhaps in a simulation sense) the situations.[4]

Architectures are also a problem for ubiquitous systems, with low-level device events needing to be marshaled and converted into higher-level events for applications. Those working in the area are talking about the need for a Seeheim-style architecture, and there has been progress with workshops dedicated to this issue (Rodden, Dix, & Abowd, 2002).

Since my earliest work in formal methods for HCI, issues of time and status phenomena have been critical (Dix 1991a, 1991b, 1996, 1998). As long as the dominant interfaces were event driven, this was largely regarded as a marginal concern. However, now we have ubiquitous devices, with physical coordinates, biomedical sensors (Allanson, 2002; Allanson & Wilson, 2002), multimedia and multimodal inputs . . . not so marginal anymore.

Although some of the work is just waiting to be reapplied, there are a number of open problems:

* nonlocalized semantics—many continuous-stream inputs such as voice or a hand gesture have meaning over a period of time, not at an instant, but there are no hard boundaries to those periods;

* multiple granularity of time—large granularity time periods (e.g., today) do not map simply onto finer grain times (do we mean working day: 8 A.M.–5 P.M.; waking day: 7 A.M.–1 A.M.; etc.). There are first steps in this area (Kutar, Britton, & Nehaniv, 2001), but it is a complex issue;

* ideas of location—in the room (does in the doorway count?), close versus far (how close?).

Note that in each case we have an apparently discrete higher-level concept (in the room, today, hand gesture for "open door"), but it has "fuzzy" edges when mapped onto lower-level features.

Perhaps this sums up the problem and the challenge of formal methods in HCI. Whenever we capture the complexity of the real world in formal structures, whether language, social structures, or computer systems, we are creating

---

[4]   Santa Fe Institute, *www.santafe.edu.*

discrete tokens for continuous and fluid phenomena. In so doing, we are bound to have difficulty. However, it is only in doing these things that we can come to understand, to have valid discourse, and to design.

14.7   FURTHER READING

There are only a few full texts explicitly on formal methods in HCI.

My own monograph covers the PIE model and many extensions and other models, including those on which status/event analysis is based.

✦ Dix, A. J. (1991). *Formal methods for interactive systems*. London: Academic Press.

The Table of Contents and some chapters are available online at *www.hiraeth.com/books/formal/*

See also my coauthored textbook, which has a detailed review of formal dialogue notations in Chapter 8 and other formal models in Chapter 9:

✦ Dix, A., Finlay, J., Abowd, G., & R. Beale (1998). *Human-computer interaction* (*2nd ed*). Hemel Hempstead, UK: Prentice Hall.

Harrison and Thimbleby's 1990 collection includes contributions from many of those working in this area at the time.

✦ Harrison, M.D., & Thimbleby, H.W. (eds.) (1990). *Formal methods in human computer interaction*. Cambridge, UK: Cambridge University Press.

Palanque and Paternó edited a more recent collection, confusingly with the same name as the above! This collection is thematic, with the contributors using their various techniques to address the Web browser as a common example.

✦ Palanque, P., & Paternó, F. (eds.) (1997). *Formal methods in human computer interaction*. London: Springer-Verlag.

Paternó has also produced a monograph looking at the whole design lifecycle and using ConcurTaskTrees as a central representation.

✦ Paternó, F. (2000). *Model-based design and evaluation of interactive applications*. London: Springer-Verlag.

Table of Contents and downloads are available online at: *giove.cnuce.cnr.it/ ~fabio/mbde.html*

For an up-to-date view of the field, probably the best source is the DSVIS conference series:

✦ Design, Verification and Specification of Interactive Systems. Vienna & Berlin: Springer-Verlag, (1995–2002).

My formal methods in HCI Web pages include a bibliography, Web links, and further resources:

www.hcibook.com/alan/topics/formal/

Also see the Web page for this chapter, which includes links to online copies of referenced papers and further information referred to in the text:

www.hcibook.com/alan/papers/theory-formal-2003/

15 Design Rationale as Theory

CHAPTER

John M. Carroll
Mary Beth Rosson Virginia Tech

A computer system does not itself express the motivations that initiated its design; the user requirements it was intended to address; the discussions, debates, and negotiations that determined its organization; the reasons for its particular features; the reasons against features it does not have; the weighing of tradeoffs; and so forth. This information comprises the *design rationale* of the system. It can be critical to the many stakeholders in a design process: customers, users, service providers, and marketers, as well as designers who want to build upon the system and the ideas it embodies.

Design rationale can contribute to theory development in human-computer interaction (HCI) in three ways. First, it provides a foundation for *ecological science* in HCI by describing the decisions and implicit causal relationships embodied in HCI artifacts. Second, it provides a foundation for *action science* in HCI by integrating activities directed at description and understanding with those directed at design and development. Finally, it provides a framework for a *synthetic science* of HCI in which the insights and predictions of diverse technical theories can be integrated.

The previous chapters illustrated how theoretical concepts and methods from a variety of sciences are used to gain insight in the context of HCI design and evaluation. This chapter inverts that train of thought to some extent. It shows how reflective HCI design practices—involving design-rationale documentation and analysis—can be used (1) to closely couple theoretical concepts and methods with the designed artifacts that instantiate them, (2) to more closely integrate theory application and theory development in design work, and (3) to more broadly integrate the insights of different technical theories.

15.1   MOTIVATION

The 1980s were exciting and productive for science and theory in HCI. To be sure, the specific content and scope of that theory was narrow from today's perspective. For example, much early theory development addressed isolated users working without errors on routine tasks, and it derived only from information-processing psychology. This early progress had three distinct effects on subsequent development of theory. First, it established a specific paradigm for theory that continues to the present (see Chapters 3 and 4, by MacKenzie and John, respectively, in this volume). Second, by clearly articulating and developing a particular approach, it helped to identify issues and opportunities for other approaches. Thus, it helped to provoke approaches addressing error recognition, diagnosis, and recovery; approaches addressing nonroutine interactions like learning by discovery or breakdowns in performance; approaches addressing interpersonal communication and cooperation; and approaches derived from other areas of cognitive science, and from anthropology and sociology.

The third and most troubling reaction to early theory work in HCI was to dismiss theory, science, and even research in general as not relevant enough to real HCI problems of system development (e.g., Whiteside & Wixon, 1987). This reaction is extreme, but understandable: The touchstone design challenge for HCI in the 1980s was to understand and address difficulties experienced by new users. This challenge was all about learning, problem solving, and error management in workplace contexts. But the most articulate theory work of that period did not address learning, problem solving, *or* errors, and it had no means of describing the dynamics of thinking and acting in workplace contexts (e.g., Suchman, 1987). The echoes of this dismissal of theory are evident still in HCI methods, many of which are grounded in raw experience and convention, not in theories or frameworks.

The late 1980s saw many debates about science and theory in HCI. Many of the issues discussed are fundamental: What is the proper balance between rigor and relevance? A model of errorless performance can be more rigorous, but it is also less relevant to real situations. What are the boundary conditions on applicability for given theories? A model of key pressing may be more useful than a model of problem solving in some circumstances. What roles can models and theories play in invention, development, and evaluation of new technology; can there be theory-based design? Studies of technology development in other fields suggest that science is more often the beneficiary than the benefactor of technology.

Our approach to design rationale as theory was directly motivated by these debates (Carroll & Rosson, 1991, 1992). Design rationale is documentation and analysis of specific designs in use. It describes the features of a design, the intended and possible use of those features, and the potential consequences of the use for people and their tasks. This involves observing or hypothesizing scenarios of user interaction, and describing their underlying design tradeoffs. For example, a scrollbar widget that appears only when pointed to takes less screen space, but it does not remind the user that scrolling is always available. It might entrain accidental scrolling more often than a permanently displayed scrollbar. And so on.

Design rationale addresses three themes from the HCI theory debates: context, applicability, and scope. Effective HCI theories guide the development of new tools and environments to support interaction, new methods to measure interaction, and new possibilities for interaction. Through our own research work, through our interactions with system developers and users, and through our exposure to ideas from anthropology and sociology, we became convinced that context must be considered directly in formulating, assessing, and applying theories. We understood context to be both the context of use and the context of system development. The context of use is the practices, the artifacts and affordances, and the constraints of the workplace, school, home, or other setting. The context of system development is the way developers work and the way technology emerges from their work. Design rationale describes and explains the "ecology" of HCI—the everyday practices and materials of users and developers.

Applying theory in HCI design involves mapping concepts across domain boundaries, and then directing descriptions and analysis to prescriptions for intervention. These are difficult translations. Theoretical terms and relations are bound to domains. Thus, applying theory from experimental psychology to HCI involves mapping the notion of "task." But tasks in experimental psychology are very different from office tasks, manufacturing tasks, military tasks, and so on. Moreover, even if a mapping of theoretical terms and relations is accomplished, we still need to direct the theory-based description to design, that is, to derive prescriptions or guidance of some sort for design actions. Design rationale helps to make theory more applicable by codifying the terms and relations of the application domain, and grounding them in design tradeoffs and decisions.

A central tension in theory or modeling is that between scope and power. In the old adage, a theory of everything is a theory of nothing. But narrow technical theories are also problematic. The early information-processing theory developed in HCI focused on minimizing user action paths to guide the design of efficient user interfaces. However, the keypress level of analysis cannot describe problems of deskilling—the feelings of diminished self-worth that people experience when their job activities and responsibilities appear to them and to others to be trivial. One way to broaden the scope of technical theory and yet avoid diluting its power is to integrate distinct sources of theory. In design rationale, the objectives of user-interface efficiency and perceptions of self-worth are considered as a tradeoff: Designers need to consider both objectives, to use both sources of theory, and to balance the upside of efficiency and the downside of deskilling.

Design rationale as an approach to theory in HCI occupies middle ground between approaches that seek to directly apply particular theories from outside the HCI domain, and approaches that dismiss such theory as narrow and irrelevant and that rely on purely heuristic usability engineering. It focuses on describing the domain of application directly in terms of design tradeoffs, but it recruits theory as necessary and possible to ground both the dimensions and positions of tradeoffs.

15.2   OVERVIEW

In the task-artifact framework (TAF; Figure 15.1) design rationale is created to guide and understand the impacts of computing technology on human behavior. Tasks are represented as *scenarios of use,* narratives in which one or more actors engage in goal-directed activity with an interactive computer system. The scenarios include the activity context, for example the social and physical setting, as well as the actors' motivations, actions, and reactions during the episode. *Claims analysis* produces a causal analysis of the actors' experience, enumerating the features of a system-in-use that are hypothesized to have positive or negative consequences (also termed *upsides* and *downsides*) for the actors. This causal analysis of current practices is used to guide the design of new technologies: New system features are envisioned to mitigate downsides and/or maintain or enhance the upsides. The new system raises new opportunities for human behavior that are documented as part of the continuing cycle of task-artifact co-evolution.

The design rationale for a system is typically built up through analysis of multiple scenarios, often over incremental versions, leading to a network of overlapping claims. Design rationale for families of artifacts also overlaps, leading to more abstract design rationale that creates a design space. Claims are

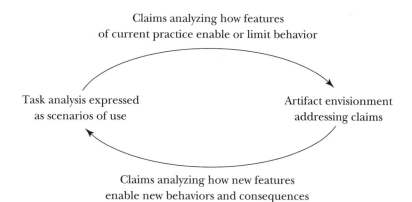

Claims analyzing how features
of current practice enable or limit behavior

Task analysis expressed
as scenarios of use

Artifact envisionment
addressing claims

Claims analyzing how new features
enable new behaviors and consequences

FIGURE

15.1

The task-artifact framework emphasizes a view of co-evolution wherein human activities raise requirements for technology, and new technology in turn raises new opportunities for human action.

theory based; they make no presumption about the intentions of a system's designers.[1]

We exemplify the TAF with the MOOsburg community network system—a system whose development has been guided and interpreted through scenario-based design and claims analysis (Carroll et al., 2001). MOOs are multi-user domains (MUD) that have an object-oriented architecture (Curtis, 1992); participants navigate a spatial model, encountering and interacting with other participants and with objects distributed throughout the structure. In MOOsburg, the spatial model is based on Blacksburg, a town in southwestern Virginia (Figure 15.2 and Plate 13 of the color insert).

Figures 15.3 and 15.4 contrast the design rationale for a central feature of MOOsburg—its underlying spatial model—in two versions that evolved over a period of six years, beginning as a course project. It was initially implemented with existing MOO software architectures and technology (Curtis, 1992). The *usage scenario* in the top of Figure 15.3 narrates the experience of Sharon, a college student interacting with friends in MOOsburg; many of the system's early users were college students using the system for relatively informal activities like this.

---

[1] The structure of a claim is suitable for expressing a variety of design tradeoffs. For example, we often use them to analyze nonfunctional requirements such as resource availability, portability, and so on (Rosson & Carroll, 2000). Here we limit the discussion to claims grounded in theoretical views of HCI.

436

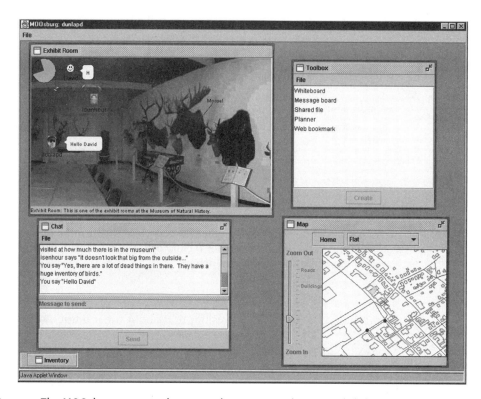

FIGURE

15.2

The MOOsburg community network system. In the upper left is an exhibit room with three visitors present; the upper right displays a list of tools that can be evoked in this place; the lower left holds a chat tool; and the lower right shows an interactive map that can be panned and zoomed to locate and enter places in MOOsburg. (See also Plate 13 of the color insert for a color version of this figure.)

The *claim* in the bottom of the figure analyzes the upsides and downsides of using a directed graph as the underlying spatial model for the MOO.

The hypothesized impacts are diverse, appealing to theories of motivation (uncertainty and exploration), problem solving (simplified next-move planning), transfer of learning (real world knowledge), and mental models (spatial imagery). The upsides and downsides raise tradeoffs that are otherwise implicit in the decision to base users' navigation on a directed-graph model. The scenario includes a usage context that helps to analyze the relationship between this design feature and Sharon's activities—she is seeking entertainment or social interaction in the MOO; she has prior knowledge of Blacksburg that helps her to

Usage scenario: **Sharon visits the science-fiction club meeting in MOOsburg.**
Sharon, a Virginia Tech physics student, visits MOOsburg for the first time. Her friend Bill has been meeting regularly with his friends at MOOsburg's science-fiction club, and he has been trying to get Sharon to join the group. Sharon has never been to a MUD before, but she knows from Bill that MOOsburg is organized by the streets and buildings of Blacksburg. When she logs on, she is told that she has arrived downtown, at the corner of College and Main; she is also given directions about where she can go from here. She chooses to go north, expecting that this will take her toward Virginia Tech. Each time she makes a move, she is given an updated description; she sees that it corresponds to what she would see if she actually walked up Main Street. After a few moves, she confirms that she is going in the right direction, though it may take her a while to get to Squires. She finally gets to the meeting and chats with the other club members. Afterwards, she decides to retrace her steps, returning to Main Street to explore other locations. She had arrived earlier by going north from Henderson Lawn, but when she exits south she is surprised to find herself in Lane Hall, not on Henderson headed back toward Main Street. She is confused for a bit, wondering if she has forgotten a step, but she is then drawn into the activities listed for this site and decides to explore here instead of going back downtown.

Claim: **A compass-based directed graph of Blacksburg's geography**
+ enables application of real-world spatial knowledge about the town
+ simplifies planning by limiting the next-move options
+ may promote feelings of uncertainty and adventure about noncontiguous locations
− but navigation to noncontiguous sites may be tedious or awkward
− but the corresponding spatial model may be difficult or impossible to envision

FIGURE   Scenario and rationale for MOOsburg compass-based navigation.

15.3

navigate the underlying space. For this physics student, the graph discontinuity is an interesting quirk that she pursues as a kind of puzzle.

As MOOsburg developed, its goals became more ambitious. It started as an experiment with familiar town-based spatial models. But as people used it, we began to recognize its potential as a more interactive front-end to the Blacksburg Electronic Village (Carroll & Rosson, 1996; Cohill & Kavanaugh, 2000). This entailed a broader view of who would participate, what background participants would have, and what activities they would pursue. These changes in usage context led us to weigh the various upsides and downsides of the directed-graph model differently. As illustrated by the more recent scenario and design rationale in Figure 15.4, MOOsburg was no longer envisioned as primarily a place for adventure and exploration, but also as a shared environment in which to collaborate on community activities (Figure 15.4).

There is considerable overlap in these two examples of scenarios and design rationale. Both spatial models leverage residents' knowledge of their town; both simplify planning and next-move selection. But the spatial hierarchy simplifies the model's internal structure by applying a consistent containment relationship

Usage scenario: **Jean visits the senior center in MOOsburg.**

Jean is a founding member of Blacksburg Electronic Village (BEV) seniors, an active group of Blacksburg retirees who have the ambition to provide information, education, and other online services to the elderly members of the town. She recently saw a demo of MOOsburg at one of their meetings at the community center, and she decides to explore a bit on her own later that night. When she arrives, she sees that she is in the middle of town, at the corner of College and Main. She also sees a line-drawing map of Blacksburg, and she can see from the highlighted dot just where she is. She easily recognizes the long slanted line of Main Street that divides the town, and the oval shape outlining the drill-field in the middle of the Virginia Tech campus. She wants to visit the seniors' room at the community center, which she knows is to the northeast of Tech. She clicks the map in that area, and it recenters around her selection point; she now is able to recognize Patrick Henry Road heading off to the east. She knows that the community center is on this road, so she zooms in to look more closely. As she zooms in, building outlines appear along the streets, and she can see that there are dots over the high school, the aquatic center, and the community center. She selects the community center dot, and the display updates with a picture of the building and its entrance. As she zooms in even further, the streets and buildings are replaced by a floor plan of the center, where she easily identifies the seniors' room. When she goes there, no one else is around, so she spends some time setting up a new discussion forum about the new access road to the Warm Hearth assisted-living development.

Claim: **A map-based spatial hierarchy of Blacksburg's geography**

$^+$ enables application of real-world spatial knowledge about the town
$^+$ simplifies the space by decomposition and containment
$^+$ supports planning via simultaneous visualization of focus plus context
$-$ but a fully detailed map may be perceptually complex

FIGURE   Scenario and rationale for the MOOsburg map-based navigation.

15.4

to parts and subparts. The resulting hierarchy also enables model visualization, minimizing the need for people to construct and imagine their own mental models of the space. Importantly, it also creates a central role for a town map, a specific visualization already familiar to most community residents.

The design rationale summarized in these two tables is at once abstract and concrete. Abstract claims are made about human-computer interaction—uncertainty about a system's functionality increases the sense of adventure and fun, limiting a person's choices simplifies planning, hierarchical decomposition simplifies a complex navigation space, and so on. But each of these abstractions is tied to concrete features of the artifact and is conditioned on the usage context provided by the scenario.

The example rationale makes a direct connection to the context of system development through its emphasis on tradeoffs. Tradeoffs are inherent in design reasoning. Claims associate the tradeoff analyses with specific usage situations; this provides a starting point for tradeoff evaluation and prioritization. The details of the setting can be discussed and varied as alternatives are considered.

Claims analysis addresses the issue of applicability directly, by creating an explicit connection between a design decision (a feature under consideration) and our knowledge of HCI (expressed as hypotheses about a feature's consequences in a situation).

This brief example also demonstrates how design rationale addresses the problem of scope in HCI theory. The causal analysis of the users' experiences in the two scenarios is grounded in multiple theory bases. Some of the consequences reflect hypotheses about theories of motivation (e.g., the effects of uncertainty and exploration); others relate to learning theory (e.g., transfer of learning, construction of mental models); others relate to theories of planning and action; and still others relate to theories of perception. In some cases the theories are complementary, providing multiple pieces of rationale for including a design feature; in other cases they suggest tradeoffs. By appealing to many different sources of knowledge, design rationale broadens the scope of the design analysis.

15.3   SCIENTIFIC FOUNDATIONS

Design rationale has three scientific foundations: ecological science, action science, and synthetic science. These correspond roughly to the three themes of context, applicability, and scope.

15.3.1   Ecological Science

Ecological science rests on the principle that systems in the natural and social world have evolved to exploit environmental regularities. This approach is well developed in perceptual psychology. And indeed there are some common themes in the history of psychology and the history of HCI with respect to the ecological science perspective.

In the late 1800s, psychology struggled to emerge as a laboratory science. Specifically, it sought to distance itself from its origins as a branch of philosophy. This effort had a long-lived effect on psychology as a discipline. Even today, psychologists often value highly controlled observations more than is appropriate, and they tend to dismiss informal experience as too complex and chaotic to analyze. This value set led to a fairly rigid approach to the study of human perception. Highly trained observers rendered extremely specific judgments about very controlled materials. In visual perception, for example, laboratory studies tended to concentrate on interpretations of simple line drawings. This approach led to many interesting studies of the visual illusions, the figure-ground distinction, impossible figures, and so on. However, the tendency of science to focus and specialize led to ever more detailed, albeit better-designed studies of the same basic set of phenomena pertaining to line drawings.

In the case of visual perception, it was World War II that got psychologists out of the laboratory and into the world. Many practical problems clamored for solution, and existing theories were not adequate. A science built upon the study of passive and controlled viewing of line drawings could contribute little to a practical understanding of the visual perception involved in landing airplanes on aircraft-carrier decks. Unfortunately for psychology, this was more than a matter of science not being ready "yet" for application. The limitations were quite fundamental: Visual perception occurs as humans *move* about in the physical world. When an observer moves, visual information is dynamic, and the dynamic relations in the information through time are critical to how we are able see the world. Sitting still is the special case. These critical dynamics depend on the optical richness of real objects—color, angle of illumination, patterns of reflection, and so forth. People can make sense of line drawings, but they typically do so through analogy and imagination. Line drawings are perceptual puzzles and not representative of ordinary perceptual interactions.

The ecological approach to visual perception was pioneered by James Gibson (1950, 1966, 1979) and Egon Brunswick (1956). Brunswick showed how some of the most perplexing perceptual phenomena identified and investigated with line drawings, like visual illusions, could be explained in terms of the ways that objects align and occlude in the physical world. He suggested that a basic method for perceptual psychology should be ecological surveys of the real world. Gibson showed that perception in movement permits direct recognition of higher-order optical properties such as the expansion pattern one sees in approaching a textured scene or surface. Gibson concluded that real-world perception typically consists of direct recognition of complex properties he called "affordances." This contradicted the most fundamental assumption of perceptual psychology, namely that higher-order properties, such as being an object or being something that can be poured, are inferred on the basis of piecemeal recognition of local features like contours, edges, and angles.

HCI can be developed as ecological science at three levels: taxonomic science, design science, and evolutionary science. The first of these, design rationale as design documentation, is quite consonant with Brunswick's (1956) notion of an ecological survey. Design rationale describes and analyzes actual designs, just as Brunswick described the layout of actual objects in the world.

Design rationale provides an inventory of the components and relationships in systems and software; it identifies potential consequences and tradeoffs associated with designs and design features, and it preserves the decision making behind designs. This provides a taxonomic science of HCI, analogous to natural sciences like comparative zoology. It can be extremely powerful: Explicitly documenting the designs already in the world can help to ensure that mistakes are made only once, and that effective ideas are reused.

Design rationale as an ecological survey of design practice provides the raw material for what might be called a design science of HCI. Descriptions of particular designs can be abstracted and generalized by categorizing designs, and the features that define the categories can be associated with general consequences for users and their tasks. As part of an ecological survey, the town map used to navigate MOOsburg can be analyzed as a specific system feature that provides a basis for classifying MOOs. But this feature might be abstracted as a containment model of space, and or even more generally as a containment model of information. The rationale for the map guides the design of MOOsburg, but it can also be part of an explanation of how people understand and use space more generally. Indeed, it could be generalized even further to analyze the link structures for nonspatial systems like Web sites and other hypertextual link structures. This concern with generalization and explanation defines a second level of ecological science in HCI.

There is also an evolutionary aspect to design: Designs react to a perceived state of affairs—tasks that people want to accomplish; distractions they want to avoid; assumptions they make about work in general and about themselves; tools and data they already understand and use, including other systems and software; and so forth. When a new artifact is designed and introduced into a given state of affairs, it changes things. It makes some tasks easier, but it may make other tasks more difficult. It makes some tasks unnecessary. It introduces some new concepts; it may extend or obviate some established concepts. In sum, tasks and the contexts of carrying out tasks create needs and opportunities for new artifacts, but those new artifacts consequently alter the tasks and eventually create new needs and opportunities for further designs. We call this the *task-artifact cycle*. Humans have always altered their own possibilities for perception, thinking, and interaction through design, but in contemporary times the rate and scope of this change has accelerated greatly. To pursue an ecological science of HCI, we must not only describe design rationales to taxonomize features, consequences, and tradeoffs, and generalize design rationales into explanations of human behavior and experience, but we must also project, understand, and manage the trajectories of change in the task-artifact cycle.

15.3.2   Action Science

Traditionally, basic or descriptive science is conceived of and carried out separately from the application of science to practical problems. The action-research paradigm integrates the traditional scientific objectives of analysis and explanation with the engineering objective of melioration. Action science is an approach to research that closely couples the development of knowledge and the application of that knowledge. The basic idea is that, if some sort of intervention is the ultimate objective of research, then the intervention itself should be a part of the research project. This is efficient: It eliminates or reduces the transfer of knowledge from scientists working in a research context to engineers and other practitioners working in an application context. It is also effective: Knowledge and technique can be lost when handed off from scientists to developers; consolidating these roles can mitigate such risks.

A second motivation for action science is that making interventions, and assessing interventions in a system, is a good method for *understanding systems.* Formally, this is analogous to applying transformations to a system in order to diagnose it. Thus, one way to understand the task of navigating in a MOO is to introduce new tool support and assess how navigation tasks are facilitated, or perhaps complicated, by use of those tools. As emphasized by Argyris, Putnam, and Smith (1985), traditional, descriptive science is conservative. Starting from careful observation, description, and analysis of the way things are tends to exaggerate the importance of the status quo, and perhaps it underemphasizes the importance of identifying possible transformations of the situation and invariants in the situation with respect to transformations. Social and technical systems are constantly evolving. The current state of affairs is important chiefly because all future trajectories must pass through that state.

In action science, strategies for change are the principal research objectives. Formulating effective strategies for change requires understanding the current state of affairs, but most critically it requires understanding the current state of affairs as the point of origin for a variety of possible futures. An appropriate way to do this is to make interventions, create new prototypes, and assess their utility in real and realistic contexts.

A third motivation for action science is that it *socially* assimilates research to practice. Beyond the efficiency of eliminating handoffs from science to application, and the insight afforded by observing systems under the transformations of design interventions, is the practical and intellectual benefit of including all stakeholders in the research. In this respect, action science is the step beyond conventional notions of participatory design in which end users are included as participants in design work on the grounds that they have a stake in the outcomes of that work and specially relevant knowledge to improve the quality of the work. In action science, end users and application developers are seen as stakeholders in the underlying research outcomes as well: Action research depends on participant involvement—even in strategic decisions about the research endeavor itself.

The effect of this is to produce knowledge that is more relevant and accessible to the broader community of people who apply knowledge. Thus, action science tends to weigh accuracy over precision, robustness with respect to incomplete information over experimental controls, and public disconfirmability over statistical rejection of the null hypothesis.

15.3.3 Synthetic Science

Technical science organizes phenomena into categories. This facilitates more coherent and detailed analysis. For example, social psychology has a lot to say about how people negotiate the meanings of actions and events, but little to say about how the articulators in their throats help them to do this. There can be debates about what phenomena should be grouped together, and there clearly are better and poorer groupings, but the overall strategy of decomposing phenomena is one key to the emergence of modern science.

In HCI design, the decompositions of technical science can be problematic. An example mentioned earlier is that of minimizing keypresses or other low-level user actions. From the standpoint of training time, asymptotic work efficiency, wear and tear on fingers and wrists, and so on, having fewer keystrokes, mouse movements, and other such actions is a sound design objective. However, at the social-organizational level, simplifying a person's job activities may not always be a good thing. It can make people think less of themselves and devalue their own skills and work knowledge, and it can also put their jobs in actual jeopardy in the sense of reduced security, salary, and opportunity.

This is a difficult sort of design tradeoff. The very same design intervention could be analyzed as a good approach with respect to one level of analysis and a bad approach with respect to another level. The problem is that the technical theories at the two levels do not concern themselves with phenomena beyond their own purviews, so they have no way of reconciling this conflict. This is not necessarily a flaw in the technical theories. But it raises the issue of how such cross-disciplinary tradeoffs can be addressed in HCI design.

Design rationale allows the insights and predictions of diverse technical theories to be integrated within a coherent analysis context. In the example of keypress efficiency versus deskilling, the resolution lies in the dimensions like overall cognitive complexity of task, the role of the particular task in the worker's overall job, and the organizational status and discretion of the workers who perform the task. These dimensions allow the tradeoff to be managed in particular design cases, and to be generalized across designs in schematic-solution strategies.

Design rationale has no "favorites" with respect to the social, cognitive, or performance theories that point to consequences for users. Indeed, designers may choose to conduct a relatively informal analysis of rationale; theoretical backing often remains implicit, with emphasis on the design guidance provided by competing concerns. But from the twin perspectives of theory-based design and design-based theory, the design rationale surfaced during a design project can be grounded in existing scientific theory, or it can instantiate predictions that would extend existing theory. This promotes attention to usage concerns at many levels, forcing consideration of tradeoffs that might otherwise be missed.

15.4   DETAILED DESCRIPTION

Applying and developing a broad range of science through design rationale is an open-ended endeavor. Even if one knows a lot of relevant science and has extensive experience in HCI design, there is no procedure to crank out design rationales, nor is it clear when to stop. In contrast, it is typically pretty clear how to apply Fitts' Law in designing or evaluating a target acquisition task. In this section, we give some general guidance for developing design rationales in the sense of scenarios and claims. At the end of the chapter, we give pointers to more detailed presentations.

The most important step in constructing a design rationale is to identify a collection of typical and critical scenarios of user interaction. It is not possible to comprehensively describe the use of a system; there are just too many things people can do with a complex tool. One should strive for balance, including scenarios in which people exercise routine functionality as well as those in which they creatively improvise, scenarios in which people are basically successful as well as those in which they recognize and recover from errors, and so forth.

One way to help ensure balance is to identify scenarios using a variety of methods. For example, field studies of users and organizations carrying out the work that a system is intended to support, and collaborative workshops with users envisioning alternative ways that work could be carried out, are two complementary ways to understand extant work situations and the design opportunities they present. The results of both kinds of investigations can be couched as scenarios. For example, one could visit the community senior center, describing its member activities and interactions in a scenario, or one could meet with a group of seniors and jointly develop a future scenario for an online senior center (recall Figure 15.4).

Designers can draw on their own prior work for ideas about possible scenarios. They can also draw on case-study reports of other design work. Scenarios from previous work may or may not be relevant to the current project. But even a scenario that is irrelevant in detail might suggest a relevant insight that could lead to a scenario. For example, the design scenario in Figure 15.3 is not about a senior center or about map-based navigation, but having it might still help a designer identify the issue of map-based navigation.

A fourth method for identifying scenarios is to try to instantiate general types of interaction scenarios in the current domain. For example, people often "search with partial information," "interact with the environment opportunistically," "follow instructions," or "seek an explanation." Designers and analysts can try to flesh out each of these general patterns with details from their design domain to generate candidate scenarios. Again, the scenarios generated could be more or less relevant; this method just facilitates generating possibilities. The scenarios in Figures 15.3 and 15.4 illustrate search with partial information.

A special case of instantiating general types involves using a technical theory. For example, typical interaction scenarios include "pointing to a target," "correcting a typo," "seeking information using proximal cues," and "negotiating goals with a collaborator." These scenario types are paradigmatic of some of the theories and frameworks described in this book (the chapters by MacKenzie, John, Pirolli, and Kraut—3, 4, 7, and 12—respectively). Indeed, it is typical that technical theories address a paradigmatic set of phenomena or interactions. Design rationale should sample across the range of these paradigmatic scenarios. The scenarios in Figure 15.3 and 15.4 are both examples of following an information scent, in Pirolli's sense.

A final method for generating scenarios is to transform existing scenarios. For example, one can ask "What could go wrong?" in a given scenario, and thereby derive a collection of error or exception scenarios. One could modify the viewpoint, the actors, the tools, and so forth in any scenario to obtain variants that might emphasize or help to raise new issues. For example, compass-based navigation in Figure 15.3 is replaced by map-based navigation in Figure 15.4. (Scenario generation methods are described in more detail in Carroll, 2000.)

Just as there are a variety of ways to identify scenarios, there are many ways to recognize claims, or tradeoffs, in scenarios. Obviously, one method for doing this would be text analysis. The claims in Figures 15.3 and 15.4 summarize upside and downside consequences of compass-based and map-based navigation as they are described in the scenario texts. In that sense, the claims are summaries that emphasize causal relations.

Often, identifying claims involves reading beyond the literal text. One way to do this is to systematically raise questions about the actions, events, goals, and experiences depicted in the scenario. For example, why did Sharon retrace her steps in Figure 15.3? Why did Jean decide to zoom in on the view when she did in Figure 15.4? How did the women carry out the actions involved in these episodes? What did each woman see and experience? General question-generation techniques have been developed in psycholinguistics (Graesser & Clark, 1985). In HCI, Carroll and Rosson (1992) described a technique based on systematically questioning Norman's (1986) stages of action.

Another approach to expanding the literal text is to jointly analyze scenarios with users—the people whose activities are described in scenarios. Scenarios can evoke domain-specific knowledge that was not explicit in the scenario but is important for accurately analyzing its causal relationships. For example, members of the seniors group would know that the proximity of the community center to the high school is a key factor in the success of their afterschool program.

While it is a useful heuristic to try to identify several upside and downside consequences for each feature, not every imaginable consequence is plausible. Some upsides are too farfetched to be considered a realistic strength of the design; some downsides are too unlikely, or perhaps of too little consequence for users, to present serious risks to the design. Ultimately, these questions are settled in real use, or, if one has a bit of luck, in user testing of a prototype. However, if upsides and downsides can be grounded in scientific principles, their plausibility can be investigated at an earlier stage. For example, the contrast between the designs in Figures 15.3 and 15.4 can be grounded in visual perception (Ware, Chapter 2, this volume) and mental models (Payne, Chapter 6, this volume). The science of how people understand and use their knowledge of geographical space is what is at issue in compass-based and map-based designs. (Claims-analysis methods are described in more detail in Carroll, 2000.)

15.5   CASE STUDY

The analysis of design rationale leads designers to reflect on the relationship between features of their design and its consequences for the system's users. These reflections may be grounded informally, in the designers' intuitive theories of human behavior, or they may have a more scientific grounding in theories of psychology, sociology, and so on. As an interactive system is developed and deployed, the design rationale associated with the system can be evaluated and refined (action science). When design rationale is generalized, the hypothesized causal regularities contribute to theory building (ecological science). To the extent that the generalized rationale is grounded in established scientific theory, the rationale serves as an integrative frame within which to understand and further investigate competing or complementary concerns (synthetic science). We now use the MOOsburg case study to illustrate the role of design rationale within each of these scientific paradigms.

15.5.1   MOOsburg as a Case Study in Action Science

Claims analyzed during design serve to document the hypotheses—and qualifications—that an artifact embodies with respect to its intended use (Carroll & Rosson, 1991, 1992). These hypotheses are then tested, refined, or transformed by examining the artifact in use. This is the essence of action science, wherein new ideas are embodied as real-world interventions and the resulting consequences are studied. In the case of MOOsburg, this cycle is in progress; prototypes are still being developed, analyzed, used, and refined.

Action science can be viewed as a process of hill climbing: An artifact is designed to embody research hypotheses about a starting state; the use of the resulting system is evaluated to assess these hypotheses; and the design is revised and fielded again, in an iterative fashion. The starting state for MOOsburg consisted of the Blacksburg Electronic Village (BEV), a conventional hierarchy of Web pages with community-related content about the town, its services and organizations, and its businesses. The fundamental transition from the BEV to our vision for MOOsburg came from *principled emulation* (Carroll, 2000; Singley and Carroll, 1996): We tried to systematically reuse concepts and techniques from MUDS in the community network in order to evoke feelings of engagement and sharing often experienced by users of MUDS. Other elements of the vision were pursued by *activity modeling:* We tried to systematically encourage and support the practices and activities—including values and norms—of the local community within MOOsburg.

Figure 15.5 presents a usage scenario for MOOsburg in which a community resident visits a location in the community network in the hopes of locating or engaging other citizens who share his concern about an ongoing community issue. In the course of his visit to this location, he interacts with friends but also discovers a creative activity underway by a group of young people. He is

Usage scenario: **John discovers the Brown Farm Park project in MOOsburg.**

John Robinette is worried. He lives on a large property right near the border of Blacksburg, and he has been following for several weeks the newspaper articles and editorials about the Brown Farm Park planned in the 20 acres next to his property. It's not that he doesn't want the park, but he has heard that it will be specially designed for Blacksburg youth, and he's worried about loud parties, teenagers cruising in cars, trash, and so on. He was thinking about writing a letter to the newspaper, but he decides to organize a discussion in MOOsburg instead. He knows that he'll be able to talk directly to other people there instead of mailing in "his view" and wondering how people are reacting.

When he logs on, he goes the new park site, which contains several plans under consideration, panoramic views of the property, and a simulation related to water pollution. He also finds other people logged on, including a neighbor whom he knows shares his concerns. He starts to chat with his neighbor, who points out a group of middle-school kids working on a park simulation. John sends a quick hello, asking the students about their project, but they are too engaged to even reply so he decides to check back later.

John browses the MOOsburg Toolbench, looking for a discussion tool. He finds a Forum-maker and creates one for the park site, "Neighborly Concerns." Just then, he notices that the kids are having a mild disagreement about the ages and activities of people using the park. He wants to record this for his discussion, but, by the time he gets their attention to ask permission to copy it into his forum, the discussion is over. He is impressed with the students' arguments, though, enough that he pulls up their personal-information files to find out who they are; he recognizes one of them as the son of a colleague at work and makes a mental note to mention the kids' project to his friend.

Before he leaves, he tries the simulation the students were working on. At first he finds the cartoonlike characters silly; they are clearly kid created and look like they belong in a video arcade. But as he tries out different ratios of kids, food, and so on, he can tell that the students have thought a lot about the impacts of different kinds of use. As he leaves, he thinks it might be fun to do something similar to demonstrate his concerns about traffic congestion and noise. Maybe he can get his friend's son to work with him on another simulation.

FIGURE	Scenario-based design as action science: envisioning community interaction
15.5	and cooperation in MOOsburg.

intrigued but unable to interrupt them to find out more, or to adapt their work to his own concerns, so he does what he can and decides to return at a later time to follow up with the students' project. This scenario integrates many aspects of our MOOsburg vision: personal identity within the community network, shared activities linked to specific locations and resources of the town, creative contributions by diverse residents, informal and spontaneous interest-based interaction.

The claims analyzed in Figure 15.6 make explicit the hypotheses about community interaction and cooperation that have become components of the MOOsburg project. For example, a central feature is the explicit connection of activities within the network to the concrete locations and resources of the town, in this case the Brown Farm Park planning site. The downside acknowledged in

Claim: **Using a community map to organize activities into interest-based groupings**
+ simplifies access to people and resources related to specific community concerns
− but not all community concerns or interests will be related to spatial locations

Claim: **Supporting synchronous chat within a community network**
+ encourages residents to interact rather than to simply gather information or work alone
− but individual efforts to initiate chat may interfere with copresent members' goals
− but problems of critical mass may convey a general sense of nonparticipation

Claim: **Restricting community-chat records to specialized "discussion" objects**
+ reassures residents that spontaneous and/or personal discussions are transient and informal
− but some spontaneous discussions that are useful will be unavailable to other residents

Claim: **Having direct access to resident's email handle and other personal information**
+ extends online characters to include information about identities and roles outside the MOO
+ reminds residents that they may also be contacted in real life, outside the MOO
− but may inhibit creative or unconventional behavior in the presence of known others

Claim: **Expecting and supporting member-developed content in the network**
+ increases the buy-in and commitment of residents, promoting the network's sustainability
+ motivates residents to develop the skills needed to make individual contributions
− but participants may experience the resulting content as too diverse or inconsistent in quality

FIGURE	Claims analysis as action science: rationale for community interaction and cooperation in MOOsburg.
15.6	

the design rationale is that not all topics or concerns may have a concrete starting point of this sort (e.g., where would one go to talk about more general ecological concerns?).

Another claim implicit in the Brown Farm scenario is that a pervasive channel for conversation will promote interaction among community residents. However, as illustrated by John's desire to interact with the students working with the simulation, there are downsides to this. If a participant arrives and attempts to chat with others already engaged in a task, he or she may be ignored or may distract them from their ongoing activities; if no one is there, the community system may appear empty or unwelcoming.

A corollary hypothesis concerns the distinction between a transient online chat and a more permanent discussion forum. It is certainly possible to store transcripts of people's informal chat, but this is not what happens in a community. Only specially marked communication media are associated with records (e.g., town meetings, newspaper letters), and these are almost always classified by topic in advance. Our analysis of how conversation is treated in the town led us to make a similar distinction in the system. This decision and its tradeoffs are evident in John's desire to capture the students' conversation, coupled with his inability to interrupt and garner permission soon enough to do so.

A third hypothesis captured in the design rationale reflects our thinking about how a resident's virtual identity in MOOsburg should be related to his or her real-world identity in the town. Participants in a virtual environment are by definition anonymous to some degree. When the feeling of anonymity is strong, social inhibitions may be reduced; this may lead to increases in creativity but also in dissension or rude behavior (Nunamaker et al., 1991; Sproull & Kiesler, 1991). Real-world communities have a low degree of anonymity—people join the community by moving into a home and establishing a postal address, a phone number, utility and tax accounts, and so on. The resident becomes visible and accountable for his or her behavior. The task of joining MOOsburg adopts a similar activity perspective: Residents should feel a sense of visibility and accountability, just as they do in Blacksburg. Thus, new users of the MOO are required to provide a working email address, along with other personal information. The analogy is with establishing a postal address or phone number, ensuring that other residents will be able to find out more about the user and to follow up directly on shared interests and concerns.

A final example comes from our design concerns related to sustainability of activities in a community network. Most proximal communities have a local government and associated staff that perform basic peacekeeping and maintenance functions. But many other town activities take place in a distributed fashion, with particular individuals taking an interest in particular topics or issues (like John in our scenario). It is important for MOOsburg to support this sort of distributed development, where interested participants can stake their claims, pursue their concerns, develop and distribute materials, and so on. Individual initiative is central to this, even if it leads to contributions that vary widely in style and quality. If we succeed at this, we expect that participants will feel responsibility for their own contributions and hence a greater commitment to the network as a whole.

The hypotheses expressed in the design rationale remain open issues within this action-science project. Not surprisingly, we have discovered that it will be very challenging to attract and support member-authored objects and content; our current approach is to identify and work closely with the "community tip-rudders" (Rheingold, 1993) who have the energy and interest to learn new technologies that will help them to address community issues (Rosson, Carroll, Seals, & Lewis, 2002). Thus far, the emphasis on interaction and on personal identity seem to be natural and appreciated, but our user population is still rather small. We do not have experience with enough online-community activities to evaluate the more specific hypotheses regarding the distinction between chat and discussion objects.

15.5.2   MOOsburg as a Case Study in Ecological Science

Design rationale supports ecological science at three levels. First, it supports taxonomic science by surveying and documenting causal regularities in the usage situation, namely the features of a designed artifact that are expected to have consequences for its users. Second, design rationale supports design-based science through abstractions that enable knowledge accumulation and application. Finally, the knowledge captured in design rationale supports the development of evolutionary science by promoting insights and development of new features and new situations. In the following, we illustrate how the MOOsburg case study illustrates each of these levels.

As previewed in Section 15.2, a central MOOsburg design issue is its spatial model for navigation. The usage scenario presented on the left of Figure 15.7, and the claims analysis presented on the left of Figure 15.8 elaborate this model with scenarios and features that articulate how activities in MOOsburg are connected to the structures and activity contexts of the real world. In the scenario, John and Nathan enrich their discussion of the park with their previous visits and use of the park land, and their interaction history in the real world. As Nathan moves from one location to another, he adopts an "appropriate" social persona, a respectful young neighbor for John Robinette and an eager but shy student in the classroom. Nathan's previous interactions with his class and teacher help him to know where and how to find the simulation tool. The design rationale summarized in Figure 15.8 analyzes the tradeoffs associated with these three facets of MOOsburg's spatial model.

The right sides of Figures 15.7 and 15.8 demonstrate how an ecological survey of this sort can guide design of related artifacts. Our research group is currently designing a place-based collaborative environment for the U.S. Navy, and in many respects this project is benefiting directly from design rationale developed for MOOsburg. For instance, the modeling of streets, buildings, and rooms has been transposed to refer to oceans, islands, ships, and so on. These are containment structures or areas likely to have similar consequences as the town structures modeled in MOOsburg. The military-planning scenario in Figure 15.7 describes how the navy commanders behave differently when in the executive meeting room versus their more informal chat room, and how the interaction with the ocean map helps to recall prior episodes or other information pertinent to the current decision process. The associated design rationale captures similar causal relations, but contextualized for the navy work setting.

Usage scenario: **Nathan and John work together on a park simulation.**

Nathan is an eighth grader and lives on the small farm next to John Robinette. He doesn't know much about the Brown Farm Park plan, though he has heard his mom and dad worrying about it and knows that they have been talking to John and his wife about organizing a meeting with other residents. Nathan is actually pretty excited about the new park, because he thinks it will have some nice open fields where he and his friends can play pick-up soccer and football.

He is surprised one afternoon to get an email from John, telling him about the Brown Farm site and asking him whether he is familiar with the simulation tool being used by the other kids, and, if so, whether he'd like to work with John on a project looking at traffic congestion and noise. Nathan knows a bit about the simulation tool from school, and he thinks this might be fun, so he sends a note back saying that he will download an example simulation that they can edit together.

After John's email, Nathan visits his MOOsburg classroom to find the tool. While he is there, his teacher arrives and asks him what he is working on. Nathan likes his teacher a lot, but, because he has never talked to her before about Brown Farm, he feels a bit shy about describing his project with Mr. Robinette. She is quickly diverted when one of her favorite students arrives. Nathan wishes he had spoken up more quickly.

Later that week, John and Nathan meet at Brown Farm in MOOsburg. They chat for a bit, exploring the town's planning map to see how it compares to what they remember about the land. Nathan thinks the wetland area has been underestimated. John agrees but suggests that the town may be projecting into the future; he's noticed a small decrease in wetland size recently. This gives them an idea for their simulation; perhaps they can show how traffic near a wetland causes its borders to contract over time.

Usage scenario: **Admiral Intony and his vice admirals finalize a training exercise.**

Admiral Intony and his vice admirals need to develop a plan for next month's Pacific training exercises. He and three of his vice admirals are located at San Diego Naval Base, but four other vice admirals are at sea—in four different ships in three fleets. The admiral's executive officer, Captain Tricoll, suggests that they meet in the Navy MOO to discuss the training options.

Captain Tricoll schedules a meeting in the admiral's virtual executive meeting room, part of the San Diego Naval Base MOO. As the others arrive, he informs them that Admiral Intony will be 15 minutes late. Several of the vice admirals are avid football fans; rather than chatting about Navy's standing in the admiral's executive room, they move to the commons area in the virtual base where they can chat informally in comfort.

Soon Admiral Intony arrives and calls the meeting to order; the officers greet each other formally according to rank and naval protocol. The admiral asks Captain Tricoll to overview the open issues. Tricoll opens the planning document he had earlier uploaded to the room, reminding them that the major open decisions are to choose fleets who will act as aggressor/defendor, and where to stage the mock battle.

Following Tricoll's lead, the group zooms out enough to see the Pacific and the four fleets of ships. As they look over the display, Vice-Admiral Smarden recalls a previous exercise staged just off Fiji. He points to an area where the ocean floor varies dramatically, making it very challenging to program and track torpedo depth. The admiral agrees, and Tricoll notes that a recent weather forecast predicts a severe storm in this area in a few weeks, likely to add further challenges. The group decides that the two fleets with greatest tonnage will play the role of defenders. This will give them a slight advantage when the storm arrives, and it will complicate the calculations of the aggressors even more.

FIGURE   Scenario-based design as ecological survey: a MOOsburg scenario inspires the
                design of a near neighbor.
15.7

Claim: **Holding teacher-student conversations in a simulated classroom**
+ instantiates the classroom community as pre-existing social context for interaction
+ encourages students and teachers to behave in ways appropriate to a classroom
+ sets up implicit boundaries that can be used as cues for changes in social behavior
− but if key aspects of the classroom are missing, interaction may be inappropriate or awkward

Claim: **Supporting naval decision making in the admiral's online conference room**
+ instantiates the executive group as pre-existing social context for interaction
+ reminds participants to exhibit appropriate protocols in arrival, departure, and utterances
+ sets up implicit boundaries that can be used as cues for changes in social behavior
− but if key aspects of real-world meeting rooms are missing, interaction may be inappropriate or awkward

Claim: **Supporting land-use discussions with a real-world zoning map**
+ enriches residents' mental experience with personal knowledge of the mapped land
+ simplifies coordination between discussion points and specific land features
− but may lead residents to adopt a too-literal or concrete approach to their land concerns

Claim: **Grounding navy executive planning activities with a real-world map**
+ enriches commanders' mental experience with personal knowledge of the mapped area
+ simplifies coordination between plan issues and specific ocean, ship, or island features
− but may lead users to adopt a too-literal or concrete approach to their planning proposals

Claim: **A virtual community organized into buildings and rooms**
+ creates a familiar structure for "storing" or "finding" things
− but information may be hidden to people not inside the building or room
− but users must navigate "into" and "out of" streets, buildings, streets, rooms, etc.

Claim: A virtual fleet visualized as an ocean populated with ships, islands, etc.
+ creates a familiar structure for "storing" or "finding" people, plans, or other resources
− but information may be hidden to people not inside a ship, on an island, etc.
− but users must explicitly choose to navigate "into" and "out of" ships, islands, etc.

FIGURE

15.8

Design rationale as ecological survey: MOOsburg claims suggest rationale for a near neighbor.

The regularities captured in design rationale can be used in a more piecemeal fashion as well. We have described the virtual-fleet project as a "near neighbor" in the design space of collaborative environments—it is based on different users, tasks, and objects, but it is otherwise quite isomorphic in structure. But any system that supports exchanges between people who share an interaction history or other social context will profit from thinking through the consequences of situating such exchanges in a place that evokes participants' interaction context. The designers might use MOOsburg rationale to develop and analyze their own project-specific scenarios of appropriate or inappropriate behavior; just as for the MOOsburg and virtual fleet projects, what-if reasoning can be explored to weigh the benefits of invoking an existing social context versus the associated costs.

Beyond encouraging a survey of specific features and their consequences, design rationale promotes cumulation and generalization. On a small scale, this happens within a single design effort, as design features are instantiated in multiple scenarios. We might reformulate the teacher-student interaction in Figure 15.7 as a teacher-parent interaction or as an organizer-volunteer interaction in other scenarios. This might then lead to a more general statement of the design feature—perhaps as "holding conversations in places that reinforce partners' contrasting roles."

More generally, design rationale cumulates across different design projects. In earlier work, we demonstrated how this was done for the case of learning tools that were designed to promote active learning while minimizing or preventing the mishaps that often accompany exploratory self-directed learning (Singley & Carroll, 1990). We also showed how features of a tool for learning to program in Smalltalk were generalized in the design of a similar tool that supported reuse of Smalltalk code (Carroll & Rosson, 1991).

In Figure 15.9, we illustrate this abstraction process within the MOOsburg case study. The scenario and claims no longer refer to the town of Blacksburg, residents of a community, or their real-world concerns. We no longer assume navigation using a local map, or a containment structure based on buildings and rooms. We have tried instead to state the "essence" of the earlier claims, so that the design space subsumes any system design that incorporates real-world places and containment structures.

The key point in this view of the case study is that the level of abstraction has been elevated. We are not just talking about community discussions, places on a town map, buildings and roads, and so on. Instead we are proposing a general-purpose design concept—a *place-based online system*—and considering its implications. The transition from a town to a navy with a fleet of ships can be seen as one step toward articulation of this more general concept. As the abstractions become more stable and refined, they express what is often referred to as *genre* in design (Carroll & Rosson, 1991; Erickson, 2000).

A design genre serves as a generator (or explanatory account) of a broad range of design issues and artifacts. Harrison & Dourish (1996) argue strongly for a distinction between "space" and "place," where a place is understood as a space that includes associated social and cultural contexts for action and interpretation. This understanding of place is highly consistent with our analysis of place-based online systems. However, our analysis of the design genre integrates with this the affordances of spatial containment and navigation, implicit social boundaries, operations with surrogates of real-world objects, and visibility and maintenance of personal identity.

Abstract usage scenario: **A group works together in a virtual world.**

Members of a real-world group meet online to discuss a shared concern. In the space, they browse and interact with virtual objects that are surrogates for objects in the real world; as part of their discussion, they point at and annotate the virtual objects. The surrogates evoke their experiences with the real-world counterparts, which enriches the online experience, helping them to remember and better articulate a range of shared and personal concerns.

As the discussion progresses, supporting information is needed. One participant remembers having used the information at another place, and navigates to this other place to retrieve it. As she enters this other online place, the images and other objects in that virtual space evoke prior history with it—the people she knows who also use it, their activities, and their various roles. She automatically adjusts behavior to meet the expectations and standards of this group. When she leaves this place and returns to the starting place, she again adjusts role and social behavior accordingly.

Claim: **Situating online interaction in a familiar place-based environment**

+ evokes and applies the interaction partners' history and common ground

+ supports social context–switching as place-based boundaries are crossed

− but important aspects of the place may be missing, making interaction inappropriate or awkward

Claim: **Online objects that refer directly to real-world objects**

+ expands mental experience of the virtual object with existing personal knowledge

− but may limit creativity with respect to virtual attributes and operations

Claim: **A virtual structure that mimics real-world physical containment relations**

+ creates a simple and extensible decomposition for storing and retrieving objects

+ leverages people's real-world skills of spatial browsing and navigation

− but highly nested structures may make search and navigation difficult

FIGURE	Design rationale as ecological generalization: abstract features and
15.9	consequences define an artifact genre.

With the design rationale for place-based virtual environments in hand, designers can apply the genre to rather different system design projects. For instance, how might an *immersive virtual reality system* be realized as a place-based environment? One key concern would be the experiences conveyed as users navigate the containment structure—magically walking "through" a wall into an adjoining room does not emphasize the associated social boundaries as much as a symbolic act like "opening a door" or making a room-switch request. Thus the social context–switching effect may be diminished. Abstract renderings of co-present users (e.g., as polygons) are less likely to emphasize personal identity than avatars adorned with personal cues like a face image, accurate information about size or shape, and so on. The abstract design rationale would help designers of the new system to raise and confront these issues more deliberately, as they consider options for avatar design and navigation.

In a rather different context, one might consider how a design genre could influence the design of a business system for *knowledge management* (i.e., a system in which the skills, knowledge, and practices of employees are captured, organized, and reused). Here the design concept suggests a spatially distributed knowledge base, and it highlights the diversity of business customs and practices across different work groups or other organizational units. Direct employee interaction would be pervasive and would make direct reference to real-world work objects. Expression and maintenance of personal identity might occur as an organizational reputation/credibility system, such as tracking and visualizing how individual employees contribute to or access the knowledge base (Kelly, Sung, & Farnham, 2002).

Figure 15.10 summarizes how the emergence of the place-based genre fits within the framework of the task-artifact cycle. The cycle begins with the activities of a real-world community, for example their desire for social interaction, shared planning, and so on. These activities engender general requirements for online support, such as intimacy, rich personal exchange, discussion and operation on shared resources, and so on. Over time, as concrete systems are envisioned, built, and analyzed in response to these needs, a genre emerges—in this case, the concept of place-based online systems. The genre's design rationale captures the essential facets of the design concept that are expected to have important consequences for the members and activities of a community. As the community responds and adapts their activities in response to these consequences, new needs may arise; these may produce further concrete system designs, elaborating or refining the design genre over time.

15.5.3 MOOsburg as a Case Study in Synthetic Science

Designers working within a problem domain are typically guided by general design goals and theoretical stances. For instance, researchers developing systems for online communities may apply theories of social psychology to promote a sense of belonging or rich interpersonal exchange. Researchers working on learning environments may hold theories of constructivist or active learning. Analysis of design rationale brings theoretical content to the surface, in the form of anticipated consequences of design features, as when the conveyance of personal identity in MOOsburg is predicted to at once increase intimacy and accountability. Furthermore, the "what-if" reasoning that generates design rationale with both positive and negative impacts promotes a synthesis of complementary or competing theoretical grounding.

Consider an example from the MOOsburg case study. One motivation for our decision to situate personal interaction within virtual renditions of real-world places was motivated by the concerns of activity theory (Bertelsen &

Claims analyzing how community supports intimacy,
history, memory, socially appropriate behavior, rich exchange

Community Interaction Scenarios:
• spontaneous discussion
• collaborative planning
• information retrieval
• manipulation of shared resources

Place-Based Online System:
• place-based interaction
• real-world surrogates
• personal identities
• spatial containment

Claims analyzing consequences of social boundaries, metaphoric
object understanding and use, personal accountability and credit,
spatial cues for navigation and object retrieval

FIGURE

15.10

A genre for place-based online systems develops through a process of co-evolution expressed as a task-artifact cycle.

Bødker, Chapter 11, this volume) and distributed cognition (Hutchins, 1995c). The actions of an individual do not occur in isolation, but rather they are always contextualized by the larger activity context(s) in which the individual participates. The community associated with the activity influences the interaction, through its norms, conventions, roles, and responsibilities. Many materials and tools mediate the interaction of individuals and their community; buildings and other aspects of the physical setting are one example that is featured in MOOsburg.

This activity-theoretic view of conversation among community members motivates the use of virtual places as a context for interaction. But at the same time, other theories emphasize contrasting impacts. For instance, a virtual place will never completely mimic a real-world place (indeed, it is not clear that one would want to do this even if possible). To the extent that some aspects are missing, social cues for interaction may be absent or diminished. Theories of computer-mediated communication (Sproull & Kiesler, 1991) would thus predict that some awkwardness or inappropriate behavior may occur. The discomfort of any such behavior might even be exacerbated by the general expectation of intimacy and appropriateness engendered by place.

Activity theory and models of computer-mediated communication have emerged from different world views and theoretical paradigms. They are not necessarily competing views, but they do emphasize different aspects and concerns of human behavior. Analysis of the design rationale for a specific system (or, more generally, for a design genre) brings such complementary views into a shared arena for discussion and debate. This might promote exchange between communities as they seek to contrast or prioritize related concerns, develop new vocabularies for predicting and measuring competing predictions, and so on.

Figure 15.11 continues the case study with additional examples of synthetic science. The benefits provided by a familiar place for interaction can also be grounded in the theory of common ground (Clark & Brennan, 1991; Monk, Chapter 10, this volume). To the extent that conversation partners have a shared history within a place, interactions within this place should evoke these memories, helping partners to anticipate and interpret the utterances of one another. McGrath (1984) offers a related theory that emphasizes the important contributions of the "standing group" to successful interaction.

The design rationale related to surrogate objects is grounded in theoretical views of users' development and reliance on mental models (Carroll & Olson, 1988; Payne, Chapter 6, this volume). For instance, theories of metaphoric reasoning (Carroll & Thomas, 1982; Gentner & Stevens, 1993) and of direct manipulation (Hutchins, Hollan, & Norman, 1986) emphasize how humans process and understand new experiences in terms of familiar experiences that have similar content or structure. Yet Vygotsky's (1962) concept of proximal zones of development points to a crucial role for entirely new conceptions that are beyond understanding and that can only be understood and assimilated with assistance. Winograd and Flores (1986) also emphasize the critical role of breakdowns (building on Heidegger's [1962] notion of "unready to hand") in noticing and making sense of novel concepts.

The grounding for design rationale concerning spatial decomposition and containment is found in theories of spatial browsing (e.g., Williamson & Shneiderman, 1992), ecological perception (Gibson, 1950, 1966, 1979), and landmark perception (Lynch, 1960), as well as in general theories of hierarchical decomposition in planning and action (Newell & Simon, 1972). At the same time, the claims analysis raises competing concerns of nesting and levels of indirection. A deeply nested user interface increases the "gulf" between a user's goal and the physical operations that achieve it (Norman, 1986). Information processing theories such as Goals, Operators, Methods, and Selection rules (GOMS) provide techniques for building precise models of negative impacts such as this (John, Chapter 4, this volume).

The treatment of personal identity within MOOsburg (or the place-based genre more generally) again recruits design rationale from activity theory, in that it emphasizes the roles and responsibilities of an individual as part of a community. It synthesizes this with rationale drawn from attribution theory (Kelly, 1955), which emphasizes maintenance of self-consistent behavior when one is

Claim: **Situating online interaction in a familiar place-based environment.**
+ evokes and applies the interaction partners' history and common ground
+ supports social context–switching as place-based boundaries are crossed
− but important aspects of the known context may be missing, making interaction inappropriate or awkward

Common ground (Clark & Brennan, 1991); Distributed cognition (Hutchins, 1995); Group dynamics (McGrath, 1984); Activity theory (Bertelsen & Bødker, Chap. 11, this volume); Computer-mediated communication (Sproull & Kiesler, 1991)

Claim: **Online objects that refer directly to real-world objects**
+ expands mental experience of the virtual object with existing personal knowledge
− but may limit creativity with respect to virtual attributes and operations

Mental models (Carroll & Olson, 1988; Payne, Chap. 6, this volume); Metaphors (Carroll & Thomas, 1982); Direct manipulation (Hutchins, Hollan, & Norman, 1986); Zone of proximal development (Vygotsky, 1962); Activity breakdowns (Winograd & Flores, 1986)

Claim: **A virtual structure that mimics real-world physical containment relations**
+ creates a simple and extensible hierarchical decomposition for storing and retrieving objects
+ leverages people's real-world skills of spatial browsing and navigation
− but highly nested structures may make search and navigation difficult

Problem-solving (Newell & Simon, 1972); Ecological psychology (Gibson, 1950, 1966, 1979); Landmarks (Lynch, 1960); Self-embedding theory (Miller & Chomsky, 1963); GOMS (John, Chap. 4, this volume)

Claim: **Direct access to user's personal information in a virtual environment**
+ emphasizes that participants are part of an existing organization, with norms and conventions
− but may inhibit display of creative or unconventional behavior

Activity theory (Bertelsen & Bødker, Chap. 11, this volume); Transfer and "working through" (Turkle, 1995); Social loafing (Kraut, Chap. 12, this volume); Process loss (Nunamaker et al., 1991)

Claim: **Expecting and supporting member-developed content in the network**
+ increases the buy-in and commitment of participants, promoting the network's sustainability
+ motivates community members to develop the authoring skills needed to make individual contributions
− but participants may experience the resulting content as too diverse or inconsistent in quality

Social capital (Putnam, 2000); Self-perception theory (Kelly, 1955); Cognitive dissonance theory (Festinger, 1957); User-interface consistency (Reisner, 1991)

FIGURE
15.11

Design rationale as synthetic science: claims grounded in complementary and/or competing theories.

observed by others. Theories of group behavior also predict that situations that emphasize personal accountability will decrease group process losses such as social loafing (Kraut, Chapter 12, this volume). The analysis of negative consequences is grounded in theories of personal interaction that consider anonymity to be a critical enabler of creative or unconventional behavior (Nunamaker et al., 1991; Turkle, 1995).

Finally, the positive rationale for distributed member-initiated content development finds grounding in theories of social capital (Putnam, 2000); individuals who make a visible contribution to an online community are helping to build social capital. From the perspective of personal motivation, cognitive dissonance theory (Festinger, 1957) suggests that, if individuals see themselves putting considerable personal effort into a task (e.g., learning to use a new authoring tool), they are more likely to see the task as intrinsically motivating and thus are more likely to attempt and enjoy the task in the future. At the same time, the design rationale for this feature includes a contrasting concern grounded in cognitive theories of perception and understanding (Norman, 1986)—widespread distribution of individually motivated and customized content may result in a diverse environment that is difficult to apprehend or appreciate.

Although we have focused here on theory bases that are familiar to work in HCI, design rationale can also synthesize scientific theories from disparate disciplines. For instance, nesting via spatial containment is formally analogous to phrase-structure embedding in natural language (Miller & Chomsky, 1963); it might display analogous constraints (Carroll, 1980). The distributed development of content has implications for models of software architecture—a centralized software infrastructure simplifies control of versions and interactions, but at the cost of decreased flexibility and the danger of a single point of failure (Greenberg & Marwood, 1994). Similarly, a software-related consequence of spatial containment is brittleness to extension and refactoring. (If a computational object is nested deep within a hierarchy, it is not clear what its status should be when a higher-level layer is removed or revised.) In general, scenarios and design rationale specify a shareable design space that can be used to raise, discuss, and arbitrate widely varying theoretical predictions and concerns (Rosson & Carroll, 2000).

15.6   CURRENT STATUS AND FURTHER READING

Our approach to design rationale as science and theory development continues to be developed primarily through action-science case studies of system development and use. Many of these are carried out in the software industry and documented only in technical reports. We have begun to collect and present some of these case studies in an Internet repository, the Usability Case Studies *(ucs.cs.vt.edu)*.

A monograph describing the early development of our approach to design rationale is J. M. Carroll, *Making use: Scenario-based design of human-computer interactions* (Cambridge, MA: MIT Press, 2000). A textbook describing our approach to design rationale as one facet of a general scenario-based methodology for managing the software development lifecycle is M. B. Rosson and J. M. Carroll, *Usability engineering: Scenario-based design of human-computer interaction* (San Francisco: Morgan-Kaufmann, 2002).

Alistair Sutcliffe's recent book, *The domain theory: Patterns for knowledge and software reuse* (Mahwah, NJ: Lawrence Erlbaum Associates, 2002), employs claims analysis as a general knowledge representation. This is an interesting and fundamental application of the approach to both cognitive science and to scientific and methodological foundations of software engineering.

A broad collection of HCI-oriented papers on design rationale is T. P. Moran and J. M. Carroll, Editors, *Design rationale: Concepts, methods and techniques* (Mahwah, NJ: Lawrence Erlbaum Associates, 1996).

ACKNOWLEDGMENTS

The development and analysis of the MOOsburg system was partially supported by grants from U.S. National Science Foundation (NSF) Information Technology Research program (IIS 0113264), the U.S. Office of Naval Research (N00014–00–1–0549), and The Hitachi Foundation Information Technology in Education Initiative. We are grateful for comments from Alan Blackwell and Andrew Monk.

Glossary

abstraction: A term in a notational system or other information artifact that is defined with reference to the primitive concepts of the system, or with reference to other abstractions that are ultimately defined by primitives. It is frequently used to aggregate many instances, so that all can be manipulated by a single action; thus, a heading style is a typical word-processor abstraction defined in terms of font properties, and all its instances can be altered by altering its definition.

abstraction hierarchy: A hierarchical description of the functional structure of a work domain, in which work-domain purposes are related to underlying physical structures. Also referred to as a *structural means-ends hierarchy* because links between adjacent levels connect ends (upper nodes) to means (lower nodes).

actions: Behavior to which meaning has been attached within a particular social/cultural context. Sometimes denotes a lower level of organization in human endeavor, including simple gestures and other motor behavior.

activity: The significant and typically collective endeavors of humans. It is the fundamental concept in activity theory, which conceives of activity as conducted through individual actions and mediated by artifacts. In the cognitive-dimensions framework, an activity is likewise a significant endeavor conducted through individual actions, but six generic types of activity are distinguished (e.g., search, design, etc.); at present, only individual interaction with information artifacts is considered.

ACT-RPM: The latest in a series of computational cognitive architectures developed by John Anderson and colleagues. ACT-RPM contains architectural mechanisms for cognitive, perceptual, and motor performance and learning. It was one of the architectures reviewed in Pew & Mavor (1998). More information about this series of architectures can be found in Anderson (1976, 1983, 1993) and Byrne & Anderson (2001).

adaptationism, adaptationist approach: The thesis that selection pressures have been the most powerful cause of evolution; a useful methodological heuristic is to assume that biological and behavioral structures are the results of adaptation to the environment.

affordance: Perceptual characteristics of an object that make it obvious what the object can do and how it can be manipulated. The concept, as used in HCI, is adapted from James J. Gibson's definition, "The affordances of the environment are what it offers the animal, what it provides or furnishes, for good or ill. . . .[affordance] implies the complementarity of the animal and the environment." (1979; p.127).

analog representations: Representations that share the structure of the things they represent. For example, a picture is an analog representation. See also **propositional representations.**

anthropology: The investigation of social structure, social relationships, and individual social action through an emphasis on culture—originally "other cultures" but increasingly the emphasis is on "home" cultures.

apex: A computational architecture using resource scheduling and reactive planning (techniques from artificial intelligence). More information can be found in Freed (1998). It has been used as a GOMS modeling tool (John, 2002; Remington et al., 2002).

artifacts: A diverse class of human-created systems, applications, tools, and conventions, including language and mathematics, that mediate human activity. Artifacts are the products of prior human activity; they both enable and constrain current human activity, and their use helps to orient the design of future artifacts. An information artifact (as used in the cognitive-dimensions framework) is an artifact designed to store, create, present, or manipulate information, whether noninteractive (e.g., a book or a map) or interactive (e.g., a spreadsheet or a heating controller).

automatic cognitive processes: Processes that are relatively quick and effortless, requiring little attention or monitoring. Well-practiced skills, like walking and driving, or signing one's name, are examples of automatic cognitive processes. See also **controlled cognitive processes.**

bounded rationality: The idea, from Herbert Simon (e.g., Simon, 1982), that human agents are rational in that they act so as to meet their goals according to their knowledge; they are only boundedly rational, however, in that they cannot necessarily compute ideal, optimal decisions. Instead, their decisions are bounded by environmental constraints on their performance (such as the need to act quickly), interacting with limits on access to knowledge and limits on the ability to process relevant information.

CCT: See **cognitive complexity theory.**

claims analysis: An analytic evaluation method involving the identification of scenario features that have significant positive and negative usability consequences.

claims feature: An element of a situation or an interactive system that has positive or negative consequences for people in this or similar situations.

CMN-GOMS: The original version of GOMS created by Card, Moran, and Newell (1980a). The "CMN" was added before "GOMS" when other versions of GOMS began to appear (e.g., CPM-GOMS and NGOMSL), to differentiate the specific representation used by Card, Moran, and Newell from the concepts in GOMS.

cognitive architecture: The fixed structure that realizes a cognitive system. It typically decribes the memories and processors in a cognitive system and how information flows between them. This is in contrast to the knowledge laid on top of an architecture to allow it to perform a task in a particular domain.

cognitive artifact: A manmade or -modified tool to support mental activity. Examples include number systems, slide rules, navigational charts, and even language itself. While generally applied to a single individual, within the framework of DCog, a cognitive artifact is also a tool that supports the coordination of information processing between entities within a functional system.

cognitive complexity theory (CCT): A computational cognitive architecture introduced by Kieras and Polson in the 1980s and used as the basis for NGOMSL. It was realized in a production system. More information can be found in Bovair, Kieras, & Polson, 1988, 1990; Kieras & Polson, 1985.

cognitive dimension: A characteristic of the way information is structured and represented—one that is shared by many notations and interaction languages of different types and, by its interaction with the human cognitive architecture, that has a strong influence on how people use the notation and determines what cognitive strategies can be pursued. Any pair of dimensions can be manipulated independently of each other, although typically a third dimension must be allowed to change (pairwise independence). (More exactly, a cognitive dimension is not solely a characteristic of the notation, but a joint characteristic of the notation and the environment in which the notation is used, whether based on paper and pencil or computer or even based on voice and sound.) Examples such as viscosity, premature commitment, and others are defined in the text. Note that in the cognitive-dimensions framework, dimensions are not evaluative *per se,* but only in relation to a particular type of activity; for example, viscosity is a problem for modification activities but not for transcription activities. See also **cognitive-dimensions framework.**

cognitive-dimensions framework: This states the pertinent values of cognitive dimensions that are required to support a given type of activity, and thereby provides a means to evaluate an information artifact.

cognitive engineering: A multidisciplinary area of research concerned with the analysis, modeling, design, and evaluation of complex sociotechnical systems. It is sometimes also called *cognitive systems engineering.*

cognitive ethnography: A qualitative method of data collection used by DCog researchers based around observation. It is "cognitive" because it focuses on computational information transformations within a functional system.

cognitive science: The scientific project dedicated to understanding the processes and representations underlying intelligent action.

cognitive work analysis: An approach to analyzing human work that focuses on how effective courses of action are constrained by both ecological and cognitive considerations.

cognitivism: Maintains a Cartesian dualism, attributing human conduct to the operation of mental predicates. Often associated with a computational theory of mind, it is a predominant paradigm within human-computer interaction (HCI).

common ground: Some piece of knowledge is common ground if all the people conversing know it and they all know that the others know it, too. (See the text for a more formal and comprehensive definition.)

complexity theory: The study of how much time or resources are required to compute things. The complexity of an algorithm or problem is typically measured relative to the size of the problem, n, and expressed in order notation. For example, a time complexity of $O(n^2)$ means that the time it takes to perform the calculation increases with the square of the problem size.

computational equivalence: Two representations that, in addition to being informationally equivalent, make the same information equally readily accessible. See also **informational equivalence.**

computational metaphor (of cognition): Hutchins (1995a, p.117) defines a "computation" as referring to "the propagation of representational state across representational media." The computational metaphor is the position taken that cognition is a form of computation, and that mental state is encoded analogously to computer representations, hence the term "metaphor." Within cognitive science, the computational metaphor is also known as the "representational theory of mind," in which computations are actions on representations. DCog claims that the computational metaphor can be applied to a unit of analysis broader than an individual's mind (i.e., the functional system).

computer-supported cooperative work (CSCW): The design of systems to support interaction and cooperative working. It emerged in the late 1980s as a result of dissatisfactions with the predominantly cognitivist paradigm employed in human-computer interaction (HCI) and in recognition of the importance of questions regarding organizations, work, and interaction for the design of computer systems.

conceptual framework: A structure describing the concepts in a cognitive system, less specific than a cognitive architecture.

constraints: In the context of cognitive work analysis, factors that limit, but do not prescribe, how effective work activity might be carried out.

controlled cognitive processes: Processes that require monitoring and effort or attention during their execution. See also **automatic cognitive processes.**

control task analysis: A way of analyzing work that focuses on the control that must be exercised over a work domain and the tasks implied to exercise such control. An analytic phase of cognitive work analysis.

conversation analysis: Originated by Harvey Sacks, this is often coupled with ethnomethodology and is the study of the way in which conversationalists order and accomplish their exchange of speech with each other as a situated and locally organized matter.

cost structure of information: An analysis of the resource and opportunity costs involved in accessing and handling information from a physical or virtual information system.

CPM-GOMS: A version of GOMS developed by John in the 1980s that explicitly joined GOMS to the model human processor. It included perceptual and motor operators as well as cognitive operators. Perceptual, cognitive, and motor operators could run in parallel, subject to resource and information dependencies. More information can be found in Gray, John, & Atwood, 1993; John 1988, 1990; John & Gray, 1992, 1994, 1995.

critical path: The path through subtasks (operators) in a PERT chart that determines the length of the total task. Used in CPM-GOMS.

CSCW: See **computer-supported cooperative work.**

DCog: The form of distributed cognition developed by Hutchins in the early 1990s. It is distinguished from other uses of the term *distributed cognition* by its explicitly computational perspective on goal-based activity systems.

descriptive model: A model that describes how a system or person behaves and that provides a framework or context for thinking about or describing a problem or situation. Usually based on data gained through empirical observation, it is often little more than a verbal or graphic articulation of categories or identifiable features in an interface.

design: Encompasses activities and actions directed at producing new artifacts. Design work is collective and multidisciplinary. It often includes professional designers, technologists, and future users of the artifacts.

design rationale: Arguments for why (or why not) a feature or set of features should be incorporated into a design.

direct perception: The theory of James J. Gibson that claims that the visual environment is perceived "directly," as opposed to being indirectly inferred from sense data.

ecological interface design: An approach to interface design that uses Rasmussen's abstraction hierarchy and skills-rules-knowledge framework to specify interfaces that support adaptive human operator behavior in the face of events or situations that systems designers did not anticipate.

EPIC: A computational cognitive architecture introduced by Kieras in the late 1990s. EPIC is known for computationally implementing perceptual and motor processes. More information can be found in Kieras & Meyer, 1997; Meyer & Kieras, 1997a, 1997b.

ethnography: Originating in the anthropology of Bronislaw Malinowski, this has come to mean the study of cultural and societal matters from inside their operations. It is associated with *fieldwork,* which emphasizes the importance of participatory methods for collecting data about social phenomena.

ethnomethodology: Founded by Harold Garfinkel, this is an alternate sociology that eschews the predominantly theoretical caste of sociology in favor of studies of the way in which social order is attested to, constituted, and used within the practical doings of societal members. *Ethnomethodological studies of work* have focused on the situated practices, methods, and interactions through which members order their work.

Fitts' Law: A predictive model of human movement developed by Paul Fitts in the 1950s. The model predicts the time for rapid aimed movements, that is, the time to acquire a target of a specified size at a specified distance.

focus: A concept used in *focus shift* analysis. It deals with the objects of work as the anchoring point of identifying the level of human action. A focus shift draws attention to the shift between one level of action and another. It indicates the dynamics of the situation that is the main point of concern.

formalism: A philosophy or practice that focuses on the manipulation of surface representations or symbols with a disregard for the underlying semantics and meaning. This may be as a strong philosophical stance or it may be because it is believed that, in a certain situation and for a particular end, the symbols capture faithfully the underlying meaning.

formal methods: In computing, this refers to the use of specification and analysis methods based on algebraic or set theoretic mathematical methods. It does not encompass all uses of mathematical analysis in computing, but it is principally applied to those concerned with the formal specification of discrete systems.

formal specification: See **formal methods.**

formative model: A model that identifies requirements that must be satisfied so that a system can behave in a new, desired way if needed.

functional system: The functional system is the unit of intelligent activity that is analyzed in DCog; it may be composed of a collection of any number of individuals and artifacts. It is bounded by the problem, and it includes all of the entities that compose the problem space and that are involved in problem solving.

goals: The "G" in GOMS, goals are what the user is trying to achieve through interaction with the computer system.

GOMS: GOMS is an analytic technique for making quantitative and qualitative predictions about skilled behavior with a computer system. The acronym stands for goals, operators, methods, and selection rules.

grounding: The process by which common ground is developed.

Guiard's model of bimanual control: A model that describes the roles of the hands in performing tasks that typically involved two hands, one being dominant or preferred and the other being nondominant or nonpreferred.

H: A standard operator in a keystroke-level model (KLM), H represents the act of homing the hands between input devices, such as between the keyboard and the mouse. It was empirically determined to take 400 msec by Card, Moran, and Newell (1980b, 1983).

halting problem: Early in computing theory, it was established that it was impossible to produce a program that can reliably tell whether any program will eventually halt (rather than run forever). As well as its intrinsic significance, this is typical of a range of impossibility results that establish the fundamental limitations of computation.

hidden dependencies: Important but invisible links between entities in the cognitive dimensions framework. Frequently the links are visible in one direction but not in the other (cell dependencies in spreadsheets, for example). See the text for more details.

informational equivalence: Two representations that contain the same information. See also **computational equivalence.**

information artifact: See **artifact.**

information-foraging theory: A framework that employs an adaptationist methodology to develop quantitative and computational psychological models of user strategies for seeking, gathering, and consuming information.

information processing: Within cognitive science, problem solving is seen as an information-processing activity [see **computational metaphor (of cognition)**], in which encoded information is acted on and transformed in the resolution of a goal held by a cognitive entity.

information psychophysics: The application of visual psychophysical techniques to perception of information conveyed through a visual representation.

information scent: The relation of environmental cues in the environment (such as bibliographic citations, or World Wide Web link text) to users' assessments of the value of information sources.

information visualizations: The use of computer-supported, interactive, visual representations of abstract data to amplify cognition.

interaction language: The commands used to instruct an interactive information artifact such as a word processor or a heating controller. These commands are a form of notation, but typically what the user can see as feedback is the effect of the command rather than the command itself. For example, in a word processor's interaction language, giving the command **Delete Word** deletes a word; in the same word processor's macro language, however, giving the same command **Delete Word** inserts the appropriate symbols into a program. See also **notation.**

joint action: Both people involved in a joint action intend to do their part and believe that the joint action includes their and the other person's part. (See the text for a more formal and comprehensive definition.)

juxtaposability: A level of visibility (in the cognitive-dimensions framework) at which any required subset of components can be viewed simultaneously. It is an essential requirement for certain cognitive strategies, such as design by modification of existing material, or for checking consistency of form across instances of similar components. See also **visibility.**

K: A standard operator in a keystroke-level model (KLM), K represents the act of striking a key on an input device like a keyboard or a mouse. The duration depends on the device and the skill of the user. A variety of quantitative estimates can be found in Card, Moran, and Newell (1980b, 1983).

keystroke-level model (KLM): The simplest GOMS technique. It provides standard keystroke-level operators (D, H, K, M, P, and R) with estimates of duration and rules for placing the M (mental) operators. It abstracts away from the goal hierarchy, multiple methods, and selection rules found in other GOMS techniques. More information can be found in Card, Moran, and Newell (1980b, 1983).

KLM: See **keystroke-level model.**

latent semantic analysis (LSA): A statistical theory and method of identifying word meaning through analysis of context of word use.

learning as development: A view of learning that emphasizes the triggering and maturation of skills (versus their acquisition through practice). Some versions construe this as biologically prefigured (Piaget), and others construe it as socially mediated (Vygotsky). From a developmental perspective, people are understood not only in terms of what they are but also in terms of what they are becoming.

LSA: *See* latent semantic analysis.

M: A standard operator in a keystroke-level model (KLM), M represents the act of mentally preparing to execute a command. M is a "catch-all" operator that may include such unobservable actions as making a decision, remembering a procedure or command, visually searching for information, and so on. Because M encompasses all such actions, it is a powerful approximation to human decision making that makes the KLM a relatively easy modeling method to use. M was empirically determined to average 1350 msec by Card, Moran, and Newell (1980b, 1983).

mediated communication: Human-to-human communication may be mediated by technology—for example, by telephone or video phone, by text chat, or by email.

mental model: A cognitive structure of concepts and procedures that users refer to when selecting relevant goals, choosing and executing appropriate actions, and understanding what happens when they interact with a computer system (or other tool).

methods: The "M" in "GOMS," methods are well-learned sequences of subgoals and operators that can accomplish a goal. There may be more than one method to accomplish a goal. If so, then selection rules are used to determine which method to use in the current task situation.

MHP: See **model human processor.**

model: A simplified expression of reality that is helpful for designing, evaluating, or understanding the behavior of a complex artifact such as a computer system.

model human processor (MHP): The information-processing cognitive architecture introduced by Card, Moran, and Newell in 1983. It was never realized in a computational form, but it sufficiently specified its memories, processors, communications, and principles of operation that some quantitative predictions of human behavior could be derived. The MHP was merged with GOMS through CPM-GOMS.

MOO (multi-user domain object-oriented): A MUD in which the characters, their behavior, and all other services are built and extended using an object-oriented programming language.

motor control: A branch of experimental psychology concerned with the study of human movement.

MUD (multi-user domain): A persistent collaborative environment that is modeled on a geographic space.

NGOMSL: A version of GOMS that is computationally realized in a tool called GLEAN. NGOMSL stands for Natural GOMS Language, and was developed by Kieras in the mid-1980s. More information can be found in Kieras (1997) and Kieras et al. (1995).

nonfunctional requirements: Qualities of a system under development that are not directly related to its function, such as maintainability or reliability.

normative model: A model that identifies one or a few best ways for a system or person to behave. The model usually offers a criterion or criteria against which to evaluate behavior.

notation: A system of symbols used in specialized fields to represent facts or values (as in a circuit diagram) or to give instructions (as in a programming language), usually subject to rules of combination and ordering ("syntax"). Although the symbols are discrete, there may be an admixture of analog features (relative placement of components in a circuit diagram, or layout of text in a program). This is a wider definition than that of Nelson Goodman's (1968), for example, but it is more typical of conventional usage. Notations may be *persistent* (written down) or *transient* (spoken or otherwise fleeting). See also **interaction language.**

operator: The "O" in "GOMS," operators are the actions that the software allows the user to take. Operators can be defined at many different levels of abstraction, but most GOMS models define them at a concrete level, like button presses and menu selections.

P: A standard operator in a keystroke-level model (KLM), P represents the act of pointing, that is, moving a cursor with a mouse. It was empirically determined to average 1100 msec by Card, Moran, and Newell (1980b, 1983), but it can also be calculated with Fitts' Law.

participatory design: A design movement primarily associated with Scandinavia, in which future users of the artifacts being designed participate in the original design work.

PERT chart: Program Evaluation Review Technique, a methodology developed by the U.S. Navy in the 1950s to manage the Polaris submarine missile program. A similar methodology, the Critical Path Method (CPM), which was developed for project management in the private sector at about the same time, has become synonymous with PERT, so that the technique is known by any variation on the names: PERT, CPM, or PERT/CPM. These methods are used in cognitive modeling to depict the parallel operation of perceptual, cognitive, and motor operators, with resource allocation and information-flow constraints.

PIE model: An example of an abstract formal model—that is, one that is used to analyze a class of systems and usability problems rather than specifying a particular system. The PIE model was developed at

York University in the mid-1980s and was one of the first steps in a new stream of formal method work in human-computer interaction (HCI) that began at that time. See: *www.hcibook.com/alan/topics/formal/*

placeholder: Something (a physical artifact, electronic record, or human memory) that explicitly or tacitly maintains the current position within a formal or informal process. See: *www.hcibook.com/alan/topics/triggers/*

practice: When being trained as a carpenter or a nurse, for example, one shares a practice. At the same time, each individual who possesses a practice keeps it up and changes it as well. It is practice that allows us to talk about more than just individual skills, knowledge, and judgment, and not just about a "generic" human being. Practice is shaped historically, which is of particular relevance for design and use of computer applications.

preattentive processing: The rapid detection of visual features theorized to occur in parallel before the operation of selective attention.

predictive model: A model that allows metrics of human performance to be determined analytically without undertaking time-consuming and resource-intensive experiments.

problem behavior graph: A graphical depiction of search through a problem space.

problem solving: Searching through a problem space from a known start state to a desired end state, or one of a set of desired end states, applying operators of uncertain outcome to move from state to state. Problem solving typically refers to a path through the problem space that includes explorations of dead-end paths and backing up to prior states. (See **skilled behavior** for a contrasting type of behavior.)

problem space: A mental representation of a problem, including the start state, the goal state, and the operators or moves that allow transitions between states. According to Newell and Simon's (1972) theory of problem solving, humans solve problems by constructing and searching a problem space.

procedural knowledge: Also called "how-to-do-it" knowledge. The knowledge of which operators to perform to move from a known start state to a desired state in a problem space.

production system: A programming language made up of conditional statements. If all conditions are satisfied, then action is taken.

profile: In cognitive-dimensions analysis, a statement of what is required (in cognitive-dimensions terms) to support a given generic activity. The profile of an activity states for each cognitive dimension whether that dimension is material and, if so, what value it should have (e.g., for modification, viscosity must be low, visibility must be high, etc.).

progressive evaluation: In the cognitive-dimensions framework, the ability to review or test a partially complete structure, to check on progress to date. It is important for novices, and becomes less so as one gains experience. Some systems allow only a complete design to be reviewed; others allow a review at any stage.

propagation of representations: A component of information-processing activity in which sequences of transformations from one representational form (or medium) to another result in information-processing activity. Hutchins claims that "representational states are propagated from one medium to another by bringing the states of the media into coordination with one another" (1995a, p.117).

propositional representations: Representations that have a more-or-less arbitrary structure; for example, a word or a sentence in a natural language. See also **analog representations.**

R: A standard operator in a keystroke-level model (KLM), R represents the time a user spends waiting for the computer to respond. Only the time actually spent waiting—beyond any mental preparation time (M)—is included in R. R must be estimated for each computer system modeled.

representation: This can be seen as encoded information, either as a symbolic abstraction of a thing (classical cognitive science), or as a distributed set of nodes (PDP) that, together, have meaning. According to the representational theory of mind, human brains operate on symbolic representations, or codes. DCog extends this to show how transformations to representations need not be entirely symbolic, but may be enacted through manipulations on physical media that have a representational status (e.g., a navigational chart or a drawing).

representational state: This is defined by Hutchins (1995a, p.117) as "a configuration of the elements in a medium that can be interpreted as a representation." Problem solving occurs by successive rerepresentations of the problem (i.e., a representation of the problem) through a series of intermediate representational states into a solution (i.e., a representation of the solution). DCog researchers attempt to make the representational state of a functional system explicit and document how changes to its representational state result in goal-directed problem-solving activity.

scenario: A narrative or story that describes the activities of one or more persons, including information about goals, expectations, actions, and reactions.

schedule chart: The graphic depiction of a PERT or CPM chart.

secondary notation: In the cognitive-dimensions framework, extra information in means other than formal syntax. Examples include layout in programs and circuit diagrams and penciled annotations on music. See the text for more details.

selection rules: The "S" in GOMS, selection rules are the rules people use to choose between multiple methods that accomplish the same goal. They typically depend on characteristics of the task or user's personal preferences or knowledge.

set theory: One of the foundations of nearly all mathematics and formalism in computing is the manipulation of sets (unordered collections of things) and functions.

situated action: One can plan to descend a set of rapids in a canoe, and one can plan and replan as one goes along, but one cannot (successfully) plan the descent and then merely execute the actions. Lucy Suchman, in her 1986 book *Plans and Situated Actions,* analyzed action as necessarily improvisational. Actions are undertaken in response to the constantly changing physical and social environment. An important consequence of this is to make plans and to plan a resource for action, and not simply as the determinant of action.

situation model: A mental model derived from a text that represents what the text is about.

skilled behavior: Movement through a problem space by applying a known operator at every state, from a known start state to a known end state. (See **problem solving** for a contrasting type of behavior.)

skills-rules-knowledge framework: A taxonomy of three qualitatively distinct levels of cognitive control. An expert human operator may exhibit any or all levels of cognitive control, depending upon the situation. This is not to be confused with models that describe stages of acquiring expertise or skill.

soar: A computational cognitive architecture developed by Allen Newel, John Laird, and Paul Rosenbloom in the early 1980s. It was used as the exemplar in Newell's 1990 book *Unified Theories of Cognition.* It has undergone continual development from its inception in many universities and has also been commercialized for complex modeling in military simulations and intelligent agents for video games. Soar was one of the architectures reviewed in Pew & Mavor (1998). More information about this series of architectures can be found in Newell (1990).

socially distributed cognition: This is the theoretical position that goal-directed group activity can be understood in computational terms.

social-organizational analysis: A way of analyzing work that focuses on how work is organized and shared across people and supporting tools. It is an analytic phase of cognitive work analysis.

sociology: The investigation of social structure, social relationships, and individual social action.

socio-organizational Church-Turing hypothesis: The recognition that organizations perform, among other things, an information-processing role, and the supposition that this means we are likely to see similar structural elements and processes in the physical and social aspects of the organizations as we do in electronic computers. See: *www.hcibook.com/alan/topics/ecology/*

spreading activation: This is a computational process that determines activation values over a set of interassociated cognitive structures. The spread of activation from one cognitive structure to another is determined by weighting values on associations among chunks. Activation values indicate degree of relevance to ongoing cognitive processes.

state: In computing, this usually refers to the inner memory of a computer at a particular point of time, but more generally it is that element in the present that encapsulates all that of the past that can affect things in the future.

state transition network (STN): A representation of dynamic systems including states (usually as labeled circles or boxes) and arcs labeled by actions that form transitions between the states.

status-event analysis: A collection of informal and formal analysis techniques that focus on the differences and relationships among discrete event phenomena (e.g., a key press, a project deadline) and more continuous status phenomena (e.g., the current mouse position, the weather, the current screen display) See: *www.hcibook.com/alan/topics/status/*

strategies analysis: A way of analyzing work that focuses on different ways that a particular control task might be carried out. An analytic phase of cognitive work analysis.

STN: See state transition network.

subgoal: A goal that must be accomplished in service of a higher-level goal. Goals are often expressed as a hierarchy of goals and several levels of subgoals. The lowest level of subgoals are accomplished through operators, which are decomposed no further.

symbolic interactionism: Originated in the social psychology of George Herbert Mead and the sociological methodology of Herbert Blumer, this places emphasis on the individual in explanations of the transactions of people and society.

syndetic modeling framework: A framework that looks at the interactions among different kinds of models—in particular, models of system behavior and models of human activity. See Barnard, May, Duke, and Duce (2000).

task analysis: Any process that identifies and examines tasks that must be performed, either by users, other agents, or the system itself, to accomplish the goals of an interactive system.

task-artifact cycle: All human artifacts both enable and constrain human activity. Human use of current artifacts thus suggests possibilities and requirements for the design of future artifacts, which in turn will ultimately both enable and constrain human activity.

tradeoff: An issue (often in design) that is understood to have competing arguments, usually contrasting positive and negative impacts of an option.

transfer of learning: A learning and memory phenomenon in which what is learned in one situation facilitates understanding and behavior in a similar situation.

use/users: Many human activities incorporate computer applications. In human-computer interaction (HCI), the terms *use* and *users* are applied to the common properties of computer applications in work activity, and to the people who use computer applications as part of their daily practice. These terms are somewhat unfortunate, as the people rarely construe their own activity as computer use *per se* or see themselves primarily as users of computer equipment.

viscosity: In the cognitive-dimensions framework, this is "resistance to change." A viscous system is one that requires many individual actions to achieve what is conceptualized as a single change. It is the opposite of fluidity. See the text for more details.

visibility: In the cognitive-dimensions framework, this is the ability to view components easily whenever necessary. See also **juxtaposability.**

visual working memory: A limited-capacity visual store that is distinct from verbal working memory. It is a core component of modern cognitive theory.

work-domain analysis: A way of analyzing work that focuses on identifying the functional structure of the work domain with which a human operator will interact (rather than identifying tasks to be performed in the work domain). An analytic phase of cognitive work analysis.

worker-competencies analysis: A way of analyzing work that focuses on the cognitive competencies required of or evident in workers, given their training, expertise, and the way information is represented to them. An analytic phase of cognitive work analysis.

yoked-state space hypothesis: The claim that users of representational devices (such as computer systems) need to mentally represent the device itself, the domain to which the device refers, and the way in which the device represents the domain. See Payne, Squibb, and Howes (1993).

Z notation: A particular notation for formal specification developed principally by the Programming Research Group, Oxford University. It is based on set theory, with mechanisms to allow large specifications to be separated into parts and structured. See Spivy (1988).

zero-parameter models: Models that can make *a priori* predictions of quantitative performance of users on an interactive system. They are called zero-parameters because no parameters need to be set from data collected on the system in question; all numeric parameters can be set through a task analysis and pre-existing data from prior research.

zone of proximal development: The inventory of capabilities people can currently demonstrate with assistance (human and material support) and therefore may, in the future, be able to achieve by themselves.

References

Abowd, G. D., & Dix, A. J. (1992). Giving undo attention. *Interacting with Computers, 4*(3), 317–342.

Abowd, G., Wang, H., & A. Monk. (1995). *A formal technique for automated dialogue development. Proceedings of designing interactive systems—DIS'95* (pp. 219–226). New York: ACM Press.

Accot, J., & Zhai, S. (1997). Beyond Fitts' law: Models for trajectory-based HCI tasks. *Proceedings of the CHI '97 Conference on Human Factors in Computing Systems* (pp. 295–302). New York: ACM Press.

Accot, J., & Zhai, S. (1999). Performance evaluation of input devices in trajectory-based tasks: An application of the Steering Law. *Proceedings of the ACM Conference on Human Factors in Computing Systems—CHI '99* (pp. 466–472). New York: ACM Press.

Accot, J., & Zhai, S. (2001). Scale effects in steering law tasks: Do device size and different motor joints matter? *Proceedings of the ACM Conference on Human Factors in Computing Systems—CHI 2001* (pp. 1–8). New York: ACM Press.

Ackerman, M. (1998). Augmenting organizational memory: A field study of answer garden. *ACM Transactions on Information Systems, 16*(3), 203–224.

Adamic, L. A., & Huberman, B. A. (2000). The nature of markets in the World Wide Web. *Quarterly Journal of Electronic Commerce, 1,* 5–12.

Agre, P. E. (1993). The symbolic worldview: A reply to Vera and Simon. *Cognitive Science, 17,* 61–69.

Allanson, J. (2002). Electrophysiological interactive computer systems. *IEEE Computer, 35*(3), 60–65.

Allanson, J., & Wilson, G. M. (2002). Physiological computing. In J. Allanson and G. M. Wilson (Eds.) *Proceedings of CHI 2002 workshop on Physiological Computing.* Lancaster University. available online *www.physiologicalcomputing.net/*

Altmann, G. T. M. (1997). *The ascent of babel.* Oxford: Oxford University Press.

Anderson, J. J., Matessa, M., & Bebiere, C. (1997). ACT-R: A theory of higher level cognition and its relation to visual attention. *Human-Computer Interaction 12,* 439–462.

Anderson, J. R. (1976). *Language, memory, and thought.* Hillsdale, NJ: Erlbaum.

Anderson, J. R. (1978). Arguments concerning representations for mental imagery. *Psychological Review, 85,* 249–277.

Anderson, J. R. (1982). Acquisition of complex skill. *Psychological Review, 89,* 369–406.

Anderson, J. R. (1983). *The architecture of cognition.* Cambridge, MA: Harvard University Press.

Anderson, J. R. (1987). Skill acquisition: Compilation of weak-method problem solutions. *Psychological Review, 94,* 192–210.

Anderson, J. R. (1990). *The adaptive character of thought.* Hillsdale, NJ: Erlbaum.

Anderson, J. R. (1993). *Rules of the mind.* Hillsdale, NJ: Erlbaum.

Anderson, J. R., & Lebiere, C. (2000). *The atomic components of thought.* Mahwah, NJ: Erlbaum.

Anderson, J. R., & Milson, R. (1989). Human memory: An adaptive perspective. *Psychological Review, 96,* 703–719.

Anderson, J. R., & Pirolli, P. L. (1984). Spread of activation. *Journal of Experimental Psychology: Learning, Memory, and Cognition, 10,* 791–798.

Anderson, J. R., Corbett, A. T., Koedinger, K. R., & Pelletier, R. (1995). Cognitive tutors: Lessons learned. *The Journal of the Learning Sciences, 4*(2), 167–207.

Anderson, R. (1996). Work, ethnography and systems design. In *Encyclopedia of Microcomputers, Vol. 20* (pp.159–183). New York: Marcel Dekker.

Anderson, R. J., Heath, C. C., Luff, P., & Moran, T. P. (1993). The social and the cognitive in human-computer interaction. *IJMMS, 38,* 999–1016.

Anzai, Y., & Simon, H. A. (1979). The theory of learning by doing. *Psychological Review, 86,* 124–140.

Apple Computer, Inc. (1987). *Human interface guidelines: The Apple desktop interface.* Reading, MA: Addison-Wesley.

Apple Computer, Inc. (1992). *Macintosh human interface guidelines.* Reading, MA: Addison-Wesley.

Argote, L. (1982). Input uncertainty and organizational coordination in hospital emergency rooms. *Administration and Society, 27*(3), 420–434.

Argyes, N. S. (1999). The impact of information technology on coordination: Evidence from the B-2 "stealth" bomber. *Organization Science, 10*(2), 162–180.

Argyris, C., Putnam, R., & Smith, D. M. (1985). *Action science.* San Francisco: Jossey-Bass.

Aronson, E., & Mills, J. (1959). The effect of severity of initiation on liking for a group. *Journal of Abnormal & Social Psychology, 59,* 177–181.

Aronson, E., Wilson, T. D., & Akert, R. M. (2002). *Social psychology (4th ed.).* Upper Saddle River, NJ: Prentice Hall.

Arsenault, R., & Ware, C. (2000). Eye-hand co-ordination with force feedback. *Proceedings of the ACM Conference on Human Factors in Computing Systems—CHI 2000* (pp.408–414). New York: ACM Press.

Asch, S. (1955). Opinions and social pressure. *Scientific American, 193*(5), 31–35.

Ashby, R. (1956). *Introduction to cybernetics*. London: Chapman and Hall.

Atwood, M. E., Gray, W. D., & John, B. E. (1996) Project Ernestine: Analytic and empirical methods applied to a real-world CHI problem. In M. Rudisill, C. Lewis, P. B. Polson, and T. D. McKay (Eds.), *Human-computer interface design: Success stories, emerging methods and real-world context* (pp.101–121). San Francisco: Morgan Kaufmann.

Bærentsen, K. (1989). Mennesker og maskiner [People and machines]. In M. Hedegaard, V. R. Hansen, & S. Thyssen (Eds.). *Et Virksomt Liv* [An active life]. (pp.142–187). Aarhus, Denmark: Aarhus Universitets Forlag.

Bærentsen, K. (2000). Intuitive user interfaces. *Scandinavian Journal of Information Systems, 12,* 29–60.

Bærentsen, K. B., & Trettvik, J. (2002). An activity theory approach to affordance. In *NordiCHI 2002, Proceedings of the Second Nordic Conference on Human-Computer Interaction, 19–23 October 2002, Aarhus, Denmark,* pp.51–60.

Bainbridge, L. (1983). Ironies of automation. *Automatica, 19,* 775–779.

Balakrishnan, R., & Hinckley, K. (2000). Symmetric bimanual interaction, *Proceedings of the ACM Conference on Human Factors in Computing Systems—CHI 2000* (pp. 33–40). New York: ACM Press.

Balakrishnan, R., & Kurtenbach, G. (1999). Exploring bimanual camera control and object manipulation in 3D graphics interfaces, *Proceedings of the ACM Conference on Human Factors in Computing Systems—CHI '99.* (pp. 56–63). New York: ACM Press.

Balakrishnan, R., Baudel, T., Kurtenbach, G., & Fitzmaurice, G. (1997). The Rockin'Mouse: Integral 3D manipulation on a plane. *Proceedings of the ACM Conference on Human Factors in Computing Systems— CHI '97,* 311–318. New York: ACM Press.

Bannon, L. (1990). A pilgrim's progress: From cognitive science to cooperative design. *AI & Society 4* (4): 259–275.

Bannon, L. (1991). From human factors to human actors: The role of psychology and human-computer interaction studies in systems design. In J. Greenbaum & M. Kyng (Eds.), *Design at work: Cooperative design of computer systems* (pp.25–44). Hillsdale, NJ: Erlbaum.

Bannon, L. and Bødker, S. (1991). Beyond the interface: Encountering artifacts in use. In J. M. Carroll (Ed.), *Designing interaction: Psychology at the human-computer interface,* pp.227–253. New York: Cambridge University Press.

Bannon, L. J., & Kuutti, K. (1993). Searching for unity among diversity: Exploring the "Interface" concept. In S. Ashlund, et al. (Eds.) *INTERCHI '93: Conference on Human Factors in Computing Systems INTERACT '93 and CHI '93 Bridges Between Worlds* (pp.263–268). New York: ACM Press.

Bardram, J. (1998). *Collaboration, coordination and computer support. An activity theoretical approach to the design of computer supported cooperative work.* Ph.d. Thesis, Aarhus, Denmark: Department of Computer Science. DAIMI PB-533.

Bardram, J. E., & Bertelsen, O. W. (1995). Supporting the development of transparent interaction. In B. Blumenthal, J. Gornostaev, & C. Unger (Eds.). *Human-computer interaction. 5th International Conference, EWHCI '95 Moscow, Russia, July 1995. Selected Papers* (pp.79–90). Berlin: Springer Verlag.

Barnard, P., May, J., Duke, D., & Duce, D. (2000). Systems, interactions, and macrotheory. *ACM Transactions on Computer-Human Interaction, 7*(2), 222–262.

Baron, R. A., & Byrne, D. E. (2000). *Social psychology* (9th ed.). Boston, MA: Allyn and Bacon.

Baron, R. S., & Kerr, N. L. (2003). *Group process, group decisions, group action* (2nd ed.). Philadelphia, PA: Open University Press.

Baskin, J. D., & John, B. E. (1998). Comparison of GOMS analysis methods. *Proceedings of ACM CHI 1998 Conference on Human Factors in Computing Systems* (Summary) (Los Angeles, CA, April 18–April 23, 1998) (pp.261–262). New York: ACM Press.

Bauer M. T., and Johnson Laird P. N. (1993). How diagrams can improve reasoning. *Psychological Science, 4,* 372–378.

Bauer, M. I., & John, B. E. (1995). Modeling time-constrained learning in a highly-interactive task. *Proceedings of ACM CHI 1995 conference on Human Factors in Computing Systems* (Denver, CO, May 7–May 11, 1995) (pp.19–26). New York: ACM Press.

Baumeister, L. K., John, B. E., & Byrne, M. D. (2000). A comparison of tools for building GOMS models. *Proceedings of ACM CHI 2000 Conference on Human Factors in Computing Systems. 1* (pp.502–509). New York: ACM Press.

Beard, D. V., Smith, D. K., & Denelsbeck, K. M. (1996). Quick and dirty GOMS: A case study of computed tomography. *Human-Computer Interaction, 11*(2), 157–180.

Beaudouin-Lafon, M. (2000). Instrumental interaction: An interaction model for designing post-WIMP user interfaces. *Proceedings of ACM CHI 2000 Conference on Human Factors in Computing Systems 2000* V. 1, 446–453.

Beaudouin-Lafon, M. Berteaud, Y., & Chatty, S (1990). Creating a direct manipulation application with Xtv. *Proceedings European X Window System Conference, EX90,* London.

Beaudouin-Lafon, M., & Lassen, M. (2000). The architecture and implementation of CPN2000, a post-WIMP graphical application. *Proc. ACM Symposium on User Interface Software and Technology, UIST 2000* San Diego, CA, 5–8 November 2000. New York: ACM Press.

Bechtel, W. (1985). Realism, instrumentalism, and the intentional stance. *Cognitive Science, 9,* 473–497.

Becker, H. (1963). *Outsiders.* New York: Free Press.

Beguin, P., & Rabardel, P. (2000). Designing for instrument mediated activity. *Scandinavian Journal of Information Systems, 12,* 173–190.

Benford, S., Bowers, J., Fahlen, L., Mariani, J., & Rodden, T. (1994). Supporting cooperative work in virtual environments. *The Computer Journal, 37*(8), 635–668.

Bentley, R., Button, G., & Pycock, J. (2001). *Lightweight computing.* PARC Forum.

Bentley, R., Hughes, J. A., Randall, D., Rodden, T., Sawyer, P., Shapiro, D., & Sommerville, I. (1992). Ethnographically-informed systems design for air traffic control. In *Proceedings of ACM CSCW'92 Conference on Computer-Supported Cooperative Work.* Toronto, Canada. pp.123–129.

Berlekamp, E. R., Conway, J. H. & Guy, R. K. (1982). *Winning ways for your mathematical plays, volume 2: Games in particular.* New York: Academic Press.

Berners-Lee, T. (1989). *Information management: A proposal.* Geneva, Switzerland: CERN.

Berscheid, E., & Reis, H. T. (1998). Attraction and close relationships. In D. T. Gilbert, S. T. Fiske, & G. Lindzey (Eds.), *The handbook of social psychology, Vol 2* (4th ed., pp.193–281). New York: McGraw-Hill.

Bertelsen, O. W. (1996). The festival checklist: Design as the transformation of artifacts. in J. Blomberg, F. Kensing, & E. Dykstra-Erickson (Eds.). *PDC '96, Proceedings of the Participatory Design Conference, Palo Alto: Computer Professionals for Social Responsibility,* pp.93–101.

Bertelsen, O. W. (1997). Understanding objects in use-oriented design. In K. Braa & E. Monteiro (Eds.). *Proceedings of the 20th Information Systems Research Seminar in Scandinavia.* Oslo, 1997, pp.311–324.

Bertelsen, O. W. (1998*). Elements to a theory of design artifacts: A contribution to critical systems development research,* Ph.D. Thesis, Aarhus University, Denmark. DAIMI PB-531.

Bertelsen, O. W., & Bødker, S. (1998) Studying programming environments in use: Between principles and praxis. *NWPER '98 The Eighth Nordic Workshop on Programming Environment Research, Bergen/Norway, Sunday June 14–Tuesday June 16, 1998.*

Bertelsen, O., & Bødker, S. (2001). Cooperation in massively distributed information spaces. *ECSCW 2001: Proceedings of the Seventh European Conference on Computer Supported Cooperative Work, Bonn, Germany, 16–20 September 2001* (pp.1–18). Dordrecht: Kluwer.

Bertelsen, O., & Bødker, S. (2002). Discontinuities. In Y. Dittrich, C. Floyd, & R. Klischewski (Eds.) *Social thinking—Software practice.* Cambridge, MA: MIT Press.

Bhavnani, S. K, & John, B. E. (1996). Exploring the unrealized potential of computer-aided drafting. *Proceedings of ACM CHI 1996 Conference on Human Factors in Computing Systems* (Vancouver, BC, April 14–April 18, 1996) (pp.332–339). New York: ACM Press.

Bhavnani, S. K, & John, B. E. (1997) From sufficient to efficient usage: An analysis of strategic knowledge. *Proceedings of CHI, 1997* (Atlanta, Georgia, March 22–27, 1997) (pp.91–98). New York: ACM Press.

Bibby, P. A., & Payne, S. J. (1993). Internalization and use-specificity of device knowledge. *Human-Computer Interaction, 8,* 25–56.

Bibby, P. A., & Payne, S. J. (1996). Instruction and practice in learning about a device. *Cognitive Science, 20,* 539–578.

Biederman, I. (1987). Recognition by components: A theory of human-image understanding. *Psychological Review, 94,* 115–147.

Bier, E., Stone, M., Pier, K., Buxton, W., & De Rose, T. (1993). Toolglass and magic lenses: The see-through interface. Proceedings of the 20th annual conference on computer graphics and interactive techniques. *ACM SIGGRAPH, 73–80.*

Birmingham, H., & Taylor, F. (1954). A design philosophy for man-machine control systems. *Proceedings of the I. R. E., XLII,* 1748–1758.

Bisantz, A., & Vicente, K. (1994). Making the abstraction hierarchy concrete. *International Journal of Human Computer Studies, 40,* 83–117.

Bisantz, A., Roth, E., Brickman, B., Gosbee, L. L., Hettinger, L., & McKinney, J. (In press). Integrating cognitive analyses in a large scale system design process. *International Journal of Human-Computer Studies.*

Blackmon, M. H., Polson, P. G., Kitajima, M., & Lewis, C. (2002). *Cognitive Walkthrough for the Web.* Paper presented at the Human Factors in Computing Systems, CHI 2002, Minneapolis, MN.

Blackwell, A. F. (1996). Metacognitive theories of visual programming: What do we think we are doing? *Proceedings IEEE Symposium on Visual Languages,* 240–246.

Blackwell, A. F. (2000). Dealing with new cognitive dimensions. Paper presented at Workshop on Cognitive Dimensions: Strengthening the Cognitive Dimensions Research Community. University of Hertfordshire, 8 December 2000.

Blackwell, A. F., & Green, T. R. G. (1999). Investment of attention as an analytic approach to cognitive dimensions. In T. Green, R. Abdullah, & P. Brna (Eds.). *Collected Papers of the 11th Annual Workshop of the Psychology of Programming Interest Group (PPIG-11),* 24–35.

Blackwell, A. F., & Green, T. R. G. (2000). A cognitive dimensions questionnaire optimised for users. In A. F. Blackwell & E. Bilotta (Eds.). *Proceedings of the Twelfth Annual Meeting of the Psychology of Programming Interest Group,* 137–152.

Blackwell, A. F., Britton, C., Cox, A., Green, T. R. G., Gurr, C., Kadoda, G., Kutar, M. S., Loomes, M., Nehaniv, C. L., Petre, M., Roast, C., Roe, C., Wong, A., & Young, R. M. (2001). In M. Beynon, C. L. Nehaniv, & K. Dautenhahn (Eds.). *Cognitive technology: Instruments of mind* (pp.325–341). Berlin: Springer Verlag

Blandford, A. E. & Green, T. R. G. (1997). OSM: an ontology-based approach to usability evaluation. *Proceedings of Workshop on Representations.* Queen Mary & Westfield College, July 1997.

Blandford, A. E., & Green, T. R. G. (2001). From tasks to conceptual structures: misfit analysis. In Proc. IHM-HCI2001.

Bødker S. (1991). *Through the interface: A human activity approach to user interface design.* Hillsdale, NJ: Erlbaum.

Bødker, S. (1993). Historical analysis and conflicting perspectives—contextualizing HCI. In L. Bass, J. Gornostaev, & C. Unger (Eds.). *Human-computer interaction. 3rd International Conference, EWHCI '93.* Springer Lecture Notes in Computer Science, vol. 753, 1–10.

Bødker, S. (1996). Applying activity theory to video analysis: How to make sense of video data in HCI. In B. Nardi (Ed.). *Context and consciousness. Activity theory and human computer interaction* (pp.147–174). Cambridge: MIT Press.

Bødker, S. (1999). *Computer applications as mediators of design and use—a developmental perspective.* Dr. Scient. Thesis, Aarhus University, Denmark.

Bødker, S. & Grønbæk, K. (1996). Users and designers in mutual activity—An analysis of cooperative activities in systems design. In Y. Engeström & D. Middleton (Eds.). *Cognition and communication at work* (pp.130–158). Cambridge, UK: Cambridge University Press.

Bødker, S., Christiansen, E., & Thüring, M. (1995). A conceptual toolbox for designing CSCW applications. In *COOP '95, International Workshop on the Design of Cooperative Systems, Juan-les-Pins, January 1995,* 266–284.

Bødker, S., Ehn, P., Kammersgaard, J., Kyng, M., & Y. Sundblad (1987). A utopian experience. In G. Bjerknes, P. Ehn, & M. Kyng (Eds.). *Computers and democracy—A Scandinavian challenge* (pp. 251–278). Aldershot, UK: Avebury.

Bødker, S., & Petersen, M. G. (2000). Design for learning in use. *Scandinavian Journal of Information Systems, 12,* 61–80.

Bødker, S., Petersen, M. G., & Nielsen, C.(2000). Creativity, cooperation and interactive design. DIS 2000. *Conference proceedings on designing interactive systems: Processes, practices, methods, and techniques,* (pp.252–261). New York: ACM Press.

Boehm, B., Clark, B. Horowitz, E., Westland, C., Madachy, R., & Selby, R. (1995). Cost models for future software life cycle processes: COCOMO 2.0. *Annals of Software Engineering, 1,* 57–94.

Booch, G., Rumbaugh J., & Jacobson I. (1999). *The unified modeling language user guide.* Reading, MA: Addison-Wesley.

Borgman, C. L., Belkin, N. J., Croft, W. B., Lesk, M. E., & Landauer, T. K. (1988). *Retrieval systems for the information seeker: Can the role of intermediary be automated?* Paper presented at the Human Factors in Computing Systems, CHI '88, Washington, DC.

Bovair, S., Kieras, D. E., & Polson, P. G. (1988). *The acquisition and performance of text-editing skill: A production–system analysis.* (Tech. Rep. No. 28). Ann Arbor: University of Michigan, Technical Communication Program.

Bovair, S., Kieras, D. E., & Polson, P. G. (1990). The acquisition and performance of text-editing skill: A cognitive complexity analysis. *Human-Computer Interaction, 5*(1), 1–48.

Bowers, J., Button, G., & Sharrock, W. W. (1995). Workflow from within and without. *Proceedings of the ECSCW'95 Fourth European Conference on Computer-Supported Cooperative Work* (pp.51–66). Dordrecht: Kluwer.

Boyle, M., Edwards, C., & Greenberg, S. (2000). The effects of filtered video on awareness and privacy. *CHI Letters: Proceedings of the CSCW'00 Conference on Computer Supported Cooperative Work, 2*(3), 1–10.

Braverman, H. (1974). *Labour and monopoly capitalism.* New York: Monthly Review Press.

Brinck, T., Gergle, D., & Wood, S. D. (2002). *Usability for the Web: Designing Web sites that work.* San Francisco: Morgan Kaufmann.

Brunswick, E. (1956). *Perception and the representative design of psychological experiments.* Berkeley: University of California Press.

Buckland, M. K. (1992). Emanuel Goldberg, electronic document retrieval, and Vannevar Bush's Memex. *Journal of the American Society for Information Science, 43,* 284–294.

Burnett, M., Cao, N., & Atwood, J. (2000). Time in grid-oriented VPLs: just another dimension? *IEEE International Symposium on Visual Languages (VL2000)* (pp.137–144). Los Alamitos, CA: IEEE Computer Society.

Burns, C. M. (2000a). Navigation strategies with ecological displays. *International Journal of Human-Computer Studies, 52* (1), 111–129.

Burns, C. M. (2000b). Putting it all together: Improving integration in ecological displays. *Human Factors, 42,* 226–241.

Burns, C., Bryant, D., & Chalmers, B. (2001). Scenario mapping with work domain analysis. *Proceedings of the Human Factors and Ergonomics Society 45th Annual Meeting, Minneapolis, MN.* (pp. 424–428). Santa Monica, CA: HFES.

Bush, V. (1945). As we may think. *Atlantic Monthly, 176,* 101–108.

Butler, B. (1999). *The dynamics of cyberspace: Examining and modeling online social structure.* Ph.D. thesis, Carnegie-Mellon University, Pittsburgh.

Button, G., & Sharrock, W. W. (1997). The production of order and the order of production: Possibilities for distributed organisations, work, and technology in the print industry. *Proceedings of the ECSCW'97* (pp.1–16). Dordrecht: Kluwer.

Buxton, W. (1983, January). Lexical and pragmatic considerations of input structures. *Computer Graphics,* 31–37.

Buxton, W. A. S. (1990). A three-state model of graphical input. *Proceedings of INTERACT '90* (pp.449–456). Amsterdam: Elsevier Science.

Buxton, W., & Myers, B. A. (1986). A study in two-handed input. *Proceedings of the ACM Conference on Human Factors in Computing Systems—CHI '87* (pp.321–326). New York: ACM Press.

Byrne, M. D., & Anderson, J. R. (2001). Serial modules in parallel: the psychological refractory period and perfect time-sharing. *Psychological Review, 108,* 847–869.

Card, S. K., English, W. K., & Burr, B. J. (1978). Evaluation of mouse, rate-controlled isometric joystick, step keys, and text keys for text selection on a CRT. *Ergonomics, 21,* 601–613.

Card, S. K., Mackinlay, J. D., & Robertson, G. G. (1990). The design space of input devices. *Proceedings of the ACM Conference on Human Factors in Computing Systems—CHI '90* (pp.117–124). New York: ACM Press.

Card, S. K., Mackinlay, J. D., & Robertson, G. G. (1991). A morphological analysis of the design space of input devices. *ACM Transactions on Office Information Systems, 9,* 99–122.

Card, S. K., Moran, T. P., & Newell, A. (1980a). Computer text-editing: An information-processing analysis of a routine cognitive skill. *Cognitive Psychology, 12,* 32–74.

Card, S. K., Moran, T. P., & Newell, A. (1980b). The Keystroke-Level Model for user performance time with interactive systems. *Communications of the ACM, 23,* 396–410.

Card, S. K., Moran, T. P., & Newell, A. (1983). *The psychology of human-computer interaction.* Hillsdale, NJ: Erlbaum.

Card, S., Pirolli, P., Van Der Wege, M., Morrison, J., Reeder, R., Schraedley, P., & Boshart, J. (2001). *Information scent as a driver of Web Behavior Graphs: Results of a protocol analysis method for web usability.* Paper presented at the Human Factors in Computing Systems, Seattle, WA.

Carroll, J. (1991). Introduction: The Kittle House manifesto. In J. M. Carroll (Ed.), *Designing interaction.* (pp.1–16). New York: Cambridge University Press.

Carroll, J. M. (1980). *Toward a structural psychology of cinema.* The Hague: Mouton.

Carroll, J. M. (1985). *What's in a name: An essay in the psychology of reference.* New York: W. H. Freeman.

Carroll, J. M. (2000). *Making use: Scenario-based design of human-computer interactions.* Cambridge, MA: MIT Press.

Carroll, J. M., & Campbell, R. L. (1986). Softening up hard science: Reply to Newell and Card. *Human-Computer Interaction, 2,* 227–249.

Carroll, J. M., Kellogg, W., & Rosson, M. B. (1991). The task artifact cycle. In J. M. Carroll (Ed.), *Designing interaction: Psychology at the human-computer interface* (pp.74–102). Cambridge, UK: Cambridge University Press.

Carroll, J. M., & Olson, J. R. (1988). Mental models in human-computer interaction: Research issues about what the user of software knows. In M. Helander (Ed.) *Handbook of human-computer interaction* (pp.45–65). Amsterdam: North Holland.

Carroll, J. M., & Rosson, M. B. (1987). The paradox of the active user. In J. M. Carroll (Ed.), *Interfacing thought: Cognitive aspects of human-computer interaction* (pp.80–111). Cambridge, MA: MIT Press.

Carroll, J. M., & Rosson, M. B. (1991). Deliberated evolution: Stalking the view matcher in design space. *Human-Computer Interaction, 6*(3&4), 281–318.

Carroll, J. M., & Rosson, M. B. (1992). Getting around the task-artifact cycle: How to make claims and design by scenario. *ACM Transactions on Information Systems, 10,* 181–212.

Carroll, J. M., & Rosson, M.B (1996). Developing the Blacksburg Electronic Village. *Communications of the ACM, 39*(12), 69–74.

Carroll, J. M., Rosson, M. B., Cohill, A. M., & Schorger, J. (1995). Building a history of the Blacksburg Electronic Village. *Proceedings of the ACM Symposium on Designing Interactive Systems: DIS'95* (pp.1–6). New York: ACM Press.

Carroll, J. M., Rosson, M. B., Isenhour, P. L., Van Metre, C., Schafer, W. A., & Ganoe, C. H. (2001). MOOsburg: Multi-user domain support for a community network. *Internet Research, 11*(1), 65–73.

Carroll, J. M., & Thomas, J. C. (1982). Metaphor and the cognitive representation of computing systems. *IEEE Transactions on Systems, Man, and Cybernetics, 12,* 107–115.

Chapanis, A., Ochsman, R., Parrish, R., & Weeks, G. (1972). Studies in interactive communication: I. The effects of four communication modes on the behavior of teams during cooperative problem-solving. *Human Factors, 14*(6), 487–509.

Cheng, P. C. (1998). AVOW diagrams: A novel representational system for understanding electricity. In *Proceedings Thinking with Diagrams 98: Is there a science of diagrams?* (pp.86–93). Aberystwyth: University of Wales Press.

Chi, E., Pirolli, P., Chen, K., & Pitkow, J. E. (2001). *Using information scent to model user needs and actions on the web.* Paper presented at the Human Factors in Computing Systems, CHI 2001, Seattle, WA.

Choudhary, R., & Dewan, P. (1995). A general multi-user undo/redo model. In H. Marmolin, Y. Sundblad, & K. Schmidt (Eds.), *Proceedings of ECSCW'95, Stockholm, Sweden* (pp.231–246). Dordrecht: Kluwer.

Chuah, M. C., John, B. E., & Pane, J. (1994). Analyzing graphic and textual layouts with GOMS: Results of a preliminary analysis. *Proceedings Companion of CHI, 1994* (Boston, MA, April 24–April 28, 1994) (pp.323–324). New York: ACM Press.

Cialdini, R. B., Borden, R. J., Thorne, R. J., Walker, M. R., Freeman, S., & Sloan, L. R. (1976). Basking in reflected glory: Three (football) field studies. *Journal of Personality & Social Psychology, 34*(3), 366–375.

Clark, H. H. (1992). *Arenas of language use.* Chicago, IL: The University of Chicago Press.

Clark, H. H. (1996). *Using language.* Cambridge, UK: Cambridge University Press.

Clark, H. H., & Brennan, S. E. (1991). Grounding in communication. In L. B. Resnick, J. Levine, & S. D. Teasley (Eds.), *Perspectives on socially shared cognition* (pp.127–149). Washington, DC: American Psychological Association.

Clarke, E. M., & J. M. Wing, (1996). Formal methods: State of the art and future directions. *ACM Computing Surveys, 28*(4), 626–643.

Clarke, S. (2001). Evaluating a new programming language. In G. Kadoda (Ed.). *Proceedings of the 13th Annual Meeting of the Psychology of Programming Interest Group.*

Coch, L., & French, J. R. P., Jr. (1948). Overcoming resistance to change. *Human Relations, 1,* 512–532.

Cockburn, A., & Jones, S. (1996). Which way now? Analysing and easing inadequacies in WWW navigation. *International Journal of Human-Computer Studies, 45,* 130–195.

Cohill, M. A., & Kavanaugh, A. L. (2000). *Community networks: Lessons from blacksburg, Virginia.* Boston: Artech House.

Cole, M. (1990). Cultural psychology: A once and future discipline. In J. Berman (Ed.), *Nebraska Symposium: Current Theory and Research in Motivation—Cross-Cultural Perspectives, 37,* 279–335.

Collins, A., & Gentner, D. (1987). How people construct mental models. In D. Holland & N. Quinn (Eds), *Cultural models in language and thought.* Cambridge, UK: Cambridge University Press.

Connolly, T., Jessup, L., & Valacich, J. (1990). Effects of anonymity and evaluative tone on idea generation in computer-mediated groups. *Management Science, 36*(6), 689–703.

Constant, D., Sproull, L., & Kiesler, S. (1996). The kindness of strangers: The usefulness of electronic weak ties for technical advice. *Organization Science, 7*(2), 119–135.

Cooper, W. H., Gallupe, R. B., Pollard, S., & Cadsby, J. (1998). Some liberating effects of anonymous electronic brainstorming. *Small Group Research, 29*(2), 147–178.

Cramton, C. D. (2001). The mutual knowledge problem and its consequences for dispersed collaboration. *Organization Science Special Issue, 12*(3), 346–371.

Cummings, J. (2001). *Work groups and knowledge sharing in a global organization.* Unpublished doctoral dissertation, Carnegie-Mellon University, Pittsburgh, PA.

Curtis, B., Sheppard, S., Kruesi-Bailey, E., Bailey, J. & Boehm-Davis, D. (1989). Experimental evaluation of software documentation formats. *J. Systems and Software 9*(2), 167–207.

Curtis, P. (1992). Mudding: Social phenomena in text-based virtual realities. *Proceedings of the 1992 Conference on the Directions and Implications of Advanced Computing,* Berkeley, CA.

Cutting, D. R., Karger, D. R., & Pedersen, J. O. (1993). *Constant interaction-time Scatter/Gather browsing of very large document collections.* Paper presented at the SIGIR '93, New York, NY.

Cutting, D. R., Karger, D. R., Pedersen, J. O., & Tukey, J. W. (1992). *Scatter/gather: A cluster-based approach to browsing large document collections.* Paper presented at the SIGIR '92, New York, NY.

Cutting, J. E. (1997). How the eye measures reality and virtual reality. *Behavior Research Methods, Instruments and Computers, 29*(1), 27–36.

Dearden, A., & Harrison, M. (1995). Modelling interaction properties for interactive case memories. In F. Paternó, (Ed.) *Eurographics Workshop on Design, Specification, Verification of Interactive Systems (Pisa 1994).* Vienna: Springer Verlag.

Dennett, D. C. (1988). *The intentional stance.* Cambridge, MA: Bradford Books, MIT Press.

Denning, P. J., Comer, D. E., Gries, D., Mulder, M. C., Tucker, A. B., Turner, A. J., & Young, P. R. (1989). Computing as a discipline. *Communications of the ACM, 32,* 9–23.

Dennis, A. R., & Valacich, J. S. (1993). Computer brainstorms: More heads are better than one. *Journal of Applied Psychology, 78*(4), 531–537.

Dennis, A. R. & Williams, M. L. (In press). Electronic brainstorming: Theory, research and future directions. In P. B. Paulus (Ed.), *Group creativity.* New York: Oxford University Press.

Dennis, A. R., & Williams, M. L. (2002). *Electronic brainstorming: Theory, research and future directions* (TR116–1). Bloomington: Kelley School of Business, Indiana University.

Devlin, K. (1994). Situation theory and the design of interactive information systems. In D. Rosenberg & C. Hutchison (Eds.), *Design Issues for CSCW* (pp.61–87). London: Springer-Verlag.

Dewan, P. (1999). Architectures for collaborative applications. In M. Beaudouin-Lafon (Ed.), *Computer Supported Co-operative Work* (pp. 169–193). Chichester, U.K.: John Wiley.

Diaper, D. (Ed.). (1989). *Task analysis for human-computer interaction.* Chicester, U.K.: Ellis Horwood.

Diehl, M., & Stroebe, W. (1987). Productivity loss in brainstorming groups: Toward the solution of a riddle. *Journal of Personality and Social Psychology, 53*(3), 497–509.

Dix, A. J. (1987). The myth of the infinitely fast machine. In D. Diaper & R. Winder (Eds.), *People and Computers III—Proceedings of HCI'87* (pp.215–228). Cambridge, UK: Cambridge University Press.

Dix, A. J. (1991a). *Formal methods for interactive systems.* London: Academic Press. Table of contents and some chapters are available online at *www.hiraeth.com/books/formal/*

Dix, A. J. (1991b). Status and events: static and dynamic properties of interactive systems. In *Proceedings of the Eurographics Seminar: Formal Methods in Computer Graphics.* Marina di Carrara, Italy. Available online at *www.comp.lanes.ac.uk/computing/users/dixa/papers/euro91/euro.91.html*

Dix, A. J. (1995a). Dynamic pointers and threads. *Collaborative Computing, 1*(3):191–216.

Dix, A. J. (1995b). LADA—A logic for the analysis of distributed action. In F. Paternó (Ed.), *Interactive systems: Design, specification and verification* (1st Eurographics Workshop, Bocca di Magra, Italy, June 1994) (pp.317–332). Vienna: Springer Verlag.

Dix, A. J. (1996). Closing the loop: Modelling action, perception and information. In T. Catarci, M. F. Costabile, S. Levialdi, & G. Santucci (Eds.), *AVI'96—Advanced Visual Interfaces* (pp.20–28). Gubbio, Italy: ACM Press.

Dix, A. (1998). Finding out—Event discovery using status-event analysis. In C. Roast & J. Siddiqi (Eds.), *Formal Aspects of Human Computer Interaction* Sheffield-Hallam University, 5–6 September 1998. Available online at *www.hcibook.com/alan/papers/fahci98/*

Dix, A. (2002a). Embodied computation. Available online at *www.hcibook.com/alan/topics/embodied-computation/*

Dix, A. (2002b). In praise of randomness. Available online at *www.hiraeth.com/alan/topics/random/*

Dix, A. (2002c). Managing the ecology of interaction. *Proceedings of Tamodia 2002—First International Workshop on Task Models and User Interface Design, Bucharest, Romania, 18–19 July 2002,* Bucharest: INFOREC Publishing House. Available online at *www.hcibook.com/alan/papers/tamodia2002/*

Dix, A. (2002d). Towards a ubiquitous semantics of interaction: Phenomenology, scenarios and traces. *Proceedings of DSV-IS 2002—Design, Specification, and Verification of Interactive Systems. Rostock, Germany, June 2002.* Berlin: Springer-Verlag.

Dix, A., & Abowd, G. (1996). Modelling status and event behavior of interactive systems. *Software Engineering Journal, 11*(6), 334–346.

Dix, A., Finlay, J., Abowd, G., & Beale, R. (1993). *Human-computer interaction.* Hempel Hempstead, U.K.: Prentice-Hall.

Dix, A., Finlay, J., Abowd, G., & Beale, R. (1998). *Human-computer interaction (2nd ed.).* Hertfordshire, U.K.: Prentice Hall. Available online at *www.hcibook.com/.*

Dix, A. J. & Harrison, M. D. (1989). Interactive systems design and formal development are incompatible? In J. McDermid (Ed.), *The theory and practice of refinement* (pp.12–26). Guildford, U.K.: Butterworth Scientific.

Dix, A., & Mancini, R. (1997). Specifying history and backtracking mechanisms. In P. Palanque and F. Paternó (Eds.), *Formal Methods in Human-Computer Interaction* (pp.1–24). London: Springer-Verlag. Available online at *www.hcibook.com/alan/papers/histchap97/*

Dix, A., Mancini, R., & Levialdi, S. (1997). The cube—extending systems for undo. *Proceedings of DSVIS'97* (pp.473–495). Granada, Spain: Eurographics. Available online at *www.hcibook.com/alan/papers/dsvis97/*

Dix, A., Ramduny, D., & Wilkinson, J. (1998). Interaction in the large. In J. Fabre & S. Howard (Eds.), *Interacting with Computers—Special Issue on Temporal Aspects of Usability, 11*(1), 9–32. Available online at *www.hcibook.com/alan/papers/IwCtau98/*

Dix, A., Ramduny-Ellis, D., & Wilkinson, J. (2002). Trigger analysis—understanding broken tasks. In D. Diaper & N. Stanton (Eds.), *The handbook of task analysis for human-computer interaction.* Hillsdale, NJ: Erlbaum. Abstract and related information is available online at *www.hcibook.com/alan/topics/triggers/*

Dix, A., Rodden, T., Davies, N., Trevor, J., Friday, A., & Palfreyman, K. (2000). Exploiting space and location as a design framework for interactive mobile systems. *ACM Transactions on Computer-Human Interaction (TOCHI), 7*(3), 285–321.

Dix, A. J., & Runciman, C. (1985). Abstract models of interactive systems. In P. Johnson & S. Cook (Eds.), *People and computers: Designing the interface* (pp.13–22). Cambridge, UK: Cambridge University Press.

Dix, A., Wilkinson, J. & Ramduny, D. (1998). Redefining organizational memory—Artifacts, and the distribution and coordination of work. In *Understanding work and designing artifacts* (York, 21st Sept., 1998). Available online at *www.hiraeth.com/alan/papers/artifacts98/*

Dobzhansky, T. (1973). Nothing in biology makes sense except in the light of evolution. *The American Bilogy Teacher, 35*(3), 125–129.

Doherty, G. J., Massink, M., & Faconti, G. (2001). Using hybrid automata to support human factors analysis in a critical system. *Formal Methods in System Design, 19*(2), 143–164.

Douglas, S. A., & Mithal, A. K. (1997). *The ergonomics of computer pointing devices.* New York: Springer Verlag.

Douglas, S. A., Kirkpatrick, A. E., & MacKenzie, I. S. (1999). Testing pointing device performance and user assessment with the ISO 9241, Part 9 standard. *Proceedings of the ACM Conference on Human Factors in Computing Systems—CHI '99* (pp.215–222). New York: ACM Press.

Dourish, P., & Button, G. (1998). On "technomethodology": Foundational relationships between ethnomethodology and system design. *Human-Computer Interaction, 13*(4), 395–432.

Dreyfus, H. L., & Dreyfus, S. D. (1986) *Mind over machine—the power of human intuition and expertise in the era of the computer.* Glasgow, UK: Basil Blackwell.

Dumais, S. T., Furnas, G. W., Landauer, T. K., Deerwester, S., & Harshman, R. (1988). *Using latent semantic analysis to improve access to textual information.* Paper presented at the Conference on Human Factors in Computing Systems, CHI '88, Washington, DC.

Eberts, R. E. (1994). *User interface design.* Englewood Cliffs, NJ: Prentice Hall.

Eckert, C. M., & Stacy, M. K. (2000). Sources of inspiration: a language of design. *Design Studies 21*(5), 523–538.

Ehn, P. (1988). *Work-oriented design of computer artifacts.* Falköping: Arbetslivscentrum/Almqvist & Wiksell International. Hillsdale, NJ: Erlbaum.

Ehn, P., & Kyng, M. (1984). A tool perspective on design of interactive computer support for skilled workers. In M. Sääksjärvi (Ed.), *Proceedings from the Seventh Scandinavian Research Seminar on Systemeering* (pp.211–242). Helsinki: Helsinki Business School.

Ehn, P., & Kyng, M. (1987). The collective resource approach to systems design. In G. Bjerknes et al. (Eds.), *Computers and democracy—A Scandinavian challenge* (pp.17–58). Aldershot, UK: Avebury.

Elkerton, J. (1993). Using GOMS models to design documentation and user interfaces: An uneasy courtship. Position paper for Workshop on Human-Computer Interaction Advances Derived from Real World Experiences, *INTERCHI'93 Conference,* Amsterdam, April 24–25.

Elkerton, J., Goldstein, S. J., & Palmiter, S. L. (1990). Designing a help system using a GOMS model: A preliminary method execution analysis. *Proceedings of the Human Factors Society 34th Annual Meeting, 1* (pp.259–263). New York: ACM Press.

Elkerton, J., & Palmiter, S. (1989). Designing help systems using the GOMS model: An information retrieval evaluation. *Proceedings of the Human Factors Society 33rd Annual Meeting, 1* (pp.281–285). New York: ACM Press.

Elkerton, J., & Palmiter, S. L. (1991). Designing help using a GOMS model: An information retrieval evaluation. *Human Factors 33*(2), 185–204.

Elkind, J. I., Card, S. K., Hochberg, J., & Huey, B. M. (1990). *Human performance models for computer-aided engineering.* San Diego, CA: Academic Press.

Ellis, C. A., & Gibbs, S. J. (1989). Concurrency control in groupware systems. *SIGMOD Record, 18*(2), 399–407, June 1989. ACM SIGMOD International Conference on Management of Data.

Ellis, C., & Wainer, J. (1994). Goal based models of collaboration. *Collaborative Computing, 1*(1), 61–86.

Ellis, G. P., Finlay, J. E., & Pollitt, A. S. (1994). HIBROWSE for hotels: Bridging the gap between user and system views of a database. *Proc. IDS '94 2nd Int'l Workshop on User Interfaces to Databases, Lancaster, UK,* (45–58). New York: Springer Verlag,

Ellis, J. (1988). Memory for future intentions: Investigating pulses and steps. In M. M. Gruneberg, P. E. Morris, & R. N. Sykes (Eds), *Practical aspects of memory: Vol 1*. Chichester, UK: Wiley.

Elwert, T., & Schlungbaum, E. (1995). Modelling and generation of graphical user interfaces in the TADEUS approach. In P. Palanque & R. Bastide (Eds.), *Design, specification and verification of interactive systems '96 (Proceedings of DSVIS'95. Toulouse, France, June 1995)*. (pp.193–208). Vienna: Springer-Verlag.

Engeström, Y. (1987). *Learning by expanding*. Helsinki: Orienta-Konsultit.

Engeström, Y., & Engeström, R. (1989). *Constructing the object in the work activity of primary care physicians*. Unpublished manuscript.

Engeström, Y., & Escalante, V. (1996). Mundane tool or object of affection? The rise and fall of the postal buddy. In B. Nardi (Ed.), *Context and consciousness. Activity theory and human computer interaction* (pp.325–374). Cambridge, MA: MIT Press.

Engeström, Y., & Miettinen, R. (1999). Introduction. In Y. Engeström, R. Miettinen, & R. L. Punamaki (Eds.) *Perspectives on activity theory*. Cambridge, UK: Cambridge University Press.

Engeström, Y., Virkkunen, J., Helle, M., Pihlaja, J., & Poikela, R. (1996). Change laboratory as a tool for transforming work. In *Lifelong Learning in Europe, 1,* no. 2.

Englebart, D. C. (1962). *Augmenting human intellect: A conceptual framework* (AFOSR-3223). Menlo Park, CA: Stanford Research Institute.

Epps, B. W. (1986). Comparison of six cursor control devices based on Fitts' law models. *Proceedings of the Human Factors Society 30th Annual Meeting* (pp. 327–331). Santa Monica, CA: Human Factors Society.

Erickson, T. (2000). Making sense of computer-mediated communication (CMC): Conversations as genres, CMC systems as genre ecologies. *Proceedings of the Thirty-Third Hawaii International Conference on Systems Science, January*. New York: IEEE Press.

Festinger, L. (1957). *A theory of cognitive dissonance*. New York: Harper & Row.

Field, D. J., Hayes, A., & Hess, R. F. (1992). Contour integration by the human visual system: Evidence for a local "association field." *Vision Research, 33*(2), 173–193.

Finholt, T. A., & Teasley, S. D. (1998). The need for psychology in research on computer-supported cooperative work. *Social Science Computer Review, 16*(1), 40–52.

Finlay, J., & Dix, A. (1996). An introduction to artificial intelligence. London: UCL Press / Taylor and Francis.

Finn, K. E., Sellen, A. J., & Wilbur, S. B. (1997). *Video-mediated communication*. Mahwah, NJ: Erlbaum.

Firby, R. J. (1989). Adaptive execution in complex dynamic world. Doctoral dissertation, Yale University. Technical Report 672.

Fish, J., & Scrivener, S. (1990). Amplifying the mind's eye: Sketching and visual cognition. *Leonardo, 23*(1), 117–126.

Fitter, M., & Green, T. R. G. (1979). When do diagrams make good computer languages? *International Journal of Man-Machine Studies, 11*(2), 235–261.

Fitts, P. (Ed). (1951). *Human engineering for an effective air-navigation and traffic-control system. Report*. Washington, D.C.: National Research Council.

Fitts, P. M. (1954). The information capacity of the human motor system in controlling the amplitude of movement. *Journal of Experimental Psychology, 47,* 381–391.

Fitts, P. M., & Peterson, J. R. (1964). Information capacity of discrete motor responses. *Journal of Experimental Psychology, 67,* 103–112.

Fitts, P. M., & Posner, M. I. (1967). *Learning and skilled performance in human performance.* Belmont CA: Brooks-Cole.

Fitzmaurice, G. W., Balakrishnan, R., Kurtenbach, G., & Buxton, B. (1999). An exploration into supporting artwork orientation in the user interface, *Proceedings of the ACM Conference on Human Factors in Computing Systems—CHI '99* (pp.167–174). New York: ACM.

Flach, J. (1995). The ecological of human machine systems: A personal history. In J. Flach, P. Hancock, J. Caird, & K. Vicente (Eds)., *Global perspectives on the ecology of human-machine systems (Vol 1).* Hillsdale, NJ: Erlbaum.

Flach, J., Hancock, P., Caird, J., & Vicente, K. (eds.). (1995). *Global perspectives on the ecology of human-machine systems (Vol 1).* Hillsdale, NJ: Erlbaum.

Flor, N., & Hutchins, E. L. (1992). Analysing distributed cognition in software teams: A case study of team programming during perfective software maintenance. In J. Joenemann-Belliveau, T. Moher, & S. Robertson (Eds.), *Empirical Studies of Programmers: 4th Workshop* (pp.36–64). Norwood, NJ: Ablex.

Floyd, C. (1987). Outline of a paradigm change in software engineering. In G. Bjerknes, P. Ehn, & M. Kyng (Eds.). *Computers and democracy—A Scandinavian challenge* (pp.191–212). Aldershot, UK: Avebury.

Foley, J. D., Wallace, V. L., & Chan, P. (1984). The human factors of computer graphics interaction techniques. *IEEE Computer Graphics and Applications, 4*(11), 13–48.

Foley, J., & Sukaviriya, P. (1995). History, results and bibliography of the user interface design environment (UIDE), an early model-based system for user interface design and implementation. In F. Paternó, (Ed.), *Eurographics Workshop on Design, Specification, Verification of Interactive Systems* (pp.3–14). Vienna: Springer Verlag.

Freed, M. (1998). *Simulating human performance in complex, dynamic environments.* Doctoral dissertation, Northwestern University.

Friedman, W. (1990). *About time.* Cambridge, MA: MIT Press.

Fulk, J., Flanagin, A., Kalman, M., Monge, P., & Ryan, T. (1996). Connective and communal public goods in interactive communication systems. *Communication Theory, 6,* 60–87.

Furnas, G. W., Landauer, T. K., Gomez, L. W., & Dumais, S. T. (1987). The vocabulary problem in human-system communication. *Communications of the ACM, 30,* 964–971.

Galbraith, J. (1977). *Organization design.* New York: Addison-Wesley Publishing.

Gallupe, R. B., Cooper, W. H., Grise, M.-L., & Bastianutti, L. M. (1994). Blocking electronic brainstorms. *Journal of Applied Psychology, 79*(1), 77–86.

Gardner, M. (1970). The fantastic combinations of John Conway's new solitaire game "life." *Scientific American, 223,* 120–123.

Garfinkel, H. (1967). *Studies in ethnomethodology.* Englewood Cliffs, NJ: Prentice-Hall.

Garfinkel, H. (Ed.). (1986). *Ethnomethodological studies of work.* London: Routledge.

Garfinkel, H., Livingston, E., Lynch, M., Macbeth, D., & Robillard, A. (1989). *Respecifying the natural sciences as discovering sciences of practical action, I & II.* Unpublished paper, Department of Sociology, University of California, Los Angeles.

Gasser, L. (1986). The integration of computing and routine work. *ACM TOIS, 4*(3), 205–225.

Gentner, D., & Stevens, A. L. (1993). *Mental models.* Mahwah, NJ: Erlbaum.

Gibson, J. J. (1950). *The perception of the visual world.* Boston, MA: Houghton-Mifflin.

Gibson, J. J. (1966). *The senses considered as perceptual systems.* Boston, MA: Houghton-Mifflin.

Gibson, J. J. (1979). *An ecological approach to visual perception.* Boston, MA: Houghton-Mifflin.

Gibson, J. J. (1986). *The ecological approach to visual perception.,* Hillsdale, NJ.: Erlbaum.

Gigone, D., & Hastie, R. (1997). Proper analysis of the accuracy of group judgments. *Psychological Bulletin, 121*(1), 149–167.

Gilbert, D. T., Fiske, S. T., & Lindzey, G. (1998). *The handbook of social psychology* (4th ed.). New York: McGraw-Hill.

Gluck, K. A., & R. W. Pew (2001). *The AMBR model comparison project: Round III—Model category learning.* Conference on Computer Generated Forces & Behavioral Representation. 10th-CGF-066.

Goffman, E. (1976). Replies and responses. *Language in Society, 5,* 257–313.

Goldschmidt, G. (1991). The dialectics of sketching. *Creativity Research Journal, 4*(2), 123–143.

Gong, R. (1993). *Validating and refining the GOMS model methodology for software user interface design and evaluation.* Doctoral dissertation, University of Michigan, 1993.

Gong, R., & Elkerton, J. (1990). Designing minimal documentation using a GOMS model: A usability evaluation of an engineering approach. *In Proceedings of ACM CHI 1990 Conference on Human Factors in Computing Systems* (Seattle, Washington, April 30–May 4, 1990) (pp.99–106). New York: ACM Press.

Gong, R., & Kieras, D. (1994). A validation of the GOMS model methodology in the development of a specialized, commercial software application. In *Proceedings of CHI, 1994, Boston, MA, USA, April 24–28, 1994)* (pp.351–357). New York: ACM Press.

Goodstein, L. (1968). An experimental computer-controlled instrumentation system for the research reactor DR-2. In *Application of on-line computers to nuclear reactors* (pp.549–566). Halden, Norway: OECD Halden Reactor Project.

Goodwin, C., & Goodwin, M. (1993). Formulating planes: Seeing as a situated activity. In Y. Engestrom & D. Middleton (Eds.), *Communities of practice: Cognition and communication at work.* Cambridge, UK: Cambridge University Press.

Gott, S. P., (1988). Apprenticeship instruction for real-world tasks: The coordination of procedures, mental models, and strategies. In E. Z. Rothkopf (Ed.), *Review of Research in Education.* Washington, D.C.: AERA.

Graesser, A. C., & Clark, L. F. (1985). *Structures and procedures of implicit knowledge.* Norwood, NJ: Ablex.

Grandjean, E. (1982). *Fitting the task to the man.* London: Taylor & Francis.

Gray, W. D. Sabnani, H., & (1994). *Why you can't program your VCR, or, predicting errors and performance with production system models of display-based action. Proceedings of ACM CHI 1994 Conference on Human Factors in Computing Systems* (Companion) (pp.79–80). New York: ACM Press.

Gray, W. D., & Boehm-Davis, D. A. (2000). Milliseconds matter: An introduction to microstrategies and to their use in describing and predicting interactive behavior. *Journal of Experimental Psychology: Applied, 6*(4), 322–335.

Gray, W. D., John, B. E., & Atwood, M. E. (1992). The precis of Project Ernestine or an overview of a validation of GOMS. In P. Bauersfeld, J. Bennett, & G. Lynch (Eds.), *Striking a balance, Proceedings of the CHI'92 Conference on Human Factors in Computing Systems* (pp.307–312). New York: ACM Press.

Gray, W. D., John, B. E., & Atwood, M. E. (1993). Project Ernestine: Validating a GOMS analysis for predicting and explaining real-world task performance. *Human-Computer Interaction, 8,* 237–309.

Gray, W. D., John, B. E., Lawrence, D., Stuart, R., & Atwood, M. E. (1989). GOMS meets the phone company, or, Can 8,400,000 unit-tasks be wrong? Poster presented at the *Proceedings of ACM CHI 1989 Conference on Human Factors in Computing Systems.* Austin, TX. New York: ACM Press.

Gray, W. D., John, B. E., Stuart, R., Lawrence, D., & Atwood, M. E. (1990). GOMS meets the phone company: Analytic modeling applied to real-world problems. In D. Diaper, D. Gilmore, G. Cockton, and B. Shackel (Eds.), *Human-computer interaction—INTERACT '90.* (pp.29–34). Amsterdam: Elsevier Science Publishers.

Green, T. R. G. (1989). Cognitive dimensions of notations. In V, A Sutcliffe and L Macaulay (Ed.). *People and computers* (pp.443–460). Cambridge, U.K.: Cambridge University Press.

Green, T. R. G. (1991). Describing information artifacts with cognitive dimensions and structure maps. In D. Diaper & N. V. Hammond (Eds.). *Proceedings of HCI'91: 'Usability Now', Annual Conference of BCS Human-Computer Interaction Group.* Cambridge, U.K.: Cambridge University Press.

Green, T. R. G. (1999). Building and manipulating complex information structures: Issues in prolog programming. In P. Brna, B. du Boulay, & H. Pain (Eds.). *Learning to build and comprehend complex information structures: Prolog as a case study* (pp.7–27). Stamford, CT: Ablex.

Green, T. R. G., & Benyon, D. (1996.) The skull beneath the skin: entity-relationship models of information artifacts. *International Journal of Human-Computer Studies, 44*(6), 801–828.

Green, T. R. G., Bellamy, R. K. E., & Parker, J. M. (1987). Parsing and gnisrap: A model of device use. In G. M. Olson, S. Sheppard, & E. Soloway (Eds.). *Empirical studies of programmers: Second Workshop* (pp.132–146). Norwood, NJ: Ablex.

Green, T. R. G. & Blackwell, A. F. (1998). Design for usability using cognitive dimensions. Tutorial session at British Computer Society conference on Human Computer Interaction HCI'98. Current revisions are maintained online at: *www.cl.cam.ac.uk/~afb21/CognitiveDimensions/CDtutorial.pdf*

Green, T. R. G., & Petre, M. (1992). When visual programs are harder to read than textual programs. In G. C. van der Veer & S. Bagnarola (Eds.). *Proceedings of ECCE-6 (European Conference on Cognitive Ergonomics).*

Green, T. R. G. & Petre, M. (1996). Usability analysis of visual programming environments: a 'cognitive dimensions' approach. *Journal of Visual Languages and Computing, 7,*131–174.

Green, T. R. G., Petre, M., & Bellamy, R. K. E. (1991). Comprehensibility of visual and textual programs: A test of superlativism against the 'match-mismatch' conjecture. In J. Koenemann-Belliveau, T. G. Moher, & S. P. Robertson (Eds.), *Empirical studies of programmers: Fourth workshop* (pp.121–146). Norwood, NJ: Ablex.

Greenbaum, J., & Kyng, M. (Eds.). (1991). *Design at work.* Hillsdale, NJ: Erlbaum.

Greenberg, S., & Marwood, D. (1994). Real time groupware as a distributed system: Concurrency control and its effect on the interface. *Proceedings of Computer-Supported Cooperative Work: CSCW '94* (pp.207–217). New York, ACM Press.

Greif, S. (1991). The role of German work psychology in the design of artifacts. In J. Carroll (Ed.). *Designing interaction: Psychological theory of the human-computer interface.* New York: Cambridge University Press.

Grice, H. P. (1957). Meaning. *Philosophical Review, 66,* 377–388.

Grossman, R. L., Nerode, A., Ravn, A. P., & Rischel, H. (Eds.). (1993) *Hybrid Systems.* Lecture Notes in Computer Science 736. Berlin: Springer Verlag.

Grudin, J. (1990a). *Interface. Proceedings of ACM CSCW'90 Conference on Computer-Supported Cooperative Work* (pp.269–278). New York, ACM Press.

Grudin, J. (1990b). The computer reaches out: The historical continuity of interface design. *Evolution and Practice in User Interface Engineering, Proceedings of ACM CHI'90 Conference on Human Factors in Computing Systems* (pp.261–268). New York: ACM Press.

Gualtieri, J., Roth, E., & Eggleston, R. (2000). Utilising the abstraction hierarchy for role allocation and team structure design. *Proceedings of the 5th International Conference on Human Interaction with Complex Systems.* April 30–May 4. Urbana, IL. US Army Research Laboratory.

Guiard, Y. (1987). Asymmetric division of labor in human skilled bimanual action: The kinematic chain as a model. *Journal of Motor Behavior, 19,* 486–517.

Hackman, R. (1987). The design of work teams. In J. Lorsch (Ed.), *Handbook of organizational behavior.* Englewood Cliffs, NJ: Prentice-Hall.

Halasz, F. G., & Moran, T. P. (1983). Mental models and problem-solving in using a calculator. In *Proceedings of CHI 83 Human Factors in Computing Systems.* New York: ACM Press.

Halverson, C. A. (1995). *Inside the cognitive workplace: new technology and air traffic control.* PhD diss. Department of Cognitive Science, University of California, San Diego.

Ham, D.-H., & Yoon, W. C., (2001a). The effects of presenting functionally abstracted information in fault diagnosis tasks. *Reliability Engineering and System Safety, 73,* 103–119.

Ham, D.-H., & Yoon, W. C., (2001b). Design of information content and layout for process control based on goal-means domain analysis. *Cognition, Technology, and Work, 3,* 205–223.

Hames, R. (1992). Time allocation. In E. A. Smith & B. Winterhalder (Eds.), *Evolutionary ecology and human behavior* (pp.203–235). New York: de Gruyter.

Hammersley, M., & Atkinson, P. (1995). *Ethnography: principles in practice. 2nd ed.* London: Routledge.

Han, B., Kim, H., Ham, D.-H., & Yoon, W. C. (2001). The role of graphical format in designing information display for process control. *Proceedings of the 2001 Conference of the Korean Human-Computer Interaction Society.* Phoenix Park. (In Korean)

Hancock, P., Flach, J., Caird, J., & Vicente, K. (1995). *Local applications of the ecological approach to human-machine systems (Vol 2)*. Hillsdale, NJ: Erlbaum.

Hargadon, A., & Sutton, R. I. (1997). Technology brokering and innovation in a product development firm. *Administrative Science Quarterly, 42*(4), 716–749.

Harpending, H. (1993). The human scenario beclouded [Review of the book *Evolutionary ecology and human behavior*]. *Science, 260*, 1176–1178.

Harrison, M. D., & Thimbleby, H. W. (Eds.) (1990). *Formal methods in human computer interaction*. Cambridge, UK: Cambridge University Press.

Harrison, S., & Dourish, P. (1996). Re-place-ing space: The roles of place and space in collaborative systems. *Proceedings of Computer-Supported Cooperative Work: CSCW '96* (pp.67–76). New York: ACM Press.

Haunold, P., & Kuhn, W. (1994). A keystroke level analysis of a graphics application: Manual map digitizing GOMS analysis. *Proceedings of ACM CHI 1994 Conference on Human Factors in Computing Systems, 1* (pp.337–343). New York: ACM Press.

Hazelhurst, B. L. (1994). *Fishing for cognition: An ethnography of fishing practice in a community on the west coast of Sweden*. PhD diss. Department of Cognitive Science, University of California, San Diego.

Heath, C., & Luff, P. (1991). Collaborative activity and technological design: Task coordination in London Underground control rooms. *Proceedings of the ECSCW'91 . . . European Conference on Computer-Supported Cooperative Work* (pp.65–79). Dordrecht: Kluwer.

Heath, C., & Luff, P. (1993). Disembodied conduct: Interactional asymmetries in video-mediated communication. In G. Button (Ed.), *Technology in working order: Studies of work, interaction and technology*. London: Routledge.

Heidegger, M. (1962). *Being and time.* (trans. by J. Macquarrie & E. Robinson). New York: Harper & Row.

Helander, M. G. (Ed.). (1988). *Handbook of human-computer interaction*. Amsterdam: North Holland.

Helander, M. G., Landauer, T. K., & Prabhu, P. V. (Eds.). (1997). *Handbook of human-computer interaction, second edition*. Amsterdam: North Holland.

Helle M. (2000). Disturbances and contradictions as tools for understanding work in the newsroom. *Scandinavian Journal of Information Systems, 12*, 81–114.

Hick, W. E. (1952). On the rate of gain of information. *Quarterly Journal of Experimental Psychology, 4*, 11–36.

Hill, G. W. (1982). Group versus individual performance. Are N = 1 heads better than one? *Psychological Bulletin, 91*, 517–539.

Hinckley, K., Pausch, R., Proffitt, D., & Kassell, N. F. (1998). Two-handed virtual manipulation. *ACM Transactions on Computer-Human Interaction, 5*(3), 260–302.

Hinckley, K., Pausch, R., Proffitt, D., Patten, J., & Kassell, N. (1997). Cooperative bimanual action. *Proceedings of the ACM Conference on Human Factors in Computing Systems—CHI '97* (pp.27–34). New York: ACM Press.

Hoare, C. A. R. (1985). *Communicating sequential process*. London: Prentice-Hall International.

Hofstadter, D. R. (1979). *Gödel, Escher, Bach: An eternal golden braid*. Harmondsworth, U.K.: Penguin Books.

Hogg, M. A., & Tindale, R. S. (2001). *Group processes*. Malden, MA: Blackwell Publishers.

Holland, J. H., Holyoak, K. J., Nisbett, R. E. & Thagard, P. R. (1986). *Induction*. Cambridge, MA: MIT Press.

Hollnagel, E., & Woods, D. (1983). Cognitive systems engineering: New wine in new bottles. *International Journal of Man-Machine Systems, 18,* 583–600.

Hori, S., Vicente, K., Shimizu, Y., & Takami, I. (2001). Putting cognitive work analysis to work in industry practice: Integration with ISO13407 on Human-Centred Design. *Proceedings of the Human Factors and Ergonomics Society 45th Annual Meeting, Minneapolis, MN* (pp.429–433). Santa Monica, CA: HFES.

Horvitz, E., Jacobs, A., & Hovel, D. (1999). *Attention-sensitive alerting*. Paper presented at the UAI '99 Conference on Uncertainty and Articial Intelligence, Stockholm, Sweden.

Huberman, B. A., & Hogg, T. (1987). Phase transitions in artificial intelligence systems. *Artificial Intelligence, 33,* 155–171.

Huberman, B. A., & Lukose, R. M. (1997). Social dilemmas and internet congestions. *Science, 277,* 535–537.

Huberman, B. A., Pirolli, P., Pitkow, J., & Lukose, R. J. (1998). Strong regularities in World Wide Web surfing. *Science, 280,* 95–97.

Hudson, S. E., John, B. E., Knudsen, K., & Byrne, M. D. (1999). A tool for creating predictive performance models from user interface demonstrations. *Proceedings of the ACM Symposium on User Interface Software and Technology* (pp.93–102).

Hughes, E. C. (1971). *The sociological eye*. Chicago: Aldine-Aterton.

Hurvich, L. M. (1981). *Color vision*. Sunderland, MA: Sinauer Associates.

Hutchins, E. (1995a). *Cognition in the wild*. Bradford: MIT Press.

Hutchins, E. (1995b). How a cockpit remembers its speeds. *Cognitive Science, 19,* 265–288.

Hutchins, E. (1995c). *Distributed cognition*. Cambridge, MA: MIT Press.

Hutchins, E. L., Hollan, J. D., & Norman, D. A. (1986). Direct manipulation interfaces. In D. A. Norman & S. W. Draper (Eds.), *User centered system design* (pp. 87–124). Hillsdale, NJ: Erlbaum.

Hutchins, E., & Klausen, T. (1996). Distributed cognition in an airline cockpit. In Y. Engeström & D. Middleton (Eds.), *Cognition and communication at work*. Cambridge, UK: Cambridge University Press.

Hydén, L.-C. (1981). *Psykologi och Materialism. Introduktion till den materialistiska psykologin*. Stockholm. Prisma. (In Swedish. *Psychology and materialism. An introduction to materialistic psychology*.)

Hyman, R. (1953). Stimulus information as a determinant of reaction time. *Journal of Experimental Psychology, 45,* 188–196.

Ingham, A. G., Levinger, G., Graves, J., & Peckham, V. (1974). The Ringelmann effect: Studies of group size and group performance. *Journal of Experimental Social Psychology, 10*(4), 371–384.

Irani, P., & Ware, C. (2000). *Diagrams based on structural object perception.* Palermo: Conference on Advanced Visual Interfaces.

Irving, S., Polson, P., & Irving, J. E. (1994). A GOMS analysis of the advanced automated cockpit GOMS analysis. *Proceedings of ACM CHI 1994 Conference on Human Factors in Computing Systems. 1* (pp.344–350). New York: ACM Press.

Isaacs, E. A., & Clark, H. H. (1987). References in conversation between experts and novices. *Journal of Experimental Psychology: General, 116*(1), 26–37.

ISO (1989). *Information processing systems, open systems interconnection, LOTOS—A formal description technique based on the temporal ordering of observational behavior, IS 8807.* Geneva: author.

ISO. (1999). *Ergonomic requirements for office work with visual display terminals (VDTs)—Part 9— Requirements for non-keyboard input devices (ISO 9241–9)* (Report Number ISO/TC 159/SC4/WG3 N147): Geneva author.

Jacko, J. & Sears, A. (Eds.). (2003). *The human-computer interaction handbook.* Mahwah, NJ: Erlbaum.

Jackson, R., MacDonald, L., & Freeman, K. (1994). *Computer generated color.* Chichester, UK: Wiley Professional Computing.

Jacob, R. J. K., Sibert, L. E., McFarlane, D. C., & Mullen Jr., M. P. (1994). Integrality and separability of input devices. *ACM Transactions on Computer-Human Interaction, 1,* 3–26.

Janis, I. L. (1972). *Victims of groupthink: A psychological study of foreign policy decisions and fiascoes.* Boston, MA: Houghton-Mifflin.

Janzen, M. J., & Vicente, K. J. (1998). Attention allocation within the abstraction hierarchy. *International Journal of Human-Computer Studies, 48,* 521–545.

Jefferson, G. (1987). On exposed and enclosed corrections in conversation. In G. Button & J. R. E. Lee (Eds.), *Talk and social organisation.* Clevedon, UK: Multilingual Matters.

Jensen, K. (1992–1997). *Coloured petri nets.* Vol 1, 1992; Vol 2, 1994; Vol. 3, 1997. Berlin: Springer Verlag.

Jessup, L. M., Connolly, T., & Galegher, J. (1990). The effects of anonymity on group process in automated group problem solving. *MIS Quarterly, 14*(3), 313–321.

Jessup, L. M., Connolly, T., & Tansik, D. A. (1990). Toward a theory of automated group work: The deindividuating effects of anonymity. *Small Group Research, 21*(3), 333–348.

John, B. E., (1988). *Contributions to engineering models of human-computer interaction.* Doctoral dissertation, Carnegie-Mellon University, Pittsburgh.

John, B. E. (1990). Extensions of GOMS analyses to expert performance requiring perception of dynamic visual and auditory information. In *Proceedings of CHI, 1990 (Seattle, Washington, April 30–May 4, 1990)* (pp.107–115). New York: ACM Press.

John, B. E. (1995). Why GOMS? *Interactions, 2*(4), 80–89.

John, B. E. (1996) TYPIST: A theory of performance in skilled typing. *Human-Computer Interaction, 11*(4), 321–355.

John, B. E., & Gray, W. D. (1992, 1994, 1995). *GOMS Analyses for Parallel Activities.* Tutorial materials presented at CHI, 1992 (Monterey, California, May 3–May 7, 1992), CHI, 1994 (Boston MA, April 24– April 28, 1994), and CHI, 1995 (Denver CO, May 7–May 11, 1995). New York: ACM Press.

John, B. E., & Kieras, D. E. (1996a). Using GOMS for user interface design and evaluation: Which technique? *ACM Transactions on Computer-Human Interaction, 3*(4), 287–319.

John, B. E., & Kieras, D. E. (1996b). The GOMS family of user interface analysis techniques: Comparison and contrast. *ACM Transactions on Computer-Human Interaction, 3*(4), 320–351.

John, B. E., & Newell, A. (1987). Predicting the time to recall computer command abbreviations. *Proceedings of CHI+ GI, 1987 (Toronto, April 5–April 9, 1987)* (pp.33–40). New York: ACM Press.

John, B. E., & Newell, A. (1989). Cumulating the science of HCI: From S-R compatibility to transcription typing. *Proceedings of CHI, 1989 (Austin, TX, April 30–May 4, 1989)* (pp.109–114). New York: ACM Press.

John, B. E., & Newell, A. (1990). Toward an engineering model of stimulus-response compatibility. In R. W. Proctor & T. G. Reeve (Eds.), *Stimulus-response compatibility: An integrated perspective.* North-Holland.

John, B. E., Rosenbloom, P. S., & Newell, A. (1985). A theory of stimulus-response compatibility applied to human-computer interaction. *Proceedings of CHI, 1985 (San Francisco, California, April 14–18, 1985)* (pp.212–219). New York: ACM Press.

John, B. E., & Vera, A. H. (1992). A GOMS analysis for a graphic, machine-paced, highly interactive task. *Proceedings of ACM CHI 1992 Conference on Human Factors in Computing Systems (Monterey, California, May 3–May 7, 1992)* (pp.251–258). New York: ACM Press.

John, B. E., Vera, A. H., Matessa, M., Freed, M., & Remington, R. (2002). Automating CPM-GOMS. *Proceedings of ACM CHI 2002 Conference on Human Factors in Computing Systems* (pp.147–154). New York: ACM Press.

Johnson, P. (1992). *Human-computer interaction. Psychology, task analysis and software engineering.* London: McGraw-Hill.

Johnson-Laird, P. N. (1983). *Mental models.* Cambridge, UK: Cambridge University Press.

Johnson-Laird, P. N. (1989). *Mental models.* In M. I. Posner (Ed), *Foundations of cognitive science.* Cambridge, MA: MIT Press.

Jones, W. P. (1986). *The memory extender personal filing system.* Paper presented at the Conference Human Factors in Computing System, CHI '86, Boston, MA.

Judge, T. A., Thoresen, C. J., Bono, J. E., & Patton, G. K. (2001). The job satisfaction–job performance relationship: A qualitative and quantitative review. *Psychological Bulletin, 127*(3), 376–407.

Kabbash, P., Buxton, W., & Sellen, A. (1994). Two-handed input in a compound task. *Proceedings of the ACM Conference on Human Factors in Computing Systems—CHI '94* (pp.417–423). New York: ACM Press.

Kabbash, P., MacKenzie, I. S., & Buxton, W. (1993). Human performance using computer input devices in the preferred and non-preferred hands. *Proceedings of the INTERCHI '93 Conference on Human Factors in Computing Systems* (pp.474–481). New York: ACM Press.

Kadoda, G., Stone, R., & Diaper, D. (1999). Desirable features of educational theorem provers—a cognitive dimensions viewpoint. In T. R. G. Green, R. Abdullah, & P. Brna (Eds.). *Collected Papers of the 11th Annual Workshop of the Psychology of Programming Interest Group (PPIG-11)* (pp.18–23). Leeds: Leeds University Press.

Kahneman, D., Triesman, A., & Gibbs, B. J. (1992). The reviewing of object files: Object-specific integration of information. *Cognitive Psychology, 24,* 175–219.

Kaptelinin, V. (1996). Computer-mediated activity: Functional organs in social and developmental contexts. In B. Nardi (Ed.). *Context and consciousness: Activity theory and human computer interaction* (pp.45–68). Cambridge, MA: MIT Press.

Kaptelinin, V., Nardi, B., & Macaulay, C. (1999). Methods & tools: The activity checklist: A tool for representing the "space" of context. *Interaction, 6* (4), 27–39.

Karau, S. J., & Williams, K. D. (1993). Social loafing: A meta-analytic review and theoretical integration. *Journal of Personality & Social Psychology, 65*(4), 681–706.

Katz, R., & Tushman, M. (1979). Communication patterns, project performance, and task characteristics: An empirical evaluation and integration in an R&D setting. *Organizational Behavior and Human Decision Processes, 23,* 139–162.

Kelly, G. (1955). *The psychology of personal constructs as a theory of personality.* New York: Norton.

Kelly, S. U., Sung, C., & Farnham, S. (2002). Designing for improved social responsibility, user participation, and content in an online community. *Proceedings of Human Factors and Computing Systems: CHI 2002* (pp.391–398). New York: ACM Press.

Kelly, T., & Littman, J. (2001). *Lessons in creativity from IDEO, America's leading design firm.* New York: Doubleday.

Kelso, J. A. S., Southard, D. L., & Goodman, D. (1979). On the coordination of two-handed movements. *Journal of Experimental Psychology: Human Perception and Performance, 5*(2), 229–238.

Kieras, D. E., & Bovair, S. (1984). The role of a mental model in learning to use a device. *Cognitive Science, 8,* 255–273.

Kieras, D. E. (1997). A guide to GOMS model usability evaluation using NGOMSL. In M. Helander, T. K. Landauer, & P. Prabhu (Eds.), *Handbook of Human-Computer Interaction* (pp.733–766). Amsterdam: Elsevier Science Publishers.

Kieras, D. E., & Meyer, D. E. (1994). *The EPIC architecture for modeling human information processing: A brief introduction.* (EPIC Tech. Rep. No. 1, TR-94/ONR-EPIC-1). Ann Arbor: University of Michigan, Department of Electrical Engineering and Computer Science.

Kieras, D. E., & Meyer, D. E. (1997). An overview of the EDIC architecture for cognition and performance with application to human-computer interaction. *Human-Computer Interaction, 12,* 391–438.

Kieras, D. E., & Polson, P. G. (1985). An approach to the formal analysis of user complexity. *International Journal of Man-Machine Studies, 22,* 365–394.

Kieras, D. E., Wood, S. D., Abotel, K., & Hornof, A. (1995). GLEAN: A computer-based tool for rapid GOMS model usability evaluation of user interface designs. *Proceedings of the ACM Symposium on User Interface Software and Technology 1995* (pp.91–100). New York: ACM Press.

Kieras, D. E., Wood, S. D., & Meyer, D. E. (1997). Predictive engineering models based on the EPIC architecture for a multimodal high-performance human-computer interaction task. *ACM Transactions on Human-Computer Interaction, 4*(3), 230–275.

Kiesler, S., Wholey, D., & Carley, K. M. (1994). Coordination as linkage: The case of software development teams. In D. H. Harris (Ed.), *Organizational linkages: Understanding the productivity paradox* (pp. 214–239). Washington, DC: National Academy Press.

Kilmister, C. (1967). *Language, logic and mathematics.* London: English Universities Press.

Kintsch, W. (1988). The role of knowledge in discourse comprehension: A construction integration model. *Psychological Review, 95*(2), 163–182.

Kintsch, W. (1992). A cognitive architecture for comprehension. In H. L. Pick, Jr., P. van den Broek, & D. C. Knill (Eds.), *Cognition: Conceptual and methodological issues* (pp.143–164). Washington, D.C.: American Psychological Association.

Kintsch, W. (1998). *Comprehension.* Cambridge, UK: Cambridge University Press.

Kirlik, A. (1995). Requirements for psychological models to support design: Toward ecological task analysis. In J. Flach, P. Hancock, J. Caird, & K. Vicente (Eds)., *Global perspectives on the ecology of human-machine systems (Vol 1).* Hillsdale, NJ: Erlbaum.

Kirsh, D. (1995). The intelligent use of space. *Artificial Intelligence, 73,* 31–68.

Kirwan, B., & Ainsworth, L. K. (Eds.). (1992). *A guide to task analysis.* London: Taylor & Francis.

Kitajima, M., & Polson, P. G. (1997). A comprehension-based model of exploration. *Human Computer Interaction, 12,* 345–389.

Koester, H., & Levine, S. P. (1994). Validation of a keystroke-level model for a text entry system used by people with disabilities. *Proceedings of the First ACM Conference on Assistive Technologies* (pp.115–122). New York: ACM Press.

Koffka, K. (1935). *Principles of gestalt psychology.* New York: Harcourt-Brace.

Koistinen, K. & Kangajosa, J. (1997). *Learning to survive, Enable '97,* Helsinki.

Korpela, M. (1994). *Nigerian practice in computer systems development.* Helsinki University of Technology TKO-A31, Helsinki.

Korpela, M., Soriyan, H. A., & Olufokunbi, K. C. (2000). Activity analysis as a method for information systems development. *Scandinavian Journal of Information Systems, 12,* 191–210.

Kosslyn, S. M. (1994). *Image and brain: The resolution of the imagery debate.* Cambridge, MA: MIT Press.

Kotze, P. (1997). The use of formal models in the design of interactive authoring support environments. DPhil Thesis. University of York, England.

Krauss, R. M., Garlock, C. M., Bricker, P. D., & McMahon, L. E. (1977). The role of audible and visible back-channel responses in interpersonal communication. *Journal of Personality & Social Psychology, 35*(7), 523–529.

Kraut, R. E., Fussell, S. R., Brennan, S. E., & Siegel, J. (2002). Understanding effects of proximity on collaboration: Implications for technologies to support remote collaborative work. In P. Hinds & S. Kiesler (Eds.) *Distributed work* (pp.137–164). Cambridge, MA: MIT Press.

Kraut, R. E., Miller, M. D., & Siegel, J. (1996). Collaboration in performance of physical tasks: Effects on outcomes and communication. In M. S. Ackerman (Ed.), *CSCW96, Boston, MA.* (pp.57–66). New York, NY: ACM Press.

Kraut, R., & Streeter, L. (1995). Coordination in large scale software development. *Communications of the ACM, 38*(3), 69–81.

Kravitz, D. A., & Martin, B. (1986). Ringelmann rediscovered: The original article. *Journal of Personality & Social Psychology, 50*(5), 936–941.

Kress, G., & van Leeuwen, T. (1996). *Reading images: The grammar of visual design.* London: Routledge.

Kuo, J., & Burns, C. M. (2000). Work domain analysis for virtual private networks. *Proceedings of the IEEE International Conference on Systems, Man and Cybernetics* (pp. 1972–1977). Piscataway, NJ: IEEE.

Kurtenbach, G., & Buxton, W. (1994). User learning and performance with marking menus. *Proceedings of Human Factors in Computing Systems, CHI '94* (pp.258–264).

Kurtenbach, G., Fitzmaurice, G., Baudel, T., & Buxton, W. (1997). The design and evaluation of a GUI paradigm based on tablets, two-hands, and transparency. *Proceedings of the ACM Conference on Human Factors in Computing Systems—CHI '97* (pp.35–42). New York: ACM Press.

Kutar, M., Britton, C., & Nehaniv, C. (2001). Specifiying multiple time granularities in interactive systems. In P. Palanque & F. Paternó (Eds.), *DSV-IS 2000 interactive systems: Design, specification and verification* (pp.169–190). Berlin: Springer Verlag.

Kuutti, K. (1991). Activity theory and its applications to information systems research and development. In H.-E. Nissen, H. K. Klein, & R. Hirschheim (Eds.). *Information systems research: Contemporary approaches & emergent traditions* (pp. 529–550). Amsterdam: North-Holland.

Kuutti, K. (1996). Activity theory as a potential framework for human-computer interaction research. In B. Nardi (Ed.), *Context and consciousness. Activity theory and human computer interaction.* Cambridge, MA: MIT Press.

Laird, J. E. (2001). Using a computer game to develop advanced AI. *Computer 34*(7), 70–75.

Landauer, T. K., & Dumais, S. T. (1997). A solution to Plato's problem: The latent semantic analysis theory of acquisition, induction, and representation of knowledge. *Psychological Review, 104*, 211–240.

Landauer, T. K., & Nachbar, D. W. (1985). Selection from alphabetic and numeric menu trees using a touch screen: Breadth, depth, and width. *Proceedings of the ACM Conference on Human Factors in Computing Systems—CHI '85* (pp.73–77). New York: ACM Press.

Lane, D. M., Napier, H. A., Batsell, R. R., & Naman, J. L. (1993). Predicting the skilled use of hierarchical menus with the keystroke-level model. *Human-Computer Interaction, 8*(2), 185–192.

Larkin, J. H., & Simon, H. A. (1987). Why a diagram is (sometimes) worth ten thousand words. *Cognitive Science, 11,* 65–100.

Larson, J., Christensen, C., Franz, T., & Abbott, A. (1996). Diagnosing groups: Charting the flow of information in medical decision-making teams. *Journal of Personality and Social Psychology, 71,* 315–330.

Larson, K., & Czerwinski, M. (1998). Web page design: Implications of memory, structure and scent for information retrieval. *Proceedings of CHI 98, Human Factors in Computing Systems (LA, April 21–23, 1998)* (pp.25–32). New York: ACM Press.

Latane, B., & Bourgeois, M. J. (2001). Dynamic social impact and the consolidation, clustering, correlation, and continuing diversity of culture. In M. A. Hogg & R. S. Tindale (Eds.), *Blackwell handbook of social psychology: Group processes.* Oxford, UK: Blackwell.

Latane, B., & L'Herrou, T. (1996). Spatial clustering in the conformity game: Dynamic social impact in electronic groups. *Journal of Personality & Social Psychology, 70*(6), 1218–1230.

Lave, J. (1988). *Cognition in practice, mind, mathematics and culture in everyday life.* Cambridge, UK: Cambridge University Press.

Lawrence, P. R., & Lorsch, J. W. (1970). *Organization structure and design.* Homewood, IL: Irwin & Dorsey.

Leavitt, H. (1951). Some effects of certain communication patterns on group performance. *Journal of Abnormal and Social Psychology, 46,* 38–50.

Lee, A. Y., Polson, P. G., & Bailey, W. A. (1989). Learning and transfer of measurement tasks. *Proceedings of ACM CHI 1989 Conference on Human Factors in Computing Systems (Austin, Texas, April 30– May 4, 1989)* (pp.115–120). New York: ACM Press.

Lee, D. (1976). A theory of the visual control of braking based on information about time-to-collision. *Perception, 5,* 437–459.

Leontiev, A. N. (1978). *Activity, consciousness, and personality.* Englewood Cliffs, NJ: Prentice-Hall.

Leontiev, A. N. (1981). The problem of activity in psychology. In J. V. Wertsch (Ed.). *The concept of activity in Soviet psychology.* Armonk, NY: Sharpe.

Lerch, F. J., Mantei, M. M., & Olson, J. R. (1989). Translating ideas into action: Cognitive analysis of errors in spreadsheet formulas. *Proceedings of ACM CHI 2000 Conference on Human Factors in Computing Systems* (pp.121–126). New York: ACM Press.

Leveson, N. G. (2000). Intent specifications: An approach to building human-centred specifications. *IEEE Transactions on Software Engineering, 26*(1), 15–35.

Lind, M. (1999). Making sense of the abstraction hierarchy. *Proceedings of the Cognitive Science Approaches to Process Control conference (CSAPC99).* September 21–24, Villeneuve d'Ascq, France.

Liu, Q., Nakata, K., & Furuta, K. (2002). Display design of process systems based on functional modeling. *Cognition, Technology, and Work, 4,* 48–63.

Locke, E. A., Latham, G. P., & Erez, M. (1988). The determinants of goal commitment. *Academy of Management Review, 13*(1), 23–39.

Luff, P., Hindmarsh, J., & Heath C. (Eds.). (2000). *Workplace studies: Recovering work practice and informing system design.* Cambridge, UK: Cambridge University Press.

Lynch, K. (1960). *The image of the city.* Cambridge, MA: MIT Press.

Lynch, M. (1993). *Scientific practice and ordinary action: Ethnomethodology and social studies of science.* Cambridge, UK: Cambridge University Press.

Lynch, M. (2001). Ethnomethodology and the logic of practice. In T. Schatzki, K. Knor-Cering, & E. von Savigny (Eds.), *The practice turn in contemporary theory* (pp.131–48). New York: Routledge.

Mackay, W. (2002). *Using video to support interaction design.* CD-ROM, ACM SigCHI/INRIA.

Mackay, W. E., Ratzer, A. V., & Janecek P. (2000). Video artifacts for design: Bridging the gap between design abstraction and detail. In *Proc. ACM Designing Interactive Systems, DIS 2000,* New York, August 2000. New York: ACM Press.

MacKenzie, I. S. (1989). A note on the information-theoretic basis for Fitts' law. *Journal of Motor Behavior, 21,* 323–330.

MacKenzie, I. S. (1991). *Fitts' law as a performance model in human-computer interaction.* Unpublished doctoral dissertation, University of Toronto *(www.yorku.ca/mack/phd.html).*

MacKenzie, I. S. (1992). Fitts' law as a research and design tool in human-computer interaction. *Human-Computer Interaction, 7,* 91–139.

MacKenzie, I. S. (2002). KSPC (keystrokes per character) as a characteristic of text entry techniques. *Proceedings of the Fourth International Symposium on Human Computer Interaction with Mobile Devices* (pp.195–210). Berlin: Springer Verlag.

MacKenzie, I. S., & Guiard, Y. (2001). The two-handed desktop interface: Are we there yet? *Extended Abstracts of the ACM Conference on Human Factors in Computing Systems—CHI 2001* (pp.351–352). New York: ACM Press.

MacKenzie, I. S., & Jusoh, S. (2001). An evaluation of two input devices for remote pointing. *Proceedings of the Eighth IFIP Working Conference on Engineering for Human-Computer Interaction—EHCI 2000* (pp.235–249). Heidelberg, Germany: Springer-Verlag.

MacKenzie, I. S., Kauppinen, T., & Silfverberg, M. (2001). Accuracy measures for evaluating computer pointing devices. *Proceedings of the ACM Conference on Human Factors in Computing Systems—CHI 2001* (pp.9–16). New York: ACM Press.

MacKenzie, I. S., & Oniszczak, A. (1997). The tactile touchpad. *Extended Abstracts of the CHI '97 Conference on Human Factors in Computing Systems* (pp.309–310). New York: ACM Press.

MacKenzie, I. S., & Oniszczak, A. (1998). A comparison of three selection techniques for touchpads. *Proceedings of the ACM Conference on Human Factors in Computing Systems—CHI '98* (pp.336–343). New York: ACM Press.

MacKenzie, I. S., Sellen, A., & Buxton, W. (1991). A comparison of input devices in elemental pointing and dragging tasks. *Proceedings of the ACM Conference on Human Factors in Computing Systems—CHI '91* (pp.161–166). New York: ACM Press.

MacKenzie, I. S., Soukoreff, W. R., & Pal, C. (1997). A two-ball mouse affords three degrees of freedom. *Extended Abstracts of the ACM Conference on Human Factors in Computing Systems—CHI '97* (pp.303–304). New York: ACM Press.

MacKenzie, I. S., Zhang, S. X., & Soukoreff, R. W. (1999). Text entry using soft keyboards. *Behaviour & Information Technology, 18,* 235–244.

Mackinlay, J. D., Card, S. K., & Robertson, G. G. (1990). A semantic analysis of the design space of input devices. *Human-Computer Interaction, 5,* 145–190.

MacNeill, D., & Blickenstorfer, C. H. (1996, May/June). Trackpads: Alternative input technologies. *Pen Computing, 3,* 42–45.

Macy, M. W. (1991). Learning to cooperate: Stochastic and tacit collusion in social exchange. *American Journal of Sociology, 97*(3), 808–843.

Maddox, M. (1996). Critique of "A longitudinal study of the effects of ecological interface design on skill acquisition" by Christoffersen, Hunter, and Vicente. *Human Factors, 38*(3), 542–545.

Malinowski, B. (1967). *Argonauts of the western pacific.* London: Routledge.

Malone T. W. (1981). Toward a theory of intrinsically motivating instruction. *Cognitive Science, 4,* 333–368.

Malone, T., & Crowston, K. (1994). The interdisciplinary study of coordination. *ACM Computing Surveys, 26*(1), 87–119.

Mancini, R. (1997). Modelling interactive computing by exploiting the Undo. Dottorato di Ricerca in Informatica, IX-97-5, Università degli Studi di Roma "La Sapienza."

Manning, H., McCarthy, J. C., & Souza, R. K. (1998). *Why most web sites fail.* Cambridge, MA: Forrester Research Inc.

March, J. & Simon, H. A. (1958). *Organizations.* New York: Wiley.

Marchionini, G., & Sibert, J. (1992). An agenda for human-computer interaction: Science and engineering serving human needs. *SIGCHI Bulletin, 23*(4), 17–32.

Marr, D. (1982). *Vision.* San Francisco: W. H. Freedman.

Marsh, S. (1994). Trust in distributed artificial intelligence. In C. Castelfranchi & E. Werner (Eds.), *Artificial social societies* (pp.94–112). Berlin: Springer Verlag.

Martinez, S. G., Bennett, K. B., & Shattuck, L. (2001). Cognitive systems engineering analyses for army tactical operations. *Proceedings of the Human Factors and Ergonomics Society 44th Annual Meeting,* Minneapolis, MN (pp.523–526).

Mathiassen, L. (1981). *Systemudvikling og systemudviklingsmetode* [Systems development and systems development method] (DAIMI PB-136). Aarhus, Denmark: University of Aarhus.

Mayhew, D. J. (1992). *Principles and guidelines in software user interface design.* Englewood Cliffs, NJ: Prentice Hall.

Mayzner, M. S., & Tresselt, M. E. (1965). Table of single-letter and digram frequency counts for various word-length and letter-position combinations. *Psychonomic Monograph Supplements, 1*(2), 13–32.

McCarthy, J. C., Miles, V. C., & Monk, A. F. (1991). An experimental study of common ground in text-based communication. *The ACM CHI'91 Conference on Human Factors in Computing Systems* (pp.209–214). New York: ACM Press.

McCarthy, J. C., & Monk, A. F. (1994). Channels, conversation, cooperation and relevance: All you wanted to know about communication but were afraid to ask. *Collaborative Computing, 1,* 35–60.

McCloskey, M. (1983). Naïve theories of motion. In D. Gentner & A. L. Stevens (Eds), *Mental models.* Hillsdale, NJ: Erlbaum.

McGrath, J. (1984). *Groups: Interaction and performance.* Englewood Cliffs, NJ: Prentice Hall.

McGrath, J. (1993). Time, task, and technology in work groups: The JEMCO workshop study. *Small Group Research (Special Issue). 24*(3), 283–421.

McGrenere J., & Ho W. (2000). Affordances: Clarifying and evolving a concept. *Proceedings of Graphics Interface 2000,* Montreal, Canada.

McLeod, P. L., Baron, R. S., Marti, M. W., & Yoon, K. (1997). The eyes have it: Minority influence in face-to-face and computer-mediated group discussion. *Journal of Applied Psychology, 82*(5), 706–718.

McNamara, J. (1982). Optimal patch use in a stochastic environment. *Theoretical Population Biology, 21,* 269–288.

Meyer, D. E., & Kieras, D. E. (1997a). A computational theory of executive cognitive processes and multiple-task performance: Part 1. Basic Mechanisms. *Psychological Review, 104,* 3–65.

Meyer, D. E., & Kieras, D. E. (1997b). A computational theory of executive control processes and human multiple-task performance: Part 2. Accounts of psychological refractory-period phenomena. *Psychological Review, 104,* 749–791.

Meyer, D. E., Smith, J. E. K., Kornblum, S., Abrams, R. A., & Wright, C. E. (1990). Speed-accuracy tradeoffs in aimed movements: Toward a theory of rapid voluntary action. In M. Jeannerod (Ed.), *Attention and performance XIII*. Hillsdale, NJ: Erlbaum.

Microsoft Corporation (1995). *The Windows interface guidelines for software design.* Redmond, WA: Microsoft Press.

Miller, G. A. (1956). The magical number seven, plus or minus two: some limits on our capacity to process information. *Psychological Review, 63*(2), 81–97.

Miller, G. A. (1983). Informavores. In F. Machlup & U. Mansfield (Eds.), *The study of information: Interdisciplinary messages* (pp.111–113). New York: Wiley.

Miller, G. A., & Chomsky, N. A. (1963). Finitary models of language users. In R. D. Luce, R. R. Bush, & E. Galanter (Eds.), *Handbook of mathematical psychology, Volume II.* New York: Wiley.

Milner, R. (1980). *A calculus of communicating systems.* Berlin: Springer-Verlag.

Mintz, A. (1951). Non-adaptive group behavior. *Journal of Abnormal & Social Psychology, 46,* 150–159.

Monk, A. F. (1998). Cyclic interaction: A unitary approach to intention, action and the environment. *Cognition, 68,* 95–110.

Monk, A. F. (1999). Participatory status in electronically mediated collaborative work. In *Proceedings of the American Association for Artificial Intelligence Fall Symposium "Psychological models of communication in collaborative systems,"* North Falmouth, MA (pp. 73–80). Menlo Park, CA: AAAI Press.

Monk, A. F., & Watts, L. A. (2000). Peripheral participation in video-mediated communication. *International Journal of Human-computer Studies, 52,* 775–960.

Moran, T. P., & Carroll, J. M. (Eds.) (1996). *Design rationale: Concepts, methods and techniques.* Mahwah, NJ: Erlbaum.

Moray, N. (1986). Monitoring behavior and supervisory control. In K. Boff, L. Kaufman, & J. Thomas (Eds.), *Handbook of perception and human performance (Vol 2).* New York: Wiley Interscience.

Moray, N. (1999). Mental models in theory and practice. In D. Gopher & A. Koriat (Eds.), *Attention and performance XVII.* Cambridge, MA: MIT Press.

Myers, B. A. (1986). Visual programming, programming by example, and program visualization: A taxonomy. *Proc. CHI 86,* 59–66.

Naikar, N, Pearce, B., Drumm, D., & Sanderson, P. (2002). A formative approach to designing teams for first-of-a-kind, complex systems. *Proceedings of the 21st European Annual Conference on Human Decision Making and Control.* July 15–16, Glasgow, Scotland.

Naikar, N., & Lintern, G. (2002). Book review of Cognitive Work Analysis: Towards Safe, Productive, and Healthy Work, by Kim J. Vicente. *International Journal of Aviation Psychology, 12,* 391–400.

Naikar, N., & Pearce, B. (2001). Analysing activity for new, complex systems with cognitive work analysis. *Proceedings of the 37th Annual Conference of the Ergonomics Society of Australia* (pp.217–222). Nov. 27–30, Sydney, Australia

Naikar, N. & Sanderson, P. (1999). Work domain analysis for training system definition and acquisition. *International Journal of Aviation Psychology, 9*(3), 271–290.

Naikar, N., & Sanderson, P. (2001). Evaluating system design proposals with work domain analysis. *Human Factors, 43*(4), 529–542.

Nardi, B. (Ed.). (1996). *Context and consciousness. Activity theory and human computer interaction.* Cambridge, MA: MIT Press

Nardi, B. A., & Miller, J. R. (1989). Twinkling lights and nested loops: Distributed problem solving and spreadsheet development. *International Journal of Man-Machine Systems, 34,* 161–184.

Navarre, D., Palanque, P., Paternó, F., Santoro, C., & Bastide, R. (2001). A tool suite for integrating task and system models through scenarios. In C. Johnson (Ed.), *DSV-IS 2001 interactive systems: Design, specification and verification.* (pp. 88–113). Berlin: Springer-Verlag.

Neisser, U. (1967). *Cognitive psychology.* New York: Appleton-Century-Crofts.

Neuwirth, C. M., Chandhok, R., Charney, D., Wojahn, P., & Kim, L. (1994). Distributed collaborative writing: A comparison of spoken and written modalities for reviewing and revising documents. In *Proceedings of ACM CHI'94 Conference on Human Factors in Computing Systems* (pp.51–57). New York: ACM Press.

Newell, A. (1982). The knowledge level. *Artificial Intelligence, 18,* 87–127.

Newell, A. (1990). *Unified theories of cognition.* Cambridge, MA: Harvard University Press.

Newell, A. (1993). Reflections on the knowledge level. *Artificial Intelligence, 59,* 31–38.

Newell, A., & Card, S. (1985). The prospects for psychological science in human-computer interaction. *Human-Computer Interaction, 1,* 209–242.

Newell, A., & Card, S. (1986). Straightening out softening up: Response to Carroll and Campbell. *Human-Computer Interaction, 2,* 251–267.

Newell, A., & Simon, H. A. (1961). Computer simulation of human thinking. *Science, 134,* 2011–2017.

Newell, A., & Simon, H. A. (1972). *Human problem solving.* Englewood Cliffs, NJ: Prentice Hall.

Newman, W. M., & Lamming, M. G. (1995). *Interactive system design.* Workingham, U.K.: Addison Wesley.

Nicols, S., & Ritter, F. E. (1995). A theoretically motivated tool for automatically generating command aliases. *Proceedings of the ACM Conference on Human Factors in Computing Systems—CHI '95* (pp.393–400). New York: ACM Press.

Nielsen, C., & Søndergaard A. (2000). Designing for mobility. *Proceedings of NordiCHI 2000.* (CD-ROM).

Nielsen, J. (2000). *Designing Web usability.* Indianapolis, IN: New Riders.

Nielsen, J., & Molich, R. (1990). Heuristic evaluation of user interfaces, *Proceedings of ACM CHI'90* Conf. (Seattle, WA, 1–5 April), pp.249–256.

Norman, D. (1980). Twelve issues for cognitive science. *Cognitive Science, 4,* 1–32.

Norman, D. A. (1980). Cognitive engineering and education. In D. T. Tuma & F. Reif (Eds.), *Problem solving and education: Issues in teaching and research.* Hillsdale, NJ: Erlbaum.

Norman, D. A. (1981). Comments on cognitive engineering, the need for clear "system images," and the safety of nuclear power plants. *Conference Record for 1981 IEEE Standards Workshop on Human Factors and Nuclear Safety* (pp.91–92, 211–212). New York: IEEE. (Workshop was held in Myrtle Beach, SC).

Norman, D. A. (1983). Some observations on mental models. In D. Gentner & A. L. Stevens (Eds), *Mental models.* Hillsdale, NJ: Erlbaum.

Norman, D. A. (1986). Reflections on cognition and parallel distributed processing. In J. L. McClelland, D. E. Rumelhart, & the PDP Research Group (Eds.) *Parallel distributed processing: explorations in the microstructure of cognition. Vol. 2, Psychological and biological models* (pp.531–546). Cambridge, MA: MIT Press.

Norman, D. A. (1986). Cognitive engineering. In D. A. Norman & S. D. Draper (Eds.), *User centered system design* (pp.31–61). Hillsdale, NJ: Erlbaum.

Norman, D. A. (1988). *The design of everyday things:* New York: Doubleday.

Norman, D. A. (1991). Cognitive artifacts. In J. M. Carroll (Ed.). *Designing interaction: psychology at the human computer interface* (pp.17–38). Cambridge, UK: Cambridge University Press.

Norman, D. A. (1993). Cognition in the head and in the world—an introduction to the special issue on situated action. *Cognitive Science, 17,* 1–6.

Norwine, A. C., & Murphy, O. J. (1938). Characteristic time intervals in telephone conversation. *Bell System Technical Journal, 17,* 281–291.

Nunamaker, J. F., Dennis, A. R., Valacich, J. S., Vogel, D. R., & George, J. F. (1991). Electronic meeting systems to support group work. *Communications of the ACM, 34*(7), 40–61.

Oh, J.-Y., & Stuerzlinger, W. (2002). Laser pointers as collaborative pointing devices. *Proceedings of Graphics Interface 2002* (pp.141–149). Toronto: Canadian Information Processing Society.

O'Leary, M., Orlikowski, W., & Yates, J. (2002). Distributed work over the centuries: Trust and control in the Hudson's Bay Company, 1670–1826. In P. Hinds & S. Kiesler (Eds.) *Distributed work* (pp.27–54). Cambridge MA.: MIT Press.

Oliver, L. W., Harman, J., Hoover, E., Hayes, S. M., & Pandhi, N. A. (1999). A quantitative integration of the military cohesion literature. *Military Psychology, 11*(1), 57–83.

Olson, G. M., & Olson, J. S. (2000). Distance matters. *Human-Computer Interaction, 15*(2–3), 139–178.

Olson, G. M., Olson, J. S., Carter, M. R., & Storrosten, M. (1992). Small group design meetings: An analysis of collaboration. *Human-Computer Interaction, 7*(4), 347–374.

Olson, J. R., & Olson, G. M. (1990). The growth of cognitive modeling in human-computer interaction since GOMS. *Human-Computer Interaction 5,* 221–265.

Olson, M. (1971). *The logic of collective action: Public goods and the theory of groups.* Cambridge, MA.: Harvard University Press.

Orlikowski, W. J. (2000). Using technology and constituting structures: A practice lens for studying technology in organizations. *Organizational Science, 11*(4), 404–428.

Osborne, A. F. (1963). *Applied imagination.* New York, NY: Scribner and Sons.

Palanque, P., & Bastide, R. (1995). Petri net based design of user-driven interfaces using the interactive cooperating objects formalism. In F. Paternó (Ed.). *Interactive Systems: Design, Specification and Verification (1st Eurographics Workshop, Bocca di Magra, Italy, June 1994)* (pp.215–228). Berlin: Springer-Verlag.

Palanque, P., & Bastide, R. (1996). Formal specification and verification of CSCW. In M. A. R. Kirby, A. J. Dix, & J. E. Finlay (Eds.). *People and computers X—Proceedings of the HCI'95 Conference* (pp. 213–231). Cambridge, UK: Cambridge University Press.

Palanque, P., & Paternó, F., (Eds.) (1997). *Formal methods in human computer interaction.* London, Springer-Verlag.

Palmer, S. E. (1992). Common region: A new principle of perceptual grouping. *Cognitive Psychology, 24,* 436–447.

Palmer, S. E., & Rock, I. (1994). Rethinking perceptual organization: The role of uniform connectedness. *Psychonomic Bulletin and Review, 1*(1), 29–55.

Parsons, T. (1937). *The structure of social action.* New York: McGraw-Hill.

Paternó, F. (2000). *Model-based design and evaluation of interactive applications.* London, Springer-Verlag. Table of contents and downloads are available online at *giove.cnuce.cnr.it/~fabio/mbde.html*

Paternó, F., & Santoro, C. (2001). Integrating model checking and HCI tools to help designers verify user interface properties. In P. Palanque & F. Paternó (Eds.), *DSV-IS 2000 interactive systems: Design, specification and verification.* (pp. 135–150). Berlin: Springer-Verlag.

Paternó, F., Mori, G., & Galimberti, R. (2001). CTTE: An environment for analysis and development of task models of cooperative applications. *Proceedings of CHI'01, Vol 2,* New York: ACM Press.

Paulus, P. B., Larey, T. S., & Dzindolet, M. T. (2000). Creativity in groups and teams. In M. E. Turner (Ed.), *Groups at work: Theory and research* (pp.319–338). Mahwah, NJ: Erlbaum.

Payne, S. J. (1991). A descriptive study of mental models. *Behaviour and Information Technology, 10,* 3–21.

Payne, S. J. (1992). On mental models and cognitive artifacts. In Y. Rogers, A. Rutherford, & P. Bibby (Eds), *Models in the mind.* London: Academic Press.

Payne, S. J. (1993). Understanding calendar use. *Human-Computer Interaction, 8,* 83–100.

Payne, S. J., & Green, T. R. G. (1986). Task-action grammars: A model of the mental representation of task languages. *Human-Computer Interaction, 2* (2), 93–133.

Payne, S. J., Howes, A., & Hill, E. (1992). Conceptual instructions derived from an analysis of device models. *International Journal of Human-Computer Interaction, 4,* 35–58.

Payne, S. J., Howes, A., & Reader, W. R. (2001). Adaptively distributing cognition: A decision-making perspective on human-computer interaction. *Behaviour and Information Technology, 20*(5), 339–346.

Payne, S. J., Squibb, H. R., & Howes, A. (1990). The nature of device models: The yoked state space hypothesis and some experiments with text editors. *Human-Computer Interaction, 5,* 415–444.

Peck, V. A., & John, B. E. (1992). Browser-Soar: A cognitive model of a highly interactive task. *Proceedings of ACM CHI 1992 Conference on Human Factors in Computing Systems (Monterey, California, May 3–May 7, 1992)* (pp.165–172). New York: ACM Press.

Pelled, L., Eisenhardt, K., & Xin, K. (1999). Exploring the black box: An analysis of work group diversity, conflict, and performance. *Administrative Science Quarterly, 44,* 1–28.

Pelz, D., & Andrews, F. (Eds.). (1966). *Scientists in organizations: Productive climates for research and development.* New York: Wiley.

Perlow, L. A. (1999). The time famine: Toward a sociology of work time. *Administrative Science Quarterly, 44*(1), 57–81.

Perry, M. J. (1997). *Distributed cognition and computer supported collaborative design: The organisation of work in construction engineering.* Unpublished PhD diss. Brunel University, London, England.

Peters, M. (1985). Constraints in the performance of bimanual tasks and their expression in unskilled and skilled subjects. *Quarterly Journal of Experimental Psychology, 37A,* 171–196.

Petri Nets World. (2002). University of Aarhus, Denmark. Accessed October 2002. *www.daimi.au.dk/ PetriNets/*

Petri, C. (1962). Kommunikation mit automaten. PhD thesis. University of Bonn, Bonn, West Germany.

Pew, R. W, & Mavor, A. S. (1998). *Modeling human and organizational behavior: Application to military simulations. Panel on modeling human behavior and command decision making: Representations for military simulations.* Washington, DC: National Academy Press.

Pfaff, G., & ten Hagen, P. J. W. (Eds.). (1985). *Seeheim workshop on user interface management systems.* Berlin: Springer-Verlag.

Pirolli, P. (1997). *Computational models of information scent-following in a very large browsable text collection.* Paper presented at the Conference on Human Factors in Computing Systems, CHI '97, Atlanta, GA.

Pirolli, P. (1998). *Exploring browser design trade-offs using a dynamical model of optimal information foraging.* Paper presented at the Conference on Human Factors in Computing Systems, CHI '98, Los Angeles, CA.

Pirolli, P. (1999). Cognitive engineering models and cognitive architectures in human-computer interaction. In F. T. Durso, R. S. Nickerson, R. W. Schvaneveldt, S. T. Dumais, D. S. Lindsay, & M. T. H. Chi (Eds.), *Handbook of applied cognition* (pp. 441–477). West Sussex, U.K.: Wiley.

Pirolli, P., & Card, S. K. (1995). *Information foraging in information access environments.* Paper presented at the Conference on Human Factors in Computing Systems, CHI '95, New York, NY.

Pirolli, P., & Card, S. K. (1999). Information foraging. *Psychological Review, 106,* 643–675.

Pirolli, P., Schank, P., Hearst, M., & Diehl, C. (1996). *Scatter/gather browsing communicates the topic structure of a very large text collection.* Paper presented at the Conference on Human Factors in Computing Systems, CHI '96, Vancouver, BC.

Plowman, L., Rogers, Y., & Ramage, M. (1995). What are workplace studies for? *Proceedings of the Fourth European Conference on Computer-Supported Cooperative Work,* pp.309–324.

Porac, C., & Coren, S. (1981). *Lateral preference and human behaviour:* New York: Springer Verlag.

Potter, S. S., Roth, E. M., Woods, D. D., & Elm, W. (2000). Bootstrapping multiple converging cognitive task analysis techniques for system design. In J. M. Schraagen, S. F. Chipman, & V. L. Shalin (Eds.), *Cognitive task analysis* (pp.317–340). Mahwah, NJ: Erlbaum.

Prakash, A., & Knister, M. J. (1992). Undoing actions in collaborative work. *Proceedings of CSCW'92. Toronto Canada* (pp.273–280). New York: ACM Press.

Prakash, A., & Knister, M. J. (1994). A framework for undoing actions in collaborative systems. *ACM Transactions on Computer Human Interaction, 1*(4), 295–330.

Preece, J. (2000). *Online communities.* New York: Wiley.

Preece, J., Rogers, Y., Sharp, H., Benyon, D., Holland, S., & Carey, T. (1994). *Human-computer interaction.* Reading, MA: Addison-Wesley.

Preece, J. Sharpe, H., & Rogers, Y. (2002). *Interaction design.* New York: Wiley.

Prentice-Dunn, S., & Rogers, R. W. (1982). Effects of public and private self-awareness on deindividuation and aggression. *Journal of Personality and Social Psychology, 43*(3), 503–513.

Pressman, R. S. (1997). *Software engineering: A practitioner's approach.* New York: McGraw-Hill.

Putnam, R. (2000). *Bowling alone: The collapse and revival of American community.* New York: Simon & Schuster.

Pylyshyn, Z. (1984). *Computation and cognition: towards a foundation for cognitive science.* Cambridge, MA: MIT Press.

Raeithel, A. (1992). An activity-theoretical foundation for design. In R. Budde, C. Floyd, R. Keil-Slawik, & H. Züllighoven (Eds.). *Software development and reality construction* (pp.391–415). Berlin: Springer Verlag.

Raeithel, A. (1996). From coordinatedness to coordination via cooperation and co-construction. Paper presented at *Workshop on Work and Learning in Transition,* San Diego, CA, January 1996.

Randall, D., Rouncefield, M., & Hughes, J. (1995). Chalk and cheese: BPR and ethnomethodologically informed ethnography in CSCW. *Proceedings of the ECSCW'95 Fourth European Conference on Computer-Supported Cooperative Work.* Dordrecht: Kluwer.

Raskin, J. (2000). *The humane interface: New directions for designing interactive systems.* Boston: Addison Wesley.

Rasmussen, J. (1974). *The human data processor as a system component: Bits and pieces of a model.* (Report No. Risø-M-1722). Roskilde, Denmark: Danish Atomic Energy Commission.

Rasmussen, J. (1976). Outlines of a hybrid model of the process plant operator. In T. B. Sheridan & G. Johannsen (Eds.), *Monitoring behavior and supervisory control* (pp.371–383). New York: Plenum.

Rasmussen, J. (1979a). *On the structure of knowledge—A morphology of mental models in a man-machine system context.* (Report No. Risø-M-2192). Roskilde, Denmark: Risø National Laboratory, Electronics Department.

Rasmussen, J. (1979b). *Preliminary analysis of human error cases in U.S. licensee event reports.* (Report No. N-8–79). Roskilde, Denmark: Risø National Laboratory, Electronics Department.

Rasmussen, J. (1980). The human as a systems component. In H. T. Smith & T. R. G. Green (Eds.), *Human interaction with computers* (pp.67–96). London: Academic Press.

Rasmussen, J. (1981). Models of mental strategies in process plant diagnosis. In J. Rasmussen & W. B. Rouse (Eds.), *Human detection and diagnosis of system failures* (pp.241–258). New York: Plenum.

Rasmussen, J. (1983). Skills, rules, and knowledge: Signals, signs, and symbols, and other distinctions in human performance models. *IEEE Transactions on Systems, Man, and Cybernetics, SMC-13*, 257–266.

Rasmussen, J. (1985). The role of hierarchical knowledge representation in decision making and system management. *IEEE Transactions on Systems, Man, and Cybernetics, SMC-15*, 234–243.

Rasmussen, J. (1986). *Information processing and human-machine interaction: An approach to cognitive engineering*. New York: North Holland.

Rasmussen, J. (1997). Merging paradigms: Decision making, management, and cognitive control. In R. Flin, E. Salas, M. E. Strub, & L. Marting (Eds.), *Decision making under stress: Emerging paradigms and applications* (pp.67–85). Aldershot, UK: Ashgate.

Rasmussen, J., & Jensen, A. (1973). *A study of mental procedures in electronic trouble shooting* (Report No. Risø-M-1582). Roskilde, Denmark: Danish Atomic Energy Commission, Research Establishment Risø.

Rasmussen, J., & Jensen, A. (1974). Mental procedures in real-life tasks: A case study of electronic trouble shooting. *Ergonomics, 17*, 293–307.

Rasmussen, J., Pejtersen, A. M., & Goodstein, L. (1994). *Cognitive systems engineering*. New York: Wiley.

Rasmussen, J., & Vicente, K. J. (1989). Coping with human errors through system design: Implications for ecological interface design. *International Journal of Man-Machine Studies, 31*, 517–534.

Reising, D. C. (1999). Book review of Cognitive Systems Engineering by Jens Rasmussen, Annelise Mark Petersen, and L. P. Goodstein. *International Journal of Aviation Psychology, 9*, 291–302.

Reising, D. C., & Sanderson, P. (1998). Designing displays under ecological interface design: Towards operationalizing semantic mapping. *Proceedings of the 42nd Annual Meeting of the Human Factors and Ergonomics Society* (pp.372–376). Santa Monica, CA: Human Factors and Ergonomics Society.

Reising, D. C., & Sanderson, P. (2000a). Testing the impact of instrumentation location and reliability on ecological interface design: Fault diagnosis performance. *Proceedings of the Joint Meeting of the Human Factors and Ergonomics Society and the International Ergonomics Association (IEA2000/HFES2000) Vol. 3* (pp.591–594). Santa Monica, CA: HFES.

Reising, D. C., & Sanderson, P. (2000b). Testing the impact of instrumentation location and reliability on ecological interface design: Control performance. *Proceedings of the Joint Meeting of the Human Factors and Ergonomics Society and the International Ergonomics Association (IEA2000/HFES2000) Vol. 1* (pp.124–127). Santa Monica, CA: HFES.

Reising, D. C., & Sanderson, P. (2002a). Work domain analysis and sensors I: Principles and simple example. *International Journal of Human-Computer Studies, 56*(6), 569–596.

Reising, D. C., & Sanderson, P. (2002b). Work domain analysis and sensors II: Pasteurizer II case study. *International Journal of Human-Computer Studies, 56*(6), 597–637.

Reising, D. C., & Sanderson, P. (2002c). Ecological interface design for pasteurizer II: A process description of semantic mapping. *Human Factors, 44*(3), 222–297.

Reisner, P. (1981). Formal grammar and human factors design of an interactive graphics system. *IEEE Transactions on Software Engineering, SE-7*(2), 229–240.

Reitman, W. R. (1965). *Cognition and thought: An information-processing approach*. New York: Wiley.

Remington, R., John, B. E., Matessa, M., Vera, A., Freed, M. (2002). Apex/CPM-GOMS: An architecture for modeling human performance in applied HCI domains. Tutorial material presented at Cognitive Science 2002.

Ren, X., & Moriya, S. (2000). Improving selection performance on pen-based systems: A study of pen-based interaction for selection tasks. *ACM Transactions on Computer-Human Interaction, 7*(3), 384–416.

Repo, A. J. (1986). The value of information: Approaches in economics, accounting, and management science. *Journal of the American Society for Information Science, 40,* 68–85.

Resnikoff, H. L. (1989). *The illusion of reality.* New York: Springer-Verlag.

Ressel, M., & Gunzenhfiuser, R. (1999). Reducing the problems of group undo. *Proceedings of Group'99. Phoenix* (pp.131–139). New York: ACM Press.

Ressel, M., Nitsche-Ruhland, D., & Gunzenhfiuser, R. (1996). An integrating, transformation-oriented approach to concurrency control and undo in group editors. *Proceedings of CSCW'96. Boston* (pp.288–297). New York: ACM Press.

Rheingold, H. (1993). *The virtual community: Homesteading on the electronic frontier.* Reading, MA: Addison-Wesley.

Rieman, J., Lewis, C., Young, R. M., & Polson, P. G. (1994). "Why is a raven like a writing desk?" Lessons in interface consistency and analogical reasoning from two cognitive architectures. *Proceedings of ACM CHI 1994 Conference on Human Factors in Computing Systems* (Boston, MA, USA, April 24–April 28, 1994). (pp.438–444). New York: ACM Press.

Roast, C., & Siddiqi, J. (1996). Formally assessing software modifiability. In C. R. Roast & J. Siddiqi (Eds.) *BCS-FACS Workshop on Formal Aspects of the Human Computer Interface, Sheffield Hallam University, 10–12 September 1996, Electronic Workshops in Computing.* New York: Springer-Verlag.

Roast, C. R., & Siddiqi, J. I. (2000). *Formal comparisons of program modification. IEEE International Symposium on Visual Languages (VL 2000).* Los Alamitos, CA: IEEE Computer Society.

Robinson, A. (1995). *The story of writing.* London: Thames and Hudson.

Rodden, T., (1996). Populating the application: A model of awareness for cooperative applications. In CSCW '96. *Proceedings of the ACM 1996 Conference on Computer Supported Cooperative Work* (pp.87–96). New York: ACM Press.

Rodden, T., Dix, A., & Abowd, G. (2002). Concepts and models for ubiquitous computing, workshop at UbiComp 2002, Göteborg, 29th Sept 2002. Available online at *www.hcibook.com/alan/conf/ubicomp-models/*

Rogers, Y., & Ellis, J. (1994). Distributed cognition: An alternative framework for analysing and explaining collaborative working. *Journal of Information Technology, 9,* 119–128.

Rosenblatt, J. K., & Vera, A. H. (1995). A GOMS representation of tasks for intelligent agents. In M. T. Cox & M. Freed (Eds.). *Proceedings of the 1995 AAAI Spring Symposium on Representing Mental States and Mechanisms.* Menlo Park, CA: AAAI Press.

Ross, E. A. (1980). *Social psychology: An outline and source book.* New York: Macmillan.

Rosson, M. B., & Carroll, J. M. (2000). Nonfunctional requirements in scenario-based development. *Proceedings of OZCHI 2000* (pp.232–239). North Ryde, Australia: CSIRO Mathematical and Information SciencVes.

Rosson, M. B., & Carroll, J. M. (2002). *Usability engineering: Scenario-based development of human-computer interaction*. San Francisco: Morgan-Kaufmann.

Rosson, M. B., Carroll, J. M., Seals, C., & Lewis, T. (2002). Community design of community simulations. *Proceedings of Designing Interactive Systems: DIS 2002* (London, June 2002). New York: ACM Press.

Rouse, W. (1980). *Systems engineering models of human-machine interaction*. New York: Elsevier.

Rouse Ball, W. (1980). *A short account of the history of mathematics (fourth edition)*. New York: Dover.

Ruddle, R. A., Payne, S. J., & Jones, D. M. (1997). Navigating buildings in "desk-top" virtual environments: Experimental investigations using extended navigational experience. *Journal of Experimental Psychology: Applied, 3,* 143–159.

Rumelhart, D. E., McClelland, J. L. & The PDP Research Group (1986). *Parallel distributed processing: explorations in the microstructure of cognition. Vol.1, Foundations*. Cambridge, MA: MIT Press.

Rumelhart, D. E., Smolensky, P., McClelland, J. L., & Hinton, G. E. (1986). Schemata and sequential thought processes in PDP models. In J. L. McClelland, D. E. Rumelhart, & the PDP Research Group (Eds.) *Parallel distributed processing: explorations in the microstructure of cognition. Vol.2, Psychological and biological models* (pp.7–57). Cambridge, MA: MIT Press.

Russo, J. E. (1978). Adaptation of cognitive processes to the eye-movement system. In J. W. Senders, D. F. Fisher, & R. A. Monty (Eds.). *Eye movements and the higher psychological functions* (pp.89–109). Hillsdale, NJ: Elbaum.

Sacks, H. (1993a). *Lectures in conversation: Vol I*. Oxford, UK: Basil Blackwell.

Sacks, H. (1993b). *Lectures in conversation: Vol II*. Oxford, UK: Basil Blackwell.

Sacks, H., Schegloff, E. A., & Jefferson, G. (1974). The simplest systematics for the organisation of turn-taking for conversation. *Language, 50,* 696–735.

Salvucci, D. D., & Macuga, K. L. (2002). Predicting the effects of cellular-phone dialing on driver performance. *Cognitive Systems Research, 3,* 95–102.

Sanderson, P. (1998). Cognitive work analysis and the analysis, design, and evaluation of human-computer interactive systems. *Proceedings of the Australian/New Zealand Conference on Computer-Human Interaction (OzCHI98)* (pp.220–227). Los Alamitos: IEEE Computer Society.

Sanderson, P. (2000). Cognitive work analysis across the system life-cycle: Achievements, challenges, and prospects. *Proceedings of the Fifth Australian Aviation Psychology Symposium*. November 20–24, Manly, Australia.

Sanderson, P., Anderson, J., & Watson, M. (2000). Extending ecological interface design to auditory displays. *Proceedings of the 2000 Annual Conference of the Computer-Human Interaction Special Interest Group (CHISIG) of the Ergonomics Society of Australia (OzCHI2000)* (pp.259–266). CSIRO: Sydney.

Sanderson, P., Eggleston, R., Skilton, W., & Cameron, S. (1999). Work domain analysis workbench: Supporting cognitive work analysis as a systematic practice. *Proceedings of the 43rd Annual Meeting of the Human Factors and Ergonomics Society* (pp.323–327). Santa Monica, CA: Human Factors and Ergonomics Society.

Sanderson, P., & Harwood, K. (1988). Skills, rules, and knowledge: A study of Rasmussen's classification. In H. B. Andersen, S. E. Olsen, & L. Goodstein (Eds.), *Tasks, errors, and mental models: Festschrift presented to Jens Rasmussen on his 60th birthday* (pp.21–34). London: Taylor & Francis.

Sanderson, P., & Naikar, N. (2000). Temporal coordination control task analysis for analysing human system integration. *Proceedings of the Joint Meeting of the Human Factors and Ergonomics Society and the International Ergonomics Association (IEA2000/HFES2000)* Vol. 1 (pp.206–209). Santa Monica, CA: HFES.

Sanderson, P., Naikar, N., Lintern, G., & Goss, S., (1999). Use of cognitive work analysis across the system life cycle: Requirements to decommissioning. *Proceedings of the 43rd Annual Meeting of the Human Factors and Ergonomics Society* (pp.318–322). Santa Monica, CA: Human Factors and Ergonomics Society.

Sandor, O., Bogdan, C., & Bowers, J. (1997). Aether: An awareness engine for CSCW. In J. Hughes, W. Prinz, T. Rodden, & K. Schmidt (Eds.) *Proceedings of ECSCW'97: The Fifth European Conference on Computer Supported Cooperative Work* (pp.221–236). Dordrecht: Kluwer.

Sandstrom, P. E. (1994). An optimal foraging approach to information seeking and use. *Library Quarterly, 64,* 414–449.

Saracevic, T. (1975). Relevance: A review of and a framework for the thinking on the notion in information science. *Journal of the American Society for Information Science, 26,* 321–343.

Sarter, N. B. (2000). The need for multisensory interfaces in support of effective attentional allocation in highly dynamic event-driven domains: the case of cockpit automation. *The International Journal of Aviation Psychology, 10*(3), 231–245.

Scaife, M., & Rogers, Y. (1996). External cognition, how do graphical representations work? *International Journal of Human-Computer Studies, 45,* 185–213.

Schamber, L., Eisenberg, M. B., & Nilan, M. S. (1990). A re-examination of relevance: Towards a dynamic situational definition. *Information Processing and Management, 26,* 755–776.

Schank, R. C., & Ableson, R. F. (1977). *Scripts, plans, goals and understanding.* Hillsdale, NJ: Erlbaum.

Schegloff, E. (1986). The routine as achievement. *Human Studies, 9*(2/3), 111–151.

Schon, D. A. (1983). *The reflective practitioner.* New York: Basic Books.

Searle, J. (1983). *Intentionality.* Cambridge, UK: Cambridge University Press.

Segerstrale, U. (2000). *Defenders of the truth: The battle for science in the sociobiology debate and beyond.* Oxford, UK: Oxford University Press.

Shannon, C. E., & Weaver, W. (1949). *The mathematical theory of communications.* Urbana: University of Illinois Press.

Shapiro, D. (1994). The limits of ethnography: Combining social sciences for CSCW. *Proceedings of the CSCW'94 Conference on Computer-Supported Cooperative Work* (pp.417–428). New York: ACM Press.

Shaw, M. (1964). Communication networks. In L. Berkowitz (Ed.), *Advances in experimental social psychology* (pp.111–147). New York: Academic Press.

Shaw, W., Mace, W., & Turvey, M. (1995). Resources for ecological psychology (Series Preface). In J. Flach, P. Hancock, J. Caird, & K. Vicente (Eds)., *Global perspectives on the ecology of human-machine systems (Vol 1).* Hillsdale, NJ: Erlbaum.

Shepard, R. N, & Metzler, J. (1971). Mental rotation of three-dimensional objects. *Science, 171,* 701–703.

Shepherd, A. (1995). Task analysis as a framework for examining HCI tasks. In A. Monk & N. Gilbert (Eds.) *Perspectives on HCI: Diverse approaches* (pp.145–174). London: Academic Press.

Sheridan, T. B. (1987). Supervisory control. In G. Salvendy (Ed.), *Handbook of human factors* (pp.1243–1268). New York: Wiley.

Sheridan, T., & Ferrell, R. (1974). *Man-machine systems.* Cambridge, MA: MIT Press.

Sherif, M., & Sherif, C. (1969). *Social psychology.* New York: Harper & Row.

Shimojima, A. (1996). Operational constraints in diagrammatic reasoning. In G. Allwein & J. Barwise (Eds). *Logical reasoning with diagrams* (pp.27–48). Oxford, UK: Oxford University Press.

Shneiderman, B. (1983). *Designing the user interface.* Reading, MA: Addison-Wesley.

Shneiderman, B. (1984). Response time and display rate in human performance with computers. *ACM Computing Surveys, 16,* (3), 265–286.

Shneiderman, B. (1998). *Designing the user interface: Strategies for effective human-computer interaction (3rd ed.).* Reading, MA: Addison Wesley.

Silfverberg, M., MacKenzie, I. S., & Kauppinen, T. (2001). An isometric joystick as a pointing device for handheld information terminals. *Proceedings of Graphics Interface 2001* (pp.119–126). Toronto: Canadian Information Processing Society.

Silfverberg, M., MacKenzie, I. S., & Korhonen, P. (2000). Predicting text entry speed on mobile phones. *Proceedings of the ACM Conference on Human Factors in Computing Systems—CHI 2000* (pp.9–16). New York: ACM Press.

Simon, H. A. (1955). A behavioral model of rational choice. *Quarterly Journal of Economics, 69,* 99–118.

Simon, H. A. (1969). *The sciences of the artificial.* Cambridge, MA: MIT Press.

Simon, H. A. (1973). The structure of ill-structured problems. *Artificial Intelligence, 4,* 181–204.

Simon, H. A. (1978). On the forms of mental representation. In C. W. Savage (Ed.) *Minnesota studies in the philosophy of science, vol. ix.* Minneapolis: University of Minnesota Press.

Simon, H. A. (1981). *The sciences of the artificial. 2nd edition.* Boston, MA: MIT Press.

Simon, H. A. (1992). What is an "explanation" of behavior? *Psychological Science, 3,* 150–161.

Singley, M. K., & Carroll, J. M. (1990). Minimalist planning tools in an instructional system for Smalltalk. In D. Diaper, D. Gilmore, G. Cockton, & B. Shackel (Eds.), *Proceedings of Third IFIP Conference on Human-Computer Interaction Interact'90* (Cambridge, UK, August 27–31) (pp.937–944). Amsterdam: North-Holland.

Singley, M. K., & Carroll, J. M. (1996). Synthesis by analysis: Five modes of reasoning that guide design. In T. P. Moran & J. M. Carroll (Eds.), *Design rationale: Concepts, techniques, and use* (pp.241–265). Mahwah, NJ: Erlbaum.

Skilton, W., Sanderson, P., & Cameron, S. (1998). Supporting cognitive work analysis with the work domain analysis workbench (WDAW). *Proceedings of the Australian/New Zealand Conference on Computer-Human Interaction (OzCHI98)* (pp.260–267). Los Alamitos: IEEE Computer Society.

Smith, W. J. (1996). *ISO and ANSI ergonomic standards for computer products: A guide to implementation and compliance:* Upper Saddle River, NJ: Prentice Hall.

Snook, S. A. (2000). *Friendly fire: The accidental shootdown of U.S. Blackhawks over northern Iraq (Vol. 280)*. Princeton, NJ: Princeton University Press.

Sommerville, I. (2000). *Software engineering (sixth ed.)*. New York, NY: Addison-Wesley.

Sommerville, I., Rodden, T., Sawyer, P., & Bentley, R. (1992). Sociologists can be surprisingly useful in interactive systems design. In A. Monk, D. Diaper, & M. Harrison (Eds.), *People and computers VII. Proceedings of HCI'92* (pp.352–352). Cambridge, UK: Cambridge University Press.

Soukoreff, W., & MacKenzie, I. S. (1995). Theoretical upper and lower bounds on typing speeds using a stylus and soft keyboard. *Behaviour & Information Technology, 14*, 370–379.

Souza, R. K. (2000). *The best of retail site design*. Cambridge, MA: Forrester Research Inc.

Spasser, M. (2000). Articulating collaborative activity. *Scandinavian Journal of Information Systems, 12*, 149–172.

Spivey, J. M. (1988). *The Z notation: A reference manual*. Hemel Hempstead: Prentice Hall International.

Spool, J. M., Scanlon, T., Schroeder, W., Snyder, C., & DeAngelo, T. (1999). *Web site usability*. San Francisco: Morgan Kaufman.

Sproull, L., & Kiesler, S. (1991). *Connections: New ways of working in the networked organization*. Cambridge, MA: MIT Press.

Stanford Encyclopedia of Philosophy, entry on The Church-Turing Thesis. Accessed October 2002. Available online at *plato.stanford.edu/entries/church-turing/*

Star, S. L. (1996). Working together: Symbolic interactionism, activity theory, and information systems. In Y. Engeström & D. Middleton (Eds.), *Cognition and communication at work* (pp. 296–318). Cambridge, UK: Cambridge University Press.

Steinberg, L. S., & Gitomer, D. H. (1993). Cognitive task analysis, interface design, and technical troubleshooting. In W. D. Gray, W. E. Hefley, & D. Murray (Eds.), *Proceedings of the 1993 International Workshop on Intelligent User Interfaces* (pp.185–191). New York: ACM Press.

Steiner, I. (1972). *Group process and productivity*. New York: Academic Press.

Stephens, D. W., & Krebs, J. R. (1986). *Foraging theory*. Princeton, NJ: Princeton University Press.

Stires, D. M., & Murphy, M. M. (1962). *PERT (program evaluation and review technique) CPM (critical path method)*. Boston, MA: Materials Management Institute.

Suchman, L. (1987). *Plans and situated action: The problem of human-machine communication*. Cambridge, UK: Cambridge University Press.

Suchman, L. (1994). Do categories have politics? The language/action perspective reconsidered. *Computer-Supported Cooperative Work, 2*, 177–190.

Sufrin, B. (1982). Formal specification of a display editor. *Science of Computer Programming, 1*, 157–202.

Sun, C. (2000). Undo any operation at any time in group editors. *Proceedings of CSCW'2000, Philadelphia* (pp.191–200). New York: ACM Press.

Sun, C., Jia, X., Zhang, Y., Yang, Y., & Chen, D. (1998). Achieving convergence, causality preservation, and intention preservation in real-time cooperative editing systems. *ACM Transactions on Computer Human Interaction, 5*(1), 63–108.

Sutcliffe, A. (2002). *The domain theory: Patterns of knowledge and software reuse.* Mahwah, NJ: Erlbaum.

Suwa, M., & Tversky, B. (1997). What do architects and students perceive in their design sketches? A protocol analysis. *Design Studies, 18,* 385–403.

Szekely, P., Sukaviriya, P., Castells, P., Muthukumarasamy, J., & Salcher, E. (1996). Declarative interface models for user interface construction tools: The MASTERMIND approach. In L. Bass & C. Unger (Eds.) *Engineering for human-computer interaction. Proceedings of the IFIP WG2.7 Working Conference. Yellowstone Park, August 1995* (pp.120–150). London: Chapman & Hall.

TACIT: Theory and Applications of Continuous Interaction Techniques, EU TMR Network ERB FMRX CT97 0133. Available online at *kazan.cnuce.cnr.it/TACIT/TACIThome.html*

Tajfel, H., Billig, M. G., Bundy, R. P., & Flament, C. (1971). Social categorization and intergroup behaviour. *European Journal of Social Psychology, Vol. 1* (20046–2772), 149–178.

Tambe, M., Johnson, W. L., Jones, R. M., Koss, F., Laird, J. E., Rosenbloom, P. S., & Schwamb, K. (1995, Spring). Intelligent agents for interactive simulation environments. *AI Magazine,* 15–39.

Tang, J. C. (1991). Findings from observational studies of collaborative work. *International Journal of Man-Machine Studies, 34,* 143–160.

Tatar, D. G., Foster, G., & Bobrow, D. G. (1991). Designing for conversation: Lessons from Cognoter. *International Journal of Man-machine Studies, 34,* 185–209.

Taylor, F. (1957). Psychology and the design of machines. *American Psychologist, 12,* 249–258.

Thimbleby, H., Cairns, P., & Jones, M. (2001). Usability analysis with markov models. *ACM Transactions on Computer-Human Interaction, 8* (2), 99–132.

Thompson, J. (1967). *Organizations in action.* New York: McGraw-Hill.

Thorndyke, P. W., & Hayes-Roth, B. (1982). Differences in spatial knowledge acquired from maps and navigation. *Cognitive Psychology, 14,* 560–589.

Timpka, T., & Sjöberg, C. (1994). Voices in design: The dynamics of participatory information systems. In R. Trigg, S. I. Anderson, & Dykstra-Ericson, E. (Eds.). *PDC'94: Proceedings of the Participatory Design Conference, Palo Alto, CA: CPSR/ACM, 1994* (pp.75–86).

Tognazzini, B. (1992). *Tog on interface.* Reading, MA: Addison-Wesley.

Toigo, J. W. (2000, May). Avoiding a data crunch. *Scientific American, 282,* 58–74.

Toleman, M. A., & Welsh, J. (1996). Can design choices for language-based editors be analysed with keystroke-level models? *Proceedings of the HCI '96 Conference on People and Computers* (pp.97–112). Surrey, UK: Springer-Verlag.

Tooby, J., & Cosmides, L. (1992). The psychological foundations of culture. In J. H. Barkow, L. Cosmides, & J. Tooby (Eds.), *The adapted mind* (pp.19–136). Oxford, UK: Oxford University Press.

Torres, J., Gea, M., Gutierrez, F., Carbrera, M., & Rodriguez, M. (1996). GRAPLA: An algebraic specification language for interactive graphic systems. In F. Bodart & J. Vanderdonckt (Eds.), *Design, specification and verification of Interactive Systems '96 (Proceedings of DSVIS'96. Namur, Belgium, June 1996)* (pp.272–291). Vienna: Springer-Verlag.

Triesman, A., & Gormican, S. (1988). Feature analysis in early vision: Evidence from search asymmetries. *Psychological Review, 95*(1), 15–48.

Triplett, N. (1898). The dynamogenic factors in pacemaking and competition. *American Journal of Psychology, 9*(4), 507–533.

Tucker, A. B. (Ed.). (1997). *The handbook of computer science and engineering.* Boca Raton, FL: CRC Press.

Tucker, A. B., & Turner, A. J. (1991). A summary of the ACM/IEEE-CS Joint Curriculum Task Force Report: Computing Curricula. *Communications of the ACM, 34,* 68–84.

Turkle, S. (1995). *Life on the screen: Identity in the age of the Internet.* New York: Simon & Schuster.

Tushman, M. (1979). Work characteristics and subunit communication structure: A contingency analysis. *Administrative Science Quarterly, 24,* 82–98.

Tweedie, L., Spence, R., Dawkes, H., & Su, H. (1995). The influence explorer. *Companion Proceedings CHI '95* (pp.129–130). New York: ACM Press.

Underwood, B. J., & Schulz, R. W. (1960). *Meaningfulness and verbal learning:* Philadelphia: Lippincott.

User Interface Engineering. (1999). *Designing information-rich web sites.* Cambridge, MA: Author.

Van de Ven, A., Delbecq, A., & Koenig, R. (1976). Determinants of coordination modes within organizations. *American Sociological Review, 41,* 322–338.

van der Veer, G. C., Lenting, B. F., & Bergevoet, B. A. J. (1996). GTA: Groupware task analysis—modelling complexity. *Acta Psychologica, 91,* 297–322.

vanRijsbergen, C. J. (1979). *Information retrieval (2nd ed.).* Boston, MA: Butterworth & Co.

Veinott, E. S., Olson, J., Olson, G. M., & Fu, X. (1999). Video helps remote work: Speakers who need to negotiate common ground benefit from seeing each other. In M. G. Williams, M. W. Altom, K. Ehrlich, & W. Newman (Eds.), *CHI'99,* Pittsburgh, PA (pp.302–309). New York: ACM Press.

Vera, A. H., & Simon, H. A. (1993). Situated action: A symbolic interpretation. *Cognitive Science, 17,* 7–48.

Vertegaal, R. (1999). The GAZE groupware system: Mediating joint attention in multiparty communiation and collabroation. In M. G. Williams, M. W. Altom, K. Ehrlich, & W. Newman (Eds.), *CHI'99,* Pittsburgh, PA (pp.294–301). New York: ACM Press.

Vicente, K. (1990). Coherence- and correspondence-driven work domains: Implications for systems design. *Behavior and Information Technology, 9,* 493–502.

Vicente, K. J. (1991). *Supporting knowledge-based behavior through ecological interface design.* Unpublished doctoral diss., University of Illinois, Urbana.

Vicente, K. J. (1996). Improving dynamic decision making in complex systems through EID: A research overview. *System Dynamics Review, 12*(4), 251–279.

Vicente, K. (1997a). Should an interface always match the operator's mental model? *CSERIAC Gateway, VIII(1),* 1–4.

Vicente, K. (1997b). Operator adaptation in process control: A three-year research program. *Control Engineering Practice, 5*(3), 407–416.

Vicente, K. J. (1999). *Cognitive work analysis: Toward safe, productive, and healthy computer-based work.* Mahwah, NJ: Erlbaum.

Vicente, K. J. (2002). Ecological interface design: progress and challenges. *Human Factors, 44,* 62–78.

Vicente, K. J., & Rasmussen, J. (1990). The ecology of human-machine systems II: Mediating "direct perception" in complex work domains. *Ecological Psychology, 2*(3), 207–249.

Vicente, K. J., & Rasmussen, J. (1992). Ecological interface design: Theoretical foundations. *IEEE Transactions on Systems, Man, and Cybernetics, 22*(4), 589–606.

von Bertalanffy, L (1968). *General systems theory.* New York: Braziller.

von Neumann, J. (1956). Probabilistic logics and the synthesis of reliable organisms from unreliable components. In C. Shannon & J. McCarthy (Eds.), *Automata studies.* Princeton, NJ: Princeton University Press.

von Neumann, J. (1966). *Theory of self-reproducing automata.* Edited and completed by A. W. Burks. Chicago: University of Illinois Press.

Vygotsky, L. S. (1962). *Thought and language.* Cambridge, MA: MIT Press.

Vygotsky, L. S., Cole, M., John-Steiner, V., & Scribner, S. (1978). *Mind in society.* Cambridge, MA: Harvard University Press.

Ware, C. (1999). *Information visualization: Perception for design.* San Francisco: Morgan Kaufman.

Ware, C., Gobrecht, C., & Paton, M (1998). Dynamic adjustment of stereo display parameters. *IEEE Transactions on Systems, Man and Cybernetics, 28*(1), 56–65.

Warren, W. (1982). Perceiving affordances: The visual guidance of stair climbing. *Journal of Experimental Psychology: Human Perception and Performance, 10,* 883–903.

Watts, L. A., & Monk, A. F. (1997). Telemedical consultation: Task characteristics. In S. Pemberton (Ed.), *CHI'97 Conference on Human Factors in Computing Systems,* Atlanta, Georgia (pp.534–535). New York: ACM Press.

Watts, L. A., & Monk, A. F. (1998). Reasoning about tasks, activity and technology to support collaboration. *Ergonomics, 41,* 1583–1606.

Watts, L. A., & Monk, A. F. (1999). Telemedicine: What happens in teleconsultation. *International Journal of Technology Assessment in Health Care, 15,* 220–235.

Wegner, P. (1997). Why interaction is more powerful than algorithms. *CACM, 40*(5), 80–91.

Welford, A. T. (1968). *Fundamentals of skill.* London: Methuen.

Wharton, C., Rieman, J., Lewis, C., & Polson, P. (1994). The cognitive walkthrough method: A practitioner's guide. In J. Nielsen & R. L. Mack (Eds.). *Usability inspection methods.* New York: Wiley.

Whiteside, J., & Wixon, D. (1987). Discussion: Improving human-computer interaction—A quest for cognitive science. In J. Carroll (Ed.), *Interfacing thought: Cognitive aspects of human-computer interaction* (pp. 353–366). Cambridge, MA: MIT Press.

Whitley, K. N., & Blackwell, A. F. (2001). Visual programming in the wild: A survey of LabVIEW programmers. *Journal of Visual Languages and Computing 12*(4), 435–472.

Wickens, C. D. (1992). *Engineering psychology and human performance, Second edition.* New York: HarperCollins.

Williams, K. E. (1993). Automating the cognitive task modeling process: An extension to GOMS for HCI. *Proceedings of the Fifth International Conference on Human-Computer Interaction Poster Sessions: Abridged Proceedings. 3,* 182.

Williams, K., & O'Reilly, C. (1998). Demography and diversity in organizations: A review of 40 years of research. *Research in Organizational Behavior, 20,* 77–140.

Williamson, C., & Shneiderman, B. (1992). The dynamic homefinder: Evaluating dynamic queries in a real estate information exploration system. *Proceedings of SIGIR '92* (pp.339–346). New York: ACM Press.

Wing, A. (1982). Timing and coordination of repetitive bimanual movements. *Quarterly Journal of Experimental Psychology, 34A,* 339–348.

Winograd, T., Bennett, J., De Young, L., & Hartfield, B. (Eds.). (1996). *Bringing design to software.* Boston, MA: Addison-Wesley.

Winograd, T., & Flores, F. (1986). *Understanding computers and cognition: A new foundation for design.* Norwood, NJ: Ablex.

Winterhalder, B., & Smith, E. A. (1992). Evolutionary ecology and the social sciences. In E. A. Smith & B. Winterhalder (Eds.), *Evolutionary ecology and human behavior* (pp.3–23). New York: de Gruyter.

Wong, W., Sallis, P., & O'Hare, D. (1998). The ecological approach to interface design: Applying the abstraction hierarchy to intentional domains. *Proceedings of the 1998 Australasian Computer Human Interaction Conference (OzCHI98)* (pp.144–151). Los Alamitos, CA: IEEE Computer Society.

Woodruff, A., Rosenholtz, R., Morrison, J. B., Faulring, A., & Pirolli, P. (2002). A comparison of the use of text summaries, plain thumbnails, and enhanced thumbnails for Web search tasks. *Journal of the American Society for Information Science and Technology, 53,* 172–185.

Woods, D. (1988). Coping with complexity: The psychology of human behavior in complex systems. In L. Goodstein, H. Andersen, & S. Olsen (Eds.), *Mental models, tasks, and errors.* London: Taylor & Francis.

Woods, D. (1993). Process tracing methods for the study of cognition outside of the experimental psychology laboratory. In G. A. Kelin, J. Orasanu, R. Calderwood, & C. Zsambok (Eds.), *Decision making in action: Models and methods.* Norwood, NJ: Ablex.

Woods, D. (1995). Towards a theoretical base for representation design in the computer medium: Ecological perception and aiding human cognition. In J. Flach, P. Hancock, J. Caird, & K. Vicente (Eds)., *Global perspectives on the ecology of human-machine systems (Vol 1).* Hillsdale, NJ: Erlbaum.

Woods, D. D., & Roth, E. M. (1988). Cognitive systems engineering. In M. Helander (Ed.) *Handbook of human computer interaction* (pp.3–43). Amsterdam: North-Holland.

Wright, P. (1988). Issues of content and presentation in document design. In. M. Helander (Ed.), *Handbook of human-computer interaction.* Amsterdam: Elsevier.

Wright, P. C., Fields, R. E., & Harrison, M. D. (2000). Analysing human-computer interaction as distributed cognition: The resources model. *Human Computer Interaction, 15* (1), 1–42.

Wûthrich, C. A. (1999). An analysis and model of 3D interaction methods and devices for virtual reality. In D. J. Duke & A. Puerta (Eds.), *DSV-IS 1999 design, specification and verification of interactive systems.* (pp.18–29). Vienna: Springer-Verlag.

Yang, S., Burnett, M. M., DeKoven, E., & Zloof, M. (1997). Representation design benchmarks: A design-time aid for VPL navigable static representations. *Journal of Visual Languages and Computing 8*(5/6), 563–599.

Young, R. M. (1983). Surrogates and mappings. Two kinds of conceptual models for interactive devices. In D. Gentner & A. L. Stevens (Eds), *Mental models*. Hillsdale, NJ: Erlbaum.

Young, R. M., Green, T. R. G., & Simon, T. (1989). Programmable user models for predictive evaluation of interface designs. *Proceedings of the ACM Conference on Human Factors in Computing Systems—CHI '89* (pp.15–20). New York: ACM Press.

Zachary, W. (1989). A context-based model of attention switching in computer-human interaction domains *Proceedings of the 33rd Annual Meeting of the Human Factors Society* (pp.286–290). Santa Monica, CA: Human Factors Society.

Zajonc, R. (1965). Social facilitation. *Science, 149 (Whole No. 3681), 269*–274.

Zhai, S., & MacKenzie, I. S. (1998). Teaching old mice new tricks: Innovations in computer mouse design. *Proceedings of Ergon-Axia '98—the First World Congress on Ergonomics for Global Quality and Productivity* (pp.80–83).

Zhai, S., Smith, B. A., & Selker, T. (1997a). Dual stream input for pointing and scrolling. *Proceedings of the ACM Conference on Human Factors in Computing Systems—CHI '97* (pp.305–306). New York: ACM Press.

Zhai, S., Smith, B. A., & Selker, T. (1997b). Improving browsing performance: A study of four input devices for scrolling and pointing tasks. *Proceedings of INTERACT '97* (pp.286–292). Amsterdam: Elsevier.

Zhang, J. (1997). The nature of external representation in problem solving. *Cognitive Science, 21*(2), 179–217.

Zhang, J., & Norman, D. A. (1994). Representations in distributed cognitive tasks. *Cognitive Science, 18,* 87–122.

Zhang, J., & Norman, D. A. (1995). A representational analysis of numeration systems. *Cognition, 57,* 271–295.

Zwaan, R. A., & Radvansky, G. A. (1998). Situation models in language comprehension and memory. *Psychological Bulletin, 123,* 162–185.

Index

L

M

About the Authors

Olav W. Bertelsen is an associate professor of human-computer interaction and systems development at the Department of Computer Science, University of Aarhus. He has been teaching human-computer interaction in the interdisciplinary multimedia education program since 1998. His Ph.D. thesis, "Elements of a Theory of Design Artifacts," was an attempt to give a systematic account, based on activity theory, on the tools, methods, techniques, etc., mediating the design of computer artifacts. Actual research interests include common information spaces; activity theory based methods and techniques in human-computer interaction; and reformation of human-computer interaction as an aesthetic discipline based in dialectical materialism.

Alan Blackwell is a lecturer in the Cambridge University Computer Laboratory, with qualifications in professional engineering and experimental psychology. He has 20 years experience designing industrial systems and software products, with current research interests in domestic and physical computing, design visualization, and psychology of programming. He teaches HCI and design courses in the Computer Laboratory and Architecture Faculty. Dr. Blackwell is a fellow of Darwin College and of the Cambridge-MIT Institute, and Co-Director of Crucible, the Cambridge network for research in interdisciplinary design.

Susanne Bødker is Professor of New Ways of Working at the Computer Science Department, University of Aarhus, Denmark. Her research areas include participatory design, computer-supported cooperative work, and human-computer interaction. She became interested in HCI while working at Xerox PARC 1982–83, and returned to Scandinavia to work on the Utopia project before turning to activity theory as a possible theoretical basis for HCI. Her Ph.D. thesis, "Through the Interface—a Human Activity Approach to User Interface Design," was an early attempt to present activity theoretical HCI to an international audience. Much of her research since can be seen as consolidation and expansion of this theoretical frame.

Graham Button is the Laboratory Director of Xerox Research Centre Europe (XRCE) Grenoble. Previously he was the Director of XRCE's Cambridge Laboratory. He joined Xerox in 1992 from the University of Plymouth where he was Principle Lecturer and where he currently holds the position of Visiting Professor. He was also visiting faculty at the University of California Los Angeles and Boston University in 1980 and 1985 respectively. Prior to joining the University of Plymouth he was Faculty Research Assistant in the sociology department at the University of Manchester where he gained his Ph.D. in 1976. His major research interests are in the organization of interaction and work, especially work involving technology; and in applying the study of work and interaction toward the design of innovative technology. In addition to his core interests in work, interaction, organizations, and technology, he also undertakes research in the philosophy of mind, and has contributed to the debates surrounding artificial intelligence and computational models of mind.

John M. Carroll is Professor of Computer Science, Education, and Psychology, and Director of the Center for Human-Computer Interaction, all at Virginia Tech. His research interests include methods and theory in human-computer interaction, particularly as applied to networking tools for collaborative learning and problem solving. He has written or edited 12 books, including *Making Use* (MIT Press, 2000), *HCI in the New Millennium* (Addison-Wesley, 2002), and *Usability Engineering* (Morgan-Kaufman, 2002, with M. B. Rosson). He serves on nine editorial boards for journals, handbooks, and series. He has received the Rigo Career Achievement Award from ACM (SIGDOC), the Silver Core Award from IFIP, and was elected to the CHI Academy. His research is supported by the US National Science Foundation, the US Office of Naval Research, and the Hitachi Foundation.

Alan Dix (D. Phil. Computing [University of York]; Dip. Mathematical Statistics [University of Cambridge]; B.A. Mathematics [University of Cambridge]) "I have long hair, a beard and am the son of a carpenter. Thereafter all pretensions to saintliness end. I began as a bearded mathematician at Cambridge, worked as a research scientist at the National Institute of Agricultural Engineering (lots of brightly painted tractors), a Cobol programmer for Cumbria County Council (lots of beige and brown ICL mainframes), then in 1984, thanks to Alvey, I became a bearded computer scientist. I worked for almost 10 years at York University before moving to become a Reader at Huddersfield in 1994, where I led the HCI Research Centre hci@hud and chaired the HCI '95 conference. I was Associate Dean of the School of Computing at Staffordshire University for two years (lots of meetings) and am now Professor of Computing at Lancaster University. I have written and edited several books (see my web pages at *www.hcibook.com/alan*), including a big textbook on human-computer interaction and a smaller textbook on artificial intelligence."

Thomas Green has degrees from Oxford and Sheffield Universities. Starting as a psycholinguist he became interested in the problems and opportunities of artificial languages such as programming languages, then in HCI more generally. As well as publishing many academic papers he has co-edited several books, including one of the first HCI books (H. T. Smith and T. R. G. Green, *Human Interaction with Computers*, Academic Press, 1981) and one specifically on *Psychology of Programming* (J.-M. Hoc, T. R. G. Green, and D. J. Gilmore and R. Samurçay, Academic Press, 1991). After working for the Medical Research Council's Applied Psychology Unit in Cambridge he retired to spend less time writing grant proposals, but is contemplating writing a book on cognitive aspects of notational design.

Bonnie John (B. Eng. 1977, The Cooper Union; M.S. 1978, Stanford University; Ph.D., 1988, Carnegie Mellon University), has been modeling human behavior to guide HCI design since 1983. She created CPM-GOMS, which explicitly links GOMS analyses to the Model Human Processor. She has created models in such domains as transcription typing, telephone call completion, using a help system, video game play, computer-aided drafting, programming, air traffic control, and launching the space shuttle. Bonnie has compared modeling across cognitive architectures and across modeling environments. She has brought this experience to bear on making modeling tools that are easier to use through automating substantial portions of the modeling process. She was a major contributor to the chapter comparing cognitive architectures in the National Research Council's book, *Modeling Human and Organizational Behavior: Application to Military Simulations* (Pew & Mavor, 1998). Bonnie is Associate Professor and a founding member of Carnegie Mellon University's Human-Computer Interaction Institute, where she directs the masters program in HCI.

Robert Kraut is Professor of Social Psychology and Human Computer Interaction at Carnegie Mellon University, with joint appointments in the Department of Social and Decision Sciences, the Human Computer Interaction Institute, and the Graduate School of Industrial Administration. He started his career as a social psychologist, but working in industry for 12 years shifted his focus from disciplines to problems. Dr. Kraut has published five books and written dozens of articles based on his research, which focuses on the design and social impacts of information technologies in small groups, in the home, and between organizations.

Scott MacKenzie joined York University in 1999 as Associate Professor in the Department of Computer Science. Before that he was professor of Computing and Information Science at the University of Guelph (1992–1999). His research is in human-computer interaction with an emphasis on human performance measurement and modeling, interaction devices, alphanumeric entry, and mobile computing. Home page: *www.yorku.ca/faculty/academic/mack/*.

Andrew Monk is Professor of Psychology at the University of York and fellow of the British Computer Society. He has published widely on Human-Computer Interaction (HCI) and electronic communication. His most recent research is concerned with the design of information and communication technology for use in the home.

Stephen Payne is a professor in the School of Psychology at Cardiff University, in Wales, UK. Payne was awarded a Ph.D. from Sheffield University in 1985 for his work on Task-Action Grammars (supervised by Thomas Green). Before moving to Cardiff he worked at Lancaster University and then in the User Interface of IBM's T. J. Watson Research Center. His current research interests are in human problem-solving and learning strategies in information-rich, interactive environments.

Mark Perry, a lecturer on interactive systems design at Brunel University in the UK, has been involved in research into human-computer interaction using distributed cognition since 1993. Parallel and related to his theoretical work on distributed cognition is Mark's supervision of several research grants in the user-centered design of ubiquitous and mobile computing, and his work as consultant to a number of leading companies in these areas. His past research includes studies in organizational memory, mobile medical device design, mobile collaboration, networked appliance design and smart homes. Mark has degrees in psychology (B.A.) and cognitive science (M.Sc.) from the University of Cardiff and was awarded his Ph.D. from Brunel University. Prior to his current position, Dr. Perry was a visiting scholar at Stanford University and a research fellow at Brunel.

Peter Pirolli is Principal Scientist in the User Interface Research Area at the Palo Alto Research Center (PARC). He received his B.Sc. in psychology and anthropology from Trent University, Canada, and earned his M.S. and Ph.D. in cognitive psychology from Carnegie Mellon University. From 1985 to 1994 he was a member of the faculty of the School of Education at the University of California, Berkeley, and a member of the Cognitive Science Institute. He is a fellow of the National Academy of Education. He joined Xerox PARC in 1991 and currently conducts studies of human-information interaction, information foraging theory, and the development of new user interface technologies.

Mary Beth Rosson is Associate Professor of Computer Science at Virginia Tech. Her research interests include scenario-based methods for the design and evaluation of interactive systems, the use of network technology to support collaboration, especially in learning contexts, and high-level programming languages and tools. She is co-author of *Usability Engineering: Scenario-Based Development of Human-Computer Interaction* (Morgan Kaufmann, 2002), along with numerous articles, book chapters and tutorials. Dr. Rosson is active in both ACM SIGCHI and ACM SIGPLAN, serving in numerous technical programs as well as conference organization roles for the CHI and OOPSLA annual conferences.

Penelope Sanderson is Professor of Cognitive Engineering and Human Factors at the University of Queensland, where she holds a joint appointment between the School of Psychology, the School of Information Technology and Electrical Engineering, and the ARC Key Centre for Human Factors. Professor Sanderson earned her Ph.D. in Engineering Psychology from the University of Toronto in 1985 and subsequently held a faculty post in the Engineering Psychology Joint Program at University of Illinois at Urbana-Champaign for 11 years. In 1997 she returned to her native Australia to take a position as Professor of Computer Science (HCI) and inaugural Director of the Swinburne University Computer Human Interaction Laboratory (SCHIL) before moving to her present post in 2001. Professor Sanderson's research interests are in cognitive engineering, with a special focus on visual display design, sonification, and applications of cognitive work analysis to medical, air defense, and process control environments. Alongside her published output she has developed software to support important cognitive engineering methodologies: the MacSHAPA program to support video and observational data analysis, and the Work Domain Analysis Workbench (WDAW) to support a key modeling approach within cognitive work analysis. Her research has been supported by NASA, Wright-Patterson AFB, the National Science Foundation, US Department of Energy, and in Australia by the Defense Science and Technology Organization (DSTO), and the Australian Research Council and Snowy Hydro Limited, among others.

Colin Ware's research focuses on applying our understanding of human perception to information display. He has published more than 100 articles on this subject and a recent book, *Information Visualization: Perception for Design* (Morgan Kaufmann, 2000). In addition to theory-based research Ware likes to build useful visualization systems. Fledermaus, a GIS visualization package originated by him and his students is now the leading 3D visualization system used in oceanography. Ware is a professor of Computer Science and Director of the Data Visualization Research Laboratory at the University of New Hampshire. He has degrees in both experimental psychology (Ph.D., University of Toronto) and Computer Science (M.Math, University of Waterloo).